*In Conflict
and Order*

Fifth Edition

In Conflict and Order
Understanding Society

D. Stanley Eitzen
Colorado State University

Maxine Baca Zinn
Michigan State University

ALLYN AND BACON
Boston   London   Toronto   Sydney   Tokyo   Singapore

Managing Editor: Susan Badger
Series Editor: Karen Hanson
Developmental Editor: Hannah Rubenstein
Senior Editorial Assistant: Laurie Frankenthaler
Cover Administrator: Linda Dickinson
Composition Buyer: Linda Cox
Manufacturing Buyer: Megan Cochran
Production Coordinator: Marjorie Payne
Editorial-Production Service: Grace Sheldrick, Wordsworth Associates
Text Designer: Karen Mason

This textbook is printed on recycled, acid-free paper.

Library of Congress Cataloging-in-Publication Data

Eitzen, D. Stanley.
  In conflict and order : understanding society / D. Stanley Eitzen,
Maxine Baca Zinn. — 5th ed.
    p.   cm.
  Includes bibliographical references.
  ISBN 0-205-12584-0
  1. Sociology. 2. Social structure. 3. Social psychology.
4. United states—Social conditions—1980–   I. Zinn, Maxine Baca,
1942–   . II. Title.
HM51.E336   1991
301—dc20   90–34160
                                                               CIP

Printed in the United States of America
10 9 8 7 6 5 4 3 2 1   96 95 94 93 92 91 90

Photo credits: *pp. 1, 16, 58, 82, 102, 171, 227, 257, 312, 347:* Robert Harbison;
pp. iii, 5, 20, 37, 51, 96, 126, 147, 183, 203, 224, 339, 357: AP/Wide World Photos;
pp. 294, 299, 482: The Christian Science Monitor/Neal Menschel; *pp. 405, 464:*

Photo credits continue on page 544, which should be considered an extension of the copyright page.

Brief Contents

Preface xiii

PART I   THE SOCIOLOGICAL APPROACH

Chapter 1   The Sociological Perspective 1
Chapter 2   The Structure of Social Groups 16
Chapter 3   The Duality of Life: Order and Conflict 37
Chapter 4   The Duality of Social Life: Stability and Change 64

PART II   THE INDIVIDUAL IN SOCIETY: SOCIETY IN THE INDIVIDUAL

Chapter 5   Culture 96
Chapter 6   Socialization 126
Chapter 7   Social Control 145
Chapter 8   Deviance 171

PART III   STRUCTURES OF SOCIAL INEQUALITY

Chapter 9   Social Stratification 203
Chapter 10   Class 224
Chapter 11   Racial and Ethnic Minorities 263
Chapter 12   Sex and Gender Stratification 299

PART IV   SOCIAL INSTITUTIONS

Chapter 13   The Economy 339
Chapter 14   Power and Politics 370
Chapter 15   Families 405
Chapter 16   Education 435
Chapter 17   Religion 464

Epilogue 494
Glossary 495
References 504
Name Index 525
Subject Index 531

Contents

Preface xiii

PART I   THE SOCIOLOGICAL APPROACH

Chapter 1   **The Sociological Perspective 1**

Assumptions of the Sociological Perspective 2
Problems with the Sociological Perspective 5
Sociological Methods: The Craft of Sociology 7
Panel 1–1   Minimizing Bias 10

Chapter 2   **The Structure of Social Groups 16**

The Micro Level 17
The Social Structure of Society 30

Chapter 3   **The Duality of Social Life: Order and Conflict 37**

Social Systems: Order and Conflict 38
Panel 3–1   Social Scientists and Values 42
Synthesis of the Order and Conflict Models 44
Panel 3–2   Anti-Asian Violence 49
Panel 3–3   The Media's Selective Perception of Race and Class 60
The Use of the Order and Conflict Models in This Book 61

Chapter 4   **The Duality of Social Life: Stability and Change 64**

Changes in Social Systems 66
Forces for Stability 66
Panel 4–1   The Bureaucracy as a Rational Tool: The Organization of
     Power 69
Panel 4–2   The Bureaucracy as an Irrational Tool: "Laws" Governing
     Behavior in Bureaucracies 70
Forces for Change 72
Panel 4–3   Winning Civil Rights for the Disabled 88
Panel 4–4   Telepower and the Global Village 90

PART II	THE INDIVIDUAL IN SOCIETY: SOCIETY IN THE INDIVIDUAL

Chapter 5 Culture 96

Culture: The Knowledge That People Share 98
Panel 5–1   Cultural Time 107

Values 110
Panel 5–2   Participation Observation 122

Values from the Order and Conflict Perspectives 123

Chapter 6 Socialization 126

The Personality as a Social Product 129
Panel 6–1   The Teaching of Prejudice 134

Similarities and Differences among Members of Society 137
Panel 6–2   The Unprepared Generation of the 1980s Faces the Future 140

Chapter 7 Social Control 145

Agents of Ideological Social Control 146
Panel 7–1   The Amish and Social Control 148
Panel 7–2   The Politics of the "Non-Partisan" Advertising Council 152

Agents of Direct Social Control 155
Panel 7–3   The Control of Illicit Sex among the Arabs 156
Panel 7–4   Big Business Is Watching You 160
Panel 7–5   Consequences of the Genome Project 166

Conclusion 168

Chapter 8 Deviance 171

What Is Deviance? 172

Traditional Theories for the Causes of Deviance 175
Panel 8–1   The Lower-Class Propensity to Criminal Behavior 179

Society as the Source of Deviance 185
Panel 8–2   The Gay Rights Movement 194

Deviance from the Order and Conflict Perspectives 197
Panel 8–3   Performance-Enhancing Drugs as Commonplace? 198

PART III	STRUCTURES OF SOCIAL INEQUALITY

Chapter 9 Social Stratification 203

Major Concepts 204

Theories of Stratification 207

Deficiency Theories 209
Panel 9–1   How Science Is Affected by the Political Climate 210
Panel 9–2   Blaming the Poor 214

Structural Theories 217
Panel 9–3   Who Benefits from Poverty? 218

Chapter 10   **Class 224**

Dimensions of Inequality 226
Panel 10–1   Equality and Progress 229

Social Classes 231

The Consequences of Social Class Position 239

Social Mobility 243

The Extent of Poverty in the United States 249
Panel 10–2   Workers, Students Teach Duke a Lesson 250

Myths about Poverty 254

A Structural Analysis of the Homeless 255

Chapter 11   **Racial and Ethnic Minorities 263**

The Characteristics of Minority Groups 266

Racial and Ethnic Groups 267

Explanations of Racial and Ethnic Inequality 276
Panel 11–1   Scientific Reasoning 284

Racial Stratification from the Conflict and Order Perspectives 285

Discrimination against Blacks and Hispanics: Continuity and Change 286

Contemporary Trends and Issues in U.S. Racial and Ethnic Relations 292
Panel 11–2   By 2010, More Than One-Third of American Children Will Be
   Black, Hispanic, or Asian 295

Chapter 12   **Sex and Gender Stratification 299**

The Roles and Ranking of Women and Men 300

Gender Stratification from the Order and Conflict Perspectives 303

The Learning of Traditional Gender Roles 306

The Reinforcement of Male Dominance 315

Structured Gender Inequality 322
Panel 12–1   Facts about Pay Equity 328

The Costs and Consequences of Sexism 331

Fighting the System 334
Panel 12–2   Women and Workforce 2000 336

PART IV   SOCIAL INSTITUTIONS

Chapter 13   **The Economy 339**

Capitalism and Socialism 341

The Corporation-Dominated Economy 343

Capitalism and Inequality 349

The Structural Transformation of the Economy 353

Capitalism in Crisis 363
Panel 13–1   Economic Planning to Solve Future Problems 366

Chapter 14   **Power and Politics 370**

Models of the National Power Structure 371
Panel 14–1   PACs Play Both Sides of Fence 374

The Consequences of the National Power Structure 391
Panel 14–2   The Framers of the Constitution: Plotters or Patriots? 392
Panel 14–3   Domestic and International Terrorism 398
Conclusion 400

Chapter 15   **Families 405**

The Mythical American Family 406

Families in Contemporary American Society 408

Changing Family Roles 416
Panel 15–1   Which Mothers Are Working: Four Profiles 423
Panel 15–2   I Want a Wife 426
Violence in Families 430

The Modern Family from the Order and Conflict Perspectives 431

Families of the Future 432

Chapter 16   **Education 435**

The Characteristics of American Education 436
Panel 16–1   Cooling Out the Failures 440
The Political Economy of Education in Corporate Society 442

Education and Inequality 445
Panel 16–2   The Cost and Consequences of a Harvard Education 454
Education from the Order and Conflict Perspectives 461

Chapter 17   **Religion 464**
Panel 17–1   The Cargo Cult of Melanesia 466

Panel 17–2   Holy Tortilla 467

Classical Sociology's Differing Interpretations of Religion 468

Some Distinctive Features of American Religion 470
Panel 17–3   Religion and Patriarchy 475

Religious Trends 479
Panel 17–4   What Does It Mean to Be Prolife 484

The Role of Mainline Churches: Conflict of Challenge? 485
Panel 17–5   Christianity's Future 488

Religion from the Order and Conflict Perspectives 491

Epilogue 494
Glossary 495
References 504
Name Index 525
Subject Index 531

Preface

This is *not a traditional* textbook for the introductory course in sociology. Several foci separate it from most mainstream books. Foremost, the book examines social organizations from a critical perspective. Far from a dispassionate description of the way things are, this book enumerates both the positive *and* negative consequences of social structure. The book introduces sociology, then shows how structure is important and necessary while simultaneously leading to social problems. This view of social life provides an integrated framework that can aid the reader in developing a sociological perspective. The book is designed to provide a coherent, consistent, and critical view of society.

Many introductory students will be exposed to sociology only once. They should leave that course with a new and meaningful way of understanding themselves, others, and society. The most fundamental goal of this book is to assist the student in developing a sociological perspective—all else is secondary.

This goal is emphasized explicitly in the first chapter and implicitly throughout the book. The sociological perspective focuses on the social sources of behavior. It requires the shedding of existing myths and ideologies by questioning all social arrangements. One of the most persistent questions of the sociologist is: Who benefits from the existing customs and social order and who does not? Since social groups are created by people, they are not sacred. Is there a better way? One editorial writer has posed a number of questions that illustrate the critical approach typical of the sociological perspective:

> Must we [Americans] try to perpetuate our global empire, maintaining far-flung military outposts, spending billions on the machinery of death, meddling in the affairs of other nations—or is there a better way? Must we continue to concentrate power and wealth in the hands of a few, preserving the income gaps that have remained virtually undisturbed through the New Deal, Fair Deal, New Frontier, and Great Society—or is there a better way? Must millions of our people be subjected to the cruel displacements of an irrational economy—or is there a better way? Must we stand by while our liberties are undermined, our resources squandered, our environment polluted—or is there a better way? Must private profit be the nation's driving force—or is there a better way? (*The Progressive*, 1976:5)

xiii

Although there will be disagreement on the answers to these questions, the answers are less important, sociologically, than the willingness to call into question existing social arrangements that many people consider sacred. This is the beginning of the sociological perspective. But being critical is not enough. The sociologist must have a coherent way to make sense of the social world, and this leads us to the second goal of this book—the elaboration of a consistent framework from which to understand and interpret social life.

This book is guided by the assumption that there is an inherent duality in all societies. The realistic analysis of any one society must include both the integrating and stabilizing forces, on the one hand, and the forces that are conducive to malintegration and change, on the other. Society in the United States is characterized by harmony *and* conflict; integration *and* division; stability *and* change. This synthesis is crucial if the intricacies of social structure, the mechanisms of social change, and the sources of social problems are to be understood fully.

This objective of achieving a balance between the order and conflict perspectives is not fully realized in this book, however. Although both perspectives are incorporated into each chapter, the scales tend to be tipped in favor of the conflict perspective. This slight imbalance is the conscious product of the way we, as authors and teachers, view the structure and mechanisms of society. In addition to presenting what we think is a realistic analysis of society, it counters the prevailing view of the order perspective with its implicit sanctification of the status quo. Such a stance is untenable to us, given the spate of social problems that persist in U.S. society. The emphasis of the conflict approach, on the other hand, questions the existing social arrangements, viewing them as sources of social problems, a position with which we agree. Implicit in such a position is the goal of restructuring society along more humane lines.

That we stress the conflict approach over the order model does not suggest that this book is a polemic. To the contrary, the social structure is also examined from a sympathetic view. The existing arrangements do provide for the stability and maintenance of the system. But the point is that by including a relatively large dose of the conflict perspective the discussion is a realistic appraisal of the system rather than a look through rose-colored glasses.

This duality theme is shown primarily at the societal level in this book. But while the societal level is the focus of our inquiry, the small group and individual levels are not ignored. The principles that apply to societies are also appropriate for the small social organizations to which we belong, such as families, work groups, athletic teams, churches, and clubs. Just as important, the sociological perspective shows how the individual is affected by groups of all sizes. Moreover, it shows how the identity of the individual is shaped by social forces and how in many important ways the individual's thoughts and actions are determined by group memberships.

The linkage of the individual to social groups is shown throughout the book. The relationship of the individual to the larger society is illustrated by special panels that examine societal changes and forces impinging on individuals and the choices available to us as we attempt to cope with these societal trends.

The book is divided into four parts. Chapters 1 through 4 introduce the reader to the sociological perspective, the fundamental concepts of the discipline, and the duality of social life. These chapters set the stage for an analysis of the structure (organization) and process (change) of U.S. society. The emphasis is on the characteristics of societies in general and the United States in particular.

Chapters 5 through 8 describe the way human beings are shaped by society. The topics include the values that direct our choices, the social bases of social identity and personality, the mechanisms that control individual and group behavior, and the violation of social expectations—deviance. Throughout these chapters we examine the forces that, on the one hand, work to make all Americans similar and those that, on the other hand, make us different.

Chapters 9 through 12 examine in detail the various forms of social inequality present in U.S. society. We examine how societies rank people in hierarchies. Also examined are the mechanisms that ensure that some people have a greater share of wealth, power, and prestige than others and the positive and negative consequences of such an arrangement. Other chapters focus on the specific hierarchies of stratification—class, race, and gender.

Chapters 13 through 17 discuss another characteristic of all societies— the presence of social institutions. Every society has developed historically a fairly consistent way of meeting its survival needs and those of its members. The family, for example, ensures the regular input of new members, provides for the stable care and protection of the young, and regulates sexual activity. In addition to the family, chapters are devoted to education, to the economy, to the polity, and to religion. The understanding of institutions is vital to the understanding of society because these social arrangements are part of its structure, resist change, and have such a profound impact on the public and private lives of people.

This fifth edition, while retaining the structure of the earlier editions, is different and improved. Of course, the latest statistical data and research findings are included. Timely topics, such as the Exxon oil spill, corporate crimes, the abortion controversy, and televangelism are discussed. More important, four themes are incorporated throughout. First, although there are separate chapters on race, class, and gender, these fundamental sources of differences are infused throughout the book. This emphasis is important when highlighting the diversity in society as well as furthering our understanding of the structural sources of inequality and injustice. Second, the tendency toward structural determinism is countered by examples of empowerment—when the powerless organize to achieve power and positive social changes (e.g., Gay rights, rights for the disabled, and better working conditions for underpaid workers). Third, the sources and consequences of the structural transformation of the economy are examined. This is a pivotal shift in the American economy with very significant implications for individuals, communities, the society, and the global economy. A final theme—anticipating the year 2000 and beyond—is incorporated in a number of panels.

These themes—inequality, the struggle by the powerless to achieve social justice, the transformation of the economy, and looking ahead to the near future—are important to consider sociologically. We see that social problems are structural in origin and that the pace of social change is increasing, yet society's institutions are slow to change and meet the challenges. The problems of U.S. society are of great magnitude, and solutions must be found. But understanding must precede action—and that is one goal of this book.

The analysis of U.S. society is a challenging task. It is frustrating because of the heterogeneity of the population and the complexity of the forces impinging on U.S. social life. It is frustrating because the diversity within the United States leads to many inconsistencies and paradoxes. Furthermore, it is difficult if not impossible for people in the United States to be objective and consistently rational about their society. Nevertheless, the sociological study of U.S. society is fascinating and rewarding. It becomes absorbing as people gain insights into their own actions and the behavior of others. Understanding the intricate complex of forces leading to a particular type of social structure or social problem can be liberating and lead toward collective efforts to bring about social change. This book attempts to give the reader just such a sociological perspective.

Finally, we are unabashedly proud of being sociologists. Our hope is that you will capture some of our enthusiasm for exploring and understanding the intricacies and mysteries of social life.

Acknowledgments

Our thanks to the following people for their thoughtful comments: Irene I. Blea, Metropolitan State College, Denver; Dean Dorn, California State University, Sacramento; Daniel Early, Central Oregon Community College; I. Eberstein, Florida State University; Dick Futrell, Eastern Kentucky University; Darlaine Gardetto, University of Missouri, Columbia; Angel Iarraza, Bowling Green State University; Patrick C. Jobes, Montana State University; Donna R. Kaufman, Humboldt State University; Kathe Lowney, Valdosta State College; Frances B. McGren, Grand Valley State University; Ginger E. Macheski, Valdosta State College; Nathalie Ostroot, Grand Valley State University; Richard A. Valencia, Fresno City College; Elizabeth Vance, Santa Monica College; and Carol Whitehurst, Humboldt State University.

Chapter One

The Sociological Perspective

*L*ife appears to be a series of choices for each of us. We decide how much schooling is important and what field to major in. We choose a job, a mate, and a life-style. But how free are we? Have you ever felt trapped by events and conditions beyond your control? Your religious beliefs may make you feel guilty for some behaviors. Your patriotism may cost you your life—even willingly. These ideological traps are powerful, so powerful that we usually do not even see them as traps.

Have you ever felt trapped in a social relationship? Have you ever continued a relationship with a friend, group of friends, lover, or spouse when you were convinced that this relationship was wrong for you? Have you ever participated in an act because others wanted you to that later seemed absolutely ridiculous, even immoral? Most likely your answers to these questions are in the affirmative because those closest to us effectively command our conformity.

At another level, have you ever felt that because of your race, gender, age, ethnicity, or social class certain opportunities were closed to you? For example, if you are a black football player certain positions on the team (usually quarterback, center, offensive guard, and kicker) will very likely be closed to you regardless of your abilities. If you are a female you may want to try certain sports or jobs but to do so is to call your "femininity" into question.

Even more remotely, each of us is controlled by decisions made in corporate boardrooms, in government bureaus, and in foreign capitals. Our tastes in style are decided on and manipulated by corporate giants through the media. High interest rates affect individual workers and their families in the housing and automobile industries by increasing unemployment. A war in the Middle East reduces the supply of oil and the price rises dramatically, restricting personal use here in the United States. That same war may mean that you will be called to action because you are the right age and sex. The weather in China and Russia affects grain prices in the United States, meaning bankruptcy or prosperity for individual farmers and high or low prices for individual consumers.

Finally, we are also trapped by our culture. We do not decide what is right or wrong, moral or immoral. These are decided for us and incorporated inside us. We do not decide what is beautiful and what is not. Even the decision on what is important and what is not is a cultural bias embedded deep inside each of us.

Sociology is the science dealing with social forces—the forces outside us that shape our very lives, interests, and personalities. As the science of society and social behavior, sociology is interesting, insightful, and important. This is because sociology explores and analyzes the ultimate issues of our personal lives, of society, and of the world. At the personal level sociology investigates the causes and consequences of such phenomena as romantic love, violence, identity, conformity, deviance, personality, and interpersonal power. At the societal level sociology examines and explains poverty, crime rates, racism, sexism, pollution, and political power. At the global level sociology researches such phenomena as war, conflict resolution, and population growth. While other disciplines are also helpful in the understanding of these social phenomena, sociology makes a unique contribution.

The insights of sociology are important for the individual because they help us understand why we behave as we do. This understanding is not only liberating but is a necessary precondition for meaningful social action to bring social change. As a scholarly discipline, sociology is important because it complements and in some cases supersedes other disciplines concerned with understanding and explaining social behavior.

ASSUMPTIONS OF THE SOCIOLOGICAL PERSPECTIVE

To discover the underlying order of social life and the principles that explain human behavior, scientists have focused on different levels of phenomena. The result of this division of labor has been the creation of scholarly disciplines, each concentrating on a relatively narrow sphere of phenomena. Biologists interested in social phenomena have focused on the organic bases for behavior. Psychological explanations assume the source of human behavior in the psyches of individuals.

The understanding of human behavior benefits from the emphases of the various disciplines. Each discipline makes important contributions to knowledge. Of the three major disciplines focusing on human behavior, sociology is commonly the least understood. The explicit goal of this book is to remedy this fault by introducing the reader to the sociological ways of perceiving and interpreting the social world. Let us begin by considering the assumptions of the sociological approach that provide the foundation for this unique, exciting, and insightful way of viewing the world.

Individuals are, by their nature, social beings. There are two fundamental reasons for this assumption. First, children enter the world totally dependent on others for their survival. This initial period of dependence means, in effect, that each of us has been immersed in social groups from birth. A second basis for the social nature of human beings is that throughout history people have found it to their advantage to cooperate with others (for defense, for material comforts, to overcome the perils of nature, and to improve technology).

Individuals are, for the most part, socially determined. This essential assumption stems from the first, that people are social beings. Individuals are products of their social environments for several reasons. During infancy, the child is at the mercy of adults, especially parents. These persons can shape the infant in an infinite variety of ways, depending on their proclivities and those of their society. The parents will have a profound impact on that child's ways of thinking about himself or herself and about others. The parents will transmit religious views, political attitudes, and attitudes toward how other groups are to be rated. The child will be punished for certain behaviors and rewarded for others. Whether that child becomes a bigot or integrationist, traditionalist or innovator, saint or sinner, depends in large measure on the parents, peers, and others who interact with him or her.

The parents may transmit to their offspring some idiosyncratic beliefs and behaviors, but most significantly they act as cultural agents, transferring the ways of the society to their children. Thus, the child is born into a family but also into a society. This society into which the individuals are born shapes their personalities and perceptions. Berger has summarized the impact of this in the following:

> Society not only controls our movements, but shapes our identity, our thoughts and our emotions. The structures of society become the structures of our own consciousness. Society does not stop at the surface of our skins. Society penetrates us as much as it envelops us. (Berger, 1963:121)

The individual's identity is socially bestowed. Who we are, how we feel about ourselves, and how others treat us are typically consequences of our location in society. Individuals' personalities are also shaped by the way we are accepted, rejected, and/or defined by others. Whether an individual is attractive or plain, witty or dull, worthy or unworthy depends on the values of society and the groups in which the individual is immersed. Although genes determine one's physiology and potential, the social environment determines how those characteristics will be evaluated.

Suggesting that human beings are socially determined is another way of saying that they are similar to puppets. They are dependent on and manipulated by social forces. A major function of sociology is to identify the social forces that affect us so greatly. Freedom, as McGee has pointed out, can come only from a recognition of these unseen forces:

> Freedom consists in knowing what these forces are and how they work so that we have the option of saying no to the impact of their operation. For example, if we grow up in a racist society, we will be racists unless we learn what racism is and how it works and then choose to refuse its impact. In order to do so, however, we must recognize that it is there in the first place. People often are puppets, blindly danced by strings of which they are unaware and over which they are not free to exercise control. A major function of sociology is that it permits us to recognize the forces operative on us and to untie the puppet strings which bind us, thereby giving us the option to be free. (McGee, 1975:3)

So, one task of sociology is to learn, among other things, what racism is and to determine how it works. This is often difficult because we typically do not recognize its existence—because we have been puppets, socialized to believe and behave in particular ways.

To say that we are puppets is too strong. This assumption is not meant to imply a total **social determinism** (the assumption that human behavior is explained exclusively by social factors).* The puppet metaphor is used to convey the idea that much of who we are and what we do is a product of our social environment. But there are nonconformists, deviants, and innovators. Society is not a rigid, static entity composed of robots. While the members of society are shaped by their social environment, they also change that environment. Human beings are the *shapers* of society as well as the *shapees*. This is the third assumption of the sociological approach.

Individuals create, sustain, and change the social forms within which they conduct their lives.   While individuals are largely puppets of society, they are also puppeteers. Chapter 2 describes this process of how people in interaction are the architects of society. In brief, the argument is that social groups of all sizes and types (families, peer groups, work groups, corporations, communities, and societies) are made by people. What interacting persons create becomes a source of control over those individuals (that is, they become puppets of their own creation). But the continuous interaction of the group's members also changes the group.

There are three important implications of this assumption that groups are human-made. First, these social forms that are created have a certain

---

*Advocates of social determinism are guilty of oversimplifying complex phenomena, just as are genetic determinists, psychological determinists, geographical determinists, and economic determinists.

Modern technology has positive and negative consequences. Automobiles provide accessible transportation, but they also produce pollution and gridlock in urban centers.

momentum of their own that defies change. The ways of doing and thinking common to the group are "natural" and "right." Although human-made, the group's expectations and structures take on a sacred quality—the sanctity of tradition—that constrains behavior in the socially prescribed ways.

A second implication is that social organizations, because they are created and sustained by people, are imperfect. Slavery benefited some segments of society by taking advantage of others. A competitive free enterprise system creates "winners" and "losers." The wonders of technology make worldwide transportation and communication easy and relatively inexpensive but create pollution and waste natural resources. These examples show that there are positive and negative consequences of the way people have organized.

A final implication is that individuals through collective action are capable of changing the structure of society and even the course of history (Anderson, 1974:3).

PROBLEMS WITH THE SOCIOLOGICAL PERSPECTIVE

Sociology is not a comfortable discipline and therefore will not appeal to everyone. To look behind the "closed doors" of social life is fraught with danger. The astute observer must ask such questions as: How does society really work? Who really has power? Who benefits under the existing social arrangements and who does not? To ask such questions means that the inquirer is interested in looking beyond the commonly accepted "official" definitions. As Berger has put it, "[the] sociological perspective involves a process of 'seeing through' the facades of social structures" (Berger, 1963:31). The underlying assumption of the sociologist is that things are *not* as they seem. Is the mayor of your town the most powerful person in the community? Is the system of justice truly just? Is professional sport free of racism? Is the United States a meritocratic society where talent and effort combine to stratify the people fairly? To make such queries is to call into question existing myths, stereotypes, and official dogma. The critical examination of society will demystify and demythologize. It sensitizes the individual to the inconsistencies present in society. Clearly that will result if you ask: Why does the United States, in the name of freedom, protect dictatorships around the world? Why do we encourage subsidies to the affluent but resent those directed to the poor? How powerful would Ted Kennedy be if his surname were Garcia? Why have more than 50 percent of the individuals killed by capital punishment in the United States been black? Why are many women opposed to the Equal Rights Amendment? Why in a democracy such as the United States are there so few truly democratic organizations?

The sociological assumption that provides the basis for this critical stance is that the social world is human-made—and therefore not sacred. The beliefs, the economic system, the law, the way power is distributed are created and sustained by people. They can, therefore, be changed by people. But if the change is to correct imperfections, then we must truly understand how social phenomena work. The central task of this book is to aid in such an understanding of United States society.

The sociological perspective is also discomforting to many because the understanding of the constraints of society is liberating. Traditional sex roles, for example, are no longer "sacred" for many persons. But while this is liberating from the constraints of tradition, it is also freedom from the protection that custom provides. The robotlike acceptance of tradition is comfortable because it frees us from choice (and therefore blame) and from ambiguity. So the understanding of society is a two-edged sword, freeing us, but also increasing the probability of frustration, anger, and alienation.

Sociology is also uncomfortable because the behavior of the subjects is not always certain. Prediction is not always accurate, because people can choose among options or can be persuaded by irrational factors. The result is that if sociologists know the social conditions, they can predict, but in terms of probabilities. In chemistry, on the other hand, scientists know exactly what will occur if a certain measure of sodium is mixed with a precise amount of chlorine in a test tube. Civil engineers armed with the knowledge of rock formations, type of soils, wind currents, and temperature extremes know exactly what specifications are needed in building a dam in a certain place. They could not, however, if the foundation and building materials kept shifting. That is the problem—and the source of excitement— for the sociologist. The political proclivities of Americans during the past few decades offer a good example of shifting attitudes. In 1964 the Republican candidate for President, Barry Goldwater, was soundly defeated, and many observers predicted the demise of the Republican Party. But in 1968, Richard Nixon, the

Republican, won. He won again in 1972 by a record-setting margin, leading to the prognostication that the Democratic Party would no longer be viable. Two years later, however, Nixon resigned in disgrace, and in 1976 the Democratic candidate, Jimmy Carter, was the victor. In 1980 President Carter was defeated by Ronald Reagan, and a number of liberal Senators were defeated by conservatives. These wide swings seemed to stop as Reagan was reelected in 1984 and he was succeeded four years later by his loyal vice-president, George Bush. Do these recent successes by political conservatives mean the demise of liberalism? History reveals otherwise. As long as human beings are not robots, their behaviors will be somewhat unpredictable. International events, economic cycles, and other occurrences will lead to shifts in political opinions and shifts in the prevailing political ideology.

SOCIOLOGICAL METHODS: THE CRAFT OF SOCIOLOGY

Sociology is dependent on reliable data and logical reasoning. These necessities are possible, but there are problems that must be acknowledged. Before we describe how sociologists gather reliable data and make valid conclusions, let us examine, in some detail, two major obstacles.

Problems in Collecting Data

A fundamental problem with the sociological perspective is that bane of the social sciences—objectivity. We are *all* guilty of harboring stereotyped conceptions of social categories such as blacks, hard hats, professors, homosexuals, fundamentalists, business tycoons, communists, jet-setters, and jocks. Moreover, we interpret people's behavior, events, and material objects through the perceptual filter of our religious and political beliefs. When fundamentalists oppose the use of certain books in school, when abortion is approved by a legislature, when the president advocates cutting billions from the federal budget by eliminating social services, or when the Supreme Court denies private schools the right to exclude certain racial groups, most of us rather easily take a position in the ensuing debate.

Sociologists are caught in a dilemma. On the one hand, they are members of society with beliefs, feelings, and biases. At the same time, though, their professional task is to study society in a disciplined (scientific) way. This latter requirement is that scientist-scholars be dispassionate, objective observers. In short, if they take sides, they lose their status as scientists.

This ideal of **value neutrality** (to be absolutely free of bias in research) can be attacked from three positions. The first is that scientists should not be morally indifferent to the implications of their research. Gouldner has argued this in the following statement:

> It would seem that social science's affinity for modeling itself after physical science might lead to instruction in matters other than research alone. Before Hiroshima, physicists also talked of a value-free science; they, too, vowed to make no value judgments. Today many of them are not so sure. If we today concern ourselves exclusively with the technical proficiency of our students

and reject all responsibility for their moral sense, or lack of it, then we may someday be compelled to accept responsibility for having trained a generation willing to serve in a future Auschwitz. Granted that science always has inherent in it both constructive and destructive potentialities. It does not follow from this that we should encourage our students to be oblivious to the difference. (Gouldner, 1962:212)

The second argument against the purely neutral position is that such a stance is impossible. Becker, among others, has argued that there is no dilemma—because it is impossible to do research that is uncontaminated by personal and political sympathies (Becker, 1967). This argument is based on several related assumptions. One is that the values of the scholar-researcher enter into the choices of what questions will be asked and how they will be answered. For example, in the study of poverty a critical decision involves the object of the study—the poor or the system that tends to perpetuate poverty among a certain segment of society. Or, in the study of the problems of youth, we can ask either: Why are some youths troublesome for adults, or alternatively: Why do adults make so much trouble for youths? In both illustrations quite different questions will yield very different results.

Similarly, our values lead us to decide from which vantage point we will gain access to information about a particular social organization. If they want to understand how a prison operates, researchers must determine whether they want a description from the inmates, from the guards, from the prison administrators, or from the state board of corrections. Each view provides useful insights about a prison, but obviously a biased one. If they obtain data from more than one of these levels, researchers are faced with making assessments as to which is the more accurate view, clearly another place in the research process where the values of the observers will have an impact.

Perhaps the most important reason the study of social phenomena cannot be value-free is that the type of problems researched and the strategies employed tend either to support the existing societal arrangements or to undermine them. Seen in this way, social research of both types is political. Ironically, however, there is a strong tendency to label only the research aimed at changing the system as political. By the same token, whenever the research sides with the underdog, the implication is that the hierarchical system is being questioned—thus, the charge that this type of research is biased. Becker has provided us with the logic of this in the following:

> When do we accuse ourselves and our fellow sociologists of bias? I think an inspection of representative instances would show that the accusation arises, in one important class of cases, when the research gives credence, in any serious way, to the perspective of the subordinate group in some hierarchical relationship. In the case of deviance, the hierarchical relationship is a moral one. The superordinate parties in the relationships are those who represent the forces of approved and official morality; the subordinate parties are those who, it is alleged, have violated that morality. . . . It is odd that, when we perceive bias, we usually see it in these circumstances. It is odd because it is easily ascertained that a great many more studies are biased in the direction of the interests of responsible officials than the other way around. (Becker, 1967:240, 242)

In summary, bias is inevitable in the study and analysis of social problems. The choice of a research problem, the perspective from which one analyzes the problems, and the solutions proposed all reflect a bias that either is supportive of the existing social arrangements or is not. Moreover, unlike biologists, who can dispassionately observe the behavior of an amoeba under a microscope, sociologists are participants in the social life they seek to study and understand. As they study race riots in cities, children living in poverty, or urban blight, sociologists cannot escape from their own feelings and values. They must, however, not let their feelings and values render their analysis invalid. In other words, research and reports of research must "tell it like it is," not as the researcher might want it to be. Sociologists must display scientific integrity, which requires recognizing biases in such a way that these biases do not invalidate the findings (Berger, 1963:5). Properly done in this spirit, an atheist can study a religious sect, a pacifist can study the military-industrial complex, a divorcee can study marriage, and a person who abhors the beliefs of the Ku Klux Klan can study that organization.

In addition to bias, people gather data and make generalizations about social phenomena in a number of faulty ways. In a sense everyone is a "scientist" seeking to find valid generalizations to guide behavior and make sense of the world. But most people are, in fact, very unscientific about the social world. The first problem, as we have noted, is the problem of bias. The second is that people tend to generalize from their experience. Not only is one's interpretation of things that happen to him or her subjective, but there also is a basic problem of sampling. The chances are that one's experience

Minimizing Bias

Social scientists must contend with the essential problem of credibility of their research. How is objectivity possible, though, when they cannot escape their personal values, biases, and opinions? The answer lies in the norms of science.

Sociologists share with other scientists **norms** for conducting research that minimize personal bias. Their research must reflect the standards of science before it is accepted in scholarly journals. These journals function as gate-keepers for a discipline. What they accept for publication is assumed by their readers to be scientific. The editors of scholarly journals send manuscripts to referees who are unaware of the identity of the authors. This system of anonymity allows the referees to make objective judgments about the credibility of the studies. They review, among other things, the methods used to assess validity and reliability. **Validity** is the degree to which a study actually measures what it purports to measure. **Reliability** is the degree to which another study repeating the same methods would yield the same results.

To guide sociologists, their professional association—the American Sociological Association—has a code of ethics, which includes a number of standards for objectivity and integrity in sociological research.*

1. Sociologists should adhere to the highest possible technical standards in their research, teaching and practice.
2. Since individual sociologists vary in their research modes, skills, and experience, sociologists should always set forth *ex ante* the limits of their knowledge and the disciplinary and personal limitations that condition the validity of findings which affect whether or not a research project can be successfully completed.
3. In practice or other situations in which sociologists are requested to render a professional judgment, they should accurately and fairly represent their areas and degrees of expertise.

4. In presenting their work, sociologists are obligated to report their findings fully and should not misrepresent the findings of their research. When work is presented, they are obligated to report their findings fully and without omission of significant data. To the best of their ability, sociologists should also disclose details of their theories, methods and research designs that might bear upon interpretations of research findings.
5. Sociologists must report fully all sources of financial support in their publications and must note any special relations to any sponsor.
6. Sociologists must not accept grants, contracts or research assignments that appear likely to require violation of the principles enunciated in this Code, and should dissociate themselves from research when they discover a violation and are unable to achieve its correction.
7. Sociologists have the obligation to disseminate research findings, except those likely to cause harm to clients, collaborators and participants, or those which are proprietary under a formal or informal agreement.
8. In their roles as practitioners, researchers, teachers, and administrators, sociologists have an important social responsibility because their recommendations, decisions, and actions may alter the lives of others. They should be aware of the situations and pressures that might lead to the misuse of their influence and authority. In these various roles, sociologists should also recognize that professional problems and conflicts may interfere with professional effectiveness. Sociologists should take steps to insure that these conflicts do not produce deleterious results for clients, research participants, colleagues, students and employees.

Source: Excerpted from American Sociological Association, "Code of Ethics," (Washington, D.C.: American Sociological Association, August 14, 1989), pp. 2–3.

will be too idiosyncratic to allow for an accurate generalization. For example, if you and your friends agree that abortion is appropriate, that does not mean that other people in the society, even those of your age, will agree with you. Very likely, your friends are quite similar to you on such dimensions as socioeconomic status, race, religion, and geographic location. Another instance of faulty sampling leading to faulty generalizations is when we make assumptions from a single case. An individual may argue that blacks can succeed economically in this country as easily as whites because he or she knows a wealthy black person. Similarly, one might argue that all Chicanos are dumb because the one you know is in the slowest track in high school. This type of reasoning is especially fallacious because it blames the victim (Ryan, 1976). The cause of poverty or crime or dropping out of school or scoring low on an IQ test is seen as a result of the flaw in the individual, ignoring the substantial impact of the economy or school.

Another typical way that we explain social behavior is to use some authority other than our senses. The Bible, for example, has been used by many persons to support or condemn activities such as slavery, capital punishment, war, or monogamy. The media provide other sources of authority for individuals. The media, however, are not always reliable sources of facts. Stories are often selected because they are unusually dramatic, giving the faulty impression of, for example, a crime wave or questionable air safety.

Finally, we use aphorisms to explain many social occurrences. The problem with this common tactic is that society supplies us with ready explanations that fit contradictory situations and are therefore useless. For instance, if we know a couple who are alike in religion, race, socioeconomic status, and political attitudes, that makes sense to us because "birds of a feather flock together." But the opposite situation also makes sense. If a couple are very different on a number of dimensions, we can explain this by the obvious explanation—"opposites attract." There are a number of other proverbs that we use to explain behavior. The only problem is that there is often a proverb or aphorism to explain the other extreme:

- Absence makes the heart grow fonder.
  Out of sight, out of mind.
- Look before you leap.
  He who hesitates is lost.
- Familiarity breeds contempt.
  To know her is to love her.
- Women are unpredictable.
  Isn't that just like a woman.
- You can't teach an old dog new tricks.
  It's never too late to learn.
- Above all, to thine own self be true.
  When in Rome, do as the Romans do.
- Variety is the spice of life.
  Never change horses in the middle of the stream.
- Two heads are better than one.
  If you want something done right, do it yourself.

- You can't tell a book by its cover.
  Clothes make the man.
- Many hands make light work.
  Too many cooks spoil the broth.
- Better safe than sorry.
  Nothing ventured, nothing gained.
- Haste makes waste.
  Strike while the iron is hot.
- Work for the night is coming.
  Eat, drink and be merry for tomorrow you may die.
- There's no place like home.
  The grass is always greener on the other side of the fence.

These contradictory explanations are commonly used and, of course, explain nothing. The job of the sociologist is to specify under what conditions certain rates of social behaviors occur.

Sources of Data

Sociologists do not use aphorisms to explain behavior nor do they speculate based on faulty samples or authorities. Because we are part of the world that is to be explained, sociologists must get evidence that is beyond reproach. In addition to observing scrupulously the canons of science, there are four basic sources of data that yield valid results for sociologists: survey research, experiments, observation, and the use of existing documents. We describe these techniques only briefly here.*

Survey Research.   Sociologists are interested in obtaining information about certain kinds of persons. They may want to know how political beliefs and behaviors are influenced by differences in sex, race, ethnicity, religion, and social class. Or sociologists may wish to know whether religious attitudes are related to racial antipathy. They may want to determine whether poor people have different values from others in society, the answer to which will have a tremendous impact on the ultimate solution to poverty.

To answer these and similar questions, the sociologist may use personal interviews or written questionnaires to gather the data. The researcher may obtain information from all possible subjects or from a selected **sample** (a representative part of a population). Because the former is often impractical, a random sample of subjects is selected from the larger population. If the sample is selected scientifically, a relatively small proportion can yield satisfactory results—that is, the inferences made from the sample will be reliable about the entire population. For example, a probability sample of only 2,000 from a total population of 1 million will provide data very close to what would

---

*See the bibliography at the end of the chapter for references on the methods of sociology. Methodological footnotes and methods panels appear occasionally throughout this book to give insight into how sociologists obtain and analyze data.

be discovered if a survey were taken of the entire 1 million (Phillips, 1971:307–313).

Typically with survey research, sociologists use sophisticated statistical techniques to control the contaminating effects of confounding variables to determine whether the findings could have occurred by chance or not, to determine whether variables are related, and whether such a relationship is a causal one. A **variable** is an attitude, behavior, or condition that can vary in magnitude and significance from case to case.

Experiments. To understand the cause-and-effect relationship among a few variables, sociologists use controlled experiments. Let's assume, for example, that we want to test whether white students in interracial classrooms have more positive attitudes toward blacks than whites in segregated classrooms have toward them. Using the experimental method, the researcher would take a number of white students previously unexposed to blacks in school and randomly assign a subset to an integrated classroom situation. Before actual contact with the blacks, however, all the white students would be given a test of their racial attitudes. This pretest establishes a benchmark from which to measure any changes in attitudes. One group, the **control group,** continues school in segregated classrooms. (The **control group** is a group of subjects not exposed to the independent variable.) The other group, the experimental group, now has blacks as classmates. (The **experimental group** is a group of subjects who are exposed to the independent variable.) Otherwise, the two groups are the same. Following a suitable period of time, the whites in both groups are tested again (posttest) for their racial attitudes. If the experimental group is found to differ from the control group in racial attitudes (the **dependent variable**), then it is assumed that interracial contact (the **independent variable**) is the source of the change. (The **dependent variable** is a variable that is influenced by the effect of another variable. The **independent variable** is a variable that affects another variable.)

As an example of a less contrived experiment, a researcher can test the results of two different treatments on the subsequent behavior of juvenile delinquents. Delinquent boys who had been adjudicated by the courts can be randomly assigned to a boys' industrial school or a group home facility in the community. After release from incarceration, records are kept on the boys' subsequent behavior in school (grades, truancy, formal reprimands) and in the community (police contacts, work behavior). If the boys from the two groups differ appreciably, then we can say with assurance, because the boys were randomly assigned to each group, that the difference in treatment (the independent variable) was the source of the difference in behavior (the dependent variable) (Phillips et al., 1973).

Observation. The researcher, without intervention, can observe as accurately as possible what occurs in a community, group, or social event. This type of procedure is especially helpful in understanding such social phenomena as the decision-making process, the stages of a riot, the attraction of cults for their members, and the depersonalization of patients in a mental hospital.

Case studies of entire communities have been very instrumental in the understanding of power structures (e.g., Hunter, 1953; Dahl, 1961) and the complex interaction patterns of cities (Whyte, 1988). Long-time participant observation studies of slum neighborhoods and gangs have been very insightful in showing the social organization present in what the casual observer might think of as very disorganized activity (e.g., Whyte, 1955; Gans, 1962; Liebow, 1967).

Existing Sources. The sociologist can also make use of existing data to test theories. The most common sources of information are the various agencies of the government. Data are provided for the nation, regions, states, communities, and census tracts on births, deaths, income, education, unemployment, business activity, health delivery systems, prison populations, military spending, poverty, migration, and the like. Important information can also be obtained from such sources as business firms, athletic teams and leagues, unions, and professional associations. Statistical techniques can be used with these data to describe populations and the effects of social variables on various dependent variables.

CHAPTER REVIEW

1. Sociology is the science dealing with social forces—the forces outside us that shape our very lives, interests, and personalities. Sociologists, then, work to discover the underlying order of social life and the principles regarding it that explain human behavior.

2. The assumptions of the sociological perspective are that (a) individuals are, by their nature, social beings; (b) individuals are socially determined; and (c) individuals create, sustain, and change the social forms within which they conduct their lives.

3. Sociology is uncomfortable for many because it looks behind the facades of social life. This requires a critical examination of society that questions the existing myths, stereotypes, and official dogma.

4. The basis for the critical stance of sociologists is that the social world is not sacred because it is made by human beings.

5. Sociology is dependent on reliable data and logical reasoning. Although value neutrality is impossible in the social sciences, bias is minimized by the norms of science.

6. Survey research is a systematic means of gathering data to obtain information about people's behaviors, attitudes, and opinions.

7. Sociologists may use experiments to assess the effects of social factors on human behavior. One of two similar groups—the experimental group—is exposed to an independent variable. If this group later differs from the control group, then the independent variable is known to have produced the effect.

8. Observation is another technique for obtaining reliable information. Various social organizations such as prisons, hospitals, schools, churches, cults, families, communities, and corporations can be studied and understood through systematic observation.

9. Sociologists also employ existing sources of data to test their theories.

10. Sociology is a science, and the rules of scientific research guide the efforts of sociologists to discover the principles of social organization and the sources of social constraints on human behavior.

KEY TERMS

Sociology	Sample	Experimental group
Social determinism	Variables	Dependent variable
Value neutrality	Control group	Independent variable

STUDY QUESTIONS

1. How would sociologists differ from psychologists in studying such phenomena as divorce or racism?
2. Peter Berger has said that "the sociological perspective involves a process of 'seeing through' the facades of social structure." What does this mean? Give examples.
3. To what extent are you shaped by your social environment? Provide examples.
4. Are you comfortable or uncomfortable with the sociological perspective? Elaborate.
5. How do sociologists minimize bias in their research activities?

FOR FURTHER READING

The Sociological Perspective

Peter L. Berger, *Invitation to Sociology: A Humanistic Perspective* (Garden City, NY: Doubleday Anchor Books, 1963).

Peter Berger and Hansfried Kellner, *Sociology Reinterpreted* (Garden City, NY: Doubleday Anchor Books, 1981).

Randall Collins, *Sociological Insight* (New York: Oxford University Press, 1982).

Randall Collins and Michael Makowsky, *The Discovery of Society*, 3rd ed. (New York: Random House, 1984).

Lewis A. Coser (ed.), *The Pleasures of Sociology* (New York: New American Library, 1980).

Sheldon Goldenberg, *Thinking Sociologically* (Belmont, CA: Wadsworth, 1987).

C. Wright Mills, *The Sociological Imagination* (New York: Oxford University Press, 1959).

Kenneth Westhues, *First Sociology* (New York: McGraw-Hill, 1982).

The Craft of Sociology

Earl R. Babbie, *The Practice of Social Research*, 5th ed. (Belmont, CA: Wadsworth, 1989).

Pauline Bart and Linda Frankel, *The Student Sociologist's Handbook*, 4th ed. (New York: Random House, 1986).

Kenneth R. Hoover, *The Elements of Social Scientific Thinking*, 3rd ed. (New York: St. Martin's, 1984).

P. McC. Miller and M. J. Wilson, *A Dictionary of Social Science Methods* (New York: John Wiley & Sons, 1983).

Gideon Sjoberg (ed.), *Ethics, Politics, and Social Research* (Cambridge, MA: Schenkman, 1967).

Robert B. Smith, *An Introduction to Social Research: Volume I of Handbook of Social Science Methods* (Cambridge, MA: Ballinger, 1983).

Chapter Two

The Structure of Social Groups

*A*n experiment was conducted some years ago when 24 previously unacquainted boys, aged 12, were brought together at a summer camp (Sherif and Sherif, 1966). For three days the boys, who were unaware that they were part of an experiment, participated in campwide activities. During this period the camp "counselors" observed the friendship patterns that emerged naturally. The boys were then divided into two groups of 12. The boys were deliberately separated in order to break up the previous friendship patterns. The groups were then totally separated for a period of five days. During this period the boys were left alone by the "counselors" so that what occurred was the spontaneous result of the boys' behavior. The experimenters found that in both groups there developed (1) a division of labor; (2) a hierarchical structure of ranks—that is, differences among the boys in power, prestige, and rewards; (3) the creation of rules; (4) punishments for violations of the rules; (5) argot—that is, specialized language such as nicknames and group symbols that served as positive in-group identifications; and (6) member cooperation to achieve group goals.

This experiment illustrates the process of social organization. The "counselors" did not insist that these phenomena occur in each group. They seemed to occur "naturally." In fact, they happen universally (see Whyte, 1943; Liebow, 1967). The goals of this chapter are to understand the components of social structure that emerge, and how these components operate to constrain behavior. Although the process is generally the same regardless of group size, we will examine it at two levels—the micro level and the societal level.

THE MICRO LEVEL

The Process of Social Organization

Social organization refers to the ways in which human conduct becomes socially organized, that is, the observed regularities in the behavior of people that are due to the social conditions in which they find themselves rather than to their physiological or psychological characteristics as individuals (Blau and Scott, 1962:2). The social conditions that constrain behavior can be divided into two types: (1) **social structure**—the structure of behavior in groups and society; and (2) **culture**—the shared beliefs of group members that unite them and guide their behavior.

Social Structure.   **Sociology** is the study of the patterns that emerge when people interact over time. The emphasis is on the linkages and network that emerge, that transform an **aggregate** of individuals into a **group.** (An **aggregate** is a collection of individuals who happen to be at the same place at the same time. A **group** is a collection of people who, because of sustained interaction, have evolved a common structure and culture.) We start, then, with **social interaction.** When the actions of one person affect another person, social interaction occurs. The most common method is communication through speech, the written word, or symbolic act (for example, a wink, a wave of the hand, or the raising of a finger). Behavior can also be altered by the mere presence of others. The way we behave (from the way we eat to what we think) is affected by whether we are alone or with others. Even physical reactions such as crying, laughing, or passing gas are controlled by the individual because of the fear of embarrassment. It could even be argued that, except in the most extreme cases, people's actions are always oriented toward other human beings whether other people are physically present or not. We, as individuals, are constantly concerned about the expected or actual reactions of others. Even when alone, an individual may not act in certain ways because of having been taught that such actions are wrong.

Social interaction may be either transitory or enduring. Sociologists are interested in the latter type because only then does patterned behavior occur. A case of enduring social interaction is a **social relationship.** Relationships occur for a number of reasons: sexual attraction, familial ties, a common interest (for example, collecting coins or growing African violets), a common political or religious ideology, cooperation to produce or distribute a product, or propinquity (neighbors). Regardless of the specific reasons, the members of a social relationship are united at least in some minimal way with the others. Most important, the members of a social relationship behave quite differently than they would as participants in a fleeting interaction. Once the interaction is perpetuated, the behavior of the participants is profoundly altered. An autonomous individual is similar to an element in chemistry. As soon as there is a chemical reaction between them, however, the two elements become parts of a new entity, as Olsen has noted:

The concepts of "elements" and "parts" are analogous to terms in chemistry. By themselves, chemical elements—sodium and chlorine, for instance—exhibit characteristics peculiarly their own, by which each can be separately identified. This condition holds true even if elements are mixed together, as long as there is no chemical reaction between them. Through a process of chemical interaction, however, the elements can join to form an entirely new substance—in this case, salt. The elements of sodium and chlorine have now both lost their individual identities and characteristics, and have instead become parts of a more inclusive chemical compound, which has properties not belonging to either of its component parts by themselves. In an emergent process such as this, the original elements are transformed into parts of a new entity. (Olsen, 1976:37)

Olsen's description of a chemical reaction is also appropriate for what arises in a social relationship. Most sociologists assume that the whole is not identical to the sum of its parts—that is, through the process of enduring interaction something is created with properties different from the component parts.* The two groups artificially formed at the summer camp, for example, developed similar structural properties regardless of the unique personalities of the boys in each group.

Although groups may differ in size or purpose, they are similar in structure and the processes that create the structure. In other words, one group may exist to knit quilts for charity while another may do terrorist bombings, but they will be alike in many important ways. Their social structure involves the patterns of interaction that emerge, the division of labor, and the linking and hierarchy of positions. The social structure is an emergent phenomenon bringing order and predictability to social life within the group.

Culture. The other component of social organization is culture—the shared beliefs of a group's members that serve to guide conduct. Through enduring social interaction common expectations emerge about how people should act. These are called **norms.** Criteria for judging what is appropriate, correct, moral, and important also emerge. These criteria are the **values** of the group. Also part of the shared beliefs are the expectations group members have of individuals occupying the various positions within the group. These are **social roles.** The elements of culture will be described briefly below for the micro and macro levels and in detail in Chapter 5.

To summarize, social organization refers to both culture and social structure. Blau and Scott describe how they operate to constrain human behavior:

The prevailing cultural standards and the structure of social relations serve to organize human conduct in the collectivity. As people conform more or less

---

*This assumption—the *realist* **position**—is one side of a fundamental philosophical debate. The *nominalists,* on the other hand, argue that to know the parts is to know the whole. In sociology the realist position is dominant and found especially in the works of Emile Durkheim (1938) and the contemporary classic by Charles Warriner (1956). The minority position in sociology is represented most prominently by George Homans (1964).

closely to the expectations of their fellows, and as the degree of their conformity in turn influences their relations with others and their social status, and as their status in turn further affects the inclinations to adhere to social norms and their chances to achieve valued objectives, their patterns of behavior become socially organized. (Blau and Scott, 1962:4–5)

Norms

All social organizations have rules (norms) that specify appropriate and inappropriate behaviors. In essence, norms are the behavioral expectations that members of a particular group collectively share. They ensure that action within social organizations is generally predictable.

Some norms are not considered as important as others and consequently are not severely punished if violated. These minor rules are called **folkways.** Folkways vary, of course, from group to group. A particular sorority may expect its members to wear formal dress on certain occasions and to never wear curlers to the library. In a church, wine may be consumed by the parishioners at the appropriate time—communion. To bring one's own bottle of wine to communion, however, would be a violation of the folkways of that church. Could you imagine an announcement in your church bulletin that communion will be next Sunday—B.Y.O.B.? These examples show that folkways involve etiquette, customs, and regulations which, if violated, do not threaten the fabric of the social organization.

The violation of the group's **mores,** on the other hand, is considered important enough so that it must be punished severely. (**Mores** are important norms, the violation of which results in severe punishment.) This type of norm involves morality—in fact, mores can be thought of as moral imperatives. In a sorority, for instance, examples of the mores might be: disloyalty, stealing from a "sister," and conduct that brings shame to the organization, such as blatant sexual promiscuity.

Status and Role

One important aspect of social structure is comprised of the positions of a social organization. If one determines what positions are present in an organization and how they are interrelated (hierarchy, reciprocal pairs, etc.), then the analyst has a structural map of that social group. The existence of positions in organizations has an important consequence for individuals—the bestowing of a social identity. Each of us belongs to a number of organizations and in each we occupy a position (**status**). If you were asked—who are you?—chances are you would respond by listing your various statuses. An individual may at the same time be a student, sophomore, daughter, sister, friend, female, Baptist, Sunday School teacher, Democrat, waitress, American citizen, and secretary-treasurer of the local chapter of Weight Watchers.

The individual's social identity, then, is a product of the particular matrix of statuses that she or he occupies. Another characteristic of statuses that has an important influence on social identity is that these positions in organi-

This scene of college students during spring break in Palm Springs illustrates the violation of societal norms and the conformity to group norms.

zations tend to be differentially rewarded and esteemed. This element of **hierarchy** (the arrangement of people in order of importance) of status reinforces the positive or negative image individuals have of themselves depending on placement in various organizations. Some individuals consistently hold prestigious positions (bank president, deacon, Caucasian, male, chairman of United Fund), while others may hold only those statuses negatively esteemed (welfare recipient, aged, Chicano, janitor) and some occupy mixed statuses (bus driver, 32nd-degree Mason, union member, church trustee).

So group memberships are vital sources of our notion of our own identity. Similarly, when they know of our status in various organizations, others assign a social identity to us. When we determine a person's age, race, religion, and occupation, we tend to stereotype that person—that is, we assume that the individual is a certain "type." This has the effect of conferring a social identity on that person, raising expectations for certain behaviors that, very often, result in a self-fulfilling prophecy.

While the mapping of statuses provides important clues about the social structure of an organization, the most important aspect of status is the behavior expected of the occupant of a status. To determine that an individual occupies the status of father does not tell us much about what the group expects of a father. In some societies, for example, the biological father has no legal, monetary, or social responsibility for his children, who are cared for by the mother and her brother. In American society, there are norms (legal and informal) that demand that the father be responsible for his children. Not only must he provide for them, but he must also, depending on the customs of the family, be a disciplinarian, buddy, teacher, Santa Claus, and tooth fairy.

The behavior expected of a person occupying a status in a group is that person's **role*** (the behavioral expectations and requirements attached to a position in a social organization). The norms of the social organization constrain the incumbents in a status to behave in prescribed and therefore predictable ways, regardless of their particular personalities. Society insists that we play our roles correctly. To do otherwise is to risk being judged by others as abnormal, crazy, incompetent, and/or immature. These pressures to conform to role demands ensure that there is stability in social groups even though member turnover occurs. For example, ministers to a particular congregation come and go, but certain actions are predictable in particular incumbents because of the demands on their behavior. These demands come from the hierarchy of the denomination, from other ministers, and most assuredly from the members of the parish. The stability imposed by role is also seen with other statuses, such as professor, janitor, police officer, student, and even President of the United States.

The organizational demands on members in the various statuses do *not* make behavior totally predictable, however. Occupants of the statuses can vary within limits. There are at least three reasons for this. First, personality variables can account for variations in the behavior of persons holding identical status. People can be conformist or unconventional, manipulated or manipulators, passive or aggressive, followers or inspirational leaders, cautious or impetuous, ambitious or lackadaisical. The particular configuration of personality traits can make obvious differences in the behavior of individuals, even though they may face identical group pressures.

A second reason role does not make social actors robots is that the occupants of a status may not receive a clear, consistent message as to what behavior is expected. A minister, for example, may find within his or her congregation individuals and cliques that make conflicting demands. One group may insist that the minister be a social activist. Another may demand that the pastor be apolitical and spend his or her time exclusively meeting the spiritual needs of the members.

Another circumstance leading to conflicting expectations—and unpredictability of action—results from multiple group memberships. The statuses we occupy may have conflicting demands on our behavior. When a black politician, for example, is elected as mayor of a large city, as has been the case in Los Angeles, Chicago, Detroit, Philadelphia, and Atlanta, he or she is faced with the constraints of the office, on the one hand, and the demands of the black constituency, on the other. Other illustrations of conflicting demands because of occupying two quite different statuses are: daughter and lover, son and peer-group member, and businessman and church deacon. Being the recipient of incompatible demands results in hypocrisy, secrecy, guilt, and most important for our consideration—unpredictable behavior.

---

*This section introduces the concept of role as it is appropriate to the context of social organization. We will elaborate on it in Chapter 5.

Although role performance may vary, stability within organizations remains. The stability is a consequence of the strong tendency of persons occupying statuses in the organization to conform. Let us look briefly at just how powerfully roles shape behavior. First, the power of role over personal behavior is seen very dramatically as one moves from one status to another. If you could observe a parent's behavior, for example, at work, at parties, at church, and at a convention in a faraway city, chances are that the behavioral patterns would be inconsistent. Or, even closer to home, what about your own behavior at home, at church, at school, in the dorm, or in a parked car? In each of these instances the same individual occupies multiple statuses and faces conflicting role expectations, resulting in overall inconsistent behavior but very likely behavior that is expected for each separate role.

The power of role to shape behavior is also demonstrated as one changes status within an organization. The Amish, for instance, select their minister by lot from among the male adults of the group. The eligible members each select a Bible. The one choosing the Bible with the special mark in it is the new pastor. His selection is assumed to be ordained by God. Now this individual has a new status in the group—the leader with God's approval. Such an elevation in status will, doubtless, have a dramatic effect on that person's behavior. Without special training (the Amish rarely attend school beyond the eighth grade), the new minister will in all likelihood exhibit leadership, self-confidence, and wisdom. Less dramatically, but with similar results nonetheless, each of us undergoes shifts in status within the organizations to which we belong—from freshman to senior, bench warmer to first team, assembly-line worker to supervisor, and from adolescent to adult. These changes in status mean, of course, a concomitant shift in the expectations for behavior (role). Not only does our behavior change but so too our attitudes, perceptions, and perhaps even our personalities.

A dramatic example of the power of role over behavior is provided by an experiment conducted by Philip Zimbardo, who wanted to study the impact of prison life on guards and prisoners. Using student volunteers, Zimbardo randomly assigned some to be guards and others to be inmates. By utilizing subjects who were unassociated with a prison, the researcher could actually study the effects of social roles on behavior without the confounding variables of personality traits, character disorders, and the like.

Zimbardo constructed a mock prison in the basement of the psychology building at Stanford University. The students chosen as prisoners were "arrested" one night without warning, dressed in prison uniforms, and locked in the cells. The "guards" were instructed to maintain order. Zimbardo found that the college students assigned the roles of guard or inmate actually *became* guards and inmates in just a few days. The guards showed brutality and the prisoners became submissive, demonstrating that roles effectively shape behavior because they have the power to shape consciousness (thinking, feeling, and perceiving). Interestingly, Zimbardo, who is a psychologist, concluded that *social factors superseded individual ones:* "Individual behavior is largely under the control of social forces and environmental contingencies rather than personality traits, character, will power or other empirically un-validated constructs (Zimbardo, 1972:6).

Finally, roles have the power to protect individuals. The constraints on behavior implied in the role provide a blueprint that relieves the individual from the responsibility for action. Thus, the certainty provided by role makes us comfortable. Gay rights and the women's movement, to name two contemporary movements, are aimed at liberation from the constraints of narrowly prescribed sex roles. But to be free of these constraints brings not only freedom but also problems. So, too, when one is freed from the constraints of a particular community, job, or marriage, the newfound liberty, independence, and excitement are countered by the frustrations involving ambiguity, choice, loneliness, and responsibility.

Social Control

Although they vary in the degree of tolerance for alternative behaviors, social groups universally demand conformity to some norms. In the absence of such demands, groups would not exist because of the resulting anarchy. The mechanisms of social control are varied. They can occur subtly in the socialization process (see Chapter 6), so that persons feel guilty or proud, depending upon their actions. They can occur in the form of rewards (medals, prizes, merit badges, gold stars, trophies, praise) by family members, peers, neighbors, fellow workers, employers, and the community to reinforce certain behaviors. Also common are negative sanctions such as fines, demerits, imprisonment, and excommunication that are used to ensure conformity. More subtle techniques, such as gossip or ridicule, are also quite successful in securing conformity because of the common fear of humiliation before one's friends, classmates, coworkers, or neighbors.

An example of a particularly devastating and effective technique is the practice of "shunning" the sinner, used by some of the Amish and Mennonite religious sects. No one in the religious community, not even the guilty party's spouse and children, is to recognize his or her existence. In one celebrated case, Robert Bear was the victim of shunning. He took the case to court on the grounds that this practice was unconstitutional because it was too severe. Since the shun was invoked, Bear's wife had not slept with him, his six children were alienated from him, and his farm operation was in ruin because no one would work for him or buy his produce. The courts ruled, however, that it was within the province of the church to punish its members for transgressions. The severity of the "shun" is an extremely effective social control device for the Amish community, guaranteeing, except in rare cases, conformity to the dictates of the group.

Whatever the mechanism used, social control efforts tend to be very effective, whether they be within a family, peer group, organization, community, or a society. Most of the people, most of the time, conform to the norms of their groups and society. Otherwise, the majority of the poor would riot, most of the starving would steal, and more young men would refuse to fight in wars. The pressure to conform comes from within us (internalization of the group's norms and values from the socialization process) and from outside us (**sanctions** or the threat of sanctions, social rewards or punishments for approved or disapproved behavior) and we obey. In fact, what we consider self-control is really the consequence of social control. These constraints are usually not oppressive to the individual. Indeed, we want to obey the rules.

Primary and Secondary Groups

A social group is an organization created through enduring and patterned interaction. It consists of people who have a common identity, share a common culture, and define themselves as a distinct social unit. Groups may be classified in a number of ways, the most significant of which involves the kind and quality of relationships that members have with each other. Sociologists have delineated two types of groups according to the degrees of intimacy and involvement among the members—primary and secondary.

Primary groups are those whose members are the most intimately involved with each other. These groups are small and display face-to-face interaction. They are informal in organization and long-lasting. The members have a strong identification, loyalty, and emotional attachment to the group and its members. Examples are the nuclear family, a child's play group, a teenage gang, and close friends. Primary groups are crucial to the individual because they provide members with a sense of belonging, identity, purpose, and security. Thus, they have the strongest influence on the attitudes and values of members.

Secondary groups, in contrast to primary groups, are much larger and more impersonal. They are formally organized, task oriented, and relatively nonpermanent. The individual member is relatively unimportant. The members may vary considerably in beliefs, attitudes, and values. Americans are greatly affected by this type of group. The government at all levels deals with us impersonally. So, too, does our school, where we are a number in a computer. We live in large dormitories or in neighborhoods where we are barely acquainted with those near us. We work in large organizations and belong to large churches.

One significant impact of their impersonal nature is that secondary groups spawn the formation of primary groups. Primary groups emerge at school, at work, in an apartment complex, in a neighborhood, in a church, or in an army. In other words, intensely personal groups develop and are sustained by their members in largely impersonal settings.

The existence of primary groups within secondary groups is an important phenomenon that has ramifications for the goals of the secondary group. Two examples from military experience make this point. In World War II the German army was organized to promote the formation of primary groups. The men were assigned to a unit for the duration of the war. They trained together, fought together, went on furloughs together, and were praised or punished as a group. This was a calculated organizational ploy to increase social solidarity in the small fighting units. This worked to increase morale, loyalty, and a willingness to die for the group. In fact, individuals often became more loyal to their fighting unit than to the nation (Shils and Janowitz, 1948).

In contrast, the U.S. army in Vietnam was organized in such a way as to minimize the possibility for forming primary groups. Instead of being assigned to a single combat unit until the war was over, soldiers were given a twelve-month tour of duty in Vietnam. This rotation system meant that in any fighting unit soldiers were continually entering and leaving. This prevented the development of close relationships and a feeling of "all for one and one for all." Since each soldier had his own departure date, his goal was not to win the war but to survive until he was eligible to go home. This individualism made morale difficult to maintain and loyalty to one's unit difficult if not impossible to achieve. It also made the goal of winning the war less attainable than would a system that fostered primary groups (Moskos, 1975).

Power of the Social Group

We have seen that primary and secondary groups structure the behavior of their members by providing rules, roles, and mechanisms of social control. The result is that most of us, most of the time, conform to the expectations of social groups. Let us examine some illustrations of the profound influence of social groups on individuals, beginning with the classic study of suicide by Emile Durkheim.

Group Affects Probability of Suicide.   One's attachment to social groups affects the probability of suicide. Suicide would appear on the surface to be one area that could strictly be left to psychological explanations. An individual is committing the ultimate individual act—ending one's own life—presumably because of excessive guilt, anxiety, and/or stress. Sociologists, however, are interested in this seemingly individual phenomenon because of the social factors that may produce the feelings of guilt or the undue psychological stress. Sociologists are not interested, however, in the individual suicide case as psychologists would be, but in a number of people in the same social situation. Let us look at how sociologists would study suicide by examining in some detail the classic study by the nineteenth-century French sociologist Emile Durkheim (1951).

Durkheim was the consummate sociologist. He reacted to what he considered the excessive psychologism of his day by examining suicide rates (the number of suicides per 100,000 people in a particular category) sociologically. Some of the interesting results of his study were that single people had higher rates than married people, childless married people had a higher rate than those with children, the rate of city dwellers exceeded that of rural people, and Protestants were more likely to be self-destructive than Catholics or Jews.

Societal conditions were also correlated with suicide rates. As expected, rates were higher during economic depressions than in periods of economic stability, although surprisingly high rates were found during economic booms.

Durkheim went an important step beyond just noting that social factors were related to suicide rates. He developed a theory to explain these facts—a theory based on the individual's relationship to a social organization. Three types of suicide—the egoistic, altruistic, and anomic—were posited by Durkheim to illustrate the effect of one's attachment to a group (society, religion, family) on self-preservation. **Egoistic suicide** occurs when an individual has minimal ties to a social group. The person is alone, lacking group goals and group supports. This explains why married people are less likely to commit suicide than single people, and why married people with children are not as likely to kill themselves as those who are childless. Being an important part of a group gives meaning and purpose to life. This lack of group supports also explains why Protestants during Durkheim's day had a higher suicide rate than Catholics. The Catholic religion provided believers with many group supports, including the belief in the authority of religious leaders to interpret the Scriptures. Catholics also believed that through the confessional, sinners could be redeemed. Protestants, on the other hand, were expected to be their own priests, reading and interpreting God's word. When guilty of sin, Protestants again were alone. There was no confessional where a priest would assure one of forgiveness. The differences in theology left individual Protestants without religious authority and with a greater sense of uncertainty. This relatively greater isolation left Protestants without the group of believers and the authority of priests in times of stress.

Altruistic suicide occurs in a completely different type of group setting. When groups are highly cohesive, the individual member of such a collectivity tends to be group oriented. Such a group might expect its members to kill themselves for the good of the group under certain conditions. Soldiers may be expected to leave the relative safety of their foxholes and attack a strategic hill even though the odds are very much against them. The strong allegiance to one's group may force such an act, which would otherwise seem quite irrational. The kamikaze attacks by Japanese pilots during World War II were suicide missions where the pilot guided the ammunition-laden plane into a target. These pilots gave their lives because of their ultimate allegiance to a social group—clearly an example of altruistic suicide. Another example of obligatory suicide for the good of the group is found among Eskimos. Because life is so tenuous in their harsh environment, Eskimos are expected to carry their full burden in providing for the survival of the group. When individuals become too old and feeble to provide their share, they provide for the survival of the group by taking their own lives.

The third type of suicide—**anomic suicide**—is also related to the individual's attachment to a group. It differs from the other two types in that it refers especially to the condition where the expectations of a group are ambiguous or they conflict with other sets of expectations. Typically, behavior is regulated by a clear set of rules (norms). But there are times when these rules lose their clarity and certainty for individuals. This is a condition of anomie (normlessness). Anomie usually occurs in a situation of rapid change. Examples of anomic situations are: emigration from one society to another, movement from a rural area to an urban one, rapid loss of status, overnight wealth, widowhood, divorce, and drastic inflation or deflation. In all these cases, people are often not sure how to behave. They are not certain of their goals. Life may appear aimless. Whenever the constraints on behavior are suddenly lifted, the probability of suicide increases. The irony is that we tend to be comfortable under the tyranny of the group and that freedom from such constraints is often intolerable. The sexual freedom of married persons in U.S. society, for example, is highly regulated. There is only one legitimate sex partner. The unmarried person is not limited. But while married persons might fantasize that such a life is "nirvana," the replacement of regulated sexual behavior with such freedom is a condition of normlessness conducive to higher suicide rates (see Cole, 1975:9).

Group Affects Perceptions.   The group may affect our perceptions. Apparently, our wish to conform is so great that we often give in to group pressure. Solomon Asch, a social psychologist, has tested this proposition by asking the subjects in an experiment to compare the length of lines on cards (Asch, 1958). The subjects were asked one at a time to identify verbally the longest line. All the subjects but one were confederates of the experimenter, coached to give the same wrong answer, placing the lone subject in the awkward position of having the evidence of his senses unanimously contradicted. Each experiment consisted of 18 trials, with the confederates giving wrong responses on 12 and correct ones on 6. For the 50 subjects going through this ordeal, the average number of times they went along with the majority with incorrect judgments was 3.84. While 13 of the 50 were independent and gave responses in accord with their perceptions, 37 (74 percent) gave in to the group pressure at least once (12 did 8 or more times). In other experiments where the confederates were not unanimous in their responses, the subjects were freed from the overwhelming group pressure and generally had confidence enough in their perceptions to give the correct answer.

Muzafer Sherif also conducted a series of experiments to determine the extent of conformity among individuals (Sherif, 1958). An individual subject was placed in a dark room to observe a pinpoint of light. The subject was asked to describe how many inches the light moved (the light appears to move, even though it is stationary, because of what is called the "autokinetic effect"). In repeated experiments each of the subjects tended to be consistent as to how far they felt the light had moved. When placed in a group, however, individuals modified their observations to make them more consistent with those of the others in the room. After repeated exposures, the group arrived at a collective judgment. The important point about this experiment is that the group, unlike the one in the Asch experiment, was composed entirely of naive subjects. Therefore, the conclusion about group pressure on individual members is more valid, reflecting natural group processes.

Group Affects Convictions.   Sectarians with group support maintain their conviction despite contrary evidence. Leon Festinger and his associates at the University of Minnesota carefully studied a group which believed that a great flood would submerge the West Coast from Seattle to Chile on December 21 of that year (Festinger, Riecken, and Schacter, 1956). On the eve of the predicted cataclysm the leader received a message that her group should be ready to leave at midnight in a flying saucer that had been dispatched to save them. The group of ten waited expectantly at midnight for the arrival of the saucer. It did not appear and finally at 4:45 A.M. leader announced that she had received another communication. The message was that the world had been spared the disaster because of the force of good found among this small band of believers. Festinger was especially interested in how the group would handle this disconfirmation of prophecy. But this group, like other millennial groups of history, reacted to the disconfirmation by reaffirming their beliefs and doubling their efforts to win converts.

Group Affects Health and Life.   Membership in a group may have an effect on one's health and even life itself. Pakistan has a caste system; children are destined to occupy the stratum of society into which they are born. Their occupation will be that of their parents with no questions asked. One of the lowest castes is that of beggar. Since the child of a beggar will be a beggar and the most successful beggars are deformed, the child will be deformed by his family (usually by an uncle). Often the method is to break the child's back because the resulting deformity is so wretched. All parents wish success for their children, and the beggar family wishing the same is forced by the constraints of the rigid social system to physically disable their child for life.

There is a religious sect in Cortez, Colorado, the "Church of the First Born," which does not believe in traditional medical care. A three-year-old boy, whose mother belonged to this sect, died of diphtheria. The boy had never been immunized for this disease. Moreover, the mother refused medical treatment for her son after the illness had been diagnosed. The mother knew the consequences of her refusal of medical treatment because her nephew had died of diphtheria, but her faith and the faith of the other members kept her from saving her son's life. This is dramatic evidence for the power of the group to curb what we erroneously call "maternal instinct."

Another example of a group demanding hazardous behavior of its members is found among some religious sects of Appalachia that encourage the handling of poisonous snakes (rattlesnakes, water moccasins, and copperheads) as part of worship. Members pick up handfuls of poisonous snakes, throw them on the ground, pick them up again, thrust them under their shirts and blouses, and even cover their heads with clusters of snakes. The ideology of the group thus encourages members to literally put their faith to the ultimate test—death. The ideology is especially interesting because it justifies death by snakebite as well as being spared the bite or recovering if bitten.

> The serpent-handlers say the Lord causes a snake to strike in order to refute scoffers' claims that the snakes' fangs have been pulled. They see each recov-

ery from snakebite as a miracle wrought by the Lord—and each death as a sign that the Lord "really had to show the scoffers how dangerous it is to obey His commandments." Since adherents believe that death brings one to the throne of God, some express an eagerness to die when He decides they are ready. Those who have been bitten and who have recovered seem to receive special deference from other members of the church. (Gerrard, 1968:23)

Group Affects Behavior.   The group can alter the behavior of members, even behaviors that involve basic human drives. Human beings are biologically programmed to eat, drink, sleep, and engage in sexual activity, but human groups significantly shape how these biological drives are met. How we eat, when we eat, and what we eat are all greatly influenced by social groups. Some groups have rigid rules that require periods of fasting. Others have festivals where huge quantities of food and drink are consumed. Sexual behavior is also controlled. Although there is a universal sex drive, mating is not a universal activity among adults. Some persons, because of their group membership, take vows of chastity. Some persons, because they have certain physical or mental traits, are often labeled by groups as undesirable and are therefore involuntarily chaste. Some societies are obsessed with sex while others are not. An example of the latter is the Dani tribe of New Guinea. Sexual intercourse is delayed between marriage partners until exactly two years after the ceremony. After the birth of a child there is a five-year period of abstinence.

These dramatic examples of the power of groups over individuals should not keep us from recognizing the everyday and continual constraints on behavior. Our everyday activities, our perceptions and interpretations, and our attitudes are the product of our group memberships. The constraints, however, are for the most part subtle and go unrecognized as such. In short, what we think of as autonomous behavior is generally not autonomous at all.

In summary, social groups undergo a universal process—the process of social organization. Through enduring social interaction a matrix of social expectations emerges which guides behavior in prescribed channels, making social life patterned and therefore predictable. Thus, social organizations tend to be stable. But this is also a process, as Figure 2–1 indicates.

Interaction among the social actors in a social organization is constant and continuous, reinforcing stability but also bringing about change. Social organizations are never static. New ideas and new expectations emerge over time. Social change, however, is generally gradual. This is because, as shown in Figure 2–1, while social organizations are human-made, the creation, like Frankenstein's monster, to an important degree controls the creator. The culture that emerges takes on a sacred quality (the sanctity of tradition) that is difficult to question. This profoundly affects the attitudes and behaviors of the social actors in the social organization and the organization itself. As Wilbert Moore, the late distinguished sociologist, has put it:

Man is an inevitably social animal, and one whose social behavior is scarcely guided by instinct. He learns social behavior, well or poorly of one sort or another. [As a member of social groups] he invents values for himself and his

Figure 2–1
Process of Social Organization

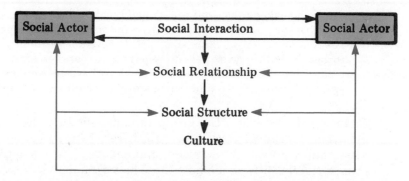

Source: This scheme is adapted from that developed by Marvin E. Olsen, *The Process of Social Organization,* 2nd ed. (New York: Holt, Rinehart and Winston, 1976).

collectivities, rules for his conduct, knowledge to aid him in predicting and controlling his environment, gods to reward and punish him, and other ingenious elements of the human condition. . . . Once [the products of this activity] are established in the human consciousness, they become, in turn, guides to behavior. (Moore, 1969:283)

THE SOCIAL STRUCTURE OF SOCIETY

Primary and secondary groups illustrate nicely the process and the components of social organization. But each of these groups exists in a larger social setting—a context that is also structured with norms, statuses, roles, and mechanisms of social control. These are the components of social structure through which society affects our attitudes and behaviors regardless of our other group memberships.

A **society** is the largest social organization to which persons owe their allegiance. It is an aggregate of people, united by a common culture, who are relatively autonomous and self-sufficient, and who live in a definite geographical location. It is difficult to imagine a society undergoing the same processes as other, smaller, social organizations because societies are typically composed of so many different persons and groups, none of whom were present at the beginning of the society. But the conceptual scheme for the process of social organization shown in Figure 2–1 is also applicable at the societal level. Continuing interaction among the members reinforces stability but also is a source of change. At any given time, the actors in the society are constrained by the norms, values, and roles that are the result of hundreds of years of evolution.

Society as a Social System

A society is a **social system,** composed of interdependent parts that are linked together into a boundary-maintaining whole. This concept of system implies that there is order and predictability within. Moreover, there are clear boundaries to a system in terms of membership and territory. Finally, the parts are independent. The economy illustrates this interdependence nicely. There is a

division of labor in society that provides a wide range of products and services meeting the needs of society's members. The presence of economic booms and depressions illustrates further the interdependence in society. For example, a depression comes about (in overly simplistic terms) when the flow of money is restricted by high taxes, high interest rates, high unemployment, and restricted buying practices by individuals. When large numbers of persons delay buying items such as a new car or refrigerator because they are uncertain of the future, the sales of these items decline dramatically. This decrease itself is a source of further pessimism, thereby further dampening sales. The price of stocks in these companies will, of course, plummet under these conditions, causing further alarm. Moreover, many workers in these industries will be laid off. These newly unemployed persons, in turn, will purchase only the necessities, thereby throwing other industries into panic as their sales decline. A depression, then, is the result of actions by individual consumers; boards of directors of corporations, banks, savings and loan associations; individual and institutional investors; and the government. Additionally, the actions of this nation and the actions of other nations greatly affect the economic conditions of each other because nations, too, form an interdependent network.

Culture of Society

Culture explains much individual and group behavior, as well as the persistence of most aspects of social life. Social scientists studying a society foreign to them must spend months, perhaps years, learning the culture of that group. They must learn the meanings for the symbols (written and spoken language, gestures, and rituals) employed by the individuals in that society. They must know the feelings people share as to what is appropriate or inappropriate behavior. Additionally, they need to know the rules of the society: which activities are considered important, the skills members have in making and using tools, as well as the knowledge members need to exist in that society. In short, analysts must discover all the knowledge that people share—that is, they must know the culture. A full discussion of culture and its transmission is found in Chapters 5–8.

Social Classes

A structural component of societies is **social stratification,** the hierarchical arrangement of people in terms of power, prestige, and resources. This universal phenomenon of social inequality is so important for the understanding of individual behavior and the structure of society that Chapters 9–11 are devoted to it. At the individual level, one's placement in the hierarchy directly affects self-perception, motivation, political attitudes, and the degree of advantage or disadvantage in school, in the economy, in the courts, and even for life itself. At the societal level, the extent of inequality affects the types and magnitude of social problems, societal stability, and economic growth.

Social Institutions

One distinguishing characteristic of societies is the existence of a set of institutions. The popular usages of this term are imprecise and omit some important sociological considerations. An institution is not anyone or anything that is established and traditional (for example, a janitor who has worked at the same school for forty-five years). An institution is not limited to specific organizations such as a school or a prison or a hospital. An institution is much broader in scope and importance than a person, a custom, or a social organization. **Institutions** are social arrangements that channel behavior in prescribed ways in the important areas of social life. They are interrelated sets of normative elements—norms, values, and role expectations—that the persons making up the society have devised and passed on to succeeding generations in order to provide "permanent" solutions to society's perpetually unfinished business.

Institutions are cultural imperatives. They serve as regulatory agencies, channeling behavior in culturally prescribed ways.

> Institutions provide procedures through which human conduct is patterned, compelled to go, in grooves deemed desirable by society. And this trick is performed by making the grooves appear to the individual as the only possible ones. (Berger, 1963:87)

For example, a society instills in its members predetermined channels for marriage. Instead of allowing the sexual partners a host of options, it is expected in American society that the couple will marry and set up a conjugal household. Although the actual options are many, the partners choose what society demands. In fact, they do not consider the other options as valid (for example, polygyny, polyandry, group marriage). The result is a patterned arrangement that regulates sexual behavior and attempts to ensure a stable environment for the care of dependent children.

Institutions arise from the uncoordinated actions of multitudes of individuals over time. These actions, procedures, and rules evolve into a set of expectations that appear to have a design, because the consequences of these expectations provide solutions that help maintain social stability. The design is accidental, however; it is a product of cultural evolution.

All societies face problems in common. Although the variety of solutions is almost infinite, there is a functional similarity in their consequence, which is stability and maintenance of the system. Table 2–1 gives a number of common societal problems and the resulting institutions. This partial list of institutions shows the type of societal problems for which solutions are continually sought. All societies, for instance, have some form of the family, education, polity, economy, and religion. The variations on each of these themes that are found in societies are almost beyond imagination. These variations, while most interesting, are beyond the scope of this book. By looking at the interrelated norms, values, and role expectations that provide "pat" solutions to fundamental societal problems, we shall begin to understand American society.

Institutions are, by definition, conservative. They are the answer of custom and tradition to questions of survival. While absolutely necessary for unity and stability, institutions in contemporary American society are often outmoded, inefficient, and unresponsive to the incredibly swift changes brought about by technological advances, population shifts, and increasing worldwide interdependence. Let us look briefly at problems within two institutions—the polity and the economy.

The polity is based on a set of norms that were for the most part appropriate for another age. Current laws, for example, penalize the cities, which

Table 2–1
Common Societal Problems and Their Institutions

Societal Problems	Institution
Sexual regulation; maintenance of stable units that ensure continued births and care of dependent children	Family
Socialization of the newcomers to the society	Education
Maintenance of order; the distribution of power	Polity
Production and distribution of goods and services; ownership of property	Economy
Understanding the transcendental; the search for meaning of life and death and the place of humankind in the world	Religion
Understanding the physical and social realms of nature	Science
Providing for physical and emotional health care	Medicine

have experienced an eroding tax base, and benefit the wealthier suburbs. The government bureaucracy is so large and unwieldy that it is unresponsive to all but the large and powerful interest groups. A final example is of ultimate importance. This is the inability to control the expansion and use of nuclear weapons throughout the world.

The American economic system, based on a philosophy of free enterprise, is also outmoded in many respects. Capitalism has always thrived in an environment when there were people to exploit (slaves, unskilled and semiskilled labor, colonies), but these exploited groups worldwide are no longer passive. The free enterprise mentality, while appropriate in an expansionist setting with seemingly inexhaustible resources, is inappropriate in a world of shortages. Consumption for its own (and profit's) sake is no longer a legitimate goal, for it hastens the end of resources and eventual chaos. The profit orientation has also meant pollution and ecological catastrophes. The resistance to government planning increases the probability of booms and busts, surpluses and shortages, and high unemployment.

As we look at the institutions of American society we must not forget that institutions are made by people and can therefore be changed. We should be guided by the insight that while institutions appear to have the quality of being "sacred," they are not. They can be changed, but critical examination is imperative. Social scientists must look behind the facades. They must not accept the patterned ways as the only "correct" ways. This is in the American heritage—as found in the Declaration of Independence. As Skolnick and Currie have put it:

> Democratic conceptions of society have always held that institutions exist to serve man, and that, therefore, they must be accountable to men. Where they fail to meet the tests imposed on them, democratic theory holds that they ought to be changed. Authoritarian governments, religious regimes, and reformatories, among other social systems, hold the opposite: in case of misalignment between individuals or groups and the "system," the individuals and groups are to be changed or otherwise made unproblematic. (Skolnick and Currie, 1970:15)

CHAPTER REVIEW

1. Social organization refers to the observed regularities in the behavior of people that are due to social conditions rather than the physiology or psychology of individuals.

2. Social organization includes both social structure and culture. These emerge through enduring social interaction.

3. Social structure involves the linkages and network that transform individuals into a group. It includes the patterns of interaction that emerge, the division of labor, and the links and hierarchy of positions.

4. Culture, the shared beliefs of a group's members, guides conduct. The elements of culture include the norms (rules), roles (behavioral expectations for the occupants of the various positions), and values (the criteria for judging of people, things, and actions).

5. Norms are rules specifying appropriate and inappropriate behaviors. The important norms are called mores and the less important ones are called folkways.

6. Each of us belongs to a number of social organizations and in each we occupy a position

(status). These statuses are a major source of identity for individuals.

7. The behavior expected of a person occupying a status in a social organization is the role. The pressures to conform to role demands ensure that there is stability and predictability in social groups even though member turnover occurs.

8. There are three reasons, however, why role expectations do not make behavior totally predictable: (a) personality differences; (b) inconsistent messages as to what behavior is expected; and (c) multiple group memberships resulting in conflicting demands.

9. Social organizations employ positive sanctions (rewards) and negative sanctions (punishments) to enforce conformity to the norms, values, and roles of the group.

10. One way to classify social groups is on the basis of size and the quality of interaction. Primary groups are those whose members are involved in intimate, face-to-face interaction, with strong emotional attachments. The organization is informal and long-lasting. The members identify strongly with each other and the group. In contrast, secondary groups are large, impersonal, and formally organized. The individual member is relatively unimportant.

11. Primary groups often emerge within secondary groups.

12. Social groups have enormous power over their members and affect their beliefs, behaviors, perceptions, and even health.

13. A society is the largest social organization to which persons owe their allegiance. The society provides the social context for primary and secondary groups. Society places constraints on these groups and their members through its own norms, values, roles, and mechanisms for social control.

14. A society is a social system composed of interdependent parts that are linked together in a boundary-maintaining whole. There is order and predictability within. There is a division of labor providing for self-sufficiency.

15. A society, like other social organizations, has a culture involving norms, roles, values, symbols, and technical knowledge.

16. Unlike other social organizations, a society has a set of institutions. These are social arrangements that channel behavior in prescribed ways in the important areas of social life.

17. Institutions are conservative, providing the answers of custom and tradition to questions of social survival. While absolutely necessary for unity and stability, institutions can be outmoded, inefficient, and unresponsive to the swift changes of contemporary life.

KEY TERMS

Social organization	Norms	Secondary group
Social structure	Values	Egoistic suicide
Culture	Social roles	Altruistic suicide
Sociology	Folkways	Anomic suicide
Aggregate	Mores	Society
Group	Status	Social system
Social interaction	Hierarchy	Social stratification
Social relationship	Role	Institution
Realist position	Sanctions	
Nominalist position	Primary group	

STUDY QUESTIONS

1. What is meant by social organization?
   Describe the social organization of a group
   to which you belong, using the appropriate
   sociological concepts.
2. Define the related concepts of status and role.
   What do they have to do with social
   organization?
3. Emile Durkheim has made a sociological
   analysis of the most private of acts—suicide.
   Describe this sociological analysis. How would
   psychologists differ in their explanation of
   this phenomenon?
4. What are social institutions? Explain the apparent anomaly that they are both sources of
   stability in society as well as sources of social
   problems.

FOR FURTHER READING

The Process of Social Organization

Robert K. Merton, *Social Theory and Social Structure* (New York: Free Press, 1968).

S. F. Nadel, *The Theory of Social Structure* (New York: Free Press, 1957).

Marvin E. Olsen, *The Process of Social Organization,* 2nd ed. (New York: Holt, Rinehart and Winston, 1976).

Max Weber, *The Theory of Social and Economic Organization,* A. M. Henderson and Talcott Parsons, trans. (New York: Free Press, 1947).

Micro Structure

Elliot Aronson, *The Social Animal,* 3rd ed. (San Francisco: W. H. Freeman, 1980).

Harold Garfinkel, *Studies in Ethnomethodology* (Englewood Cliffs, NJ: Prentice-Hall, 1967).

Erving Goffman, *Presentation of Self in Everyday Life* (Garden City, NY: Doubleday Anchor Books, 1957).

A. Paul Hare, Robert F. Bales, and Edward Borgatta, eds., *Small Groups* (New York: Alfred A. Knopf, 1965).

Macro Structure

Graham C. Kinloch, *Society as Power* (Englewood Cliffs, NJ: Prentice-Hall, 1989).

Gerhard Lenski and Jean Lenski, *Human Societies: An Introduction to Macrosociology,* 5th ed. (New York: McGraw-Hill, 1987).

Stephen K. Sanderson, *Macrosociology: An Introduction to Human Societies* (New York: Harper and Row, 1988).

Robin Williams, Jr., *American Society: A Sociological Interpretation,* 3rd ed. (New York: Alfred A. Knopf, 1970).

Chapter Three

The Duality of Social Life: Order and Conflict

What is violence? The answer depends on one's vantage point in the power structure because violence is defined as such if the act threatens the power structure. Protesting blacks in South Africa, for example, are perceived by whites as violent whereas the actions of the police to maintain order are seen as violent by the protestors. Similarly, the students in Tiananmen Square in Beijing in the spring of 1989 who demonstrated for increased freedoms were viewed by the Chinese government as a threat and forcibly defeated. The students' actions were depicted on government television as illegitimate (violent) whereas the actions to maintain order were defined as legitimate. From the perspective of the victimized group, however, the actions of the police were illegitimate and, therefore, amounted to "police brutality."

Violence always refers to a disruption of some condition of order, but order, like violence, is also politically defined. "Order" itself can be very destructive to some categories of persons. In South Africa the normal way that society is organized does harm to blacks (poor health care, low wages, segregated facilities, inferior education). Somehow the term *violence* is not applied to high infant mortality and rates of preventable disease that prevail among the poor and powerless in every society. Critics of this type of societal violence might call such harmful outcomes "institutional violence," to imply that the system itself injures and destroys (Skolnick, 1969:3–8).

Violence is also defined politically through the selection process. Some acts of force (to injure persons or to destroy property) are not always forbidden or condemned in U.S. society. Property damaged during celebrations (winning the Super Bowl, on Hallowe'en, or during Mardi Gras) is often overlooked. Even thousands of drunken, noisy, and sometimes destructive college students on the Florida beaches during spring break are allowed for the most part because they are just boisterous youth on a binge (and the money they spend helps the local economy). But if those same thousands of students were to destroy the same amount of property in a demonstration of which the goal was to change the system, then the acts would be defined as "violent" and the police would be called to restore order by force if necessary (which, of course, would not be defined as violence by the authorities). Thus, violence is condemned or condoned through political pressures and decisions. The basic criterion is whether the act is in approved channels or is supportive of existing social and political arrangements. If not supportive, then the acts are, by definition, to be condemned and punished.

In sum, there is a relationship between the power structure and violence. The perception of how violence is defined provides insight toward a greater understanding of the role of conflict and order in society.

The analyst of society begins with a mental picture of its structure. This image (or **model**) influences what scientists look for, what they see, and how they explain the phenomena that occur within the society.

SOCIAL SYSTEMS: ORDER AND CONFLICT

Among the characteristics of societies is one—the existence of segmentation—that is the basis for the two prevailing models of society. Every society is composed of parts. This differentiation may result from differences in age, race, sex, physical prowess, wisdom, family background, wealth, organizational membership, type of work, or any other characteristic considered to be salient by the members. The fundamental question concerning differentiation is this: What is the basic relationship among the parts of society? The two contradictory answers to this question provide the rationale for the two models of society—order and conflict.

One answer is that the parts of society are in harmony. They cooperate because of similar or complementary interests and because they need each other to accomplish those things beneficial to all (for example, production and distribution of goods and services, protection). Another answer is that the subunits of society are basically in competition with each other. This view is based on the assumption that the things people desire most (wealth, power, autonomy, resources, high status) are always in short supply; hence, competition and conflict are universal social phenomena.

The Order Model

The **order model*** attributes to societies the characteristics of cohesion, consensus, cooperation, reciprocity, stability, and persistence. Societies are viewed as social systems, composed of interdependent parts that are linked together into a boundary-maintaining whole. The parts of the system are basically in harmony with each other. The high degree of cooperation (and societal integration) is accomplished because there is a high degree of consensus on societal goals and on cultural values. Moreover, the different parts of the system are assumed to need each other because of complementary interests. Because the primary social process is cooperation and the system is highly integrated, all social change is gradual, adjustive, and reforming. Societies are therefore basically stable units.

For order theorists, the central issue is: What is the nature of the social bond? What holds groups together? This was the focus of one of the most important figures in sociology, Emile Durkheim, the French social theorist of the early 1900s. The various forms of integration were used by Durkheim to explain differences in suicide rates, social change, and the universality of religion (Durkheim, 1933; 1951; 1961).

One way to focus on integration is to determine the manifest and latent consequences of social structures, norms, and social activities. Do these consequences contribute to the integration (cohesion) of the social system? Durkheim, for example, noted that the punishment of crime has the **manifest** (intended) **consequences** of punishing and deterring the criminal. The **latent consequence** (unintended) of punishment, however, is the societal reaffirmation of what is to be considered moral. The society is thereby integrated through belief in the same rules (Durkheim, 1938:64–75).

Taking Durkheim's lead, sociologists of the order persuasion have made many penetrating and insightful analyses of various aspects of society. By focusing on *all* the consequences of social structures and activities—intended and unintended, as well as negative (malintegrative)—we can see behind the facades and thereby understand more fully such disparate social arrangements and activities as ceremonials (from rain dances to sporting events), social stratification, fashion, propaganda, and even political machines.†

The Conflict Model

The assumptions of the **conflict model** (the view of society that posits conflict as a normal feature of social life, influencing the distribution of power, and the direction and magnitude of social change) are opposite from those of the order model. The basic form of interaction is not cooperation but competition,

---

*This model is most often referred to in sociology as *functionalism* or the structural-functional model. It is the basis for the analysis of American society by Robin M. Williams, Jr. (1970).

†See Robert K. Merton's *Social Theory and Social Structure* for an excellent discussion of sociological research from the order (functionalist) perspective (1957:19–84).

which often leads to conflict. Because the individuals and groups of society compete for advantage, the degree of social integration is minimal and tenuous. Social change results from the conflict among competing groups and therefore tends to be drastic and revolutionary. The ubiquitousness of conflict results from the dissimilar goals and interests of social groups. It is, moreover, a result of social organization itself.

The most famous conflict theorist was Karl Marx, who, after examining history, theorized that there exists in every society (except, Marx believed, in the last historical stage of communism) a dynamic tension between two groups—those who own the means of production and those who work for the owners. The powerful will use and abuse the powerless, thereby "sowing the seeds" of their own destruction. The destruction of the elite is accomplished when the dominated unite and overthrow the dominants.

Ralf Dahrendorf, a contemporary conflict theorist, has also viewed conflict as a ubiquitous phenomenon, not because of economic factors as Marx believed, but because of other aspects of social organization. Organization means, among other things, that power will be distributed unequally. The population will therefore be divided into the "haves" and the "have-nots" with respect to power. Because organization also means constraint, there will be a situation in all societies where the constraints are determined by the powerful, thereby further ensuring that the "have-nots" will be in conflict with the "haves"—thus, the important insight that conflict is endemic to social organization.*

One other emphasis of conflict theorists is that the unity present in society is superficial because it results not from consensus but from coercion. The powerful, it is asserted, use force and fraud to keep society running smoothly, with benefits mostly accruing to those in power.

The Duality of Social Life

The basic duality of social life can be seen by summarizing the opposite ways in which order and conflict theorists view the nature of society. If asked, "What is the fundamental relationship among the parts of society?" the answers of order and conflict theorists would disagree. This disagreement leads to and is based upon a number of related assumptions about society. These are summarized in Table 3–1.

One interesting but puzzling aspect of Table 3–1 is that these two models are held by different scientific observers *of the same phenomenon.* How can such different assumptions be derived by experts on society? The answer is that both models are correct. Each focuses on reality—but only part of that reality. Scientists have tended to accept one or the other of these models, thereby focusing on only part of social reality, for at least two reasons: (1) one model or the other was in vogue at the time of the scientist's intellectual

---

*This description is a very superficial account of a complex process that has been fully described by Ralf Dahrendorf (1959).

Table 3–1
Duality of Social Life: Assumptions of the Order and Conflict Models of Society

	Order Model	Conflict Model
Question:	What is the fundamental relationship among the parts of society?	
Answer:	Harmony and cooperation.	Competition, conflict, domination, and subordination.
Why:	The parts have complementary interests. Basic consensus on societal norms and values.	The things people want are always in short supply. Basic dissensus on societal norms and values.
Degree of integration:	Highly integrated.	Loosely integrated. Whatever integration is achieved is the result of force and fraud.
Type of social change:	Gradual, adjustive, and reforming.	Abrupt and revolutionary.
Degree of stability.	Stable.	Unstable.

development*; or (2) one model or the other made the most sense for the analysis of the particular problems of interest—for example, the interest of Emile Durkheim, who devoted his intellectual energies to determining what holds society together, or the fundamental concern of Karl Marx, who explored the causes of revolutionary social change. The analyses of sport and social problems are two important areas where sociologists have been influenced by the order and conflict models. Let us turn to these contrary ways to view these two social phenomena before examining a synthesis of the two models.

Sport from the Order and Conflict Perspectives.   Order theorists examining any aspect of society emphasize the contribution that aspect makes to the stability of society (this section is dependent on Coakley, 1986:24–33). Sport, from this perspective, preserves the existing social order in several ways. To begin, sport symbolizes our way of life—competition, individualism, achievement, and fair play. Not only is sport compatible with basic American values but it also is a powerful mechanism for socializing youth to adopt desirable character traits, to accept authority, and to strive for excellence. Sport also supports the status quo by promoting the unity of society's members through

---

*Order theorists have dominated American sociology since the 1930s. This has led to the charge by "radical" sociologists that the contemporary sociology establishment has served as the official legitimator of the system—not the catalyst for changing the system. This radical challenge to order theory gained momentum in the 1960s and has generated a great deal of subsequent conflict theorizing.

Social Scientists and Values

Social scientists are not value neutral. Whether they admit it or not, they take sides by adopting a way of perceiving and interpreting the social world. This does not render social science useless, as the late Michael Harrington, a highly esteemed social scientist and political activist, has argued in the following excerpt:

> Truths about society can be discovered only if one takes sides. . . . You must stand somewhere in order to see social reality, and where you stand will determine much of what you see and how you see it. The data of society are, for all practical purposes, infinite. You need criteria that will provisionally permit you to bring some order into that chaos of data and to distinguish between relevant and irrelevant factors or, for that matter, to establish that there are facts in the first place. These criteria cannot be based upon the data for they are the precondition of the data. They represent—and the connotations of the phrase should be sa-vored—a "point of view." That involves intuitive choices, a value-laden sense of what is meaningful and what is not. . . .
>
> The poor, I suggest, see a different social world from the rich—and so do those who think, whether consciously or not, from the vantage point of the poor or the rich. I was born into and have lived my life in the middle class. But I have tried to write from the point of view of the poor and excluded, those in the United States and elsewhere. I am therefore a deeply biased man, a taker of sides; but that is not really distinctive at all. Everyone else is as biased as I am, including the most "objective" social scientist. The difference between us is that I am frank about my values while many other analysts fool both themselves and their audiences with the illusion that they have found an intellectual perch that is free of Earth's social field of gravity.

Source: From *Taking Sides* by Michael Harrington © 1985 by Michael Harrington. Reprinted by permission of Henry Holt and Company, Inc.

patriotism (e.g., national anthem, militaristic displays, and other nationalistic rituals accompanying sports events). Can you imagine, for example, a team that espouses antiestablishment values in its name, logo, mascot, and pageantry? Would we tolerate a major league team called the Atlanta Atheists? the Boston Bigamists? the Pasadena Pacifists? or the Sacramento Socialists? Finally, sport inspires us through the excellent and heroic achievements of athletes, the magical moments in sport when the seemingly impossible happens, and the feelings of unity in purpose and of loyalty of fans.

Clearly, then, sport from the order perspective is good. Sport socializes youth into proper channels; sport unites; and sport inspires. Thus, to challenge or criticize sport is to challenge the very foundation of our society's social order.

Conflict theorists argue that the social order reflects the interests of the powerful. Sport is organized at whatever level—whether youth, high school, college, or professional—to exploit athletes and meet the goals of the powerful (e.g., public relations, prestige, and profits).

Sport inhibits the potential for revolution by society's "have-nots" in three ways. First, sport validates the prevailing myths of capitalism such as anyone can succeed if he or she works hard enough. If a person fails, it's his or her fault and not that of the system. Second, sport serves as an "opiate of the masses" by diverting attention away from the harsh realities of poverty, unemployment, and dismal life chances by giving them a "high" (Hoch, 1972). And, third, sport gives false hope to blacks and other oppressed members of society as they see sport as a realistic avenue of upward social mobility. The high visibility of wealthy athletes provides "proof" that athletic ability translates into monetary success. The reality, of course, is that only an extremely small percentage of aspiring athletes ever achieves professional status. In basketball, for example, there are about 500,000 high school players in any one year, about 3,667 college seniors playing, and only about 50 of them will play as rookies at the professional level (Coakley, 1986:290).

Conflict theorists agree with order theorists on many of the facts but differ significantly in interpretation. Both agree that sport socializes youth but conflict theorists view this negatively, since they see sport as a mechanism to get youth to learn to follow orders, work hard, and fit into a system that is not necessarily beneficial to them. Both agree that sport maintains the status quo. But instead of this being interpreted as good as the order theorists maintain, conflict theorists view this as bad because it reflects and reinforces the unequal distribution of power and resources in society.

Social Problems from the Order and Conflict Perspectives. There is a general agreement among sociologists that a **social problem** reflects a violation of normative expectations. It is a situation that is incompatible with the values of a significant number of people, who agree that the situation should be altered. Under this rubric fall such different phenomena as poverty, homelessness, crime, discrimination, drug addiction, political extremism, and mental illness.

The order and conflict perspectives constrain their adherents to view the causes, consequences, and remedies of social problems in opposing ways. The order perspective focuses on deviants themselves. This approach (which has been the conventional way of studying social problems) asks: Who are the deviants? What are their social and psychological backgrounds? With whom do they associate? Deviants somehow do not conform to the standards of the dominant group; they are assumed to be out of phase with conventional behavior. This is believed to occur most often as a result of inadequate socialization. In other words, deviants have not internalized the norms and values of society because they either are brought up in an environment of conflicting value systems (as are children of immigrants or the poor in a middle-class school) or are under the influence of a deviant subculture such as a gang. Because the order theorist uses the prevailing standards to define and label deviants, the existing practices and structures of society are accepted implicitly. The remedy is to rehabilitate the deviants so that they conform to the societal norms.

The conflict theorist takes quite a different approach to social problems. The adherents of this perspective criticize order theorists for blaming the victim (Ryan, 1976). To focus on the individual deviate is to locate the symptom, not the disease. Individual deviants are a manifestation of a failure of society to meet the needs of individuals. The sources of crime, poverty, drug addiction, and racism are found in the laws, the customs, the quality of life, the distribution of wealth and power, and in the accepted practices of schools, governmental units, and corporations. In this view, then, the schools are the problem, not the dropouts; the quality of life, not mental illness; the maldistribution of wealth, not the poor; the roadblocks to success for minority-group members, not apathy on their part. The established system, in this view, is not "sacred." Because the system is the primary source of social problems, it, not the individual deviant, must be restructured.

Although most of this book attempts to strike a balance between the order and conflict perspectives, the conflict model is clearly favored when social problems are brought into focus. This is done explicitly for three reasons: (1) the focus on the deviant has dominated sociology and there is a need for balance; (2) the subject matter of sociology is not individuals, who are the special province of psychology, but society. If sociologists do not make a critical analysis of the social structure, who will? Also, (3) we are convinced that the source of social problems is found within the institutional framework of society. Thus, a recurrent theme of this book is that social problems are societal in origin and not the exclusive function of individual pathologies.

SYNTHESIS OF THE ORDER AND CONFLICT MODELS

The assumptions of both models are contradictory for each comparison shown in Table 3–1, and their contradictions highlight the duality of social life. Social interaction can be harmonious or acrimonious. Societies are integrated or divided, stable or unstable. Social change can be fast or slow, revolutionary or evolutionary.

Taken alone, each of these perspectives fosters a faulty perception and interpretation of society, but taken together, they complement each other and present a complete and realistic model. A synthesis that combines the best of each model would appear, therefore, to be the best perspective for understanding the structure and process of society (see van den Berghe, 1963; Lenski, 1966).

The initial assumption of a synthesis approach is that the *processes of stability and change are properties of all societies.* There is an essential paradox to human societies: they are always ordered; they are always changing. These two elemental properties of social life must be recognized by the observer of society. Within any society there are forces providing impetus for change *and* there are forces insisting on rooted permanence. Allen Wheelis (1958) has labeled these two contrary tendencies as the instrumental process and the institutional process, respectively.

The **instrumental process** is based on the desire for technological change—to find new and more efficient techniques to achieve goals. The **institutional process,** on the other hand, designates all those activities that are dominated by the quest for certainty. We are bound in our activities, often by customs, traditions, myths, and religious beliefs. So there are rites, taboos, and mores that persons obey without thinking. So, too, are there modern institutions such as monotheism, monogamy, private property, and the sovereign state, all of which are coercive in that they limit freedom of choice, but they are assumed proper by almost all individuals in American society.

These two processes constitute the **dialectic** (opposing forces) of society. As contrary tendencies, they generate tension because the instrumental forces are constantly prodding the institutions to change when it is not their nature to do so.

The second assumption is that *societies are organized but the very process of organization generates conflict.* Organization implies, among other things, differential allocation of power. Inequalities in power are manifested in at least two conflict-generating ways: differentials in decision making, and inequalities in the system of social stratification (social classes and minority groups). Scarce resources can never be distributed equally to all persons and groups in society. The powerful are always differentially rewarded and make the key decisions as to the allocation of scarce resources.

A third basic assumption for a synthesis model is that *society is a social system.* The term *social system* has several important implications: (1) that there is not chaos but some semblance of order—that action within the unit is, in a general way, predictable; (2) that boundaries exist which may be in terms of geographical space or membership; and (3) that there are parts which are interdependent—thus conveying the reality of differentiation and unity. A society is a system made up of many subsystems (for example, groups, organizations, communities). Although these are all related in some way, some are strongly linked to others, while others have only a remote linkage. The interdependence of the parts implies further that events and decisions in one sector may have a profound influence on the entire system. A strike in the transportation industry, for example, eventually impinges upon all individuals and groups. But some events have little or no effect upon all of American society. Most important for the synthesis approach is the recognition that the parts of the system may have complementary interests with other parts but may also have exclusive, incompatible interests and goals. There is generally some degree of cooperation and harmony found in society because of consensus over common goals and because of similar interests (for example, defense against external threats). Some degree of competition and dissensus is also present because of incompatible interests, scarcity of resources, and unequal rewards. Societies, then, are imperfect social systems.

A fourth assumption is that *societies are held together by complementary interests, by consensus on cultural values, but also by coercion.* Societies do cohere. There are forces that bind diverse groups together into a single entity. The emphasis of both order and conflict models provides twin bases for such integration—consensus and coercion.

Finally, *social change is a ubiquitous phenomenon in all societies. It may be gradual or abrupt, reforming or revolutionary.* All social systems change. Order theorists have tended to view change as a gradual phenomenon occurring either because of innovation or because of differentiation (for example, dividing units into subunits to separate activities and make the total operation more efficient within the society). This view of change is partially correct.

Change can also be abrupt; it can come about because of internal violence, or it may result from forces outside the society (that is, reaction to events outside the system, or accepting the innovations of others).

To summarize, a synthesis of the order and conflict models views society as having "two faces of equal reality—one of stability, harmony, and consensus and one of change, conflict, and constraint" (Dahrendorf, 1968:127).

The remainder of this chapter illustrates the duality of social life by examining American society from the perspectives of the conflict and order theorists. We consider the sources of disunity in the United States and the major instances of violence that have occurred throughout American history. Despite the existence of division and violence, the United States is unified at least minimally. We therefore also consider the factors that work to unify.

Division and Violence

Societies are integrated but disunity and disharmony also exist to some degree in all societies. It is especially important to examine the segmenting influences in American society, for they aid in explaining contemporary conflict and social change.

Social scientists studying the divisive forces in American society have found that in small groups, the more heterogeneous the group, the more likely cliques will form. A group composed of members of one religion, for example, cannot form cliques on the basis of religion, but one with three religions represented has the potential of subdividing into three parts (Davies, 1966). This principle applies to larger organizations as well, including societies. The United States, then, has the potential of many, many subgroups since it is so diverse. The United States is, in effect, a mosaic of different groups—different on a number of dimensions, such as occupation, racial background, education, and economic circumstances. Let us briefly examine these and other dimensions and the manner in which they bring about segmentation in American society.

Size.   The United States is large in size, in both number of people and expanse of land. Both these facts have a segmenting influence in U.S. society. With respect to population size, there is an accepted sociological proposition that states: "As the population of a social organization increases, the number of its parts and the degree of their specialization also increases" (Mott, 1965:50). If, as in the United States, there is not only a large population (over 250 million) but also a high level of technology, then the division of labor becomes very refined. This division is so refined that there are over 30,000 different occupations recognized and catalogued by the Bureau of the Census.

If they have specialized occupations, they will probably interact most often with persons like themselves. Because of similar interests, they will tend to cooperate with each other and perhaps compete with other groups for advantage. An important social theorist of the early 1900s, Robert Michels, wrote about this tendency for exclusion and conflict as a universal tendency in all social organizations.

> By a universally applicable social law, every organ of the collectivity, brought into existence through the need for the division of labor, creates for itself, as soon as it becomes consolidated, interests peculiar to itself. The existence of these special interests involves a necessary conflict with the interests of collectivity. (Michels, 1966:389)

A second segmenting factor related to size has to do with land rather than population. The United States, excluding Alaska and Hawaii, has an area of 3,615,123 square miles. Found within this large territory is a wide range in topography and climate. Some areas are sparsely settled, others not. Some regions are attracting new residents at a much faster rate than others.

Traditionally there have been pronounced regional differences (and sometimes rivalries) because each region had its own economic specialization (that is, its own industry and agriculture) and each was relatively isolated from the influences of the others. The revolutions in manufacturing, transportation, and communication have helped to break down this regionalism.

Although regionalism has been declining, it remains a force that sometimes divides Americans. As evidence of this, many votes in Congress show that regional considerations often outweigh national ones. Many nonsouthern Americans have stereotyped ideas of southerners. Consequently, communication within American society is often blocked and interaction stifled because persons from one region feel not only physically separate from but also superior to persons from other regions.

Social Class.   Economic differences provide important sources of division in American society. There is a natural resentment of persons without the necessities of life toward those with a bountiful supply of not only the necessities but luxuries as well. There is also hostility toward a system that provides excessive benefits (or excessive hurdles) to persons not on the basis of demonstrated skills but on family background.

Status (prestige) differentials also divide Americans. Organizations, residential areas, and social clubs sometimes exclude certain persons and groups because of their social "inferiority."

Race.   Throughout human history race has been used as a criterion for differentiation. If any factor makes a difference in American society, it is race. Blacks, Native Americans, Mexican Americans, Asian Americans, and other minority racial groups have often been systematically excluded from residential areas, occupations, and organizations, and even sometimes denied equal rights under the law. Although the overt system of racial discrimination has changed, racist acts continue in American society, with the result that these disadvantaged groups continue to be treated as second-class citizens.

Racial strife has occurred throughout American history. Slave revolts, Indian battles, race riots, and lynchings have occurred with regularity. Racial conflict continues today not only in the ghettos of large cities but in most neighborhoods where the minority group is large enough to be perceived by the majority as a threat, in universities and secondary schools, in factories and other places of work, and in the armed forces.

Many members of racial minorities want justice now. It is equally clear that many majority-group members will do virtually anything to keep the status quo (that is, to retain an advantageous position for themselves). Some minority persons seeking to shake the status quo may participate in various acts of violence. This violence brings repression by the powerful, which further angers and frustrates the minority—thus a treadmill of violence and division.

The racial composition of the United States is changing and this will likely lead to increased tension and conflict. The two largest racial minorities are increasing in number faster than the rest of the population. By 2000, blacks will number nearly 36.4 million (13.0 percent of the population) and Hispanics, the fastest growing minority, will likely number 30.3 million (10.8 percent of the population—up from 4 percent in 1970) (Davis, Haub, and Willette, 1983:39). Also in recent years refugees in great numbers have fled to the United States. In 1987, for example, a total of 601,000 legal immigrants entered the United States, including 258,000 from Asia and 249,000 from Latin America (U.S. Bureau of the Census, 1989:10). Not classified as refugees are the million or so undocumented immigrants mostly from Mexico and South America who enter the country illegally each year. These refugees have brought problems that have led to growing hostility. Jobs are in short supply. Taxes are already high, and these groups require large amounts of aid. The poor fear that these new refugees will take jobs, increase demands on cheap housing, and decrease welfare currently allocated to them. Schools and other public agencies cannot meet the demands of these new groups.

Ethnic Groups.   The United States is inhabited by a multitude of ethnic groups that migrated to this country in different waves and that continue to do so. These groups have distinctive lifestyles and customs. One reason for this is that they have retained a cultural heritage brought to this country from another society. Another, and very important for their continued distinctiveness, is the structure of American society. The persistence of subordination, discriminatory housing and work patterns, and other forms of structured inequality encourages solidarity among the disadvantaged (see Taylor, 1979; Yancey, Ericksen, and Juliani, 1976). The uniqueness and strong ethnic identification of immigrant groups is a source of internal strength for them but causes resentment, negative stereotypes, competition, hatred, and conflict as other ethnic groups or members of the dominant majority question their loyalty, resent their success, fear being displaced by them in the job market, and worry about maintaining the integrity of their schools and neighborhoods (Panel 3–2).

Religion.   A wide variety of religious beliefs is found in the United States (see Figure 3–1). Although 59 percent of Americans are Protestants, the variations

Population Today

A pattern of "activity [against Asian Americans] in the form of violence, vandalism, harassment, and intimidation continues to occur across the Nation," the U.S. Civil Rights Commission says in a new draft report. "Incidents were reported in every jurisdiction visited by Commission staff and in other parts of the country as well."

Violence against minorities has an unfortunate history in the U.S., but Asian-directed violence has not been studied until recently. It ranges in seriousness from anti-Asian bumper stickers to assault and homicide. Its victims include such diverse groups as Hmong tribespeople, Korean shopkeepers, and Vietnamese fishermen.

"No single factor has produced current Anti-Asian behavior. Rather it appears to be a combination of many factors of which race is one," says the Commission in its draft report. Among other things, the report reveals economic resentment of, and also profound ignorance about, Asian Americans; for example, the shocking 1982 murder of Vincent Chin in Detroit. Chin, a Chinese American, was fatally beaten in a parking lot by two unemployed auto workers, reportedly because they thought he was Japanese and they were expressing resentment over U.S. sales of Japanese cars.

(The defendants received probatory sentences for manslaughter, but one of them was subsequently convicted under federal law for violating Chin's civil rights and sentenced to 25 years in prison. The Chin case was instrumental in drawing national attention toward Asian-directed violence.)

According to the Commission, one problem is that many citizens evidently do not see people of Asian or Pacific Island origin as the diverse groups they are, even though they come from many different societies and in many cases have been a component of the U.S. population for generations.

Asian Americans number about 5.1 million, about 2.1 percent of the U.S. population as of 1985, according to PRB estimates. Since immigration law reform in 1965 and the influx of Southeast Asian refugees following the Vietnam War, this population group has grown more rapidly. . . . In 1985, 264,691 immigrants to the U.S. i.e., 46 percent of legal immigrants, were Asians. They are concentrated more in some areas than others, but even in the San Francisco area, where Asians are considered concentrated, they account for only 1.12 percent of the total metro area population.

Statistics on the level of violence against Asians are hard to come by, a situation the Commission hopes its findings will help correct. An independent fact-finding agency of the Executive Branch, the Commission has been researching the dilemma since 1984, with field investigations in eight states.

Source: "Anti-Asian Violence Pattern Probed," *Population Today* 14 (No. 7/8, July–August 1986): 9–11.

among them include snake handlers in Appalachia, the Amish who refuse modern conveniences, sects that refuse medical help, literalists who are dogmatic in their narrow views of the Scriptures, and other groups that accept religious pluralism. Among the 28 percent of Americans who are Roman Catholics, great differences exist in beliefs and lifestyles. The same is true when comparing Orthodox, Conservative, and Reformed Jews. And, outside the Judeo-Christian tradition are Buddhists, Muslims, and many other religious organizations and faiths.

Religion, like race and ethnicity, evokes an emotional response in individuals. It is difficult to be neutral about religion. It is almost impossible to accept the idea that religious beliefs other than one's own are equally legitimate. Religion also has a polarizing effect because it is often the basis for selecting

Figure 3–1
**The Clusters
of American
Religion: 1987**

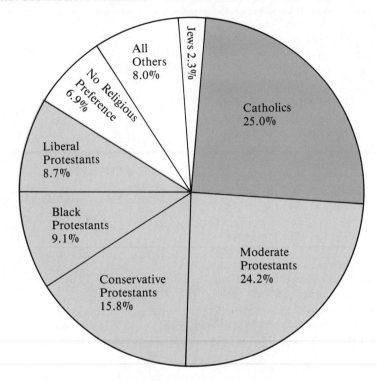

Source: Martin E. Marty, "The Years of the Evangelicals," *The Christian Century* 106 (February 15, 1989): 173.

(or rejecting) mates, friends, neighbors, schools, and employees. Therefore, religious differences in the United States not only differentiate persons but also may provide the basis for conflict.

Religious intolerance is not unknown in American history. Although the nation was founded on the principle of religious freedom, at various times and places Jews, Catholics, Quakers, Mennonites, and atheists have been targets of religious bigotry.

There have been political parties (Know-Nothing Party), organizations (Ku Klux Klan and the American Nazi Party), and demagogues (Louis Farakhan and Lyndon La Rouche) that have been anti-Catholic and anti-Semitic. Their moderate success in attracting followers demonstrates that some Americans are susceptible to such appeals. The effect has been to lessen the probability of interfaith cooperation and enhance the likelihood of conflict.

These segmenting factors create some groups in society that are advantaged and others that are disadvantaged. The former work to perpetuate their advantages while the latter sometimes organize to protest and change the system they consider unfair. But how can these persons change the system if they are self-defined as powerless? A first step is legitimate, polite protest, which usually takes the form of voting, petitions, or writing public officials.

A second option is to use impolite, yet legitimate forms of protest (for example, peaceful demonstrations, picket lines, boycotts, and marches). The third alternative, used when others fail, is to employ illegitimate forms of protest (for example, civil disobedience, riots, bombings, and guerrilla warfare).

Illegitimate protest is selected by dissident groups because of the intransigence of those in power toward change. The dissident groups consider their actions legitimate because they are for a just cause ("the ends justify the means"), but these protests are perceived as illegitimate by those in power. Those in authority resort to force, often intensifying the zeal and purpose of the protester, and frequently rallying previously uncommitted persons to the cause of the dissidents.

Implicit in this section is the notion that highly differentiated social systems, like that in the United States, must cope with the realities of disharmony, conflict of interest, and even violence. There is no alternative to conflict because of the diverse conditions of the American social structure. This is not to say that conflict is altogether bad. There can be positive consequences of conflict for both parties to the conflict and for society as well (Coser, 1966).

All societies have the potential for cleavage and conflict because of the differential allocation of power. Concomitant with having power is the holding of other advantages (prestige, privilege, and economic benefits). Persons with advantage almost invariably wish to keep it, and those without typically want to change the reward system.

This Vietnam veteran renounces his Congressional Medal in protest of U.S. aid to the Contras. Both of these issues—the Vietnam War and U.S. aid to the Contras—divided Americans.

Coupled with the stratification system (the structured inequality of categories of people, see Chapter 9) in the United States are other aspects of social structure that increase the probability of conflict. The United States, perhaps more than any other society, is populated by a multitude of ethnic groups, racial groups, and religious groups. The diversity is further increased by the existence of regional differences and a generation gap. Although assimilation has occurred to some degree, the different groups and categories have not blended into a homogeneous mass, but continue to remain separate—often with a pride that makes assimilation unlikely and conflict possible.

Violence and the Myth of Peaceful Progress

There are two beliefs held typically by Americans that combine to make the **myth of peaceful progress**—the incorrect belief that throughout U.S. history disadvantaged groups have gained their share of power, prosperity, and respectability without violence (see Skolnick, 1969; Graham and Gurr, 1969; Rubenstein, 1970). First, there is a widely held notion that the United States is made up of diverse groups that have learned to compromise differences in a peaceful manner. Second, there is the belief that any group in the United States can gain its share of power, prosperity, and respectability merely by playing the game according to the rules. Hence, there is no need for political violence in the United States, since the system works for the advantage of all.

Because these beliefs are widely shared most Americans do not understand dissent by minority groups. These are believed to be aberrations and are explained away by saying that they are communist inspired, or that some groups are exceptions to the rule because they are basically immoral and irrational. Perhaps the most prevalent explanation locates the source of all violence in the individual psyches of the persons involved.

These explanations are incomplete because they locate the blame outside the system itself. American history shows that, with but few exceptions, powerless and downtrodden groups seeking power have not achieved it without a struggle. American institutions, Rubenstein has noted, are better designed to facilitate the upward mobility of talented individuals than of oppressed groups. "Most groups which have engaged in mass violence have done so only after a long period of fruitless, relatively nonviolent struggle in which established procedures have been tried and found wanting" (Rubenstein, 1970:8). The problem is that the United States, like all other societies, has not and does not allow for the nonviolent transfer of power.

Throughout American history groups that were oppressed resorted to various legitimate and illegitimate means to secure rights and privileges which they believed to be rightfully theirs. Those in power typically reacted either by doing nothing or by repression—the choice depending upon the degree to which the minority groups' actions were perceived as a real threat. The following is a partial list of groups which at various times in American history have resorted to violence to achieve social, economic, or political objectives.

Revolutionary Colonists.   The most notable case of violence by a minority in early American history was the Revolutionary War. The United States was literally born through violence. The American colonists first petitioned the King of England to redress grievances, and when this failed they turned to acts of civil disobedience and finally to eight years of war. "The Declaration of Independence," clearly a revolutionary document, provided the rationale for mass violence:

> We hold these truths to be self-evident, that all men are created equal, that they are endowed by their Creator with certain unalienable Rights, that among these are Life, Liberty, and the pursuit of Happiness. That to secure these rights, Governments are instituted among Men, deriving their just powers from the consent of the governed. That whenever any Form of Government becomes destructive of these ends, it is the Right of the People to alter or to abolish it, and to institute new Government, laying its foundation on such principles and organizing its powers in such form as to them shall seem most likely to effect their Safety and Happiness. Prudence, indeed, will dictate that Governments long established should not be changed for light and transient causes; and accordingly all experiences hath shewn that mankind are more disposed to suffer, while evils are sufferable, than to right themselves by abolishing the forms to which they are accustomed. But when a long train of abuses and usurpations, pursuing invariably the same Object evinces a design to reduce them under absolute Despotism, it is their right, it is their duty, to throw off such Government, and to provide new Guards for their future security.

This document, a cornerstone of American heritage, legitimates the use of violence by oppressed peoples. It could have been written by a modern-day revolutionary. While still revered, its content is no longer taken literally by the bulk of the American citizenry.

Native Americans.   Long before the Revolutionary War and continuing to the present day, Indians attempted to change the order established by whites. When white settlers took their land, ruined their hunting, and imprisoned them on reservations, the Indians fought these occurrences and were systematically suppressed by the United States government (Brown, 1971). In recent years Indians have occasionally boycotted, used violence, or used legal offensives to regain former Indian lands. The last tactic has become especially popular. More than half of the 266 federally recognized tribes have claims in various federal courts.

Exploited Farmers.   Farmers have used violence on occasion to fight economic exploitation. Between the Revolutionary War and 1800, for example, three such revolts took place—Shays's Rebellion, the Whiskey Rebellion, and Fries's Rebellion. The protesting farmer has used various forms of violence (destruction of property, looting, and killing) throughout American history. Some modern farmers have resorted to acts of violence to publicize their demands and to terrorize other farmers in order to present a united front against their opponents.

Slaveholders.   Feeling the threat of the abolitionist movement, white southerners beginning in about 1820 used violent means to preserve slavery. In the early stages this amounted to civil disobedience and later it burst out into fighting in places like "bleeding Kansas." Eventually the South seceded and the Civil War was waged—a classic example of a minority group using violence to force a change and being suppressed by the power of the majority.

WASP Supremacists.   Following the Civil War and continuing to the present day, some whites have engaged in guerrilla warfare, terrorism, and lynching in order to maintain the subjugation of blacks. From 1882 to 1903, for example, 1,985 blacks were killed by southern lynch mobs (Cutler, 1905:177).

Riots, lynchings, and mob actions are not solely southern phenomena. Many Americans from other sections of the country have used these techniques against various "alien" groups (usually Catholics and immigrants from non-Teutonic Europe) in order to maintain their superiority. American history is rife with examples of this phenomenon: "Native Americans" tore apart the Irish section of Philadelphia in 1844; a Roman Catholic church and homes of Irish Catholics were destroyed in Boston in 1854; Chinese and Japanese immigrants were victims of both riots and discrimination, particularly on the West Coast; Japanese, even those who were American citizens, were put in "concentration camps" during World War II because their patriotism was suspect; and Jews have been the objects of physical attack, boycotts, intimidation, and discrimination throughout American history. Perhaps the best contemporary example of mob violence against intruders can be seen in some communities where an all-white neighborhood is faced with one or more Haitian or Vietnamese families moving in. Threats, burning crosses, ostracism, and occasional physical violence have occurred with alarming regularity where black "invasion" of previously all-white areas has taken place. This is not a southern phenomenon but an American one.*

Ethnic Minorities. Immigrant groups (that is, those groups most recently immigrant) as well as racial groups, because they have been the target of discrimination, threats, and physical violence, have themselves participated in violence. Sometimes gangs have attacked the groups responsible for their deprived condition. Most often, however, hostility by immigrants has been aimed at groups with less power, either toward blacks or toward more newly arrived immigrants.

Violence by blacks has occurred throughout American history. Always the victims, they have sometimes responded to violence in kind. During the years of slavery more than 250 insurrections took place. Mass black violence has occurred in many major cities (for example, Chicago and Washington, D.C., in 1919, Detroit in 1943, and again in 1967, Los Angeles in 1965, Newark in 1967, and Miami in 1987).

The rage that racial minorities must feel against whites has surfaced sporadically in small and diffuse ways as well. Most commonly it has been manifested in individual crimes (murder, theft, and rape) or gang assaults on whites or in destruction of property owned by whites.

Labor Disputants. Another relatively powerless group resorting to violence to achieve its aims has been American labor. The workers of the 1870s attempted to organize for collective action against unfair policies of the industrialists. Unions, such as the Knights of Labor, American Federation of Labor, and the Industrial Workers of the World, formed. Their primary tactic was the strike, which in itself is nonviolent. But strikers often used force to keep persons from crossing the picket lines. Nor were the owners blameless. Their refusal to change existing wages, hours, and working conditions was the source of grievance. They sometimes turned to violence themselves to suppress the unions (for example, threats and hiring persons to physically break up picket lines).

The intransigent refusal of the owners to change the truly awful conditions of nineteenth-century workers resulted in considerable violence in many industries, particularly in the coal mining, steel, timber, and railroad industries. Labor violence, as in other cases mentioned previously, was ultimately effective. Working conditions, wages, and security of the workers improved. Legislation was passed providing for arbitration of differences, recognition of unions, and so on. Clearly, the use of force was necessary to gain advances for laboring men and women.

---

*Ironically, this type of violence usually occurs in white ethnic blue-collar areas (black "invasion" is not a threat in the more expensive neighborhoods) where individuals are more prone toward "law-and-order" political candidates. Apparently when individuals feel personally threatened, "law and order" becomes vigilantism.

Given the evidence just cited, it is remarkable that people still believe in the myth of peaceful progress. Violence was necessary to give birth to the United States. Violence was used both to keep the blacks in servitude and to free them. Violence was used to defeat rebellious Indians and to keep them on reservations. Additionally, violence has been a necessary means for many groups in American society to achieve equality or something approaching parity in power and in the rights that all Americans are supposed to enjoy.

The powerful have not been munificent in giving a break to the powerless. To the contrary, much effort has been expended by the powerful to keep the powerless in that condition. Many times in American history, violence has been the only catalyst for change. Minority groups in the United States (for example, blacks, women, farmers) have repeatedly gone outside of existing law. To these groups, the use of force was justified because of the need to right insufferable wrongs—the very reason the colonists gave for breaking from England. We should note, however, that violence does not always work. The Indian revolts were not beneficial in any way to the Indians. Moreover, some groups, such as the Jews, have advanced with comparatively little violence. Historically, however, "violence is as American as cherry pie." The Presidential Commissions on Civil Disorders and Violence have laid bare the inaccuracies of the "peaceful progress" idea held by so many Americans. The uniform remedy suggested by these commissions for minimizing violence is to solve the cause of social unrest and perceived injustice. It cannot be a surprise that minority groups occasionally use violence because they are reacting against a system that systematically disadvantages them with little hope for change through peaceful means.

The Integrative Forces in Society

Most order theorists recognize that conflict, disharmony, and division occur within societies, particularly in complex, heterogeneous societies. They stress, however, the opposite societal characteristics of cooperation, harmony, and unity. They see American society as "We the people of the United States . . ." rather than a conglomerate of sometimes hostile groups.

In particular, order theorists focus on what holds society together. What are the forces that somehow keep anarchy from becoming a reality—or as the philosopher Hobbes asked long ago, "Why is there not a war of all against all?" The answer to this fundamental question is found in the combined effects of a number of factors.

Functional Integration. Probably the most important unifying factor is the phenomenon of **functional integration** (unity among divergent elements of society resulting from a specialized division of labor). In a highly differentiated society such as the United States with its very specialized division of labor, interaction among different segments occurs with some regularity. Interdependence often results because no group is entirely self-sufficient. The farmer needs the miller, the processor, and retail agents, as well as the fertilizer manufacturer and the agricultural experimenters. Manufacturers need raw materials, on the one hand, and customers, on the other. Management needs workers and the workers need management.

These groups, because they need each other, because each gains from the interaction, work to perpetuate a social framework that maximizes benefits to both parties and minimizes conflict or the breaking of the relationship. Written and unwritten rules emerge to govern these relationships, usually leading to cooperation rather than either isolation or conflict, and to linkages between different (and potentially conflicting) groups.

Consensus on Societal Values.   A second basis for the unification of diverse groups in American society is that almost all Americans hold certain fundamental values in common. Order theorists assume that commonly held values are like social glue binding otherwise diverse people in a cohesive societal unit. Unlike functional integration, unity is achieved here through similarity rather than through difference.

Most Americans believe that democracy is the best possible government. Americans accept the wishes of the majority on election day. Defeated candidates, for example, do not go off into the hills with their followers to blow up bridges and otherwise harass the government. Most Americans are patriotic. They revere American heritage and believe strongly in individualism and free enterprise, and the Judeo-Christian ethic.

There are many symbols that epitomize the consensus of Americans with respect to basic values. One such unifying symbol is the American flag. Although a mere piece of cloth, the flag clearly symbolizes something approaching the sacred. Reverence for the flag is evidenced by the shock shown when it is defiled and by the punishment given to defilers. The choice of the flag as an object to spit on, or burn, is a calculated one by dissident groups. They choose to defile it precisely because of what it represents and because most Americans revere it so strongly.

In 1989, the Supreme Court ruled that an individual who had desecrated the flag was guaranteed the right to do so because the Constitution protects the freedom of political expression. This decision outraged the majority of Americans, and politicians seized the opportunity to pass legislation making flag desecration an illegal act.

Similarly, such documents as the Declaration of Independence and the Constitution are held in high esteem and serve to unify Americans. The American heritage is also revered through holidays such as Thanksgiving and Independence Day. Consensus is also achieved through the collective "worship" of such American heroes as George Washington, Abraham Lincoln, and John F. Kennedy.

The Social Order.   A third factor that unifies all Americans, at least minimally, is that they are all subject to similar influences and "rules of the game." Americans are answerable to the same body of law (at the national level) and they are under the same government. Additionally, Americans use the same language, the same system of monetary exchange, the same standards for measurement, and so on. The order in society is evidenced by the fact that

Order in society is evidenced by members taking for granted such processes as obeying traffic lights.

Americans take for granted such assorted practices as obeying traffic lights, the use of credit, and the acceptance of checks in lieu of money.

Group Membership.   A source of unity (as well as cleavage) is group memberships. Some groups are exclusive, since they limit membership to a particular race, ethnic group, income category, religion, or other characteristic. The existence of exclusive organizations creates tension if persons are excluded who want to be included, because exclusiveness generally implies feelings of superiority. Country clubs, fraternities, some churches, and some neighborhoods are based on the twin foundations of exclusiveness and superiority. In American society, however, there are groups whose membership consists of persons from varying backgrounds (that is, the membership includes rich and poor or black and white). Consequently, heterogeneous organization such as political parties, religious denominations or churches, and veterans' organizations allow members the chance not only to interact with persons unlike themselves but also to join together in a common cause.

Many, if not most, Americans who belong to several organizations belong to organizations with different compositions by race, religion, or other salient characteristics. To the extent that these crosscutting memberships and allegiances exist, they tend to "cancel out" potential cleavages along social class, race, or other lines. Individuals belonging to several different organizations will probably feel some "cross-pressures" (that is, pulls in opposite directions), thereby preventing polarization.

Additionally, most Americans belong to at least one organization such as a school, church, or civic group with norms that support those of the total society. These organizations support the government and what it stands for and they expect their members to do the same.

International Competition and Conflict.   External threats to the society's existence unify. The advice Machiavelli gave his "prince" is a regrettable truth: "if the Prince is in trouble he should promote a war." This was the advice that Secretary of State Seward gave to President Lincoln prior to the Civil War. Although expedient advice from the standpoint of preserving unity, it was, Lincoln noted, only a short-term solution.

A real threat to security unifies those groups, no matter how diverse, who feel threatened. Thus, a reasonable explanation for lack of unity in America's involvement in an Indochina war was that the Viet Cong were not perceived by most Americans as a real threat to their security. The Soviet buildup in armaments in the 1980s, on the other hand, was perceived as a real threat, unifying many Americans in a willingness to sacrifice in order to catch up with and surpass the Russians.

The Mass Media.   The world is in the midst of a communications revolution. Television, for example, has expanded to encompass virtually every home in the United States. This phenomenon—universal exposure to television—has been blamed, among other things, for rising juvenile delinquency, lowering cultural tastes, declining test scores, contributing to general moral deterioration, and suppressing creativity. These criticisms are countered by order theorists, who see television and the other forms of mass media as performing several integrative functions. Government officials, for example, can use the media to shape public opinion (for example, to unite against an "enemy" or to sacrifice by paying higher taxes). The media also reinforce the values and norms of society. Newspaper editorials extol certain persons and events while decrying others. Soap operas are stories involving moral dilemmas, with virtue winning out. Newspaper and magazine stories under the caption, "It Could Only Have Happened in America," abound. The media do not, except for a few exceptions, "rock the boat." American heroes are praised and its enemies vilified. The American way is the right way; the ways of others are considered incorrect, or downright immoral. See Panel 3–3 for an example of how the media tend to ignore the realities of race and class.

Planned Integration.   Charismatic figures or other persons of influence may work to unite segmented parts of the system (conversely, they can promote division). Thus, a union leader or the archbishop of a Catholic diocese can, through personal exhortation or by example, convince group members to cooperate rather than compete, or to open membership requirements rather than maintain exclusiveness.

Public officials on the local, state, and national levels can use their power to integrate the parts of the society in three major ways: (1) by passing laws to eliminate barriers among groups; (2) by working to solve the problems that

The Media's Selective Perception of Race and Class

From the window that I wake at, most of my city is untouched. Houses stand stately after the 7.1 earthquake.

Everyone knows from watching television that earthquake damage in the Bay Area has been restricted to a relatively few neighborhoods. But not everyone may realize that considerations of race and class shaped the images that Americans saw on their TV screens.

The Marina district of San Francisco is a stately, upper-middle-class neighborhood. Homes sit alongside the Bay. People here lived well, and they faced tragedy with dignity after their neighborhood was devastated. Marina residents on TV were articulate, focused. No wonder television crews set up their cameras at this neighborhood's periphery and interviewed the residents who, even in anger and frustration, remained gentle.

But why have so few of the television crews chosen to go to the Moscone Center where those who lost homes in the city's low-income neighborhoods are now bedded down? Many of those who sleep at Moscone do not speak in tones modulated with good humor. Many of them possessed little to begin with, and they lost that little bit with the earthquake. Some had nothing and now have to redefine what nothing means.

Why were so few of the camera crews talking to people who live in West Oakland's projects, a stone's throw away from the Interstate 880 freeway that collapsed? These people now live under the same sort of stress that affects those of the Marina district.

Despite the fact that the stench of dead bodies permeates the air around the Cypress projects, help was slow in coming to those people. Not until I–880 was threatened with further collapse did the social service system that sheltered the Marina even reach out to those who lived in the midst of the Cypress deaths.

Why didn't Bryant Gumbel and Jane Pauley venture down to Watsonville, where the population is mostly Mexican and poor, where average family income is about $15,000 a year? Are the losses there less painful, the survival tales less moving?

Or do the media value white life over all by ignoring the fact that the lives of far too many people of color were also shattered by the earthquake?

TV's silence about the earthquake's impact on the non-white and the poor is reminiscent of the Depression when aid was more available to whites than to blacks; when the employment expansion resulting from World War II only included blacks after a March on Washington was threatened.

At every tragedy we are told to pull together and ignore our differences. We should not complain that the Marina was more televised than the Cypress neighborhoods because earthquake relief will finally assist both areas. We must not point out that Hispanics in Watsonville have been largely ignored because they, too, will gain from regional awareness.

But when the urgency abates, we become separate again: black, white, yellow, brown. Some have the skills to lobby for press attention or emergency aid, while others merely have the fortitude to survive and pray for help.

This is not the time to speak of race and class, a friend of mine cautions. Our television anchors reflect this point with pithy cliches: "We are all in this together." Together or not, it rankles that some people's suffering generates more concern than that of others.

The fact is that the earth shrugged, concrete tumbled and people lost their lives. But once again, race and class determined the focus of the news and our national concern.

Source: Julianne Malveaux, "Race and Class Shape TV Images of Earthquake," *Rocky Mountain News* (November 4, 1989): 57.

segment the society; (3) by providing mediators to help negotiate settlements between such feuding groups as management and labor (Mott, 1965:283–284). High officials such as the President utilize various means of integration. First, there is the technique of **co-optation** (appointing a member of a dissident group to a policy-making body to appease the dissenting group). Second, they can use their executive powers to enforce and interpret the laws in such a way as to unite groups within the society. Finally, the president and other high officials may use the media to persuade the people. The president, for example, can request television time on all networks during prime time, thereby reaching most of the adult population in order to use full presidential powers of persuasion to unite diverse groups.

False Consciousness.   Most Americans do not feel oppressed. Even many persons who do not have many material blessings tend to believe in the American creed that anyone can be upwardly mobile—if not themselves, then at least their children (Sennett and Cobb, 1973). According to the Marxian theory, when oppressed people hold beliefs damaging to their interests, they have **false consciousness.**

Thus, contrary to Karl Marx's prediction more than a century ago that capitalism would be overthrown by an oppressed majority, most Americans today consider themselves as "haves" rather than as "have-nots." There has been little polarization along purely economic lines because of a relatively large middle-class. This may be changing, however, as more and more of the middle-class are moving downward (see Chapter 10).

THE USE OF THE ORDER AND CONFLICT MODELS IN THIS BOOK

There are two contradictory models of society—the order and conflict models. The order model views society as basically cooperative, consensual, and stable. The system works. Any problems are the faults of people, not society. At the other extreme, the adherents of the conflict model assume that society is fundamentally competitive, conflictual, coercive, and radically changing. Social problems are the faults of society, not individuals, in this view.

The order and conflict models of society are both significant, and they will be utilized in the remainder of this book. While each, by itself, is important, a realistic analysis must include both. The order model must be included because there is integration, order, and stability; because the parts are more or less interdependent; and because most social change is gradual and adjustive. The conflict model is equally important because society is not always a harmonious unit. To the contrary, much of social life is based on competition. Societal integration is fragile; it is often based on subtle or blatant coercion.

A crucial difference between the two models is the implicit assumption of each as to the nature of the social structure (rules, customs, institutions, social stratification, and the distribution of power). The order perspective assumes that the social structure is basically right and proper because it serves the fundamental function of maintaining society. There is, therefore, an implicit acceptance of the status quo, assuming that the system works. As we examine the major institutions of society in this book, one of the tasks will be to determine how each of these institutions aids in societal integration.

Although order theorists also look for the **dysfunctions** of institutions, rules, organizations, and customs (dysfunctions refer to negative consequences), the critical examination of society is the primary thrust of conflict theorists. While this book will describe the way American society is structured and how this arrangement works for society integration, a major consideration will center around the question, "who benefits under these arrangements and who does not?" Thus, the legitimacy of the system will always be doubted.

CHAPTER REVIEW

1. Sociologists have a mental image (model) of how society is structured, how it changes, and what holds it together. There are two prevailing models—order and conflict—that provide contradictory images of society.

2. Order model theorists view society as ordered, stable, and harmonious, with a high degree of cooperation and consensus. Change is gradual, adjustive, and reforming. Social problems are seen as the result of problem individuals.

3. Conflict model theorists view society as competitive, fragmented, and unstable. Social integration is minimal and tenuous. Social change, which can be revolutionary, results from clashes among conflicting groups. Social problems are viewed as resulting from society's failure to meet the needs of individuals. Indeed, the structure of society is seen as the problem.

4. The order and conflict models present extreme views of society. Taken alone, each fosters a faulty perception and interpretation of society. A realistic model of society combines the strengths of both models. The assumptions of such a synthesis are: (a) the processes of stability and change are properties of all societies; (b) societies are organized but the very process of organization generates conflict; (c) society is a social system, with the parts linked through common goals and similar interests, *and* competitive because of scarce resources and inequities; (d) societies are held together by both consensus on values and by coercion; and (e) social change may be gradual or abrupt, reforming or revolutionary.

5. The divisive forces bringing about segmentation in American society are size, social class, race, ethnic groups, and religion. Thus, society has the potential for cleavage and conflict.

6. Americans tend to believe in the "myth of peaceful progress"—that disadvantaged groups throughout history have gained prosperity and equality without violence. The evidence, however, is that oppressed groups have had to use force or the threat of force to achieve gains.

7. There are a number of integrative forces in American society. These are functional integration, consensus on values, the social order, group memberships, threats from other societies, the mass media, planned integration, and false consciousness.

KEY TERMS

Model
Order model (functionalism)
Manifest consequences
Latent consequences
Conflict model

Social problem
Instrumental process
Institutional process
Dialectic
Myth of peaceful progress

Functional integration
Co-optation
False consciousness
Dysfunctions

STUDY QUESTIONS

1. What is the order model of society? What kinds of social phenomena does it focus on? What social phenomena are neglected from this perspective?

2. What is the conflict model of society? What kinds of social phenomena does it focus on? What social phenomena are neglected from this perspective?

3. What are the potentially divisive forces in society?

4. Contrary to popular belief, throughout much of U.S. history, oppressed groups have used violence to achieve progress. What is the evidence to support this refutation of the "myth of peaceful progress"?

5. What are the integrative forces of society?

FOR FURTHER READING

Sociological Theories: General

Thomas J. Bernard, *The Consensus-Conflict Debate* (New York: Columbia University Press, 1983).

Tom Campbell, *Seven Theories of Human Society* (New York: Oxford University Press, 1981).

Randall Collins, *Three Sociological Traditions* (New York: Oxford University Press, 1985).

R. P. Cuzzort, *Using Social Thought: The Nuclear Issue and Other Concerns* (Mountain View, CA: Mayfield, 1989).

George Ritzer, *Sociological Theory* (New York: Knopf, 1983).

The Order Model

Mark Abrahamson, *Functionalism* (Englewood Cliffs, NJ: Prentice-Hall, 1978).

Kingsley Davis, *Human Society* (New York: Macmillan, 1937).

Robert K. Merton, *Social Theory and Social Structure*, rev. ed. (New York: Free Press, 1968).

Talcott Parsons, *Sociological Theory and Modern Society* (New York: Free Press, 1967).

Jonathan Turner and Alexandra Maryanski, *Functionalism* (Menlo Park, CA: Benjamin-Cummings, 1979).

Robin Williams, Jr., *American Society: A Sociological Interpretation*, 3rd ed. (New York: Knopf, 1970).

The Conflict Model

Charles H. Anderson and Jeffry R. Gibson, *Toward a New Sociology*, 3rd ed. (Homewood, IL: Dorsey Press, 1978).

William J. Chambliss, ed., *Sociological Readings in the Conflict Perspective* (Reading, MA: Addison-Wesley, 1973).

Ralf Dahrendorf, *Class and Class Conflict in Industrial Society* (Stanford: Stanford University Press, 1958).

Graham C. Kinloch, *Society as Power: An Introductory Sociology* (Englewood Cliffs, NJ: Prentice-Hall, 1989).

Karl Marx and Friedrich Engels, *The Communist Manifesto*, Eden Paul and Cedar Paul, trans. (New York: Russell and Russell, 1963).

C. Wright Mills, *The Power Elite* (New York: Oxford University Press, 1956).

Michael Parenti, *Power and the Powerless* (New York: St. Martin's Press, 1978).

Chapter Four

The Duality of Social Life: Stability and Change

*T*echnological breakthroughs are a major source of social change. In modern society these occur with ever greater rapidity and often with dramatic impact on individuals. These impacts are often positive but there is a dark side to technological change as well. Consider, for example, the possible implications of the following technology-related incidents for individuals and society:

- Cancer kills about 469,400 Americans every year (Census Bureau, 1989:78). According to Russell Mokhiber, "of the 38 million workers in manufacturing industries, 1.7 million are exposed to a potential carcinogen each year. Workplace carcinogens are believed to cause an estimated 23 to 38 percent of all deaths resulting from cancer each year" (Mokhiber, 1988:16–17).
- The Coast Guard reported to Congress that it recorded 6,700 oil spills during 1988, 10 of which involved at least 100,000 gallons (reported in Rudolph 1989). These paled in comparison to the 11 million gallon spill of the *Exxon Valdez* in Alaska in March 1989. Just three weeks after the spill, the oil had spread to 3,000 square miles of water and covered 1,300 miles of formerly pristine coastline. The dangers caused by the intrusion of oil to the habitat of fish, mollusks, sea otters, marine microorganisms, and waterfowl are incalculable.
- In the past 15 years there have been 151 "significant" nuclear accidents in nuclear plants in 14 countries. The most notable of these, the core meltdown of a Soviet nuclear reactor at Chernobyl in 1986, had devastating effects throughout Russia and Europe, and even raised radioactive levels as far away as the United States. The United States had 101 operational nuclear plants in

1986, 9 of which have a design flaw similar to the one causing the Chernobyl accident (Diamond, 1986).

- The Supreme Court has ruled that gene-splicing technology can be patented. This ruling opened the door for patenting new life forms with genetic information never before in existence. According to one critic, Jeremy Rifkin, "These genetically engineered microbes are alive and are inherently unpredictable. Unlike chemicals, they reproduce, migrate, grow. If something goes wrong, you can't recall them, seal them up, clean them up or do anything about them" (quoted in Chaze, 1986:21).

There are some major economic and social problems that appear inevitable for the early 1990s. Some of these are: (1) underemployment will be a problem; (2) the standard of living will decline; (3) competing business and political interest groups will make planning to meet societal goals difficult, if not impossible, to achieve; (4) huge government expenditures to bail out failed Savings and Loans (as much as $500 billion) will reduce the monies spent for social projects; (5) the gap between the "haves" and the "have nots" will widen; (6) the large cities will be increasingly unable to meet their needs; (7) resources will grow short; and (8) businesses will continue to resist pollution control.

Given the strong probability of these and other problems escalating in proportion and severity, will the system adapt and stabilize or change, even dramatically? There are adaptive mechanisms and trends that may neutralize or at least minimize the potential for social unrest and tumultuous change. These are: (1) the state's ability to adapt by increasing benefits such as unemployment compensation in times of crisis (see Piven and Cloward, 1971); (2) the tendency of unrest by minorities and other groups to be localized and segmented; (3) the increasing frequency with which both spouses are in the labor force to offset declining personal incomes; (4) patriotism's ability to unify people in times of international tensions; and (5) patriotism's ability to foster a spirit of sacrifice in times of scarcity.

There is an alternative scenario. The problems could reach unprecedented proportions. The government could become more and more ineffective in solving problems. The masses or a significant number of people could focus on a major national problem whose source was clearly identified. Leaders could emerge. The people could become committed to activism with the goal of major structural changes.

The question, then, is just how resilient is our social system? Will the 1990s be a time of turmoil and major change or will this period be characterized by adaptation and relative stability? The answer is not easy because there are structural forces that work to achieve change and there are others that operate to promote stability. The dialectic between these opposing forces is the subject of this chapter.

CHANGE IN SOCIAL SYSTEMS

Social systems, if they are to survive, require two opposite tendencies—stability and change. They require stability so that interaction and behaviors will be relatively predictable for goods and services to be produced and distributed, for work to be coordinated, and for chaos in everything from traffic to politics to be averted.

But while societies and their members need stability and predictability, social change is both inevitable and necessary. To say that change is inevitable is another way of saying that it is normal. Inevitable changes in the environment or within a social system require changes in the social system. Changes occur in response to external forces that impinge on the system such as war, flood, famine, and economic conditions. Changes occur also because of conditions within the social system such as shortages or surpluses, technological innovations, population growth or decline, conflict between factions, and economic booms or declines. Because societies are never completely stable and tranquil, adjustments (minor or major) are necessary to meet members' needs. These changes may be gradual or abrupt, reforming or revolutionary, deliberate or accidental.

Thus, the duality of social systems introduced in the last chapter includes not only order and conflict but also the related conditions of stability and change. This chapter is organized to describe how society is buffeted by these two seemingly contrary tendencies. We will begin by examining the structural sources for stability, and follow by examining the sources of change.

FORCES FOR STABILITY

Societies strain toward persistence. We are bound in our activities, for example, by the constraints of customs, traditions, myths, and ideologies that we have been taught to accept, without thinking. Some of these are so important that we will sacrifice—even our lives, if necessary—to perpetuate them. Religious beliefs and nationalism evoke this kind of response in most of us. Clearly, perceived threats to religious dogma and to the foundations of our political heritage will be resisted by most. We consider four especially important impediments to social change—institutions, bureaucracy, ideology, and organizations bent on preserving the status quo—in addition to the values and ideologies held by the members of society.

Institutions

All institutions are by definition reactionary. They provide answers from tradition and thus preserve stability. Each institution, whether it be the family, education, religion, the economy, or the polity, channels behavior in prescribed ways. Any deviation from these demands is punished, either formally or informally. For example, we do not have the option in American society to marry more than one spouse at a time. Similarly, school districts rarely hire those who are known homosexuals. Let's look briefly at the institution of the polity and some other elements of society and see how they operate to resist change in American society.

The government is structured to inhibit change. For example, the choices of decision makers are often limited by various **systemic imperatives** (the economic and social constraints on decision makers that promote the status quo). In other words, there is a bias that pressures the government to do certain things and not to do other things. Inevitably, this bias favors the status quo, allowing those with power to continue as they are, because no change is always easier than change. The current political and economic systems have worked and generally are not subject to question, let alone change. In this way the laws, customs, and institutions of society resist change. Thus the propertied and the wealthy benefit while the propertyless and the poor continue to be disadvantaged. As Parenti has argued, the law has such a bias:

> The law does not exist as an abstraction. It gathers shape and substance from a context of power, within a real-life social structure. Like other institutions, the legal system is class-bound. The question is not whether the law should or should not be neutral, for as a product of its society, it *cannot* be neutral in purpose or effect. (Parenti, 1978:188)

In addition to the inertia of institutions, there are other systemic imperatives. One such imperative is for the government to strive to provide an adequate defense system against our enemies, which stifles any external threat to the status quo. Domestically, government policy is also shaped by the systemic imperative for stability. The government promotes domestic tranquility by squelching dissidents. This last point is significant. The job of the government is to keep order. By definition, this function works against change. The "enemies" of societies therefore are harassed by the FBI, the CIA, and other government agencies.

The very way that the government is organized promotes stability. For example, the requirement that three-fourths of the state legislatures, each by a two-thirds vote, must ratify proposed amendments, makes it extremely difficult to amend the Constitution. Thus, though a majority of the Congress, the people, and the state legislators favor the Equal Rights Amendment, this proposed amendment has failed to be ratified. Similarly the law resists change because the courts use the principle of precedent to determine current cases. The way Congress is organized is another example. Committee chairs are selected on the basis of seniority, not expertise. Longevity in public office is rarely achieved by taking radical stances. Thus the very powerful positions of committee chairs are occupied by people oriented toward the status quo.

As a final example, the two-party system is organized to preserve the status quo. A multiparty system, as is common in Western Europe, means that each party has a narrow appeal because of its principles. Our system of two parties, in contrast, requires that both parties have wide appeal. A radical position is not acceptable in this system. Although there is no mention of political parties in the Constitution, our two-party system has evolved in such a way as to make third parties inconsequential. Attempts to add parties are thwarted by the election laws, which make it difficult for candidates other than Republicans and Democrats to get on the ballots in each state. At the presidential level third-party candidates find it difficult to qualify for public campaign funds. They also have difficulty being allowed to participate in televised debates and receiving equal time on television. Finally, the way Congress is organized, one must be a Republican or a Democrat to be effective.

Bureaucracy

The process of **bureaucratization** refers to the changes within organizations toward greater rationality—that is, improved operating efficiency and more effective attainment of common goals (see Panel 4–1). As the size and complexity of an organization grow, there is a greater need for coordination if efficiency is to be maintained or improved. Organizational efficiency would be maximized (ideally) under the following conditions:

- When the work is divided into small tasks performed by specialists;
- When there is a hierarchy of authority (chain of command) with each position in the chain having clearly defined duties and responsibilities;
- When behaviors are governed by standardized, written, and explicit rules;
- When all decisions are made on the basis of technical knowledge, not personal considerations;
- When the members are judged solely on the basis of proficiency, and discipline is impartially enforced. (Weber, 1947:329–341)

In short, a bureaucracy is an organization designed to perform like a machine.

The push toward increased bureaucratization pervades nearly all aspects of American life including the government (at all levels), the church (the Catholic Church, the Methodist Church), education (all school systems), sports (NCAA, athletic departments at "big time" schools, professional teams), corporations (General Motors, IBM), and even crime ("mafia").

The majority of social scientists have viewed with alarm what they conceive to be the trend toward greater and greater bureaucratization. Individuals will, it is typically predicted, increasingly become small cogs in very big machines. Narrowly defined tasks, a rigid chain of command, and total impersonality in dealing with others will be our organizational lot in the future. Human beings will be rigid conformists—the prototype of the organization man or woman.

Several aspects of bureaucracies as they operate in reality work to promote the status quo.* First, the blind obedience to rules and the unquestioned following of orders means that new and unusual situations cannot be handled efficiently because the rules do not apply. Rigid adherence to the rules creates automatons. Second, bureaucracies tend to be stagnant in selecting people for

---

*These forces promoting the status quo may actually foster change when bureaucracies are unable to adapt. Thus, individuals may subvert the bureaucracy or form new organizations to meet new conditions. Bureaucracies, then, provide the interesting paradox that in their quest for rationality, they may actually accomplish irrationality (Merton, 1968).

The Bureaucracy as a Rational Tool: The Organization of Power

Bureaucracy is a remarkable product of gradual, halting, and often unwitting social engineering. Most elements were in place before the spurt of industrialization in the nineteenth century; it was this spurt and the associated control over employees that destroyed most other forms of large-scale organized activity. Without this form of social technology, the industrialized countries of the West could not have reached the heights of extravagance, wealth, and pollution that they currently enjoy. . . .

First . . . I would like to state my own biases. After twenty years of studying complex organizations, I have come to two conclusions that run counter to much of the organizational literature. The first is that the sins generally attributed to bureaucracy are either not sins at all or are consequences of the failure to bureaucratize sufficiently. In this respect, I will defend bureaucracy as the dominant principle of organization in our large, complex organizations. My second conclusion is that the extensive preoccupation with reforming, "humanizing," and decentralizing bureaucracies, while salutary, has served to obscure from organizational theorists the true nature of bureaucracy and has diverted us from assessing its impact upon society. The impact upon society in general is incalculably more important than the impact upon the members of a particular organization, that most critics concern themselves with. . . .

By its very nature, and particularly because of its superiority as a social tool over other forms of organization, bureaucracy generates an enormous degree of unregulated and often unperceived social power; and this power is placed in the hands of a very few leaders. As bureaucracies satisfy, delight, and satiate us with their output of goods and services, they also shape our mentality, control our life chances, and define our humanity. They do so not so much in our role as members of one or more of these organizations, but as members of a society that is truly an organizational society. Those who control these organizations control the quality of our life, and they are largely self-appointed leaders.

Let me be quite clear about my position. . . . In my view, bureaucracy is a form of organization superior to all others we know or can hope to afford in the near and middle future; the chances of doing away with it or changing it are probably nonexistent in the West in this century. Thus, it is crucial to understand it and appreciate it. But it is also crucial to understand not only how it mobilizes social resources for desirable ends, but also how it inevitably concentrates those forces in the hands of a few who are prone to use them for ends we do not approve of, for ends we are generally not aware of, and more frightening still, for ends we are led to accept because we are not in a position to conceive alternative ones.

Source: Charles Perrow, *Complex Organizations: A Critical Essay, Second Edition* (Glenview, IL: Scott, Foresman, 1979): 5–7. Copyright © 1972, 1979 Scott, Foresman and Company. Reprinted by permission.

leadership roles. Leaders in bureaucracies typically follow two principles when choosing new leaders. The first is to select from the pool of potential leaders those who in addition to being competent have not "rocked the boat"; have proved their loyalty to the organization; and are likely to continue the policies of the current leadership. The second has been labeled *The Peter Principle* (Peter and Hull, 1969). When a vacancy occurs, the leadership tends to choose an individual who has been successful at the lower level. That person will continue to advance in the hierarchy until he or she has reached his or her level of incompetence. A good teacher and researcher in college may not be a good department administrator, yet that is often the basis for selection. The Peter Principle taken to the extreme means that a bureaucracy

The Bureaucracy as an Irrational Tool: "Laws" Governing Behavior in Bureaucracies

Boren's Laws of the Bureaucracy. (1) When in doubt, mumble. (2) When in trouble, delegate. (3) When in charge, ponder.

Robertson's Second Order Rule of Bureaucracy. The more directives you issue to solve a problem, the worse it gets.

Dyer's Law. A continuing flow of paper is sufficient to continue the flow of paper.

Evelyn's Rules for Bureaucratic Survival. (1) A bureaucrat's castle is his desk . . . and parking place. Proceed cautiously when changing either. (2) On the theory that one should never take anything for granted, follow up on everything, but especially those items varying from the norm. The greater the divergence from normal routine and/or the greater the number of offices potentially involved, the better the chance a never-to-be-discovered person will file the problem away in a drawer specifically designed for items requiring a decision. (3) Never say without qualification that your activity has sufficient space, money, staff, etc. (4) Always distrust offices not under your jurisdiction which say that they are there to serve you.

Fowler's Law. In a bureaucracy, accomplishment is inversely proportional to the volume of paper used.

Hacker's Law of Personnel. It is never clear just how many hands—or minds—are needed to carry out a particular process. Nevertheless, anyone having supervisory responsibility for the completion of the task will invariably protest that his staff is too small for the assignment.

Imhoff's Law. The organization of any bureaucracy is very much like a septic tank—the really big chunks always rise to the top.

Parkinson's Laws. (1) Work expands so as to fill the time available for its completion. (2) Expenditure rises to meet income. (3) Expansion means complexity and complexity, decay; or to put it even more plainly—the more complex, the sooner dead.

Peter Principle and Corollaries. In every hierarchy, whether it be government or business, each employee tends to rise to his level of incompetence; every post tends to be filled by an employee incompetent to execute its duties. *Corollaries:* (1) Incompetence knows no barriers of time or place. (2) Work is accomplished by those employees who have not yet reached their level of incompetence. (3) If at first you don't succeed, try something else.

Rayburn's Rule. If you want to get along, go along.

Riesman's Law. An inexorable upward movement leads administrators to higher salaries and narrower spans of control.

Rigg's Hypothesis. Incompetence tends to increase with the level of work performed. And, naturally, the individual's staff needs will increase as his level of incompetence increases.

Smith's Principles of Bureaucratic Tinkertoys. (1) Never use one word when a dozen will suffice. (2) If it can be understood, it's not finished yet. (3) Never do anything for the first time.

Vail's First Axiom. In any human enterprise, work seeks the lowest hierarchical level.

Work Rules. (1) The boss is always right. (2) When the boss is wrong, refer to Rule 1.

Source: Paul Dickson, *The Official Rules: The Definitive, Annotated Collection of Laws, Principles, and Instructions for Dealing with the Real World* (New York: Delta, 1978). Reprinted with permission.

will ultimately be staffed with people who have reached the level just above where they are competent. The result, noted by organizational researchers Blau and Meyer, is that people who realize they are "over their heads" will tend to relieve their feelings of insecurity by overemphasizing rules and regulations (Blau and Meyer, 1971:104; see Panel 4–2).

In sum, the bureaucratic form of organization inhibits social change because it tends to encourage sameness. Office holders and those who replace them tend to be very much alike in expertise, outlook, and attitudes. As Leslie, Larson, and Gorman have put it: "Bureaucrats tend strongly to resemble past, present, and future bureaucrats (Leslie, Larson, and Gorman, 1980:283).

Ideology

Ideology—the shared beliefs about the physical, social, or metaphysical world—can be a prime mover or an impediment to change. The following are a few examples from history of how ideological beliefs stifled change (from Lauer, 1973:120–122):

- In China, Confucian thought acted as a barrier to change by idealizing the past.
- During the Middle Ages, economic progress was retarded by the Christian belief that usury (the loaning of money for interest) was sinful. The Church also channeled surplus wealth into building religious monuments rather than investing in trade and commercial development.
- The Church at various times has enforced rigid conformity through the Inquisition, heresy trials, and witchcraft trials.
- New scientific ideas challenging religious orthodoxy have routinely been fought by religious groups. Galileo's trial for heresy and the Scopes trial in Tennessee for teaching evolution are two blatant examples of this strong tendency.
- In Russia biological breakthroughs were retarded because the government insisted on a biological theory congruent with Marxian ideology—that socially acquired traits are genetically transmitted to the next generation. Thus, the insights of Mendelian genetics were ignored.

Groups Organized to Resist Change

A **social movement** is a collective attempt to promote or resist change. Such movements arise when people are sufficiently discontented that they will work for a better system. A social movement develops organization with leaders, a division of labor, an ideology, and a set of roles and norms for the members (see Blumer, 1951; Smelser, 1962). One type of social movement is explicitly organized to resist change. These **resistance movements** are organized to reinforce the old system by preventing change. Later in this chapter we will examine reform and revolutionary social movements. For now, let's look at those movements that work to resist change or are reactionary in that they want to reverse change that has already occurred.

Since periods of rapid change foster resistance movements, there are numerous contemporary examples of this phenomenon. There are current efforts to stop the trend toward the use of nuclear power for energy. People have organized to resist the damming of rivers because they want to protect the environment. The move to make the Equal Rights Amendment part of the Constitution has met with considerable organized resistance. Pro-abortion groups have formed to reverse legislation and judicial acts making abortion illegal or difficult to obtain. These resistance movements are, by definition, political in nature. This is illustrated by the contemporary movement fostered by evangelicals to use their political clout to reverse trends they consider opposite to Christian principles.

FORCES FOR CHANGE

There are a variety of important forces converging in contemporary American society that heighten the questioning of traditional behavior patterns, alter roles and rules, and shift modes of thought and action. These reforming and revolutionary forces—population dynamics, technology, the government, and social movements—are the subjects of this section.

Population Dynamics

The size, geographical distribution, and other characteristics of a society's population have obvious effects on people's lives. Too many people, for example, increase the potential for unemployment, exacerbate pollution, increase the use of natural resources, strain schools, health facilities, and other services, and may cause tensions and conflicts among individuals and groups. This section examines six **demographic** (population) factors that especially affect contemporary American life: (1) population growth, (2) urbanization, (3) migration, (4) the new immigration, (5) the changing racial composition, and (6) the aging population.

Population Growth.   The United States has experienced a rapid population growth in this century. The 1900 population of 76 million grew to 250 million by 1990, an increase of 174 million persons (and 329 percent) in just 90 years. This surge in population was the result of two factors. The first was that medical advances significantly decreased the mortality (death) rate, resulting in extending life expectancy dramatically from 47 years in 1900 to 74.9 years in 1987. The second reason for this growth was immigration. During this span approximately 30 million more people moved to the United States than out of it. Remarkably, however, this great growth in population occurred despite a downward trend in fertility (the birth rate). In 1900, for example, women averaged 3.5 children in their lifetimes, but by 1987 this average had fallen to 1.8 children. In this section we will examine fertility rates in recent American history, determining the reasons for the rises and falls and the consequences of differing rates for the society. We will then project the population growth into the future to determine the eventual stable population size and the consequences of having a stable population of that magnitude.

Despite the more than tripling in U.S. population from 1900 to 1990, the United States does not have the population problem of the developing countries. Whereas the population of some countries is increasing at an annual rate of more than 3 percent, the United States is growing at a 0.6 percent rate. While some African nations have 51 births per 1,000 people, the U.S. rate is below 16 births per 1,000 people. In fact, as we will document shortly, the United States has achieved a birth rate below the replacement level. In other words, a zero population growth rate has been achieved. So the population problem that faces the world would appear to have bypassed the United States. We would argue that this is a false premise in two regards. First, population pressures anywhere affect the United States because of the resulting shortages in resources, ecological imbalances, and increased international tensions. Second—and a point that is stressed at the end of this section—population changes affect social life in a number of important ways.

Fertility in recent American history.   Table 4–1 documents the dramatic fall in birth rates in recent United States history. In 1800 there were 58 live births per 1000 population (higher than the current rate in Africa, 46 per 1000, that makes it the fastest-growing continent) and this has steadily declined to 15.6 per 1000 in 1987. What is most significant about this current rate is that it is *below* the replacement rate and therefore will, if maintained, produce a stationary population—zero population growth (ZPG). The ZPG rate is 2.11 children per woman and, as Table 4–1 shows, the rate dipped below this in 1972 and continues to decline. However, actual zero population growth did not occur at this point and will not for a number of years. A rate of 2.11 children per woman must be maintained for 70 years before a stationary population is accomplished (a consistent rate of 1.9 children per woman would take 50 years, and a rate of 1.0 would bring population growth to an immediate halt). The reason for the growth in population after the ZPG rate has been reached is that it takes the age structure several generations to change so that it reflects the birth rates and death rates at each age that would produce a replacement level of children. In other words, the current age structure is so comprised that there is a relatively large proportion of persons of reproductive age. In 1956, for example, there were about 10 million women

Table 4–1			

Table 4–1
Declining Birth Rates in America: 1800–1989

Year	Births per 1000 Population	Average Number of Births per Adult Woman (15–44)
1800	58	7.0
1850	48	5.4
1900	32	3.5
1936	18	2.1
1950	24	3.2
1957	25	3.8
1970	18	2.4
1975	14.7	1.75
1980	15.8	1.9
1985	15.8	1.8
1989	15.9	1.9

in the high-fertility age group (age 20–29) but in 1980 there were about 20 million in this age category. So while women on the average may have fewer babies, this low rate will still mean an increasingly large number of children until the number of women in this category is substantially fewer.

Consequences of the birth dearth.   Predicting the population at some future time based on current fertility trends is a faulty enterprise. However, let us assume that the birth rate will continue at the current 1.8 children per woman until the year 2000 instead of a rate of 2.8 (the rate in the early 1960s). What will be the consequences at the family and societal levels?

At the family level smaller size will have very positive consequences. Families will have more wealth to spend on health and educational benefits for their children. But more than just spending more money on their children for doctors or college expenses, small family size is related to physical and intellectual endorsements. Hartley has summarized the research findings in the following two areas:

1. *Health* is better on the average for persons in small families than those in large families. Height, weight, vital capacity, and strength all decline as the number of children goes up. There is a tenfold increase in mental deficiency as one moves from first child to sixth. Even with father's occupation constant, short stature is related to large family size.
2. *Intelligence* tests have indicated that children from small families consistently score higher on the average than children from large families. We have tended to disregard these early studies because of the possible spuriousness of the relationship, since both are related to social class. However, when family income, social class, or the occupation of the father is held constant, there is still a substantial decline in IQ with increasing numbers of children in the family. The greatest differences are found in verbal intelligence, with declines noted even from the first to later children (Hartley 1973:195).

Other benefits that would tend to accrue to small families are increased marital satisfaction (absence of unwanted children, fewer economic troubles), less complicated divorces for families with few or no children, and persons living longer, healthier lives.

Resources will also be saved because most families will be small. Families, therefore, will need less land, smaller dwellings, fewer clothes, smaller appliances, smaller cars, and less electricity, heat, and fuel.

Another saving for the society would be the smaller amount that the government (and therefore taxpayers) would have to pay for infrastructure services (roads, sewage disposal, water, schools, police and fire protection).

The boom generation.   Birth rates in this century, while showing a definite downward trend, had one period that reversed the trend, resulting in a baby boom. This aberration has had and will continue to have a profound effect on American society.

The depression period was a time of low fertility as families postponed having children or restricted their family size because of economic difficulties and uncertainties. These uncertainties were compounded further by World War II. Again fertility was kept low by the conscious acts of families or now because many husbands and wives were physically separated. So following 15 years of depression and war persons who had delayed child bearing began to make up for lost time. The result was a period of rising fertility from 1947 through 1960. Between 1947 and 1957, for example, 43 million babies were born—10 million more than in the previous decade—and one fifth of the present population. This created a 10-million-person bulge in the age structure. Like a pig that has been swallowed by a python, this bulge has been slowly moving through the age structure, creating problems and dislocations at every stage (see Figure 4–1). It will continue to create problems of adjustment for the duration of the 70-year life span of the baby boom—until 2020 or so.

The immediate effect of the baby boom was to reduce the number of women in the labor force. By 1950 there were 858,000 fewer women working than in 1945 and the proportion of working women was below that of 1940. Increased family size also increased the need for room, hence the trend to move to the suburbs. In the 1950s the suburbs grew by nearly 20 million, and homeownership increased.

In the mid-fifties this bulge in the age structure created a crisis for elementary schools—a tremendous shortage in classrooms and teachers. By 1960 the nation had 1.4 million classrooms, about half of which had been built since 1950 to accommodate the boom generation. In the early 1960s these shortages hit the secondary schools and by the end of that decade the colleges faced up to these problems. During this time, for example, one new institution of higher learning opened *every week*. The baby boom had caused a rapid expansion of facilities and teachers at every level but when the population bulge moved on the schools faced another problem—empty classrooms and a surplus of teachers. The colleges that had geared up to the teacher shortage continued to graduate teachers with the jobs rapidly drying up. Then the colleges themselves faced a difficult adjustment period as the number of their students declined sharply.

As the new wave of humanity entered adolescence, the society faced new problems. Traffic accidents increased because of the tremendous number of young drivers. The volume of crime increased dramatically because of the larger proportion of individuals in the high-crime-prone years.

Employment opportunities will be a continuing problem into the next century because of the boom generation. Promotions for the baby boomers and the workers following them will be much more limited than in earlier generations because the baby boomers dominate the middle-management ranks. The problem is exacerbated further by (1) the increasing number of women who seek employment and who are now competing for management positions and (2) the increased demands by minorities for better jobs.

The members of the boom generation will, as they move through the age structure, also affect the economy in a number of ways. For example, their large numbers will ensure a growing market for housing, furniture, and other items. There will be a continual problem of economic dislocations. Companies

Figure 4–1
**Progress of
Depression
Cohort, Baby
Boom Cohort,
and Baby Bust
Cohort Through
U.S. Population
Age-Sex
Pyramid:
1960–2050**

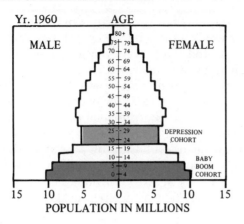

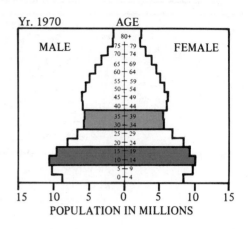

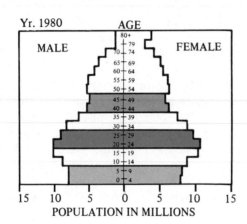

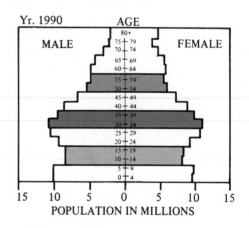

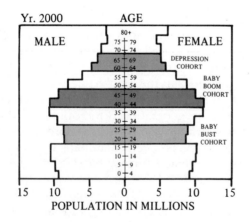

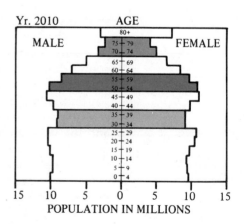

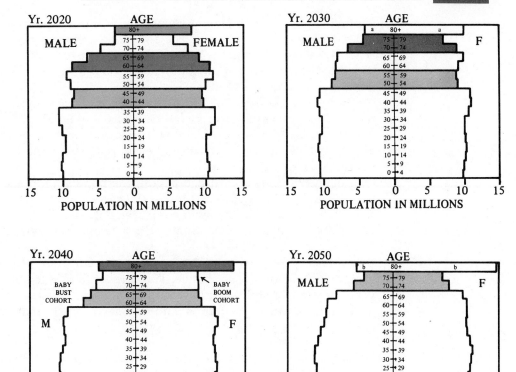

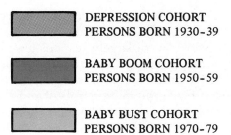

DEPRESSION COHORT
PERSONS BORN 1930–39

BABY BOOM COHORT
PERSONS BORN 1950–59

BABY BUST COHORT
PERSONS BORN 1970–79

Source: Leon F. Bouvier, "America's Baby Boom Generation: The Fateful Bulge," *Population Bulletin* Vol. 35, No. 1 (Population Reference Bureau, Inc., Washington, D.C., 1980), Figure 4. Reprinted by permission.

supplying goods for the boom generation will face expansion followed by a rapid decline as the "boomers" age and move on to another stage, just as the schools built rapidly and then found themselves overbuilt. These dislocations added to the problems of unemployment could be a continual source of economic booms and recessions.

In the decade from 2010 to 2020 the boom generation will reach retirement. The number of persons over 65 in 2030 will be 52 million (compared to 23 million in 1977). The problem, of course, is that these people on pensions and Social Security will have to be supported by the younger working population.

Finally, 70 years after it had begun, the population bulge created by the baby boom will have passed through the age structure. By then, presuming a steady birth rate at or below the replacement rate, the U.S. population will have stabilized at about 270 million with a balanced age structure.

Urbanization.   Here we consider how the concentration of people in limited geographical areas affects change. The cities of the United States have undergone three major shifts that have important social consequences: accelerated growth, the growth of suburbs, and the racial transformation of the central cities. These are the topics of this section.

Population implosion.   As the United States grew from a tiny nation of several million in 1790 to one of 250 million in 1980 there was a related trend of an ever greater concentration of the people in urban places. Using the Census Bureau's definition of an urban place as an incorporated area exceeding 2,500 in population, the United States has moved steadily from a rural to an urban nation—the 1790 population was 5 percent urban, while the population in 1900 was 40 percent urban, and 75 percent urban in 1988. Looked at another way, in 1800 there were only 6 cities in excess of 8000 people, while in 1987 there were 37 metropolitan areas exceeding 1,000,000 in population (48.9 percent of the U.S. population lived in those 37 metropolitan areas in 1988) (Forstall and Starsinic, 1989).

This fantastic growth is the result of several factors: population increase (births over deaths), immigration, and the internal migration from rural to urban. Changes in technology were largely responsible for many rural persons leaving farms. The mechanization of agriculture, for example, significantly reduced the rural job market, resulting in a farm population decline from 32 million persons in 1940 to 10 million in 1970 and 4.95 million in 1988. The cities were also attractive to migrants because they offered a variety of jobs, entertainment, and the like. This trend had some negative consequences. Certainly many small rural towns declined and decayed as their population base eroded. Rural bankruptcy increased. Towns once served by doctors, dentists, lawyers, and other professionals were now denied these services at the local level. Also, many rural persons who moved to the city found that environment difficult and alien. Many of their skills were not transferable to urban jobs. This urban trend, then, was the source of dislocations for many newcomers and for their rural sources of origin. Also, of course, the cities undergoing this rapid growth had difficulty providing adequate housing, sewage disposal, and other services for the hordes of newcomers.

The suburban explosion.   Whereas the long-term strong trend has been from rural to urban, there has also been a recent trend outward from the central cities to separate communities contiguous with the large city. The growth of the suburbs is a twentieth-century phenomenon accompanying the building of the highway system, and the increased use of the automobile, commuter trains, and buses. The 1970 Census revealed that for the first time the suburban population of metropolitan areas exceeded that of the central city.

The population composition of the suburbs points to several problems. The suburbanites, when compared to the residents of the central city, are usually white and relatively affluent. Thus, there is the problem that suburbs constitute a white ring around an ever-blacker inner city. This homogenization also results in the services (including education) being superior in the suburbs because the tax revenues are relatively higher. Thus arise the inequality of educational opportunity and the cry by some for busing and other integration plans.

Another trend that tends to strangle the inner city is that places of work are increasingly being located in the suburbs. This loss of jobs in the central city reflects the trend of businesses and plants to relocate in the suburbs, where land may be cheaper, taxes lower, and traffic congestion and parking less of a problem.

The negative consequences of this trend for the central city are obvious. Foremost is that job opportunities are increasingly limited. High unemployment results in financial hardship for the city because of the decreased tax revenues but also because of increased welfare needs. Decreased tax revenues are also a consequence of the movement of taxpaying individuals and businesses away from the city.

Racial transformation of the central cities.   The 1960s and 1970s were decades of great growth for the suburbs and concomitant loss in population for the central cities. This fact, at first glance, would seem to reveal that the central cities were only losing people—that there was relatively little in-migration. Such an interpretation is incorrect, however. What occurred was a **white flight**—that is, whites leaving the cities for the suburbs and blacks, usually from the rural South, moving in. This trend continued in the 1980s but with the racial mix not only more and more black but also Hispanic and in some locations Asian as well.

This racial transformation of large cities has several implications. First, it reflects the rapid urbanization of the black and Hispanic populations. A second consequence is that an increasing number of cities have racial minorities with more voting power than whites. From 1968 to 1987, for example, the number of black mayors increased from 48 to 303, with most of the largest cities included (Zinsmeister, 1988). Hispanics have been less successful, but their members have been mayors of such cities as San Antonio and Denver.

Third, increasingly nonwhite cities will have de facto segregation in neighborhoods and schools, despite Supreme Court rulings to the contrary. Finally, as the central cities have become increasingly populated by racial minorities, the affluent of all races have left for the suburbs, leaving the cities without an adequate tax base and increasingly unable to provide services to those most in need of them (education, welfare, health care, and housing).

Geographic Mobility within the United States.   In addition to the movement of people to the cities and suburbs, another major migration trend has been toward the sunbelt states. These states, especially California, Arizona, Florida, and Texas, are growing rapidly not only because of the favorable geographical climate but more importantly because businesses are moving there due to a favorable business climate (including lower taxes, lower wages, and less entrenched unions). This increases employment opportunities in these areas and encourages many to go where the jobs are more plentiful. The mountain states are also growing rapidly because of the vast energy resources located there, the growth of new industries, and the aesthetic appeal of the region.

These migration patterns represent profound shifts in the population, leaving some areas of the country stagnant, with declining tax bases, and relatively high unemployment, while other regions are experiencing vigorous development and relative prosperity. Politically, this internal migration has important implications as well. It is estimated that the reapportionment based on the 1990 Census will move eighteen Congressional seats from the urban and politically liberal Northeast and Midwest to the politically conservative South and West (Barringer, 1989).

The New Immigration.   Historically, immigration has been a major source of population growth and ethnic diversity in the United States. Immigration waves from northern and southern Europe, especially from 1850 to 1920, brought many millions of foreigners, mostly Europeans, to the United States. In the 1920s the United States placed limits on the number of immigrants it would accept, with the operant principle that the new immigrants should resemble the old ones. The "national origins" rules were designed to limit severely the immigration of Eastern Europeans and to deny the entry of Asians.

The Immigration Act amendments of 1965 abandoned the quota system that had preserved the European character of the United States for nearly half a century. The new law encouraged a new wave of immigrants, only this time they arrived not from Northern Europe but from the Third World, especially Asia and Latin America (Friedrich, 1985:26).

> Europeans made up 90 percent of immigrants 100 years ago when the Statue of Liberty was dedicated and more than half still in 1965 when a new influx was prompted by the law change that lowered barriers than had been based largely on race. Only 11 percent of the 570,000 legal immigrants recorded in 1985 came from Europe. Asians accounted for 46 percent of the legal total and Latin Americans—mainly Mexicans and almost all Spanish-speaking—made up 37 percent. (Bouvier and Gardner, 1986:4)

Reprinted by
permission of United
Feature Syndicate.

In addition to the legal immigrants (500,000 to 600,000 each year in the 1980s), many people enter the United States illegally. The number who enter clandestinely is impossible to determine. Roughly 2 million undocumented migrants were counted in the 1980 census, but this is an obvious undercount because people illegally in the country will avoid the census if possible. Also, many illegal aliens move to the United States only for periods of employment and then return home, usually to Mexico. The Immigration and Naturalization Service apprehends about 1.8 million illegal immigrants each year, many more than once, which confounds the estimates further. Although the statistics about these undocumented settlers are illusive, the best estimate by the Census Bureau is that there were about 4.7 million illegal aliens in 1987 (Robey, 1987). Other estimates are as high as 6 to 10 million. Whatever the estimate, there is agreement that roughly 60 percent were Hispanic (and two-thirds of these were Mexicans).

Undocumented immigrants face special problems. Because they are considered illegal, they live as fugitives, constantly in fear of getting caught. They are sometimes exploited by unscrupulous employers and landlords, but they cannot complain to the authorities because they have criminal status. They are not eligible for welfare benefits, and they often do not seek medical attention when needed because it is either too costly or because they fear being identified and sent back home. The 1986 Immigration and Reform and Control Act sought to redress some of the problems of undocumented immigrants by trying to reduce their number by making those people who employ them subject to criminal penalties, and by granting amnesty and legal residency to those immigrants who had entered the United States illegally before 1982 and who had been continuous residents since. This second provision affected approximately 2 million directly and many more indirectly. When the migrants who obtain legal status eventually become citizens, their immediate family members in their country of origin will be eligible to join them in the United States without restrictions.

Many of the new immigrants (legal and illegal) work as migrant workers for low wages and few, if any, worker benefits.

The settlement patterns of this new migration differ from previous flows into the United States. Whereas previous immigrants settled primarily in the industrial states of the Northeast and Mideast, or in the farming areas of the Midwest, immigrants today are much more dispersed geographically. Recent migrants have tended to converge in the largest cities in six states: California (where 64 percent of the nation's Asians live as do 35 percent of the country's Hispanics), followed by New York, Texas, Florida, Illinois, and New Jersey. Asians have tended to settle on the West Coast whereas Mexicans are most likely found in the Southwest, with other Hispanics widely scattered (e.g., Cubans in Florida and Puerto Ricans in New York).

Southern California has been uniquely affected by migration settlement. Between 1970 and 1980, the Hispanic population in southern California doubled to 2.8 million. Hispanics now make up nearly 25 percent of the total population of nearly 12.3 million. During the same period, the Asian population more than tripled while the number of whites declined by 500,000. The population influx has changed the face of the region, creating a patchwork of barrios, Koreatowns, Little Tokyos, Little Taipeis, and Little Saigons, many of them in neighborhoods once predominantly white or black (Conklin, 1986:5). The diverse population of southern California speaks 88 languages and dialects, which, when coupled with cultural differences, cause incredible problems for the schools, governmental service agencies, and businesses (Edmondson, 1985). The racial and ethnic diversity will continue. By the year 2000, it is estimated that only 42 percent of southern California's residents will be Caucasian whereas 41 percent will be Hispanic, 9 percent Asian, and 8 percent black (Conklin, 1985:5). In short, Caucasians will be in the minority.

Immigrants, whether legal or illegal, are resented by many Americans. They are seen as reducing the chances of the current residents. Immigrants are often perceived as threats to jobs, and their willingness to work for low wages is believed to depress wages and working conditions for others. They are thought to be a drain on taxpayers because of the social services they require, such as health care and education. These resentments are especially acute where migrants are a significant part of the population. Yet studies challenge the notion that immigrants are an economic drain on a region. Mexican immigrants, both legal and illegal, pay more in taxes than they cost in government services, with the exception of education. On the basis of the 1980 census of California, a study by the Rand Corporation found that less than 5 percent of all Mexican immigrants received any cash public assistance, and a vast majority of them paid payroll and Social Security taxes. Overall, Mexican immigration has probably been an economic asset to California in that it stimulated employment growth and kept wages competitive (Conklin, 1986:5). Furthermore, certain industries such as the garment industry, agriculture, restaurants, hotels, and other service industries depend largely on immigrant labor. Thus, the immigrants actually provide benefits to the economy.

The Changing Racial and Ethnic Landscape.   The recent migration is rapidly and permanently changing the face of America: "It is altering its racial makeup, its landscapes and cityscapes, its taste in food and clothes and music, its entire perception of itself and its way of life" (Friedrich, 1985:26–27). Let's examine, briefly, the two categories whose numbers dominate the recent migrants—Hispanics and Asians.

Hispanics.   As recently as 1980, Hispanics were 6.4 percent of the total U.S. population. By 1988 they had increased by 34 percent (five times the population growth rate in the United States) to 8.1 percent of the population (19.4 million). By the year 2000, Hispanics are expected to total 30.3 million (10.8 percent of the total population) and by 2020 they will be the largest minority group (see Table 4–2).

Asians.   In 1970 Asian Americans numbered 1.4 million (1.5 percent of the total U.S. population). Since then, they have migrated in large numbers to the United States, including more than 700,000 Indochinese refugees after the Vietnam War, swelling their numbers to 5.1 million (2.1 percent of the population) in 1985. It is estimated that they will more than double in size in the year 2000 to about 12.1 million (see Table 4–2).

The Aging Population: The Graying of America

The age distribution of the population has been shifting significantly in this century, with more Americans living past the arbitrary line of 65 years of

Table 4–2
Population 1980 and as Projected for 2000 and 2020: Four Main Racial/Ethnic Groups (Assuming an Annual Net Immigration of 1 Million)

Racial/Ethnic Group	1980 Number (millions)	1980 Percent of Total	2000 Number (millions)	2000 Percent of Total	2020 Number (millions)	2020 Percent of Total
White	181.0	79.9	200.3	71.7	205.6	64.9
Black	26.5	11.7	36.4	13.0	44.4	14.0
Hispanic	14.6	6.4	30.3	10.8	46.6	14.7
Asian and other	4.4	2.0	12.1	4.3	20.3	6.4
Total U.S. population	226.5	100.0	279.1	100.0	316.9	100.0

Source: Leon F. Bouvier and Cary B. Davis, *The Future Racial Composition of the United States* (Washington, D.C.: Population Reference Bureau, Inc., 1982). Reprinted by permission.

age. In 1900, about 4.1 percent of the population was over 65 years of age (3.1 million), whereas more than 29.8 million Americans (12.2 percent) were in that category in 1987 (U.S. Bureau of the Census, 1989:13). The average life expectancy in 1900 was 49 years of age and in 1987 was 74.9 years of age. Even as the average life expectancy gradually levels off, the number of elderly will continue to swell, as Figure 4–2 shows. Moreover, the proportion will grow steadily—to an estimated 16 percent in 2020 and 21.7 percent by 2050. A surge in the number and proportion of elderly will occur between 2010 and 2025, when the baby boom generation reaches retirement age.

As the aged population grows in size, societal problems of providing for the needs of the elderly will be heightened. Older people have specialized medical problems that are expensive to treat. They are retired, so they must live on pensions. And the problems of financial support are exacerbated as the nonold become proportionately smaller, creating a "piggyback" problem of too many nonproductive people being supported by two few productive workers. As the number of elderly increases, the tax burden on the nonold will be extremely high—or benefits to the aged will decrease dramatically. How will the old react to the increased strain and pressure on the community and institutional social service delivery systems? Will they increase political pressures on the government? But the burdened nonold may also pressure politicians to reduce services to the elderly.

Elderly people have become politically active in an attempt to change some of the social conditions especially damaging to them. Not only are they the age group most likely to vote, but they also are joining in collective efforts to bring about changes beneficial to them. Several national organizations are dedicated to political action that will benefit the elderly, such as the American Association for Retired Persons (AARP), with 30 million members in 1989 and growing by 8,000 every day (it is the nation's largest special-interest organization), the National Committee to Preserve Social Security and Medicare, the National Council of Senior Citizens, the National Council on Aging (a confederation of some 1400 public and private social welfare agencies), the National Caucus on Black Aged, and the Gerontological Society. Collectively,

Figure 4–2
**Number of
Elderly for
1950–2020**

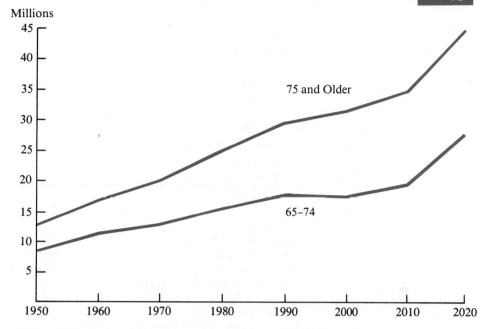

Sources: Bureau of the Census, "Historical Statistics of the United States: Colonial Times to 1970"; "Projections of the Population of the United States: 1977–2050." *Current Population Reports,* Series P-25, No. 704. Reprinted from Mary Barberis, "America's Elderly: Policy Implications," policy supplement to *Population Bulletin* 35 (January 1981): 4.

these organizations have many millions of members. They work through lobbyists, mailing campaigns, advertising, and other processes to improve the lot of the elderly in American society.

Just how effective these organizations are is unknown. But as the elderly continue to increase in numbers, their sphere of influence is likely to increase as well. Since they now account for about 15 percent of the voting public, elderly citizens could be a significant voting bloc if they developed an age consciousness and voted alike. Politicians from states with a high concentration of old people are increasingly aware of their potential voting power, and legislation more sympathetic to the needs of the elderly may be forthcoming. It is probably only a matter of time before the elderly will focus their concerns and become an effective pressure group that demands equity.

Technology

Technological change in the United States has been so rapid that it could be characterized as revolutionary. As Sykes has said, paraphrasing Michael Harrington:

> Our lives are becoming drastically transformed not by any self-conscious plan or the machinations of a few, but by the unanticipated consequences of economic and technological development in which we are all implicated. It is the

man of business and industry, especially with his goal of productivity and his skillful allocation of resources, who has been the great revolutionary of our era. He has remade our existence far more than any ideologist, smashing institutions, shifting the landscape, stuffing some regions with people and depopulating others—all without a policy or overall purpose. (Sykes, 1971:30; see Harrington, 1965)

Technological breakthroughs (for example, the assembly line, computers, robots) are indeed revolutionary since they create and destroy occupations. They may make some products obsolete and increase the demand for others. They alter behavior, and may even cause a shift in values. Thus, technology solves some problems but creates some new ones. As Charles Silberman has said:

> Economic growth reduces poverty, but it also produces congestion, noise, and pollution of the environment. Technological change widens the individual's range of choice and makes economic growth possible; it also dislocates workers from their jobs and their neighborhoods. Affluence plus new technology frees men from slavery to the struggle for existence, from the brutalizing labor that had been man's condition since Adam; it thereby forces them to confront the questions of life's meaning and purpose even while it destroys the faith that once provided answers. (Silberman, 1970:22)

The industrial techniques of the early 1900s, for instance, had a number of profound effects. They created a need for a large working class of semi-

Technological breakthroughs are indeed revolutionary; they both create and destroy occupations.

skilled workers whose tasks were largely repetitive. They fostered the growth of cities (and conversely the decline of rural areas). They created products at a relatively low cost, thereby causing the decline of many skilled craftspersons. The high influx of goods through mass production increased the probability of economic booms and depressions, since production and distribution were not always synchronized.

As technology advances many of the jobs created in an earlier era are displaced. There is no longer the need for huge masses of semiskilled workers. The present demand is for educated white-collar workers with narrow specialties. In 1956 there were for the first time more white-collar workers than blue-collar workers. The problem now is that having a narrow specialty ensures obsolescence, since new techniques and knowledge undoubtedly will alter present arrangements very quickly.

Technological changes are the cause of many social problems as well as the source of varied blessings. The paradoxical nature of this trend is important to consider, because both aspects are real and have profound effects upon individuals, groups, and the society as a whole. Much of the current unrest is in reaction to the "bad" qualities engendered by these trends.

Contemporary technology has replaced tedious tasks and backbreaking tasks with labor-saving devices and more leisure time. Life without electricity, television, central heating, air conditioning, and other "necessities" would be difficult for most Americans to accept. For many Americans, however, people are viewed as victims of technology. In the words of Philip Slater:

> We talk of technology as the servant of man, but it is a servant that now dominates the household, too powerful to fire, upon whom everyone is helplessly dependent. We tiptoe about and speculate upon his mood. What will be the effects of such-and-such an invention? How will it change our daily lives? We never ask, for example, if the trivial conveniences offered by the automobile could really offset the calamitous disruption and depersonalization of our lives that it brought about. We simply say "You can't stop progress" and shuffle back inside. (Slater, 1970:44–45)

Technological advances in communications and transportation have had profound liberating consequences for Americans. Transoceanic flights, space travel, instantaneous worldwide communications, color television from Neptune or Rangoon have had the effect of emancipating human beings from the provinciality of their local communities. We have seen alternatives. Dogma has less of a hold on our thinking. We have participated vicariously in historical events. The old customs, the status quo are brought into question as never before.

Television has had an especially important impact on American life. The exact nature of this impact is difficult to assess, however, since young adults today are the first to have been exposed to television from birth. The average American child by age 18 has watched 22,000 hours of television, 500,000 commercials, 18,000 murders, and countless acts of aggression (Public Broadcasting System, 1984). The same average viewer has watched thousands of

Winning Civil Rights for the Disabled

In 1989 Congress passed historic legislation to protect the civil rights of disabled people. This bill, the Americans with Disabilities Act, extends to the disabled the same protections against discrimination that were given blacks and women in the 1960s and 1970s.

There are 43 million disabled Americans, defined as anyone with a physical or mental impairment that "substantially limits" everyday living. In other words, this category includes a wide range of people, such as the mentally retarded, paraplegics, the blind, those with cerebral palsy, and those with AIDS. Before this legislation, disabled people faced discrimination in jobs, social situations, and transportation. The new law prohibits stores, hotels, restaurants, and theaters from denying access to disabled persons. Employers can no longer reject qualified workers just because they are disabled. Moreover, employers must modify the workplace to make it accessible to their disabled workers. Public buildings under construction or undergoing remodeling must be made accessible to wheelchair users

under the new legislation. So, too, must public transportation vehicles be equipped with lifts to accommodate wheelchair users. Finally, telephone companies must now have operators who can take messages typed by deaf persons on a Telecommunications Device for the Deaf and then relay it orally to a hearing person on another phone.

The disabled are one of the last minority groups to win their civil rights. They were behind racial minorities and women because they did not mobilize a vast movement with highly visible protests. They also lacked a charismatic leader, as had blacks with Martin Luther King, Jr., and women with Betty Friedan. Nevertheless, they achieved some early victories with a 1973 law that protected the disabled from discrimination by institutions receiving federal funding (similar to Title IX legislation prohibiting discrimination against women in education) and 1975 legislation that ensured all disabled children access to schools.

The sweeping victory for the disabled in 1989 was won despite the contrary efforts of many in the business community who argued that the

hours of inane situation comedy, fantasy, game shows, and music videos. He or she also has watched great drama, debates, music, and has been educated to the wonders of nature. Additionally, the television medium has been used to persuade him or her to "need" certain products, to form certain opinions, and to vote for particular candidates. But more important, television has forced persons to broaden their horizons. One's experience is no longer limited to the local community. Through television we participate vicariously in wars, riots, demonstrations, assassinations, coronations, United Nations debates, festivals, famines, summit meetings, the Olympic Games, national disasters, and international crises. Whereas persons once were exposed to a consistent set of expectations and constraints, television (as well as the modern means of transportation) presents us with a variety of lifestyles and ideologies.

In sum, the technological revolution has an immense impact upon individuals and institutions because it is responsible for internal migration, changes in the occupational structure, and the freeing of individuals from the provinciality of localism.

provisions were too costly to businesses. Success was achieved over this considerable opposition through a number of means. Foremost, the disabled have developed a common identity ("class consciousness") through a shared outrage at the discrimination they experience. Now, instead of feelings of isolation, feelings of a common bond and empowerment have emerged among the disabled. Even though more disabled people now receive an education (a result of greater access fostered by the 1973 and 1975 federal laws), they continue to face severe discrimination in the job market.

The resulting frustration has led many to become active in the disabilities movement. Some of these people joined advocacy groups while others joined together to employ tactics of civil disobedience, such as disrupting public transportation or blocking access to city hall, in order to make their plight more visible. In one celebrated case, the students at Gallaudet University, a college for the deaf, protested the selection of a hearing president in 1988. They refused to go to classes, occupied the administration building, and eventually forced the newly appointed president to resign and the governing board to appoint the university's first deaf president. The 1989 victory was also fueled by increased numbers of disabled people, including the aged, who had become disabled with blindness, deafness, arthritis, and the like (it is estimated that the number of elderly Americans with at least one disability increased from 5 million in 1984 to 6.2 million in 1990) and those with AIDS. With the realization that about one-fifth of Americans are disabled, politicians have found it difficult to vote against them. As a cohesive group, the disabled have considerable potential political clout. Their growing sense of a shared condition and common identity have made their voting as a bloc on certain issues more likely than ever. The result has been, finally, legislation guaranteeing their civil rights.

Source: The content of this essay has been taken from a number of sources, especially, Joseph P. Shapiro, "Liberation Day for the Disabled," *U. S. News & World Report* (September 18, 1989): 20–24; and Jason De Parle, "Realizing the Rights of the Disabled," *The New York Times* (December 17, 1989), Section 4, pp. 1, 5.

The Government

Although the government can resist change, it can also be a powerful force for change (Lauer, 1973:153–159). For example, in the United States the government has fought wars and made peace, been imperialistic, opened the West, subsidized the transcontinental railroad, seized land from the native Americans, built dams and canals, harnessed the atom, and initiated space travel. Through laws the government has stimulated farming (the Homestead Act of 1862 gave farmers tracts of land), encouraged education (the Morrill Act of 1862 instituted land grant colleges in each state), desegregated schools (*Brown* v. *Board of Education*), and attempted to eliminate sexism in the schools (Title IX).

The government has been active in all major changes in American history. It has not been a disinterested bystander but rather an impetus for change in a particular direction. Most important, the government has tended to promote changes that benefited those already affluent segments of society. Those actions providing equity for the lower strata of society generally have occurred when there was a threat of social unrest (Lauer, 1973:156–157; Piven and Cloward, 1971).

Telepower and the Global Village

The human use of communications contains the key to the future of our species. The linking of our optical and electronic technologies in new and different ways is not only the key to a new golden age, but a high-risk gamble as well. Our new telepower technologies can make us or break us.

The "global electronic machine" is where it all starts. This machine is far bigger than a nuclear aircraft carrier, a C5A cargo jetliner, or even a continuous-process automobile-manufacturing plant. It contains hundreds of millions of tons of coaxial cable buried underground and beneath the oceans. It includes electronic switches and exchange equipment with enough gold and silver to fully stock a large jewelry store. Parts of the machine are invisible because they are flying in space—orbiting in circles a tenth of the way to the moon. Over a hundred of these space communications devices are relaying billions of messages around the world every year. The parts of the global electronic machine are now so numerous that no one can count them. Billions of telephones, television sets, facsimile devices, telexes, computers, and radios are linked to this massive network. Each year, the colossal machine grows by leaps and bounds as fiber-optic cables, new electronic switches, and new "ports" are added to accommodate more users around the world.

The machine is making the global village a reality. Soon, people in remote Tuvalu and Niue in the South Pacific will be able to call Chicago, Toulouse, or Chiang Mai, Thailand. In the 20 years since the moon landing, the number of people able to see global events on television has expanded sixfold from 500 million to 3 billion people. Our ability to share information and knowledge is today creating global trade and culture. Tomorrow, it will begin to form a global brain—a global consciousness. . . .

THE NEW GLOBALISM

Increasingly, there will be a global economy and a global market, where remoteness largely disappears. Everyone, even in Burkina Faso and Borneo, will "plug in" to the global electronic machine.

Examples of the electronic global village today are everywhere. Television coverage of the 1988 Summer and Winter Olympics reached an estimated global audience of 3 billion, or 60 percent of the world. Close to $100 trillion in electronic fund transfers occur globally via satellite or cable connection every year. Everything from weather forecasting and scientific data exchange to commodity trading, airline reservations, and global marketing are tied to the global electronic machine . . . .

JOBS IN THE TELEPOWER ECONOMY

Both labor and patterns of work face a period of great turmoil in the age of telepower. Changes to be faced include perennial and lifelong job retraining, technological unemployment, the 168-hour workweek, telecommuting to work, and "electronic immigrants" competing for local service jobs.

The global electronic machine cannot help but redefine work and reshape the world's economies. One change already emerging is the 168-hour workweek. With a global society, the movement of the sun and of the economy never stops. Airline booking systems, global

Social Movements Oriented to Changing Society

There are three types of social movements that are political in nature. There are those that are organized to prevent changes, the resistance movements discussed earlier. There are **reform movements,** which seek to alter a specific part of society. These movements commonly focus on a single issue such as women's rights, gay liberation, or the environment. Typically there is an

electronic-fund-transfer systems, satellite-system controls, and hundreds of computer systems, robotic manufacturing units, and power and tele-communications networks run day and night, seven days a week, 365 days a year. Our electronic servants do not need to eat or sleep and usually are most productive if they work every hour of the week—168 hours. This means more shift work, more automation, and even more telerobotics so so that many plants and facilities can be monitored and controlled from remote locations . . . .

CONVERGING TECHNOLOGIES

The new telepower technologies will affect more than just jobs. The scope, structure, and marketing strategies of high-technology corporations will also be greatly affected. It seems likely, based on current trends, that we will see the consolidation of many key technologies, particularly computers, robotics, artificial intelligence, tele-communications, advanced transportation, aerospace, and advanced energy systems. This combination of converging technologies is called, for lack of a better name, "tele-computer-energetics." The parallels in technology that result from computer chips, solar cells, digital telecommunications, artificial intelligence, and advanced software development create a powerful incentive to create economies of scale, density, technology, and scope in these increasingly interrelated fields . . . .

"ELECTRONIC IMMIGRANTS"

The key element in charting corporate and economic activity in the age of the global brain is that no important trend can or will be "local." Tele-computer-energetics, technological unemployment, and the 168-hour workweek will be experienced around the world. The global electronic machine will serve to make these changes happen more quickly as the constraints of time are overcome. One trend will happen as a direct result of the global machine: the creation of a new type of global worker, called the "electronic immigrant."

This new worker will telecommute to work over great distances, perhaps even many thousands of miles. People in the relatively cheaper labor markets—such as Jamaica, Barbados, the Philippines, India, and China—will be recruited and trained to perform a variety of services that can be performed remotely, such as computer programming, word processing, inventory control and management, or telephone sales.

The ability to recruit and electronically import cheap professional services into the United States, Japan, and Europe could become the top international trade issue of the twenty-first century. Beyond the trade and job impacts of electronic immigrants, there will also be political impacts. If more and more jobs in a developing country are those held by electronic immigrants working for a wealthier country, there could come a time when the economic ties begin to dictate political relationships. This is to suggest that if the electronic-immigrant trend continues unchecked, we could see the creation of "telecolonies," whose local finances and politics are largely controlled from an overseas capital.

Source: Joseph N. Pelton, "Telepower: The Emerging Global Brain," *The Futurist* 23 (September/October 1989): 9–13. Reprinted by permission.

---

aggrieved group such as blacks, native Americans, homosexuals, farmers, or workers that focuses its strategy on changing the laws and customs to improve its situation (see Panel 4–3). As noted in the previous chapter, at various times in American history oppressed groups have organized successful drives to change the system to provide more equity. The Civil Rights Movement of the 1950s and 1960s provides an example. Blacks had long been exploited in American society. A series of events in this period, such as the jailing of Rosa Parks (a black woman) for not giving her seat on a bus to a white man as was the custom, raised the consciousness of blacks and whites. A leader emerged, Martin Luther King, Jr., who inspired blacks to stand up against oppression. He and others organized marches, sit-ins, boycotts, and court cases, which eventually succeeded in destroying the racist laws and customs of the South. King's reform movement was bent on tearing down existing norms and values and substituting new ones. Many individuals and groups resisted these efforts.

The third type of social movement—**revolutionary movements**—seeks radical changes. Such movements go beyond reform by seeking to replace the existing social structure with a new one. For example, a shift from a socialist to a capitalist economy would dramatically change all areas of social life, as is occurring throughout eastern Europe.

Several categories of persons are particularly susceptible to the appeal of social movements. Obvious candidates for recruits are the disadvantaged. The American economic system, because it encourages private property, profit, and accumulation, divides people into rich and poor, powerful and powerless (Wolfe, 1977). The result, as suggested by the theory of Karl Marx, is a class which bears all the burdens of society without sharing its advantages (Marx, 1967). At the other end of the scale there is a class that lives in affluence at the expense of the oppressed. The antagonism between these two groups will ultimately result in the attempt by the oppressed to change the system. Clearly, individuals who define themselves as oppressed are ripe for appeals to change a system they consider unjust.

There are other categories of persons who, because of their status in the social system, are also candidates for involvement in social movements (Lauer, 1973:159–165). These types share a condition called **status anguish**—a fundamental concern with the contradictions in the individual's status set. One type of status anguish results from **marginality** (the condition resulting from taking part in two distinct ways of life without belonging fully to either) (see Hughes, 1944–1945). Some examples of categories experiencing marginality are second-generation immigrants, recent migrants from rural areas to urban centers, and interracial couples. These people are in two different worlds but not fully part of either. The result, commonly, is psychic stress which may manifest itself in attempts by the marginal group to seek change that would allow them to be accepted.

Another form of status anguish that occurs is the condition of **status inconsistency** (when a person ranks high on one status dimension and low on another). A black physician, for example, has high occupational status in American society but ranks low on the racial dimension of status. Such an individual is accepted and treated according to his or her high status by some while others ignore the occupational dimension and consider only his or her race. Faced with this kind of contradiction, individuals may react by withdrawal from painful situations, accommodation, or aggression.

The third form of status anguish—**status withdrawal**—occurs as a result of losing status. Those individuals whose occupations have lost out to new technology are included in this category. Another example would be small entrepreneurs who cannot compete with huge corporations. These downwardly mobile persons are typically going to blame outside conditions for their problems and seek reforming or revolutionary means to restore their lost status.

CHAPTER REVIEW

1. Within societies there are structural forces that work to achieve change while there are others that operate to promote stability. Both change and stability are inevitable and necessary for the survival of societies. These contradictory forces present another inherent duality in social systems.

2. The forces for stability are the constraints of customs, traditions, myths, and ideologies.

3. Institutions are barriers to social change because they provide answers from tradition. The institution of the government inhibits change because of systemic imperatives (the necessity of order, the stifling of dissent, enforcing the law, and promoting the political and economic systems). Also the organization of the government preserves the status quo.

4. Bureaucracies are complex organizations designed to increase efficiency by dividing work into small tasks performed by specialists; by having a chain of command in which each position has clearly defined responsibilities; by making decisions based on technical knowledge; and by judging performance by proficiency.

5. Bureaucracies promote the status quo in several ways. Unquestioned following of rules and orders means that new and unusual situations cannot be handled because the rules do not apply. Promotions within the hierarchy are made on the basis of conformity, loyalty, and productivity.

6. Ideological beliefs can stifle change. Religious beliefs, for example, have rejected new ideas and technologies throughout history.

7. A social movement is a collective attempt to promote or resist change. A resistance movement is explicitly organized to resist change.

8. Population growth is another source of socie-

tal change. The baby boom generation provides an excellent example. This bulge of an extra 10 million people has had dramatic effects on society as it moves through the age structure.

9. Urbanization, the concentration of people in limited geographical areas, is another force for social change. The growth of cities and suburbs, and the racial transformation of the central cities in this century have greatly affected changes in American society.

10. Migration is having a profound effect on contemporary life. Migration patterns away from central cities to suburbs and from the industrial Northeast to the sunbelt are bringing economic problems to the abandoned areas and increased economic and political power to the growing regions.

11. Immigration, legal and illegal, is adding as it always has to the ethnic diversity of the United States. It is also bringing problems, such as increased hostilities among competing groups and increased costs for social services.

12. New immigration patterns and the growth of blacks, Hispanics, and Asians are changing the racial proportions of many areas. These changes have paralleled conservative economic strategies and political setbacks in the progressive legislation affecting racial-ethnics. New forms of racial oppression and racial conflict signal a resurgence of a repressive racial order.

13. The proportion of the U.S. population aged 65 and over is growing. This trend will increase during the next 50 years. The problems faced by the old now and in the future increase the likelihood of political activity by them to solve their problems.

14. Technology is a major force for change, altering roles, rules, ideas, and behaviors. A

few examples are the automobile, television, contraceptives, and computers, which have affected the family, created and destroyed occupations, and changed perceptions.

15. The government, although it can resist change, can also be a prime mover by financing new technologies, opening or closing trade with other nations, stimulating the economy, and the like.

16. There are two types of social movements organized to promote change. A reform movement seeks to alter a specific part of society such as discrimination against a certain category. The goal of a revolutionary movement is more ambitious, seeking the transformation of the entire society.

17. Social movements to enhance or inhibit change appeal to certain categories of persons. These are the disadvantaged and oppressed and those who share a condition called "status anguish." These persons are marginal in status (such as children of immigrants, recent migrants from rural to urban areas, and interracial couples), have inconsistent status, or have lost status.

KEY TERMS

Systemic imperatives	Resistance movement	Revolutionary movement
Bureaucratization	Demographic factors	Status anguish
Peter Principle	Fertility	Marginality
Ideology	White flight	Status inconsistency
Social movement	Reform movement	Status withdrawal

STUDY QUESTIONS

1. Using the information from this and the last chapter, what are the contradictory forces in social systems that work toward stability *and* change; integration *and* conflict?
2. How do population changes affect societal changes? Give specific examples using change in fertility rates, migration, distribution by race, and the changing age structure.
3. What are the benefits of bureaucracy? What are its deficiencies?
4. Immigration has always been a major source of ethnic diversity in the United States. Currently, the influx of Hispanics and Asians is having a dramatic impact on American society. What are the consequences of this "new immigration"?
5. Discuss how technological change has positive *and* negative consequences for individuals and society.

FOR FURTHER READING

Social Change: General

Charles L. Harper, *Exploring Social Change* (Englewood Cliffs, NJ: Prentice-Hall, 1989).

Barry Jones, *Sleepers Awake! Technology and the Future of Work* (Melbourne: Oxford University Press, 1982).

William Kornhauser, *The Politics of Mass Society* (New York: Free Press, 1959).

Alvin Toffler, *The Third Wave* (New York: Morrow, 1980).

Steven Vago, *Social Change* (New York: Holt, Rinehart and Winston, 1980).

Forces for Social Change

Daniel Bell, *The Cultural Contradictions of Capitalism* (New York: Basic Books, 1976).

Barry Bluestone and Bennett Harrison, *The Deindustrialization of America* (New York: Basic Books, 1982).

Herbert Blumer, "Collective Behavior," in Alfred M. Lee (ed.), *Principles of Sociology,* 2nd ed. (New York: Barnes and Noble, 1955), pp. 165–198.

Lawrence G. Brewster, *The Public Agenda: Issues in American Politics* (New York: St. Martin's, 1984).

Hugh Davis Graham and Ted Robert Gurr (eds.), *Violence in America: Historical and Comparative Perspectives,* rev. ed. (Beverly Hills, CA: Sage, 1979).

Michael Harrington, *Decade of Decision* (New York: Simon and Schuster, 1980).

Bennett Harrison and Barry Bluestone, *The Great U-Turn: Corporate Restructuring and the Polarizing of America* (New York: Basic Books, 1988).

Landon Y. Jones, *Great Expectations: America and the Baby Boom Generation* (New York: Ballantine, 1980).

Frank Levy, *Dollars and Dreams: The Changing American Income Distribution* (New York: Russell Sage Foundation, 1987).

Michael Parenti, *Power and the Powerless* (New York: St. Martin's, 1978).

Max Weber, *The Theory of Social and Economic Organization,* A. M. Henderson and Talcott Parsons (trans.), (New York: Free Press, 1947).

Chapter Five

Culture

What is the meaning of a kiss? The meaning varies within a society depending on the situation and differs widely from society to society. As argued in the following excerpt, the kiss is a cultural creation.

Nothing seems more natural than a kiss. Consider the French kiss, also known as the soul kiss, deep kiss, or tongue kiss (to the French, it was the Italian kiss, but only during the Renaissance). Western societies regard this passionate exploration of mouths and tongues as an instinctive way to express love and to arouse desire. To a European who associates deep kisses with erotic response, the idea of one without the other feels like summer without sun.

Yet soul kissing is completely absent in many cultures of the world, where sexual arousal may be evoked by affectionate bites or stinging slaps. Anthropology and history amply demonstrate that, depending on time and place, the kiss may or may not be regarded as a sexual act, a sign of a friendship, a gesture of respect, a health threat, a ceremonial celebration, or disgusting behavior that deserves condemnation . . . .

One of the first modern studies to dispel the belief that sexual behavior is universally the same (and therefore instinctive) was *Patterns of Sexual Behavior,* written in 1951 by Clellan Ford and Frank Beach. Ford and Beach compared many of the sexual customs of 190 tribal societies that were recorded in the Human Relations Area Files at Yale University.

Unfortunately, few of the field studies mentioned kissing customs at all. Of the 21 that did, some sort of kissing accompanied intercourse in 13 tribes—the Chiricahua, Cree, Crow, Gros Ventre, Hopi, Huichol, Kwakiutl, and Tarahumara of North America; the Alorese, Keraki, Trobrianders, and Trukese of

Oceania; and in Eurasia, among the Lapps. Ford and Beach noted some variations: The Kwakiutl, Trobrianders, Alorese, and Trukese kiss by sucking the
lips and tongue of their partners; the Lapps like to kiss the mouth and nose at
the same time. (I would add Margaret Mead's observation of the Arapesh. They
"possess the true kiss," she wrote; they touch lips, but instead of pressing,
they mutually draw the breath in.)

But sexual kissing is unknown in many societies including the Balinese,
Chamorro, Manus, and Tinguian of Oceania; the Chewa and Thonga of Africa;
the Siriono of South America; and the Lepcha of Eurasia. In such cultures the
mouth-to-mouth kiss is considered dangerous, unhealthy, or disgusting, the
way most Westerners would regard a custom of sticking one's tongue into a
lover's nose. Ford and Beach report that when the Thonga first saw Europeans
kissing they laughed, remarking, "Look at them—they eat each others saliva
and dirt."

Deep kissing apparently has nothing to do with the degree of sexual inhibi-
tion or repression in a culture. Donald S. Marshall, an anthropologist who
studied a small Polynesian island he called Mangaia, found that all Mangaian
women are taught to be orgasmic and sexually active; yet kissing, sexual and
otherwise, was unknown until Westerners (and their popular films) arrived on
the island. In contrast, John C. Messenger found that on a sexually repressed
Irish island where sex is considered dirty, sinful, and, for women, a duty to be
endured, tongue kissing was unknown as late as 1966 . . . .

Small tribes and obscure Irish islanders are not the only groups to eschew
tongue kissing. The advanced civilizations of China and Japan, which regard
sexual proficiency as high art, apparently cared little about it. In their volumi-
nous production of erotica—graphic displays of every possible sexual position,
angle of intercourse, variation of partner and setting—mouth-to-mouth kissing
is conspicuous by its absence. Japanese poets have rhapsodized for centuries
about the allure of the nape of the neck, but they have been silent on the
mouth; indeed, kissing is acceptable only between mother and child. (The Japanese have no word for kissing—though they recently borrowed from English to
create "kissu.") Intercourse is "natural"; a kiss, pornographic. When Rodin's
famous sculpture, *The Kiss*, came to Tokyo in the 1920s as part of a show of
European art, it was concealed from public view behind a bamboo curtain.

Among cultures of the West, the number of nonsexual uses of the kiss is
staggering. The simple kiss has served any or all of several purposes: greeting
and farewell, affection, religious or ceremonial symbolism, deference to a
person of higher status. (People also kiss icons, dice, and other objects, of
course, in prayer, for luck, or as part of a ritual.) Kisses make the hurt go away,
bless sacred vestments, seal a bargain. In story and legend a kiss has started
wars and ended them, and awakened Sleeping Beauty and put Brunnhilde to
sleep.

Source: Excerpts from Leonore Tiefer, "The Kiss," *Human Nature* (July 1978): 28,30. Copyright © 1978 by Human Nature, Inc. Reprinted by permission of the publisher.

An important focus of sociology is on the social influences on human behavior. As people interact over time two fundamental sources of constraints on individuals emerge—social structure and culture. As noted in Chapter 2, *social structure* refers to the linkages and network among the members of a social organization. **Culture,** the subject of this chapter, is the knowledge that the members of a social organization share. Because this shared knowledge includes ideas about what is right, how one is to behave in various situations, religious beliefs, and communication, culture constrains not only behavior but how people think about and interpret their world.

This chapter is divided into two parts. The first describes the nature of culture and its importance for understanding human behavior. The second part focuses on one aspect of culture—values. This discussion is especially vital for understanding the organization and problems of society, in this case, American society.

CULTURE: THE KNOWLEDGE THAT PEOPLE SHARE

Social scientists studying a society foreign to them must spend months, perhaps years, learning the culture of that group. They must learn the meanings for the symbols (written and spoken language, gestures, and rituals) the individuals in that society employ. They must know the feelings people share as to what is appropriate or inappropriate behavior. Additionally, they need to know the rules of the society: which activities are considered important, the skills members have in making and using tools, as well as the knowledge members need to exist in that society. In short, the analyst must discover all the knowledge that people share—that is, he or she must know the culture. Let us examine each of the characteristics of this important social concept.

Characteristics of Culture

An Emergent Process.　As individuals interact on any kind of sustained basis, they exchange ideas about all sorts of things. In time they develop common ideas, common ways of doing things, and common interpretations for certain actions. In so doing, the participants have created a culture. The emergent quality of culture is an ongoing process; it is built up slowly rather than being present at the beginnings of social organization. The culture of any group is constantly undergoing change because the members are in continuous interaction. Culture, then, is never completely static.

A Learned Behavior.　Culture is not instinctive or innate in the human species; it is not part of the biological equipment of human beings. The biological equipment of humans, however, makes culture possible. That is, we are symbol-making creatures capable of attaching meaning to particular objects and actions and communicating these meanings to others. When a person joins a new social organization, she or he must learn the culture of that group. This is true for the infant born into a society as well as for a college woman joining a sorority or a young man inducted into the armed forces, or for immigrants to a new society. This process of learning the culture is called **socialization.**

A Channel for Human Behavior.   Culture, since it emerges from social interaction, is an inevitable development of human society. More important, it is essential in the maintenance of any social system because it provides two crucial functions—predictability of action and stability. To accomplish these functions, however, culture must restrict human freedom (although as we shall see, cultural constraints are not normally perceived as such); through cultural patterns the individual is expected to conform to the expectations of the group.

How does culture work to constrain individuals? Or put another way, how does culture become internalized in people so that their actions are controlled? Somehow culture operates not only outside individuals but also inside them. Sigmund Freud recognized this process when he conceptualized the **superego** as that part of the personality structure that internalizes society's morals and thus inhibits people from committing acts considered wrong by their parents, a group, or the society.

The process of **internalization** (where society's demands become part of the individual, acting to control his or her behavior) is accomplished mainly in three ways. First, culture becomes part of the human makeup through the belief system into which a child is born. This belief system, provided by parents and those persons immediately in contact with youngsters, shapes their ideas about the surrounding world as well as giving them certain ideas about themselves. The typical American child, for example, is taught to accept Christian beliefs without reservation. These beliefs are literally "force fed," since alternative belief systems are considered unacceptable by the "feeders." It is interesting to note that after Christian beliefs are internalized by the child, they are often used by the "feeders" as levers to keep the child in line.

Second, culture is internalized through psychological identification with the groups to which individuals belong (membership groups), or to which they want to belong (**reference groups**). Individuals want to belong; they want to be accepted by others. Therefore, they tend to conform to the behavior of their immediate group as well as to the wishes of society at large.

Finally, culture is internalized by providing the individual with an identity. People's age, sex, race, religion, and social class have an effect upon the way others perceive them and the way they perceive themselves. Berger has said, "in a sociological perspective, identity is socially bestowed, socially sustained, and socially transformed" (Berger, 1963:98; see also Cuzzort, 1969:203–204).

Culture, then, is not freedom but rather constraint. Of the entire range of possible behaviors (which probably are considered appropriate by some society somewhere), the person of a particular society can choose only from a narrow range of alternatives. The paradox, as Peter Berger has pointed out, is that while society is like a prison to the persons trapped in its cultural demands and expectations, it is not perceived as limiting to individual freedom. Berger has stated it well in the following passage:

> For most of us the yoke of society seems easy to bear. Why? . . . because most of the time we ourselves desire just what society expects of us. We *want* to obey the rules. We *want* the parts that society has assigned to us. (Berger, 1963:93)

Individuals do not see the prisonlike qualities of culture because they have internalized the culture of their society. From birth children are shaped by the culture of the society into which they are born. They retain some individuality because of the configuration of forces unique to their experience (gene structure, peers, parents' social class, religion, and race), but the behavioral alternatives deemed appropriate for them are narrow.

Culture even shapes thought and perception. What we see and how we interpret what we see is determined by culture. CBS News staged an experiment several years ago that illustrates this point. A black man with something in his hand ran down a crowded city street. White bystanders were asked what they saw. The typical response was that they had perceived the black as carrying a gun, knife, or stolen property, and running from the authorities. In fact, the man was running to catch a bus with a rolled-up newspaper in his hand. Would the respondents have interpreted the actions differently if the person were white? Many white Americans believe that blacks tend toward criminal activity. This stereotype can, therefore, affect negatively the interpretation of a socially acceptable act.

For a dramatic illustrative case of the kind of mental closure that may be determined by culture, consider the following riddle about a father and son driving down a highway:

> There is a terrible accident in which the father is killed, and the son, critically injured, is rushed to a hospital. There the surgeon approaches the patient and suddenly cries, "My God, that's my son!"

How is it possible that the critically injured boy is the son of the man in the accident as well as the son of the surgeon? Answers might involve the surgeon being a priest, or a stepfather, or even artificial insemination. The correct answer to this riddle is that the surgeon is the boy's mother. Americans, male and female alike, have been socialized to think of women as occupying roles less important than physician/surgeon. If Russians were given this riddle, they would almost uniformly give the correct answer since approximately three-fourths of Russian physicians are women. So culture may be confining—not liberating. It constrains not only actions but also thinking.

A Maintainer of Boundaries.   Culture not only limits the range of acceptable behavior and attitudes but it instills in its adherents a sense of "naturalness" about the alternatives peculiar to a given society (or other social organization). Thus there is a universal tendency to deprecate the ways of persons from other societies as wrong, old-fashioned, inefficient, or immoral, and to think of the ways of one's own group as superior (as the only right way). The concept for this phenomenon is **ethnocentrism.** The word combines the Greek word *ethnikos,* which means nation or people, and the English word for center. So one's own race, religion, or society is the center of all and therefore superior to all.

Ethnocentrism is demonstrated in statements such as "My fraternity is the best," "Reincarnation is a weird belief," "We are God's chosen people," or "Polygamy is immoral." To name the playoff between the American and National Leagues the "World Series" implies that baseball outside the United States (and Canada) is inferior. Religious missionaries provide a classic example of one among several typical groups convinced that their own faith is the only correct one.

A resolution passed at a town meeting in Milford, Connecticut, in 1640 is a blatant example of ethnocentrism. It stated:

> Voted, the earth is the Lord's and the fulness thereof
> Voted, the earth belongs to the saints
> Voted, we are the saints.

Further examples of ethnocentrism taken from U.S. history are: "manifest destiny," "white man's burden," exclusionary immigration laws such as the Oriental Exclusion Act, and "Jim Crow" laws. A current illustration of ethnocentrism can be seen in the activities of the United States as it engages in exporting the "American way of life," because it is believed that democracy and capitalism are necessities for the good life and therefore best for all peoples.

Ethnocentrism, because it implies feelings of superiority, leads to division and conflict among subgroups within a society and among societies, each of which feels "superior."

Ethnocentric ideas are real because they are believed and they influence perception and behavior. Analysts of U.S. society (whether they are Americans or not) must recognize their own ethnocentric attitudes and the way these affect their own objectivity.

To summarize, culture emerges from social interaction. The paradox is that although culture is human-made, it exerts a tremendous complex of forces that *constrain* the actions and thoughts of human beings. The analyst of any society must be cognizant of these two qualities of culture, for they combine to give a society its unique character; culture explains social change as well as stability; culture explains existing social arrangements (including many social problems); culture explains a good deal of individual behavior because it is internalized by the individual members of society and therefore has an impact (substantial but not total) on their actions and personalities.

Types of Shared Knowledge

The concept of culture refers to knowledge that is shared by the members of a social organization. In analyzing any social organization and, in this case, any society, it is helpful to conceive of culture as combining six types of

The flag is an especially important symbol, and this is why political protesters choose to defile it.

shared knowledge—symbols, technology, ideologies, societal norms, values, and roles.

Symbols. By definition, language refers to symbols that evoke similar meanings in different people. Communication is possible only if persons attribute the same meaning to stimuli such as sounds, gestures, or objects. Language, then, can be written, spoken, or unspoken. A shrug of the shoulders, a pat on the back, the gesturing with a finger (which finger can be *very* significant), a wink, or a nod are examples of unspoken language and vary in meaning from society to society. Consider the varying meaning for two common gestures:

> When displayed by the Emperor, the upright-thumb gesture spared the lives of gladiators in the Roman Coliseum. Now favored by airline pilots, truck drivers and others who lean out of windows, it means "all right" in the United States and most of Western Europe. In other places, including Sardinia and Northern Greece, it is the insulting "up yours." . . . [The "A-Okay" gesture with the thumb and forefinger making a circle means "everything-is-fine" in the United States but it] has very different meaning in parts of Europe. In Southern Italy, for instance, it means "you asshole" or signifies that you desire anal sex. It can mean "you're worth nothing" in France and Belgium. (Ekman, Friesen, and Bear, 1984:67–68)

Technology.   Technology refers to the information, techniques, and tools used by people to satisfy their varied needs and desires. For analytic purposes two types of technology can be distinguished—material and social. **Material technology** refers to knowledge of how to make and use things. It is important to note that the things produced are not part of the culture but represent rather the knowledge that people share and that make it possible to build and use the object. The knowledge is culture, not the object.

Social technology is the knowledge about how to establish, maintain, and operate the technical aspects of social organization. Examples of this are procedures for operating a university, a municipality, or a corporation through such operations as Robert's Rules of Order, bookkeeping, or the kind of specialized knowledge citizens must acquire to function in society (knowing the laws, how to complete income tax forms, how to vote in elections, how to use credit cards and banks) (Olsen, 1976:60; Lenski, 1970:37–38).

Ideologies.   These are shared beliefs about the physical, social, and metaphysical worlds. They may, for example, be statements about the existence of supernatural beings, the best form of government, or racial pride.

Ideologies help individuals interpret events. They also provide the rationale for particular forms of action. They can justify the status quo or demand revolution. A number of competing ideologies exist within American society—for example, fundamentalism and atheism, capitalism and socialism, and white supremacy and black supremacy. Clearly, ideology unites as well as divides and is therefore a powerful human-made (cultural) force within societies.

Societal Norms.   Norms are societal prescriptions for how one is to act in given situations—for example, at a football game, concert, restaurant, church, park, or classroom. We also learn how to act with members of the opposite sex, with our elders, with social inferiors, and with equals. Thus, behavior is patterned. We know how to behave and we can anticipate how others will behave. This allows interaction to occur smoothly.

There is a subdiscipline in sociology called **ethnomethodology,** which is the scientific study of the commonplace activities of daily life. The goal is to discover and understand the underpinnings of relationships (the shared meanings that implicitly guide social behavior). The assumption is that much of social life is "scripted"; that is, the players act according to society's rules (the script). The conduct in the family, in the department store between customer and salesperson, between doctor and patient, between boss and secretary, between coach and player is, in a very real sense, determined by societal scripts.

But what happens when persons do not play according to the common understandings (the script)? The ethnomethodologist Harold Garfinkel (1967) has used this technique to discover the implicit bases of social interaction. Examples of possible rule breaking include: (1) when answering the phone, you remain silent; (2) when selecting a seat in the audience, you ignore the empty seats and choose rather to sit next to a stranger (violating that person's privacy and space); (3) you act as a stranger in your family; (4) in talking with a friend, you insist that that person clarify the sense of commonplace remarks; and (5) you bargain with clerks over the price of every item of food you wish to purchase. Now these behaviors violate the rules of interaction in American society. When they are violated, the other persons in the situation do not know how to respond. Typically, they become confused, anxious, and angry. This buttresses the notion that most of the time social life is very ordered and orderly. We behave in prescribed ways and we anticipate that others will do the same. The norms are strong and we tend to follow them automatically.

In addition to being necessary for the conduct of behavior in society, societal norms vary in importance, as we saw in our discussion of norms at the micro level. There are those norms that are less important—the *folkways*—that are not severely punished if violated. Examples of folkways in American society are: it is expected that men should rise when a woman enters the room (unless she is the maid); women should not wear curlers to the opera; and one does not wear a business suit but go barefoot.

Violation of the *mores* of society is considered important enough by society to merit severe punishment. This type of norm involves morality. Some examples of mores are: one must have only one spouse at a time; "thou shalt not kill" (unless defending one's country or one's own property); and one must be loyal to the United States.

There is a problem, however, for many Americans in deciding the degree of importance for some norms. Figure 5–1 shows the criteria for deciding whether norms should be classified as folkways or mores.

Figure 5–1 shows that on the basis of the two defining criteria there are four possibilities, not just two. It is difficult to imagine cases that would be located in cell (b). The only possibilities are activities that have only recently been designated as very harmful but against which laws have not yet been passed for strict punishment (either because of the natural lag in the courts and legislatures or because powerful groups have been influential in blocking the necessary legislation). The best current example of cases that would fall in cell (b) would be the pollution of lakes, streams, and air by large commercial enterprises. These acts are recognized as having serious consequences for present and future generations, but either go unpunished or receive only minor fines.

Figure 5–1
Classification of Norms

		Severity of Punishment	
		High	Low
Degree of Importance	High	Mores (a)	(b)
	Low	(c)	Folkways (d)

Cell (c), on the other hand, is interesting because there are acts not important to the survival of society or the maintenance of its institutions that receive severe punishments (at least relative to the crime). Some examples would be a male student being suspended from school until he gets his hair cut; persons caught smoking marijuana being sentenced to a jail term; young men burning their draft cards being jailed or drafted; and a woman being fired from her job for not wearing a bra.

Both criteria used to delineate types of norms—degree of importance and severity of the punishments—are determined by those in power. Consequently, activities that are perceived by the powerful as being disruptive of the power structure or institutional arrangements that benefit some and not others are viewed as illegitimate and punished severely. For example, if 10,000 young persons protest against the political system with marches, speeches, and acts of civil disobedience, they are typically perceived as a threat and jailed, beaten, gassed, and harassed by the police and the National Guard. Compare the treatment of these young people with another group of 10,000 on the beaches of Florida during their annual spring break. These people often drink to excess, are sexually promiscuous, and are destructive of property. Generally, the police consider these behaviors as nonthreatening to the system and therefore treat them relatively lightly.

Norms are also situational. Behavior expected in one societal setting may be inappropriate for another. Several examples should make this point clear. One may ask for change from a clerk, but one would not put money in a church collection plate and remove change. Clearly, behavior considered acceptable by fans at a football game (yelling, booing authority figures, even destroying property) would be inexcusable behavior at a poetry reading. Behavior allowable in a bar probably would be frowned upon in a bank. Or doctors may ask patients to disrobe in the examining room but not in the subway.

Finally, because they are properties of groups, norms vary from society to society and from group to group within societies. Thus, behavior appropriate in one group of society may be absolutely inappropriate in another. Some examples of this are:

- *Item:* The "couvade" is a practice surprisingly common throughout the world, but in sharp contrast to what occurs in the United States. This refers to the time when a woman is in childbirth. Instead of the wife suffering, the husband moans and groans and is waited on as though he were in greater pain. After his wife has had the baby she will get up and bring her husband food and comfort. The husband is so incapacitated by the experience that in some societies he stays in bed for as many as 40 days.
- *Item:* Among the Murgin of Australia, a woman giving birth to twins kills one of the babies because it makes her feel like a dog to have a litter instead of one baby. A tribe along the Niger Delta puts both the mother and the twins to death. With the Bankundo of the Congo valley, on the other hand, the mother of twins is the object of honor and veneration.
- *Item:* In some Latin American countries high-status males are expected to have a mistress. This practice is even encouraged by their wives because it

implies high status (given the cost of maintaining two households). In the United States, such a practice is grounds for divorce. American wives would never find such a circumstance something to brag about.

- *Item:* In Pakistan one never reaches for food with his or her left hand. To do so would make the observers physically sick. The reason is that the left hand is used to clean oneself after a bowel movement. Hence, the right hand is symbolically the only hand worthy of accepting food.

Values.   Another aspect of society's structure are its **values,** which are the bases for the norms. These are the criteria used in evaluating objects, acts, feelings, or events as to their relative desirability, merit, or correctness. Values are extremely important, for they determine the direction of individual and group behavior, encouraging some activities and impeding others. For example, efforts to get Americans to conserve energy and other resources run counter to the long-held American values of growth, progress, and individual freedom. Consequently, the prevailing values have thwarted the efforts of various presidents and others to plan carefully about future needs and restrict usage and the rate of growth now.

Roles.   Societies, like other social organizations, have social positions (**statuses**) and behavioral expectations for those who occupy these positions (*roles*). There are family statuses (son or daughter, sibling, parent, husband, wife); age statuses (child, adolescent, adult, aged); sex statuses (male, female); racial statuses (black, Chicano, Indian, white); and socioeconomic statuses (poor, middle class, wealthy). For each of these statuses there are societal constraints on behavior. To become 65 years old in American society is an especially traumatic experience for many. The expectations of society dramatically shift when one reaches this age. The aged are forced into a situation of dependence rather than independence. To be a male or female in American society is to be constrained in a relatively rigid set of expectations. Similarly, blacks and other minorities, because of their minority status, have been expected to "know their place." The power of the social role is best illustrated, perhaps, by the person who occupies two relevant statuses—for example, the black physician or the woman airline pilot. Although each of these persons is a qualified professional, both will doubtless encounter many situations where persons will expect them to behave according to the dictates of the traditional role expectations of their **ascribed status** (race or sex, statuses over which the individual has no control) rather than their **achieved status** (that is, their occupation).

The Social Construction of Reality

A society's culture determines how the members of that society will interpret their environment (Berger and Luckman, 1967). Language, in particular, influences the ways in which the members of a society perceive reality. Two linguists, Edward Sapir and Benjamin Whorf, have shown this by the way the Hopi Indians and Anglos differ in the way each speak about time (Carroll,

Cultural Time

To find social time it is necessary to look beyond the individual perceptions and attitudes, to the temporal construct of the society or culture. Temporal constructs are not to be found in human experience, but rather in the cultural symbols and institutions through which human experience is construed. Our own Indo-European language imposes the concept of time on us at a very early age, so it is difficult to identify with the concept of timelessness. Societies do exist without a consciousness of time. But most societies possess a concept of time. Conceptualizations of time are as varied as the cultures, but most can be categorized by one of three images. Time in the broad sense is viewed as a line (linear), a wheel (cyclical), or as a pendulum (alternating phenomenon). But within these central images, numerous other distinctions must be made. One is tense. Is there a past or present or future, or all three? If more than one, to which is the society oriented and in what way? Another is continuity. Is time continuous or discontinuous? Does the continuity or hiatus have regularity? Another is progressiveness. Is evolutionary transformation expected with the passage of time? Still another is use. Is time used for measuring duration or is it for punctuality? The metaphysical distinctions are numerous. Is there a mode for measuring time? Is it reversible or irreversible? Subjective or objective, or both? Unidirectional? Rectilinear?

These distinctions come into focus when one studies various cultures. The Pawnee Indians, for example, have no past in a temporal sense; they instead have a timeless storehouse of tradition, not a historical record. To them, life has a rhythm but not a progression. To the Hopi, time is a dynamic process without past, present, or future. Instead, time is divided vertically between subjective and objective time. Although Indo-European languages are laden with tensed verbs and temporal adjectives indicating past, present, and future, the Hopi have no such verbs, adjectives, or any other similar linguistic device. The Trobriander is forever in the present. For the Trobriander and the Tiv, time is not continuous throughout the day. Advanced methods of calculating sun positions exist for morning and evening, but time does not exist for the remainder of the day. For the Balinese, time is conceived in a punctual rather than a durational sense. The Balinese calendar is marked off, not by even duration intervals, but rather by self-sufficient periods which indicate coincidence with a period of life. Their descriptive calendar indicates the *kind* of time, rather than what time it is. The Maya had probably the most complicated system of time yet discovered. Their time divisions were regarded as burdens carried by relays of divine carriers—some benevolent, some malevolent. They would succeed each other, and it was very important to determine who was currently carrying in order to know whether it was a good time or a bad time.

Source: Excerpted from F. Gregory Hayden, "A Critical Analysis of Time Stream Discounting for Social Program Evaluation." *The Social Science Journal 17* (January 1980): 26–27. Reprinted by permission.

1956). The Hopi language has no verb tenses and no nouns for times, days, or years. Consequently the Hopi think of time as continuous—without breaks. The English language, in sharp contrast, divides time into seconds, minutes, hours, days, weeks, months, years, decades, centuries, and the like. The use of verb tenses in English clearly informs everyone whether an event occurred in the past, present, or future (see Panel 5–1 for other examples of how time is conceived of in various societies). Clearly precision regarding time is important to English-speaking peoples while unimportant to the Hopi.

There is an African tribe that has no word for the color gray. This implies that they do not see gray even though we "know" that there is such a color and readily see it in the sky and in hair. The Navajo do not distinguish between *blue* and *green* yet they have two words for different kinds of *black*.

The Aimore tribe in eastern Brazil has no word for *two*. The Yancos, an Amazon tribe, cannot count beyond *poettarrarorincoaroac*, their word for *three*. The Temiar people of West Malaysia also stop at three (McWhirter and McWhirter, 1972:167). Can you imagine how this lack of numbers beyond two or three affects the way these people perceive reality?

Our language helps us to make order out of what we experience. Our particular language allows us to perceive differences among things or to recognize a set of things to be alike even when they are not identical. Language permits us to order these by what we think they have in common. As Bronowski has put it:

> Habit makes us think the likeness obvious: it seems to us obvious that all apples are somehow alike, or all trees, or all matter. Yet there are languages in the Pacific Islands in which every tree on the island has a name, but which have no word for tree. To these islanders, trees are not at all alike; on the contrary, what is important to them is that the trees are different. (Bronowski, 1978:21)

The social interpretation of reality is not limited to language. For example, some people believe that there is such a thing as "holy water." Now there is no chemical difference between water and holy water but some people believe that the differences in properties and potential are enormous. To understand holy water we must examine priests and parishioners, not water (Szasz, 1974:17). Similarly, consider the difference between spit and saliva (Turner, n.d.). There is no chemical difference between them, the only difference being that in one case the substance is inside the mouth and in the other it is outside. We swallow saliva continuously and think nothing about it yet one would not gather his or her spit in a container and then drink it. Clearly saliva is defined positively and spit negatively, yet the only difference is a social definition.

There is a debate in philosophy and sociology on this issue of reality. One position—**ontology**—accepts the reality of things because their nature cannot be denied (a chair, a tree, the wind, a society). The opposite side—**epistemology**—argues that all reality is socially constructed. In this view all meaning is created out of a world that generates no meanings of its own (Edgley and Turner, 1975:6). The world is absurd and humans make sense out of it to fit their situation. This extreme position is expressed by two sociologists in the following quotation:

> Fundamental to our view is the assumption that the universe has no intrinsic meaning—it is, at bottom, absurd—and that the task of the sociologist is to discover the various imputed or fabricated meanings constructed by [people] in society. Or, to put it another way, the sociologist's job is to find out *by what illusions people live*. Without these artifacts, these delicately poised fantasies,

most of us would not survive. Society, as we know it, could not exist. Meaninglessness produces terror. And terror must be dissipated by participating in, and believing in, collective fictions. They constitute society's "noble lie," the lie that there is some sort of inherent significance in the universe. It is the job of sociology to understand [how people] impute meaning to the various aspects of life. (Farberman and Goode, 1973:2)

Cultural Relativity

A number of customs from around the world have been described in this chapter. These typically seem to us weird, cruel, or stupid. Anthropologists, though, have helped us to understand that in the cultural context of a given society, the practice may make considerable sense. For example, anthropologist Marvin Harris has explained why sacred cattle are allowed to roam the countryside in India while the people may be starving (Harris, 1975). Outsiders see cow worship as the primary cause of India's hunger and poverty, because cattle do not contribute meat while eating crops that would otherwise go to humans. Harris, however, argues that cattle must not be killed for food because they are the most efficient producer of fuel and food. To kill them would cause the economy to collapse. Cattle contribute to the Indian economy in a number of significant ways. They are the source of oxen, which are the principal traction animals for farming. Their milk helps to meet the nutritional needs of many poor families. India's cattle annually excrete 700 million tons of recoverable manure, half of which is used for fertilizer and the rest for fuel. Cow dung is also used as a household flooring material. If cows were slaughtered during times of famine, the economy would not recover in good times. To Western experts it looks as if the Indian would rather starve to death than to eat his cow. But as Harris has argued, "They don't realize that the farmer would rather eat his cow than starve, but that he will starve if he does eat it" (Harris, 1975:21). The practice of cow worship also allows for a crude redistribution of wealth. The cattle owned by the poor are allowed to roam freely. In this way the poor are able to let their cows graze the crops of the rich and come home at night to be milked. As Harris has concluded:

> The sacredness of the cow is not just an ignorant belief that stands in the way of progress. Like all concepts of the sacred and the profane, this one affects the physical world; it defines the relationships that are important for the maintenance of Indian society.
>
> Indians have the sacred cow; we have the "sacred" car and the "sacred" dog. It would not occur to us to propose the elimination of automobiles and dogs from our society without carefully considering the consequences, and we should not propose the elimination of zebu cattle without first understanding their place in the social order of India.
>
> Human society is neither random nor capricious. The regularities of thought and behavior called culture are the principal mechanisms by which we human beings adapt to the world around us. Practices and beliefs can be rational or irrational, but a society that fails to adapt to its environment is doomed to extinction. Only those societies that draw the necessities of life

from their surroundings, inherit the earth. The West has much to learn from the great antiquity of Indian civilization, and the sacred cow is an important part of that lesson. (Harris, 1978:36)

This extended example is used to convey the idea that the customs of a society should be evaluated in the light of the culture and their functions for that society. These customs should *not* be evaluated by our standards, but by theirs. This is called **cultural relativity.** The problem with cultural relativity, of course, is ethnocentrism—the tendency for the members of each society to assume the rightness of their own customs and practices and the inferiority, immorality, or irrationality of those found in other societies.

VALUES

Even though all of the components of culture are essential for an understanding of the constraints on human behavior, perhaps the quickest way to reach this understanding is to focus on its values. These are the criteria used by the members of society to evaluate objects, ideas, acts, feelings, or events as to their relative desirability, merit, or correctness.

Human beings are valuing beings. They continually evaluate themselves and others. What objects are worth owning? What makes people successful? What activities are rewarding? What is beauty? Of course, different societies have distinctive criteria (values) for evaluating. People are considered successful in the United States, for example, if they accumulate many material things as a result of hard work. In other societies people are considered to be successful if they attain total mastery of their emotions or if they totally reject materialism.

One objective common to any social science course is the hope that students will become aware of the various aspects of social life in an analytical way. For Americans studying their own society this means that while immersed in the subject matter, they also become participant observers. This implies an objective detachment (as much as possible) so that one may understand better the forces which in large measure affect human behavior, individually and in groups.

The primary task for the participant observer interested in societal values is to determine what the values are. There are a number of clues that are helpful for such as task.* The first clue is to determine what most preoccupies people in their conversations and actions. So one might ask: Toward what do people most often direct their action? Is it, for example, contemplation and meditation or physical fitness or the acquiring of material objects? In other words, what gives individuals high status in the eyes of their fellows?

A second technique that might help delineate the values is to determine the choices that people make consistently. The participant observer should ascertain what choices tend to be made in similar situations. For example,

---

*A good but partial list of methods to determine empirically the values of American society has been developed in a text by Robin M. Williams Jr. (1970:444–446).

how do individuals dispose of surplus wealth? Do they spend it for self-aggrandizement or for altruistic reasons? Is there a tendency to spend it for the pleasure of the present, save it for security in the future, or spend it on others?

A third procedure is used typically by social scientists—that is, to find out through interviews or written questionnaires what people say is good, bad, moral, immoral, desirable, or undesirable. There is often a difference between what people say and what people do. This is always a problem in the study of values because there will sometimes be a discrepancy between values and actual behavior. Even if there is a difference between what they write on a questionnaire or say in an interview and their actual behavior, people will probably say or write those responses they feel are appropriate, and this by itself is a valid indicator of what the values of the society are.

One may also observe the reward-punishment system of the society. What behavior is rewarded with a medal, or a bonus, or public praise? Alternatively, what behavior brings condemnation, ridicule, public censure, or imprisonment? The greater the reward or the punishment, the greater the likelihood that important societal values are involved. Consider, for example, the extraordinary punishment given to Americans who willfully destroy the private property of others (for example, a cattle rustler, a thief, a looter, or a pyromaniac).

Closely related to the reward-punishment system are the actions that cause individuals to feel guilt or shame (losing a job, living on welfare, declaring bankruptcy) or those actions which bring about ego enhancement (a better-paying job, getting an educational degree, owning a business). Individuals feel guilt or shame precisely because they have internalized the norms and values of society. When values and behavior are not congruent, feelings of guilt will be a typical response.

Another technique is to examine the principles that are held as part of "the American way of life." These principles are enunciated in historical documents such as the Constitution, the Declaration of Independence, and the Bible. We are continually reminded of these principles in speeches by elected officials, by editorials in the mass media, and from pulpits. The United States has gone to war to defend such principles as democracy, equality, freedom, and the free enterprise system. One question the analyst of values should ask, therefore, is, "For what principles will the people fight?"

The remainder of this chapter is devoted to the description of the American system of values. Understanding American values is essential to the analysis of American society, for they provide the basis for America's uniqueness as well as the source of many of its social problems.

Values as Sources of Societal Integration and Social Problems

American society, while similar in some respects to other advanced industrial societies, is also fundamentally different. Given the combination of geographical, historical, and religious factors found in the United States, it is not surprising that American cultural values are unique.

Geographically, the United States has remained relatively isolated from other societies for most of its history. Americans have also been blessed with an abundance of rich and varied resources (land, minerals, and water). Until only recently, Americans were unconcerned with conservation and the careful use of resources (as many societies must be to survive) because there was no need. The country provided a vast storehouse of resources so rich they were often used wastefully.

Historically, the United States was founded by a revolution that grew out of opposition to tyranny and aristocracy. Hence, Americans have verbally supported such principles as freedom, democracy, equality, and impersonal justice.

Another historical factor that has led to American culture having its particular nature is that the United States has been peopled largely by immigrants. This fact has led, on the one hand, to a blending of many cultural traits, such as language, dress, and customs; and alternatively, to the existence of ethnic enclaves that resist assimilation.

A final set of forces that has affected American culture stems from its religious heritage. First is the Judeo-Christian ethic that has prevailed throughout American history. The strong emphases on humanitarianism, the inherent worth of all individuals, a morality based on the Ten Commandments, and even the Biblical injunction to "have dominion over all living things" have had a profound effect upon how Americans evaluate each other.

Another aspect of America's religious heritage, the **Protestant ethic,** has been an important determinant of the values that are believed to typify most Americans (see Weber, 1958). (The Protestant ethic is the religious belief espoused by Martin Luther emphasizing hard work and continual striving to prove that one is "saved.") The majority of early European settlers in America tended to believe in a particular set of religious beliefs that can be traced back to two individuals, Martin Luther and John Calvin. Luther's contribution was essentially twofold: each person was considered to be his or her own priest (stressing the person's individuality and worth), and each person was to accept his or her work as a "calling." To be "called" by God to do a job, no matter how humble, was to give the job and the individual dignity. It also encouraged everyone to work very hard to be successful in that job.

The contribution of John Calvin was based on his belief in "predestination." God, because He is all-knowing, knows who will be "saved." Unfortunately, individuals do not know whether they are "saved" or not, and this is very anxiety-producing. Calvinists came to believe that God would look with more favor upon those preordained to be "saved" than those who were not. Consequently, success in one's business became a sign that one was "saved," and this was therefore anxiety-reducing. Calvinists worked very hard to be successful. As they prospered, the capital they accumulated could be spent only on necessities, for to spend on luxuries was another sign that one was not "saved." The surplus capital was therefore invested in the enterprise (purchasing more property or better machinery, hiring a larger work force, or whatever).

Reprinted courtesy of the *Rocky Mountain News.*

Luther and Calvin produced an ethic that flourished in America. This ethic stressed the traits of self-sacrifice, diligence, and hard work. It stressed achievement, and most importantly, it stressed a self-orientation rather than a collectivity orientation. Indirectly, this ethic emphasized private property, capitalism, rationality, and growth.

Thus geography, religious heritage, and history have combined to provide a distinctive set of values for Americans. However, before we describe these dominant American values, several caveats should be mentioned. First, the tremendous diversity of the United States precludes any universal holding of values. There are persons and groups that reject the dominant values. Moreover, there are differences in emphasis for the dominant values by region, social class, age, and religion. Second, the system of American values is not always consistent with behavior. Third, the values themselves are not always consistent. How does one reconcile the coexistence of individualism with conformity? or competition and cooperation? Robin Williams, an eminent analyst of American society, has concluded that:

> We do not find a neatly unified "ethos" or an irresistible "strain toward consistency." Rather, the total society is characterized by diversity and change in values. Complex division of labor, regional variations, ethnic heterogeneity, and the proliferation of specialized institutions and organizations all tend to insulate differing values from one another. (Williams, 1970:451)

To minimize the problem with inconsistencies, we will present only the most dominant of American values in this section. Let's examine these in turn.

Success (Individual Achievement).   The highly valued individual in American society is the self-made person—i.e., one who has achieved money and status through his or her own efforts in a highly competitive system. Our culture heroes are persons like Abe Lincoln and John D. Rockefeller, each of whom rose from humble origins to the top of his profession.

Success can be achieved, obviously, by outdoing all others, but it is often difficult to know exactly the extent of one's success. Hence, economic success (one's income, personal wealth, and type of possessions) is the most commonly used measurement. Economic success, moreover, is often used to measure personal worth. As Robin Williams has put it, "The comparatively striking feature of American culture is its tendency to identify standards of personal excellence with competitive occupational achievement" (Williams, 1970:454–455).

Competition.   Competition is highly valued in U.S. society. Most people believe it to be the one quality that has made the United States great because it motivates individuals and groups to be discontented with the status quo and with being second best. Motivated by the hope of being victorious in competition, or put another way, by fear of failure, Americans must not lose a war or the Olympics or be the second nation to land men on the moon.

Competition pervades almost all aspects of U.S. society. The work world, sports, courtship, organizations like the Cub Scouts, and schools all thrive on competition. The pervasiveness of competition in schools is seen in how athletic teams, cheerleading squads, debate teams, choruses, bands, and casts are composed. In each case competition among classmates is used as the criterion for selection. Of course, the grading system is also often based on the competition of individuals with each other.

The Cub Scouts, because of its reliance on competition, is an all-American organization. In the first place, individual status in the den or pack is determined by the level one has achieved through the attainment of merit badges. Although all boys can theoretically attain all merit badges, there is competition as the boys are pitted against each other to see who can obtain the most. Another example of how the Cub Scouts use competition is their annual event—the Pinewood Derby. Each boy in a Cub pack is given a small block of wood and four wheels that he is then to shape into a racing car. The race is held at a pack meeting with one boy eventually being the winner. The event is rarely questioned even though nearly all of the boys go home disappointed losers. Why is such a practice accepted—indeed publicized? The answer, simply, is that it is symbolic of the ways things are done in virtually all aspects of American life.

An important consequence of this emphasis on the "survival of the fittest" is that some persons take advantage of their fellows to compete "successfully." In the business world we find theft, fraud, interlocking directorates, and price-fixing are techniques used by some individuals to "get ahead" dishonestly. A related problem, abuse of nature for profit, while not a form of cheating, nevertheless takes advantage of others, while one pursues economic success. The current ecology crisis is caused by individuals, corporations, and communities that find pollution solutions too expensive. Thus, in looking out for themselves, they ignore the short- and long-range effects on social and biological life. In other words, competition, while a constant spur for individuals and groups to succeed, is also the source of some illegal activities and hence social problems in American society.

Similar scandals are also found in the sports world. The most visible type of illegal activity in sports is illegal recruiting of athletes by colleges and universities. In the quest to succeed (i.e., win), some coaches have felt it necessary to violate NCAA regulations by altering transcripts to ensure an athlete's eligibility, allowing substitutes to take admissions tests for athletes of marginal educational ability, paying athletes for nonexistent jobs, illegally using government work-study monies for athletes, and offering money, cars, and clothing to entice athletes to their schools (Eitzen and Sage, 1989: 128–129).

The Valued Means to Achieve.   There are three related highly valued ways to succeed in U.S. society. The first is through hard work. Americans, from the early Puritans to the present day, have elevated persons who were industrious and denigrated those who were not. Most Americans, therefore, assume that poor people deserve to be poor because they are allegedly unwilling to work as hard as persons in the middle and upper classes. This type of explanation places the blame on the victim rather than on the social system that systematically thwarts efforts by the poor. Their hopelessness, brought on by their lack of education, or by their being black, or by their lack of experience, is interpreted as their fault and not as a function of the economic system.

The two remaining valued means to success are continual striving and deferred gratification. Continual striving has meaning for both the successful and the not-so-successful. For the former, one should never be content with what he or she has; there is always more land to own, more money to make, or more books to write. For the poor, continual striving means a never-give-up attitude, a belief that economic success is always possible through hard work, if not for yourself, at least for your children.

Deferred gratification refers to the willingness to deny immediate pleasure for later rewards. The hallmark of the successful person in American society is just such a willingness—to stay in school, to moonlight, or to go to night school. One observer has asserted that the difference between the poor and the nonpoor in this society is whether they are future or present-time oriented (Banfield, 1974). Superficially, this assessment appears accurate, but we would argue that this lack of a future-time orientation among the poor is not a subcultural trait but basically a consequence of their hopeless situation.

Progress.   Societies differ in their emphasis on the past, the present, and the future. American society, while giving some attention to each time dimension, stresses the future. Americans neither made the past sacred nor are they content with the present. They place a central value on progress—on a brighter tomorrow, a better job, a bigger home, a move to the suburbs, college education for their children, and on self-improvement.

Americans are not satisfied with the status quo; they want growth (bigger buildings, faster planes, bigger airports, more business moving into the community, bigger profits, and new world's records). They want to change and conquer nature (dam rivers, clear forests, rechannel rivers, seed clouds, and spray insecticides).

Although the implicit belief in progress is that change is good, some things are not to be changed, for they have a sacred quality (the political system, the economic system, American values, and the nation-state). Thus, Americans while valuing technological change, do not favor changing the system (revolution).

The commonly held value of progress has also had a negative effect on contemporary American life. Progress is typically defined to mean either growth or new technology. Every city wants to grow. Chambers of Commerce want more industry and more people (and incidentally more consumers). No industry can afford to keep sales at last year's figures. Everyone agrees that the gross national product (GNP) must increase each year. If all these things are to grow as Americans wish, then concomitant with such growth must be increased population, more products turned out (using natural resources), more electricity, more highways, and more waste. Continued growth will inevitably throw the tight ecological system out of balance since there are but limited supplies of air, water, and places to dump waste materials. Not only are these limited but they diminish as the population increases.

Progress also means a faith in technology. It is commonly believed by Americans that scientific knowledge will solve problems. Scientific break-throughs and new technology have solved some problems and do aid in saving labor. But often new technology creates problems that were unantici-pated.* Although the automobile is of fantastic help to humankind, it has polluted the air, and it kills about 60,000 Americans each year in accidents. It is difficult to imagine life without electricity, but the creation of electricity pollutes the air and causes the thermal pollution of rivers. Insecticides and chemical fertilizers have performed miracles in agriculture but have polluted food and streams (and even "killed" some lakes). Obviously, the slogan of the DuPont Corporation—"better living through chemistry"—is not entirely correct.

Material Progress.   An American belief holds that "work pays off." The payoff is not only success in one's profession but also in economic terms—income and the acquisition and consumption of goods and services that go beyond adequate nutrition, medical care, shelter, and transportation. The superflu-

---

*Sociologists have a term for this phenomenon—*latent functions*—which means, in effect, unintended consequences. The intended consequences of an activity or social arrangement are called *manifest functions*.

ous things that we accumulate or strive to accumulate, such as country club memberships, jewelry, lavish homes, boats, second homes, pool tables, electric toothbrushes, and season tickets to the games of our favorite teams are symbols of success in the competitive struggle. But these have more than symbolic value because they are elements of what Americans consider the "good life" and, therefore, a right.

This emphasis on *having* things has long been a facet of U.S. life. This country, the energy crisis notwithstanding, has always been a land of opportunity and abundance. Although many persons are blocked from full participation in this abundance, the goal for most is to accumulate those things that bring status and that provide for a better way of life by saving labor or enhancing pleasure in our leisure.

Individual Freedom.   Americans value individualism. They believe that people should generally be free from government interference in their lives and businesses and free to make their own choices. Implied in this value is the responsibility of each individual for his or her own development. The focus on individualism places responsibility on the individual for his or her acts— not on society or its institutions. Being poor is blamed on the individual, not on the maldistribution of wealth and other socially perpetuated disadvantages that blight many families generation after generation. The aggressive behavior of minority youth is blamed on them, not on the limits placed on their social mobility by the social system. Dropping out of high school before graduation is blamed on individual students, not on the educational system that fails to meet their needs. This attitude helps to explain the reluctance by persons in authority to provide adequate welfare, health care, and compensatory programs to help the disadvantaged. This common tendency of individuals to focus on the deviant rather than the system that produces deviants has also been true of American social scientists analyzing social problems.

Individual freedom is, of course, related to capitalism and private property. The economy is supposed to be competitive. Individuals, through their own efforts, business acumen, and luck can (if successful) own property and pyramid profits.

The belief that private property and capitalism are not to be restricted has led to several social problems: (1) unfair competition (monopolies, interlocking directorates, price fixing); (2) a philosophy by many entrepreneurs of *caveat emptor* ("Let the buyer beware"), whereby the aim is profit with total disregard for the welfare of the consumer; and (3) the current ecology crisis, which is due in great measure to the standard policy of many Americans and most corporations to do whatever is profitable—thus a total neglect for conservation of natural resources.

All these practices have forced the federal and state governments to enact and enforce regulatory controls. Clearly, Americans have always tended to abuse nature and their fellows in the name of profit. Freedom if so abused must be curtailed, and the government (albeit somewhat reluctantly, given the pressures from various interest groups) has done this.

The related values of capitalism, private property, and self-aggrandizement (individualism) have also led to an environmental crisis. Industries fouling the air and water with refuse, farmers spraying pesticides that kill weeds and harm animal and human life, are but two examples of how individual persons and corporations look out for themselves with an almost total disregard for the short- and long-range effects of their actions on life. As long as Americans hold a narrow self-orientation rather than a collectivity orientation this crisis will not only continue but steadily worsen. The use people make of the land (and the water on it or running through it, and the air above it) has traditionally been theirs to decide because of the American belief in private property. This belief in private property has meant, in effect, that individuals have had the right to pave a pasture for a parking lot, tear up a lemon grove for a housing development, put down artificial turf for a football field, dump waste products into the air and water, and so on. Consequently, individual decisions have had the collective effect of taking millions of acres of arable land out of production permanently, polluting the air and water, covering land where vegetation once grew with asphalt, concrete buildings, and astroturf even though green plants are the only source of oxygen.

Values and Behavior

The discrepancy between values and behavior has probably always existed in American society. Inconsistencies have always existed, for example, between the Christian ethic of love, brotherhood, and humanitarianism, on the one hand, and the realities of religious bigotry, the maximization of self-interest, and property rights over human rights on the other. The gap may be widening because of the tremendous rate of social change taking place (the rush toward urbanization, the increased bureaucratization in all spheres of social life). Values do not change as rapidly as do other elements of the culture. Although values often differ from behavior, they remain the criteria for evaluating objects, persons, and events. It is important, however, to mention behaviors that often contradict the values because they demonstrate the hypocrisy prevalent in U.S. society that so often upsets young people (and others) who, in turn, develop countercultures (a topic that we shall cover shortly).

Perhaps most illustrative of the inconsistency between values and behavior is the belief in the American Creed held by most Americans—generally assumed to encompass equality of all persons, freedom of speech and religion, and the guarantees of life, liberty, and prosperity—as against the injustices perpetuated by the system and individuals in the system on members of minority groups.

Americans glorify individualism and self-reliance. These related traits, however, are not found in bureaucracies, where the watchword is "to get along you have to go along." Rather than individualism, the way to get ahead in corporations and other large bureaucracies is to be a team player.

There is a myth that successful persons in the United States have always been self-made. Of course some individuals have achieved wealth, fame, and power through their own achievements, but many have inherited their advantages. The irony is that the wealthy are considered successful whether they made the money or not. Americans tend to give great weight to the opinions expressed by the wealthy, as evidenced by the electorate's tendency to elect them to public office.

Americans have always placed high value on the equality of all persons (in the courts or in getting a job). This value is impossible to reconcile with the racist and superiority theories held by some individuals and groups. It is also impossible to reconcile with many of the formal and informal practices on jobs, in the schools, and in the courts.

Related to the stated belief in equality are the other fundamental beliefs enunciated by the Founding Fathers: the freedoms guaranteed in the Bill of Rights and the Declaration of Independence. Ironically, although the United States was founded by a revolution, the same behavior (called for by the Declaration of Independence) by dissident groups is now squelched (in much the same way as by King George III).

Americans value "law and order." This reverence for the law has been overlooked throughout American history whenever "law-abiding" groups, such as vigilante groups, took the law in their own hands (by threatening that anyone who disobeys vigilante law will by lynched). Currently, the very groups to make the loudest demands for "law and order" are ones who disobey certain laws—for example, southern politicians blocking federal court orders to integrate schools, American Legion posts that notoriously ignore local, state, and federal laws about gambling and liquor, and school administrators allowing prayer in public schools despite the ruling of the Supreme Court.

A final example of disparity between American values and behavior involves the pride Americans have in solving difficult problems. Americans are inclined to be realists. They are pragmatic, down-to-earth problem solvers ready to apply scientific knowledge and expertise to handle such technical problems as getting human beings to and from the moon safely. This realism tends to be replaced by mere gestures, however, when it comes to social problems. Americans have a compulsive tendency to avoid confrontation with chronic social problems. They tend to think that social problems will be solved if one has "nice" thoughts, such as "just say no" (Nancy Reagan's solution to the problem of substance abuse). Somehow the verbal level is mistaken for action. If we hear our favorite television personality end the program with a statement against pollution or crime, we think the problem will somehow be solved. This is evidenced at another level by proclaiming a "war on drugs," or by setting up a commission to study stock-market fraud, cost overruns in the Pentagon, or youth gangs. Philip Slater has said that the typical American approach to social problems is to decrease their visibility—out of sight, out of mind.

When these discarded problems rise to the surface again—a riot, a protest, an expose in the mass media—we react as if a sewer has backed up. We are shocked, disgusted, and angered. We immediately call for the emergency plumber (the special commission, the crash program) to ensure that the problem is once again removed from consciousness. (Slater, 1970:15)

The examples just presented make clear that while Americans express some values, they often behave differently. The values do, however, still provide the standards by which individuals are evaluated. These inconsistencies are sometimes important in explaining individual behavior (guilt, shame, aggression), and the emergence of insulating personal and social mechanisms such as compartmentalization and racial segregation.

Not only is there an inconsistency between values and behavior, but there is also a lack of unity among some of the values themselves. Some examples of this phenomenon, which has been called "ethical schizophrenia," are individualism vs. humanitarianism, materialism vs. idealism, and pragmatism vs. utopianism (Record and Record, 1965).

Cultural Diversity

Americans are far from unanimous on a number of public issues (e.g., gun control, the death penalty, or prayer in schools). Despite inconsistencies and ambiguities, Americans do tend to believe in certain things—for example, that democracy is the best form of government; that capitalism is the best economic system; that success can be defined in terms of hard work, initiative, and the amassing of wealth and property; that Christianity should be the country's dominant religion; and that there should be equality of opportunity and equal justice before the law. It is important to note that while these values are held generally by the U.S. populace, there is never total agreement on any of them. The primary reason for this is the tremendous diversity found within the United States.

It is composed of too many people who differ on important social dimensions: age, sex, race, region, social class, ethnicity, religion, rural/urban, and so on. These variables suggest that groups and categories will differ in values and behavior because certain salient social characteristics imply differential experiences and expectations. These are noted often in the remainder of this book.

Let us examine a few differences held by various groups and categories to illustrate the lack of consistency among Americans. Values are the criteria used to determine, among other things, morality. A Gallup survey asked a national sample in 1988 their opinions on abortion. Table 5–1 breaks down the data by sex, race, age, income, and education. Clearly on this issue Americans differ. The differences are systematic rather than random. The lower his or her income or education, the more likely to be antiabortion.

There are rural-urban differences in American society that are well known. An interesting example is the probability that rural people are more humanitarian, yet more intolerant of deviance among their neighbors than are urban dwellers. But there are variations among rural communities as there are among urban places on these and other differences.

Region of the country accounts for some variation in values held. But the generalizations made about southerners, easterners, and midwesterners, while having some validity, gloss over many real differences. Within any one

Table 5–1
**Attitudes
toward
Abortion**

Question: Do you think abortions should be legal under any circumstances, legal only under certain circumstances, or illegal in all circumstances?

Characteristic	Legal in Any Circumstance	Legal in Certain Circumstances	Illegal in All Circumstances
National	24%	57%	17%*
Sex			
Men	24	56	17
Women	23	58	17
Age			
18–29 years	22	60	16
30–49 years	28	54	17
50 and older	19	60	17
Education			
College graduates	39	50	10
Some college	23	61	14
High school graduates	20	59	7
Not high school graduates	13	59	26
Household Income			
$40,000 and over	37	53	9
$25,000–$39,999	22	63	14
$15,000–$24,999	18	58	20
Under $15,000	13	58	26

*The row totals do not add to 100% because those with "no opinion" are not included here.

Source: The Gallup Report, No. 281 (February 1989):17. (This survey was conducted September 25–October 1, 1988.) Reprinted by permission.

region there are differences among rural and urban people, among different religious groups, among different ethnic groups, and so on. Perhaps the best study of cultural variation within the United States (and even within one geographical region) was done by Kluckhohn and Strodtbeck (1961). These researchers studied five small communities in the same general area in the American southwest—a Mormon settlement, a Texan settlement, a village of Spanish-Americans, a Zuñi reservation, and a Navajo reservation. They found that these groups were quite different with respect to individual versus collective orientation, time dimension, the relationship of human beings to nature, and so on. Because each of these communities differed in their answers to various human dilemmas, their values also differed significantly.

Kluckhohn and Strodtbeck, of course, did not choose American communities at random. They were very selective, hoping to demonstrate the existence of real cultural differences within the United States. What they found

Participant Observation

A common method of data collection is **participant observation** the direct observation of social phenomena in natural settings. One way to accomplish this is for the researcher to become part of what he or she is studying. There are several roles that observers may take in this regard. One is to hide the fact that one is a researcher and participate as a member of the group being studied. Another is to let the subjects know that you are a scientist but remain separate and detached from the group. A third option is to identify oneself as a researcher and become friends with those being studied. Each of these alternatives has its problems, such as the ethics of deceiving subjects and the fundamental problem of subjects altering their behavior if they know they are being investigated.

Elliot Liebow—a white, Jewish, and middle-class researcher—investigated the **subculture** of poor black males in one section of the Washington, D.C. ghetto.* From the beginning Liebow identified himself as a researcher. He became deeply involved with his subjects. He partied with them, visited in their homes, gave them legal advice, and just generally "hung around" with them in their leisure hours. As the research progressed he became more and more a part of the streetcorner life he was investigating. As a white, though, he never escaped completely being an outsider.

At first Liebow's field notes concentrated on individuals: what they said, what they did, and the contexts in which they said or did them. Through this beginning he ultimately saw the patterns of behavior and how the subjects perceived and understood themselves. He was able to understand the social structure of streetcorner life. More important, his research enabled him to see the complexity of the social network of society's "losers" and how they continuously slip back and forth between the values and beliefs of the larger society and those of their own social system.

*Tally's Corner (Boston: Little, Brown, 1967).

were four subcultures (all but the Texas community) within one geographical region within the United States.

The concept **subculture** has been defined typically as a relatively cohesive cultural system that varies in form and substance from the dominant culture. Under the rubric "subculture," then, there are ethnic groups, delinquent gangs, and religious sects. Milton Yinger (1962) has proposed that the concept "subculture" be defined more precisely. He has suggested that it be used for one type of group and "counterculture" for another type that has been previously called a subculture. For Yinger the concept "subculture" should be limited to relatively cohesive cultural systems that differ from the dominant culture in such things as language, values, religion, and style of life. Typically, a group that is a subculture differs from the larger group because it has immigrated from another society and because of physical or social isolation has not been fully assimilated. The cultural differences, then, are usually based on ethnicity. Tradition keeps the culture of this group somewhat unique from the dominant culture. There are a number of examples of such subcultures in the United States—the Amish, the Hutterites, some Orthodox Jewish sects, many Indian tribes, Appalachian snake handlers, and Poles, Croatians, Hungarians, Italians, Greeks, and Irish groups at one time or another in American history. The existence of numerous subcultures within the United States explains much of the lack of consistency with respect to American values.

A **counterculture,** as defined by Yinger, is a culturally homogeneous group that has developed values and norms that differ from the larger society because the group opposes the large society. This type of group is in conflict with the dominant culture. The particular values and norms can be understood only by reference to the dominant group.

The values held by delinquent gangs such as the Cripps and the Bloods, are commonly believed to be a reaction against the values held by the larger society (and hence would represent a counterculture). Albert K. Cohen (1955) has noted, for example, that lower-class juvenile gangs not only reject the dominant value system but they exalt opposite values. These boys, Cohen argues, are ill-equipped because of their lower-class origins and other related drawbacks to be successful in the game as it is defined by the dominant society. They, therefore, repudiate the commonly held values for new values that have meaning for them and under which they can perform satisfactorily. These values differ from the values of the larger culture because the delinquents actually want the larger values but cannot attain them. If Cohen's thesis is correct, then delinquent gangs indeed form a counterculture (although Cohen specifically names them subcultures).

VALUES FROM THE ORDER AND CONFLICT PERSPECTIVES

Values are sources of both societal integration and social problems. Order theorists assume that sharing values solves the most fundamental problem of societal integration. The values are symbolic representations of the existing society and therefore promote unity and consensus among Americans. They must, therefore, be preserved.

Conflict theorists, on the other hand, view the mass acceptance of values as a form of cultural tyranny that promotes political conservatism, inhibits creativity, and gets people to accept their lot because they believe in the system rather than joining with others to try and change it. Thus, conflict theorists believe that slavish devotion to society's values inhibits necessary social change. Moreover, American values are assumed by conflict theorists to be the actual source of social problems such as crime, conspicuous consumption, planned obsolescence, the energy crisis, pollution, and the artificial creation of winners and losers.

Regardless of which side one may take on the consequences of American values, most would agree that the traditional values of individual freedom, capitalism, competition, and progress have made America relatively affluent. The future, however, will very likely be very different from the past, requiring a fundamental change in these values. The future of slow growth or no growth, lower levels of affluence, and resource shortages will require that Americans adapt by adopting values that support cooperation rather than competition, that support group goals over individual goals, and a mode of "making do" rather than the purchasing of unnecessary products and the relentless search for technological solutions.

CHAPTER REVIEW

1. Culture, the knowledge the members of society or other social organizations share, constrains behavior and how people think about and interpret their world.

2. Culture emerges as a result of continued social interaction.

3. Culture is learned behavior. The process of learning the culture is called socialization.

4. Through the socialization process, individuals internalize the culture. Thus the control that culture has over individuals is seen as natural.

5. Culture channels behavior by providing the rules for behavior and the criteria for judging.

6. Culture is boundary maintaining. One's own culture seems right and natural. Other cultures are considered inferior, wrong, or immoral. This tendency to consider the ways of one's own group superior is called ethnocentrism.

7. Six types of shared knowledge constitute the culture—symbols, technology, ideologies, norms, values, and roles.

8. Norms are divided into two types by degree of importance and severity of punishment for their violation. Folkways are less important while the mores are considered more vital and thereby more severely punished if violated.

9. Roles are the behavioral expectations of those who occupy the statuses in a social organization.

10. Through language and other symbols culture determines how the members of a society will interpret their environment. The important point is that through this "construction of reality" the members of a society make sense out of a world that has no inherent meaning.

11. The variety of customs found throughout the world is staggering. The members of one society typically view the customs found elsewhere as weird, cruel, and immoral. If we understand the cultural context of a given society, however, their practices generally make sense. This is called cultural relativity.

12. Knowing the values (the criteria for evaluation) of a society is an excellent way of understanding that society.

13. American values are the result of three major factors: (a) geographical isolation and being blessed with abundant resources; (b) founding of the nation in opposition to tyranny and aristocracy and supporting freedom, democracy, equality, and impersonal justice; and (c) a religious heritage based on the Judeo-Christian ethic and the Protestant work ethic.

14. The dominant American values are: success through individual achievement, competition, hard work, progress through growth and new technology, material progress, and individual freedom.

15. These American values are the sources of societal integration as well as social problems.

16. Despite the power of culture and American values over individual conduct, the diversity present in American society means that for many there are inconsistencies between values and actual behavior. There are clear variations in how Americans feel on public issues based on their different social situations.

17. A major source of cultural variation in the United States is the existence of subcultures. Because of different religions and ethnicity some groups retain a culture different from the dominant one. Other groups form a culture because they oppose the larger society. The latter are called countercultures.

18. Order theorists assume that the sharing of values promotes unity among the members of society. The values therefore must be preserved.

19. Conflict theorists view the mass acceptance of values as a form of cultural tyranny that promotes political conservatism, inhibits creativity, and encourages false consciousness.

KEY TERMS

Culture
Socialization
Superego
Internalization
Reference group
Ethnocentrism
Material technology
Social technology

Ethnomethodology
Values
Status
Ascribed status
Achieved status
Social construction of reality
Ontology
Epistemology

Cultural relativity
Protestant ethic
Deferred gratification
Subculture
Participant observation
Counterculture

STUDY QUESTIONS

1. Because individuals internalize the culture, they tend to assume that its control over one's behavior is not control but "natural." Assess your ideas and behaviors to determine which, if any, of them are culture free.
2. What is meant by the social construction of reality? Provide examples.
3. How are U.S. values sources of both societal integration *and* social problems?
4. How do order theorists and conflict theorists differ in their interpretation of values?

FOR FURTHER READING

Culture: General

Ruth Benedict, *Patterns of Culture* (Baltimore: Penguin, 1946).

Peter L. Berger and Thomas Luckman, *The Social Construction of Reality* (Garden City, NY: Doubleday Anchor Books, 1967).

Marvin Harris, *Cows, Pigs, Wars, and Witches: The Riddles of Culture* (New York: Random House Vintage Books, 1974).

Jeremy Rifkin, *Time Wars: The Primary Conflict in Human History* (New York: Henry Holt, 1987).

American Values

Robert N. Bellah, Richard Madsen, William M. Sullivan, Ann Swidler, and Steven M. Tipton, *Habits of the Heart: Individualism and Commitment in American Life* (Berkeley: University of California Press, 1985).

Marvin Harris, *America Now: The Anthropology of a Changing Culture* (New York: Simon and Schuster, 1981).

Florence Kluckhohn and Fred L. Strodtbeck, *Variations in Value Orientations* (New York: Harper & Row, 1961).

Philip Slater, *Wealth Addiction* (New York: E. P. Dutton, 1980).

Robin Williams, *American Society: A Sociological Interpretation*, 3rd ed. (New York: Alfred A. Knopf, 1970).

Daniel Yankelovich, *New Rules: Searching for Self-Fulfillment in a World Turned Upside Down* (New York: Bantam, 1982).

Subcultures

Rosabeth M. Kanter, *Commitment and Community: Communes and Utopias in Sociological Perspective* (Cambridge; MA: Harvard University Press, 1972).

William M. Kephart, *Extraordinary Groups: The Sociology of Unconventional Life-Styles* (New York: St. Martin's, 1976).

Elliot Liebow, *Tally's Corner* (Boston: Little, Brown, 1967).

Jay MacLeod, *Ain't No Makin' It* (Boulder, CO: Westview, 1987).

J. Milton Yinger, *Countercultures: The Promise and Peril of a World Turned Upside Down* (New York: Free Press, 1982).

Chapter Six

Socialization

Oscar Stohr and Jack Yufe are identical twins separated as babies by their parents' divorce. Oscar was raised by his maternal grandmother in the Sudetenland of Czechoslovakia. He was a strict Catholic. As a loyal Nazi, he hated Jews. His brother, Jack, was raised by his Jewish father in Trinidad. During World War II he was loyal to the British and hated the Germans.

The twins were united briefly in 1954, but Jack was warned by the translator to not tell his brother that he was Jewish. In 1979, at age 47, the brothers were reunited by scientists who wished to establish the degree to which environment shapes human behavior. Because they had the same genes, any differences between the brothers must result from how they were raised.

The scientists found not only that they were physically alike but that the twins were strikingly similar in temperament, tastes, tempo, and the way that they did things. Both had been excellent athletes. Both had had trouble in school with mathematics. But the twins also differed in many important respects. Jack is a workaholic, while Oscar enjoys his leisure time. Jack is a political liberal while Oscar is a traditionalist. This difference is seen in Jack's tolerance of feminism and Oscar's resistance to that movement. Jack is proud of being Jewish while Oscar never mentions his Jewish heritage.

In this chapter we examine this process of socialization that is so powerful in shaping human thought and behavior as to make identical twins different.

Every day thousands of newborns arrive in American society. How do these savages become members of society? How do they lose their "savageness"? How do they become "human"? The answer to these questions is that they learn to be human by acquiring the meanings, ideas, and actions appropriate for that society. This process of learning the culture is called *socialization*.*

Children are born with the limits and potential established by their unique genetic compositions. Their physical features, size and shape, rate of physical development, and even temperament will unfold within predetermined boundaries (Franklin, 1989). The limits of their intellectual capabilities are also influenced by biological heritage. But, while children are biologically human, they do not have the instincts or the innate drives that will make them human. They acquire their "humanness" through social interaction. Their concepts of themselves, personality, conception of love, freedom, justice, right and wrong, and interpretation of reality are all products of social interaction. In other words, human beings are essentially the social creations of society.

Evidence for this assertion is found by examining the traits and behaviors of children raised without much human contact. There have been occasional accounts of **feral children** throughout history—children believed to have been raised by animals. When found, they look human but act like the animals with whom they have had contact. One case involved a Tarzan-like child reported to have been raised by monkeys in the jungles of central Africa. The boy was discovered in 1974 at about the age of six with a troop of gray monkeys. Two years later after painstaking efforts to "rehabilitate" him, he remained more monkey than human. "He is unable to talk and communicates by 'monkey' grunts and chattering. He will eat only fruit and vegetables, and when excited or scared jumps up and down uttering threatening monkey cries" (Associated Press, May 15, 1976). If a child's personality were largely determined by biological heritage, this child would have been much more human than simian. But, there is a consistent finding in all cases that feral children are not normal. They cannot talk and have great difficulty in learning human speech patterns. They do not walk or eat like human beings. They express anger differently. In essence, the behavior that arises in the absence of human contact is not what we associate with human beings.

The most famous case of a child who was raised with only minimal human contact was a girl named Anna (Davis, 1940, 1948). Anna was an illegitimate child. Her grandfather refused to acknowledge her existence, and to escape his ire, the mother put her in an attic room and, except for minimal feeding, ignored her. Anna was discovered by a social worker at about age six and she was placed in a special school. When found, Anna could not sit up or walk. She could not talk and was believed to be deaf. She was immobile and completely indifferent to those around her. Staff members worked with

---

*That this chapter focuses on how children learn the culture should *not* be interpreted to mean that the socialization process stops at the end of adolescence. To the contrary, socialization is a lifelong process occurring within each social group within the society.

Anna (during one year a single staff member had to receive medical attention more than a dozen times for bites she received from Anna), and eventually Anna learned to take care of herself, walk, talk, and play with other children.

> By the time Anna died of hemorrhagic jaundice approximately four and a half years [after she was found], she had made considerable progress as compared with her condition when found. She could follow directions, string beads, identify a few colors, build with blocks, and differentiate between attractive and unattractive pictures. She had a good sense of rhythm and loved a doll. She talked mainly in phrases but would repeat words and try to carry on a conversation. She was clean about clothing. She habitually washed her hands and brushed her teeth. She would try to help other children. She walked well and could run fairly well, though clumsily. Although easily excited, she had a pleasant disposition. Her involvement showed that socialization, even when started at the late age of six, could still do a great deal toward making her a person. Even though her development was no more than that of a normal child of two or three years, she had made noteworthy progress. (Davis, 1948:205)

The conclusion from those who had observed Anna and other cases of isolated children is that being deprived of social interaction during one's formative years deprives individuals of their humanness.

The second essential to socialization is language. Language is the vehicle through which socialization occurs. In Anna's case, what little human contact she had during her first six years was physical and not communicative interaction. As Kingsley Davis has noted, Anna's case illustrates "that communicative contact is the core of socialization" (Davis, 1948:205). This principle is also illustrated by Helen Keller. This remarkable person became deaf and blind as a result of illness during infancy. She was locked into her own world until her teacher, Anne Sullivan, was able to communicate to her that the symbol she traced on Helen's hand represented water. That was the beginning of language for Helen Keller and the beginning of her understanding of who she was and the meaning of the world and society in which she was immersed (Keller, 1954).

Learning language has profound effects on how individuals think and perceive. Through their languages societies differ in the way they conceive of time, space, distance, velocity, action, and specificity. To illustrate this last dimension—specificity—let's consider the Navajo language. With respect to rain, the Navajo makes much finer distinctions than the English, who generally leave it to: "It has started to rain;" "It is raining;" and "It has stopped raining." When the Navajo reports his or her experiences

> he uses one verb form if he himself is aware of the actual inception of the rain storm, another if he has reason to believe that the rain has been falling for some time in his locality before the occurrence struck his attention. One form must be employed if rain is general round about within the range of vision; another if, though it is raining about, the storm is plainly on the move. Similarly, the Navaho must invariably distinguish between the ceasing of rainfall (generally), and the stopping of rain in a particular vicinity because the rain clouds have been driven off by the wind. The [Navaho] people take the con-

sistent noticing and reporting of such differences. . . . as much for granted as the rising of the sun. (Kluckhohn and Leighton, 1946:194)

In short, the languages of different societies are not parallel methods for expressing the same reality. Our perception of reality depends on our language. In this way experience itself is a function of language. As the distinguished linguist B. L. Whorf has put it: "no individual is free to describe nature with absolute impartiality but is constrained to certain modes of interpretation even while he thinks himself most free" (Whorf, 1956:1).

In learning language we discover the meaning of symbols not only for words but also for objects, such as the cross, the flag, and traffic lights. Through language we can think about the past and the future. Language symbolizes the values and norms of the society, thus enabling the user to label and evaluate objects, acts, individuals, and groups. The words we use in such instances can be positive, such as beautiful, wise, moral, friend, and appropriate, or negative, such as ugly, dumb, immoral, enemy, or inappropriate. Moreover, the description of the same act can portray a positive or a pejorative image. This can be seen in the sports world, as reported by syndicated columnist Jim Murray:

"On our side, a guy is 'colorful.' On their side, a 'hotdog'."
"Our team is 'resourceful.' Theirs is 'lucky'."
"Our guys are 'trusted associates.' Theirs are 'henchmen'."
"Our team gives rewards. Theirs, bribes."
"Our team plays 'spirited' football. Theirs plays 'dirty'."
"Our team is 'opportunistic.' Theirs gets all the breaks."
"Our guy is 'confident.' Theirs is an egotist." (Murray, 1976:150)

Thus, language is a powerful labeling tool, clearly delineating who is "in" and who is "out." Finally, children learn who they are by using words to describe themselves. The words they use are those that others, in turn, have used in talking about them and their actions.

THE PERSONALITY AS A SOCIAL PRODUCT

In Chapter 2 we noted the dialectic character of society. Society is at once a product of social interaction, yet that product continuously acts back on its producers. As Berger (1975:234) has put it, "Society is a product of man. . . . Yet it may also be stated that man is a product of society." In this section, the emphasis is on this second process—human beings as a product of society. In particular, we shall examine the emergence of the human personality as a social product.

We develop a sense of **self** (our personality) in interaction with others. Newly born infants have no sense of self-awareness. They are unable to distinguish between themselves and their surroundings. They cry spontaneously when uncomfortable. They eventually become aware that crying can be controlled and that its use can bring a response from others. In time, and especially with the employment of language, the child begins to distinguish between "I" and "you" and "mine" and "yours"—signs of self-awareness. But this is just the beginning of the personality-formation process. Let us look now at several classical theories of how children develop personalities and how they learn what is expected of them in the community and society.

Charles H. Cooley: The Looking-Glass Self

Cooley (1864–1929) believed that children's conceptions of themselves arise through interaction with others (Cooley, 1964). He used the metaphor of a **"looking glass self"** to convey the idea that all persons understand themselves through the way in which others act toward them. They judge themselves on how they think others judge them. Cooley believed that each of us imagines how we look to others and what their judgment of us is. Bierstedt has summarized this process: "I am not what I think I am and I am not what you think I am. I am what I think you think I am" (Bierstedt, 1974:197).

The critical process in Cooley's theory of personality development, then, is the feedback the individual receives from others. Others behave in particular ways with regard to an individual. The individual interprets these behaviors positively or negatively. When the behaviors of others are perceived as consistent the individual accepts this definition of self, which in turn has consequences for his or her behavior. In sum, there is a self-fulfilling prophecy—the individual is as defined by others. Suppose, for example, that whenever you entered a room and approached a small knot of people conversing with each other, they promptly melted away with lame excuses. Clearly, this experience, repeated many times, would affect your feelings about yourself. Or, if wherever you appeared, a conversational group quickly formed around

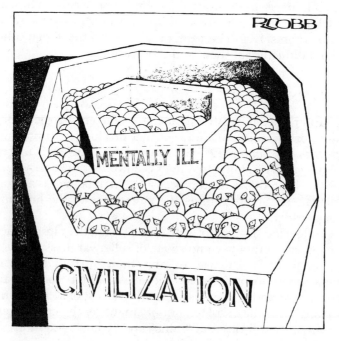

you, would not such attention tend to give you self-confidence and ego strength?

Cooley's insight that our self-concepts are a product of how others react to us is important in understanding behavior. Why are some categories of persons more likely to be school dropouts or criminals or malcontents or depressed while others fit in? As we see in Chapter 8, deviance is the result of the successful application of a social label, a process akin to the "looking-glass self." So, too, does this concept help us to understand the tendency of minority-group members to have low self-esteem. If black children, for example, receive a consistent message from whites that they are inferior, that they are incapable of success in intellectually demanding tasks, and that they are not trustworthy, the probability is that they will have these traits. Many black children and adults fulfill this prophecy, thereby reinforcing the stereotypes of the majority and the low self-esteem of the blacks.

George Herbert Mead: Taking the Role of the Other

Mead (1863–1931) theorized about the relationship of self and society (Mead, 1934). In essence, he believed that children find out who they are as they learn about society and society's expectations. This occurs in several important stages. Infants learn to distinguish between themselves and others from the actions of their parents. By the age of two or so, children have become self-conscious. By this Mead meant that the children are able to react to themselves as others will react to them. For example, they will tell themselves "No-No," as they have been told many times by their parents, and not touch the hot stove. The importance of this stage is that the children have internalized the feelings of others. What others expect has become a part of them. They have become conscious of themselves by incorporating the way others are conscious of them.

The next stage is the play stage. Children from ages four to seven spend many hours a day in a world of play. Much of this time is spent in pretending to be mothers, teachers, doctors, police officers, ministers, grocers, and other roles. Mead called this form of play "taking the role of the others." As they play at a variety of social roles, children act out the behavior associated with these social positions and thus develop a rudimentary understanding of adult roles and why people in those positions act the way they do. They also see how persons in these roles interact with children. Thus, children learn to look at themselves as others see them. As McGee has put it, "he learns who he is by 'being' who he is not" (McGee, 1975:74–75). The play stage, then, accomplishes two things. It provides further clues for children as to who they are and it prepares them for later life.

The game stage occurs at about age eight and is the final stage of personality development in Mead's scheme. In the play stage the children's activities were fluid and spontaneous. The game stage, in contrast, involves activities that are structured. There are rules that define, limit, and constrain the participants. Mead used the game of baseball to illustrate what occurs in the game stage. In baseball children must understand and abide by the rules.

Children "take the role of others" by pretending to occupy various adult roles.

They must also understand the entire game—that is, when playing second base what they and the other players must do if there is a player on first, one out, and the batter bunts down the first base line. In other words, the various individuals in a game must know the roles of all the players and adjust their behavior to that of the others. The assessment of the entire situation is what Mead called the discovery of the "generalized other." In the play stage, children learned what was expected of them by **significant others** (parents, relatives, teachers). The game stage provides children with constraints from many others, including people they do not know. In this way children incorporate and understand the pressures of society—the **generalized other.** By passing through these stages children have finally developed a social life from the expectations of parents, friends, and society.

Sigmund Freud: The Psychoanalytic View

Freud (1856–1939) emphasized the biological dimension along with social factors in personality development (Freud, 1946). For Freud, the infant's first years are totally egocentric, with all energies directed toward pleasure. This is an expression of a primitive biological force—the **id**—that dominates the infant. The id, although a force throughout life, is gradually stifled by society. Parents, as the agents of society, hamper children's pleasure seeking by imposing schedules for eating, punishing them for messy behavior and masturbation, forcing them to control their bowels, and the like.

The process of socialization is, in Freud's view, the process of society controlling the id. Through this process children develop egos. The **ego** is the rational part of the personality that controls the id's basic urges, finding realistic ways of satisfying these biological cravings. The individual also develops a **superego** (conscience) which regulates both the id and ego. The superego is the consequence of the child's internalizing the parents' morals. A strong superego represses the id and channels behavior in socially acceptable ways.

Freud presents a view of socialization that differs significantly from the theories of Mead and Cooley. Whereas Mead and Cooley saw the socialization process as a complete and nonconflictual one, Freud believed the process to be incomplete and accomplished by force. Freud saw the person pulled by two contradictory forces—the natural impulses of biology and the constraints of society—resulting in the imperfection and discontent of human beings. Mead and Cooley, in contrast, did not view the child as one who is repressed, led kicking and screaming into adulthood. For Mead the child passed through natural stages as a willing apprentice to become a conforming member of society. Thus, Mead's conception of the socialization process is deterministic—the individual is a creature of society. Freud's view is quite different.

> To Freud man is a *social* animal without being entirely a *socialized* animal. His very social nature is the source of conflicts and antagonisms that create resistance to socialization by the norms of any of the societies which have existed in the course of human history. (Wrong, 1969: 130)

Society's Socialization Agents

Two themes stand out in this section. First, the personality of the child is, to a large degree, socially created and sustained. Second, through the process of socialization, the child internalizes the norms and values of society. In a sense, the child learns a script for acting, feeling, and thinking that is in tune with the wishes of society. Before we leave this topic, let us look briefly at the special transmitters of the cultural patterns—the family, the schools, and the media.

The Family.   Aside from the obvious function of providing the child with the physical needs of food, clothing, and shelter, the family is the primary agent of socialization. The family will indoctrinate the child in the ways of society. The parents equip the child with the information, etiquette, norms, and values necessary for the functioning member of society. Parents in blatant and subtle ways emit messages of what is important, appropriate, moral, beautiful, correct, and what is not. There is no option for young children.

The Teaching of Prejudice

A southern child's basic lessons were woven of such dissonant strands as these; sometimes the threads tangled into a terrifying mess; sometimes archaic, startling designs would appear in the weaving; sometimes a design was left broken while another was completed with minute care. Bewildered teachers, bewildered pupils in homes and on the street, driven by an invisible Authority, learned their lessons:

The mother who taught me what I know of tenderness and love and compassion taught me also the bleak rituals of keeping Negroes in their "place." The father who rebuked me for an air of superiority toward schoolmates from the mill and rounded out his rebuke by gravely reminding me that "all men are brothers," trained me in the steel-rigid decorums I must demand of every colored male. They who so gravely taught me to split my body from my mind and both from my "soul," taught me also to split my conscience from my acts and Christianity from southern tradition.

Neither the Negro nor sex was often discussed at length in our home. We were given no formal instruction in these difficult matters but we learned our lessons well. We learned the intricate system of taboos, of renunciations and compensations, of manners, voice modulations, words, feelings, along with our prayers, our toilet habits, and our games. I do not remember how or when, but by the time I had learned that God is love, that Jesus is His Son and came to give us more abundant life, that all men are brothers with a common Father, I also knew that I was better than a Negro, that all black folks have their place and must be kept in it, that sex has its place and must be kept in it, that a terrifying disaster would befall the South if ever I treated a Negro as my social equal and as terrifying a disaster would befall my family if ever I were to have a baby outside of marriage. I had learned that God so loved the world that He gave His only be-gotten Son so that we might have segregated churches in which it was my duty to worship each Sunday and on Wednesday at evening prayers. I had learned that white southerners are a hospitable, courteous, tactful people who treat those of their own group with consideration and who carefully segregate from all the richness of life "for their own good and welfare" thirteen million people whose skin is colored a little differently from my own.

I knew by the time I was twelve that a member of my family would always shake hands with old Negro friends, would speak graciously to members of the Negro race unless they forgot their place, in which event icy peremptory tones would draw lines beyond which only the desperate would dare take one step. I knew that to use the word "nigger" was unpardonable and no

They must accept the messages of their parents of what is and what ought to be. As Everett Wilson has put it:

> But when he [the child] enters the human group, he is quite at the mercy of parents and siblings. They determine both what and when he shall eat and wear, when he shall sleep and wake, what he shall think and feel, how he shall express his thoughts and feelings (what language he shall speak and how he shall do it), what his political and religious commitments shall be, what sort of vocation he shall aspire to. Not that parents are ogres. They give what they have to give: their own limited knowledge, their prejudices and passions. There is no alternative to this giving of themselves; nor for the receiver is there any option. Neither can withhold the messages conveyed to the other. (Wilson, 1966:92)

well-bred southerner was quite so crude as to do so; nor would a well-bred southerner call a Negro "mister" or invite him into the living room or eat with him or sit by him in public places.

I knew that my old nurse who had cared for me through long months of illness, who had given me refuge when a little sister took my place as the baby of the family, who soothed, fed me, delighted me with her stories and games, let me fall asleep on her deep warm breast, was not worthy of the passionate love I felt for her but must be given instead a half-smiled-at affection similar to that which one feels for one's dog. I knew but I never believed it, that the deep respect I felt for her, the tenderness, the love, was a childish thing which every normal child outgrows, that such love begins with one's toys and is discarded with them, and that somehow— though it seemed impossible to my agonized heart—I too, must outgrow these feelings. I learned to use a soft voice to oil my words of su- periority. I learned to cheapen with tears and sentimental talk of "my old mammy" one of the profound relationships of my life. I learned the bitterest thing a child can learn: that the human relations I valued most were held cheap by the world I lived in.

From the day I was born, I began to learn my lessons. I was put in a rigid frame too intricate, too twisting to describe here so briefly, but I learned to conform to its slide-rule measure-

ments. I learned it is possible to be a Christian and a white southerner simultaneously; to be a gentlewoman and an arrogant callous creature in the same moment; to pray at night and ride a Jim Crow car the next morning and to feel comforta- ble in doing both. I learned to believe in freedom, to glow when the word *democracy* was used, and to practice slavery from morning to night. I learned it the way all of my southern people learn it; by closing door after door until one's mind and heart and conscience are blocked off from each other and from reality.

I closed the doors. Or perhaps they were closed for me. One day they began to open again. Why I had the desire or the strength to open them, or what strange accident or circumstance opened them for me would require in the an- swering an account too long, too particular, too stark to make here. And perhaps I should not have the wisdom that such an analysis would de- mand of me, nor the will to make it. I know only that the doors opened, a little; that somewhere along that iron corridor we travel from babyhood to maturity, doors swinging inward began to swing outward, showing glimpses of the world beyond, of that bright thing we call "reality."

Source: Selection is reprinted from *Killers of the Dream* by Lillian Smith, by permission of W. W. Norton & Company, Inc. Copyright 1949, © 1961 by Lillian Smith. Copyright renewed 1977 and 1989 by Paula Snelling.

Thus, the children learn from their parents. They learn from them the meaning of physical objects such as the Bible, poison, and the police officer's badge. They also learn the relative worth of social groups such as Jews or blacks. Panel 6–1 provides an example of how one southern white girl was raised to hate blacks.

The Schools: In contrast to families who may differ somewhat in their atti- tudes, interests, and emphases, the schools provide a more uniform indoctri- nation of youth in the culturally prescribed ways. Formal education in any society serves to enculturate young persons. The schools have the avowed goal of preparing persons for their adult roles. Youngsters in school must learn appropriate skills and incorporate character traits and attitudes (such as patriotism) that pay off. In the United States some of the character traits are competitiveness, ambition, and conformity.

As we see in Chapter 15, the formal system of education is most conservative—transmitting the attitudes, values, and training necessary for the maintenance of society. Thus, schools are preoccupied with order and control. This emphasis on order teaches the norms and prepares the youth for the organizational life they are expected to experience as adults. Unlike the family, where the child is part of a loving relationship, the school is impersonal. The rules are to be obeyed. Activities are regimented rather than spontaneous. Thus, the child learns how to function in the larger society by learning the formal prescriptions of society and by learning that to get along one must go along.

The Media.   The mass media—consisting of newspapers, magazines, movies, radio, and television—play a vital role in promoting the existing values and practices of society. For example, the mass media provide us with most of the information that helps us to define sociopolitical reality. As Parenti has suggested:

> How we view issues, indeed, what we even define as an issue or event, what we see and hear, and what we do *not* see and hear are greatly determined by those who control the communications world. . . . Even when we don't believe what the media say, we are still hearing or reading their viewpoints rather than some other. They are still setting the agenda, defining what it is we must believe or disbelieve, accept, or reject. The media exert a subtle, persistent influence in defining the scope of respectable political discourse, channeling public attention in directions that are essentially supportive of the existing politico-economic system. (Parenti, 1986:ix)

The media promote traditional American values. In his study of *CBS Evening News, NBC Nightly News, Newsweek,* and *Time,* sociologist Herbert Gans found that these news sources portrayed eight clusters of enduring values: ethnocentrism, altruistic democracy, responsible capitalism, small-town pastoralism, individualism, moderatism, social order, and national leadership (Gans, 1979). The promotion of these values is especially effective because it appears to the consumers as independent and objective.

Television, through its entertainment shows, also functions to promote the status quo. Stereotypes of the aged, women, and minorities are promoted on these programs. Crime shows, for example, provide a series of morality plays in which

> wrongs are righted, victims avenged, and victimizers awarded for just deserts. The timing is the same, the rhythm, the choreography, the cast, the denouement—everyone has learned just what to expect. On the top of the heap are television's Good Guys, for years mainly mature white males. On the bottom of the heap lie the Victims—piled up bodies of children, old people, poor people, nonwhites, young people, lone women—all done in by Bad Guys recruited principally from the lower social strata many of the so-called victims come from. . . . Our modern morality plays . . . point the finger at the social strata from which evil emanates and signal the conditions that make it

Television has tremendous power to influence youth. The messages they receive from this medium promote ideological control.

quite proper to shoot, kill, maim, hurt, rip, smash, slash, crush, tear, burn, bury, excise. What starts out as shocking becomes routine then is converted into ritual. (Goldsen, 1977:223–224, 234)

The impact of television is of special importance because youth are so exposed to this medium, as shown by these examples:

- Three-year-old children watch 26 to 30 hours of TV a week.
- Young people see some 12,000 acts of televised violence a year.
- "By the time an American child graduates from high school, he or she will have spent more time in front of the tube than in class." (Aufderheide, 1989)

The messages children receive are consistent: they are bombarded with materialism and consumerism, what it takes to be a success, violence, and the value of law and order. In short, the media have tremendous power to influence us all, but particularly our youth. This influence can be in the direction of acceptance or criticism of the system. Overwhelmingly, the media are supportive of that system.

SIMILARITIES AND DIFFERENCES AMONG MEMBERS OF SOCIETY

Modal Personality Type

In Chapter 2 we described the condition that Durkheim called *anomie.* This refers to a situation where an individual is unsure of his or her social world—the norms are ambiguous or conflicting. In other words, an anomic situation lacks consistency, predictability, and order. Since this condition is upsetting, individuals and groups seek order. Every society provides a common **nomos** (meaningful order) for its members (Berger and Luckman, 1967). "Every society has its specific way of defining and perceiving reality—its world, the universe, its overarching organization of symbols" (Berger and Kellner, 1975:219). Through the socialization process, the newcomer to society is provided a reality that makes sense. By learning the language and the ready-made definitions of society, the individual is given a consistent way to perceive the world. The order that is created for each of us is taken for granted by us; it is the only world that we can conceive of; it is the only system in which we feel comfortable.

> This order, by which the individual comes to perceive and define his world, is thus not chosen by him, except perhaps for very small modifications. Rather it is discovered by him as an external datum, a ready-made world that simply is *there* for him to go ahead and live in, though he modifies it continually in the process of living in it (Berger and Kellner, 1975:220)

Each society has its unique way of perceiving, interpreting, and evaluating reality. This common culture, and nomos, is internalized by the members of society through the process of socialization—thus, people are a product of their culture. It follows, then, that the members of a society will be similar in many fundamental respects. Although there are individual exceptions and subcultural variations, we can say that Americans differ fundamentally from Mexicans, Germans, the French, and others. Let us illustrate how people in a society will develop similarly by briefly characterizing two categories of Native Americans of North America (taken from Barnouw, 1979:59–75):

1. *The Pueblo of the southwest.* The Zuñi and Hopi are submissive and gentle peoples. Children are treated with warmth and affection. They live in highly cooperative social structures where individualism is discouraged. One who thirsts for power is ridiculed.

Life in these societies is highly structured. The rules are extremely important and order is highly valued. They never brew intoxicants and reject the use of drugs. In these orderly and cooperative settings, people are trusted. Life is pleasant and relatively free from hatred. The kind of person that develops in these societies tends to be confident, trusting, generous, polite, cooperative, and emotionally controlled.

2. *The northern plains.* The Native Americans of this area are aggressive peoples. They are fierce warriors exhibiting almost suicidal bravado in battle. They stress individuality with fierce competition for prestige. They boast of their exploits. They stress individual ecstasy in their religious experiences, brought about by fasting, self-torture, and the use of drugs (peyote and alcohol).

The Plains tribes, in contrast to the Pueblo, are more individualistic, competitive, and aggressive. They are more expressive as individuals and less orderly in group life.

These examples show that each society tends to produce a certain type of individual—a **modal personality type.** The individual growing up in

American society, with its set of values, will tend to be individualistic, competitive, materialistic, and oriented toward work, progress, and the future. While this characterization of Americans is generally correct, there are some problems with the assumption that socialization into a culture is so all-powerful. First, the power of socialization can vary by the type of society. Small, homogeneous societies like those of Native American tribes provide the individual member of society with a consistent message, while in a heterogeneous society like the United States, individuals are confronted with a number of themes, variations, and counterthemes. More fundamental, though, is the second problem—is the socialization process completely deterministic? The views of Cooley and Mead noted earlier would seem to suggest this. Dennis Wrong has criticized this position. He has argued that, from a Freudian position, the individual and society are never completely in harmony. While individuals are socialized and generally comply with the demands of society, the process is never complete (Wrong, 1969:130). The distance from complete socialization is maximized in modern, heterogeneous societies.

Why We Aren't All Alike

Every society has its deviants. Clearly, people are not robots. Given the power of society, through the socialization process, what are the forces that allow for differences in people in the United States? We begin with a discussion of the major agencies of socialization.

Family.   We have said that the family is the ultimate societal agency for socialization. Families teach their children the language, etiquette, skills, and the like that will enable the child to find his or her niche in society. But families differ in a variety of important ways (for example, in religion, political views, optimism, and affluence). Socioeconomic status is an especially important variable. In Chapter 14 we provide the details as to how the different social classes tend to rear children and the consequences. Two examples suffice for the present discussion. Working-class parents tend to be authoritarian, demanding control of their youngsters and providing punishment for failure to comply. Authority figures are to be obeyed without questions. In contrast, upper-middle-class parents have tended to allow their children to explore, experiment, and question. The family is democratic. Rules are not necessarily absolute. Clearly, children growing up in authoritarian and permissive families will differ in their acceptance of authority, political proclivities, and views of the world.

The family may have little influence on the child if the parents disagree on politics, religion, values, and the like. Or, if they are consistent, the parents' views may be neutralized by contrary values held by friends. This is facilitated by the decreasing amount of time that the parents spend with the children compared to the time spent in previous generations (Boocock, 1975). As parents spend less and less time raising and influencing their children,

The Unprepared Generation of the 1980s Faces the Future

It's like being strapped naked into a roller coaster as it inches toward an unseen precipice. Stripped of protective illusions that comforted my parents, I am approaching the brink of a century guaranteed to bring change of cataclysmic proportions. All I can do is hang on for the ride and remind myself that there is no shame in screaming.

To my parents, that seems overly pessimistic, the bleak view of a child grown world-weary before his time. I disagree; this is my time. And it is not weariness but anticipation that fills me as I look to the future. Whatever else happens, I have the satisfaction of knowing that the decades my generation will live through sure won't be boring.

We are the first generation to enter adulthood faced with undeniable evidence that the foundations of America's most cherished beliefs are shaken and crumbling. The reverberations, too large to measure now, will surface in our lifetimes in ways no one can predict.

How can you quantify the discovery that your country is no longer No. 1? Or how massive load debt will strain a population brought up believing theirs is the land of milk and honey? What will happen when the people of a nation grown used to calling the tune have to pay the piper?

I can't blame my parents for not understanding how I look to the future. They are children of the '50s. The worst bogeymen they were taught to fear were Communists and the Bomb. The children who came of age in the '80s got those lessons with their first Crayolas. After milk and cookies, we were introduced to a cast of bogeymen that left the Bomb begging for respect. Global warming. The disappearing ozone layer. Nuclear waste piling up. Toxins in every bite. Our parents blamed our listlessness on too many bowls of Froot Loops and not enough exercise.

We learned nice things in school, too. History class gave us lessons on representative democracy and the American tradition of world leadership. In science class we learned about elemental forces of the universe and how our nation's mastery of those forces led to America's technological superiority. Economics class centered on the evolution of American capitalism and how it provided a high standard of living for all.

I know my teachers meant well. But the curriculum tended to be like an armadillo: slow-moving and largely ignorant of the world around it. The world of the '80s, I found, was disturbingly dissimilar to the pictures in the textbooks.

In 1983 I graduated from high school, and the U.S. invaded Grenada, a flyspeck island nation that no one ever heard of. This puzzled me.

In grade school I avidly read every book in the library about the American military, from the French and Indian Wars to Vietnam. There was plenty about invasions. But I couldn't reconcile the tales of brave men storming the beaches of

their youngsters are influenced more and more by not only their peers but also baby sitters, schools, and television.

Some families may have little or negative influence on their children because they are hopelessly disorganized. One or both parents may be alcoholics, unstable, or uncommunicative.

In sum, although children raised in American society are affected by a common culture, family experiences and emphases can vary enough to result in behavioral and attitudinal differences. That children and families can be fundamentally different is seen in the occasional value conflicts between parents and school authorities on sex education, the use of certain literature, rules, and the proper way to enforce rules. But the schools themselves also vary, resulting in different products by type of school.

Normandy with the stories from Grenada. A few dozen construction workers with rifles against an invasion fleet? This was new.

Saving Grenada apparently had something to do with restoring esprit de corps after hundreds of Marines had been blown up in a Beirut barracks by a car bomb. I learned later that a high school friend, who'd dropped out to join up, lost a leg in Beirut, while America saved face in Grenada.

Before Grenada, politics ranked up there with calculus on my list of things best left to others. But news of the invasion was accompanied by another disturbing picture—an aging ex-actor named Ronald Reagan enthusiastically telling the cameras what a splendid victory this was for democracy.

Ah, democracy. So that's what my teachers were making such a fuss over. I was too young to vote and I was already wondering if I should bother.

Eventually I did vote, when I got a chance. But most people my age still think politics is better left to others. I've had dozens of discussions on the subject. They all end the same way. My friends ask, "What difference does it make?" And I cannot find an answer that satisfies them.

Watergate, the political scandal for the previous generation, ended in the resignation of President Richard Nixon. The congressional investigation of our generation probed the Iran-contra affair. It produced reams of evidence implicating the president, vice president, attorney general and other top government officials in crimes far worse than Watergate.

The result? Oliver North became a hero, the vice president became president and the nation turned back to its soap operas. Nixon, rehabilitated, returned to the front pages. It's discouraging. Try to get people to look up from their beer and care about politics after that.

More Americans ignored the last election than voted for president. What can reverse the trend? What happens to democracy when it becomes an instrument of the minority? We shall see.

My generation will find the answers to many questions in the years to come, but not because we asked. The decisions will be forced upon us by default. Sooner or later, there will be too many homeless people, too many highways and bridges crumbling under decades of neglect, too many industries bankrupt or bought by the Japanese. Sooner or later, the bill for this last decade will come due.

That's what makes the future so exciting. The problems we face have begun to reveal themselves, but the answers remain hidden. It will be up to us—the unprepared, ill-equipped, uncaring children of the '80s—to shoulder the burden or collapse. Either way, it's going to be a hell of a show.

Source: Andrew Galarneau, "Coming of Age in the 80s," *In These Times* (November 1–7, 1989): 5. Reprinted by permission of *In These Times,* 2040 N. Milwaukee, Chicago, IL 60647 (312–772-0100).

Schools.   American schools, as are schools in all societies, are conservative. But there are differences that have a substantial impact on students. There are schools, for example, where the curriculum, schedule, and philosophy are very rigid. Children sit in straight rows, may talk only with permission, wear the prescribed clothing, and accept without question the authority of the teacher. There are other schools, however, where the curriculum, schedules, teachers, and rules are flexible. The products of these two types of schools are likely to differ in much the same way as do the children of autocratic or permissive homes.

Religion.   In general, organized religion in the United States reinforces American values and the policies of the government (see Chapter 16). But there are significant differences among and within the various religious bodies. There are religious disagreements on morality, birth control, abortion, capital punishment, evolution, and other volatile issues. Moreover, religious ideas can conflict with those of one's peers, and with what is taught in school. The more salient one's religion, then, the more likely one will differ from those who do not share one's religious views.

Social Location.   Each of us is located in society, not only geographically, but also socially. Depending on our wealth, occupation, education, ethnic or racial heritage, and family background, we see ourselves and others see us as being superior to some persons and inferior to others. Our varying positions in this hierarchy will have an effect on our attitudes and perceptions. In particular, those who are highly placed will tend to be supportive of the status quo, while those who are less advantaged will likely be more antagonistic to the way things are and desirous of changes beneficial to them.

Contradictory Influences.   We have seen that youngsters may experience pulls in opposite directions from family, church, and school. Other sources of contradictory attractions are peer groups and the media. Parents may insist, for instance, that their children not fight. Yet, their peers might demand such behavior. Moreover, children are bombarded by violence (much of which is considered appropriate) in the movies and on television. How are these children to behave, faced with such opposing and powerful stimuli? Some will follow their parents' dictates, while others will succumb to other pressures.

Conflicts in Role Definition.   Some societies are clear and consistent in their expectations for members' behavior. There is no such consensus in American society. An examination of a few fundamental social roles illustrates the disagreement on the expectations of the occupants. Adolescents are often unsure of what is expected of them. The law sometimes defines them as children and at other times as adults. Parents and other adults often lack consistency in what they expect of teenagers. The aged are another category that experiences ill-defined expectations. At times they are treated as adults and at other times they are not taken seriously. Some must retire from work at age 65 while others may continue.

Gender roles provide another example of varying expectations depending on the individual, audience, and community. Traditional masculine and feminine roles are in flux. What precisely is expected of a man and woman as they enter a building? Does the man open the door for the woman? This was appropriate behavior in the past and it may be now, but one is never sure, for some women find such behavior offensive. What are the expectations of a newly married husband and wife? How will they divide the household chores? Who is to be the breadwinner? And later, if there is a divorce, who will take the children? Twenty years ago, or even five years ago, the answers to these questions were much more certain.

To conclude, the emphasis of this chapter is on how the individual is shaped by powerful social forces, but we must not forget that people are not utterly predictable. Moreover, human beings are actively involved in shaping the social landscape. In sum, the person is, as Kenneth Westhues has said, "a two-sided being, at once created and creating, predictable and surprising" (Westhues, 1982:viii).

Both order and conflict theorists acknowledge the power of the socialization process. They differ, however, in their interpretation of this universal process. The order theorists view this as necessary to promote stability and law-abiding citizens. Conflict theorists, on the other hand, view the process as one in which persons are led to accept the customs, laws, and values of society uncritically and therefore become willing participants in a society that may be in need of change. In other words, the members of society are taught to accept the ways things are, even though the social order benefits some and disadvantages others. This process is so powerful that most of the powerless and disadvantaged in our society do not rebel because they actually believe in the system that systematically keeps them down. Karl Marx explained this irony through the concept of *false consciousness*.

CHAPTER REVIEW

1. Socialization is the process of learning the culture. Children must learn the culture of the society in which they are born. Socialization, however, is a lifelong process and occurs in all social groups.

2. Infants become human only through learning the culture.

3. The socialization of youth requires social interaction.

4. Another essential to socialization is language, which has profound effects on how individuals think and perceive.

5. The personality emerges as a social product. We develop a sense of self only through interaction with others.

6. One theory of how personality develops is Cooley's "looking-glass self." Through interaction children define themselves according to how they interpret how others think of them.

7. Mead's theory of self-development involves several stages. Through interaction with their parents, infants are able to distinguish between themselves and others. By age two they are able to react to themselves as others react to them. In the play stage (from age four to seven) children pretend to be in a variety of adult roles (taking the role of the other). In the game stage (about age eight) children play at games with rigid rules. They begin to understand the structure of the entire game with the expectations for every-

one involved. This understanding of the entire situation is called the "generalized other."

8. According to Freud's theory, socialization is the process by which society controls the id (the biological needs for pleasure). Through this process children develop egos (the control of the id by finding appropriate ways to satisfy biological urges). A superego also emerges which is the internalization of the morals of the parents, further channeling behavior in socially acceptable ways.

9. Through interaction children internalize the norms and values of society. There are three special transmitters of the cultural patterns—the family, the schools, and the media.

10. Because the socialization agents of society present a relatively consistent picture, the members of a society tend to be alike in fundamental ways (modal personality type). The smaller and more homogeneous the society, the more alike the members of that society will be.

11. Despite the tendency for the members to be alike, people, especially in large, heterogeneous societies, are not all similar. The sources of deviation are the differences found in families (e.g., in social class, religion, ethnic background); schools with differing philosophies (rigid or flexible, public or sectarian); religions, social locations, contradictory influences, and conflicts in role definitions.

12. Both order and conflict theorists acknowledge the power of the socialization process. They differ in their interpretation of this universal process. Order theorists view socialization as necessary to promote stability and law-abiding citizens. Conflict theorists, in contrast, view the process as one in which persons are led to accept the customs, laws, and values of society uncritically. This process is so powerful that the disadvantaged may accept the system that disadvantages them (false consciousness).

KEY TERMS

Feral children	Generalized other	Superego
Self	Id	Nomos
Looking-glass self	Ego	Modal personality type
Significant others		

STUDY QUESTIONS

1. To what extent is "humanness" a social product rather than instinctual?
2. What is meant by the assertion "humans are *social* animals"?
3. How do order and conflict theorists differ in their evaluation and interpretation of the role of the media in the socialization process?
4. While the forces that socialize us are powerful, they are not totally deterministic. Why aren't they?

FOR FURTHER READING

The Socialization Process

Charles Horton Cooley, *Human Nature and the Social Order* (New York: Schocken, 1964).

Frederick Elkin and Gerald Handel, *The Child and Society,* 4th ed. (New York: Random House, 1984).

Erik Erikson, *Childhood and Society* (New York: W. W. Norton, 1950).

Frances Fitzgerald, *America Revised* (Boston: Atlantic-Little Brown, 1979).

Sigmund Freud, *Civilization and Its Discontents,* Joan Riviere, trans. (London: Hogarth, 1946).

Herbert J. Gans, *Deciding What's News* (New York: Pantheon, 1979).

Erving Goffman, *The Presentation of Self in Everyday Life* (Garden City, NY: Doubleday, 1959).

Rose K. Goldsen, *The Show and Tell Machine: How Television Works and Works You Over* (New York: Delta, 1977).

George Herbert Mead, *Mind, Self and Society* (Chicago: University of Chicago Press, 1934).

Michael Parenti, *Inventing Reality: The Politics of the Mass Media* (New York: St. Martin's Press, 1986).

Jean Piaget and Barbara Inhelder, *The Psychology of the Child* (New York: Basic Books, 1969).

Gail Sheehy, *Passages: Predictable Crises in Adult Life* (New York: Dutton, 1976).

Modal Personality

Victor Barnouw, *Culture and Personality,* 3rd ed. (Homewood, IL: Dorsey, 1979).

Ruth Benedict, *Patterns of Culture* (Baltimore: Penguin Books, 1946).

Urie Bronfenbrenner, *Two Worlds of Childhood: U.S. and U.S.S.R.* (New York: Simon & Schuster [Pocket Books], 1973).

Stanley Elkins, *Slavery: A Problem of American Institutional and Intellectual Life* (New York: Universal Library, 1963).

Margaret Mead, *Sex and Temperament in Three Primitive Societies* (New York: William Morrow, 1935).

David Reisman, *The Lonely Crowd* (New York: Doubleday, 1953).

Chapter Seven

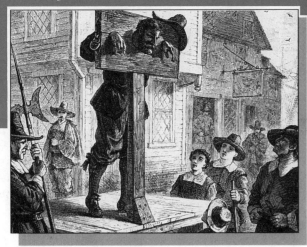

Social Control

At 9:34 P.M. on July 13, 1977, the electricity went out in New York City and in some areas did not work again for twenty-five hours. Under the cover of darkness many areas of the city were pillaged. More than two thousand stores were broken into with property losses estimated at $1 billion. The plunderers were of all ages. They stole appliances, jewelry, shoes, groceries, clothes, furniture, liquor, and automobiles (fifty new Pontiacs from one dealer). The atmosphere was a mixture of revenge, greed, and festival. Observers characterized the looting binge as a carnival atmosphere in which the actors had no concept of morality. It was as if they were immune from the law and from guilt. All of society's constraints were removed resulting in anarchy. When the lights went out, the social controls on behavior left as well for many citizens.

All social groups have mechanisms to ensure conformity—mechanisms of **social control.** The socialization process is one of these ways by which individuals internalize the norms and values of the group. Persons are taught what is proper, moral, and appropriate. This process is generally so powerful that individuals conform, not out of fear of punishment, but because they *want* to. In other words, group demands *out there* become demands *inside* us.

But socialization is never perfect—we are not all robots. As we see in Chapter 8, people deviate. To cope with this, social groups exert external control—that is, rewards and punishments. These controls are the subject of this chapter.

The focus of this chapter is on social control at the societal level. The dominant modes of socialization vary by type of society. Small, homogeneous societies, for example, are dominated by tradition, while large, modern societies are very much less affected by the force of tradition. Traditional societies tend to have an overriding consensus on societal values; therefore, the family, religion, and the community convey to each individual member a consistent message on which behaviors are appropriate and which ones are not. Although the formal punishment of norm violators does occur in traditional societies, informal controls are usually quite effective and more typical.

In a complex society such as the United States, social control is more difficult to attain because of the existence of different groups with values that are often competing. Therefore, social control tends to be more formal and appears more repressive (because it is more overt) than that which is found in traditional societies. It occurs in many forms and disguises. Social control is accomplished in the home and school and through various other institutions. It is attained through the overt and covert activities of political agencies, psychotherapists, and even genetic engineers. Efforts to manipulate the masses through various techniques of persuasion also keep deviance in check.

The remainder of this chapter is devoted to an extensive examination of the various agents of social control in American society. These are divided into two types by the means used to achieve social control: ideological and direct intervention. The former aims at control through manipulation of ideas and perceptions, while the latter controls the actual behavior of citizens.

AGENTS OF IDEOLOGICAL SOCIAL CONTROL

Ideological social control is the attempt to manipulate the consciousness of citizens so that they accept the ruling ideology and refuse to be moved by competing ideologies. Other goals are to persuade the members of society to comply willingly with the law and to accept without question the existing distribution of societal power and rewards. These goals are accomplished in at least three ways. First, ideological social control is accomplished through the socialization of youth. Young people, for example, are taught the values of individualism, competition, patriotism, and respect for authority at home, in school, in scouting organizations, in sports, and through the media. The socialization process could be referred to as cultural control, since the individual is given authoritative definitions of what should and should not be done, which make it appear as if there were no choice (Stivers, 1975). Second, ideological conformity occurs by frontal attacks on competing ideologies by politicians, ministers, teachers, and other persons in authority. Finally, there are propaganda efforts by political authorities to persuade the public what actions are moral, who the enemies are, and why certain courses of governmental action are required. Let us examine these in detail by describing the agents of social control that are especially important in accomplishing the goal of ideological conformity.

Family

The primary responsibility of parents is to teach their children the attitudes, values, and behaviors considered appropriate by the parents (and society). Parents universally want their children to succeed. Success is not only measured in terms of monetary achievement but also in whether the child fits in society. This requires that the child learn to behave and think in the ways that are deemed "proper." Although, as noted in Chapter 6, there is a wide latitude in the actual mode of socialization in the family, most children do behave in acceptable ways (Bronfenbrenner, 1958; Kohn, 1959).

Education

The formal system of education is an important societal agent for conformity. The school insists that the behavioral standards of the community be maintained in speech, dress, and demeanor. More than this, the schools indoctrinate their pupils in the "correct" attitudes about work, respect for authority, and patriotism. The textbooks used in schools have typically not provided an accurate account of history, for example, but rather an account that is biased in the direction the authorities wish to perpetuate. The treatment given minorities in these texts is one indicator of the bias. Another is the contrast

An important function of schools is to promote ideological conformity.

The Amish and Social Control

The Amish are a religious sect found mainly in Pennsylvania, Indiana, and Kansas. They are farmers who resist modern technology. They forbid the use of motorcycles, automobiles, and electricity. They wear simple clothes of the nineteenth century. They believe that they are only temporary visitors on earth, and hence remain aloof from it. This explains why they insist on being different. Most important, the Amish insist on conformity within their community.

The Amish descend from Jacob Amman, a Mennonite preacher in Switzerland. The Mennonites and other Anabaptists of that day differed from mainstream Protestants because they believed in the separation of church and state, adult baptism, refusal to bear arms and take oaths. Amman and his followers split away from the Mennonites in 1700 over an issue of church discipline—the *Meidung*. Amman felt that the Mennonites were too lax in their discipline of deviants and that the *Meidung* must be enforced in severe cases. The *Meidung* is one of the most potent of all social control mechanisms. The following is a description by William Kephart of this device used by the Amish to ensure conformity within the community.

The ultimate sanction is imposition of the *Meidung*, or ban, but because of its severity, this form of punishment is used only as a last resort. The Amish community relies heavily on the individual's conscience to tell him what is right and wrong. And since the typical Amishman has a finely developed conscience, actions like gossip or reprimand are usually sufficient to bring about conformity. The *Meidung* would be imposed only if a member were to leave the church, or marry an outsider, or break a major rule (such as buying an auto) without being repentant.

Although the *Meidung* is imposed by the bishop, he will not act without the near unanimous vote of the congregation. The ban, however, is total. No one in the district is permitted to talk or associate with the errant party, including members of his own family. Even normal marital relations are forbidden. Should any member of the community ignore the *Meidung*, that person would also be placed under the ban. As a matter of fact, the *Meidung* is honored by *all Amish districts*, including those which are not in full fellowship with the district in question. There is no doubt that the ban is a mighty weapon. Jacob Amman intended it to be.

On the other hand, the ban is not irrevocable. If the member admits the error of his ways—and asks forgiveness of the congregation in person—the *Meidung* will be lifted and the transgressor readmitted to the fold. No matter how serious the offense, the Amish never look upon someone under the ban as an enemy, but only as one who has erred. And while they are firm in their enforcement of the *Meidung*, the congregation will pray for the errant member to rectify his mistake.

Although imposition of the ban is infrequent, it is far from rare. Males are involved much more often than females, the younger more frequently than the old. The *Meidung* would probably be imposed on young males more often were it not for the fact that baptism does not take place before age sixteen, and sometimes not until eighteen. Prior to this time, young males are expected to be—and often are—a little on the wild side, and allowances are made for this fact. The prebaptismal period thus serves as a kind of safety valve.

Baptism changes things, however, for this is the rite whereby the young person officially joins the church and makes the pledge of obedience. Once the pledge is made, the limits of tolerance are substantially reduced. More than one Amish youth has been subjected to the *Meidung* for behavior which, prior to his baptism, had been tolerated.

Source: Copyright © 1976 by St. Martin's Press, Inc. From *Extraordinary Groups: The Sociology of Unconventional Life-Styles.* By William M. Kephart. Reprinted with permission of St. Martin's Press, Inc.

between descriptions of the behavior of the United States and the behavior of its enemies in wars (see Fitzgerald, 1979).

One critic of the schools is concerned with the problem of conformity, which taken to the extreme results in blind obedience to such malevolent authority figures as Adolph Hitler, Charles Manson, and the Rev. Jim Jones. Rather than turning out conformists, the schools should be turning out individuals with the courage to disobey false prophets.

> The power of socialization can conceivably be harnessed so as to develop individuals who are rational and skeptical, capable of independent thought, and who can disobey or disagree at the critical moment. Our society, however, continues systematically to instill exactly the opposite. The educational system pays considerable lip service to the development of self-reliance, and places huge emphasis on lofty concepts of individual differences. Little notice is taken of the legions of overly obedient children in the schools; yet, for every overly disobedient child, there are probably twenty who are obeying too much. There is little motivation to encourage the unsqueaky wheels to develop as noisy, creative, independent thinkers who may become bold enough to disagree. (McCarthy, 1979:34)

Religion

Established religion in America tends to reinforce the status quo. Few clergy and their parishioners work actively to change the political and economic system. Instead they preach sermons extolling the virtues of "the American Way of Life," and "giving unto Caesar the things which are Caesar's." Directly or indirectly there has been a strong tendency for religious groups throughout American history to accept existing government policies, whether they are slavery, war, or the conquest of the Native Americans.

Religious groups also preserve the status quo by teaching that people should accept an imperfect society (poverty, racism, and war) because they are born sinners. In this way, religion, as Marx suggested, *is* an opiate of the masses because it convinces them to accept an unjust system rather than work to change it. The downtrodden are advised to accept their lot because they will be rewarded in the next life. Thus, they have no need to change the system from below. As Szymanski has argued:

> The doctrine of the omnipotence of God and total submission to His will pervades the general world views of religious people, and hence is sublimated as submission to political rulers and the upper class. Religion provides a consolation for the suffering of people on earth and a deflection of one's hopes into the future. Combined with its advocacy of the earthly status quo, religion thus typically serves as a powerful legitimatizing force for upper-class rule. Further, most religions, especially the religions of the working class and the poor—Baptism, Methodism, the Messianic sects, and Catholicism—in their sermons typically condemn radical political movements and preach instead either political abstention or submission to government authority. (Szymanski, 1978:253)

Sport

School and professional sports work to reinforce conforming attitudes and behaviors in the populace in several ways (Eitzen and Sage, 1989). First, there is the strong relationship between sport and nationalism. Success in international sports competition tends to trigger pride among that nation's citizens. The Olympics and other international games tend to promote an "us vs. them" feeling among athletes, coaches, politicians, the press, and fans. It can be argued, then, that the Olympic Games is a political contest, a symbolic world war in which nations win or lose. Because this interpretation is commonly held, citizens of the nations involved unite behind their flag and their athletes.

The integral interrelationship of sport and nationalism is easily seen in the blatantly militaristic pageantry that surrounds sports contests. The playing of the national anthem, the presentation of the colors, the jet aircraft flyovers, the band forming a flag or a liberty bell, are all political acts supportive of the existing political system.

For whatever reason, sport competition and nationalism are closely intertwined. When American athletes compete against those of another country, national unity is the result (for both sides, unless one's athletes do poorly). Citizens take pride in their representatives' accomplishments, viewing them as collective achievements. This identification with athletes and their cause of winning for the nation's glory tends to unite a nation's citizens regardless of social class, race, and regional differences. Thus, sport can be used by political leaders whose nations have problems with divisiveness.

As mentioned in Chapter 3, sport can serve as an opiate of the masses in several ways. Virtually all homes have television sets, making it possible for almost everyone to participate vicariously in and identify with local and national sports teams. Because of this, their minds and energies are deflected away from the hunger and misery that are disproportionately the lot of the lower classes in American society.

Sport also acts as an opiate by perpetuating the belief that persons from the lowest classes can be upwardly mobile by success in sports. Clearly this is a myth since for every major leaguer who has come up from poverty, tens of thousands have not. The point, however, is that most Americans *believe* that sport is a mobility escalator and that it is merely a reflection of the opportunity structure of the society in general. Again, poor youth who might otherwise invest their energies in changing the system, work instead on a jump shot. The potential for revolution is thus impeded by sport.

Another way that sport serves to control persons ideologically is by reinforcing American values among the participants. Sport is a vehicle by which the American values of success in competition, hard work, perseverance, discipline, and order are transmitted. This is the explicit reason given for the existence of Little League programs for youngsters and the tremendous emphasis on sports in American schools.

One explicit goal of sports is to build character. The assumption is that participation in sports from the Little Leagues through the Big Leagues (professional ranks) provides the athletes with those values that are American: achievement in competitive situations through hard work, materialism, progress, and respect for authority. As David Matza (1964:207) has put it: "The substance of athletics contains within itself—in its rules, procedures, training, and sentiments—a paradigm of adult expectations regarding youth." Schools want individuals to follow rules, be disciplined, to work hard, to fit in; and sports accomplish these goals.

Not only do schools insist that athletes behave a certain way during practice and games, but they also strictly monitor the behavior of the athletes in other situations as well. The athletes must conform to the school's norms in dress, speech, demeanor, and grades if they want to continue to participate. In this way, school administrators use athletes as models of decorum. If others in the school and community admire athletes, then athletes serve to preserve the community and school norms.

Media

The movies, television, newspapers, and magazines also serve basically to reinforce the system. There is clearly a conservative bias among the various corporations involved because their financial success depends on whether the public will buy their product and whether advertisers will use their vehicles. As Parenti has argued:

> Along with products, the corporations sell themselves. By the 1970s, for the first time since the Great Depression, the legitimacy of big business was being called into question by large sectors of the public. Enduring inflation, unemployment, and a decline in real wages, the American people became increasingly skeptical about the blessings of the corporate economy. In response, corporations intensified their efforts at the kind of "advocacy advertising," designed to sell the entire capitalist system rather than just one of its products. Between 1971 and 1977, the spending on "nonproduct-related" advertisements more than doubled, from $230 million to over $474 million, showing a far greater growth rate than advertising expenditures as a whole. *Today, one-third of all corporate advertising is directed at influencing the public on political and ideological issues as opposed to pushing consumer goods.* (That portion is tax deductible as a "business expense," like all other advertising costs.) Led by the oil, chemical, and steel companies, big business fills the airwaves and printed media with celebrations of the "free market," and warnings of the baneful effects of government regulation. (Parenti, 1986:67)

That the media reinforce the values and norms of society is seen in newspaper editorials that extol certain persons and events while decrying others and in stories under the caption, "It Could Only Have Happened in America." Soap operas also accomplish this since they are stories involving moral dilemmas with virtue winning out. Television, in particular, has had a significant impact on the values of Americans. The average American child, prior to the first grade, will watch television as much as the time required to obtain

The Politics of the "Non-Partisan" Advertising Council

The nation's second-largest advertiser is not Sears, Roebuck & Company, as the trade statistics indicate, nor is it General Foods, General Motors, or McDonald's. The number-two huckster does not peddle autos, cigarettes, washing machines, or hamburgers. Rather, it hawks ideas and causes to Americans, and it does so without ever purchasing an inch of space in newspapers or magazines or a second of broadcast time.

The Advertising Council, a New York-based nonprofit corporation, ranks second among advertisers (behind Procter & Gamble) thanks to about $650 million worth of space and time the media donate each year for its "public service" campaigns. Though the Council itself is relatively unknown, its work is ubiquitous: Smokey the Bear, Crime Dog McGruff, television spots for the Red Cross and the United Way, and the slogans "Take stock in America," "Give to the college of your choice," and "A mind is a terrible thing to waste" are some of the Council's creations.

Founded in 1942 by a group of leading advertising executives, the Council promotes voluntary, individual actions "to help solve national problems." Each year it conducts about two dozen "non-partisan public service campaigns in the interest of Americans generally," some in cooperation with government agencies, others in conjunction with private organizations. In each case, an ad agency volunteers to produce a campaign for the Council and its client; the client pays agency out-of-pocket expenses, estimated at $150,000 to $200,000. Major corporations contribute just under $1 million annually to sustain Council operations.

The Council's campaigns include pitches on behalf of the Peace Corps, the national Endowment for the Arts, the Alliance to Save Energy, and the National Alliance of Business. It promotes the prevention of child abuse, support for colleges and universities, education about high blood pressure, "equality for all," and other ways to make "our system work better."

Through its television and radio spots, billboards, subway and bus signs, and advertisements in the press, the Council dominates the public service advertising (PSA) market—and reaches millions with its diverse but remarkably consistent set of messages which, taken together, make up a distinct view of what American society is and ought to be. Without exception, Council ads and Council-based organizations convey one theme: Personal charity can untangle any mess, solve any problem; collective or governmental action is never necessary in a land of good neighbors.

"They are promoting a vision of America that is not susceptible to solutions by government, that solves its problems through volunteerism, and is very middle-class in its orientation," says Andrew Schwartzman, executive director of the Media Access Project, a public-interest law firm in Washington, D.C.

G. William Domhoff, professor of sociology and psychology at the University of California—Santa Cruz, says of the Advertising Council, "They feel that we're one big happy family, that there are no serious differences among people of different social classes. They present the image that solving every problem is a matter of good will, that no group of class has to make any particular sacrifice."

Indeed, the preeminent partisan of national consensus and diminished government, Ronald Reagan, has called the Council "indispensable." "You know," he told the organization last November, "those words, 'the Ad Council,' evoke for me the whole idea of what our American spirit and volunteerism are all about."

The American spirit—the bootstrap ideology—was more accurately described as the myth of individual influence, the illusion of individual political competence" by the authors of a 1977 study, *Politics in Public Service Advertising on Television*. "PSAs encourage pseudo-participation," the Duke University political scientists wrote, "by exhorting Americans to act in a limited and pre-determined manner."

"We're directing our message to individual people around the country, telling what they can do," says Council spokesman Benjamin Greenberg. "It's like in commercial advertising they're telling you that you can buy aspirin to get rid of a headache."

Of course, people do not embrace a particular view of the world—or purchase aspirin—simply because a television spot urges them to do so, "but a message gets repeated over and over and it becomes part of the lexicon of images we're exposed to," notes Michael Singsen, media director of the San Francisco-based Public Media Center, which prepares PSAs for social-action organizations. "Who hasn't heard of Smokey the Bear or 'Don't be a litterbug'? It's more of an insidious nature than an overt one."

According to both Singsen and Domhoff, the Advertising Council does not induce direct changes in attitude or behavior; it simply reinforces existing conceptions of acceptable civic activity. As University of California—Berkeley sociologist Todd Gitlin puts it, the Council "contributes to the general cultural stock of symbols." But more important, all three emphasize, is the Council's role in keeping alternative—more systemic—visions from gaining access to the media.

"Simply by occupying this [PSA] space, the Council has enabled television stations to argue that they've discharged their public service responsibility," Gitlin points out.

"Because of its dominance," Singsen says, "a lot of other ideas do not get out. And because of the way they've been able to set the tone for public-service announcements, by making them noncontroversial and nonpolitical, they've been able to get a lot of stations to buy into the notion that PSAs *should* be noncontroversial and nonpolitical."

By refusing to back controversial causes, the Council has persuaded most media enterprises that its products are safe because they are non-partisan, nondenominational, and noncommer-cial—and in a literal sense that is correct. But the Council's campaigns are, in fact, intensely if subtly political, for they assert that private interests can invariably meet the demands of the public interest. The faith in charitable stop-gap measures as a substitute for structural reform sustains the status quo and the entrenched position of American business.

What's more, some of the Council's work renders direct assistance to specific segments of corporate America. For example, the familiar antipollution ads featuring an Indian shedding tears over roadside trash have been employed for more than two decades to persuade Americans that pollution is primarily a problem of careless littering. The damage done by litter is, of course, inconsequential compared to the damage done by industrial pollution, but the images and the Ad Council's slogan—"People start pollution, people can stop it"—suggest that individuals, not government or industry, are responsible for the foul condition of the environment, and are therefore personally responsible for finding a solution.

People who watch conventional television, read magazines, ride mass transit, or listen to the radio—in essence, most of us—will continue to be exposed to large doses of the Council's individualist vision of America, indeed, according to a recent issue of the Council's *Bulletin*, the Ad Council is undertaking the largest number of new campaigns in its history.

And Smokey will still be with us, and Mc-Gruff, and all the other cute or compelling critters in the Council's stable, assuring us that all is well in America or, if it isn't, that we can fix it by sending a dollar here, ordering a pamphlet there, doing something, anything, except rocking the boat.

Source: Excerpts from Keenen Peck, "Ad Nauseam," *The Progressive* 47 (May 1983): 43–47. Reprinted by permission from *The Progressive*, 409 East Main Street, Madison, Wisconsin 53703. Copyright © 1983, *The Progressive,* Inc.

a college degree (Public Broadcasting System, 1984). What are the consistent messages that television emits? One study has concluded that:

> Television influences the way children think about jobs, job values, success and social surroundings. It stresses the prestige of upper-middle-class occupations: the professions and big business. It makes essentially middle-class value judgments about jobs and success in life. (Himmelweit, Oppenheim, and Vance, 1958)

In short, the media shape how we evaluate ourselves and others. Just as important, they affect directly the way viewers or readers perceive and interpret events. The media, therefore, have tremendous power to influence us to accept or question the system (see Panel 7–2). Although the media do investigative reporting and occasionally question the system, the overall impact of the media is supportive of the system.

Government

Governmental leaders devote a great deal of energy toward ideological social control. One governmental effort is to convince the public that capitalism is good and communism is bad. This is done in political speeches and books. Blatant examples are noted earlier in this chapter of how state legislatures have tried to control the ideological content (patriotism, procapitalism, anticommunism) in schools. Another example of ideological control is seen in government agencies such as the Defense Department and the departments of Agriculture, Commerce, and Education. Each maintains active public relations programs which spend millions of dollars to persuade the public of their views.

The public can also be manipulated by being convinced that their security is threatened by an enemy. This could be done to unify a nation troubled by internal strife. The advice Machiavelli gave his "prince" is a regrettable truth: "if the Prince is in trouble, he should promote a war." This was the advice that Secretary of State Seward gave to President Lincoln prior to the Civil War. Although expedient advice from the standpoint of preserving unity, it was, Lincoln noted, only a short-term solution. Similar efforts to unite by suggesting an external threat, although short of declaring war, have been tried by various American political leaders or candidates for office.

Perhaps the most obvious way that government officials attempt to shape public opinion is through speeches, especially on television. The President can request free prime-time television to speak to the public. These efforts are typically intended to unite the American people against an enemy (inflation, deflation, the energy crisis, communism).

We have described how the various agents of ideological social control operate. Perhaps the best evidence that they are successful is that few of the downtrodden in American society question the legitimacy of the political and economic system. Karl Marx theorized that the "have-nots" in a capitalist society (the poor, the minority group members, the workers) would eventually feel their common oppression and unite to overthrow the owners of capital. That this has not happened in America is due, in large part, to the success of the various agents of ideological social control (Parenti, 1978).

AGENTS OF DIRECT SOCIAL CONTROL

Direct social control refers to attempts to punish or neutralize (render powerless) organizations or individuals who deviate from society's norms. The deviant targets here are essentially four: the poor, the mentally ill, criminals, and political dissidents. This section is devoted to three agents of social control whose efforts are directed at these targets—social welfare, sciences/ medicine, and the government.

Welfare

Piven and Cloward, in their classic study of public welfare, have argued that public assistance programs serve a social control function in times of mass unemployment by defusing social unrest (Piven and Cloward, 1971). When large numbers of people are suddenly barred from their traditional occupations, the legitimacy of the system itself may be questioned. Crime, riots, looting, and social movements bent on changing the existing social and economic arrangements become more widespread. Under this threat, relief programs are initiated or expanded by the government. Piven and Cloward show how during the Great Depression, for example, the government remained aloof from the needs of the unemployed until there was a great surge of political disorder. The function of social welfare, then, is to defuse social unrest through direct intervention of the government. Added proof for Piven and Cloward's thesis is the contraction or even abolishment of public assistance programs when political stability is restored.*

The conditions of the 1990s should provide an interesting test of Piven and Cloward's theory. Current trends indicate that the middle-class is shrinking and that the gap between the "haves" and the "have nots" is increasing (see Chapters 10, 11, and 13). As long as these increasing numbers of the deprived are docile, government programs to alleviate their suffering will be

---

*The second function of welfare mentioned by Piven and Cloward is more subtle (and fits more logically as an agent of ideological social control). Even in good times some people must live on welfare (the disabled, the husbandless who must care for dependent children). By having a category of persons on welfare who live in wretched conditions and who are continuously degraded, work is legitimized. Thus, the poor on welfare serve as an object lesson—keeping even those who work for low wages relatively satisfied with their lot. As Piven and Cloward have concluded:

> In sum, market values and market incentives are weakest at the bottom of the social order. To buttress weak market controls and ensure the availability of marginal labor, an outcast class—the dependent poor—is created by the relief system. This class, whose members are of no productive use, is not treated with indifference, but with contempt. Its degradation at the hands of relief officials serves to celebrate the virtue of all work and deters actual or potential workers from seeking aid. (Piven and Cloward, 1971:52)

The Control of Illicit Sex among the Arabs

In the kinship culture of the Arab world . . . family bonds are so strong that all members suffer "blackening of the face" after the dishonorable act of any one. However, within this general context, there is for the Arab mind a sharp distinction between those shameful events that do involve women and those that do not. In the Arab world, the greatest dishonor that can befall a man results from the sexual misconduct of his daughter or sister, or *bint 'amm* (one's father's brother's daughter). The marital infidelity of a wife, on the other hand, brings to the Arab husband only emotional effects and not dishonor.

The roots of this particular view of male honor go deep into the structure and dynamics of the Arab kin group. The ties of blood, of patrilineal descent, can never be severed, and they never weaken throughout a person's life. This means that a woman, even though she marry into a different kin group, never ceases to be a member of her own paternal family. Her paternal family, in turn, continues to be responsible for her. This has beneficial effects for the married woman, especially during that difficult period in her life which precedes the time when her sons reach maturity and become her supporters and defenders. Prior to that time, the young wife, who is considered something of an outsider by her husband's family, can always count on the aid and sympathy of her own father and brothers. The very knowledge that these men are lined up solidly behind her, and are ready, if need be, even to fight for her, puts a restraint on her husband's family in their treatment of a young daughter-in-law.

Whatever credit or discredit a woman earns reflects back on her own paternal family. This continuing responsibility comes powerfully into play if a woman becomes guilty of a sexual indiscretion, or if her behavior arouses as much as a suspicion that she may be tempted to do something forbidden by the traditional code. The most powerful deterrent devised by Arab culture against illicit sex (which means any sexual relations between a man and a woman who are not married to each other) is the equation of family honor with the sexual conduct of its daughters, single or married. If a daughter becomes guilty of the slightest sexual indiscretion (which is defined in various terms in various places), her father and brothers become dishonored also. Family honor can be restored only by punishing the guilty woman; in conservative circles, this used to mean putting her to death.

That the sexual conduct of women is an area sharply differentiated from other areas of the honor-shame syndrome is reflected in the language. While honor in its non-sexual, general connotation is termed "*sharaf,*" the specific kind of honor that is connected with women and depends on their proper conduct is called "'*ird.*" *Sharaf* is something flexible: depending on a

meager; but should the outrage of the oppressed be manifested in urban riots, acts of terrorism, or in social movements aimed at political change, then, if Piven and Cloward are correct, government welfare programs to aid the poor will become more generous.

Science and Medicine

The practitioners and theoreticians in science and medicine (physicians, psychotherapists, geneticists, electrical engineers, and public health officials) have devised a number of techniques for shaping and controlling the behavior of nonconformists. In the words of Michael Parenti:

man's behavior, way of talking and acting, his *sharaf* can be acquired, augmented, diminished, lost, regained, and so on. In contrast, *'ird* is a rigid concept: every woman has her ascribed *'ird*; she is born with it and grows up with it; she cannot augment it because it is something absolute, but it is her duty to preserve it. A sexual offense on her part, however slight, causes her *'ird* to be lost, and once lost, it cannot be regained. It is almost as if the physical attribute of virginity were transposed in the *'ird* to the emotional-conceptual level. Both virginity and *'ird* are intrinsically parts of the female person; they cannot be augmented, they can only be lost, and their loss is irreparable. The two are similar in one more respect: even if a woman is attacked and raped, she loses her *'ird* just as she loses her virginity. Where the two differ, of course, is in the circumstance that the legal, approved, and expected loss of virginity during the wedding night has no counterpart in the *'ird*: a good woman preserves it, guards it jealously until her dying day.

What is even more remarkable is that the *sharaf* of the men depends almost entirely on the *'ird* of the women of their family. True, a man can diminish or lose his *sharaf* by showing lack of bravery or courage, or by lack of hospitality and generosity. However, such occurrences are rare because the men learn in the course of their early enculturation to maintain at all cost the appearances of bravery, hospitality, and generosity. Should a man nevertheless become guilty of an open transgression of any of these, he will, of course, lose his honor, but this is not accompanied by any institutionalized and traditionally imposed physical punishment. Over crimes which are outside the focus of the code of ethics, such as killing, stealing, breaking promises, accepting bribes, and other such misdeeds, Arab opinion is divided; some say such acts would affect a man's *sharaf*, others feel they would not. But as to the results of a woman's transgression of the *'ird* there is complete and emphatic unanimity: it would destroy the *sharaf* of her menfolk. This led one student of Arab ethics to the conclusion that the core of the *sharaf* is clearly the protection of one's female relatives' *'ird*." To which we can add that this attitude is characteristic of the Arab world as a whole, and that, moreover, a transgression of the *'ird* by a woman and by her paramour is the only crime (apart from homicide) which requires capital punishment according to the Arabic ethical code. Since any indiscretion on her part hurts her paternal family and not her husband's, it is her paternal family—her father himself, or her brothers, or her father's brother's son—who will punish her, by putting her to death, which is considered the only way of repairing the damage done to the family honor.

Source: Reprinted with permission of Charles Scribner's Sons, an imprint of Macmillan Publishing Company from *The Arab Mind* by Raphael Patai. Copyright © 1973, 1976, 1983 Raphael Patai.

In their never-ending campaign to contain the class struggle and control behavior unacceptable to the existing order, authorities have moved beyond clubs, bullets, and eavesdropping devices and are resorting to such things as electroshock, mind-destroying drugs, and psychosurgery. Since the established powers presume that the present social system is virtuous, then those who are prone to violent or disruptive behavior, or who show themselves to be manifestly disturbed about the conditions under which they live, must be suffering from *inner* malfunctions that can best be treated by various mind controls. Not only are political and social deviants defined as insane, but sanity itself has a political definition. The sane person is the obedient one who lives in peace and goes to war on cue from his leaders, is not too much troubled by the inhumanities committed against people, is capable of fitting into one of the mindless job slots of a profit-oriented hierarchical organization, and does not challenge the established rules and conventional wisdom. Since authorities accept the present politico-economic system as a good one, then anything that increases its ability to control dissident persons is also seen as good. (Parenti, 1988:150–151)*

Psychologists and psychotherapists are clearly agents of social control. Their goal is to aid persons who, in the patient's eyes and the eyes of others, do not follow the expectations of the society. In other words, they attempt to treat persons considered "abnormal" in order to make them "normal." By focusing on the individual and his or her adjustment, the mental health practitioners validate, enforce, and reinforce the established ways of society. The implicit assumption is that the individual is at fault and needs to change, not that society is the root cause of mental suffering.

More generally, the labeling of mental illness works as a system of social control. As Scarpitti and Andersen have argued,

> Those who are labeled mentally ill are often the outgroups of society. In fact, labeling groups or individuals as mentally ill can work to contain social and political protest, if those who are disturbed are institutionalized, treated with drug therapy, or otherwise incapacitated. The historic identification of homosexuality with mental illness is a case in point. As long as gay men and women were defined as "sick," then it was less likely that other people in society would challenge the heterosexual privilege characteristic of economic, social, and political institutions. (Scarpitti and Andersen, 1989:352)

In short, this application of the medical model to individuals exhibiting certain behaviors personalizes the problem and deflects attention *away* from the social sources for the behaviors.

Psychosurgery is yet another method with important implications for social control. As with drug therapy or psychotherapy, individuals who are considered abnormal are treated to correct the problem, but this time through brain surgery. With modern techniques, surgeons can operate on localized portions of the brain that govern particular behaviors (for example, sex, aggression, appetite, or fear).

An extreme example of how psychosurgery might be used for social control was presented by a former Colorado state legislator in 1989. In a letter sent to the governor and all 100 legislators he proposed that violent criminals be given frontal lobotomies to reduce Colorado's prison population. He argued:

> There is a new medical procedure which is humane, safe and permanent; one which will eliminate the violent criminals from our society, reduce our prison population by 10 to 15 percent and provide for early release of all individuals. This procedure is "frontal lobotomy, a procedure done through the eye cavity, leaving no scars and rendering the patient docile, yet able to follow simple

commands and to function on their [sic] own. It is accepted as standard medical practice for the violently insane in our sanitariums today. Why not for violent and dangerous criminals? (quoted in Associated Press, June 22, 1989)

Eugenics, the improvement of the human race through control of hereditary factors, is an ultimate form of social control. That is, if society decided that certain types of people should be sterilized, then those types would be eliminated in a generation. This practice was tried in Nazi Germany, where Jews, gypsies, and the "feebleminded" were sterilized. It has also occurred in the United States. From 1907 to 1964, for instance, more than 64,000 persons in 30 states were legally sterilized for perceived abnormalities such as drunkenness, criminality, sexual perversion, and "feeblemindedness."

The sterilization of the poor, especially racial minorities, has also occurred. Parenti, summarizing recent findings, asserts:

> One of every four Native American women of childbearing age is sterilized. One of every three women in Puerto Rico has been sterilized, most of them involuntarily. In Los Angeles and parts of the southwest, Chicano women have been forcibly sterilized. And in parts of the South, Black girls whose mothers are on welfare are routinely sterilized when they turn fifteen. While the federal government limits funding for Medicaid abortions, thus depriving low-income women of access to medically safe abortions, the government continues to fund sterilization operations for low-income people. (Parenti, 1988:152–153)*

The potential for eugenics will progress dramatically in the near future through biotechnology. Scientists are now capable of manipulating, recombining, and reorganizing living tissue into new forms and shapes. Cells have been fused from different species. Genes have been isolated and mapped, that is, the genes responsible for various physical traits have been located at specific sites on specific chromosomes. Moreover, scientists have been able to change the heredity of a cell. These breakthroughs have positive consequences. Prospective parents, for example, can have the genes of their unborn fetus checked for abnormalities. If an hereditary disorder such as hemophilia or sickle-cell anemia is found, the fetus could be aborted or the genetic makeup of the fetus could be altered before birth. While this new technology has useful applications, it raises some serious questions. Will parents, doctors, and scientists only correct genetic defects, or will they intervene to make genetic "improvements"? Should dark skin be eliminated? Should aggression be omitted from the behavior traits of future people? If so, passive subjects could be totally controlled without fear of revolution. The social-political-economic system, whatever its composition, would go unchallenged, and society would be tranquil. The logic of genetic engineering, while positive in the sense of ridding future generations of hereditary diseases, is frightening in its basic assumption that problems arise, not from the faults of society, but from the genes of individuals in society (see Panel 7–4).

Big Business Is Watching You

If you're looking for Big Brother these days, don't limit your search to the municipal building, police department or courthouse. He's come to work now, too. Big business has become Big Brother. With technological advances originally designed to lessen workers' loads, business has begun spying on its employees.

Workers have only recently begun to realize this. In its November 1985 report on the dangers of technological advances to workers, the International Labor Office in Geneva states: "The tremendous advance in computer technology has substantially contributed to developing [worker] control techniques. Personnel control . . . has become far more efficient."

Particularly useful is the marriage of phones and computers. New technology helps promote an old management objective: dominating workers in order to control them. . . . All surveillance methods—as yet fairly limited—collect information about the employee. Some of the information relates directly to work performance. Some does not. Only the imagination of management can constrain the eventual scope of workplace surveillance. . . .

Modern surveillance methods generally are technically advanced, computer-enhanced and often software-based. In one of the oldest surveillance methods, now enhanced by computer technology, managers bug employee-customer conversations. Companies euphemistically call the practice "service observation." Others call it phone monitoring.

Supervisors can monitor workers simply by sitting next to a telephone rep, but more commonly they link employee lines to a listening device in their office. Several popular telecommunications products such as PBX systems and automatic-call distributors, both of which help an office receive and route incoming calls, have as side benefits this monitoring capability.

Some products allow supervisors to listen in on employees from remote locations—even different cities and states. Jack Mahoney, one union representative for a Seattle local of the Communications Workers of America, says he knows of a case in which 11 people in disparate West Coast locations simultaneously monitored a Seattle operator. Mahoney says, "You get a little paranoid after a while."

But phone monitoring is just one brand of workplace surveillance. Other kinds include the following:

- Pen registers track the time, destination and length of outgoing employee calls. They've been used, for example, to build records of calls made by employees.
- Software packages can produce detailed reports on the quantity and quality of an employee's performance—the number of keystrokes per hour in the case of a typist or the accuracy of a spot welder in an auto assembly plant.
- A small computer module keeps track of a trucker's speed during a cross-country trip. At trip's end, if the computer tape shows that the driver exceeded the speed limit, he can be reprimanded, suspended and finally fired.

Growing consensus among privacy experts, labor leaders and industry analysts suggests a nearly ubiquitous pattern of worker watching. There seems to be more surveillance of more employees in more forms by more employers than ever before. . . .

The adverse effects of workplace surveillance—both physical and psychological—are well-documented. Researchers at the University of Toronto have uncovered a wide range of problems. On the physical side, says Toronto researcher and computer science professor Andrew Clement, monitoring can produce the usual panoply of stress-related illnesses, including ulcers, heart disease and high blood pressure. . . .

Clement says his research has uncovered other, more insidious ill effects as well: monitoring can create a climate of distrust, a breakdown in employee relationships, degradation of employee self-worth and loss of dignity and confidence.

He quotes an airline reservation agent as saying, "I feel that the company doesn't trust me, that's why they have this machine that watches me. It sure doesn't do much for my self-esteem."

But it's more than mere stress harming electronically monitored workers. It's a feeling of powerlessness. "After a while, you think they are your mother and father and you have to do what they say," says one New Jersey Bell worker. "It's like you're not on a job at all; it's like you're in kindergarten."

Another New Jersey Bell worker puts it more succinctly: "They manipulate people's lives. I'm not my own person when I work for them." . . .

By whatever name, in whatever company, the goal of such management practices remains the same: achieving a high level of control over employees through an authoritarian management style that emphasizes maximizing worker production and minimizing worker paychecks. In the context of workplace surveillance, this means intimidating the employee into toeing the company line and working harder.

The approach has been partly successful. Employees are intimidated. . . .

Control is the name of the game. And in the eyes of Stanley Aronowitz, a University of California professor of social sciences, such management is actually more ideological than practical. He points to one of the great ironies of workplace surveillance: it may provide management with greater control, but it isn't good business.

In a recent *Wall Street Journal* story, Harley Shaiken, a labor and technology expert at the Massachusetts Institute of Technology, said workplace spying is not a cure for productivity problems. "In the overwhelming majority of cases,

monitoring degrades the quality of the job and, ironically, can actually impair productivity."

Clement came to a similar conclusion at the University of Toronto about how worker-watching affects customer service: "As work is speeded up and employees are made more conscious of the imperative to produce quantifiable results, telephone operators and reservation agents report that they are less able to devote their attention to providing good quality service." British Columbia Telephone operator Linda Rolufs supported that position in testimony before a Canadian regulatory commission: "When you are monitored or evaluated you are admonished to keep customer contact to a minimum. We actually had one operator called down for being too nice to customers."

The evidence clearly incriminates workplace surveillance: it doesn't boost productivity or improve customer service, it costs thousands of dollars and it harms workers physically, mentally and emotionally.

Yet managers like the control it gives them. . . . Control means first defining the proper place of employees—subservient—and then putting them there. It also is the means by which management gets a grip on that most capricious cog in production—the human worker.

The use of technology to achieve greater control in the workplace threatens to change fundamental relationships between employers and employees, making employees more dominated and powerless than ever before. The irony is that the working public tacitly approves of this shift by not demanding a halt to workplace surveillance. And the more an activity like workplace surveillance continues, the more it becomes, over time, "normal."

Source: Excerpts from Tim Healy and Peter Marshall, "Big Business Is Watching You," *In These Times* (February 26, 1986): 12–13. Reprinted from *In These Times,* a weekly newspaper based in Chicago.

Similar questions can be raised about the other techniques in this section. The creativity of the scientific community has presented the powerful in society with unusually effective means to enforce conformity. The aggressive in schools, prisons, mental hospitals, and in society can be anesthetized. But what is aggressive behavior? What is violence?

Recently, the Justice Department proposed a test of 2,000 boys ages 9 to 12 who have already had their first contact with the police. The goal of this test is to identify the chronic offender. Proponents of the proposal argue that chronic offenders have certain characteristics that the tests could identify— such as left-handedness, dry or sweaty palms, below normal reactions to noise and shocks, high levels of the male hormone testosterone, abnormalities in alpha waves emitted by their brains, and physical anomalies such as mal-formed ears, high steepled palate, furrowed tongue, curved fingers, and a wide gap between the first and second toes (reported in Anderson, 1983). Such a plan, if implemented, has frightening implications. Will these tests actually separate chronic offenders from one-time offenders? Is criminal be-havior actually related to the formation of one's tongue, ears, and toes? And, if the tests do identify potential problem people accurately, should such per-sons be punished for their potential behaviors rather than their actual behav-iors? Most significant, what are the negative effects of being labeled a chronic offender? Such a label would doubtless have a self-fulfilling prophecy effect as those who interact with labeled persons do so on the basis of that label.

Government

The government, as the legitimate holder of power in society, is directly involved in the control of its citizens. A primary objective of the government is to provide for the welfare of its citizens. This includes protection of their lives and property. It requires, further, that order be maintained within the society. There is a clear mandate, then, for the government to apprehend and punish criminals. Not so clear, however, is the legitimacy of a government in a democracy to stifle dissent, which is done in the interests of preserving order. The U.S. heritage, best summed up in the Declaration of Indepen-dence, provides a clear rationale for dissent:

> Governments are instituted among men, deriving their just powers from the consent of the governed. That whenever any form of government becomes destructive of these ends [the rights of life, liberty, and the pursuit of happi-ness], it is the right of the people to alter or to abolish it, and to institute a new government, laying its foundation on such principles and organizing its powers in such form as to them shall seem most likely to effect their safety and happiness.

The American government, then, is faced with a dilemma. American tradition and values affirm that dissent is appropriate. Two facts of political life work against this principle, however. First, for social order to prevail, a society needs to ensure that existing power relationships are maintained over time (otherwise anarchy will result). Second, the well-off in society benefit from the existing power arrangements so they use their influence (which is considerable, as noted in the previous chapter) to encourage the repression of challenges to the government. The evidence is strong that the American government has opted for repression of dissent. Let us examine this evidence.

To begin with, we must peruse the processes of law enactment and law enforcement. These two processes are both directly related to political authority. Some level of government determines what the law will be (that is, which behaviors are to be allowed and which ones are to be forbidden) and the agents of political authorities then apprehend and punish violators. Clearly, the law is employed to control behaviors that might otherwise endanger the general welfare (for example, the crimes of murder, rape, and theft). But laws also promote certain points of view at the expense of others (for example, the majority instead of the minority, or the status quo rather than change). With this in mind, let us turn to the two schools of thought on the function of the law—the prevailing liberal view and the Marxist interpretation (Quinney, 1970:18–25; 1973).

The dominant view in American society is based on liberal democratic theory and is congruent with the order model. The state exists to maintain order and stability. Law is a body of rules enacted by representatives of the people in the interests of the people. The state and law, therefore, are essentially neutral, dispensing rewards and punishments without bias. A basic assumption of this view is that the political system is pluralistic—that is, the existence of a number of interest groups of more-or-less equal power. The laws, then, reflect compromise and consensus among these various interest groups. In this way the interests of all are protected.

Contrary to the prevailing view of law based on consensus for the common good is the view of the radical criminologists, which is based on conflict theory. The assumptions of this model are (1) the state exists to serve the ruling class (the owners of large corporations and financial institutions); (2) the law and the legal system reflect and serve the needs of the ruling class; and (3) the interests of the ruling class are served by the law when domestic order prevails and challenges to changing the economic and political system are successfully thwarted. In other words, the law does not serve society as a whole, but the interests of the ruling class prevail.

Closely related to the Marxian view of the role of law in capitalist societies is the interest-group theory of Richard Quinney (1970:29–42). The essence of this theory is that a crime is behavior that conflicts with the interests of those segments of society that have the power to shape criminal policy.

> Law is made by men, representing special interests, who have the power to translate their interests into public policy. Unlike the pluralist conception of politics, law does not represent a compromise of the diverse interests of society, but supports some interests at the expense of others. (Quinney, 1970:35)

Quinney's view is in the conflict model tradition. Society is held together by some segments coercing other segments. Interest groups are unequal in power. The conflict among interest groups results in the powerful getting their way in determining public policy. Evidence for this position is seen in the successful efforts of certain interest groups to get favorable laws: the segregation laws imposed by whites on blacks, the repression of political dissidents whose goal is to transform society, and the passage of income tax laws that benefit the rich at the expense of wage earners.

Quinney's model makes a good deal of sense. The model is not universally applicable, however, because certain crimes—burglary, murder, and rape—would be regarded as crimes no matter which interest group was in power. A very important part of his theory that does fit almost universally is his proposition that: *"The probability that criminal definitions will be applied varies according to the extent to which the behaviors of the powerless conflict with the interests of the power segments"* (Quinney, 1970:18).

The law, of course, provides the basis for establishing what is criminal behavior. Enforcement of the law is accomplished by the police and the courts. The evidence is overwhelming that the law is unequally enforced in American society. Let us direct our attention here, rather, to the efforts of other agencies in the political system to control deviance, especially political deviance.

Government agencies have a long history of surveillance of citizens. The pace quickened in the 1930s and increased further with the Communist threat in the 1950s. Surveillance reached its peak during the height of antiwar and civil rights protests of the late 1960s and early 1970s. The FBI's concern with internal security, for example, dates back to 1936, when President Roosevelt directed J. Edgar Hoover to investigate domestic Communist and Fascist organizations in the United States. In 1939, as World War II began in Europe, President Roosevelt issued a proclamation that the FBI would be in charge of investigating subversive activities, espionage, and sabotage, and directed that all law enforcement offices should give the FBI any relevant information

Reprinted by permission of the United Feature Syndicate.

I CAN'T TAKE IT ANYMORE... THE BURGLARIES..THE BREAK-INS.. RUNNING FROM THE COPS...HIDING OUT IN FLEA-RIDDEN MOTELS... CHARLIE, YOU'VE GOT TO QUIT THE FBI.

on suspected activities. These directives began a pattern followed by the FBI under the administrations of Presidents Truman, Eisenhower, Kennedy, Johnson, Nixon, Ford, Carter, Reagan, and Bush.

The scope of these abuses by the FBI and other government agencies such as the CIA, the National Security Agency, and the Internal Revenue Service, is incredible. In the name of "national security" the following actions have been taken against American citizens:

- The Internal Revenue Service (IRS) monitored the activities of 99 political organizations and 11,539 individuals during the period 1969–1973. During and since that period the IRS has used a variety of methods to invade the private lives of individuals, including the use of seizure-liens, assessments, penalties, wiretaps, and even hiring prostitutes to occupy suspects while agents photocopied the contents of briefcases (Fleetwood, 1980; Burnham, 1989).
- From 1967 to 1973 the NSA (National Security Agency) monitored the overseas telephone calls and cables of approximately 1650 Americans and U.S. organizations, as well as almost 6000 foreign nationals and groups (*Newsweek*, November 10, 1975).
- The CIA opened and photographed nearly 250,000 first class letters in the United States between 1953 and 1973 (Ermann and Lundman, 1978:18).
- As Director of the CIA, William Colby acknowledged to Congress that his organization has opened the mail of private citizens and accumulated secret files on more than 10,000 Americans (Ermann and Lundman, 1978).
- The FBI over the years conducted about 1,500 break-ins of foreign embassies and missions, mob hangouts, and the headquarters of such organizations as the Ku Klux Klan and the American Communist Party (*Newsweek*, July 28, 1979).
- Beginning in 1957 the FBI monitored the activities of civil rights leader Martin Luther King, Jr. The efforts included physical and photographic surveillance and the placement of electronic listening devices in his living quarters.
- In its annual report for 1982 an electronic surveillance by Federal and state officials, the Office of the U.S. Courts stated that the FBI and the Drug Enforcement Administration installed 129 taps and bugs in 1981 (Schwartz, 1983).
- The FBI consistently monitored the activities of hundreds of American writers including Nelson Algren, Pearl Buck, Truman Capote, William Faulkner, Ernest Hemingway, Sinclair Lewis, Archibald MacLeish, Carl Sandburg, John Steinbeck, Thornton Wilder, Tennessee Williams, and Thomas Wolfe (Mitgang, 1987). The question is why? Was it because the most acclaimed writers in the United States were part of a conspiracy or were individual lawbreakers, or was it because, as has been suggested by Natalie Robins, an *unconscious* effort on the FBIs part to control writers with a chilling effect that really adds up to intimidation?" (Robins, 1987:367).
- To support the Reagan Administration's support of the contras in Nicaragua, several government agencies used questionable tactics. For example, Americans returning from visits to Nicaragua had their belongings searched, seized, and photocopied by customs officials (Donner, 1985). Also, the General Accounting Office reported that a unit of the State Department "engaged in prohibited, covert propaganda activities designed

Consequences of the Genome Project

The National Institutes of Health have funded ($3 billion) a massive effort to decipher the three-billion-digit genetic sequence that encodes the recipe for making a human being. Called the Human Genome Project, this endeavor has enormous potential positive and negative effects. The following essay enumerates some of them.

The initial round of human genetic therapies is expected in medicine. First come cures for single-gene disorders, such as cystic fibrosis, muscular dystrophy, sickle cell anemia, kidney disease, and Huntington's disease. In five years: insertion of therapeutic genes into human cancer patients. In 10 years: genetic therapies for a wide variety of cancers. In 20 years: cures for autoimmune disorders and rheumatoid arthritis. In 40 to 50 years: cures for diabetes, Alzheimer's and multiple sclerosis. Then, at some point, we're expected to confront a realm of cancers, heart disease, arthritis, and mental disorders that, while genetically treatable, involve so many genetic or environmental variables that a sure-fire genetic cure is impossible.

It's hard to decide how seriously to take these sunny forecasts, since scientists both in and out of the business sector find it in their interests to make them. In any event, the really big issues will come in the next generation of DNA technology. If the frontiers of genetic engineering can advance from one-gene to three-gene traits within a few years, what stands in the way of discovering the larger gene combinations that influence height, weight, and skin color? For that matter, won't we eventually be able to identify the genetic roots of intelligence, ambition, courage, and altruism? And if so, whose children will be permitted to benefit? . . . Questions of practice arise: Will science ever be able to *specify* genes that make a person more likely to be smart, ambitious, emotionally stable, etc.? Here complexity rears its ugly head. There are three billion genes in the human genome, and they can interact in astoundingly diverse ways. To take the simplest case: children of dwarves who inherit one normal gene and one dwarf gene turn out more normal than those who inherit two dwarf genes. So a child who inherits only one gene for Huntington's disease will be better off than one who inherits two bad genes, right? Wrong. Each case is different. This kind of variation may seriously limit our ability to extrapolate from one gene-trait relationship to another, and vastly complicate attempts to alter whole complexes of genes to predictable effect.

The three billion genes in the genome—many of which affect the expression of others—are nothing compared to the multiplicity of environmental factors that affect genetic expression. Keeping track of the resulting chains of causality is probably hopeless. Granted, the same exact collision of genetic and environmental factors, if replayed, would produce the same result. But even if you know all of the factors involved, you couldn't predict the outcome unless you had seen the same situation play out before. That's unlikely, and arguably impossible. Wait, it gets worse. The

---

to influence the media and the public to support the administration's Latin American policies" (quoted in Zaldivar, 1987).

These are but a few examples of government abuses against its citizens. Actually the extent of the government's monitoring of its citizens is much greater than these examples indicate. A survey of 142 federal agencies by the Office of Technology found that one-fourth of them conducted some form of electronic surveillance. The Drug Enforcement Administration, for example, uses 10 separate surveillance technologies while the FBI uses 17. The report

central factor in every collision, the person, is a function not just of three billion genes but also of a history of gene-environment collisions . . . .

The ensuing problems are obvious. Such gene therapy, if it became available, would at first be so expensive that only the rich could afford it. Even the purest free marketer would have to think twice about that. And if society chooses not to let the market allocate this resource, should we pay to make gene therapy available to everyone, or should we ban it? (And will Congress ban it if Japan doesn't?) Before you decide, answer these questions: Certainly parents should have access to genetic therapies for alleviating serious diseases, right? Including mental retardation? And if that's fair game, then how about below-average intelligence? Similarly: Certainly parents should be allowed to head off severe manic-depressive illness (the genetic roots of some variants of this are now coming to light). So what's wrong with making your child less prone to more subtle mood swings? To playground violence? To temper tantrums? . . .

The ethical questions that may grow out of all this 30 or 40 years down the road will be colored in more ways than one by the question of the complexity of genetic causation. Rifkin has been talking for years about the ethics of parents choosing one trait over its alternatives; tall over short, for example, or white over black. But choices may also involve deciding whether some whole categories of traits are more important than others. The reason is that a single gene or group of genes can exert simultaneous effects on more than one trait. The same gene that contributes to your hooked nose may reduce your chances of tooth decay, for all we know, or even limit your fluency in foreign languages. So you can't order everything from the trait menu, and you sometimes can't order even one item without worrying about a bunch of others. Now the question is, do you care more about your kid's nose or her linguistic facility? And if there's any downside at all, should society let you choose?

The other problem is, the more nuanced your definition of a mental strength or virtue, the less likely you are to find consistent genetic correlates for it. So the tendency will be to design a standard that weeds out nuance. In the case of intelligence, you ask multiple-choice questions instead of essay questions. you eliminate from the test those subjects in which scientists can't agree on an objective standard. You're left with IQ, a decent predictor of professional success. You compare genomes and IQ scores and discover a strong link. In your scholarly journal article, you stipulate that IQ measures only one aspect of intelligence. But alert entrepreneurs are already hyping the story on TV. Expectant parents are lining up to get into pilot IQ gene "therapy" programs. The danger, it turns out, is not that these IQ genes will explain the subtlety of intelligence, but that they will replace it.

Source: William Saletan, "Genes 'R' Us," *The New Republic* 201 (July 17 and 24, 1989): 18–20. Reprinted by permission of the publisher.

identified 85 separate computerized record systems used for law-enforcement, investigative and intelligence purposes, with a total of 288 million records concerning 114 million people (*New York Times,* October 25, 1985).

One should remember that the government *must* exert some control over its citizens. There must be a minimum of control if the fabric of society is to remain intact. But in exerting control, there are serious problems that came to the forefront during the Nixon years. First, there is the problem of the violation of individual rights as guaranteed in the Constitution. Under what conditions can these be violated by the government—if ever? A closely related problem can be framed in the form of a question: Who monitors the monitors? The problem inherent in this question is not only the tactics of the monitors but also the criteria used to assess who should be controlled or who should not.

A most serious charge is that the government squelches protest, which Thomas Jefferson said is the hallmark of a democracy. The implication is that the government is beyond questioning—the dissidents are the problem. But as Donner has put it:

> To equate dissent with subversion, as intelligence officials do (the FBI, CIA, IRS, Justice Department, and the Department of Defense), is to deny that the demand for change is based on real social, economic, or political conditions (Donner, 1971:35).

CONCLUSION

In 1949 George Orwell wrote a novel about life as he envisioned it to be in 1984. The essence of his prediction was that every word, every thought, and every facial expression of citizens would be monitored by government using sophisticated electronic devices. The computer age has fulfilled in part Orwell's prophecy. The federal government has an average of 18 computer files on each American; each state has an average of 15 files per person, and local governments average 6 files. In the private sector (e.g., credit, insurance, banks, employers) we have another 40 files. The average citizen's name emerges in computers 35 times a day and gets passed among computers 5 times a day (Hillkirk, 1983). Not only is such computer knowledge an invasion of one's privacy, but it provides the government with the technology to monitor closely the activities of those who threaten it. And, as we have seen in this chapter, the government is strongly inclined to do so. But the political dissident is not the only person whose freedoms are being threatened. As Howard Zinn has put it:

> Our actual freedom is determined . . . by the power the policeman has over us on the street, or that of the local judge behind him; by the authority of our employers; by the power of teachers, principals, university presidents, and boards of trustees if we are students; by parents if we are children; by children if we are old; by the welfare bureaucracy if we are poor; by prison guards if we are in jail; by landlords if we are tenants; by the medical profession or hospital administration if we are physically or mentally ill. (quoted in Wicker, 1973)

The technology for "1984" exists in drugs, psychosurgery, and telemetry. Currently, various arms of the government have used some of these techniques in their battle to fight crime, recidivism, political dissidence, and other forms of nonconformity. But at what point does the government go too far in its control of nonconformity? The critical question, as stated earlier, is who monitors the monitors? One can easily envision a future when the government, faced with anarchy or political revolution, might justify ultimate control of its citizens—in the name of national security. If this were to take place, then obviously, the freedoms rooted in 200 years of history will have been washed away.

The future may resemble Orwell's vision, however, not because of a tyrannical government, but rather because it is in the interests of society that people be controlled. The time may come when people, because human survival depends on it, will not have the freedom to have as many children as they want or the freedom to squander energy on eight-cylinder cars or air-conditioned homes or to own a gun. B. F. Skinner, the famous behavioral psychologist, has argued that we must give up our outmoded notions of freedom and dignity and build a society in which the behavior of people will be controlled for their own good—for the sake of their survival, happiness, and satisfaction (Skinner, 1972). In other words, if not enough people exercise self-control, the government, for the common good, may be forced to impose controls from the outside. And with the technology available to the government, absolute control is a real threat.

CHAPTER REVIEW

1. All societies have mechanisms to ensure conformity—mechanisms of social control.

2. The socialization process through which the demands of the group become internalized is a fundamental mechanism of social control. This process is never complete, however; otherwise we would be robots.

3. Ideological social control is the attempt to manipulate the consciousness of citizens so they accept the status quo and ruling ideology.

4. The agents of ideological social control are the family, education, religion, sport, and the media.

5. Direct social control refers to attempts to punish or neutralize organizations or individuals who deviate from society's norms, especially the poor, the mentally ill, criminals, and political dissidents.

6. According to Piven and Cloward, public assistance programs serve a direct social control function in times of mass unemployment by defusing social unrest.

7. Science and medicine provide the techniques for shaping and controlling the behavior of nonconformists. Drugs, psychosurgery, and genetic engineering are three such techniques.

8. The government is directly involved in the control of its citizens. It apprehends and punishes criminals. It is also involved in the suppression of dissent, which, while important for preserving order, runs counter to the American democratic heritage. Order theorists argue that the state exists to maintain order. The state and the law in this view are neutral, dispensing rewards and punishments without bias. Conflict theorists, however, believe that the state and the law exist to serve the ruling class. Squelching political dissent, therefore, benefits the powerful.

KEY TERMS

Social control
Ideological social control

Direct social control

Eugenics

STUDY QUESTIONS

1. How do order and conflict theorists differ in their interpretation of the role of sport and social control?
2. What is the relationship of ideological social control to what we learned about socialization in the last chapter?
3. What is Piven and Cloward's thesis concerning the social control function of welfare assistance programs?
4. How do order theorists and conflict theorists differ in their views of the state and the law?

FOR FURTHER READING

Ideological Social Control

Martin Carnoy, *Education as Cultural Imperialism* (New York: Longman, 1974).

Jules Henry, *Culture against Man* (New York: Random House (Vintage Books), 1963).

Donald B. Kraybill, *Our Star-Spangled Faith* (Scottsdale, PA: Herald Press, 1976).

Michael Parenti, *Inventing Reality: The Politics of the Mass Media* (New York: St. Martin's Press, 1986).

Alan Wolfe, *The Seamy Side of Democracy: Repression in America*, 2nd ed. (New York: Longman, 1978).

Direct Social Control

Ward Churchill and Jim Vander Wall, *Agents of Repression: The FBI's Secret Wars against the Black Panther Party and the American Indian Movement* (Boston: South End Press, 1988).

Frances Fox Piven and Richard A. Cloward, *Regulating the Poor: The Functions of Public Welfare* (New York: Random House, 1971).

Richard Quinney, *Critique of Legal Order: Crime Control in Capitalist Society* (Boston: Little, Brown, 1973).

Jeremy Rifkin, *Algeny* (New York: Penguin Books, 1984).

David R. Simon and D. Stanley Eitzen, *Elite Deviance*, 3rd ed. (Boston: Allyn and Bacon, 1990).

B. F. Skinner, *Beyond Freedom and Dignity* (New York: Alfred A. Knopf, 1972).

Thomas Szasz, *The Manufacture of Madness* (New York: Harper & Row, 1970).

Chapter Eight

Deviance

Who are the deviants in American society? There is considerable evidence that most of us at one time or another break the laws. For example:

- Surveys by the Internal Revenue Service consistently find that three out of ten persons cheat on their income taxes. This does *not* include the monies received from the selling of goods or services for cash and tips received that go unreported to the government. An estimated 25 percent of the total labor force does not report all or part of its income from these otherwise legal practices.
- A study found that one-third of job applicants lied about their work experiences to prospective employers (reported in Associated Press, September 3, 1987).
- U.S. employees "steal" an average of 4.5 hours per worker per week—almost six weeks a year (Dessler, 1987).
- Marijuana may be the country's largest cash crop, with annual harvests valued at anywhere between $10 billion and $33 billion. The Justice Department's Drug Enforcement Agency (DEA) estimates the number of commercial growers at between 90,000 and 150,000 with another million people growing marijuana for their personal use (Wise, 1989).

These illustrations indicate that many of us are guilty of cheating and stealing—behaviors clearly considered wrong. But are those of us who commit these illegal or immoral acts deviant? The complexities of the designation of "deviant" are the topics of this chapter.

The previous three chapters have analyzed the ways in which human beings, as members of society, are constrained to conform. We have seen how society is not only outside of us coercing us to conform but also inside of us making us *want* to behave in the culturally prescribed ways. But despite these powerful forces, people deviate from the norms. These acts and actors are the subjects of this chapter.

WHAT IS DEVIANCE?

Deviance is that behavior which does not conform to social expectations. It violates the rules of a group (custom, law, role, or moral code). *Deviance, then, is socially created* (Becker, 1963:8–9). Social organizations create right and wrong by originating *norms*, the infraction of which constitutes deviance. This means that nothing inherent in a particular act makes it deviant. Whether an act is deviant or not depends on how others react to it. As Kai Erikson has put it: "Deviance is not a property *inherent* in any particular kind of behavior; it is a property *conferred upon* that behavior by the people who come into direct or indirect contact with it" (Erikson, 1966:6). This means that *deviance is a relative, not an absolute notion.* Evidence for this is found in two sources: inconsistencies among societies as to what is deviance, and inconsistencies in the labeling of behavior as deviant within a single society.

There is abundant anthropological evidence that what is right or wrong varies from society to society. The following are a few examples:

- The Ila of Africa encourage sexual promiscuity among their adolescents. After age ten girls are given houses of their own during harvest time, where they can play at being husband and wife with boys of their choice. In contrast the Tepoztlan Indians of Mexico do not allow girls to speak to or encourage a boy after the time of the girl's first menstruation.
- Egyptian royalty were required to marry their siblings, whereas this was prohibited as incestuous and sinful for European royalty.
- Young men of certain Native American tribes are expected, after fasting, to have a vision. This vision will be interpreted by the tribal elders to decide that young man's future occupation and status in the tribe. If an Anglo youth were to tell his elders that he had had such a vision, he would likely be considered mentally ill.

Differential treatment for similar behavior by different categories of persons within a single society provides further proof that deviance is *not* a property of the act but depends upon the reaction of the particular audience. Several examples illustrate that it is not the act but the situation that determines whether the behavior is interpreted by others as deviant or not:

- Unmarried fathers escape the severe censure that unmarried mothers typically receive.
- Sexual intercourse between consenting adults is not deviant except if one partner pays another for his or her services and then the deviant is the recipient of the money, not the donor.

- Murder is a deviant act but the killing of an enemy during wartime is rewarded with praise and medals.
- A father would be considered a deviant if he removed his bathing suit at a public beach but his two-year-old son could do this with impunity. The father can smoke a cigar and drink a martini every night, but if his young son did, the boy (and his parents, if they permitted this) would be considered deviant (Weinstein and Weinstein, 1974:271).
- Women smokers were once considered deviants but are no longer considered so.

In a heterogeneous society there will often be widespread disagreement on what the rules are and therefore what constitutes deviance. There are differences over, for example, sexual activities between consenting adults (regardless of sex, marital status), smoking marijuana, public nudism, pornography, drinking alcohol, remaining seated during the national anthem, and refusal to fight in a war. Concerning this last instance, who is the deviant in a war, for example, the person who kills the enemy or the person who refuses to kill them? There is a difference of opinion among Americans on this with the majority likely to define the draft evaders and protesters as the deviants.

This leads to a further insight about deviance: *the majority determines who is a deviant.* If most people believe that the Viet Cong are the enemy, then napalming them and their villages is appropriate and refusal to do so is deviant. If most people believe there is a God you may talk to, then such a belief is not deviance (in fact, the refusal to believe in God may then be deviant). But if the majority are atheists, then those few who believe in God would be deviant and subject to ridicule, job discrimination, and mental treatment.

Another example of this "safety in numbers" principle is the effort by some parents to deprogram their children if they have adopted a different religion—for example, pentecostal Christian, Children of God, or Hare Krishna. These parents had their children kidnapped. The children were confined for days with little food or sleep and badgered by hired experts into recanting their beliefs. As Mewshaw has described it:

Euphemistically called "deprogramming," the process amounts to little more than a methodical and sometimes violent attempt to exorcise not Satan, but unpopular, misunderstood, or inarticulate notions about God. (Mewshaw, 1976:32)

Erikson has summarized how deviance is a relative rather than an absolute notion in the following statement:

Definitions of deviance vary widely as we range over the various classes found in a single society or across the various cultures into which mankind is divided, and it soon becomes apparent that there are no objective properties which all deviant acts can be said to share in common—even within the confines of a given group. *Behavior which qualifies one man for prison may qualify another for sainthood, since the quality of the act itself depends so much on the cir-*

cumstances under which it was performed and the temper of the audience which witnessed it [italics added]. (Erikson, 1966:5–6)

An insight of the order theorists is important to note. Deviance is an integral part of all healthy societies (Durkheim, 1958; 1960; Dentler and Erikson, 1959). Deviant behavior according to Durkheim, actually has positive consequences for society because it gives the nondeviants a sense of solidarity. By punishing the deviant, the group expresses its collective indignation and reaffirms its commitments to the rules.

> Crime brings together upright consciences and concentrates them. We have only to notice what happens, particularly in a small town, when some moral scandal has just been committed. They stop each other on the street, they visit each other, they seek to come together to talk of the event and to wax indignant in common. From all the similar expressions which are exchanged, for all the temper that gets itself expressed, there emerges a unique temper . . . which is everybody's without being anybody's in particular. That is the public temper. (Durkheim, 1960: 102)

Durkheim believed that the true function of punishment was not the prevention of future crimes. He asserted, rather, that the basic function of punishment is to reassert the importance of the rule being violated. It is not that a murderer is caught and put in the electric chair to keep potential murderers in line. That argument assumes people to be more rational than they really are. Instead, the extreme punishment of a murderer reminds each of us that murder is wrong. In other words, the punishment of crimes serves to strengthen our belief as individuals and as members of a collectivity in the legitimacy of society's norms. This enhances the solidarity of society as we unite in opposition to the deviant.

Crime, seen from this view, has positive functions for society. In addition to reaffirming the legitimacy of the society, defining certain acts as crimes creates the boundaries for what is acceptable behavior in the society.

Deviance, from the order perspective, is not only a consequence of social order (a violation of society's rules) but also is necessary for social order. As Rubington and Weinberg have said: "Each [social order and deviance] presupposes the other. And from studying one, sociologists frequently learn more about the other" (Rubington and Weinberg, 1973:1).

The conflict theorists have pointed out that all views of rule violations have *political* implications (Becker, 1963:4). When persons mistreat rule breakers they are saying, in effect, that the norms are legitimate. Thus, the bias is conservative, serving to preserve the status quo, which includes the current distribution of power. The opposite view, that the norms of society are wrong and should be rejected, is also political. When people and groups flout the laws and customs (for example, the draft, segregation, and marijuana smoking) they are not only rejecting the status quo but also questioning the legitimacy of those in power. As Edwin Schur has argued:

> Deviance issues are inherently political. They revolve around some people's assessments of other people's behavior. And power is a crucial factor in determining which and whose assessments gain an ascendancy. Deviance policies,

likewise, affect the distribution of power and always have some broad political significance. (Schur, 1980:xi)

TRADITIONAL THEORIES FOR THE CAUSES OF DEVIANCE

The Individual as the Source of Deviance

Biological, psychological, and even some sociological theories have assumed that the fundamental reason for deviance is a fatal flaw in certain people. The criminal, the dropout, the addict, the schizophrenic, have something wrong with them. These theories are deterministic, arguing that the individual ultimately has no choice but to be different.

Biological Theories.   Biological explanations for deviance have focused on physiognomy (the determination of character by facial features), phrenology (the determination of mental abilities and character traits from the configuration of the skull), somatology (the determination of character by physique), genetic anomalies (for example, XYY chromosome in males), and brain malfunctions.

Some of these theories have been discredited (for example, Lombroso's theory that some distinct body types are more likely to be criminal because they are throwbacks to an earlier stage of human development—closer to the ape stage than nondeviants). Other biological theories have shown a statistical link between certain physical characteristics and deviant behavior. Chances are, though, that when such a relationship is found, it is also related to social factors. The learning disability known as dyslexia, for example, is related to school failure, emotional disturbance, and juvenile delinquency. This disability is a brain malfunction where visual signs are scrambled. Average skills in reading, spelling, and arithmetic are impossible to attain if the malady remains undiagnosed. Teachers and parents often are unaware that the child is dyslexic and assume, rather, that she or he is retarded, lazy, or belligerent. The child (who actually may be very bright—Thomas Edison and Woodrow Wilson were dyslexic) finds school frustrating. Such a child is

Reprinted by permission of United Feature Syndicate.

therefore much more likely than those not affected to be a troublemaker, to be alienated, to be either pushed out of school or a dropout, and to never reach full intellectual potential.

Psychological Theories.   These theories also consider the source of deviance to reside within the individual, but they differ from the biological theories in that they assume conditions of the mind or personality to be the fault. Deviant individuals, depending on the particular psychological theory, are psychopaths (asocial, aggressive, impulsive) as a result of a lack of affection during childhood, Oedipal conflict, psychosexual trauma, or other early life experience (Cohen, 1966:41–45). Using Freudian assumptions, the deviant is one who has not developed an adequate *ego* to control deviant impulses (the *id*). Or, alternatively, deviance can result from a dominating *superego*. Persons with this condition are so repulsed by their own feelings (such as sexual fantasies, or ambivalence toward parents and siblings) that they may commit deviant acts in order to receive the punishment they deserve. Freudians, therefore, place great stress on the relationship between children and their parents. The parents, in this view, can be too harsh or too lenient, or too inconsistent in their treatment of the child. Each situation leads to inadequately socialized children and immature, infantile behavior by adolescents and adults.

Since the fundamental assumption of the biological and psychological theories of deviance is that the fault lies within the individual, the solutions are aimed at changing the individual. Screening of the population for those individuals with the presumed flaws is considered the best preventative. Doctors could routinely determine which boys had the XXY or XYY chromosome pattern. Psychological testing in the schools could find out which persons were unusually aggressive, guilt-ridden, or fantasy-oriented. Although the screening for potential problem people may make some sense (to detect dyslexics, for example), there are some fundamental problems with this type of solution. First, the screening devices likely will not be perfect, thereby mislabeling some persons. Second, screening is based on the assumption that there is a direct linkage between certain characteristics and deviance. If identified as a predeviant by these methods, the subsequent treatment of that individual and his own new definition of self would likely lead to a self-fulfilling prophecy and a false validation of the screening procedures, increasing their usage and acceptability.

A related problem with these screening procedures is the tendency to overpredict. In one attempt to identify predelinquents, a panel of experts examined a sample of youths already in the early stages of troublemaking and made predictions regarding future delinquency. Approximately 60 percent of the cases were judged to be predelinquents. A follow-up twenty years later revealed, however, that less than one-third actually became involved with the law (Powers and Witmer, 1951).

For those identified as potential deviants or those who are actually deviants, the "kinds-of-people" theorists advocate solutions aimed at changing the individuals. The person is treated by drug therapy, electrical stimulation of the brain, electronic monitoring, surgery, operant conditioning, counseling, psychotherapy, probation with guidance of a psychiatric social worker, or incarceration. The assumption is clearly that deviants are troubled and sick persons who must be changed to conform to the norms of society.

The Sociological Approach.   There are a number of sociological theories that are also "kinds-of-people" explanations for deviance. Instead of individual characteristics distinguishing the deviant from the nondeviant, these focus on differing objective social and economic conditions. These are based on the empirical observations that crime and mental illness rates, to name two forms of deviance, vary by social class, ethnicity, race, place of residence, and sex.

> From these gross differences, the sociologist infers that something beyond the intimacy of family surroundings is operative in the emergence of delinquent patterns; something in the cultural and social atmosphere apparent in certain sectors of society. (Matza, 1964:17)

Let us look at some of these theories, which emphasize that certain social conditions are conducive to the internalization of values that encourage deviance.

Cultural transmission.   Sutherland's theory of differential association sought to explain why some persons are criminals while others are not, even though both may share certain social characteristics such as social class position (Sutherland and Cressey, 1966:81–82). Sutherland believed that through interaction, one learns to be a criminal. If our close associates are deviants, there is a strong probability that we will learn the techniques and the deviant values that make criminal acts possible. In sum:

> the significant feature of Sutherland's theory is his claim that procriminal sentiments are acquired, as are all others, by association with other individuals in a process of social interaction. Criminal orientations do not, thus, stem from faulty metabolism, inadequate superego development, or even poverty. (Hartjen, 1974:51)*

Societal goals and differential opportunities.   Robert Merton (1957) has presented an explanation for why the lower classes (who coincidentally live in the cities) disproportionately commit criminal acts. In Merton's view, societal values determine both what are the appropriate goals (success through the acquisition of wealth) as well as the approved means for achieving these goals. The problem, however, is that some people are denied access to the legitimate means of achieving these goals. The poor, especially those from certain racial and ethnic groups, in addition to the roadblocks presented by negative stereotypes, often receive a second-class education or they have to drop out of

---

*From *Crime and Criminalization* by Clayton A. Hartjen. Copyright © 1974 by Praeger Publishers. Reprinted by permission of Praeger Publishers, A Division of Holt, Rinehart and Winston.

school prematurely because of financial exigencies, all of which effectively exclude them from high-paying and prestigious occupations. Because legitimate means to success are inaccessible to them, they often resort to certain forms of deviant behavior to attain success. Viewed from this perspective, deviance is a result of social structure and not the consequence of individual pathology. McGee makes this point in his analysis of Merton's scheme.

> [In each of the deviant adaptations] the individuals are behaving as they have been taught by their societies. They are not sinful or weak individuals who choose to deviate. They are, in fact, doing what they have learned they are supposed to do in order to earn the rewards which their society purports to offer its members. But either because their positions in the social structure do not permit them access to the means through which to seek the rewards they have learned to want, or because the means do not in fact guarantee goal attainment, they become frustrated and experience loss of self-esteem. In a final attempt to do and be what they have been taught they must, they engage in what is called deviant behavior. Such behavior is simply an attempt to gain the same self-esteem which others are presumed to have and which the society has made it intolerable to be without. (McGee, 1975: 211–212)

Although Merton's analysis provides many important insights, the emphasis is on the adjustments people make to the circumstances of society. Deviance is a property of people because they cannot adapt to the discrepancy between the goals and the means of society. The problem is that Merton accepts the American success ethic. In the words of Doyle and Schindler:

> What is missing is the perspective that the winner, firster, money mentality could be a pathology rather than a value in America, a pathology that so powerfully corrupts our economy, polity, and way of life that it precludes any possibility of a cohesive, healthy, community. Certainly it is valid and worthwhile to explore the situation of the deprived in a success oriented society, but it is also valid to question the viability of a social system with such a "value" at its core. The sociology of deviance has turned too quickly and too exclusively to hypotheses about "bad" people. The analysis of "bad" societies has been neglected. (Doyle and Schindler, 1974:2)

Subcultural differences by social class.   We explore the **culture of poverty** hypothesis in Chapter 9. (The culture of poverty is the view that the poor are qualitatively different in values and life-styles from the rest of society and that these cultural differences explain their poverty.) Since it has special relevance for explaining differential crime rates, we will briefly characterize it here with that emphasis. The argument is that people because of their social class position differ in resources, power, and prestige and hence have different experiences, lifestyles, and ways of life. The lower-class culture has its own values, many of which run counter to the values of the middle and upper classes. There is a unique morality (a "right" action is one that works and can be got away with) and a unique set of criteria that make one successful in the lower-class community (being tough, willingness to take risks) (Miller, 1958; Banfield, 1974). Panel 8–1 provides what Banfield considers the elements of

The Lower-Class Propensity to Criminal Activity

The elements of propensity (toward criminal activity) seem to be mainly these:

Type of morality. This refers to the way in which an individual conceptualizes right and wrong and, therefore, to the weight he gives to legal and moral rules in making choices. One whose morality is "preconventional" understands a "right" action to be one that will serve his purpose and that can be gotten away with; a "wrong" action is one that will bring ill success or punishment. An individual whose morality is preconventional cannot be influenced by authority (as opposed to power). One whose morality is "conventional" defines "right" action as doing one's "duty" or doing what those in authority require; for him, laws and moral rules have a constraining effect even in the absence of an enforcement apparatus. One whose morality is "postconventional" defines "right" action as that which is in accord with some universal (or very general) principle that he considers worthy of choice. Such an individual is constrained by law as such only if the principle that he has chosen requires him to be; if it requires him to obey the law only when he thinks that the law in question is just, he is, of course, not under the constraint of law at all.

Ego strength. This refers to the individual's ability to control himself—especially to his ability to adhere to and act on his intentions (and therefore to manage his impulses) and to his ability to make efforts at self-reform. One who is radically deficient in ego strength cannot conceive or implement a plan of action; he has a succession of fleeting resolves, the last of which eventuates in action under the pressure of circumstances.

Time horizon. This refers to the time perspective an individual takes in estimating costs and benefits of alternative courses of action. The more present-oriented an individual, the less likely he is to take account of consequences that lie in the future. Since the benefits of crime tend to be immediate and its costs (such as imprisonment or loss of reputation) in the future, the present-oriented individual is *ipso facto* more disposed toward crime than others.

Taste for risk. Commission of most crimes involves a certain amount of risk. An individual who places a very low (perhaps even a negative) value on the avoidance of risk is thereby biased in the direction of crime.

Willingness to inflict injury. Most crimes involve at least the possibility of injury to others and therefore a certain willingness on the part of the actor to inflict injury. It may be useful to distinguish among (a) individuals with a distaste for inflicting any injury ("crimes without victims" would still be open to them, of course); (b) those with a distaste for injuring specifiable individuals (they might steal from a large enterprise, but they would not cheat the corner grocer); (c) those with a distaste for doing bodily (but not necessarily other) injury to people; and (d) those with no distaste for inflicting injuries, along with those who positively enjoy inflicting them.

These several elements of propensity tend to exist in typical combinations. In general, an individual whose morality is preconventional also has little ego strength, a short time horizon, a fondness for risk, and little distaste for doing bodily harm to specifiable individuals. The opposites of these traits also tend to be found together.

It also happens that individuals whose propensity toward crime is relatively high—especially those with high propensity for violent crime—tend to be those whose situation provides the strongest incentive to crimes of common sorts. The low-income individual obviously has much more incentive to steal than does the high-income one. Similarly, a boy has much more incentive to "prove he is not chicken" than does a girl. In general, then, high propensity and high inducement go together.

Source: Edward C. Banfield, *The Unheavenly City Revisited* (Boston: Little, Brown, 1974): 182–183. Copyright © 1968, 1970, 1974 by Edward C. Banfield. Reprinted by permission of the author.

propensity to crime by the lower class. Banfield may be correct in his assertions about the "lower-class culture," but there is strong evidence that it is incorrect (see Chapter 9). Assuming that Banfield's characterization of the lower-class propensity to crime is correct, the critical question is whether these differences are durable or not. Will a change in monetary status or peer groups make a difference because the individual has a dual value system—one that is a reaction to his deprived situation and one that is middle class? This is a key research question because the answer determines where to attack the problem—at the individual or the societal level.

The "Blaming-the-Victim" Critique of the Individual-Oriented Explanations for Deviance

Although the socialization theories focus on forces external to individuals that push them toward deviant behavior, they, like the biological and psychological theories, are "kinds of people" theories that find the fault within the individual. The deviant has an acquired trait—the internalization of values and beliefs favorable to deviance—that is social in origin. The problem is that this results in *blaming the victims,* as William Ryan has forcefully argued:

> The new ideology attributes defect and inadequacy to the malignant nature of poverty, injustice, slum life, and racial difficulties. The stigma that marks the victim and accounts for his victimization is acquired stigma, a stigma of social, rather than genetic origin. But the stigma, the defect, the fatal difference—though derived in the past from environmental forces—is still located *within* the victim, inside his skin. With such an elegant formulation, the humanitarian can have it both ways. He can, all at the same time, concentrate his charitable interest on the defects of the victim, condemn the vague social and environmental stresses that produced the defect (some time ago), and ignore the continuing effect of victimizing social forces (right now). It is a brilliant ideology for justifying a perverse form of social action designed to change, not society, as one might expect, but rather society's victim. (Ryan, 1976:7)*

Let us contrast, then, two ways to look at deviance—blaming the victim or blaming society. The fundamental difference between these two approaches to deviance is whether the problems emanate from the pathologies of individuals or because of the situation in which deviants are immersed. The answer is doubtless somewhere between these two extremes, but since the individual blamers have held sway, let us look carefully at the critique of this approach (Ryan, 1976; Caplan and Nelson, 1973).

Let us begin by considering some victims. One group of victims is composed of children in slum schools who are failures. Why do they fail? Victim

---

*William Ryan, *Blaming the Victim,* rev. ed. (New York: Pantheon, 1976) p. 7. Reprinted by permission of the publisher.

blamers point to the children's **cultural deprivation.*** They do not do well in school because their families speak a different dialect, because their parents are uneducated, because they have not been exposed to all the education experiences of middle-class children (for example, visits to the zoo, extensive travel, attendance at cultural events, exposure to books). In other words, the defect is in the children and their families. System blamers, however, look elsewhere for the sources of failure. They ask: what is there about the schools that make slum children more likely to fail? The answer for them is found in the irrelevant curriculum, the class-biased IQ tests, the tracking system, the overcrowded classrooms, the differential allocation of resources within the school district, and insensitive teachers whose low expectations for poor children comprise a prophecy that is continually fulfilled.

Another victim is the criminal. Why is the **recidivism** rate (reinvolvement in crime) of criminals so high? The individual blamer would point to the faults of the individual criminals: their greed, feelings of aggression, weak impulse control, and lack of a conscience (superego). The system blamers' attention is directed to very different sources for this problem. They would look, rather, at the penal system, the employment situation for ex-criminals, and the schools. For example, studies have shown that 20 to 30 percent of inmates are functionally illiterate. This means they cannot meet minimum reading and writing demands in U.S. society such as filling out job applications. Yet these persons are expected to leave prison, find a job, and stay out of trouble. Because they are illiterate and ex-criminals, they face unemployment or at best the most menial jobs (where there are low wages, no job security, and no fringe benefits). The system blamer would argue that these persons are not to blame for their illiteracy but rather that the schools at first and later the penal institutions have failed to provide these people with the minimum requirements for citizenship. Moreover, the lack of employment and the unwillingness of potential employers to train functional illiterates forces many to return to crime in order to survive.

Blacks (and other racial minorities) constitute another set of victims in American society. What accounts for the greater probability for blacks than whites to be failures in school, to be unemployed, to be criminals, and to be heroin addicts? The individualistic approach places the blame on the blacks themselves. They are "culturally deprived," they have high rates of illegitimacy, a high proportion of transient males, and a relatively high proportion of black families have a matriarchal structure. This approach neglects the pervasive effects of racism in American society, which limits the opportuni-

---

*The term *cultural deprivation* is a loaded ethnocentric term. It implies that the culture of the group in question is not only deficient but that it is inferior. This label is applied by members of the majority to the culture of the minority group. It is not only a malicious "putting down" of the minority, but the concept itself is patently false because no culture can be inferior to another; it can only be different. The concept does remind us, however, that people can and do make invidious distinctions about cultures and subcultures. Furthermore, they act on these definitions as if they were true.

ties for blacks, provides them with a second-class education, and renders them powerless to change the system through approved channels.

Why is there a strong tendency to place the blame for deviance on individuals rather than on the social system? The answer lies in the way that persons tend to define deviance. Most people define deviance as behavior that deviates from the norms and standards of society. Because people do not ordinarily question the norms or the way things are done in society, they tend to question the exceptions. The system is not only taken for granted, but it has, for most people, an aura of sacredness because of the traditions and customs behind it. Logically, then, those who deviate are the source of trouble. The obvious question, then, is why do these people deviate from the norms? Because most persons abide by society's norms, the deviation of the exceptions must be the result of some kind of unusual circumstance—accident, illness, personal defect, character flaw, or maladjustment (Ryan, 1976:10–18). The key to this approach, then, is that the flaw is within the deviant and not a function of societal arrangements.

The position taken in this debate has serious consequences. Let us briefly examine the effects of interpreting social problems solely within a person-blame framework (Caplan and Nelson, 1973). First, this interpretation of social problems frees the government, the economy, the system of stratification, the system of justice, and the educational system from any blame. The established order is protected against criticism, thereby increasing the difficulty encountered in trying to change the dominant economic, social, and political institutions. A good example is found in the strategy of social scientists studying the origins of poverty. Since the person blamer studies the poor rather than the nonpoor, the system of inequality (buttressed by the tax laws, welfare rules, and employment practices) goes unchallenged. A related consequence of the person-blame approach, then, is that the relatively advantaged segments of society retain their advantages.

Not only is the established order protected from criticism by the person-blame approach, but the authorities can control dissidents under the guise of being helpful. Caplan and Nelson have provided an excellent illustration of this in the following quote:

> Normally, one would not expect the Government to cooperate with "problem groups" who oppose the system. But if a person-blame rather than system-blame action program can be negotiated, cooperation becomes possible. In this way, the problem-defining process remains in the control of the would-be benefactors, who provide "help" so long as their diagnosis goes unchallenged.
>
> In 1970, for example, while a group of American Indians still occupied Alcatraz Island in San Francisco Bay, a group of blacks took over Ellis Island in New York Harbor. Both groups attempted to take back lands no longer used by the Federal Government. The Government solved the Ellis Island problem by getting the blacks to help establish a drug-rehabilitation center on it. They solved the Alcatraz problem by forcibly removing the Indians. Had the Indians been willing to settle for an alcoholism-treatment center on Alcatraz, thereby acknowledging that what they need are remedies for their personal

problems, we suspect the Government would have "cooperated" again.
(Caplan and Nelson, 1973:104)

Another social control function of the person-blame approach is that troublesome individuals and groups are controlled in a publicly acceptable manner. Deviants, whether they be criminals, homosexuals, or social protesters are controlled by incarceration in prison or mental hospital, drugs, or other forms of therapy. In this manner, not only is blame directed at individuals and away from the system, but the problems (individuals) are in a sense eliminated.

A related consequence is the manner in which the problem is to be treated. A person-blame approach demands a person-change treatment program. If the cause of delinquency, for example, is defined as the result of personal pathology, then the solution lies clearly in counseling, behavior modification, psychotherapy, drugs, or some other technique aimed at changing the individual deviant. Such an interpretation of social problems provides and legitimates the right to initiate person-change rather than system-change treatment programs. Under such a scheme, norms that are racist or sexist, for example, will go unchallenged.

The person-blame ideology not only invites person-change treatment programs but also programs for person control. The typical result is that the overwhelming emphasis of government programs is on more police, courts, and prisons rather than on changing criminogenic social conditions.

The person-blame approach advocates the control of criminals by placing them in prison.

A final consequence of person-blame interpretations is that they reinforce social myths about the degree of control we have over our fate. It provides justification for a form of **Social Darwinism**—that is, a person's placement in the stratification system is a function of ability and effort. By this logic, the poor are poor because they *are* the dregs of society. In short, they deserve their fate, as do the successful in society. Thus, there is little sympathy for governmental programs to increase welfare to the poor.

We should recognize, however, that the contrasting position—the system-blame orientation—also has its dangers. First, it is only part of the truth. Social problems and deviance are highly complex phenomena that have both individual and systemic origins. Individuals, obviously, can be malicious and aggressive for purely psychological reasons. Perhaps only a psychologist can explain why a parent is a child abuser, or why a sniper shoots at cars passing on the freeway. Clearly, society needs to be protected from some individuals. Moreover, some persons require particular forms of therapy, remedial help, or special programs on an individual basis if they are to function normally. But much that is labeled deviant is the end product of social conditions.

A second danger in a dogmatic system-blame orientation is that it presents a rigidly deterministic explanation for social problems. Taken too far, this position views individuals as robots controlled totally by their social environment. A balanced view of people is needed, since human beings have autonomy most of the time to choose between alternative courses of action. This raises the related question as to the degree to which people are responsible for their behavior. An excessive system-blame approach absolves individuals from the responsibility of their actions. To take such a stance would be to argue that society should never restrict deviants. This extreme view invites anarchy.

Despite the problems just noted, the system-blame approach will be emphasized in this chapter. The rationale for this is, first, that the contrasting view (individual-blame) is the prevailing view in U.S. society. Since average citizens, police personnel, legislators, judges, and social scientists tend to interpret social problems from an individualistic perspective, a balance is needed. Moreover, as was noted earlier, to hold a strict person-blame perspective has many negative consequences, and citizens must realize the effects of their ideology.

A second basis for the use of the society-blaming perspective is that the subject matter of sociology is not the individual, who is the special province of psychology, but society. If sociologists do not emphasize the social determinants of behavior and if they do not make a critical analysis of the social structure, then who will? As noted in Chapter 1, an important ingredient of the sociological perspective is the development of a critical stance toward societal arrangements. The job of the sociologist is to look behind the facade to determine the positive and negative consequences of societal arrangements. The persistent question is: Who benefits under these arrangements and who does not? This is why there should be such a close fit between the sociological approach and the societal blaming perspective. Unfortunately, this has not always been the case.

SOCIETY AS THE SOURCE OF DEVIANCE

We have seen that the traditional explanations for deviance, whether they be biological, psychological, or sociological, have found the source of deviance in individual deviants, their families, or their immediate social settings. The basic assumption of these theories is that because deviants do not fit in society, something is wrong with them. In this section we shall provide an antidote to the medical analogy implicit in those theories by focusing instead on two theories that place the blame for deviance on the role of society—labeling theory and conflict theory.

Labeling Theory

All the explanations for deviance described so far assume that deviants differ from nondeviants in behavior, attitude, and motivation. This is buttressed by the commonly held belief that deviance is the actions of a few weird people who are either criminals, insane, or both. In reality, however, most persons break the rules of society at one time or another. The evidence is that the members of all social classes commit thefts, assaults, and use illegal drugs. Summarizing a number of studies on the relationship between socioeconomic class and crime, Hirschi has said:

> While the prisons bulge with the socioeconomic dregs of society, careful quantitative research shows again and again that the relation between socio-economic status and the commission of delinquent acts is small, or nonexistent. (Hirschi, 1969:66)

These studies do not mesh with our perceptions and the apparent facts. Crime statistics do show that the lower classes are more likely to be criminals. Even data on mental illness demonstrate that the lower classes are more likely than the middle classes to have serious mental problems (Hollingshead and Redlich, 1958; Myers and Bean, 1968). The difference is that most persons break the rules at one time or another, even serious rules for which they could be placed in jail (for example, theft, statutory rape, vandalism, violation of drug or alcohol laws, fraud, violations of the Internal Revenue Service), but only some get the *label* of deviant (Becker, 1963:14). As one adult analyzed his ornery but normal youth:

> I recall my high school and college days, participating in vandalism, entering locked buildings at night, drinking while under age—even while I made top grades and won athletic letters. I was normal and did these things with guys who now are preachers, professors, and businessmen. A few school friends of poorer families somehow tended to get caught and we didn't. They were failing in class, and we all believed they were too dumb not to know when to have fun and when to run. Some of them did time in jail and reformatories. *They* were "delinquents" and *we* weren't. (Janzen, 1974:390; see also Chambliss, 1973)

This chapter began with the statement that society creates deviance by creating rules, the violation of which constitutes deviance. But rule breaking itself does "not a deviant make." The successful application of the label "deviant" is crucial (Schur, 1971). This is the essence of **labeling theory,** the view of deviant behavior that stresses the importance of the society in defining what is illegal and in assigning a deviant status to particular individuals, which in turn dominates their identities and behaviors.

Who gets labeled as a deviant (criminal, psychotic, faggot, or junkie) is not just a matter of luck or random selection but the result of a systematic societal bias against the powerless. Chambliss has summarized the empirical evidence for criminals:

> The lower class person is (1) more likely to be scrutinized and therefore be observed in any violation of the law, (2) more likely to be arrested if discovered under suspicious circumstances, (3) more likely to spend the time between arrest and trial in jail, (4) more likely to come to trial, (5) more likely to found guilty, (6) if found guilty, more likely to receive harsh punishment than his middle- or upper-class counterpart. (Chambliss, 1969:86)

We can see how the well-to-do tend to avoid the criminal label by examining the disposition of those persons actually found guilty of a felony (major crime) by their socioeconomic characteristics. The judicial procedures in Florida provide a revealing glimpse of this bias. For persons accused of a felony but placed on probation, Florida law allows a judge the option of withholding adjudication of guilt. The importance of avoiding this label is that such persons lose none of their civil rights and may truthfully assert that they have never been convicted of a felony. To be a "convicted felon," on the other hand, means that one loses the rights to vote, hold public office, serve on juries, and possess certain firearms. The stigma of "felon" also makes employment more difficult as well as acceptance in other situations. A study of the legal and social characteristics of 2,419 consecutive felony probation cases found that defendants who were older, black, poorly educated, had a prior record, and were defended by a court-appointed attorney were the most likely to be labeled (Chiricos, Jackson, and Waldo, 1972). Clearly, the judges reflected the bias present in society by formally imposing criminal labels on those persons *expected* to be the most criminal (the poor, the uneducated, racial minorities), who coincidentally are the least powerful segments in society.

Not only are the more well-to-do less likely to receive a punishment of imprisonment, but those who are imprisoned receive advantages over the lower-class and minority inmates. The most blatant example of this is found by examining what type of person actually receives the death penalty. A former Attorney General has summarized the findings in the following quote:

> The poor and the black have been the chief victims of the death penalty. Clarence Darrow observed that "from the beginning, a procession of the poor, the weak, the unfit, have gone through our jails and prisons to their deaths. They have been the victims." It is the poor, the sick, the ignorant, the powerless and the hated who are executed.
>
> Racial discrimination is manifest from the bare statistics of capital punishment. Since we began keeping records in 1930, there have been 2,066 Negroes and only 1,751 white persons put to death. Hundreds of thousands of rapes

have occurred in America since 1930, yet only 455 men have been executed for rape—and 405 of them were Negroes. There can be no rationalization or justification of such clear discrimination. It is outrageous public murder, illuminating our darkest racism. (Clark, 1970:335)

The social class of the prisoner on death row is also related to whether an individual receives the ultimate punishment or not. In a study of death row in Pennsylvania from 1914 to 1958, those offenders with court-appointed counsel were much more likely to be executed than offenders with private counsel. Likewise, there is a greater probability of the death penalty being imposed on persons of low-prestige occupations than for those of higher prestige (Wolfgang, Kelly, and Nolde, 1962).

Who gets paroled is another indicator of a bias in the system. Parole is a conditional release from prison that allows prisoners to return to their communities under the supervision of a parole officer before the completion of their maximum sentence. Typically, parole is granted by a parole board set up for the correctional institution or for the state. Often the parole board members are political appointees without training. The parole board reviews a prisoner's social history, past offenses, and behavior in prison and makes its judgment. The decision is rarely subject to review and can be made arbitrarily or discriminatorily.

The bias that disadvantages minorities and the poor throughout the system of justice continues as parole board members, corrections officers, and others make judgments that often reflect stereotypes. What type of prisoner represents the safest risk, a black or a white? An uneducated or an educated person? A white-collar worker or a chronically unemployed unskilled worker? The evidence is overwhelming and consistent—the parole system, just as the rest of the criminal justice system, is biased against people of color and those of low socioeconomic status.

At the beginning of 1989, the state and federal prisons held 627,402 inmates. This amounted to 244 inmates per 100,000 U.S. residents (up from 139 per 100,000 in 1980, and 79 per 100,000 in 1925 when these statistics were first determined).

We have shown that the underdogs in society (the poor and the minorities) are disproportionately represented in the prison population. An important consequence of this is that it reinforces the negative stereotypes already present in the majority of the population. The large number of blacks and the poor in prison "prove" that they have criminal tendencies. This belief is reinforced further by the high recidivism rate of 70 percent of ex-prisoners.

At least four factors relative to the prison experiences operate to fulfill the prophecy that the poor and the black are likely to behave criminally. The first is that the entire criminal justice system is viewed by the underdogs as unjust. There is a growing belief among prisoners that because the system is biased against them, all prisoners are, in fact, political. This "consciousness raising" increases the bitterness and anger among them.

A second reason for the high rate of crime among those processed through the system of criminal justice is the accepted fact that prison is a brutal, degrading, and altogether dehumanizing experience. Mistreatment by guards, sexual assaults by fellow prisoners, overcrowding, unsanitary conditions, are commonplace in American prisons. Prisoners cannot escape the humiliation, anger, and frustration. These feelings, coupled with the knowledge that the entire system of justice is unjustly directed at certain categories of persons, creates within many ex-cons the desire for revenge.

A third factor is that prisons provide learning experiences for prisoners in the art of crime. Through the interaction of the inmates, individuals learn the techniques of crime from the masters and develop the contacts that can be used later.

Finally, the ex-con faces the problems of finding a job and being accepted again in society. Long-termers face problems of adjusting to life without regimentation. More important, since good-paying jobs, particularly in times of economic recession, are difficult for anyone to find, the ex-con who is automatically assumed to be untrustworthy is faced with either unemployment or those jobs nobody else will take. Even the law works to his disadvantage by prohibiting certain jobs to ex-cons.

The result of nonacceptance by society is often to return to crime. Previous offenders, on the average, are arrested for crime within six weeks after leaving prison. This, of course, justifies the beliefs by police officers, judges, parole boards, and other authorities that certain categories of persons should receive punishment while others should not.

The Consequences of Labeling.   We have just seen that the labeling process is a crucial factor in the formulation of a deviant career. In other words, the stigma of the label leads to subsequent deviance. This is what Lemert (1951) meant by the concept of secondary deviance. **Primary deviance** is the rule-breaking that occurs prior to labeling. **Secondary deviance** is that behavior resulting from the labeling process. Being labeled a criminal means being rejected by society, by employers, by friends, and even by relatives. There is a high probability that such a person will turn to behavior that fulfills the prophecies of others. Put another way, persons labeled as deviants tend to become locked into a deviant behavior pattern. Looking at deviance this way turns the tables on conventional thought.

> Instead of assuming that it is the deviant's difference which needs explanation, [the labeling perspective] asks why the majority responds to *this* difference as it does. This shift of the question reverses the normal conception of causation; the labeling school suggests that the other person's peculiarity has not caused us to regard him as different so much as our labeling hypothesis has caused his peculiarity. (Nettler, 1974:203)

Ex-mental patients, like ex-convicts, usually have difficulty in finding employment and establishing close relationships because of the stigma of the label. This, of course, leads to frustration, anger, low self-esteem, and other symptoms of "mental illness." Moreover, the consistent messages from others (remember Cooley's looking-glass self) that one is sick will likely lead the individual to behavior in accord with these expectations. Even while a patient is in the mental hospital, the actions of the staff may actually foster in the person a self-concept of "deviant" and behavior consistent with that definition. Patients who show insight about their "illness" confirm the medical and societal diagnosis and are positively rewarded by psychiatrists and other personnel (see Scheff, 1966). The opposite also occurs, as illustrated so vividly by the character R. P. McMurphy in *One Flew over the Cuckoo's Nest* (Kesey, 1962). Although the mythical McMurphy fought this tendency to confirm the expectations of powerful others, the pressures to conform were great. Cole has summarized this process of how the deviant role is sustained in the following:

> After someone is labeled as deviant, he often finds it rewarding to accept the label and act deviant. Consider, for example, a patient in a mental hospital who has been diagnosed as a schizophrenic. If the patient refuses to accept the diagnosis, claims that he is not mentally ill, and demands to be immediately released, the staff will consider him to be hostile and uncooperative. He may be denied privileges and treated as hopelessly insane. After all, the person who cannot even recognize that he is ill must be in a mental state in which he has no perception of reality! On the other hand, if the patient accepts the validity of the diagnosis, admits his illness, and tries to cooperate with the staff in effecting a cure, he will be rewarded. He will be defined as a good cooperative patient who is sincerely trying to get better. Any weird or unusual behavior he engages in will be ignored; after all, he is mentally ill, and such types of behavior should be expected from a person in his mental state. He may even be rewarded for engaging in behavior which is considered to be characteristic of schizophrenia. Such behavior serves to reassure the staff that the patient is indeed mentally ill and that the social organization of the mental hospital makes sense. (Cole, 1975:141–142)

The labeling perspective is especially helpful in understanding the bias of the criminal justice system. It shows, in summary, that when society's underdogs are disproportionately singled out for the criminal label, the subsequent problems of stigmatization and segregation they face result in a tendency toward further deviance, thereby justifying the society's original negative response to them. This tendency for secondary deviance is especially strong when the imposition of the label is accompanied by a sense of injustice. Lemert (1967) argued that a stronger commitment to a deviant identity is greatest when the label (stigma) is believed by the individual to be inconsistently applied by society. The evidence of such inconsistency is overwhelming.

From this perspective, then, the situations which show that society's underdogs engage in more deviance than persons from the middle and upper classes are invalid, since they reflect the differential response of society to the deviance by them at every phase in the process of criminal justice. Hartjen has provided an excellent statement that summarizes this process.

> Criminal sanctions are supposedly directed toward a person's behavior—
> what he does, not what kind of person he is. Yet, the research on the adminis
> tration of criminal justice . . . reveals that just the opposite occurs. A person
> is likely to acquire a social identity as a criminal precisely because of what he

is—because of the kind of personal or social characteristics he has the misfortune to possess. Being black, poor, migrant, uneducated, and the like increases a person's chances of being defined as a criminal. . . . What I am suggesting here is that the very structure and operation of the judicial system, which was created to deal with the problem called crime, are not only grounded in an unstated image of the criminal but also—merely because the system exists—serve to produce and perpetuate the "thing" it was created to handle. That is to say, the criminal court (and especially the juvenile court) does not exist in its present form because the people it deals with are what they are. Rather, the criminals and delinquents become the way they are characterized by others as being because the court (and the world view it embodies) exists in the form that it does. *The criminal, thus, is a "product" of the structural and procedural characteristics of the judicial system.* (Hartjen, 1974:120–121)*

"Solutions" for Deviance from the Labeling Perspective.   The labeling theorist's approach to deviance leads to unconventional solutions (Schur, 1971). The assumption is that deviants are not basically different—except that they have been processed (and labeled) by official sources (judges and courts; psychiatrists and mental hospitals). The primary target for policy, then, should be neither the individual nor the local community setting, but the process by which some persons are singled out for the negative label. From this approach, organizations produce deviants. Speaking specifically about juvenile delinquency, Schur has argued that the solution should be what he has called **radical nonintervention** (the strategy of leaving juvenile delinquents alone as much as possible rather than giving them a negative label).

> We can now begin to see some of the meanings of the term "radical nonintervention." For one thing, it breaks radically with conventional thinking about delinquency and its causes. Basically, radical nonintervention implies policies that accommodate society to the widest possible diversity of behaviors and attitudes, rather than focusing as many individuals as possible to "adjust" to supposedly common societal standards. This does not mean that anything goes, that all behavior is socially acceptable. But traditional delinquency policy has proscribed youthful behavior well beyond what is required to maintain a smooth-running society or to protect others from youthful depredations.
>
> Thus, the basic injunction for public policy becomes: *leave kids alone wherever possible.* This effort partly involves mechanisms to divert children away from the courts but it goes further to include opposing various kinds of intervention by diverse social control and socializing agencies. . . . Subsidiary policies would favor collective action programs instead of those that single out specific individuals; and voluntary programs instead of compulsive ones. Finally, this approach is radical in asserting that major and intentional sociocultural change will help reduce our delinquency problems. Piecemeal socioeconomic reform will not greatly affect delinquency; there must be through-

---

*From *Crime and Criminalization* by Clayton A. Hartjen. Copyright © 1974 by Praeger Publishers. Reprinted by permission of Praeger Publishers, A Division of Holt, Rinehart and Winston.

going changes in the structure and the values of our society. If the choice is between changing youth and changing society (including some of its laws), the radical noninterventionist opts for changing the society. (Schur, 1973: 154–155)

One way to accomplish this "leave the deviants alone whenever possible" philosophy would be to treat fewer acts as criminal or deviant. For adults this could be accomplished by decriminalizing victimless crimes, such as gambling, drug possession, prostitution, and homosexuality. Youth should not be treated as criminals for behavior that is legal if one is old enough. Truancy, running away from home, curfew violations, and purchasing alcohol are acts for which persons below the legal age can receive the label "delinquent," yet they are not crimes for adults. Is there any wonder, then, why so many youthful rule breakers outgrow their "delinquency," becoming law-abiding citizens as adults?

Acts dangerous to society do occur, and these must be handled through legal mechanisms. But when a legal approach is required, justice must be applied evenly. Currently, the criminal label is disproportionately applied to individuals from the "other side of the tracks." This increases the probability of further deviance by these persons because of "secondary deviance" and justifies further stern punishment for this category. This unfair cycle must be broken.

The strengths of labeling theory are: (1) that it concentrates on the role of societal reactions in the creation of deviance, (2) the realization that the label is applied disproportionately to the powerless, and (3) that it explains how deviant careers are established and perpetuated. There are problems with the theory, however (see Warren and Johnson, 1973; Gibbs, 1966; Davis, 1975; Liazos, 1972). First, it avoids the question of causation (primary deviance). Labeling, by definition, occurs after the fact. It disregards undetected deviance. As McCaghy has put it,

> By minimizing the importance of explaining initial (primary) deviance, whatever meaning the behavior originally had for the deviant is ignored as a contributor to subsequent behavior. Although societal reaction may become a crucial factor in behavior, it is questionable that whatever purpose of reward the behavior first held is invariably replaced. For example, if a person first steals for thrills, do thrills fail to be a factor once societal reaction has taken its toll? (McCaghy, 1976:87)

Another problem with labeling involves the assumption that deviants are really normal—because we are all rule breakers. Thus, it overlooks the possibility that some persons are unable to cope with the pressures of their situation. Some people are dangerous. Individuals who are disadvantaged tend to be more angry, frustrated, and alienated than their more fortunate fellows. The result may be differences in quantity and quality of primary deviance.

This perspective also relieves the individual deviant from blame. The underdog is seen as victimized by the powerful labelers. Further, individuals enmeshed in the labeling process are so constrained by the forces of society that they are incapable of choice. Once again, McCaghy has put it well: "Although it is true that deviants may be pawns of the powerful, this does not mean that deviants are powerless to resist, to alter their behavior, or to acquire power themselves" (McCaghy, 1976:88).

Perhaps its most serious deficiency, though, is that labeling theory focuses on certain types of deviance but ignores others. The attention is directed at society's underdogs, which is good. But those forms of deviance emanating from the social structure or from the powerful are not considered a very serious omission. As Liazos has put it, the themes of labeling theory focus attention on those who have been successfully labeled as deviants ("nuts, sluts, and perverts"), the deviant subculture, and the self-fulfilling prophecy that perpetuates their deviant patterns (Liazos, 1972). While this is appropriate and necessary, it concentrates on the powerless. The impression is that deviance is an exclusive property of the poor in the slum, the minorities, and street gangs.

But what of the deviance of the powerful members of society and even society itself? Liazos (1972) has chronicled these for us:

1. The unethical, illegal, and destructive actions found in the corporate world, such as robbery through price fixing, low wages, pollution, inferior and dangerous products, deception, and outright lies in advertising.
2. The covert institutional violence committed against the poor by the institutions of society: schools, hospitals, corporations, and the government.
3. The political manipulators who pass laws that protect the interests of the powerful and disadvantage the powerless.
4. The power of the powerful is used to deflect criticism, labeling, and punishment even when deserved.

In short, labeling overlooks the deviant qualities of the society and its powerful members. Although social structure should be central to sociologists, the labeling theorists have minimized its impact on deviance. Liazos has summarized the problem this way:

> We should banish the concept of "deviance" and speak of oppression, conflict, persecution, and suffering. By focusing on the dramatic forms, as we do now, we perpetuate most people's beliefs and impressions that such "deviance" is the basic cause of many of our troubles, that these people (criminals, drug addicts, political dissenters, and others) are the real "troublemakers"; and, necessarily, we neglect conditions of inequality, powerlessness, institutional violence, and so on, which lie at the bases of our tortured society. (Liazos, 1972:119)

Another way deviance is explained—conflict theory—extends labeling theory by focusing on social structure, thereby overcoming the fundamental criticisms of Liazos and others.

Conflict Theory

Why is certain behavior defined as deviant? The answer, according to conflict theorists, is that powerful economic interest groups are able to get laws passed and enforced that protect their interests (Quinney, 1970, 1974). We must begin, then, with the law.

Of all the requirements for a just system, the most fundamental is the foundation of nondiscriminatory laws. Many criminal laws are the result of a consensus among the public as to what kinds of behaviors are a menace and should be punished (for example, murder, rape, theft). The laws devised to make these acts illegal and the extent of punishment for violators are nondiscriminatory (although, as we have seen, the administration of these laws is discriminatory) since they do not single out a particular social category as the target.

There are laws, however, that discriminate because they result from special interests using their power to translate their interests into public policy. These laws may be discriminatory because some segments of society (for example, the poor, minorities, youth, renters, debtors) rarely have access to the lawmaking process and therefore often find the laws unfairly aimed at them. Vagrancy, for example, is really a crime that only the poor can commit.

Not only is the formation of the law political, but so, too, is the administration of the law. This is because at every stage in the processing of criminals, choices are made by authorities based on personal bias, pressures from the powerful, and the constraints of the status quo. Some examples of the political character of law administration are: (1) the attempt by the powerful to coerce others to their view of morality, hence laws against homosexuality, pornography, drug usage, and gambling; (2) the powerful may exert pressure on the authorities to crack down on certain kinds of violators, especially those individuals and groups who are disruptive (protesters); (3) there may be

One consequence of the Gay Rights Movement is the open demonstration by gays for civil rights and acceptance of their life-style.

The Gay Rights Movement

The forces of society converge to restrict the behavior of individuals to those activities considered socially acceptable. But occasionally some who find these demands too confining organize to change society. One contemporary example is the Gay Rights Movement.

Experts agree that about 10 percent of adult Americans (about 17 million persons) are homosexuals. Although homosexuals have been accepted by some societies (e.g., ancient Greece and Rome), they have never been accepted in the United States. The erotic sexual attraction and behaviors between members of the same sex have always been severely santioned in our society. Formal laws forbidding such behaviors have been enacted. Employers, typically, have not knowingly hired homosexuals. Persons assumed to have such aberrant proclivities have been the objects of ridicule throughout society—in the media, on playgrounds, in factories, and in boardrooms. Because of discrimination against them, fear of social ostracism, and other forms of rejection even by friends and family, most homosexuals have felt it necessary to conceal their sexual preference.

These compelling fears have kept homosexuals for most periods of American history from organizing to change a repressive situation. A few homosexual organizations were formed (the first in 1925 and others in the 1950s) for mutual support, but a relatively few homosexuals were willing at these times to declare publicly their deviance from the norm of society.

The 1960s provided a better climate for change as youths, Blacks, women, pacifists, and other groups questioned the norms and ideologies of the dominant society. This time clearly was one of heightened awareness among the oppressed of their oppression and of the possibility that through collective efforts they could change what seemed before as unchangeable.

The precipitating event for homosexual unity occurred at 3 A.M. on June 28, 1969 when police raided the Stonewall Inn of New York's Greenwich Village. But instead of dispersing, the 200 homosexual patrons, who had never collectively resisted the police before, threw objects at the police and set fire to the bar. The riot lasted 45 minutes, but it gave impetus to a number of col-

political pressure exerted to keep certain crimes from public view (embezzlement, stock fraud, the Iran-contra affair); (4) there may be pressure to protect the party in power, the elected officials, the police, CIA, and FBI; and (5) any effort to protect and preserve the status quo is a political act. Hartjen has summarized why the administration of justice is inherently political in the following quote:

> Unless one is willing to assume that law-enforcement agents can apply some magic formula to gauge the opinions of the public they serve, unless one is willing to assume that citizens unanimously agree on what laws are to be enforced and how enforcement is to be carried out, unless one is willing to assume that blacks, the poor, urbanites, and the young are actually more criminalistic than everyone else, it must be concluded, at least, that discriminatory law enforcement is a result of differences in power and that actual decisions as to which and whose behavior is criminal are expressions of this power. One need only ask himself why some laws, such as those protecting

lective efforts by gays to publicize police harassment of the gay community, job discrimination, and other indignities that homosexuals face. Gay liberation groups emerged in numerous cities and on university campuses. By 1980 over 4,000 homosexual organizations existed in the United States. Many neighborhoods in major cities became openly homosexual—most notably the Castro district in San Francisco, New Town in Chicago, and Greenwich Village in New York City. Gay organizations now include: churches, associations of professionals, health clinics, and networks of gay-owned businesses to supply the gay community's needs. The proliferation of these organizations for homosexuals has provided a supportive climate allowing many of them to "come out of the closet."

The increased numbers of "public" homosexuals have provided the political base for changing the various forms of oppression that homosexuals experience. A Gay Media Task Force promotes accurate and positive images of gays in television, films, and advertising: a Gay Rights National Lobby promotes favorable legislation; and a National Gay Task Force serves to further gay interests by attacking the minority group status of homosexuals in a variety of political and ideological arenas.

The positive results of these political activities, although limited, have been encouraging to the gay community. Since 1983, Wisconsin and most of the larger cities in the United States have enacted gay-rights laws. The Civil Service Reform Act of 1978 prohibits federal agencies from discriminating against gays in employment practices. And, although still rare, a few avowed homosexuals have been elected to public office.

The successes of gay-rights political activists have not yet achieved their ultimate goal—the full acceptance of homosexuality as an alternative lifestyle. Homosexuals are still not allowed to marry. Discrimination in housing and jobs still occurs. Polls show that only about one-third of Americans consider it an acceptable lifestyle. And gay-rights movements have met fierce resistance by fundamentalist religious groups such as the Moral Majority who believe homosexuality to be morally offensive and dangerous. But clearly during the past 20 years, the collective efforts of homosexuals have had an enormous and positive impact for homosexuals.

the consumer from fraud, go largely unenforced while the drug addict, for example, is pursued with a paranoiac passion. (Hartjen, 1974:11)*

The conflict approach is critical of the "kinds-of-people" explanations of order theorists and the focus of labeling theorists because both center on individual deviants and their crimes. Order theorists and labeling theorists tend to emphasize street crimes and ignore the crimes of the rich and powerful, such as corporate crimes (which go largely unpoliced) and crimes by governments (which are not even considered crimes).

Conflict theorists, in contrast, emphasize corporate and political crimes, which do many times the economic damage and harm to people than do

*From *Crime and Criminalization* by Clayton A. Hartjen. Copyright © 1974 by Praeger Publishers. Reprinted by permission of Praeger Publishers, A Division of Holt, Rinehart and Winston.

street crimes. **Corporate crime** refers to the "illegal and/or socially harmful behaviors that result from deliberate decision making by corporate executives in accordance with the operative goals of their organizations" (Kramer, 1982:75). This definition focuses attention on corporations, rather than individuals, as perpetrators, and it goes beyond the criminal law to include "socially harmful behaviors." Both of these elements are critical to conflict theorists. First, deviance is not limited to troubled individuals, as is the traditional focus in sociology. Organizations, too, can be deviant. Moreover, research has shown that corporations have a higher criminality rate than do individuals, (and the law does not define most harmful corporate behavior as illegal). For example, one study of the 1000 largest U.S. corporations found that 11 percent had been convicted of at least one illegal act over a ten-year period (Ross, 1980). As Simon and Eitzen have commented:

> Imagine for a moment that, in a ten-year period, 11 percent of the adult population of the United States had been convicted of some illegal offense and sentenced to prison. As a result, approximately 12 million people would be placed in a prison system that is overcrowded with a mere half million inmates. At such a point, liberals and conservatives alike would call crime an epidemic—an institutionalized phenomenon in U.S. society. However, when the same level of corporate crime is discussed, the problem is not considered to be serious. (Simon and Eitzen, 1990:349)

The second part of the definition of corporate crime stresses "socially harmful behaviors" whether criminal or not. This means that conflict theorists ask such questions as:

> What about selling proven dangerous products (e.g., pesticides, drugs, or food) overseas, when it is illegal to do so within the United States? What about promoting an unsafely designed automobile such as the Ford Pinto? Or, what about being excessively slow to promote a safe work environment for workers? (Timmer and Eitzen, 1989:85)

The definition of **political crime** separates order and conflict theorists. Because order theorists assume that the law and the state are neutral, they perceive political crimes as activities against the government, such as acts of dissent and violence whose purpose is to challenge and change the existing political order. Conflict theorists, in sharp contrast, assume that the law and the state are tools of the powerful. Thus, the political order itself may be criminal since it can be unjust. Moreover, government, like a corporation, may follow policies that go against democratic principles and that do harm. Examples of political crimes from this perspective are CIA interventions in the domestic affairs of other nations, Watergate, the Iran-contra affair, war crimes, slavery, imperialism (such as forcibly taking the land from the Indians), police brutality, and using citizens experimentally without their knowledge and consent. An extreme example of human subjects as "guinea pigs" is a study that was begun in 1932 by the U.S. Public Health Service. The subjects were 400 black male syphilis patients in Macon County, Alabama. The patients did not know that they had syphilis and were never informed of that fact. Because the purpose of the study was to assess the consequences of not treating the disease, the men were not treated, nor were their wives—and when their children were born with congenital syphilis, they, too, were not treated. The experiment lasted forty years, until 1972 (Jones, 1981).

In sum, the focus of the conflict perspective is on the political and economic setting in society. The power of certain interests determines what gets defined as deviance (and who, then, is a deviant), and how this "problem" is to be solved. Since the powerful benefit from the status quo, efforts to reform society are vigorously thwarted by them. The solution, from the conflict theorists, however, requires not only reform of society but its radical transformation. *The structure of society is the problem.*

The strengths of the conflict perspective on deviance are (Sykes, 1974): (1) its emphasis on the relationship between political order and nonconformity; (2) the understanding that the most powerful groups use the political order to protect their interests; (3) that it emphasizes how the system of justice is unjust, and that the distribution of rewards in society is skewed; and (4) the realization that the institutional framework of society is the source of so many social problems (for example, racism, sexism, pollution, unequal distribution of health care, poverty, and economic cycles).

There are some problems with this perspective, however. First, there is the tendency to assume a conspiracy by the well-to-do. Because the empirical evidence is overwhelming that the poor, the uneducated, and the members of minority groups are singled out for the deviant label, some persons make the too facile imputation of motive.

Second, the answer of the conflict theorists is too utopian. The following quotation by Quinney is representative of this naivete:

> The alternative to the contradictions of capitalism is a truly democratic society, a socialist society in which human beings no longer suffer the alienation inherent in capitalism. When there is no longer the need for one class to dominate another, when there is no longer the need for a legal system to secure the interests of a capitalist ruling class, then there will no longer be the need for crime. (Quinney, 1974:25)

But, would crime and other forms of deviance disappear under such a socialist system? This, like Marx's final stage of history, is a statement of faith rather than one based on proof.

DEVIANCE FROM THE ORDER AND CONFLICT PERSPECTIVES

The two contrasting theoretical perspectives in sociology—the order model (functionalism) and the conflict model—constrain their adherents to view the causes, consequences, and remedies of deviance in opposing ways (see Table 8–1).

The order perspective focuses on deviants themselves. This approach (which has been the conventional way of studying social problems) asks: Who are the deviants? What are their social and psychological backgrounds? With whom do they associate? Deviants somehow do not conform to the standards of the dominant group; they are assumed to be out of phase with conventional

Performance-Enhancing Drugs as Commonplace?

Every society gets the drug problem it deserves. Drug-hunger is essential to our modern way of life; it's a constant, like electricity, or air pollution. We lie to ourselves about drugs and the nature of their attraction for us. Because of that, we risk being blindsided in the 21st century—when the hidden cultural logic of drug use will reach a bizarre crescendo.

Not long ago, President Bush told an audience of astonished Amish that Wall Street yuppies use cocaine. That uncomfortable truth discredits the silly myth that drugs are the exclusive province of derelicts, teen-agers, bohemians and the lumpen. Those well-heeled professionals do cocaine, not because it's fun (although it is), but because it gives them a vital short-term edge that helps them prosper in the crazed environment of a futures pit.

The coming thing in drugs is not intoxicants but performance enhancers. In the future, we won't use drugs to "escape reality," but to lash ourselves to superhuman effort.

You can see this trend coming already. The cozy, dreamy days of marijuana and LSD are history; what people want now is crack, amphetamine and anabolic steroids—headlong speed and muscle by order. Steroids provide no pleasurable "high"—in fact, they ruin your sleep, your tem-

per and your complexion—but it's estimated that 1 million Americans abuse them. The market is vast and growing, and the steroids scandal of the last Olympics perversely gave this market a tremendous popular boost.

The reasons are obvious. Ben Johnson is, in fact, the fastest man in the world.

Put yourself in Ben Johnson's place. (It will happen soon enough, so you might as well get used to it.) Steroids enhance strength, but soon we are going to discover substances that will enhance memory, enhance intelligence, enhance mood, enhance sexuality. The drugs we have today already do this, in halting ways—amphetamine, for instance, has been found to raise the IQ by about 10 points, though for short periods, at great cost to health.

As we come to understand the nature of our own neurochemistry, we are going to discover a galaxy of extremely potent substances with greater specificity and fewer side effects. The drugs we use today are mostly vegetable extracts that crudely mimic human biochemistry. But betaendorphin, for instance, is a natural human brain chemical, an analgesic 10,000 times more potent than morphine. The high-tech development of drugs will eventually lead us to abuse our own body chemistry.

With the advent of monoclonal antibodies and genetic engineering, we are learning to produce pure biochemicals cheaply, artificially, by the

behavior. This is believed to occur most often as a result of inadequate socialization. In other words, deviants have not internalized the norms and values of society because they are either brought up in an environment of conflicting value systems (as are children of immigrants or the poor in a middle-class school) or are under the influence of a deviant subculture such as a gang. Since the order theorist uses the prevailing standards to define and label deviants, the existing practices and structures of society are accepted implicitly. The remedy is to rehabilitate the deviants so that they conform to the societal norms.

The conflict theorist takes a quite different approach to social problems. The adherents of this perspective criticize order theorists for "blaming the victim." To focus on the individual deviant is to locate the symptom, not the

198

ton. Imagine the vast coca fields of South America reduced to a few stainless steel vats neatly hidden in a basement in Medellin or San Francisco. Cheaper drugs, better quality, less risk, more profit—the logic of industrial commerce is very powerful. We have found no way to date to defeat the black-market drug industry, and the social, financial and technological factors are all very strongly on its side.

Now imagine yourself as a 21st century student, taking entrance exams for the law, or for medicine perhaps, while your competing fellow students enjoy the secret luxury of eidetic memory, enhanced IQ and perfect concentration. Could you resist that temptation when "everyone else is doing it"—and the cost of failure means the humiliating sacrifice of your ambitions?

Or imagine yourself as a failing TV journalist, when the stringers on the other networks can instantly remember every campaign promise the president ever made.

The irresistible logic of drugs confounds all attempts at repression, creating a maelstrom of money, guns and violence that has turned our inner cities into unprecedented war zones. The problem isn't stopping there, and it's not going to stop anywhere else in our society, either, because it is part of us, and inherent in the way we live and think.

Drugs are a technology like others. Like nuclear power, for instance, the tremendous potency of high-tech pharmacology has fearsome side effects.

That is the milieu in which we were born and raised; it is part and parcel of the culture all around us—the culture that invented cosmetic surgery, genetic engineering, antibiotics, telephones, jet travel and a thousand other glittering shortcuts to the Artificial Paradise. Our unstoppable cultural hunger for drugs is overwhelming evidence for this simple fact.

Already, today, we are busily investing billions in the basic medical research that will open a Pandora's box. The alternative is Luddism, to virtuously ignore this medical knowledge and plod on with the burdens of schizophrenia, cancer, AIDS, Alzheimer's disease and the simple God-given limits of what we used to call "the human condition." Ladies and gentlemen, we are not going to accept those limits, under any circumstances. We may give them pious lip service, but when it comes to the crunch, we will vote otherwise with our bloodstreams.

Sooner or later, we will stop trying to bail back the sea with a fork, and come to terms with this horrifically powerful transformation in our lives. The war against drugs is a lost cause; the only question is how many will die in the service of empty rhetoric.

Source: Bruce Sterling, "Addictions Undreamed of: The New Drug Technology," *New York Newsday* (September 5, 1989). Reprinted by permission.

disease. Individual deviants are a manifestation of a failure of society to meet the needs of individuals. The sources of crime, poverty, drug addiction, and racism are found in the laws, the customs, the quality of life, the distribution of wealth and power, and in the accepted practices of schools, governmental units, and corporations. The established system, in this view, is not "sacred." Since it is the primary source of social problems, it, not the individual deviant, must be restructured.

Since this is a text on society, we have emphasized and will continue to emphasize the conflict approach. The insights of this approach will be clarified further in the remainder of this book as we examine the structure and consequences of social inequality in the next four chapters, followed by five chapters describing the positive and negative effects of institutions.

TABLE 8–1
Assumptions of the Order and Conflict Models about Deviance*

Order Model	Conflict Model
Who is deviant? Those who break the rules of society.	Those who break the rules but also those who make the rules. Deviance is created by the powerful, who make the rules. Enactment and enforcement of these rules are used by the powerful to control potentially dissident groups and to maintain their own interests at the expense of those being ruled.
The legitimacy of deviance: Deviance is illegitimate, by definition.	Deviance of rule breakers can be legitimate because the rules are arbitrarily made and reflect a class bias. Deviance is also necessary to change an unjust society.
The causes of deviance: People are deviant because they have not been socialized to accept and obey the customs of society.	Deviance is caused by society, which makes the rules, the violation of which constitutes deviance. The inequities of society generate the behavior that the powerful label as deviant.
The solutions for deviance: Control by punishment and rehabilitation of deviant individuals (therapy, behavior modification, incarceration).	Restructure society (eliminate inequities, provide adequately for the needs of all members, a fair system of justice, laws that reflect the interest of all groups).

*(See Davis, 1975; Sykes, 1974; Horton, 1966; Skolnick and Currie, 1970; Chambliss, 1974, 1976).

CHAPTER REVIEW

1. Deviance is behavior that violates the laws and expectations of a group. This means that deviance is not a property inherent in a behavior but a property conferred upon that behavior by others. In short, deviance is socially created.

2. What is deviant varies from society to society and within a society the same behavior may be interpreted differently as it is done by different categories of persons.

3. The norms of the majority determine what behaviors will be considered deviant.

4. Order theorists point out that deviant behav-

ior has positive consequences for society because it gives the nondeviants a sense of solidarity and it reaffirms the importance of society's rules.

5. Conflict theorists argue that all views of rule violations have political implications. Punishment of deviants reflects a conservative bias by legitimating the norms and the current distribution of power. Support of the deviant behavior is also political because it rejects the legitimacy of those in power and their rules.

6. There are several traditional theories for the causes of deviance that assume the source as a fatal flaw in certain people. These are theories

that focus on physical or psychological reasons for deviant behavior.

7. "Kinds-of-people" explanations for deviance also apply to some theories by sociologists. One theory argues that crime results from the conditions of city life. Another places the blame on the influences of peers. A third focuses on the propensity of the poor to be deviants because of the gap between the goal of success and the lack of the means for these people to attain it. Finally, some have argued that lower-class culture is responsible.

8. These "kinds-of-people" theories have been criticized for blaming the victim. Because they blame the victim, the society (government, system of justice, education) is freed from blame. Because the established order is protected from criticism, necessary social change is thwarted.

9. An alternative to person-blame theories is labeling theory. This approach argues that while most people break the rules on occasion, the crucial factor in establishing a deviant career is the successful application of the label "deviant."

10. Who gets labeled as a deviant is not a matter of luck but the result of a systematic societal bias against the powerless.

11. Primary deviance is the rule breaking that occurs prior to labeling. Secondary deviance is that behavior resulting from the labeling process.

12. Labeling theorists argue that because de-

viants are not much different from nondeviants, the problem lies in organizations that label. Thus, these organizations should: (a) leave the deviants alone whenever possible; and (b) apply justice fairly when the legal approach is required.

13. Labeling theory has been criticized because it: (a) disregards undetected deviance; (b) assumes that deviants are really normal because we are all rule-breakers; (c) relieves the individual from blame; and (d) focuses on certain types of deviance but ignores deviance by the powerful.

14. Conflict theory focuses on social structure as the source of deviance. There is a historical bias in the law that favors the powerful. The administration of justice is also biased. In short, the state is a political organization controlled by the ruling class for its own advantage. The power of powerful interests in society determines what and who is deviant.

15. From the conflict perspective the only real and lasting solution to deviance is the radical transformation of society.

16. Order theorists focus on individual deviants. Because this perspective uses the prevailing standards to define and label deviants, the existing practices and structures of society are accepted implicitly. The remedy is to rehabilitate the deviants so they conform to the societal norms.

KEY TERMS

Deviance
Culture of poverty
Cultural deprivation
Recidivism

Social Darwinism
Labeling theory
Primary deviance
Secondary deviance

Radical nonintervention
Corporate crime
Political crime

STUDY QUESTIONS

1. Are there universal criteria that determine what is deviant at all times and places? Explain.
2. Most of us at one time or another behave in deviant ways. Why, then, aren't we considered deviants?
3. Explain how deviant behavior has *positive* social consequences for the group.

4. What is labeling theory? What are its strengths and weaknesses in understanding deviant behavior?
5. Contrast the order and conflict interpretations of deviance.

FOR FURTHER READING

Howard S. Becker, *The Outsiders: Studies in the Sociology of Deviance,* 2nd ed. (New York: Free Press, 1973).

D. Stanley Eitzen and Doug A. Timmer, *Criminology: Crime and Criminal Justice* (New York: John Wiley, 1985).

Kai Erikson, *Wayward Puritans: A Study in the Sociology of Deviance* (New York: John Wiley, 1966).

Erving Goffman, *Stigma: Notes on the Management of Spoiled Identity* (Englewood Cliffs, NJ: Prentice-Hall, 1963).

Edwin M. Lemert, *Human Deviance, Social Problems, and Social Control,* 2nd ed. (Englewood Cliffs, NJ): Prentice-Hall, 1972).

Harold E. Pepinsky and Paul Jesilow, *Myths That Cause Crime,* 2nd ed. (Cabin John, MD: 1985).

Richard Quinney, *The Social Reality of Crime* (Boston: Little, Brown, 1970).

Jeffrey H. Reiman, *The Rich Get Richer and the Poor Get Prison: Ideology, Class, and Criminal Justice,* 3rd ed. (New York: Macmillan, 1990).

Earl Rubington and Martin S. Weinberg, *The Study of Social Problems: Six Perspectives,* 4th ed. *(New York: Oxford University Press, 1989).*

William Ryan, Blaming the Victim, rev. ed. (New York: Vintage Books, 1976).

Edwin M. Schur, *The Politics of Deviance* (Englewood Cliffs, NJ: Prentice-Hall, 1980).

David R. Simon and D. Stanley Eitzen, *Elite Deviance,* 3rd ed. (Boston: Allyn and Bacon, 1990).

Chapter Nine

Social Stratification

The rewards in society are not distributed randomly. Consider, for example, these facts from 1987 (Census Bureau, 1989:446–448):

- The richest 20 percent of American families had 43.7 percent of the nation's income, while the poorest fifth had only 4.6 percent.
- The median family income for white families was $32,274; for Hispanic families it was $20,306; and for black families it was $18,098.
- Among year-round fulltime workers, the median income was $26,722 for males and $17,504 for females.

These data indicate a wide disparity in the distribution of economic resources in American society by class, race, and gender. The pattern of these structured inequities is called *social stratification*, the subject of this and the following three chapters.

Inequality is a fact of social life. All known societies have some system of ranking individuals and groups along a superiority-inferiority scale. This chapter examines these ranking systems. These structured systems of inequality are crucial to our understanding of human groups because they are important determinants of human behavior and because they have significant consequences for society and its members.

This chapter is divided into three sections. First, the important concepts are introduced. Second, the three major hierarchies—class, race, and gender—are described briefly. The third section describes and critiques the theories used to explain the universality of stratification systems and how hierarchies of dominant and subordinate groups are established and maintained.

MAJOR CONCEPTS

People differ in age, physical attributes, and in what they do for a living. The process of categorizing persons by age, height, occupation, or some other personal attribute is called **social differentiation.** When people are ranked in a vertical arrangement (hierarchy) that differentiates them as superior or inferior, we have **social stratification.** The key difference between differentiation and stratification is that the process of ranking or evaluation occurs only in the latter. What is ranked and how it is ranked are dependent upon the values of the society.

Social stratification refers, in essence, to structured social inequality. The term "structured" refers to stratification being socially patterned. This implies that inequalities are not caused by biological differences (for example, sex or race). Biological traits do not become relevant in patterns of social superiority or inferiority until they are socially recognized and given importance by being incorporated into the beliefs, attitudes, and values of the people in the society. Americans, for example, tend to believe that sexual and racial characteristics make a difference—therefore they do.

The social patterning of stratification is also found in the distribution of rewards in any community or society, since that distribution is governed by social norms. In American society few individuals seriously question the income differential between medical doctors and primary school teachers because the norms and values of society dictate that such inequalities are just.

Patterned behavior is also achieved through the socialization process. Each generation is taught the norms and values of the society and of its social class. The children of slaves and the children of the ruling family in a society are each taught the behavior "proper" for persons of their station in life.

Finally, the system of stratification is always connected with other aspects of the society. The existing stratification arrangements are affected by and have effects upon such matters as politics, marriage and the family, economics, education, and religion.

Harold Kerbo has summarized what is meant by social stratification:

> *Social stratification* means that inequality has been hardened or *institutionalized,* and there is a *system* of social relationships that determines who gets what, and why. When we say *institutionalized* we mean that a system of layered hierarchy has been established. People have come to expect that individuals and groups with certain positions will be able to demand more influence and respect and accumulate a greater share of goods and services. Such inequality

may or may not be accepted equally by a majority in the society, but it is recognized as the way things are. (Kerbo 1983:11)

The hierarchies of stratification—class, race, and gender—"place" groups, individuals, and families in the larger society. The crucial consequence of this "placement" is that the rewards and resources of society such as wealth, power, and privilege are unequally distributed. And, crucially, differential access to these societal resources and rewards produces different life experiences and different life chances. **Life chances** refer to the chances throughout one's life cycle to live and to experience the good things in life. Life chances are the most critical because they are those things that "(1) better-off people can purchase (good education, good medical care, comfortable homes, fine vacations, expert services of all kinds, safe and satisfying occupations) and which poor people would also purchase if they had the money; (2) . . . make life easier, longer, healthier, and more enjoyable" (Tumin, 1973:104). The converse, of course, is that people at the low end of the stratification hierarchies will have inadequate health care, shelter, and diets. Their lives will be more miserable and they will die sooner.

To understand American society we must understand the hierarchies of class, race, and gender. These structures of inequality array the resources and advantages of society in patterned ways. These hierarchies are also structured systems of exploitation and discrimination where the affluent dominate the poor, men dominate women, and whites dominate people of color (Feagin, 1986:21).

The hierarchies of class, race, and gender are interrelated systems of stratification. Economic resources, the bases of class, are not randomly distributed but vary systematically by race and sex. For example, people of color and women have fewer occupational choices than do white males. People of color and women often experience separate and unequal education and receive less income for the work they do resulting in different life chances.

Traditionally, the family has been viewed as the principal unit in the class system because it passes on wealth and resources from generation to generation. While the family is basic in maintaining stratification, life chances are affected by race and gender inequalities as well as social class. In most families, men have greater socioeconomic resources and more power and privileges than women even though all family members are viewed as members of the same social class. While a family's placement in the class hierarchy does determine rewards and resources, hierarchies based on sex create different conditions for women and men even within the same family (Acker, 1973). Systems of sex stratification cut across class and racial divisions to distribute resources differently to men and women (Baca Zinn and Eitzen, 1990, Chapter 4).

Class

When a number of persons occupy the same relative economic rank in the stratification system, they form a **social class.** Social class "implies having or not having the following: individual rights, privileges, power, rights over others, authority, life style choices, self-determination, status, wealth, access to services, comfort, leisure, etc." (Comer, 1978:171). Persons are socially located in a class position on the basis of income, occupation, and education, either alone or in combination. In the past, the occupation, income, and education of the husband determined the class location of the family. But family behavior is better explained by locating families according to the more prestigious occupation, regardless of whether it is the husband's or the wife's (Yorburg, 1983:189). Occupations are part of the larger opportunity structure of society. Those that are highly valued and carry high income rewards are unevenly distributed. The amount of income determines how well a given household can acquire the resources needed for survival and perhaps for luxury. The job or occupation which is the source of that paycheck connects families with the opportunity structure in different ways. This connection generates different kinds of class privileges for families. **Privilege** refers to the distribution of goods and services, situations, and experiences that are highly valued and beneficial (Jeffries and Ransford, 1980:68). Class privileges are those advantages, prerogatives, and options that are available to those in the middle and upper class. They involve help from "the system": banks, credit unions, medical facilities, and voluntary associations. Class privileges are based on the systematic linkages between families and society. Class privilege creates many differences in family patterns.

Race

Racial and ethnic stratification refers to systems of inequality in which some fixed group membership such as race, religion, or national origin is a major criterion for ranking social positions and their differential rewards. Like the class system, this hierarchy represents institutionalized power, privilege, and prestige. Racial and ethnic hierarchies generate domination and subordination, often referred to as majority-minority relations. Minority groups are those that are dominated by a more powerful group and are stigmatized and singled out for differential treatment.

A **racial group** is socially defined on the basis of a presumed common genetic heritage resulting in distinguishing physical characteristics. **Ethnicity** refers to the condition of being culturally rather than physically distinctive. Ethnic peoples are bound together by virtue of a common ancestry and a common cultural background.

A racial group that has a distinctive culture or subculture, shares a common heritage, and has developed a common identity is also an ethnic group. Both race and ethnicity are traditional bases for systems of inequality, although there are historical and contemporary differences in the societal placement of racial-ethnics and white-ethnics in this society. We will examine how racial stratification deprives people of color of equal access to society's resources and thereby creates family patterns that are different from the idealized family model.

The most important feature of racial stratification is the exclusion of people of color from equal access to society's valued resources. People of color or racial-ethnics have less power, wealth, and social status than other Americans. Blacks, Hispanics, and Asian Americans constitute the largest of the racial minorities in American society.

Gender

The stratification system that assigns women's and men's roles unequally is the **sex-gender system.** It consists of two complementary yet mutually exclusive categories into which all human beings are placed. The sex-gender system combines biologically based sex roles with socially created gender roles. In everyday life, the terms "sex role" and "gender role" are used interchangeably. This obscures important differences and underlying issues in the study of women's and men's experiences. **Sex roles** refer to behaviors determined by an individual's biological sex. **Gender roles** are social constructions; they contain self-concepts, psychological traits, as well as family, occupational, and political roles assigned dichotomously to each sex. For example, the traditional female gender role includes expectations for females to be passive, nurturant, and dependent. The standard male gender role incorporates alternative expectations—behavior that is aggressive, competitive, and independent (Lipman-Blumen, 1984:1–2).

Patriarchy is the term for forms of social organization in which men are dominant over women. As we see in Chapter 12 patriarchy is infused throughout American society. Generally, men have more power than women and they also tend to have greater power over women as well. While there is considerable class and racial variation here, men in general gain some privilege at the expense of women. In sum, the sex-gender system distributes power, resources, prestige, and privilege unequally.

THEORIES OF STRATIFICATION

There are two fundamental questions about stratification that sociologists and other observers of society have pondered. The first is, "Why are societies stratified?" The second is, "Within stratified societies, why are certain categories ranked as superior while others are considered inferior?" There are alternative theoretical explanations for each of these important questions and each has important implications. Let's begin with the two sociological theories for the more general and logically prior question.

All societies have some form of stratification. How is this universal phenomenon to be explained? Sociologists answer this question from either the order or the conflict perspective. The position of the order theorists is basically supportive of inequality, since the unequal distribution of rewards is assumed to be not only inevitable but necessary. Conflict theorists, on the other hand, tend to denounce the distributive system as basically unjust, unnecessary, and the source of many social problems.

Order Theory

Adherents of the order model begin with the fact that social inequality is a ubiquitous and apparently unavoidable phenomenon. They reason that inequality must, therefore, serve a useful function for society. The argument, as presented in the classic statement by Davis and Moore, is as follows (Davis and Moore, 1945): The smooth functioning of society requires that various tasks be accomplished through a division of labor. There is a universal problem, then, of allocation—of getting the most important tasks done by the most talented people. Some jobs are more important for societal survival than others (typically persons involved in decision making, medicine, religion, teaching, and the military). The societal problem is how to get the most talented people motivated to go through the required long periods of training and to do these important tasks well. The universally found answer, according to Davis and Moore, is differential rewards. Society must provide suitable rewards (money, prestige, and power) to induce individuals to fill these positions. The rewards must, it is argued, be distributed unevenly to various positions because the positions are not equally pleasant or equally important. Thus, a differential reward system guarantees that the important societal functions are fulfilled, thereby ensuring the maintenance of society. In this way, differential ranks actually serve to unify society through a division of labor (functional integration) and through the socialization of persons to accept their positions in the system. Although there probably is some truth to this argument, the analyst of American society must also ask: Is inequality primarily integrative or divisive? Is it necessary? Must the poor always be with us? (see Tumin, 1953; Huaco, 1966).

Conflict Theory

Conflict theorists view stratification in a wholly different manner from the order theorists. Rather than accepting stratification as a source of societal integration, the conflict perspective assumes that stratification reflects the distribution of power in society and is therefore a major source of discord and coercion. It is a source of discord because groups compete for scarce resources and because the powerless, under certain conditions, resent their lowly position and lack of rewards. Coercion results from stratification as the powerful (who are coincidentally male, white, and wealthy) prey on the weak. From this view, then, the unequal distribution of rewards reflects the interests of the powerful and not the basic survival needs of society as the order theorists contend.

A major contention of the conflict theorists is that the powerful use ideology to make their value system paramount. Karl Marx argued that the dominant ideology in any society is always the ideology of the ruling class. The ruling class uses the media, schools, religion, and other institutions to legitimate systems of inequality. So powerful is this socialization process that even oppressed peoples tend to accept their low status as "natural." Marx called this tendency of the oppressed to accept their oppression **false consciousness** (see Marx and Engels, 1959; and Parenti, 1978:15–18). The working class and the poor in the United States, for example, tend to accept their lack of monetary rewards, power, and prestige because they believe that the system is truly meritocratic—and that they lack the skills and brains to do the better-rewarded tasks in society. In short, they believe that they deserve their fate (see Sennett and Cobb, 1973). Consequently, they accept a differential reward system and the need for supervision and decision making left to "experts." False consciousness thus inhibits efforts by the disadvantaged to change an oppressive system. Marx argued, however, that when the oppressed became aware of their common oppression and that they have been manipulated by the powerful to serve the interests of the powerful, they will develop a **class consciousness**—an objective awareness of their common exploitation—thus becoming unified in a cause to advance their class interests.

While it is true that social stratification is an important source of societal friction, conflict theorists have not answered the important question as to its necessity (neither have the order theorists for that matter, although they address themselves directly to that question). Both models have important insights that we must consider. The order theorists see stratification serving the useful function of societal maintenance by providing a mechanism (differential rewards) to ensure that all the slots in the division of labor are filled. Conflict theorists are equally valid in their contention that stratification is unjust, divisive, and a source of social instability or change.

DEFICIENCY THEORIES

Some categories of people are systematically disadvantaged in American society, most especially the poor, nonwhites, and women. Is there some flaw within these groups—perhaps biological or cultural—that explains their inferiority? Or is it the structure of society that blocks their progress while encouraging the advancement of others? To answer these questions we will examine the various explanations for poverty. The specific explanations for inequities by race and gender are addressed in detail in the appropriate chapter, using the same explanatory categories used to understand poverty. Who or what is to blame for poverty? There are two very different answers to these questions (Barrera, 1979:174–219). One is that the poor are in that condition because of some deficiency: either they are biologically inferior or their culture fails them by promoting character traits that impede their progress in society. The other response places the blame on the structure of society: some persons are poor because society has failed to provide equality in educational opportunity, because institutions discriminate against minorities, because private industry has failed to provide enough jobs, because automation has made some jobs obsolete, and so forth. In this view, society has worked in such a way as to trap certain persons and their offspring in a condition of poverty.

Biological Inferiority

In 1882 the British philosopher and sociologist Herbert Spencer came to the United States to promote a theory later known as *Scial Darwinism.* He argued

How Science Is Affected by the Political Climate

The following essay is by Stephen Jay Gould, Harvard professor of evolutionary biology. Gould argues that scientists—all scientists—are enmeshed in a web of personal and social circumstances that affect their science. Leftist geneticists, for example, are more likely to combat biological determinism just as politically conservative geneticists favor interpretations of inequality as the reflection of genetic inadequacies of people.

Social disparities as "a product of nature"

The rise and fall in popularity of scientific theories correlates with changes in the political and social climate. That's why, as the nation moves to the right politically, arguments for biological determinism are bound to become popular. The determinists' message is that existing inequalities in society are a reflection of the intrinsic character of people and are not the fault of social institutions. Determinists are saying that disparities are a product of nature and therefore cannot be alleviated by very expensive social programs.

Similarly, the hereditarian version of IQ, which holds that you are measuring something that's inherited and unchangeable, flourished in the 1920s, the age of Sacco and Vanzetti and of jingoism inspired by World War I. The hereditarians argued that the single number called IQ could capture the multifarious and complexities of the concept of intelligence and that you could rank races, classes and sexes on the basis of their average scores. To think that a whole host of abilities could be encompassed in a meaningful way by a single number is fundamentally fallacious. An approach which recognizes that *intelligence* is a word we give to an irreducible set of multifarious abilities might lead to a more adequate assessment.

The "grievous consequences" of IQ testing

I don't deny there is biology involved in some human abilities. I'd never be a marathon runner no matter how hard I trained, and I'll certainly never be a basketball player, because I am too short. But it is one thing to acknowledge that there is biology behind a lot of what we do; it is quite another to say that abilities are the result of intrinsic and unalterable heredity.

Yet today there are still many people, including some scientists, who think, in their heart of hearts, that IQ tests are measuring that the poor were poor because they were unfit. Poverty was nature's way of "excreting . . . unhealthy, imbecile, slow, vacillating, faithless members" of society in order to make room for the "fit," who were duly entitled to the rewards of wealth. Spencer preached that the poor should not be helped through state or private charity, because such acts would interfere with nature's way of getting rid of the weak (*The Progressive*, 1980; see also Hofstadter, 1955). Social Darwinism has generally lacked support in the scientific community, although it has continued to provide a rationale for the thinking of many individuals. Recently, however, the concept has resurfaced in the work of two respected scientists. Both suggest that the poor are in that condition because they do not measure up to the more well-to-do in intellectual endowment.

Arthur Jensen, professor of educational psychology at the University of California, has argued that there is a strong possibility that blacks are less

something intrinsic and permanent. That kind of thinking has had grievous social consequences for many groups in American society.

"Scientists reflect the prejudices of their lives" In evaluating these and other arguments by scientists, it is important that people be wary of the claim that science stands apart from other human institutions because its methodology leads to objective knowledge. People need to realize that scientists are human beings like everybody else and that their pronouncements may arise from their social prejudices, as any of our pronouncements might. The public should avoid being snowed by the scientist's line: "Don't think about this for yourself because it's all too complicated."

I wish scientists scrutinized more rigidly the sources of justification for their beliefs. If they did, they might realize that some of their findings do not derive from a direct investigation of nature but are rooted in assumptions growing out of experience and beliefs.

But don't draw from what I have said the negative implication that science is a pack of lies—that it's merely social prejudice. On the one hand, science is embedded in society, and scientists reflect the social prejudices of their own lives and those of their class and culture. On the other hand, I believe that there are correct answers to questions, and science, in its own bumbling, socially conditioned manner, stumbles toward those answers.

Gauging "the truth value of an idea" In evaluating science, a distinction has to be drawn between where an idea comes from and how worthy it is. The truth value of an idea is independent of its source, but when you know its source, you might get more suspicious about its potential truth value.

Darwin's theory of natural selection, for example, came directly out of a social context: It was essentially Adam Smith's economics read into nature. Without Adam Smith and the whole school of Scottish economics, I doubt that Darwin would ever have thought of it. Yet Darwin was right, in large measure. So social conditioning doesn't make an idea wrong; it does mean you have to scrutinize it.

Source: Stephen Jay Gould, "How Science Changes With the Political Climate." Reprinted from *U.S. News & World Report* issue of March 1, 1982. Copyright 1982, U.S. News & World Report, p. 62. Reprinted by permission of the publisher.

well endowed mentally than whites. From his review of the research on IQ, he claimed that approximately 80 percent of IQ is inherited, while the remaining 20 percent is attributable to environment. Since blacks differ significantly from whites in achievement on IQ tests and in school, Jensen claimed that it is reasonable to hypothesize that the sources of these differences are genetic as well as environmental (Jensen, 1969; 1980).

Richard Herrnstein, a Harvard psychologist, agrees with Jensen that intelligence is largely inherited, and goes one step further positing the formation of hereditary castes based on intelligence (Herrnstein, 1971; 1973). For Herrnstein, social stratification by inborn differences occurs because: (1) mental ability is inherited, and (2) success (prestige of job and earnings) depends on mental ability. Thus, a meritocracy (social classification by ability) develops through the sorting process. This reasoning assumes that persons close in mental ability are more likely to marry and reproduce, thereby ensuring castes by level of intelligence. According to this thesis, "in times to

Social Darwinists would argue that this person is advantaged because of superior inherited intellectual capacity.

come, as technology advances, the tendency to be unemployed may run in the genes of a family about as certainly as bad teeth do now" (Herrnstein, 1971:63). This is another way of saying that the bright people are in the upper classes and the dregs are at the bottom. Inequality is justified just as it was years ago by the social Darwinists.

To buttress their claim for the overwhelming primacy of heredity over environment in intelligence, both Jensen and Herrnstein used data from the classic studies of identical twins by the famous British psychologist Sir Cyril Burt. These studies from the 1940s and 1950s have come under a cloud of suspicion. Burt, who died in 1971, has been accused of fraud, of having faked much of his research, of reporting tests that were never done, and of signing fictitious names as coauthors.

Notwithstanding the flaws in the logic and in the evidence used by Jensen and Herrnstein, it is important to consider the implications of this thesis for dealing with the problem of poverty.

Jensen and Herrnstein have argued that dispassionate study is required to determine whether intelligence is inherited to the degree that they state. Objectivity is the *sine qua non* of scientific inquiry, and one cannot argue with its merits. We should recognize, however, the important social consequences implied by the Jensen-Herrnstein argument. First, this argument is a classic example of blaming the victim. The individual poor person is blamed instead of schools, culturally biased IQ tests, or social barriers of race, religion, or nationality. By blaming the victim, this thesis claims a relationship between lack of success and lack of intelligence. This is a spurious relationship because it ignores the advantages and disadvantages of ascribed status. According to William Ryan, "Arthur Jensen and Richard Herrnstein confirm regretfully that black folks and poor folks are born stupid, that little rich kids grow up rich adults, not because they inherited Daddy's stock portfolio, but rather because they inherited his brains" (Ryan, 1972b:54).

A second implication is the belief that poverty is inevitable. The "survival of the fittest" capitalist ideology is reinforced, justifying both discrimination against the poor and privilege for the privileged. Inequality is rationalized so that little will be done to aid its victims. The acceptance of this thesis, then, has obvious consequences for what policy decisions will be made or not made in dealing with poverty.

This thesis divides Americans further by appealing to bigots. It provides scientific justification for their beliefs in the racial superiority of some groups and the inferiority of others. By implication, it legitimates segregation and unequal treatment of "inferiors." The goal of integration and the fragile principle of egalitarianism are seriously threatened to the degree that members of the scientific community give this thesis credence or prominence (McGahey, 1981).

Another serious implication of the Jensen-Herrnstein argument is the explicit validation of the IQ test as a legitimate measure of intelligence. The IQ test attempts to measure "innate potential," but to do this is impossible, because the testing process must inevitably reflect some of the skills that develop during the individual's lifetime. For the most part, intelligence tests measure educability—that is, the prediction of conventional school achievement. Achievement in school is, of course, also associated with a cluster of other social and motivational factors, as Joanna Ryan observes.

> The test as a whole is usually validated, if at all, against the external criterion of school performance. It therefore comes as no surprise to find that IQ scores do in fact correlate highly with educational success. IQ scores are also found to correlate positively with socio-economic status, those in the upper social classes tending to have the highest IQs. Since social class, and all that this implies, is both an important determinant and also an important consequence of educational performance, this association is to be expected. (Ryan, 1972a:54)

The Jensen-Herrnstein thesis, however, overlooks the important contribution of social class to achievement on IQ tests. This oversight is crucial, since most social scientists feel that these tests are biased in favor of those who have had a middle- and upper-class environment and experience. IQ tests discriminate against the poor in many ways. They discriminate obviously in the language that is used, in the instructions that are given, and in the experiences they assume the subjects have had. The discrimination can also be more subtle. For minority-group examinees, the race of the person administering the test influences the results. Another, less well-known fact about IQ tests is that in many cases they provide a self-fulfilling prophecy, as this observer notes:

Blaming the Poor

A continuing controversy is what to do about the urban poor. Edward Banfield, a distinguished professor of urban government at Harvard and chairperson of President Nixon's task force on model cities, has written a highly controversial book that presents the conservative assessment of the urban condition.

In Banfield's view, the urban poor have a culture of poverty that dooms them and their descendants to the lowest social class. The essence of the poor subcultures is a present-time orientation.

> The lower-class individual lives from moment to moment. If he has any awareness of a future, it is of something fixed, fated, beyond his control: things happen to him, he does not make them happen. Impulse governs his behavior, either because he cannot discipline himself to sacrifice a present for a future satisfaction or because he has no sense of the future. He is therefore radically improvident: whatever he cannot consume immediately he considers valueless. His bodily needs (especially for sex) and his taste for "action" take precedence over everything else—and certainly over any work routine. He works only

as he must to stay alive, and drifts from one unskilled job to another, taking no interest in his work.

The poor are doomed by their hedonism. But according to Banfield, the culture of poverty is such that it makes the slums actually desirable to the slum dwellers.

> Although he has more "leisure" than almost anyone, the indifference ("apathy" if one prefers) of the lower-class person is such that he seldom makes even the simplest repairs to the place that he lives in. He is not troubled by dirt and dilapidation and he does not mind the inadequacy of public facilities such as schools, parks, hospitals, and libraries; indeed, where such things exist he may destroy them by carelessness or even by vandalism. Conditions that make the slum repellent to others are serviceable to him in several ways. First, the slum is a place of excitement— "where the action is." Nothing happens there by plan and anything may happen by accident—a game, a fight, a tense confrontation with the police; feeling that something exciting is about to happen is highly congenial to people who live for the present and for whom the present is often empty. Second, it is a place

---

> IQ scores obtained at one age often determine how an individual is subsequently treated, and, in particular, what kind of education he receives as a consequence of IQ testing will in turn contribute to his future IQ, and it is notorious that those of low and high IQ do not get equally good education. (Ryan, 1972a:44)

The Jensen-Herrnstein thesis also provides justification for unequal schooling. Why should school boards allot comparable sums of money for similar programs in middle-class schools and lower-class schools if the natural endowments of children in each type of school are so radically different? Why should teachers expect the same performance from poor children as from children from the more well-to-do? The result of such beliefs is, of course, a self-fulfilling prophecy. Low expectations beget low achievement.

Finally, the Jensen-Herrnstein thesis encourages policymakers either to ignore poverty or to attack its effects rather than its causes in the structure of society itself.

of opportunity. Just as some districts of the city are specialized as a market, for, say, jewelry or antiques, so the slum is specialized as one for vice and for illicit commodities generally. Dope peddlers, prostitutes, and receivers of stolen goods are all readily available there, within easy reach of each other and of their customers and victims. For "hustlers," the slum is the natural headquarters. Third, it is a place of concealment. A criminal is less visible to the police in the slum than elsewhere, and the lower-class individual, who in some parts of the city would attract attention, is one among many there. In the slum one can beat one's children, lie drunk in the gutter, or go to jail without attracting any special notice; these are things that most of the neighbors themselves have done and that they consider quite normal.

As Banfield sees it, the poor are the cause of urban problems:

So long as the city contains a sizeable lower class, nothing basic can be done about its most serious problems. Good jobs may be offered to all, but some will remain chronically unemployed. Slums may be demolished, but if the housing that replaces them is occupied by the lower class it will shortly be turned into new slums. Welfare payments may be doubled or tripled and a negative income tax substituted, but some persons will continue to live in squalor and misery. New schools may be built, new curricula devised, and the teacher-pupil ratio cut in half, but if the children who attend these schools come from lower-class homes, they will be turned into blackboard jungles, and those who graduate or drop out from them will, in most cases, be functionally illiterate. The streets may be filled with armies of policemen, but violent crime and civil disorder will decrease very little. If, however, the lower classes were to disappear—if say, its members were overnight to acquire the attitudes, motivations, and habits of the working class—the most serious and intractable problems of the city would all disappear with it. . . . The lower-class forms of all problems are at bottom a single problem: the existence of an outlook and style of life which is radically present-oriented and which therefore attaches no value to work, sacrifice, self-improvement, or service to family, friends, or community.

Source: Edward C. Banfield, *The Unheavenly City Revisited* (Boston: Little, Brown, 1974):61, 72, 234–235. Copyright © 1968, 1970, 1974 by Edward C. Banfield. Reprinted by permission of the author.

Cultural Inferiority

One prominent explanation of poverty, called the **culture of poverty** hypothesis, contends that the poor are qualitatively different in values and lifestyles from the rest of society *and that these cultural differences explain continued poverty.* In other words, the poor, in adapting to their deprived condition, are found to be more permissive in raising their children, less verbal, more fatalistic, less apt to defer gratification, and less likely to be interested in formal education than the more well-to-do. Most important is the contention that this deviant cultural pattern is transmitted from generation to generation. Thus, there is a strong implication that poverty is perpetuated by defects in the lifeways of the poor. If poverty itself were to be eliminated, the former poor would probably continue to prefer instant gratification, be immoral by middle-class standards, and so on. Panel 9–2 provides an illustration by Edward Banfield, an eminent political scientist, who views the poor in this manner. Banfield presents a classic example of *blaming the victim.* To him, the poor have a subculture with values that differ radically from the other social classes. He does not see the present-time orientation of the poor as a function of the hopelessness of their situation. Yet it seems highly unlikely that the poor see little reason to complain about the slums: What about the filth, the rats, the overcrowded living conditions, the high infant mortality? What about the lack of jobs and opportunity for upward mobility? This feeling of being trapped seems the primary cause of hedonistic present-time orientation. If the structure were changed so that the poor could see that hard work and deferred gratification really paid off, they could adopt a future-time orientation.

Critics of the culture of poverty hypothesis argue that the poor are an integral part of American society; they do not abandon the dominant values of the society, but rather, retain them while simultaneously holding an alternative set of values. This alternative set is a result of adaptation to the conditions of poverty. Elliot Liebow, in his classic study of lower-class black men, has taken this view. For him, streetcorner men strive to live by American values but are continually frustrated by externally imposed failure:

> From this perspective, the streetcorner man does not appear as a carrier of an independent cultural tradition. His behavior appears not so much as a way of realizing the distinctive goals and values of his own subculture, or of conforming to its models, but rather as his way of trying to achieve many of the goals and values of the larger society, of failing to do this and of concealing his failure from others and from himself as best he can. (Liebow, 1967:222; see also Rodman, 1963; Hannerz, 1969)

Most Americans, however, believe that the poor are poor because they have a deviant system of values that encourages behaviors leading to poverty (Feagin, 1972; *Socioeconomic Newsletter,* 1978). Current research shows that this prevailing view is a myth. If there were a culture of poverty, then there would be a relatively large proportion of the poor that would constitute a permanent "underclass." The deviant values and resulting behaviors of the poor would doom them and their children to continuous poverty. But the University of Michigan's Panel Study of Income Dynamics (Duncan, 1984) followed 5000 representative households for ten years and found that only 2.6 percent fit the stereotype of permanent poverty. Contrary to common belief, most poor people are poor only temporarily; their financial fortunes rise and fall with widowhood, divorce, remarriage, acquiring a job with decent pay or losing one, or other changes affecting economic status. The 2.6 percent who are persistently poor are different from the temporarily poor: 62 percent are black, compared with 19 percent; 39 percent are disabled, compared with 17 percent; one-third are elderly compared with 14 percent; and 61 percent were female heads of households compared with 28 percent of the temporarily poor. Examining just the two-thirds of the persistently poor who are not elderly, 65 percent live in households headed by women and almost three-quarters of these women are black (Duncan, 1984:48–52). These facts show once again the interconnections of race and gender in understanding inequality in American society and, as we will see in the next section, how inequality

is structured by race and gender. The other important implication of these findings is that inequality negates the culture of poverty. Duncan and his colleagues find little evidence that poverty is a consequence of the way poor people think. Economic success is not a function of "good" values and behaviors and failure the result of "bad" ones. Thus, the solution to poverty is not to change the attitudes of "flawed persons" but to change the opportunity structures in society (Duncan, 1984:65).

STRUCTURAL THEORIES

In contrast to blaming the biological or cultural deficiencies of the poor, there is the view that the way in which society is organized creates poverty and makes certain kinds of people especially vulnerable to being poor.

Institutional Discrimination

Michael Harrington, whose book *The Other America* was instrumental in sparking the federal government's War on Poverty, has said, "The real explanation of why the poor are where they are is that they made the mistake of being born to the wrong parents, in the wrong section of the country, in the wrong industry, or in the wrong racial or ethnic group" (Harrington, 1963:21). This is another way of saying that the society is to blame for poverty, not the poor. Customary ways of doing things, prevailing attitudes and expectations, and accepted structural arrangements work to the disadvantage of the poor. Let us look at several examples of the way in which the poor are trapped.

Most good jobs require a college degree, but the poor cannot afford to send their children to college. Scholarships go to the best-performing students. Children of the poor most often do not perform well in school, largely because of low expectations for them among teachers and administrators.

Who Benefits from Poverty?

Herbert Gans, a sociologist, has some interesting insights about the benefits of poverty. He begins with the assumption that if some social arrangement persists, it must be accomplishing something important (at least in the view of the powerful in society). What, then, does the existence of a relatively large number of persons in a condition of poverty accomplish that is beneficial to the powerful?

1. Poverty functions to provide a low-wage labor pool that is willing (or unable to be unwilling) to do society's necessary "dirty work." The middle and upper classes are subsidized by the existence of economic activities that depend on the poor (low wages to many workers in restaurants, hospitals, and in truck farming).
2. The poor also subsidize a variety of economic activities for the affluent by supporting, for example, innovations in medicine (as patients in research hospitals or as guinea pigs in medical experiments) and providing servants, gardeners, and house cleaners who make life easier for the more well-to-do.
3. The existence of poverty creates jobs for a number of occupations and professions that serve the poor or protect the rest of society from them (penologists, social workers, police, pawn shop owners, numbers racketeers, and owners of liquor stores). The presence of poor people also provides incomes for doctors, lawyers, teachers, and others who are too old, poorly trained, or incompetent to attract more affluent clients.
4. Poor people subsidize merchants by purchasing products that others do not want (seconds, dilapidated cars, deteriorated housing, day-old bread, fruit, and vegetables) and that otherwise would have little or no value.
5. The poor serve as a group to be punished in order to uphold the legitimacy of conventional values (hard work, thrift, honesty, and monogamy). *The poor provide living proof that moral deviance does not pay,* and thus, an indirect rationale for blaming the victim.
6. Poverty guarantees the status of those who are not poor. The poor, by occupying a position at the bottom of the status hierarchy, provide a reliable and relatively permanent measuring rod for status comparison, particularly by those just above them (that is, the working

This is reflected in the system of "tracking" by ability as measured on class-biased examinations. Further evidence is found in the disproportionately low amounts of money given to schools in impoverished neighborhoods. All of these acts result in a self-fulfilling prophecy—the poor are not expected to do well in school and they do not. Since they are failures as measured by "objective" indicators (such as the disproportionately high number of dropouts and discipline problems and the very small proportion who desire to go to college), the school feels justified in its discrimination toward the children of the poor.

The poor are also trapped because they get sick more often and stay sick longer than the more well-to-do. The reasons, of course, are that they cannot afford preventive medicine, proper diets, and proper medical attention when ill. The high incidence of sickness among the poor means either that they will be fired from their jobs or that they will not receive money for the days missed from work (unlike the more well-to-do, who usually have jobs with such fringe benefits as sick leave and paid-up medical insurance). Not receiving a paycheck for extended periods means that the poor will have even less money

class, whose politics, for example, are often influenced by the need to maintain social distance between themselves and the poor).

7. The poor aid in the upward mobility of others. A number of persons have entered the middle class through the profits earned from providing goods and services in the slums (pawn shops, second-hand clothing and furniture stores, gambling, prostitution, and drugs).

8. The poor, being powerless, can be made to absorb the costs of change in society. In the nineteenth century they did the backbreaking work that built the railroads and the cities. Today they are the ones pushed out of their homes by urban renewal, the building of expressways, parks, and stadia. Many economists assume that a degree of unemployment is necessary to fight inflation. The poor, who are "first to be fired and the last to be hired," are the ones who make the sacrifice for the economy.

Gans notes:

This analysis is not intended to suggest that because it is often functional, poverty *should* exist, or that it *must* exist. For one thing, poverty has many more dysfunctions than func-

tions; for another, it is possible to suggest functional alternatives. For example, society's dirty work could be done without poverty, either by automation or by paying "dirty workers" decent wages. Nor is it necessary for the poor to subsidize the many activities they support through their low-wage jobs. This would, however, drive up the costs of these activities, which would result in higher prices to their customers and clients. . . .

In sum, then, many of the functions served by the poor could be replaced if poverty were eliminated, but almost always at higher costs to others, particularly more affluent others. Consequently a functional analysis [equivalent to the order model] must conclude that poverty persists not only because many of the functional alternatives to poverty would be quite dysfunctional for the affluent members of society. . . . Poverty can be eliminated only when they become dysfunctional for the affluent or powerful, or when the powerless can obtain enough power to change society. (p. 24)

Source: Herbert J. Gans, "The Uses of Power: The Poor Pay All." *Social Policy* 2 (July-August 1971):20–24. Copyright © 1971 by Social Policy Corporation. Reprinted by permission of the publisher.

for proper health care—thereby ensuring an even higher incidence of sickness. Thus, there is a vicious cycle of poverty. The poor will tend to remain poor, and their children tend to perpetuate the cycle.

The traditional organization of schools and jobs in American society has limited the opportunities of racial minorities and women. Chapters 11 and 12 describe at length how these groups are systematically disadvantaged by the prevailing laws, customs, and expectations of society. Suffice it to say in this context that:

- Racial minorities are deprived of equal opportunities for education, jobs, and income.
- Women typically work at less prestigious jobs than men and when working at equal status jobs receive less pay and fewer chances for advancement.

The Political Economy of Society

The basic tenet of capitalism—that who gets what is determined by private profit rather than collective need—explains the persistence of poverty (Parenti, 1978:54–55). The primacy of maximizing profit works to promote poverty in several ways. First, employers are constrained to pay their workers the least possible in wages and benefits. Only a portion of the wealth created by the laborers is distributed to them; the rest goes to the owners for investment and profit. This means that it is important for employers to keep wages low. That they are successful in this is demonstrated by the millions of poor people who work full-time but remain under the poverty level. Second, since the price of labor is determined by the supply, it is in the interest of employers to have a surplus of laborers (Smith, 1981:299–331). It is especially important to have a supply of undereducated and desperate people who will work for very low wages. A large supply of these marginal people (such as minorities, women, undocumented workers) aid the ownership class by depressing the wages for all workers in good times and provide the obvious category of people to be laid off from work in economic downturns.

A third impact of the primacy of profits in capitalism is that employers make investment decisions without regard for their employees (potential or actual). If costs can be reduced, employers will purchase new technologies to replace workers (such as robots to replace assembly line workers and word processors to replace secretaries). Similarly, owners may shut down a plant and shift their operations to a foreign country where wages are significantly lower.

In sum, the fundamental assumption of capitalism is individual gain without regard for what the resulting behaviors may mean for others. The capitalist system, then, should not be accepted as a neutral framework within which goods are produced and distributed, but rather as an economic system that perpetuates inequality.

A number of political factors complement the workings of the economy to perpetuate poverty. Political decisions to fight inflation with high interest rates, for example, will hurt several industries, particularly automobiles and home construction, causing high unemployment.

The powerful in society also use their political clout to keep society unequal.

> Poverty exists in America because the society is unequal, and there are over-whelming political pressures to keep it that way. Any attempt to redistribute wealth and income will inevitably be opposed by powerful interests. Some people can be relatively rich only if others are relatively poor, and since power is concentrated in the hands of the rich, public policies will continue to reflect their interests. (Robertson, 1981:271)

Clearly, the affluent in a capitalist society will resist efforts to redistribute their wealth to the disadvantaged. Their political efforts are, rather, to increase their benefits at the expense of the poor and the powerless (see Panel 9–3). In short, they work for laws beneficial to them, sympathetic elected and appointed officials, policies based on "trickle-down" economics, and favorable tax laws such as low capital gains taxes and regressive taxes.

In sum, we have examined three stratification systems—the social class system, the system based on race and ethnicity, and the sex-gender system. By definition, in each stratification system certain categories of people are

TABLE 9–1
Varying Explanations of Inequality by Class, Race, and Gender

Explanations for Inequality	Structures of Inequality		
	Class	Race	Gender
Biological inferiority	Social Darwinism, the poor are unfit.	Jensen/Herrnstein: Blacks are less endowed mentally than whites.	Women are biologically different from men: weaker, less aggressive, more nurturant, less able in mathematics and spatial relationships but better in language.
Cultural inferiority	Culture of poverty, the poor have a maladaptive value system that dooms them and their children.	Blacks have loose morals, unstable families, do not value education, and lack motivation.	Gender role socialization leads females to accept society's devalued roles, to be passive, and to be secondary to males.
Structural discrimination	The dominant use their power to maintain advantage. The poor are trapped by segmented labor markets, tracking in schools, and other structural arrangements.	Institutional racism blocks opportunities. Segmented labor markets, use of biased tests for jobs, school placement, residential segregation.	Institutional sexism limits women's chances in legal system, job markets, wages, etc. Patriarchy where men are dominant over women through organizational norms.

considered inferior and treated unfairly. Various theories have provided the rationales for this alleged inferiority. A review of these explanations is found in Table 9–1, which summarizes the theories used to explain why the poor are poor as discussed in this chapter, and which anticipates the discussion of racial and gender inequalities found in Chapters 11 and 12.

CHAPTER REVIEW

1. The process of categorizing people on some dimension(s) is called social differentiation.
2. When people are ranked in a hierarchy that differentiates them as superior or inferior this is called social stratification.
3. The three hierarchies of stratification—class, race, and gender—"place" groups, families, and individuals in the larger society. The rewards and resources of society are unequally distributed according to this "placement." Most crucially, this social location determines for people the chances for a longer, healthier, and more enjoyable life.

4. Order model theorists accept social inequality as universal and natural. They believe that inequality serves a basic function by motivating the most talented people to perform the most important tasks.

5. Conflict theorists tend to denounce social inequality as basically unjust, unnecessary, and the source of many social problems. The irony is that the oppressed often accept their deprivation. Conflict theorists view this as the result of false consciousness—the acceptance through the socialization process of an untrue belief that works to one's disadvantage.

6. The explanations for why some categories of people are ranked at the bottom of the various hierarchies of stratification are biological, cultural, or structural.

7. The biological explanation for poverty is that the poor are innately inferior. Arthur Jensen and Richard Herrnstein, for example, have argued that certain categories of people are disadvantaged because they are less well endowed mentally (a theoretical variation of social Darwinism).

8. Another explanation that blames the poor for their poverty is the culture of poverty hypothesis. This theory contends that the poor are qualitatively different in values and lifestyles from the successful and that these differences explain the persistence of poverty from generation to generation.

9. Critics of innate inferiority and culture of poverty explanations charge that, in blaming the victim, both theories ignore how social conditions trap individuals and groups in poverty. The source of the problem lies not in the victims but in the way society is organized to advantage some and disadvantage others.

KEY TERMS

Social differentiation
Social stratification
Life chances
Social class
Privilege

Racial group
Ethnicity
Sex-gender system
Sex roles

Gender roles
Patriarchy
False consciousness
Class consciousness

STUDY QUESTIONS

1. Explain what is meant by this statement: "The structures of inequality—class, race, and gender—array the resources and advantages of society in patterned ways."
2. Within your college community is there a system of stratification? What appear to be the criteria used in this ranking of individuals and groups on your campus?
3. Contrast the views of order theorists and conflict theorists on social stratification.

4. What are the sociological criticisms of the deficiency theories of social inequality? How do structural theories of inequality meet these criticisms?
5. Summarize Gans's argument in Panel 9–3 concerning who benefits from poverty. Is this analysis from the order or conflict perspective?

FOR FURTHER READING

Greg J. Duncan, *Years of Poverty, Years of Plenty* (Ann Arbor: Institute for Social Research, University of Michigan, 1984).

Stephen Jay Gould, *The Mismeasure of Man* (New York: W. W. Norton, 1981).

Celia Heller, *Structured Social Inequality*, 2nd ed. (New York: Macmillan, 1987).

Vincent Jeffries and H. Edward Ransford, *Social Stratification: A Multiple Hierarchy Approach* (Boston: Allyn and Bacon, 1980).

Harold R. Kerbo, *Social Stratification and Inequality* (New York: McGraw-Hill, 1983).

Gerhard Lenski, *Power and Privilege: A Theory of Social Stratification* (New York: McGraw-Hill, 1966).

R. C. Lewontin, Steven Rose, and Leon J. Kamin, *Not in Our Genes: Biology, Ideology, and Human Nature* (New York: Pantheon, 1984).

Melvin Tumin, *Social Stratification: The Forms and Functions of Social Inequality*, 2nd ed. (Englewood Cliffs, NJ: Prentice-Hall, 1985).

Chapter Ten

Class

*I*t was in autumn 1964, fresh from Harvard College, from a term at Oxford, and from the indulgence of three years as an expatriate and social dropout on the fringes of the literary life on the Left Bank of Paris, that I returned to the United States and chose, for reasons which I do not wholly understand, to find a job within a fourth grade classroom of the Boston Public Schools. I had never read the works of Gunnar Myrdal, Michael Harrington, or Robert Coles. But it was in that year in Boston that I saw before my eyes a world of suffering, of hopelessness and fear, that I could never have imagined in the privileged and insulated decades of my childhood and schooling.

Up until 1964 I had been to Roxbury on very few occasions. Sometimes, on a Wednesday night, I had accompanied my father as we drove into the city to drop off the live-in maid who cleaned our house and cooked my meals and cared for me and for my sister six days out of seven. Thursday was the maid's day off. I used to wonder what she did, whether she had children and a household of her own, whether she suffered for the time in which she could not see them, how they could manage with no mother in their home. I knew that she was both a competent and gentle-hearted woman. She could clean and she could cook and she could offer love unstinted. I knew she couldn't read or write. That didn't seem to count. She did not need to read in order to perform the work of polishing the silverware and scrubbing kitchen floors.

When I asked her one day whether she had children, she replied that she had three. They lived in Roxbury with their grandmother. I worried about this sometimes, but not often. Not by the intention of my mother and my father, but by the enormous distance that divided my suburban life from anything that happened on that distant street of darkened houses where we dropped her off on Wednesday nights, I was inoculated against pangs of conscience. My curiosity about her children and about their lives was rapidly dissolved as I proceeded to evolve the plans for my career.

In 1964 I learned at last, and with a wave of shame and fear that turned before long into an unbounded and compensatory rage, that the children of our colored maid had been denied the childhood and happiness and care that had been given to me by their mother. I knew now that these children had been robbed of childhood. I had not robbed them: I had been recipient of stolen goods. What had been stolen from them seemed unspeakable: a crime, an evil past imagination.

Source: Excerpts from *Illiterate America* by Jonathan Kozol, copyright © 1985 by Jonathan Kozol. Used by permission of Doubleday, a division of Bantam, Doubleday, Dell Publishing Group, Inc.

The democratic ideology that "all men are created equal" has been a central value throughout American history. We are often reminded by politicians, editorial writers, and teachers that ours is a society where the equality of every person is highly valued. This prevailing ideology, however, does not mesh with reality. Slavery was once legal and racial discrimination against blacks was legal until the 1960s. Women were not permitted to vote until this century. Native Americans had their land taken from them and were then forced to locate on reservations. Japanese Americans were interned against their will during World War II. And, at a time when the richest 400 Americans in 1987 had an average net worth of $550 million (*Forbes,* 1987), there were 33 million Americans living below the official poverty line. Clearly, as George Orwell wrote in his classic, *Animal Farm,* "all . . . are equal but some are more equal than others" (1946:123).

The previous chapter considered some general principles and theories of social stratification. This chapter focuses on one hierarchy of stratification—the social class system, which is the ranking based primarily by economic resources. The chapter is divided into several parts, which describe (1) the dimensions of socioeconomic inequality; (2) the American class structure; (3) the degree to which people can move from one class to another—social mobility; (4) the consequences of class position; (5) poverty in the midst of plenty; and (6) a structural analysis of homelessness.

DIMENSIONS OF INEQUALITY

There is a great deal of evidence that Americans rank differently from one another on a number of socioeconomic dimensions. Let us examine some of the documentation of the existence of these differences in the United States.

Wealth

Wealth is unquestionably maldistributed in the United States. There exists unbelievable wealth in the hands of a few and wretched poverty for millions. At the top there were 26 billionaires in 1986 with the richest—Samuel Walton, owner of Wal-Mart Stores—worth an estimated $4.5 billion (*Forbes*, 1986). Just as dramatic, the top one-half of 1 percent of households—419,550—had an average net worth of $8.85 million and as a group controlled 35.1 percent of the nation's wealth (see Table 10–1). This small group of the "super-rich" owned 58 percent of the unincorporated businesses, 46.5 percent of the individually owned corporate stock, 77 percent of the value of all trusts, and 62 percent of state and local bonds (Joint Economic Committee of Congress, reported in *In These Times*, 1986). At the bottom end, 90 percent of American households owned 28.2 percent of the nation's wealth in 1986. Most significant, the gap is widening. The top 0.5 percent increased their share from 25.4 percent in 1963 to 35.1 percent in 1983, while the bottom 90 percent during those 20 years dropped from 36.0 percent of the wealth to 32.1 percent.

Personal wealth is also badly skewed by race. Whites had a median wealth of $39,135, which as noted in the last chapter was nearly eight times greater than the wealth for Hispanics, and twelve times the wealth for blacks (Eskey, 1986; see also Oliver and Shapiro, 1989). Among households headed by a woman, white women had median assets totalling $22,500, compared

Table 10–1
The Distribution of American Wealth, 1983

Group	% Households	No. Households	% Total Wealth	Wealth Range	Average Wealth
"Super-rich"	0.5	419,590	35.1	$2.5 million or more	$8.85 million
"Very rich"	0.5	419,590	6.7	$1.4 million to $2.5 million	$1.70 million
"Rich"	9.0	7,552,620	29.9	$206,341 to $1.4 million	$419,616
"Everyone else"	90.0	75,526,200	28.2	less than $206,341	$ 39,584

Source: Joint Economic Committee of Congress, 1986; "Scandal at the Fed? Doctoring the Numbers on Wealth Concentration," *Dollars & Sense*, No. 125 (April 1987):10–11, 22. Reprinted by permission.

Wealth and the material benefits that accompany it are maldistributed in the United States.

with just $671 for black women, and $478 for Hispanics (Census Bureau, reported by United Press International, July 19, 1986).

Income

The distribution of income is also very unequal and widening. From 1970 to 1986, for example, the proportion of total income received by the top 20 percent increased from 40.9 percent to 43.7 percent while the bottom 20 percent of Americans reduced its income from 5.4 percent of the total to 4.6 percent (see Table 10–2).

The data from Table 10–2 show that income inequality is increasing in American society. Especially noteworthy is the sharp gain in the ratio, which is a crude measure of income concentration, from 1980 to 1986.

> The data show that the wealthiest fifth of all families had about $40 billion more in income [in 1986] than it would have had if its share of the national income simply remained the same as in 1980. Correspondingly, the other four-fifths of all American families had about $40 billion less in income [in 1986] than they would have had if they had received the same proportion of national income as in 1980. (Wilkins, 1988:56)

Table 10–2
**Income
Inequality,
1970–1987**

Year	Income Share of Highest Fifth	Income Share of Lowest Fifth	Ratio Highest Fifth: Lowest Fifth
1987	43.7%	4.6%	9.50
1986	43.7	4.6	9.50
1985	43.5	4.6	9.46
1984	42.9	4.7	9.13
1983	42.8	4.7	9.11
1982	42.7	4.7	9.09
1981	41.9	5.0	8.38
1980	41.6	5.1	8.16
1979	41.7	5.2	8.02
1978	41.5	5.2	7.98
1977	41.5	5.2	7.98
1976	41.1	5.4	7.61
1975	41.1	5.4	7.61
1974	41.0	5.5	7.45
1973	41.1	5.5	7.47
1972	41.4	5.4	7.67
1971	41.1	5.5	7.47
1970	40.9	5.4	7.57

Source: Bureau of the Census, "Money Income of Households, Families, and Persons in the United States: 1987," *Current Population Reports,* Series P–60, No. 162 (February 1989), p. 42.

This relative gain in income by the upper 20 percent reflects the increased tax benefits received by the affluent from Congress and the administration during the 1980s and the concurrent lowering of tax benefits to the middle-class and the decrease in welfare programs for the poor. Another important explanation for this increasing inequality gap is the changing job structure as the economy shifts from manufacturing to service and as American jobs are exported (Reich, 1989). (Chapter 13 describes the changing economy and its effects.) See Panel 10–1 for a comparison of income inequality in the United States with other industrial nations.

Education

Americans also vary considerably in educational attainment. The amount of formal education an individual achieves is a major determinant of his or her occupation, income, and prestige. Despite the standard belief by Americans in free mass education and the almost uniform requirement that persons complete at least eight years of formal schooling, very real differences in

Equality and Progress

Traditionally, the United States has been considered to be the country in which the democratic vision of economic equality has come closest to realization. And, as we've seen, it has even been argued that the American commitment to equality has gone too far, with unfortunate consequences for economic growth and well-being. In this view, the wealthy need the lure of potential riches in order to maintain the incentive to invest in profitable enterprises. And, at the other end of the scale, coddling by the welfare state makes people too content with their lot in life, reduces their motivation for hard work, and ultimately weakens the economy as a whole.

But if we compare the United States with other industrial countries, these arguments seem unconvincing. Most of those countries have gone further than we have in reducing inequality of incomes—*and* are outperforming the United States economically. It's apparent that there is a wide variation among these countries, both in the share of income held by the relatively wealthy and, even more strikingly, in the share held by the relatively poorest people. The income share of the most affluent fifth of the population ranges from just over a third in Sweden to nearly half in France, with the United States toward the more unequal end of the scale. The share of the lowest income fifth shows a similar but sharper pattern. The most unequal countries are Spain and France, with the United States, Canada, and Australia not far behind. The poorest fifth of the Dutch population gets, proportionately, twice the share of income as their Spanish and French counterparts, and nearly twice the share of the poorest fifth of Americans.

Dividing the share of the richest by the share of the poorest gives a ratio of rich to poor that can serve as a shorthand guide to the width of the income gap in these countries. In the relatively egalitarian Netherlands, the most affluent fifth receives only about four times the income of the poorest. Sweden, Norway, and Japan also rank high on income equality. Only Spain and France, among these countries, have a more unequal distribution of income than the United States.

Does the greater income equality in countries like Sweden, Holland, or Japan interfere with economic efficiency? Simply mentioning a country like Japan is enough to suggest the limits of this argument. The evidence, in fact, supports the opposite conclusion: Greater equality and a stronger economy most often go hand in hand. Measured by gross national product per capita, *most* of the countries with a smaller income gap have moved ahead of the United States in economic performance. Those with similar or greater income inequality remain behind. There are exceptions; England has relatively high income equality and a smaller GNP per capita. Japan does, too, but in this case, the measure is misleading since Japan is simply moving up from further behind—and at a pace that has become the envy of other industrialized countries. (The French data are somewhat misleading, too; France has an unusually large agricultural population, which tends to make its income data less directly comparable with those of other advanced countries and masks a lower spread of inequality in its urban population.)

The reasons for this positive relationship between equality and economic progress are complex. One of the most important is the amount of unemployment a society is willing to tolerate. High unemployment is part of the explanation for the very low share of income earned by the lowest fifth in the United States. Full employment policies are one of the most important reasons why countries like Sweden or Japan have a more equal spread of income. At the same time, of course, full employment means that these countries are making better and more productive use of their human resources, leading to a stronger, more competitive economy.

Source: Elliott Currie and Jerome H. Skolnick, *America's Problems: Social Issues and Public Policy* (Boston: Little, Brown and Co., 1984) pp. 120–21.

educational attainment exist. In 1987 the data for adults 25 and over revealed that 12.7 million Americans had an eighth-grade education or less.

Perhaps the best indicator of inequality in education is the number of Americans who are illiterate or marginally illiterate. Jonathan Kozol summarizes these dismal data:

> Twenty-five million American adults cannot read the poison warnings on a can of pesticide, a letter from their child's teacher, or the front page of a daily paper. An additional 35 million read only at a level which is less than equal to the full survival needs of our society.
>
> Together, these 60 million people represent more than one third of the entire adult population.
>
> The largest numbers of illiterate adults are white, native-born Americans. In proportion to population, however, the figures are higher for blacks and Hispanics than for whites. Sixteen percent of white adults, 44 percent of blacks, and 56 percent of Hispanic citizens are functional or marginal illiterates. Figures for the younger generation of black adults are increasing. Forty-seven percent of all black seventeen-year-olds are functionally illiterate. That figure is expected to climb to 50 percent by 1990.
>
> Fifteen percent of recent graduates of urban high schools read at less than sixth grade level. One million teenage children between twelve and seventeen cannot read above the third grade level. Eighty-five percent of juveniles who come before the courts are functionally illiterate. Half the heads of households classified below the poverty line by federal standards cannot read an eighth grade book. Over one third of mothers who receive support from welfare are functionally illiterate. Of 8 million unemployed adults, 4 to 6 million lack the skills to be retrained for hi-tech jobs. (Kozol, 1985:4–5)

There is an obvious correspondence between being inadequately educated and receiving little or no income. There is not only a generational correlation between these two variables but an intergenerational one as well. The children of the poor and uneducated tend not to do well in school and eventually drop out (regardless of ability), while the children of the educated well-to-do tend to continue in school (regardless of ability). Thus, the cycle of inequality is maintained.

Occupation

Another demonstration that persons diverge in status is that occupations vary systematically in prestige. The degree of prestige and difference accorded to occupations is variable. A justice of the Supreme Court obviously enjoys more prestige than a bartender. But society makes much more subtle prestige distinctions. There is a rather uniform tendency to rate physicians slightly higher than college professors, who in turn are somewhat higher in rank than dentists. Further down the prestige scale, mail carriers outrank carpenters, who in turn have higher prestige than automobile mechanics.*

---

*C. C. North and Paul K. Hatt, the two sociologists who gathered these prestige rankings in 1947, found some degree of variation but a substantial agreement among a cross section of American adults ($N = 3000$) (North and Hatt, 1947). This study was replicated in 1963 to

The culture provides a ready-made and well-understood ranking system. It provides a relatively uniform system based on several related factors: (1) the importance of the task performed (that is, how vital the consequences of the task are for the society), (2) the degree of authority and responsibility inherent in the job, (3) the native intelligence required, (4) the knowledge and skills required, (5) the dignity of the job, and (6) the financial rewards of the occupation.

But society also presents us with warped images of occupations, which leads to the acceptance of stereotypes. The media, for example, through advertisements, television, and movie portrayals, evoke positive images for middle- and upper-class occupations and negative ones for lower-prestige occupations. Professional and business leaders are white, male, cultured, and physically attractive. They are decisive, intelligent, and authoritative. At the other end of the occupational spectrum very different characteristics are portrayed:

> It is the incumbents of the lowest-prestige occupations who are portrayed in the least enhancing light. Blue-collar workers of all kinds are either the butt of comedy or the embodiment of ignorance or deviance. They are often ethnic, always lower class, sometimes immoral, generally unattractive, frequently bigoted, and not-too-bright. They are not superhuman; they are subhuman, often with personalities bent by a warp that evokes laughter or disgust. (Nilson and Edelman, 1979:60)

Occupation, then, is a very important variable that sorts people into hierarchically arranged categories. It is highly correlated with income level but as the data in Table 10–3 indicate, the gender of the worker makes a tremendous difference. Regardless of the occupational category, women make considerably less, on average, than men employed in the same category.

SOCIAL CLASSES

Social class is a complex concept that centers on the distribution of economic resources. That is, when a number of individuals occupy the same relative economic rank in the stratification system, they form a **social class.** There are no clear class boundaries, except perhaps those delineating the highest and lowest classes. A social class is not a homogeneous group, given the diversity within it, yet there is some degree of identification with other people in similar economic situation. Also, people have a sense of who is "superior," "equal," and "inferior" to them. This is evidenced in patterns of deference and feelings of comfort or uneasiness during interaction. Similarly, there tend to be commonalities in life-styles and tastes (e.g., consumption patterns,

---

ascertain if Americans had changed their ranking of occupations. The correlation between the two studies of 0.99 suggests that the rating of occupations by Americans has remained remarkably stable (Hodge, Siegel, and Rossi, 1964). Incidentally, sociologists have found a high correlation in the ratings for occupations for a number of industrialized nations (Hodge, Freiman, and Rossi, 1966).

Table 10–3
Income Differentials by Occupation and Gender

(1987, median incomes for full-time, year-round workers)

Occupation Category	Women	Men	Ratio Women:Men
Executive, administrators, and managerial	$21,874	$36,155	.61
Professional specialty	24,565	36,098	.68
Technical and related support	19,559	29,170	.67
Sales	14,277	27,880	.51
Administrative support, including clerical	16,346	23,896	.68
Precision production (craft and repair)	17,190	24,931	.69
Machine operators, assemblers	13,028	20,821	.63
Transportation and material moving	12,770	22,472	.57
Handlers, cleaners, helpers, laborers	13,118	16,730	.78
Private household service workers	7,053	*	*
Service	11,214	17,335	.65
Farming, forestry, and fishing	7,034	12,389	.57
Averages for totals	$16,909	$26,008	.65

*Too few men in these occupations for a comparison
Source: Bureau of the Census, *Statistical Abstract of the United States: 1989* (109th ed.).
(Washington, D. C.: U. S. Government Printing Office, 1989), Table no. 668, p. 408.

childraising patterns, the role of women) among people in a similar economic position. But while we can make fairly accurate generalizations about people in a social class, the heterogeneity within it precludes accurate predictions about each of those included. In the words of Barbara Ehrenreich:

> Class is a notion that is inherently fuzzy at the edges. When we talk about class, we are making a generalization about large groups of people, and about how they live and make their livings. Since there are so many borderline situations, and since people do move up and down between classes, a description like middle class may mean very little when applied to a particular individual. But it should tell us something about the broad terrain of inequality, and about how people are clustered, very roughly, at different levels of comfort, status, and control over their lives. (Ehrenreich, 1989:13)

Sociologists agree that there are social classes and that money is a central criterion for classification, but they disagree on the importance of other criteria to delineate them. Although this oversimplifies the debate, we examine the two main ways to conceptualize social class. These contrasting views correspond with the order and conflict approaches. Let's examine these two positions and the resulting social class structure that results from each approach (the following is dependent on Wright et al., 1982; Liazos, 1985:228–234; Vanneman and Cannon, 1987; and Sanderson, 1988:191–195).

The Order Model's Conception of Social Class

Order theorists use *income, occupation,* and *education* as the fundamental indicators of social class, with occupation as central. Occupational placement determines income, interaction patterns, opportunity, and life-style. Life-style is the key dependent variable. Each social class is viewed as having its distinct culture. There are believed to be class-specific values, attitudes, and motives that distinguish its members from other classes. These orientations stem from income level and especially from occupational experiences (Collins, 1988:29). From this perspective, "*how* people get the money and *what* they do with it is as important (perhaps even more important than) as *how much* they have" (Liazos, 1985:230).

The typical class system from the order perspective has these classes.

1. Upper-Upper Class. Sometimes referred to as "the old rich," the members of this class are wealthy, and because they have held this wealth for several generations, they have a strong in-group solidarity. They belong to exclusive clubs and attended equally exclusive boarding schools. Their children intermarry and the members vacation together in posh, exclusive resorts around the world (Domhoff, 1970; Baltzell, 1958; Mills, 1959).

2. Lower-Upper Class. The wealth of the members is of relatively recent origin (hence, the term "the new rich"). The new rich differ from the old rich in prestige, not necessarily wealth. Great wealth alone does not ensure acceptance by the elite as a social equal. The new rich are not accepted because they differ from the old rich in behaviors and life-styles. The new rich is composed of the self-made wealthy. These families have amassed fortunes typically through business ventures, or because of special talent in music, sport, or other form of entertainment. Additionally, some professionals (doctors, lawyers) may become wealthy because of their practice and/or investments. Finally, a few persons may become very wealthy by working their way to the top executive positions in corporations, where high salaries and lucrative stock options are common.

3. Upper-Middle Class. The key distinguishing feature of this class is high-prestige (but not necessarily high-income) jobs that require considerable formal education and have a high degree of autonomy and responsibility. This stratum is composed largely of professional people, executives, and business people. They are self-made, having accomplished their relatively high status through personal education and occupational accomplishments.

4. Lower-Middle Class. These are white-collar workers (as opposed to manual workers) who work primarily in minor jobs in bureaucracies. They work, for example, as secretaries, clerks, salespeople, police officers, and teachers.

5. Upper-Lower Class. These people work at repetitive jobs with little autonomy that require no creativity. They are blue-collar workers who, typically, have no education beyond high school. They are severely blocked from up-ward mobility.

6. Lower-Lower Class.   This class is composed of unskilled laborers whose formal education is often less than high school. The chronically unemployed are in this class. When they do work, it is for low wages, no fringe benefits, and no job security. Minority-group members—blacks, Puerto Ricans, Mexi-can Americans, Native Americans—are disproportionately found in this cat-egory. These persons are looked down on by all others in the community. They live "on the other side of the tracks." They are considered by others to be undesirable as playmates, friends, organization members, or marriage partners. Lower-lowers are thought to have a "culture of poverty"—that is, their presumed traits of laziness, dependence, and immorality, which because they are opposite of "good middle-class virtues," lock them into their "inferiority."

The Conflict Model's Conception of Social Class

The conception of social class presented by the order theorists has important insights. As Liazos, a conflict theorist, has put it:

> Only a fool would deny that occupation, education, and the various "life-style" qualities (speech, dress, leisure activities, etc.) define a person's class. They do matter to people, and we do distinguish one person or family from another by the kind of work they do, where they went to school, and so on. (Liazos, 1985:230–231)

Conflict theorists, however, argue that order theorists understate the central-ity of money in determining where people fall in the class system. "Where people live, how much education they receive, what they do to earn an in-come (or if they do not need to earn an income), who they associate with, and so forth, depend on how much money their families earn or have" (Liazos, 1985:231). Conflict theorists, in contrast to order theorists, focus on money and power, rather than on life-style. Again, turning to Liazos:

> In capitalist societies, the greatest class division is between the few who own and run corporations . . . and the rest of the people. This is not to say that all other people belong to one class; obviously they do not. But it is to say that the one million or so people who belong to the families that own, control, and profit by the largest corporations differ fundamentally from the rest of us. It is their *power and wealth* that essentially distinguish them from the rest of soci-ety, not their speech, dress, education, leisure activities, and so on. (Liazos, 1985:231)

Conflict theorists also differ from order theorists in how they view occu-pation as a criterion for social class. A social class, in this view, is not a cluster of similar occupations but, rather, a number of individuals who occupy a similar position within the social relations of economic production (Wright et al., 1982). In other words, what is important about social classes is that they involve relationships of domination and subordination that are made possible by the systematic control of society's scarce resources. The key, then, is not the occupation itself but the control one has over one's own work, the work of others, decision making, and control over investments. People who own, manage, oppress, and control must be distinguished from those who are managed, oppressed and controlled (Eshleman, 1988:216).

Using these three criteria—money, relation to the means of production, and power—conflict theorists tend to distinguish five classes.

1. Ruling Class.   The people in this class hold most of the wealth and power in society. They control the corporations, banks, media, and politics. The members are only a small percentage of individuals and families. Domhoff (1979) and Parenti (1988) say that the top 0.5 percent of society owns more than 45 percent of the privately held wealth. At the apex are the 400 wealthiest families, as listed annually by *Forbes*. According to the 1989 list, there were 66 billionaires; the 400 richest Americans had a combined net worth of $269 billion (up $50 billion from 1988); and the minimum required to make the list was $275 million (*Forbes*, 1989). The key is that the families and individuals in the ruling class own, control, govern, and rule the society. They control capital, markets, labor, and politics. In Marxist terms, the great wealth held by the ruling class is extracted from the labor of others.

2. Professional-Managerial Class.   Four categories of persons are included in this class—managers, supervisors, and professionals in business firms, and professionals outside business but whose mental work aids business.

The most powerful managers are those near the top of the organizational charts who have broad decision-making powers and responsibilities. They have considerable power over the workers below them. In the words of Vanneman and Cannon:

> As firms grew, an army of managers, professionals, and white-collar employees took over some of the managerial functions previously reserved for capitalists alone. These salaried officials work for owners of productive property, just as blue-collar workers do, but earn generous incomes and enjoy substantial prestige. And—what is crucial for a *class* analysis—the new middle class also shares in some of the *power* that capital has exercised over workers. (Vanneman and Cannon, 1987:53)*

There are also lower-level managers, forepersons, and other supervisors. They have less training than do the organizational managers, have limited authority, and are extensively controlled by top and middle managers. These people hold a contradictory class position. They have some control over others, which places them in this category, but their limited supervision of the routine work of others puts them close to the working class. The key for inclusion in this class, though, is that the role of supervisor places the individual with the interests of management in opposition to the working class (Vanneman and Cannon, 1987:55; see also Poulantzas, 1974:14). As Randall Collins has argued:

> The more one gives orders, the more one identifies with the organizational ideals in whose name one justifies the orders, and the more one identifies with one's formal position. (Collins, 1988:31)

Another social category within this class includes professionals employed by business enterprises. These professionals (doctors, lawyers, engineers, accountants, inspectors) have obtained their position through educational attainment, expertise, and intellect. Unlike the ruling class, these professionals do not own the major means of production, but rather they work for the ruling class. They do not have supervisory authority, but they influence how workers are organized and treated within the organization. They are dominated by the ruling class although this is mediated somewhat by the dependence of the elite on their specialized knowledge and expertise (for an extended discussion of this growing class, see Ehrenreich, 1989).

Finally, there are those professionals who have substantial control over workers' lives but who are not part of business enterprises. Their mental labor exists outside the corporation but nonetheless their services control workers. Included in this category are social workers, who are responsible for ensuring that the unemployed and poor do not disrupt the status quo (Piven and Cloward, 1971). Educators serve as gatekeepers, sifting and sorting people for good and bad jobs, which gives them enormous power over workers and their children (Vanneman and Cannon, 1987:76). Doctors keep workers healthy, and psychologists provide help for troubled people and seek to bring

---

deviants back into the mainstream where they can function "normally." Vanneman and Cannon argue that these professionals outside business belong in the same social class as those professionals working directly for business.

> If [this class] is defined by the control it exerts over other people, then, it necessarily incorporates the social worker, teacher, and doctor as well as the first-line supervisor and plant manager. What the social worker, teacher, and doctor share with the engineer, accountant, and personnel officer is a specialization of mental labor: they all plan, design, and analyze, but their plans, designs, and analyses are largely executed by others. (Vanneman and Cannon, 1987:76)*

3. *Small Business Owners.*   The members of this class are entrepreneurs who own businesses that are not major corporations. They may employ no workers (thus, exploiting no labor power) or a relative few. The income and power over others by members of this class varies considerably.

4. *Working Class.*   The members of this class are the workers in factories, restaurants, offices, and stores. They include both "white collar" and "blue collar" workers. White collar workers are included because they, like blue collar workers, do not have control over other workers or even their own lives (Vanneman and Cannon, 1987:11). The distinguishing feature of this class is that they sell their labor power to capitalists and earn their income through wages. Their economic well-being depends on decisions made in corporate board rooms and by managers and supervisors. They are closely supervised by other people. They take orders. This is a crucial criterion for inclusion in the working class because "the more one takes orders, the more one is alienated from organizational ideals. . . ." (Collins, 1988:31). Thus, they are clearly differentiated from those classes whose members identify with the business firms for which they work.

5. *Poor.*   These people work for minimum wages and/or are unemployed. These people do society's dirty work for low wages. At the bottom in income, security, and authority, they are society's ultimate victims of oppression and domination.

Erik Olin Wright and his colleagues (1982) made an empirical investigation of the American class structure using the conflict approach. Among their results are several interesting findings. First, it is incorrect to rank occupations, as order theorists do, because within the various occupational categories there are managers/supervisors *and* workers. In other words, workers in white-collar jobs can be divided into managers and workers (proletariat). So, too, in jobs for laborers, operatives, and unskilled services.

> There is a long tradition in sociology of arguing over whether or not lower white-collar jobs should be considered in the working-class or the "middle-

---

class." Usually it is assumed in such debates that occupations as such can appropriately be grouped into classes, the issue being where a specific occupation ought to be located. . . . If classes are conceptualized in relational terms, this is not even the correct way to pose the problem. Instead, the empirical question is the extent of proletarianization within different occupational categories. (Wright et al., 1982:720)

Second, social class is closely related to gender and race. Wright and his associates found that women are more proletarianized, regardless of occupational category, than are men (54 percent occupying working class locations compared with only 40 percent for men).* Similarly, 64 percent of all blacks are in the working class compared with only 44 percent of whites.

If we examine the combined race-sex-class distributions, we see that black women are the most proletarianized of all: 65 percent of black women in the labor force are in the working class, compared to 64 percent of black men, 52 percent for white women, and only 38 percent for white men. (Wright et al., 1982:724)

Summary: Class from the Order and Conflict Perspectives

Vanneman and Cannon have summarized the fundamental differences between the order and conflict views of social class.

In the [conflict] vision, class divides society into two conflicting camps that contend for control: workers and bosses, labor and capital, proletariat [workers] and bourgeoisie [middle class]; in this dichotomous image, classes are bounded, identifiable collectivities, each one having a common interest in the struggle over control of society. In the [order] vision, class sorts out positions in society along a many-runged ladder of economic success and social prestige; in this continuous image, classes are merely relative rankings along the ladder: upper class, lower class, upper-middle class, "the Toyota set," "the BMW set," "Brahmins," and the dregs "from the other side of the tracks." People are busy climbing up (or slipping down) these social class ladders, but there is no collective conflict organized around the control of society. (Vanneman and Cannon, 1987:39)

These radically different views on social class should not obscure the insights that both provide for the understanding of this complex phenomenon. Occupation is critical to both but for very different reasons. For the order theorist, occupations vary in how people evaluate them; some are clearly superior to others in status (recall the research on occupational prestige noted earlier in this chapter). Thus, the perceptions of occupations within a population indicate clearly that there is a prestige hierarchy among them and the individuals identified with them. The conflict theorist also focuses on occupations but without reference to prestige. Where a person is located in the work process determines the degree of control that individual has over others and oneself.

---

*For an extended discussion of the complexities of gender differences in social class placement, see Collins, 1988.

The key to determine class position is whether one gives orders or takes orders. Moreover, this placement determines one's fundamental interests, because one is either advantaged (living off the labor of others) or is disadvantaged (oppressed). Empirically, both of these views mesh with reality.

Second, order theorists focus on commonalities in life-styles among individuals and families similar in education, income, and occupation. These varying life-styles are real. There are differences in language use, tastes for music and art, interior decorating, dress, childrearing practices, and the like (see Fussell, 1983). Although real, the emphasis on life-style misses the essential point, according to conflict theorists. For them, life-style is not central to social class; giving or taking orders is. This is why there is disagreement on where, for example, to place lower-level white-collar workers, such as clerks and secretaries. Order theorists place them in the middle class because the prestige of their occupations is higher than those of blue-collar workers and because their work is mental rather than manual. Conflict theorists, on the other hand, place them with workers who take orders, that is, in the worker class. Conflict theorists also point to two important implications of the emphasis on life-style. First, although culture is a dependent variable, that is, it is a consequence of occupation, income, and education, the culture of a social class is assumed to have a power over its members that tends to bind them to their social class (e.g., the culture of poverty is believed to keep the poor poor—see Chapters 8, 9, and 11). A second implication is the implicit assumption that these "cultures" are themselves ranked with the culture of the higher classes, the more valued. Conflict theorists have the opposite bias— they view the denigration of society's losers as "blaming the victim." From this perspective, the higher the class, the more the members are guilty of oppressing and exploiting the labor of those below. In short, there is a strong tendency among conflict theorists to identify with the plight of "underdogs" and to label pejoratively the behaviors of "topdogs."

Finally, each of these views of social class are useful for the understanding of social phenomena. The order model's understanding of inequality in terms of prestige and life-style differences have led to research that has found interesting patterns of behaviors by social location, which is one emphasis of sociology. Similarly, the focus of the order model has resulted in considerable research on mobility, mobility aspirations, and the like, which are helpful for the understanding of human motivation as well as the constraints on human behavior. The conflict model, on the other hand, examines inequality from differences in control—control over society, community, markets, labor, others, and oneself. The resulting class division is useful for understanding conflict in society—strikes, lockouts, political repression, social movements, and revolutions.

THE CONSEQUENCES OF SOCIAL CLASS POSITION

Regardless of the theoretical position, there is no disagreement on the proposition that one's wealth is the determining factor in a number of crucial areas, including the chance to live and the chance to obtain those things (for example, possessions, education) that are highly valued in society. As we saw in Chapter 9, the term *life chances* refers to the chances throughout one's life cycle to live and to experience the good things in life. This is dependent almost exclusively on the economic circumstances of the family to which one is born. Gerth and Mills have contended that life chances refer to

> everything from the chance to stay alive during the first year after birth to the chance to view fine art, the chance to remain healthy and grow tall, and if sick to get well again quickly, the chance to avoid becoming a juvenile delin- quent—and very crucially, the chance to complete an intermediary or higher educational grade. . . . (Gerth and Mills, 1953:313)

Life Expectancy

Economic position has a great effect upon how long one will live or in a crisis who will be the last to die. For instance, the official casualty lists of the trans-Atlantic luxury liner, the *Titanic,* which rammed an iceberg in 1912, listed 3 percent of the first-class female passengers as lost; 16 percent of the second-class female passengers drowned, and among the third-class females 45 percent were drowned (Lord, 1955:107). Apparently, even in a disaster, socioeconomic position makes a very real difference—the higher the eco-nomic status of the individual, the greater the probability of survival.

The greater advantage toward longer life by the well-to-do is not limited to disasters such as that of the *Titanic.* A consistent research finding is that health and death are influenced greatly by social status.*

Probably the most complete and valid (methodologically) study in this area was conducted by Kitagawa and Hauser, who matched 340,000 death certificates (for deaths occurring during the months May–August, 1960) to the 1960 Census records (Kitagawa and Hauser, 1968). Using educational attainment level as an indicator of socioeconomic status, the researchers found the expected strong inverse correlation between mortality and educa-tional attainment. Among white women between the ages of 25 and 64 years, for example, the mortality rate for those with less than eight years of school was 61 percent higher than among college-educated women. Among white males in this age bracket, the mortality rate for those with less than eight years of school was 48 percent higher than for the college-educated men.

Principal Cause of Death

The data from Kitagawa and Hauser show very clearly the relationship be-tween socioeconomic status (as measured by educational attainment) and the principal cause of death. The most striking finding was for white males be-tween 25 and 64; those with less than eight years of education had a mortality

---

*There is an excellent summary article (by Aaron Antonovsky) surveying more than thirty studies done prior to 1950 in the United States and elsewhere that lead to the conclusion that socioeconomic status influences one's chance of staying alive (Antonovsky, 1967).

rate from tuberculosis of more than 800 percent higher than the college-educated. This relationship, although not as strong as found for tuberculosis, was also noted for death from influenza, pneumonia, accidents (motor vehicle and all others), and cancer of the stomach, lung, bronchus, and trachea.

The American Cancer Society has reported that the cancer survival rates are 25 percent lower for those below the official poverty line than for those above it. Moreover, lower-income people have higher rates for certain cancers, including cancers of the lung, cervix, and esophagus (Findlay, 1986). The American Heart Association has found that the higher the income, the lower the risk of dying of coronary diseases such as heart attacks, strokes, and hypertension. Poor blacks, for example, were found to be 53 percent more likely to die of heart disease than wealthier blacks, and poor whites were 33 percent more likely than more affluent whites to die of heart disease (Stewart, 1985).

Physical Health

The physical health of poor persons is more likely to be impaired than is the health of the more well-to-do because of differences in diet, sanitation facilities, adequate shelter, and proper medical treatment. Consider the following facts concerning differential medical care for the poor:

- 37 million Americans (18 percent of the population) have no medical insurance (Gold, 1989). "Regardless of income or employment status, black children were significantly less likely than whites to be protected against medical costs. Compared with whites, black children in employed families were 70 percent more likely to be uninsured" (Hughes et al., 1989:xi).
- The percentage of babies born to mothers who received late or no prenatal care increased in 1986, the seventh year in a row of no improvement or worsening (Hughes et al., 1989:xi).
- A study by the American Cancer Society revealed that people living below the poverty level have a relative cancer survival rate 10 to 15 percent below that of the nonpoor. Among the reasons for this are that the poor who develop cancer do not receive an early diagnosis and treatment because they cannot afford medical care, they have no medical insurance, and less than 45 percent are eligible for Medicaid (reported in Cimons, 1989).

Family Instability

Research relating socioeconomic status to family discord and marital disruption has found an inverse relationship—the lower the status, the greater the proportion of divorce or desertion. An explanation for this relationship is that lower-class families experience greater economic and job insecurity. Given the tremendous emphasis in the United States on success and achievement, lower-class persons (particularly men) will tend to define themselves and be perceived by others in the society as a failure. Such a belief will, doubtless, hinder rather than help a marriage relationship.

The Draft

Involuntary conscription into the U.S. Army—the draft system—works to the disadvantage of the uneducated. In 1969 only 10 percent of the men drafted were college men—yet over 40 percent of college-age men go to college. The Supreme Court has further helped the educated by ruling that a person can be a conscientious objector on a basis of either religion or philosophy. Young intellectuals can use their knowledge of history, philosophy, and even sociology to argue that they should not serve. The uneducated will not have the necessary knowledge or sharpened intellect to make such a case.

For those educated young men who end up in the armed services, there is a greater likelihood of their serving in noncombat supply and administrative jobs than for the non-college-educated. Persons who can type, do bookkeeping, or know computer programming will generally be selected to do jobs where their skills can be used. Conversely, the nonskilled will generally end up in the most hazardous jobs. The chances for getting killed while in the service are greater, therefore, for the less educated than for the college educated (Zeitlin, Lutterman, and Russell, 1977; Baskir and Strauss, 1978; Useem, 1983; Feigelson, 1982).

Justice

Chapter 8 provided strong evidence that the administration of justice is unequal in the United States. Low-income persons are more likely to be arrested, to be found guilty, and to serve longer sentences for a given violation than are persons in the middle and upper classes.

Why is the system of justice unjust? The affluent can afford the services of the very best lawyers for their defense, detectives to gather supporting evidence, and expert witnesses such as psychiatrists. The rich can afford to appeal the decision to a series of appellate courts. The poor, on the other hand, cannot afford bail and must await trial in jail, and they must rely on court-appointed lawyers, who are usually among the least experienced lawyers in the community and who often have heavy case loads. All the evidence points to the regrettable truth that a defendant's wealth makes a significant difference in the administration of justice.

There is a class bias held by most citizens, including arresting officers, prosecuting attorneys, judges, and jury members, that affects the administration of justice. This bias is revealed in a set of assumptions about persons according to their socioeconomic status. The typical belief is that the affluent or the children of the affluent, if lawbreakers, are basically "good" people whose deviance is an aberration, a momentary act of immaturity. Thus, a warning will suffice or, if the crime is quite serious, a short sentence is presumed to cause enough humiliation to bring back their "naturally" conforming ways. Lawbreaking by the poor, on the other hand, is much more troublesome and must be punished harshly, because these are essentially "bad" people and their deviance will persist if tolerated or mildly punished by the authorities.

Education

In general, life chances are dependent on wealth—they are purchased. The level of educational attainment (except for the children of the elite, where the best in life is a birthright) is the crucial determinant of one's chances of income.

Inequality of educational opportunity exists in all educational levels in many subtle and not so subtle ways. It occurs in the quality of education when schools are compared by district. The districts with a better tax base have superior facilities, better motivated teachers (because the districts can pay more), and better techniques than do the poorer districts. Within each school, regardless of the type of district, children are given standardized tests that have a middle-class bias. Armed with these data, children are placed in "tracks" according to "ability." These tracks thus become discriminatory, because the lowest track is composed disproportionately of the lower socioeconomic category. These tracks are especially harmful in that they structure the expectations of the teacher.

SOCIAL MOBILITY

This section analyzes the degree of social mobility in society. This emphasis fits with the order model. It assumes that status (as opposed to class) differences are gradations, corresponding with occupation. Moreover, there is the assumption that a high degree of social mobility exists in U.S. society, with a growing middle mass of workers enjoying a high standard of living (Knottnerus, 1987).

Societies vary in the degree to which individuals may move up in status. Probably the most rigid stratification system ever devised was the **caste system** of India. In brief, this system (1) determined status by heredity, (2) allowed marriage to occur only within one's status group (endogamy), (3) determined occupation by heredity, and (4) restricted interaction among the status groups. Even the Indian caste system, however, was not totally rigid, for some mobility has been allowed under certain conditions.*

In contrast to the closed stratification system of India, the United States has a relatively open system. Social mobility is not only permitted, but it is part of the American value system that upward mobility is good and should be the goal of all Americans.

The United States, however, is not a totally open system. All American children have the social rank of the parents while they are youths. As we shall see in Chapters 11 and 12, the social class of parents has a tremendous influence on whether the child can be mobile (either upward or downward).

---

*Some observers have charged that the stratification system of the United States is castelike with reference to race. Race, in many ways, presents a barrier that determines status, range of marriage partners, and discriminatory treatment of all kinds (see Berreman, 1960).

Concepts

Social mobility refers to an individual's movement within the class structure of society. **Vertical mobility** is movement upward or downward in social class. **Horizontal mobility** is the change from one position to another of about equal prestige. The shift in occupations from being an electrician to a plumber is an example of horizontal mobility.

Social mobility occurs in two ways. **Intergenerational mobility** refers to vertical movement comparing a daughter with her mother or a son with his father. **Intragenerational mobility** is the vertical movement of the individual through his or her adult life.

Societal Factors Affecting Social Mobility.   There are societal factors that increase the likelihood of people's vertical mobility regardless of their individual efforts. The availability of cheap and fertile land with abundant resources gave many thousands of Americans in the nineteenth century opportunities for advancement no longer present. Similarly, the arrival of new immigrants to the United States from 1880 to 1920 provided a status boost for those already here. Economic booms and depressions obviously affect individuals' economic success. Technological changes too can provide increased chances for success as well as diminish the possibilities for those trained in occupations now obsolete. Finally, the size of one's age cohort can limit or expand opportunities for success.

The Extent of Vertical Mobility in the United States.   The most comprehensive study of intergenerational mobility has been conducted by Peter Blau and Otis Dudley Duncan (1967). Some of their conclusions are that: (1) few sons of white-collar workers become blue-collar workers; (2) most mobility moves are short in distance; (3) occupational inheritance is highest for sons of professionals (physicians, lawyers, professors); and (4) the opportunities for the sons of nonprofessionals to become professionals are very small. Another study, this one by the Carnegie Council on children, found that only one male in five exceeds his father's social status through individual effort and achievement (De Lone, 1979).

The commonly accepted belief of Americans that ours is a meritocratic society is largely a myth. Equality of opportunity does not exist because (1) employers may discriminate on the basis of race, sex, or ethnicity of their employees or prospective employees; (2) educational and job training opportunities are unequal; and (3) the family has great power to enhance or retard a child's aspirations, motivation, and cognitive skills (Jencks, 1979; Gintis, 1979).

Education and Social Mobility

The schools play a major part in both perpetuating the meritocratic myth and legitimizing it by giving and denying educational credentials on the basis of "open and objective" mechanisms that sift and sort on merit (Bowles and

Gintis, 1976). The use of IQ tests and tracking, two common devices to segregate students by cognitive abilities, are highly suspect because they label children, resulting in a positive self-fulfilling prophecy for some children and a negative one for others. Moreover, the results of the tests and the placement of children in "tracks" because of the tests, are biased toward middle- and upper-class experiences.

Educational attainment, especially receiving the college degree, is the most important predictor of success in America. Bowles and Gintis have shown, for example, that those in the lowest tenth of the population in years of schooling have a 3.5 percent chance of being in the top fifth of the population in monetary income. At the other end, though, those in the highest tenth of the population in education have a 45.9 percent chance of being in the top 20 percent in income. Moreover, among people with identical IQ test scores, those in the top tenth in schooling are eight times more likely to be in the top fifth in income than those in the lowest tenth in education (Bowles and Gintis, 1976:110–113). Clearly, mental skills alone are not enough. They must be coupled with formal schooling to maximize the likelihood of economic success.

Just as important, Bowles and Gintis have also shown that family socioeconomic background determines how much education one receives: those in the lowest tenth in socioeconomic family background *with the same average IQ scores* as those in highest tenth in socioeconomic family background will receive an average of 4.9 *fewer years of education* (Bowles and Gintis, 1976:31). In short, educational level determines socioeconomic position—and one's family's socioeconomic background determines one's educational opportunities. Thus, the ascribed status of family background has a profound impact on the probability of educational achievement and upward mobility.

Christopher Jencks and his associates have added to the work of Bowles and Gintis, providing the most current and methodologically sophisticated analysis of the determinants of upward mobility in their book *Who Gets Ahead?* (Jencks, 1979). Their findings, summarized, show the following as the most important factors leading to success.

1. Family background is the most important factor. Children coming from families in the top 20 percent in income will, as adults, have incomes of 150 to 186 percent of the national average whereas those from the bottom 20 percent will earn 56 to 67 percent of the national average.
2. Educational attainment—especially graduating from college—is very important to later success. It is not so much what one learns in school but obtaining the credentials that counts. The probability of high educational attainment is closely tied to family background.
3. Scores from intelligence tests are by themselves poor predictors of economic success. Intelligence test scores are related to family background and educational attainment. The key remains the college degree. If high IQ people do not go to college they will tend *not* to succeed economically.
4. Personality traits of high school students, more than grades and IQ, have an impact on economic success. No single trait emerges as the decisive determinant of economic success but rather the combined effects of many different traits are

found to be important. These are self-concept, industriousness (as rated by teachers), and the social skills or motivations that lead students to see themselves as leaders and to hold positions of leadership in high school.

The picture drawn by Jencks and other experts on social mobility in America is of a relatively rigid society in which being born to the right family has a profound impact, especially on the probability of graduating from college. There are opportunities for advancement in society but they are clustered among the already advantaged. If the stratification system were open with equality of opportunity it would make sense that people, even the disadvantaged, would support it. The irony is that although the chances of the poor being successful are small indeed, the poor tend to support the inequality generated by capitalism—truly a case of false consciousness. This irony will become clearer as we see the consequences of inequality for individuals.

The New Downward Mobility and the Shrinking Middle Class.   Throughout most of American history children expected to do better economically than their parents, and many did. Upward mobility in every generation was a higher probability than downward mobility, but at some point in the 1970s the odds shifted.

> In the decades prior to the 1970s, children expected early on to live better than their parents. Such is not now the case. A father-son example illustrates this dramatically. Suppose a young man of 18 or 19 is preparing to leave his parents' home. As he leaves, he sees what his father's salary would buy and he keeps the memory as a personal yardstick. In the 1950s or 1960s, the young man would have quickly measured up. By age 30, he already would have been earning one-third more than his father earned when the young man left home. But today, a 30-year-old man is earning about 10 percent less than his father earned when the young man left home. (Levy and Michel, 1986:36)

Figure 10–1 shows this another way, by presenting the median earnings for full-time workers from 1960 through 1987 by gender in constant 1987 dollars. These data show that income rose for males until 1972 and has declined since, whereas income for females rose slightly throughout the same period (with women in 1987 making, on average, 65 percent of what men make).

As relative income for men has declined in the past 15 years or so, who is being affected adversely? Figure 10–2 shows, first, that the income distribution in the United States is skewed with most people toward the bottom. Moreover, it shows that the middle class, defined here as those with incomes ranging from $19,000 to $47,000 (in 1986 dollars) fell from 52.3 percent of the population in 1978 to 44.3 percent in 1986. This shrinkage in the middle was offset by a 2.8 percent gain in the top income group and in a 5.2 percent gain in the bottom income category. In short, the middle shrank, as two-thirds of those leaving fell in income status and one-third rose (Rose, 1986:9).

In addition to a falling level of income in the last decade, the cost of some items has increased, which further shrinks the standard of living for many.

Figure 10–1
Median Earnings: 1960-87

(In 1987 dollars. Year-round, full-time workers)

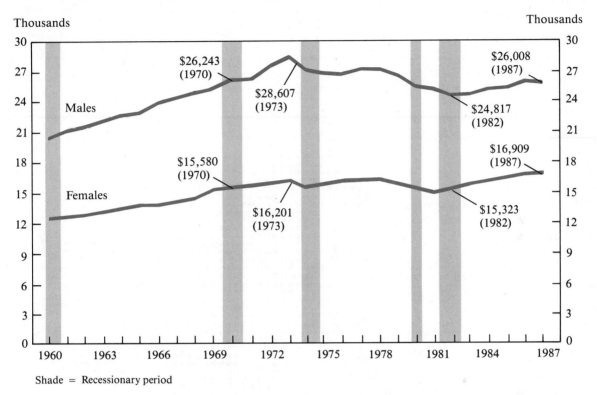

Thousands

Thousands

$26,243
(1970)

$28,607
(1973)

$26,008
(1987)

$24,817
(1982)

Males

$15,580
(1970)

$16,201
(1973)

$16,909
(1987)

$15,323
(1982)

Females

Shade = Recessionary period

Source: Bureau of the Census, "Money Income of Households, Families, and Persons in the United States: 1987," *Current Population Reports,* Series P–60, No. 162 (February 1989), p. 6.

The high inflation rate that characterized the 1970s increased dramatically the cost of automobiles, college education, health care, and housing. The typical 30-year-old male in 1973, for example, spent 21 percent of his monthly income on the costs to carry a mortgage on a median-priced home. This more than doubled to 44 percent of monthly income for the average 30-year-old male in 1983 (Levy and Michel, 1986:37; see also Brophy, 1986). As a result, among people under 35 years the rate of home ownership has fallen from 43.3 percent in 1981 to 39.7 percent in 1986 (Greenhouse, 1986:10).

There are two fundamental reasons explaining why the current period is the first in American history where the rate of downward mobility exceeds the rate of upward mobility. The first is demographic—the baby-boom generation and the many women entering the workforce have crowded the labor market. The unprecedented numbers competing for scarce jobs in the past ten to fifteen years have depressed wages and family income. Although this

Figure 10–2
**The Shrinking
Middle Class:
1978–1986**

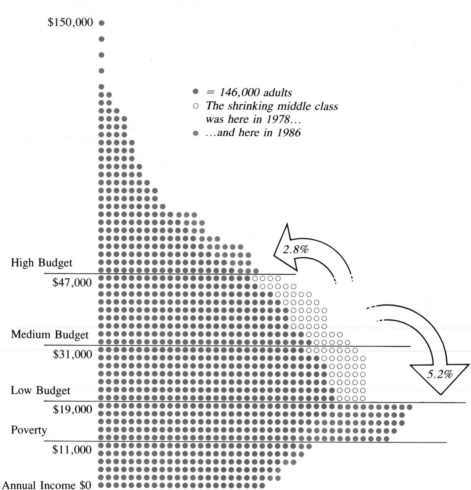

Source: From *The American Profile Poster,* by Stephen J. Rose. Copyright © 1986 by Social Graphics Co. Reprinted by permission of Pantheon Books, a division of Random House Inc.

accounts for some of the problem, the more important source of downward pressure is the structural transformation of the economy (Harrison, Tilly, and Bluestone, 1986). The massive shift away from traditional manufacturing to high technology and service industries has tended to eliminate relatively high-wage jobs and created job opportunities in low-wage jobs. As this shift has accelerated, the share of jobs providing a middle-class standard of living has shrunk (Kuttner, 1983). The moving of plants to low-wage regions of the country or to other countries further depresses wages. So, too, the overseas competition that produces goods that undersell American products results in lower wages. Unions have acquiesced to these pressures by lowering their demands, making concessions, and even in some instances accepting a two-tiered wage scale where the newly hired are paid considerably lower wages than earlier workers for the same work. There are exceptions to this, however, as described in Panel 10–2.

THE EXTENT OF POVERTY IN THE UNITED STATES

What separates the poor from the nonpoor? In a continuum there is no absolute standard for wealth. The line separating the poor from the nonpoor is necessarily arbitrary. The Social Security Administration (SSA) sets the official poverty line based on what it considers the minimal amount required for a subsistence level of life. To determine the poverty line, the SSA computes the cost of a basic nutritionally adequate diet and multiplies that figure by three. This figure is based on a government research finding that poor people spend one-third of their income on food. If we use this standard, in 1987, 13.5 percent of the population (32.5 million persons) were defined as living in poverty.*

In this chapter we consider the poor as those below this arbitrary line. However, the government procedure is not only arbitrary; it actually minimizes the extent of poverty in America. Some economists have argued that a more realistic figure would be 50 percent of the median income. In 1987, for example, the official poverty line was $11,611 for a nonfarm family of four. If the 50 percent of median income standard were used, the line would have been $15,425, adding many millions to the poverty category. Such a procedure might shock the government into more action to alleviate suffering in this country. In effect, though, "the poor" is anyone denied adequate health, diet, clothing, and shelter because of lack of resources.

Exact figures on the number of poor are difficult to determine. For one thing, the amount of money needed for subsistence varies drastically by locality. Compare, for example, the money needed for rent in New York City with that needed in rural Arkansas. Another difficulty is that those most likely to be missed by the U.S. Census are the poor. People most likely to be missed in the census live in ghettos (where several families may be crowded into one apartment) or in rural areas, where some homes are inaccessible and where some workers follow the harvest from place to place and therefore have no permanent home. Transients of any kind may well be missed by the census. The conclusion is inescapable that the proportion of the poor in the United States is underestimated, because the poor tend to be invisible, even to the government. This underestimate of the poor has important consequences, since U.S. Census data are the basis for political representation in Congress. These data are also used as the basis for instituting new governmental programs or abandoning old ones. Needless to say, an accurate count of the total population is necessary if the census is so used.

---

*The 1987 data on poverty used throughout this section are taken from Bureau of the Census, "Poverty in the United States: 1987," *Current Population Reports*, Series P–60, No. 163 (February 1989).

Workers, Students Teach
Duke a Lesson

The high school seniors who, along with their parents, toured the grounds of Duke University here this past May saw an archetypal image of the scholarly community: wide lawns, gothic stonework, students with books slung casually from their arms, tweed-jacketed professors. But campus employees at Duke—those working on the loading docks and in the boiler rooms, laundries and bathrooms—were all but invisible.

The students who enroll or come back this fall, however, will learn that, invisible or not, Duke University can no longer overlook the vital role played by such workers. But the Duke workers, members of American Federation of State, County and Municipal Employees (AFSCME) Local 77—virtually all of them black and most of them women—were not generously granted respect and acknowledgment from corporate boardrooms on high. They won it for themselves through a vigorous and spirited struggle.

Last spring, housekeeping workers at Duke, with take-home salaries running below $200 a week, challenged and defeated ServiceMaster, an enormous corporation whose annual income exceeds $1.5 billion.

The Duke fight is not only a good lesson about how determined workers can win even in a period when Southern labor is taking its lumps: it also demonstrates how a university workers' movement led by black women, with strong support from student activists, can emerge victorious.

ServiceMaster is the nation's leading institutional cleaning company, specializing in hospitals, office buildings, and schools. It has been convicted twice for firing employees in a racially discriminatory manner and brags in its own promotional literature of its capabilities as a union buster. ServiceMaster's name is derived from the phrase "in service to the Master," which alludes to the putatively Christian philosophy of this monolith. After Duke's contract with ServiceMaster was canceled, one university administrator remarked, "They come off like 'Janitorial Services by Jerry Falwell'—I have no idea why we hired them."

Other administrators might not have such fuzzy memories. Duke signed a contract with ServiceMaster in December 1988 for the management of the school's housekeeping staff. There were several reasons for the move, including a national trend by institutional management to farm out cleaning work to service conglomerates. Although Duke's buildings were immaculate, there was a feeling within the administration that the job could be done more cheaply. Duke's new Capital Campaign, an arguably overambitious endowment effort with a stated goal of $400 million, put a premium on thrift. ServiceMaster's sales rep had promised to bring down costs. The company is renowned for "low-balling"—offering low initial bids and then raising the price once the institution becomes dependent on its services.

ServiceMaster's opening act at Duke was to call a meeting on a half hour's notice at which employees were notified of their new overseer. Racism and condescension set the tone. "He [the ServiceMaster executive] said the first thing we need to do is to go to the chapel and pray," said one housekeeper, "because, he said, things were going to get rough on us."

"He kept telling us how his sister was a doctor and how much his suits cost, and how we need to better ourselves, shine our shoes and all," one worker reported. "It was 'boys' this and 'girls' that, and we didn't appreciate it one bit."

THE BARBER OF SERVILE

The ServiceMaster man, employees noticed, was particularly obsessed with their hair. "He said, 'If you come in here with that hair all fried, dyed and laid to the side in those jeri-curls, you are wearing a hair net.' " This decree was expanded to include a strict prohibition against hats. Hats and hair nets perform the same function, of course, but hair nets are a traditional mark of servitude. How hats might interfere with mopping floors and scrubbing toilets was never explained.

Hair, however, was not the most outrageous expression of racism in the new dress code. Each of the workers I interviewed repeated Service-Master's contention that "beige and brown don't look good on black people" and that new blue uniforms would be in order. "The way I see it," one woman said bluntly, "they're trying to take us back to slavery, this ServiceMaster."

Submission and discipline were also on the agenda. ServiceMaster told its new workers that their performance would be monitored by company observers dressed as students and faculty. "We don't know who they are," said one employee with 14 years service. "Are we that bad of people that they have to spy on us?" The evident purpose of the anonymous spying was intimidation since, as one worker noted, "with this type of work, all they have to do is check our areas and see if they are clean."

The most troublesome rumor for many workers was ServiceMaster's intention to create a work shift starting at 2 a.m., an effort to keep cleaning people invisible as well as silent.

"It does something to you—it ages you, working that graveyard shift," said one experienced janitor. For workers with children, a 2 a.m. shift presents obvious problems. In a workforce that is 85 percent women, there is also danger in having to work in isolated areas of a university plagued by rape and assault. "They don't care about that," said one woman. "What do they care about us? Nothing."

Workers began to talk about changing their situation. They first notified their union business manager, who was strangely unresponsive. Then workers began to recruit students to their cause, and an awkward but dynamic coalition was formed.

The workers soon discovered that students enjoy special freedoms that make them excellent allies. As everyone who has ever had a job knows, freedom of speech has a way of stopping at the time clock. Students, however, have a special, temporary leeway to freely express themselves, a fact the workers used to great advantage.

Because several of the most able and energetic activist student leaders were African-Americans, it was difficult for the Duke administration to split the worker-student alliance along obvious class lines. It was also plain that Duke was sensi-

tive to the negative image it had in Durham's black community and did not want to add fuel to that particular fire. There was fear in some quarters that retaining ServiceMaster would induce black students to carry out their explicit threat to "tell it like it is" at minority recruitment time.

The alliance between workers and students was mutually beneficial; students who participated learned much about the real world in the struggle against ServiceMaster, and friendships were forged among people who had not always seen each other as full human beings.

THE INFERNAL PATERNAL

The student-worker alliance faced unavoidable difficulties. There was no way for students to speak out for workers without seeming paternalistic. This was especially true because the students were mostly white and the workers were virtually all black. At Duke, the biggest reason for the success of the coalition was that student activists stayed in constant touch with their worker allies and listened attentively each step of the way. Political skills and savvy were important, but the bottom line was remembering whose fight this was.

Publicity and protest from the ranks forced the union leadership to take a tougher stand. This pressure made it clear that the union was more than just one or two leaders. Shop stewards and the rank and file initiated and led the fight. In the end, Local 77 officials came around and behaved responsibly and capably.

After two weeks of public outcry by workers and students, direct communication between the Duke administration and the workers came at last. Students arranged a meeting with President H. Keith H. Brodie in late March. They convinced him to come to a nearby seminar room where several of the workers waited. The workers then said their piece, recounting for Brodie the abuse that ServiceMaster had heaped on them. They showed Dr. Brodie the whisk brooms the corporation had issued them in place of long-handled brooms, a punishment for talking to the press. And they offered several reasonable alternative management structures.

A few days later, Brodie announced the university's decision to abandon the contract with ServiceMaster. That weekend, workers and students held a celebration picnic. It was a glorious occasion that none would have predicted given the cultural and political obstacles to such a triumph.

The victory over ServiceMaster energized Local 77. The union recently negotiated a pay increase more than double the usual 1 percent to 3 percent raise, mainly because it was able to negotiate from a position of strength. With strong rank-and-file leadership and renewed morale, the union can now, with its proven achievements, actively recruit more members. Student activism at Duke, in turn, received a tremendous boost, accelerating a two-year upswing and giving rise to previously undreamed-of possibilities for mobilizations with campus workers.

More broadly, it is encouraging that 180 service workers can shake themselves free from domination by a giant multinational corporation. The Duke University housekeepers' victory confirms that democracy can be a daily reality when people learn to cooperate across social barriers.

As one cleaning woman told President Brodie, "We do all the dirty work, and we should have some say-so."

Source: Tim Tyson, "Workers, Students Teach Duke a Lesson," *In These Times* (September 20–26, 1989), p. 2. Reprinted by permission of *In These Times*, 2040 N. Milwaukee, Chicago, IL 60647 (312–772–0100).

Despite these difficulties and the understanding of actual poverty by the government's poverty line, we do know some facts about the poor.

Racial Minorities

Income in the United States, as we have seen, is maldistributed by race. Not surprisingly, then, 33.1 percent of all blacks were poor in 1987 as were 28.2 percent of all Hispanics compared to only 10.5 percent of all whites. Hispanics will soon replace blacks as the racial group with the highest poverty rate. This prediction is based on several facts regarding the Hispanic population. First, Hispanics tend to be far younger than whites or blacks generally, making them more likely to be newer to the work force and therefore among the lowest paid. Second, they tend to be concentrated in the lowest segment of the labor market, where pay is at or near the minimum wage regardless of longevity. Whereas the minimum has not increased since 1981, workers in jobs above the bottom tier have experienced raises in pay. Third, high unemployment is prominent in those geographical areas heavily populated by Hispanics. Finally, Hispanics tend to have larger families than whites or blacks, and Hispanic two-parent families are more likely than those in the other two racial groups to have just one wage-earner.

Women

Two out of three impoverished adults in the United States are women, a consequence of the prevailing institutional sexism in society that provides with few exceptions poor job and earnings opportunities for women. This combined with the high frequency of marital disruption and the number of never-married women with children has resulted in the high probability of women who head families being poor.

This trend, termed the "feminization of poverty" (see Pearce, 1978; Ehrenreich and Stallard, 1982; Stallard, Ehrenreich, and Sklar, 1983) implies that the relatively large proportion of poor women is a new phenomenon in American society. Thus, the term obscures the fact that women have always been more economically vulnerable than men, especially older women and women of color. But when women's poverty was mainly limited to these groups their economic deprivation was mostly invisible. The plight of women's poverty became a visible problem when the numbers of white women in poverty increased rapidly in the past decade or so with rising marital disruption. Even with the growing numbers of poor white women the term "feminization of poverty" implies that all women are at risk when actually the probability of economic deprivation is much greater for certain categories of women. The issue, then, is not gender but class, race, and gender (Burnham, 1986).

Children

Children make up about 27 percent of the nation's population, but 40 percent of those who are poor. Put another way, while the nation's poverty rate was 13.5 percent, the rate for children was 22 percent (20.6 percent for children under 18 and 22.6 percent for those under three years of age). The Children's Defense Fund provides the following facts and projections:

> All groups of children are poorer today than they were at the beginning of the decade—especially white children, whose poverty rates have increased by almost a third. If present trends persist, white children may eventually face the same savage levels of poverty in the future that now afflict black and Hispanic children. Today nearly one in two black and one in three Hispanic children is poor.

Danziger in *Used Cartoons* © 1988 TCSPS.

If we do not rise off our national rear end and mobilize to prevent and reduce child poverty, between now and the year 2000 *all* of the growth in our child population will consist of poor children and our children in the next century will be poorer than today.

- In the year 2000, one in four of all American children, 16 million children, will be poor—3 million more than in 1987.
- By the year 2030, one in three, or 25 million American children, will be poor—about double the number today. (Children's Defense Fund, 1989:xvi–xvii)

MYTHS ABOUT POVERTY

What should be the government's role in caring for its less fortunate citizens? Much of the debate on this important issue among politicians and citizens is based on erroneous assumptions and misperceptions. "These myths need to be dispelled in order to direct public policy intelligently" (O'Hare, 1986:22).

Refusal to Work

Several facts belie the faulty assumption that poor people refuse to work. About one-half of poor adults under age sixty-five (47.2 percent in 1987) work at least part of the time. Actually, the main increase in the number of poor since 1979 has been among the working poor (Whitman, 1988). This increase is the result of declining wages, the increase in working women who head households, and a minimum wage of $3.35, unchanged since 1981. A report by the Joint Economic Committee of Congress (reported in Rowley, 1986) has noted that in 1969 a full-time worker earning the minimum wage to support a three-member family earned 109.4 percent of the 1969 poverty level. A similar worker in 1979 earned 100.3 percent, but in 1985 he or she earned only 78.2 percent of the poverty level for a family of three.

Welfare Dependency

We should recognize, first, that most poor people do *not* receive welfare. In 1984 only about one-third of poor families received public assistance payments, and only about 40 percent of the poor received noncash benefits such as food stamps, free or reduced school lunches, public housing, or Medicaid (O'Hare, 1986:24). Second, the previous section documented that the "life chances" of the poor are clearly negative. There is considerable evidence of misery among America's poor. We know, for example, that economic hardships increase the likelihood of pathologies such as alcoholism, suicide, and spouse and child abuse (Horwitz, 1984; Brenner, 1973). We also know that millions of Americans are seriously hungry and/or homeless (see McGeary and Lynn, 1988; Kozol, 1988; Wright, 1989; and Rossi, 1989). The numbers who are hungry and/or homeless are growing rapidly precisely because of the reduction in or elimination of governmental assistance programs to the economically deprived.

There is a fundamental misunderstanding by the American public about where most governmental benefits are directed. We tend to assume that government monies and services go mostly to the poor (**welfare,** the receipt of financial aid and/or services from the government) when in fact by far the greatest government aid goes to the nonpoor (**"wealthfare"**, the receipt by the nonpoor of financial aid and/or services from the government). In fiscal 1984 over three-fourths of the federal outlays for human resources went to all children in education programs and to most of the elderly through Social Security Retirement and Medicare. In effect, government programs that helped mainly the middle class received about $363 billion in fiscal 1984 while those aimed directly at helping the poor received about $70 billion (O'Hare, 1985:29).

The "upside-down" welfare system, with aid mainly helping the already affluent, is also accomplished by two hidden welfare systems. The first is through tax loopholes (called "tax expenditures"). Through these legal mechanisms the government officially permits certain individuals and corporations to pay lower taxes or no taxes at all. In 1975, tax expenditures amounted to about a $93 billion saving for the already fortunate. By 1985, the amount was about $355 billion (Currie and Skolnick, 1988:128). In an interesting and telling irony, the government tax breaks to homeowners who were able to deduct interest and taxes amounted to a housing subsidy of $43.8 billion in 1988 (*Statistical Abstract*, 1989:308), whereas the amount the poor received in public and subsidized housing in that year amounted to only about $7 billion.

The second hidden welfare system to the nonpoor is in the form of direct subsidies and credit to assist corporations, banks, agribusiness, defense industries, and the like. These subsidy programs, which may have noble purposes such as helping an ailing industry (e.g., a $500 billion bailout of Savings and Loans begun in 1989), do transfer substantial sums primarily from the middle class upward to large corporations and individuals who own stock in them. Elliott Currie and Jerome Skolnick argue that this is

> "socialism for the rich"—that is, they supply money and support to corporate businesses, not according to the much-applauded principles of the free market, but according to need as determined by the government. . . . [We should recognize that government welfare to a corporation or an industry may be necessary to avert an economic disaster. This is also the principle that] underlies government spending for *individuals* who have floundered in the "free" market. There, the government seeks to maintain the individual as a productive member of society. Applauding the government's commitment to corporate welfare while condemning its support for individuals facing economic difficulties seems less than consistent. (Currie and Skolnick, 1984:139–140)

A STRUCTURAL ANALYSIS OF THE HOMELESS

The homeless are the poorest of the poor. Estimates vary from a low of 350,000 Americans to a high exceeding 3 million Americans. Whatever the actual number, two points must be underscored. First, the proportion of Americans who are homeless is the highest since the Great Depression, *with a rapid rise in the past ten years or so.* Second, the numbers actually minimize the seriousness of the problem because many poor people are on the *brink* of homelessness and many who lack housing are hidden by doubling or tripling up with relatives or friends. Jonathan Kozol estimates that there are more than 300,000 hidden homeless in New York City alone, and nationwide more than 3 million families are living doubled up. When these households are added to those poor people paying more than half of their monthly income for rent, more than 10 million families are living near the edge of homelessness in the United States (Kozol, 1988:1, 14).

Even though the number of homeless in the United States is disputed by politicians, activists, case workers, and social scientists, there is widespread agreement that the number has increased dramatically in the past decade or so. The question is why? What factors explain this spreading social problem now? The current and expanding crisis of homelessness results from the convergence of two incompatible forces: (1) the rapidly dwindling supply of low-income housing; and (2) the increased economic vulnerability among the poor and the near poor. Let us examine these forces in turn.

The Low-Income Housing Shortage

The homeless problem is fundamentally a housing problem, that is, there is not enough low-cost housing available for the economically marginal in U.S. society. Low-income housing has shrunk dramatically in recent years. Inflation is one source of this shrinkage. The cost of housing at all levels has risen rapidly. The median price of a single-family dwelling sold in 1970 was $23,000; in 1980 it was $62,200; and in 1989 it was $92,900. This price varies by locality, of course, with the median 1989 cost in San Francisco $265,700; Los Angeles, $218,000; Boston, $188,600; and New York City, $185,200. The cost of renting has followed this inflationary trend. This inflation in the housing market at all levels has placed increased pressures on the low-income population, who simply cannot afford the increased rents or they must sacrifice in other areas to pay the relatively high rents. Data from 1985, for example, showed that 6.1 million households below the poverty line spent more than 50 percent of their incomes for housing. Paying such a high proportion of a low income each month places these poor people in jeopardy of not making their rent and being evicted. In short, they are extremely vulnerable to becoming homeless.

Although inflation is an important reason for the loss of low-income housing, other factors are more important. Foremost, there has been an absolute decrease in the number of low-income units. Most conspicuous has been the loss of single-room occupancy (SRO) boarding houses, the housing of last resort for the economically marginal population. In New York City, for example, the stock of SROs shrunk from 127,000 units in 1975 to 14,000 in 1985.

The number of SROs and other low-cost rental units has decreased because of two related trends. One trend is gentrification—the process of converting low-income housing to condominiums or upscale apartments for the

The number of homeless people is rising as a result of the at-risk population's facing an ever-shrinking supply of low-cost housing.

middle- and upper-middle classes (Kasinetz, 1984). Another trend has been the demolition of low-income housing and replacement with office buildings, apartments, and stores to revitalize downtown centers. Both of these actions—gentrification and demolition—by developers to increase their profits result in removing affordable rental housing from the market, driving up rents in the remaining apartments, and uprooting tenants from their homes and communities.

These actions by the private sector, which have decimated the supply of low-cost housing, have not been overcome by governmental policies. Federal housing programs, which provide government subsidies for the construction of low-cost housing, declined dramatically during the Reagan presidency. Federal support for subsidized housing dropped from $32.2 billion in 1981 to $6 billion in 1989. Put another way, the Department of Housing and Urban Development (HUD) authorized the construction of 183,000 subsidized dwellings in 1980 but only 20,000 in 1989. Moreover, the relatively meager federal budget for housing was mismanaged by HUD with outright fraud and monies that were targeted for the poor actually often being allocated for housing for the nonpoor. Ameliorating the problems of the poor was clearly not a priority of the Reagan administration.

> When Reagan came to office in 1981, the federal government spent seven dollars on defense for every dollar on housing. When he left office in 1989, the ratio was forty-six to one. (Appelbaum, 1989:9)

The Swelling of the At-Risk Population

A common belief among politicians, journalists, and other people is that the recent rise in the homeless is a consequence of the trend to deinstitutionalize mental patients that began in the 1950s. The data appear on the surface to support this notion, because the average daily census of psychiatric institutions dropped from 677,000 in 1955 to 151,000 in 1984. That the number of former mental patients swelled as a result of deinstitutionalization does not necessarily explain the increased number of homeless in the 1980s. In fact, almost all of the reduction of the number of mental patients in institutions had occurred by 1978, yet the homeless only began overflowing the shelters after 1983.

Several other cautions must be raised concerning the emphasis on the homeless as mentally ill. First, although some homeless people are mentally disturbed and incapable of sustaining personal relationships and steady work, most are capable of functioning in society. Yet the myth is perpetuated in the media that the majority of the homeless have a history of chronic mental illness.

A second caution has to do with cause and effect. Does mental illness cause homelessness or do the stresses induced by extreme poverty and homelessness cause mental dysfunction? Doubtless, homelessness is both a cause and effect of mental illness, but we need to emphasize that a stable life leads to stability and an unstable one to instability.

A third caution is that the emphasis on the personal sources of homelessness blames the victims for their problem by deflecting attention away from its structural sources. To do so leads to faulty generalizations and public policies doomed to fail. In the words of David Snow and his associates:

> It is demeaning and unfair to the majority of the homeless to focus so much attention on the presumed relationship between mental illness, deinstitutionalization, and homelessness. To do so not only wrongfully identifies the major problems confronting the bulk of the homeless, it also deflects attention from the more pervasive structural causes of homelessness, such as unemployment, inadequate income for unskilled and semi-skilled workers, and the decline in the availability of low-cost housing. (Snow et al., 1986:422)

Since the late 1960s some dramatic changes in families have increased the probability of poverty and homelessness, especially for women and their dependent children. One change has been the rapid rise in divorce. Beginning in the mid-1960s, the divorce rate has risen sharply, reaching a peak in 1981 with a very slight decline since then. In effect, about one-half of marriages now end in divorce. The lower the economic resources of the couple, the greater the likelihood of separation and divorce. In terms of race, black couples have a much greater probability of divorce than either do whites or Hispanics. This fact is related to low income (this should also be true of Hispanics, but the strong prohibition against divorce by the Catholic Church tends to temper the power of low income for them). Research has shown, for example, that if black men have the same employment and income as whites, the proportion of stable families between the two races is comparable. But blacks and whites are not comparable in income, with the unemployment rate consistently more than twice as high for blacks as whites and the proportion below the government's poverty line exceeding one in three blacks but only about one in ten whites. For families in economic distress that divorce, the woman suffers most. This is especially true for divorced mothers who retain custody of the children, which is the case nine times out of ten. Their former husbands do not have resources for child support. And there probably was little, if any, marital property to divide. Thus, divorced poor women with children are prime candidates for homelessness.

Even middle-class women with children who divorce may find themselves in serious economic difficulty. Many of them do not have the skills for a middle-class life-style. With divorce they are left with the children and, typically, a low-paying job (female workers in American society make, on average, 70 cents for every dollar a male worker makes). Moreover, many absent fathers, even those who can afford it, do not pay child support.

In sum, the economic situation for most divorced women is grim. The "feminization of poverty" is a reality that reflects the high divorce rate and is a consequence of a sexist society in which women earn much less than what men earn. All this, plus the added burden of women almost always ending up with the children.

The changing economy is another force that has made certain segments of the population especially vulnerable to extreme poverty. Four interrelated forces have been transforming the American economy (Eitzen and Baca Zinn, 1989; this transformation is examined in detail in Chapter 13). These factors are (1) technological breakthroughs in microelectronics, which means, for example, robots replacing workers; (2) the globalization of the economy, which means competition from abroad; (3) capital flight (overseas investment by U.S. firms, the relocation of U.S. businesses in other countries, and mergers); and (4) a shift from an economy dominated by producing goods to one based on services (e.g., banking, insurance, health care, education, custodial work, restaurants, security, and transportation). These trends have combined to transform the American economy in a generation. The result has been millions of lost jobs because of plant closings and layoffs. Many of the unemployed have found new jobs but often at lesser wages and benefits, but 1.5 million of the 10 million who lost jobs from 1983 to 1988 did not find new employment (*New York Times*, 1988).

The structural transformation of the U.S. economy has been especially difficult for racial minorities. Blacks, for example, are overrepresented in the manufacturing sector, which has undergone such a severe contraction. Also, they are concentrated in the industrial cities of the Northeast and Great Lakes regions, which have experienced economic decline. These cities have changed from centers of production and distribution of goods to centers of administration, information exchange, and higher-order services (Kasarda, 1985). This shift has reduced the overall number of jobs available and has changed the requirements for obtaining employment, with education being the critical requirement. There is a mismatch in inner cities, as most blacks and other minorities do not have the education for the increasing number of high-tech jobs. Thus, the changing economy, which has transformed jobs and cities, has left in its wake many disadvantaged individuals and families who have either become homeless in the past decade or are on the edge of homelessness.

Finally, at the time in U.S. history when powerful forces were converging to lead more and more people to the brink of real poverty, government policies shifted dramatically toward more austere social programs. In essence, the government "jerked away the safety net," leaving more and more poor vulnerable to the ravages of poverty. Each of the Reagan budgets lowered programs that helped the needy in society by tightening eligibility requirements and reducing the monies allocated. All told, during the Reagan administration, government monies for the poor were *reduced* by $51 billion.

The problems of the poor who depend on welfare were compounded by the Reagan plan to reduce the scope of the federal government by shifting funds to the states to be used at their discretion. This "home rule" strategy, based on the assumption that local governments know what is best for their constituents, has several important negative consequences for the poor. First, it allows local patterns of discrimination against women, blacks, Hispanics, Native Americans, and other relatively powerless minorities to flourish unhindered by federal restrictions. And second, the states vary markedly in their ability and/or willingness to provide welfare for the needy. Data from 1987 show, for example, that the average monthly payment (AFDC) for a family of three ranged from $120 in Mississippi to $617 in California (O'Hare, 1987).

This section has provided an integrated theory of homelessness in American society. The dramatic rise in the new homelessness of the past decade or so is the result of two countervailing trends—as the supply of low-income housing was being drastically reduced, increasing numbers of Americans, especially women, children, and minorities were becoming more and more economically vulnerable. The housing supply dwindled as entrepreneurs (speculators and developers) made decisions that changed low-cost housing into more profitable ventures. The numbers of the poor increased at the same time because of societal forces such as the transformation of the economy, changes in family structure, and public policies that have cut back programs to help the needy.

CHAPTER REVIEW

1. Americans vary greatly on a number of socioeconomic dimensions. Wealth and income are maldistributed. Educational attainment varies. Occupations differ greatly in prestige and pay.

2. Order theorists place individuals into social classes according to occupation. Each social class is composed of social equals who share a similar life-style. Each class-specific culture is assumed to have a power over its members.

3. Conflict theorists focus on money, relation to the means of production, and power as the determinants of class position. Crucial to this place-

ment is not occupational prestige as the order theorists posit, but whether one gives orders or takes orders in the work process.

4. The consequences of one's socioeconomic status are best expressed in the concept of "life chances," which refers to the chances to obtain those things highly valued in society. The data show that the higher one's economic position: the longer one's life; the healthier (physically and mentally) one will be; the more stable one's family; the less likely one will be drafted; the less likely one will be processed by the criminal justice system; and the higher one's educational attainment.

5. Societies vary in the degree to which individuals may move up in status. The most rigid are called caste systems which are essentially closed to hereditary groups. Class systems are more open, permitting vertical mobility.

6. Although the United States is a relatively open class system, the extent of intergenerational mobility (a son or daughter surpassing his or her parents) is limited.

7. The prime determinants of upward mobility appear to be: (a) family background; (b) educational attainment; (c) graduation from college; and (d) personality traits.

8. In the past decade downward mobility has, for the first time in American history, exceeded upward mobility, resulting in a shrinking middle class. The two reasons for this shift are (a) the unprecedented numbers of "baby boomers" and women competing for scarce jobs; and (b) the structural transformation of the economy.

9. According to the government's arbitrary line, which minimizes the actual extent of poverty, in 1987, 13.5 percent of the U.S. population was officially poor. Disproportionately represented in the poor category are blacks, Hispanics, women, and children.

10. The poor are *not* poor because they refuse to work. Most adult poor either work at low wages, cannot find work, work part-time, are homemakers, are ill or disabled, or are in school.

11. Government assistance to the poor is *not* sufficient to eliminate their economic deprivation. Less than half of the poor actually receive any federal assistance. When compared with the nonpoor, their life chances are negative, with a higher incidence of health problems, malnutrition, social pathologies, and homelessness.

12. Most government assistance is targeted to the affluent rather than the poor. The nonpoor receive three-fourths of the federal monies allocated to human services. Tax expenditures and other subsidies provide enormous economic benefits to the already affluent, which further redistributes the nation's wealth upward.

13. The homeless are the poorest of the poor. The proportion of Americans who are homeless is the highest since the Great Depression, and the number has risen rapidly in the past decade or so. The structural reasons for this sudden rise in the homeless population are (1) the sudden dwindling of low-income housing and (2) the increased economic vulnerability among the poor and the near poor resulting from the transformation of the economy, changes in family structure, and public policies that have reduced substantially programs to help the needy.

KEY TERMS

Social class	Vertical mobility	Intragenerational mobility
Life chances	Horizontal mobility	Welfare
Caste system	Intergenerational mobility	Wealthfare
Social mobility		

STUDY QUESTIONS

1. What are the key differences in the conception of social class by order model and conflict model theorists?

2. What are the consequences of social class position in terms of life chances?

3. What is the evidence that the gap between the

"haves" and the "have-nots" is increasing in the United States?

4. To what extent is upward social mobility difficult for poor youth?

5. Which social categories are most likely to be poor? Referring to the discussion in Chapter 9, what are the fundamental reasons for the overrepresentation of these categories in the poor classification?

6. Why has the homeless population increased so rapidly in the past ten years or so?

FOR FURTHER READING

Children's Defense Fund, *A Vision for America's Future* (Washington, DC: Children's Defense Fund, 1989).

Peter W. Cookson, Jr. and Caroline Hodges Persell, *Preparing for Power: America's Elite Boarding Schools* (New York: Basic Books, 1985).

Barbara Ehrenreich, *Fear of Falling: The Inner Life of the Middle Class* (New York: Pantheon, 1989).

David T. Ellwood, *Poor Support: Poverty in the American Family* (New York: Basic Books, 1988).

Michael Harrington, *The New American Poverty* (New York: Holt, Rinehart and Winston, 1984).

Charles Hoch and Robert A. Slayton, *New Homeless and Old* (Philadelphia: Temple University Press, 1989).

Harold R. Kerbo, *Social Stratification and Inequality: Class Conflict in the United States* (New York: McGraw-Hill, 1983).

Jonathan Kozol, *Rachel and Her Children: Homeless Families in America* (New York: Crown, 1988).

Rochelle Lefkowitz and Ann Withorn (eds.), *For Crying Out Loud: Women and Poverty in the United States* (New York: Pilgrim Press, 1986).

Frank Levy, *Dollars and Dreams: The Changing American Income Distribution* (New York: Russell Sage Foundation, 1987).

Physician Task Force on Hunger in America, *Hunger in America: The Growing Epidemic* (Middletown, CT: Wesleyan University Press, 1985).

Karin Stallard, Barbara Ehrenreich, and Holly Sklar, *Poverty in the American Dream.* Institute for New Communications, pamphlet no. 1. (Boston: South End Press, 1983).

Reeve Vanneman and Lynn Weber Cannon, *The American Perception of Class* (Philadelphia: Temple University Press, 1987).

James D. Wright, *Address Unknown: The Homeless in America* (New York: Aldine de Gruyter, 1989).

Chapter Eleven

Racial and Ethnic Minorities

*A*t the University of Wisconsin in Madison, the brothers of Phi Gamma Delta fraternity are known as Fijis, and each spring they throw what they call a Fiji Island Party. For the festivities of May 1987, they painted themselves in blackface and set up, on the lawn outside their fraternity house, a large caricatured cutout of a black man with a bone through his nose.

At about the same time, black students at the University of Michigan found fliers slipped under their doors declaring "open hunting season on jigaboos and porch monkeys." At the University of Massachusetts, white students attacked an interracial couple and several black students on campus.

These incidents and others like them have been widely reported as evidence of a resurgence of racism on campus. University administrators have responded to the outcry by announcing plans to combat the problem.

But for minorities, the news is old. Long after the civil-rights movement and desegregation, black students worry about their safety at universities all over the country. Name-calling and even violent threats are routine. And campus racism is no new phenomenon. The Fiji party, for example, had been going on every spring for years before anyone called attention to it.

But tensions between black and white students are just the most visible part of the problem. Hispanics, Asians, and native Americans, as well as blacks, struggle against racism deeply rooted in the universities. It starts when they apply for admission and financial aid, continues in the classroom, and extends to daily life on campus.

Fewer nonwhites are enrolling in college these days, and fewer can stay. Blacks and Hispanics are increasingly underrepresented on campus—26,000 fewer blacks attend college now than in 1980—because cuts in financial aid and the shift from grants to loans under the Reagan Administration make tuition unaffordable for most minorities.

More black students graduate from high school now than ten years ago, but more and more blacks and Hispanics join the military or enroll in vocational schools instead of going to college.

Enrollment by Asians has not declined, but in the last few years it has leveled off. Students charge that some admissions policies are deliberately designed to keep them out. Berkeley awards extra points, for example, to students who pass achievement tests in European foreign languages, but no points are awarded to students who know Chinese or Vietnamese. Asian students, like Hispanics and blacks, also say they feel alienated and receive inadequate support while at the university.

Institutional callousness to nonwhites fosters an atmosphere among students that is hostile to minorities in several ways:

- White students don't see or know much about other cultures and ethnic groups because groups are underrepresented on campus.
- White culture dominates the curriculum, and that reinforces white students' assumption that theirs is the only legitimate culture.

Many of the gains achieved by the civil-rights movement in the 1960s and 1970s are slipping away. Cultural centers and special programs set up to accommodate nonwhite students have dwindled or disappeared.

Although student activists have made some gains recently in the struggle against campus racism, it will take a deep revision of universities' structures and values to make a lasting change.

Mandatory ethnic-studies programs, which would teach students about a variety of cultures, are a big item among the reforms student activists are demanding and university administrators are discussing on various campuses, including Stanford, Berkeley, Wisconsin, Michigan, and Massachusetts.*

---

*Source: Ruth Conniff, "Racism 101" The Progressive (December, 1988):30–33. Reprinted by permission of The Progressive, 409 East Main Street, Madison WI 53703.

Race relations in the United States have once again captured national attention, exposing the myth that civil rights victories would bring an end to racial inequality. Recent trends and events reveal that instead of racial progress, new problems of race have emerged in the past two decades. They include the increasing isolation of minorities in central cities, growing minority unemployment, a steady influx of immigration, and an epidemic of racially motivated violence. Created in large part by national and global economic changes, these conditions are making race a central social and political issue of the 1980s and 1990s.

The United States is a mosaic of different social groups and categories. However, they are not equal in power, resources, prestige, or presumed worth. They are differentially ranked on each of these dimensions. But why is one group alleged to be superior to another? The basic reason is differential power—power derived from superior numbers, technology, weapons, property, or economic resources. Those holding superior power in a society establish a system of inequality by dominating less powerful groups, and this system of inequality is then maintained and perpetuated by power (Yetman and Steele, 1971:4).

Racial and ethnic groups are among those that are disadvantaged by society's institutions. Racial and ethnic stratification is a basic feature of American society. It is built into society's policies and practices that may appear neutral but systematically exclude people on the basis of race and ethnicity, thus creating majority and minority relations. "Normal" arrangements provide privileges for whites at the expense of blacks, Hispanics, and other people of color. Racial privilege, like class privilege, reaches far back into America's past. The racial hierarchy with white groups of European origin at the top and people of color at the bottom serves important functions for society and for certain categories of people. It ensures that some people are available to do society's dirty work at low wages. Racial hierarchy has positive consequences for the status quo: It enables the powerful to retain their control and their advantages. Racial stratification also offers better occupational opportunities, income, and education to white people. These advantages constitute racial privilege.

This chapter examines racial inequality from several different vantage points. First, the characteristics of minority groups and racial and ethnic groups are presented. Then, the historical victimization of blacks, Chicanos, Asian Americans, and Native Americans is discussed. Explanations of racial inequality are followed by a look at its effect on blacks and Hispanics in terms of income, jobs, education, and health. Finally, the chapter turns to contemporary trends in racial and ethnic relations in order to reveal growing racial polarization.

The theme of the chapter is that the unequal placement of minority groups is the result of structured systems of discrimination. While patterns of discrimination have changed over time, racial domination remains a persistent feature of American society. Today, old forms of inequality thrive alongside new and more subtle forms of discrimination. The problems of race relate to broader issues of social organization. The oppressed people are not the problem; the structure of society that distributes resources unequally is the problem. Furthermore, minorities are not always passive victims of racial oppression. Their histories reveal varied strategies of survival, resistance, and coping in the face of overwhelming odds. Nevertheless, the magnitude of discrimination in America has maintained the subordination of people of color.

THE CHARACTERISTICS OF MINORITY GROUPS

Because majority-minority relations operate basically as a power relationship, conflict (or at least the potential for conflict) is always present. Overt conflict is most likely when the subordinate group attempts to alter the distribution of power. Size is not crucial in determining whether or not a group is the most powerful. A numerical minority may in fact have more political representation than the majority, as is the case in the Union of South Africa and in most colonial situations. Thus, the most important characteristic of a subordinate "minority" group is that it is dominated by a more powerful group.

A second characteristic of a minority group is that it is composed of people with similar characteristics that differ significantly from the dominant group. These characteristics are salient: They are visible, though not necessarily physical, and they make a difference.

The behavior and/or characteristics of minority group members are stereotyped and systematically condemned by the dominant or majority group. Minority groups typically inspire stereotypes in the minds of the dominant group, presumably because these negative generalizations keep them "down."

One last characteristic that all minority groups have in common is that they are singled out for differential and unfair treatment. The discrimination may be subtle or blatant, but it is always detrimental. A sizable portion of this chapter will focus on the various manifestations of discrimination toward minority groups in the United States.

These criteria—relative powerlessness, visible differentiation from the majority, negative stereotyping, and unfair discrimination—determine what social categories are **minority groups.** Typically, eight categories of people are commonly designated as minority groups. Each type is described in the paragraphs that follow.

Race is a social category that serves as a basis for differential treatment. Although the concept of race defies biological definition, in most societies it is socially significant. Racial groups are set apart and singled out for unequal treatment.

A second category, *ethnicity,* is also a traditional basis for inequality. An ethnic group has a culture distinctive from the dominant one. An Amish rural community and an Italian neighborhood in Boston are examples of ethnic groups. Of course, racial groups may also differ culturally from the dominant group—say, the Chinese in San Francisco's Chinatown or any tribe of Native Americans.

The third classification, *religion,* also places some categories in inferior positions. Throughout most of their history Jews have been persecuted because of their religion (or assumed religious ties) in one country after another. Much of the unrest in Northern Ireland stems from religious differences. The Protestants in that country are dominant, and the Catholics are the objects of discrimination.

Another category, the *impoverished,* constitutes a minority group in all societies. As we found in Chapter 10, the American poor are powerless and victims of varied forms of discrimination.

One basis for differentiation, *gender,* has only recently been recognized as a basis for minority status. Women in American society are relatively powerless, perceived in terms of stereotyped qualities (e.g., incapable of leadership because of being highly emotional), and victimized by discrimination, as you see in Chapter 12.

Certain *deviant* groups also have the characteristics of minority groups (see Chapter 8). Unmarried mothers (and their offspring), homosexuals, ex-criminals, and ex-mental patients are examples of deviant groups with minority status.

A seventh category, the *aged,* meets the criteria for a minority group in many societies. The elderly in the United States are clearly objects of discrimination, possess negative stereotypes, and are relatively powerless.

The *physically different* also have minority group status. The deformed, the handicapped, the obese, the ugly, and the short experience discrimination because they are different.

RACIAL AND ETHNIC GROUPS

Both race and ethnicity are very significant in U.S. society. Groups labeled as races by the wider society are bound together by their common conditions. As a result, they develop distinctive cultural or ethnic characteristics. Groups with common national origins or common religious traditions also develop separate cultural or ethnic characteristics. **Ethnicity** is the condition of being culturally distinct on the basis of race, religion, or national origin. Ethnic groups such as Jews, Poles, and Italians have distinguishing cultural characteristics that are rooted in national origin and religion. Racial groups also have distinctive ethnic or cultural characteristics. Therefore, they may be referred to as racial-ethnics. Blacks, Chicanos, Vietnamese, Puerto Ricans, and Native Americans are examples of racial-ethnics because each of these groups has a distinctive culture or subculture, shares a common heritage, and has developed a common identity. Crucial to an understanding of these groups is that their racial characteristics have acquired meaning in a given social context that has changed over time. The meaning of race is shaped politically. What happens, according to Luhman and Gilman, is that "when people become convinced that two or more races exist, then those races do, in fact, exist in the everyday lives of the people who are labeled accordingly" (Luhman and Gilman, 1980:6).

Both race and ethnicity are traditional bases for systems of inequality, although there are historical and contemporary differences in society's placement of racial-ethnics and white-ethnics in this society.

Differences among Ethnic Groups

Some ethnic groups have moved into the mainstream of society while others have remained in a subordinate status. The Germans, Italians, and Irish, for example, experienced discrimination when they migrated here in the late nineteenth century but have been accepted into the dominant majority. Native Americans, blacks, Chicanos, and others, however, have not become assimilated and continue to be objects of discrimination. Two factors combine to explain much of this apparent anomaly.

The most obvious reason is color. Those groups easily identified by physical characteristics find it difficult if not impossible to escape the devalued label. Second, the conditions under which the ethnic groups came into contact with the dominant majority appear to be crucial. A key to the way ethnic groups were ultimately treated is whether or not they migrated to the United States voluntarily. (The following discussion is adapted from Luhman and Gilman, 1980:8–27.) Voluntary migrants came to the New World to enhance their inferior status or to market their skills in a land of opportunity. They came with hope and sometimes with resources to provide a foundation for their anticipated upward mobility. Most also had the option of returning if they found the conditions here unsatisfactory.

The voluntary migrants came to the United States in several waves. In colonial times the English, Scotch-Irish, and Germans were the most notable ethnic groups. The Catholic Irish came in great numbers just before the Civil War as a result of the great potato famine in Ireland. They were rural, unskilled, Catholic, and anti-English in sentiment. They settled in urban areas and experienced a good deal of discrimination. During this same period Chinese and later the Japanese migrated to western states. They experienced great discrimination by whites apprehensive about jobs.

From about 1870 to 1920 a great wave of voluntary migrants came to America, mainly from the Catholic areas of Europe—Poland, Italy, and Eastern Europe. These new immigrants were different from the dominant English Protestant culture. As a result, they experienced more discrimination than many of the earlier immigrants. The antimigrant feeling was exposed in a 1924 federal law, the National Origins Act, which restricted immigration from southern and eastern Europe and stopped it altogether for Asians.

The voluntary migrants came to America and experienced varying forms of labor exploitation and other forms of discrimination. In general, though, they fared better than those who came involuntarily. The different consequences were due in large part to the labor that racial-ethnics did when they were forced into the United States. Unlike European-ethnics, who began work mostly in industry or at least in industrial sectors of the economy, racial-ethnics could not move about as families or individuals in response to the needs of an industrializing economy. Instead, blacks, Chicanos, and Asians were forced into preindustrial work that was low in pay, status, and chances for upward mobility. To understand the plight of the involuntary migrants, let us look briefly at the historical experiences of four such groups—blacks, Chicanos, Asians, and Native Americans.

Blacks

The slave trade brought blacks to America from Africa from 1619 until the Civil War, when they constituted one-eighth of the population. The slaves were defined as property and denied the rights given to other members of society. Families could be broken up for economic or punitive reasons. The slave owners used their power in several ways to maintain their dominance over their slaves. They demanded absolute obedience; to question the authority of the master meant physical punishment, often severe. Second, blacks were taught to defer to their masters and to accept their own inferiority. Third, the masters used public displays of power to create in slaves a sense of awe. Fourth, slaves were taught to identify with their masters' economic success. Finally, slaves were made to feel dependent on their masters, primarily by restrictions on their education. Typically, it was illegal in the South to teach a slave to read or write.

Following Emancipation the newly freed blacks, except for the brief period of Reconstruction, remained powerless. They did not have the skills and resources to break away from their dependence on whites. Because whites owned the land, blacks were forced to enter into sharecropping agreements, where they would farm the land, take all the risks, and return a percentage of the crops harvested to the owner. Typically, the sharecroppers would borrow on the next year's crop to purchase equipment, food, and clothing. Thus, a cycle of indebtedness was set up that bound the sharecroppers as if they were slaves.

During this same period many states passed "Jim Crow" laws mandating racial segregation in almost all areas of life (separate schools, transportation, neighborhoods, drinking fountains, and public eating establishments). These laws, which legalized white domination, remained in effect until about 1965.

The hallmark of representative democracy is that all citizens have the fundamental right to vote for those who will administer and make the laws. Those in power have often defied this principle of democracy by minimizing, neutralizing, or even negating the voting privileges of blacks (Simon and Eitzen, 1990:231–232). Although the Fourteenth Amendment gave blacks the right to vote after the Civil War, the white majority in the southern states used a variety of tactics to keep them from voting. Most effective was the strategy of intimidation. Blacks who tried to assert their right to vote were often beaten, sometimes lynched, or their property was destroyed. A more subtle approach, however, was quite effective in eliminating the black vote in the southern states: Through legal means laws were passed to achieve illegal discrimination. One tactic was the white primary, which excluded blacks from the party primary (Key, 1949:619–643). The Constitution prohibited the states from denying the vote on the basis of race. A political party, however, because it was a private association, *could* discriminate. The Democratic party throughout most of the South chose the option of limiting the primary to whites. Blacks could legally vote in the general election, but only for the candidates already selected by whites. And since the Democratic party in the South was supreme, whoever was selected in the primary would be the victor in the general election. This practice was nullified by the Supreme Court in 1944.

Other legal obstacles for blacks in the South were the literacy test and the poll tax, which were finally prohibited by the Twenty-Fourth Amendment, passed in 1964. Both obstacles were designed as southern suffrage requirements to admit whites to the electorate and exclude blacks (without mentioning race). The literacy test and its related requirements were blatantly racist.

Its object was to allow all adult white males to vote while excluding all Blacks. The problem with this test was that many whites would also be excluded because they were illiterate. Legislators in various southern states contrived alternatives to the literacy requirements that would allow the illiterate whites to vote. One loophole was the "grandfather clause." This provision, based on Louisiana law, "exempted persons from the literacy test who were registered voters in any state prior to or on January 1, 1867, the sons and grandsons of such persons, and male persons of foreign birth naturalized before January 1, 1898" (Key, 1949:577). Obviously, the use of these dates prevented blacks from voting and thereby served to maintain white domination.

Beginning with World War I, a time of labor shortage and industrial expansion, blacks began to move from the rural South to the urban North. After the war, blacks in the North experienced large-scale discrimination as jobs became scarce. World War II brought another great wave of migrants to the industrial cities of the North, and again after the war blacks faced unemployment and discrimination from many fronts.

Several conditions following World War II made the black experience different the second time. Blacks were now concentrated in cities more than ever, increasing the likelihood of group actions to alter their oppression. Also, more blacks were educated and could provide leadership. More important, many blacks had served the country in the war and now were unwilling to accept continued inferiority. The result of these factors and others was the civil rights movement of the 1960s. Although there were significant positive changes for blacks resulting from this movement, including favorable legislation and court decisions, these gains have faltered due to economic conditions and continued racial discrimination.

Chicanos

The growing Hispanic presence in the United States has blinded many Americans to the real diversity that exists within this community. Hispanics or Latinos have diverse origins and diverse histories. In 1988, 62 percent of all Hispanic Americans were Chicanos or Mexican Americans, about 13 percent were Puerto Rican, 5 percent were Cuban, 12 percent were Central American and South American, and 8 percent "other Hispanic" (Valdivieso and Davis, 1988:4). Even though all groups have made major numerical impact on the United States since World War II, in this section we focus on Chicanos who involuntarily became part of the United States largely because of military conquest (Estrada et al., 1981; Moore, 1976).

Beginning about 1600 the southwestern part of the present United States was controlled by Spain. Mexico gained control over this area when it gained independence from Spain in 1821. Mexico permitted immigrants to settle in this territory (primarily in what is now Texas), and by 1830 there were some 20,000 Anglo* settlers (Barrera, 1979:1, 4). By 1835 these settlers were hostile

---

*Anglos, as used by Chicanos, refers to all Caucasian Americans, not just those who trace their origins to the British Isles.

toward Mexico and Mexicans. As one historian has described it, "The Texans saw themselves in danger of becoming the alien subjects of a people to whom they deliberately believed themselves morally, intellectually, and politically superior" (Baker, 1965:52). This feeling of superiority, Mexico's abolition of slavery, and other factors led to the Texas revolt of 1835 and an independent Texas republic. When the United States granted statehood to Texas in 1845, despite the fact that Mexico still claimed it, war was inevitable. Many U.S. politicians and business interests supported the war because of the high probability of winning and of subsequent territorial expansion (Acuña, 1972). As a result of the war, which lasted from 1846 to 1848, Mexico lost half its national territory and the United States increased its area by a third (Arizona, California, Colorado, New Mexico, Texas, Nevada, Utah, and parts of Kansas, Oklahoma, and Wyoming).* Under the Treaty of Guadalupe Hidalgo (1848), Mexicans living on the U.S. side of the new border who decided to remain would have all the rights of U.S. citizens according to the Constitution.

Despite the guarantees to the Mexicans who remained, their status under the new regime was clearly secondary. Their civil and property rights were routinely violated. Most importantly, the U.S. military, judicial system, and government were used to establish Anglos in positions of power in the economic structures that Mexicans had developed in mining, ranching, and agriculture (McWilliams, 1949). The techniques used to accomplish this control were taxation; a court system unfamiliar with Mexican and Spanish landowning laws, traditions, and customs; and the appropriation of land for the National Forest Service with little if any compensation. In short, Mexican Americans were largely dispossessed of power and property. With the coming of the railroads and the damming of rivers for irrigation, the Southwest became an area of economic growth, but the advantages accrued mainly to Anglos. Mexican Americans no longer owned the land; now they were the source of cheap labor, an exploited group at the bottom of the social and economic ladder. As Barrera has summarized:

> Dispossession from the land . . . depleted the economic base of Chicanos and put them in an even less favorable position to exercise influence over the political process. In addition, it had other far-ranging consequences, including facilitating the emergence of a colonial labor system in the Southwest, based in large part on Chicano labor. (Barrera, 1979:33)

What emerged in the nineteenth-century Southwest was a segmented labor force, which Barrera refers to as a colonial labor system: "A colonial labor system exists where the labor force is segmented along ethnic and/or racial lines, and one or more of the segments is systematically maintained in a subordinate position" (Barrera, 1979:39).

The twentieth century has been a period of large-scale immigration from Mexico to the Southwest. The number of persons born in Mexico living in the United States was 103,393 in 1900, 221,915 in 1910, and 639,017 in 1930.

---

*In 1853 the United States purchased from Mexico (the Gadsden Purchase) an additional 45,000 square miles in Arizona and New Mexico.

The Great Depression was an especially difficult time for Chicanos. Not only were they vulnerable because of their marginal jobs, they were also the object of hostility from many Anglos, who believed they were flooding an overcrowded labor market, depressing wages, and functioning as a drain on the welfare system. As a result, from 1929 to 1934 more than 400,000 Mexicans, many of them U.S. citizens, were forced to repatriate in Mexico. Those who applied for welfare benefits were the most likely to be victims: "Those who applied for relief were referred to 'Mexican Bureaus,' whose sole purpose was to reduce the welfare rolls by deporting the applicants. Indigence, not citizenship, was the criterion used in identifying Mexicans for repatriation" (Estrada et al., 1981:117).

In contrast, after World War II, when the economy was booming and jobs were plentiful, the U.S. government instituted the bracero program, which permitted Mexicans to migrate to the United States to work in agriculture. Farmers favored such a program because it assured them of a steady supply of cheap labor. This program was terminated in 1964, after nearly 5 million Mexicans had come to the United States, and a total annual immigration quota of 120,000 was imposed on all nations in the Western Hemisphere.

Since World War II there has been another source of migrants—"illegals" or "undocumented workers"—who came to the United States in great numbers seeking work. A current estimate is that perhaps more than a million people a year cross the border to work in the United States without legal permission. These immigrants are especially vulnerable to low wages and other abuses by employers and landlords.

The Census Bureau estimates the current Hispanic population at 20 million with perhaps another 7 million "undocumented workers" (Valdivieso and Davis, 1988). Both figures are likely to be too low, since the Census Bureau misses a significant portion of those who are poor, work in migrant jobs, live in overcrowded conditions; and, of course, those who are in the United States illegally do everything they can to avoid detection.

Currently, Chicanos experience discrimination not only in jobs and wages but also through segregated schools, the use of Anglo-oriented tests for placement in schools, residential segregation, and exclusionary policies by private organizations.

Asian Americans

Asian-American groups are different from other racial ethnics. Their characteristics vary widely according to their national origins and time of entry in the United States.

The history of Asian Americans begins with the arrival after 1848 of Chinese men recruited to work in California, the beginning of a large influx touched off by the gold rush. The numbers grew rapidly, with thousands working on construction of the transcontinental railroads in the 1860s. Agitation against the Chinese during the 1870s included rioting, special taxes, and an anti-Chinese law passed in 1887. In 1882 Congress passed the Chinese

Exclusion Act, which essentially banned immigration of Chinese into the United States. One result of such anti-Chinese sentiment was the substitution of Japanese workers for Chinese. (Gardner, Robey, and Smith, 1985:8).

Strict immigration laws of the 1920s (e.g., the National Origins Act of 1924) virtually halted Asian immigration into the United States. Immigration was also low during the depression of the 1930s. After 1952, some easing of Asian immigration was permitted with the McCarran-Walter Act. Asian immigration then skyrocketed with liberalized immigration policy in 1965 (Gardner, Robey, and Smith, 1985).

In 1970, Asian Americans numbered 4.1 million (1.5 percent of the total U.S. population). Since then, Asian Americans have migrated in larger numbers to the United States, including more than 700,000 Indochinese refugees after the Vietnam War, swelling their numbers to 5.1 million (2.1 percent of the population) in 1985. It is estimated that the number of Asian Americans will double in size by the year 2000 to about 10 million (Gardner, Robey, and Smith, 1985).

Asian Americans are often characterized as the "model minority," a label that masks great disparities among them. The largest Asian-American groups are Chinese (21 percent), Filipinos (20.4 percent), Japanese (14.9 percent), Vietnamese (12.3 percent), Korean (10.5 percent), and Asian Indian (10.2 percent). There are also such ethnic groups as Laotians, Kampucheans, Thais, Pakistanis, Indonesians, and Hmongs.

Whereas most of the pre-World War II Asian immigrants were peasants, the recent immigrants vary considerably by education and social class. On the one hand, many arrived as educated middle-class professionals with highly valued skills and some knowledge of English. Others, such as the Indochinese, arrived as uneducated, impoverished refugees. These differences are reflected in the differences in income and poverty level by ethnic category. Asian Americans taken together have higher average incomes than do other Americans. Some categories, however, do significantly less well. Two-thirds of the Indochinese, for example, who arrived from 1978 through 1981, were below the poverty line two years after arrival, and that figure was still 30 percent after four years (Gardner, Robey, and Smith, 1985:35).

Native Americans

Native Americans, formerly known as American Indians, have lived continuously in North America for at least 30,000 years (Dorris, 1981). The tribes located in North America were and are extremely heterogeneous, with major differences in physical characteristics, language, and social organization. There were theocracies, democracies, and hereditary chiefdoms; matrilineal and patrilineal systems; hunters and farmers; nomads and villagers. Some tribes were basically cooperative; others were fiercely competitive.

> In 1492, when Columbus landed at Watling's Island in the Bahamas, the North American continent was an area of astonishing ethnic and cultural diversity. North of the Rio Grande was a population of 12 million people, something

like 400 separate and distinct cultures, 500 languages, and a dazzling variety of political and religious institutions and physical and ethnic types. (Cook, 1981:118)

Native Americans, then, lived in a pluralistic world, with tribes of quite different cultures and social organizations coexisting. In contrast, the Europeans who settled in the New World were quite similar: They spoke some variant of Indo-European language; they had a common religious tradition—Christianity; political and social conventions were similar (patrilineal descent, male dominance, property rights, and political organization as a nation-state). They shared a belief in what they considered the international law of the right of discovery. This belief held that the European nation first landing on and claiming the right to territory not formerly held by other Europeans had the exclusive authority to negotiate with the natives for the absolute ownership of the land. This ethnocentric notion was buttressed further by the Europeans' belief that they represented the highest level of civilization. They were convinced of their superiority to the natives of the New World, whom they considered to be not only infidels but inferior beings.

From the beginning, the Europeans took the land once owned by the natives. One way they took land was through treaties. The English and the French offered inducements to tribes to cede some of their land in exchange for the promise of material goods, health benefits, and the guaranteed security of Indian lands. Often these treaties included a perpetuity clause—that the treaty would remain in effect and the Indians could live in peace, security, and independence in their lands "as long as the waters flow and the grasses grow." The Indians accepted the treaties but were quickly disillusioned; "virtually all were broken by the European signatories" (Dorris, 1981:49).

As new waves of settlers moved westward, the lands the Indians had been promised were forcibly taken. Native Americans protecting their lands fought battles with settlers and with U.S. troops. Always the result was that Native Americans were forced to move farther west to remote areas.

Native Americans were also forced to move to other places against their will. Although the Supreme Court ruled that the Cherokees had legal title to their lands in the South, President Andrew Jackson forcibly evicted them and forced them to walk 1,000 miles in midwinter from Carolina and Georgia to Oklahoma. Four thousand died in this forced march. They had been promised that the land that they settled in the Indian territory would never be made part of a state; yet this area became part of Oklahoma in 1907.

As the population of European origin in the United States began to surge west of the Mississippi in the late 1800s, there was increasing pressure on the recently removed groups, such as the Cherokee, to give up some of their new land and on the indigenous groups to the west, such as the Sioux, to give up large amounts of land traditionally under their control. Some of this further expansion was accomplished in a relatively peaceful manner through treaties, and some was accomplished through violent military confrontation. The lands reserved for Native Americans were generally regarded as the least desirable by whites and were almost always located far from major population

SOME DAY, SON...
NONE OF THIS
WILL BE YOURS.

Reprinted by
permission of United
Feature Syndicate.

centers, trails, and transportation routes that later became part of the modern system of metropolitan areas, highways, and railroads. In sum, for most of the nineteenth century the policy of the U.S. government was to isolate and concentrate Native Americans in places with few natural resources, far from contact with the developing U.S. economy and society (Sandefur, 1989).

In 1871 all Native Americans were made "wards" of the federal government and were placed on federal reservations on lands considered of little value. As wards, Native Americans had no control of their communities and no power to effect federal policies over them. They were under the jurisdiction of the Bureau of Indian Affairs, which decided "what they would eat, where they would live, and ultimately what style of living they would adopt" (Luhman and Gilman, 1980:37). Thus, they were stripped of their political rights and even their culture.

Native Americans were first granted U.S. citizenship and the right to vote in 1924. Some states, including New York and North Carolina, disputed their right to vote even into the 1970s. Recent legislation and court decisions have restored some rights and powers to Native American tribes. This legislation is significant in two major respects. First, various tribes are claiming in the courts that they have the legal rights to millions of acres of land. Second, Native American lands are teeming with riches that the Indians also claim. According to Cook:

> It is one of history's more stunning ironies. The 51.9 million acres in the U.S. reserved for the Indians were lands the white man could not see any conceivable reason to reserve for himself. They were too wet or too dry, too barren or too remote. Now, at a time when the U.S. seems to be running out of practically everything, the 272 federally recognized Indian reservations constitute one of the largest and least known mineral repositories on the continent— nearly 5 percent of the U.S.'s oil and gas, one-third of its strippable low-sulfur coal, one-half of its privately owned uranium. (Cook, 1981:108)

We do not yet know how the powerful will decide on these claims. If history is a guide, Native Americans will not receive their share.

The treatment of Native Americans throughout their history of contact with Europeans and Caucasian Americans has been brutal. From a population of 12 million at the time of Columbus, their numbers were reduced to an estimated 210,000 in 1910.* This remarkable decrease was the result of three major factors: death in battle; death from such Old World diseases as smallpox, cholera, and measles, to which they lacked immunity; and the poverty and misery forced on them by the decisions of the powerful.

Today, Native Americans are the poorest, the least educated, least employed, unhealthiest, and worst-housed ethnic group in the United States. A few statistics confirm their appalling condition:

- More than one-third live below the poverty line. In some areas of Arizona and Utah the proportion below this line is as high as 65 percent.
- Only about one-third of Indian males are high school graduates.
- Sixty-two percent of all housing units on Indian reservations are substandard, compared with 12.9 percent in the general U.S. population.
- Deaths from tuberculosis, dysentery, and accidents are four times higher for Indians than for non-Indians.
- For 1976–1978 the Indian Health Service reported 16.1 infant deaths per 1000 live births, compared with 14.1 per 1000 for the total population (Cabib, 1981:3).
- The life expectancy of the average Indian is ten years below that of the nation as a whole.
- Unemployment generally ranges between 45 and 55 percent.
- The suicide rate is double the national average, and the alcoholism rate is at least eight times as high (Huntley, 1983).

Blacks, Latinos, Asian Americans, and Native Americans, then, have been and are subordinated. Some important characteristics help to explain their continued secondary status in American society. Each of these groups is set apart from the majority on the basis of race—a quality that has social and political rather than biological significance. The next section elaborates on the explanations given for this phenomenon.

EXPLANATIONS OF RACIAL AND ETHNIC INEQUALITY

Why have some racial and ethnic groups been consistently disadvantaged throughout American history? Some ethnic groups, such as the Irish and Jews, have experienced discrimination but managed to overcome their initial disadvantages (Sowell, 1981a). Others, such as the blacks, Chicanos, and Native Americans, have not been able to cast off their secondary status. Three types of theories have been used to explain why some groups are consistently singled out for discrimination: deficiency theories, bias theories, and structural discrimination theories. The following discussion is based on Barrera, 1979:174–219.

---

*The 1980 Census counted as Indians all who identified themselves as such—1,418,195.

Deficiency Theories

A number of analysts have argued that some groups are inferior because they *are* inferior. That is, when compared with the majority, they are deficient in some important way. There are three varieties of deficiency theory.

Biological Deficiency.   This classical explanation for the inferiority of certain groups maintains that their inferiority is the result of flawed genetic—and, therefore, hereditary—traits. This is the position of Arthur Jensen and Richard Herrnstein, as we saw in Chapter 9, that blacks are mentally inferior to whites. Despite the work of these and others of their persuasion, there is no definitive evidence for the thesis that racial groups differ in intelligence. Biological deficiency theories are generally not accepted in the scientific community.

Cultural Deficiency.   Many varieties of explanations for racial subordination center on cultural characteristics thought to be inherited from the past and handed down from generation to generation. Cultural differences treated as cultural deficiencies are the reason that racial minorities are disproportionately found in subordinate positions. **Cultural deficiency** explanations argue that some flaw within the minority way of life is responsible for that minority group's secondary status.

From this perspective minorities are culturally disadvantaged because of their heritage and customs. For example, some analysts have argued that Chicano culture has held members of this group back (Kluckhohn and Strodtbeck, 1961; for the opposing position, see Baca Zinn, 1981, 1982). From this perspective, Chicanos are viewed as disadvantaged because their culture values the present rather than the future, dependency rather than independence, and low rather than high motivation for achievement. These traits, coupled with the difficulty that many have with the English language, mean that Chicanos will be less likely to be successful in Anglo schools and Anglo work settings.

Cultural deficiency provides the basis for the famous 1967 report of Daniel Patrick Moynihan who charged that the tangle of pathology within black ghettos was rooted in the deterioration of the Negro family (U.S. Department of Labor, 1965). High rates of marital dissolution, female-headed households, out-of-wedlock births, welfare dependency, and the resulting family structure were explained as the residuals of slavery and discrimination, a complex web of pathological patterns passed down through successive generations. This work was guided and shaped by assumptions about poverty that found cultural patterns of the poor to be defective and self-perpetuating.

The Moynihan report was widely criticized for contending that deviant family forms are part of black culture rather than being an adaptation to socioeconomic conditions. The main objection to the Moynihan report is that it is a classic case of blaming the victim. It locates the cause of pathology within blacks, not in the racially stratified society.

In effect, culture deficiency theorists blame the victim and ignore the structural constraints that deny certain groups the same opportunities that others have. During the 1960s and 1970s there was extensive refutation of cultural deficiency theories. Many scholars documented various strengths within minority communities and showed how their unique ways of life were "adaptations" to the conditions of poverty and racism. Recently, however, cultural deficiency as a theory has been used to explain rising poverty and the growth of female-headed households in U.S. inner cities. According to some scholars, policy makers, and social commentators, declining economic conditions in black ghettos are created by culture, the deteriorating family, and welfare. For example, Charles Murray in his book *Losing Ground* (1984) has charged the welfare state with responsibility for family decline and poverty. He has argued that increased welfare benefits have made it profitable for black women to have children out of wedlock. In his view, welfare also encourages black men to escape family responsibilities, which creates poverty in the long run. Another disturbing example of the "ghetto pathology" theme was illustrated in Bill Moyers's 1986 television documentary "The Vanishing Black Family." We return to this theme in the last section of the chapter.

Bias Theories

The deficiency theories just discussed blame the minorities for their plight. **Bias theories,** on the other hand, blame the members of the majority—in particular, they blame the prejudiced attitudes of majority members. Gunnar Myrdal, for example, argued in his classic, *An American Dilemma,* that prejudiced attitudes are the source of discriminatory actions, which in turn keep minorities subordinate (Myrdal, 1944). The inferior status of minorities reinforces negative stereotypes that in turn justify the prejudice of the majority; the process is a vicious cycle that perpetuates the secondary status from generation to generation.

David Wellman has made an extensive critique of bias theories and presented an alternative (Wellman, 1977). He has raised a number of objections to the traditional view that the attitudes of white Americans are the major cause of racism. The typical view is that whites, particularly lower-class whites, have hostile feelings toward and make faulty generalizations about minorities. Minorities are thus prejudged and misjudged by the majority, and the result is discrimination. Prejudiced attitudes, however, do not explain the behaviors of unprejudiced whites who defend the traditional arrangements that negatively affect minorities. Unbiased persons fight to preserve the status quo by favoring, for example, the seniority system in occupations, or they oppose affirmative action, quota systems, busing to achieve racial balance, and open enrollment in higher education. As Wellman has argued:

> The terms in which middle-class professionals defend traditional institutional arrangements are, strictly speaking, not examples of racial prejudice. They are neither overtly racial nor, given these people's *interests,* misrepresentations of facts. However, while the sentiments may not be prejudiced, they

> justify arrangements that in effect, if not in intent, maintain the status quo and thereby keep blacks in subordinate positions. (Wellman, 1977:8)

Thus, to focus strictly on prejudice is to take too narrow a view. This view presents an inaccurate portrayal of racism because it concentrates only on the bigots and ignores the discriminating acts of those who are not prejudiced. Moreover, according to Wellman, prejudice is not the cause of discrimination. Rather, it is the racial organization of society that is the cause of people's racial beliefs. The determining feature of majority-minority relations is not prejudice, but rather the superior position of the majority and the institutions that maintain this superiority. "The subordination of people of color is functional to the operation of American society as we know it and the color of one's skin is a primary determinant of people's position in the social structure" (Wellman, 1977:35). Thus, institutional and individual racism generate privilege for whites. Discrimination provides the privileged with disproportionate advantages in the social, economic, and political spheres. Racist acts, in this view, are not only based on hatred, stereotyped conceptions, or prejudgment but are rational responses to the struggle over scarce resources by individuals acting to preserve their advantage.

Structural Discrimination Theories

Critics of the deficiency and bias theories argue that these explanations focus, incorrectly, on individuals—the characteristics and attitudes of the prejudiced majority and the flaws of the minority. Both kinds of theory ignore the politico-economic system that dominates and oppresses minorities. Parenti has criticized those who ignore the system as victim-blamers. "Focusing on the poor and ignoring the system of power, privilege, and profit which makes them poor, is a little like blaming the corpse for the murder" (Parenti, 1978:24). **Structural discrimination theories** correct this error by focusing on institutionalized patterns of discrimination that operate independently of people's attitudes. These themes are based on the power, domination, and conflict that are institutionalized in the American racial order.

Institutional racism refers to the established, customary, and respected ways in which society operates to keep the minority in a subordinate position. For Carmichael and Hamilton (1967) there are two types of racism— individual and institutional. Individual racism consists of overt acts by individuals that harm other individuals or their property. This type of action is usually publicly decried and is probably on the decline in the United States. Institutional racism is more injurious than individual racism to more minority group members, but it is not recognized by the dominant-group members as racism. Carmichael and Hamilton illustrated the two types as follows:

> When a black family moves into a home in a white neighborhood and is stoned, burned or routed out, they are victims of an overt act of individual racism which many people will condemn—at least in words. But it is institutional racism that keeps black people locked in dilapidated slum tenements,

subject to the daily prey of exploitative slumlords, merchants, loan sharks, and discriminatory real estate agents. . . . Respectable individuals can absolve themselves from individual blame: *they* would never plant a bomb in a church: *they* would never stone a black family. But they continue to support political officials and institutions that would and do perpetuate institutionally racist policies. Thus *acts* of overt, individual racism may not typify the society, but institutional racism does. (Carmichael and Hamilton, 1967:4–5)

We have noted that some individuals and groups discriminate whether or not they are bigots. These individuals and groups operate within a social milieu that is also discriminatory. The social milieu includes laws, customs, religious beliefs, social stratification, the distribution of power, and the stable arrangements and practices through which things get done in society. These social arrangements and accepted ways of doing things may consciously or unconsciously disadvantage some social categories while benefiting others. The major sectors of society—the system of law and the administration of justice, the economic system, the formal educational structure, and health care—are all possible discriminators. Thus, the term *institutional discrimination* is a useful one. As Knowles and Prewitt have said, the institutions of society

have great power to reward and penalize. They reward by providing career opportunities for some people and foreclosing them for others. They reward as well by the way social goods and services are distributed—by deciding who receives training and skills, medical care, formal education, political influence, moral support and self-respect, productive employment, fair treatment by the law, decent housing, self-confidence, and the promise of a secure future for self and children. (Knowles and Prewitt, 1965:5)

Analysts of society, pursuing the phenomenon of discrimination, need to ask, How are things normally done in the society? Who gets preferential treatment under these normal arrangements? Who is automatically excluded because of these arrangements? The answers to these questions are not always easy because the arrangements are "natural" and the discrimination often unintentional or disguised. The task is especially difficult because the exact placement of responsibility is often impossible to pinpoint. Who is responsible for the low scores of ghetto children on standard IQ tests? Who is responsible for residential segregation? Who is responsible for the high unemployment rate of minority group members?

There are four basic themes of institutional discrimination (Benokraitis and Feagin, 1974). First is the importance of history in determining present conditions and affecting resistance to change. Historically, institutions defined and enforced norms and role relationships that were racially distinct. The American nation was founded and its institutions established when blacks were slaves, uneducated, and different culturally from the dominant whites. From the beginning blacks were considered inferior (the original Constitution, for example, counted a slave as three-fifths of a person). Religious beliefs buttressed this notion of the inferiority of blacks and justified the differential allocation of privileges and sanctions in society. Laws, customs, and traditions usually continue to reinforce current thinking. Institutions have an inertial quality: Once set in motion, they tend to continue on the same course. Thus, institutional racism is extremely difficult to change without a complete overhaul of society's institutions.

The second theme of institutional discrimination is that discrimination can occur *without* conscious bigotry. All it takes for institutional discrimination to continue is for employers to insist that prospective employees take aptitude or IQ tests that are based on middle-class experiences, or for decisions on who must be fired in times of financial exigency to be based on seniority, or for employers to stress educational requirements for hiring. These conditions, seemingly fair and neutral, are biased against minorities.

Institutional discrimination is also more invisible than individual discrimination. Institutional discrimination is more subtle and less intentional than individual acts of discrimination. As a result, establishing blame for this kind of discrimination is extremely difficult.

Finally, institutional discrimination is reinforced because institutions are interrelated. The exclusion of minorities from the upper levels of education, for example, is likely to affect their opportunities in other institutions (type of job, level of remuneration). Similarly, being poor means that your children will probably receive an inferior education, be propertyless, suffer from bad health, and be treated unjustly by the criminal justice system. These inequities are cumulative. As Benokraitis and Feagin have argued:

> Once a minority is excluded from one institution, chances are greater that it will also be excluded from other institutional privilege. Thus, institutional racism theorists agree that once, historically, institutions have evolved differential opportunities for wealth, power, prestige, privilege, and authority based on racial criteria, unequal resources will produce unequal qualifications to compete for goods and services, unequal qualifications will limit access to goods and services and unequal access to goods and services will result in unequal resources. (Benokraitis and Feagin, 1974:6)

Let us examine some illustrations of how various aspects of the society work to derogate minority groups, deny them equality, and even do them violence. Institutional derogation occurs when minority groups and their members are made to seem inferior or possess negative stereotypes through legitimate means by the powerful in society. The portrayal of minority group members in the media (movies, television, newspapers, and magazines) is often derogatory. Only recently has there been an effort to thwart the negative images of minorities in the media. The "Amos n' Andy" radio program that was popular in the 1940s and 1950s used almost all the black stereotypes—and America laughed. The early Shirley Temple movies had an adult black man by the name of Stepin Fetchit whose role was to be more childlike than Miss Temple. The traditional roles of blacks, Native Americans, and women in movies, novels, and television have typically focused on the negative stereotypes of these groups. These stereotypes are similarly reinforced in textbooks.

The system (customs, practices, expectations, laws, beliefs) also works to deny equality to minority group members—most often without malicious intent. Because it is the system that disadvantages, discrimination would continue even if tomorrow all Americans were to awake with all animosity toward minority groups obliterated from their hearts and minds. All that is needed for minorities to suffer is that the law continue to favor the owners of property over renters and debtors. All that is needed for job opportunities to remain unequal is for employers to hire those with the most conventional training and experience and to use machines when they seem more immediately economical than manual labor. All that is needed to ensure that poor children get an inferior education is to continue "tracking," using class-biased tests, making education irrelevant in their work, rewarding children who conform to the teachers' middle-class concepts of the "good student," and paying disproportionately less for their education (buildings, supplies, teachers, counselors) (Steinberg, n.d.:3). In other words, all that is needed to perpetuate discrimination in the United States is to pursue a policy of "business as usual."

Skolnick has described institutional discrimination as it applies to blacks, but the same could be said for the treatment of other minority groups as well:

> It is theoretically possible to have a racist society in which most of the individual members of that society do not express racist attitudes. A society in which most of the good jobs are held by one race, and the dirty jobs by the people of another color, is a society in which racism is institutionalized, no matter what the beliefs of its members are. For example, the universities of America are probably the least bigoted of American institutions. One would rarely, if ever, hear an openly bigoted expression at schools like Harvard, Yale, the University of Chicago, the University of California. At the same time, university faculties and students have usually been white, the custodians black. The universities have concerned themselves primarily with the needs and interests of the white upper middle and upper classes, and have viewed the lower classes, and especially blacks, as objects of study rather than of service. In this sense, they have, willy-nilly, been institutionally "white racist." (Skolnick, 1969:180)

Approximately 5 percent of lawyers, 17 percent of all physicians, 7 percent of dentists, and 5 percent of architects are racial minorities (*Monthly Labor Review,* 1985:50). Racial minority groups are underrepresented in the professions because they receive a "disadvantaged" education for the reasons given above. This underrepresentation brings about the conditions that the dominant group considers proof of the minority's inferiority. The great British playwright George Bernard Shaw is reported to have said, "The haughty American nation . . . makes the Negro clean its boots, and then proves the . . . inferiority of the Negro by the fact that he is a bootblack."

One structural theory, colonial theory, directly addresses the question of why some ethnic groups have overcome their disadvantaged status while others have not. This issue is important, because it challenges the myth that the United States is a melting pot. **Colonial theory** argues that there are fundamental differences between the experiences of racial ethnics and European ethnics. Racial ethnics were colonized within the boundaries of the United States, but Europeans immigrated to this society. Internal colonialism determined the asymmetrical relations of people of color within the dominant society, and it shaped their continuing experiences in America. Using this framework, we can see that despite certain similarities (such as poverty and discrimination) the experiences of racial minorities contrasted sharply with those of European immigrants. These conditions make assimilation into the larger society a myth for people of color because the colonial experiences embedded them in a system of racial domination. The key ingredient in internal colonialism is that the racial control that began as the result of conquest is institutionalized in social, economic, and political spheres.

The colonial model assigns fundamental importance to the labor that people of color did when they were brought into the United States. European ethnics began work mostly in industry, or at least in industrial sectors of the economy, where they could move about as families or individuals in response to the needs of an industrializing economy. In contrast, blacks and Chicanos were forced into certain types of work. Blauner has noted the consequences of preindustrial work:

> Like European overseas colonialism, America has used African, Asian, Mexican, and to a lesser degree Indian workers for the cheapest labor, concentrating people of color in the most unskilled jobs, the least advanced sectors of the economy and the most industrially backward regions of the nation. In an historical sense, people of color provided much of the hard labor (and the technical skills) that built up the agricultural base and the mineral-transport-communications infrastructure necessary for industrialization and modernization, whereas the Europeans worked primarily within the industrialized, modern sectors. The initial position of European ethnics, while low, was therefore strategic for movement up the economic and social pyramid. The placement of nonwhite groups, however, imposed barrier upon barrier on such mobility, freezing them for long periods of time in the least favorable segments of the economy. (Blauner, 1972:62)

Today the labor market continues to trap minority group members. Job opportunities are segmented in American society into a dual labor market. (The following discussion is adapted from Moore, 1978:27–34.) There are essentially two types of employers, with the labor market operating differently for each. Employers in the primary core enterprises are heavily capitalized and unionized; they offer jobs with relatively high wages, good working conditions, security, fringe benefits, and the chance for advancement. The other type, the marginal employers, pay the lowest wages and often have deplorable working conditions (such as in the garment industry, restaurants, and farming). These jobs require few skills. Employers are interested in workers who will make minimal demands. Workers who agitate for better wages and working conditions are soon replaced because they have no job security and there is generally a large pool of persons available to take over their jobs (teenagers, ex-convicts, recent migrants from rural areas, recent immigrants, and the poor). Very few people at the bottom of the labor market ever have access to the jobs considered part of the "American dream"—those

Scientific Reasoning

Science uses methods that are logical, systematic, and verifiable. It is exactly opposite to forms of analysis using dogma, intuition, and revelation. The objective of science is to search for facts. This quest is guided by a number of postulates that scientists agree maximize the chances for finding facts. These are:

1. All behavior is naturally determined.
2. Human beings are part of the natural world.
3. Nature is orderly and regular.
4. Nature is uniform.
5. Nature is permanent.
6. All objective phenomena are eventually knowable.
7. Nothing is self-evident.
8. Truth is relative; absolute or final truth may never be achieved.
9. All perceptions are achieved through the senses.
10. People can trust their perceptions, memory, and reasoning as reliable agencies for acquiring facts.

Once they are obtained, verifiable facts must be assembled and arranged into useful structures. It requires the use of logic (valid reasoning) to achieve reliable conclusions about facts. There are a number of rules and prescriptions for logical reasoning that have been established over the course of twenty-five centuries of Western thought.

As an example of the role that *faulty* logic plays in our interpretations, let's consider the following discussion:

[Blacks] have a proportionately higher crime rate than do Whites. This common contention (made even by chiefs of police, prison officials and legislators) illustrates several facets of faulty logic: (a) It implicitly infers that *all* [blacks] have a higher potential for committing crimes; and this is not a fact—only some classes of urban [blacks] in the United States exhibit a higher rate of some types of popularly-noticed crimes. (b) It also infers that [blacks]—even if they should in fact commit proportionately more crimes—do so *because*

they are [blacks]. This implication is also false in fact, as any social psychologist well knows. Without elaborating this example, it is interesting to note that here is a case of a partially-true assertion which is valid for the wrong reason (i.e., wrong in the sense of popular attribution or causative reasoning). In the cases where [blacks] have a proportionately higher crime rate than do Whites, they apparently do so because (1) crime rates are proportionately higher in urban than in rural areas; and the [black]-criminal allegation is largely an outgrowth of [black] immigration into urban areas; (2) popularly-noted crimes are generally of a lower criminal class variety (e.g., rape, robbery, burglary and assault); and [blacks] predominate in the lower classes due to the racial discrimination exhibited against them in jobs, housing, etc.; and because (3) crime rates as indicated by the population of penal establishments (where [blacks] are proportionately high) simply reflect disproportionate social (i.e., police, the courts, the press) sensitivity to lower-class crimes. There is no substantial evidence, for example, that [blacks] commit proportionately as many (let alone more) upper-class crimes (e.g., embezzlement, big-time gambling, forgery, espionage) than do Whites; in fact, growing evidence strongly suggests that they commit proportionately fewer of such kinds of crimes. If, however, it is clearly established as a matter of fact that one's criminal-behavior potential is in no way a direct and necessary consequence of his racial inheritance, then it may be validly deduced that—if and when [blacks] achieve complete social, economic, political and legal equality with Whites—they probably will commit the same proportion of all types of crimes as will Whites.

The foregoing argument suggests the fundamental role that sound reasoning plays in the scientific approach.

Source: Carlo L. Lastrucci, *The Scientific Approach: Basic Principles of the Scientific Method* (Cambridge, MA: Schenkman, 1967). An elaboration of the postulates of science is found on pp. 37–47, and the excerpt is from pp. 50–51. Reprinted by permission of the publisher.

with security, good pay, and chances for advancement. Low educational attainment and lack of skills keep minority group members in jobs that are unstable, below average in wages, and a dead end. The poor black or Chicano is most likely to end up in these jobs because the institutions of society are programmed for sifting and sorting individuals, usually according to predetermined categories such as age, race, sex, and socioeconomic background (see Chapter 13).

Structural theories view race as a basis for the formation of power and resource inequality. Most structural theories recognize that class discrimination and racial discrimination work with and through each other to produce social inequality. The roots of racial discrimination lie deep within the American economy. Racial stratification theories emphasize the deep-lying roots of racial and ethnic inequalities in the U.S. economy.

RACIAL STRATIFICATION FROM THE CONFLICT AND ORDER PERSPECTIVES

Order perspectives of race and ethnic relations have assumed that the United States is a land of opportunity and that all groups—ethnic and racial—would eventually be assimilated into the mainstream. This would occur as minorities abandoned their distinctive ethnic characteristics and adopted "American" traits. As they learned the skills and acquired the education required by the larger society, minorities would achieve equality. In assimilating, they would give up their ethnicity. "**Assimilate**" comes from the Latin word, assimulare, meaning to make similar (Feagin, 1984:26). Assimilation theories underscore value consensus as maintaining order in the existing social structure as assimilation proceeds. However, racial ethnics were placed in the larger society in ways that precluded their assimilation. The American economy did not provide equal opportunities for them. The melting pot did not apply to people of color. Differences between whites and racial peoples produced conflict not consensus across race lines.

Conflict theories are critical of assimilation theories for failing to recognize that race is a basis for the formation of power and resource inequality. Most conflict theories emphasize the deep-lying roots of racial and ethnic inequalities in the U.S. economy. Assimilation or order theories tend to neglect these economic issues. They are concerned primarily with how minorities adapt in the larger society. They propose that, with the proper attitudes, minorities could solve their own problems, competing and succeeding in the American mainstream.

Assimilation theories see the situations of blacks and other nonwhites as similar to those of earlier white immigrants. Just as white ethnics have made a place for themselves in the land of opportunity, so could racial minorities. All it takes is "self-help" to end subordination. Conflict theories recognize that racial ethnics were never meant to assimilate. Racial stratification exists because certain segments of society benefit from it. Employers can turn racism into higher profits by paying less than average wages to people of color. In 1980, employers' direct gain from wage discrimination—the amount extra they would have to pay if black workers earned the same as whites—reached $25 billion, a substantial fraction of corporate profits. Employers also benefit indirectly when they are able to keep a divided labor force in a weak bargaining position. This, however, harms white workers as well as black workers. Nevertheless, white workers also benefit from racism. If there is a certain amount of unemployment to be "shared" by workers, and a given number of good jobs to go around, white workers benefit from their relatively lower unemployment, their better access to good jobs, and a higher income relative to workers who face discrimination (Zarsky and Bowles, 1986:54).

DISCRIMINATION AGAINST BLACKS AND HISPANICS: CONTINUITY AND CHANGE

The treatment of blacks and Hispanics* has been disgraceful throughout American history. Members of both categories have been denied equality in money, jobs, services, housing, and even the right to vote. Since World War II, however, under pressure from civil rights advocates, the government has led the way in breaking down these discriminatory practices. The 1960 Civil Rights movement overturned segregation laws, opened voting booths, created new job opportunities, and renewed hope for racial equality. Public policies and economic growth improved the situation of racial minorities. However, most of the gains made by Civil Rights legislation, increased education opportunities, affirmative action programs, and increased black political participation, have been short-lived. Although many well-educated people of color in the past quarter century have made considerable gains, the well-being of blacks and Hispanics has, in many respects, deteriorated.

A comprehensive four-year National Research Council study on the state of black America over the past fifty years has found that there is a continuing gap in status between blacks and whites in the United States. The 1989 report has revealed that on virtually every indicator of well-being—income and living standards, health and life expectancy, and residential opportunities, as well as political and social participation—blacks remained substantially behind whites (Jaynes and Williams, 1989).

Hispanics, too, fall well behind whites on most indicators of status. Even though levels of well-being vary widely among Hispanic groups, they face common obstacles to becoming incorporated into the economic mainstream of society. The basic point of the next section is that inequalities faced by racial minorities reflect the routine operation of the political economy and the basic patterns of institutional discrimination.

---

*Unless otherwise noted, this section uses statistics on Hispanics rather than Chicanos. Lumping Hispanics into one group obscures diversities within this category. However, the data supplied by the government provides information only on the total Spanish-speaking population. Hispanics, although they share the Spanish language and Roman Catholicism, vary in many respects so that few generalizations are possible.

Income

Table 11–1 shows clearly that the average income for white families is greater than the average income for black and Hispanic families. The median 1987 income of black families was $18,098, about 56 percent of white families. Median family income for Hispanics in 1987 was only $20,300, two-thirds of the non-Hispanic median income of $31,600. Even though the median family income for blacks is still below that of Hispanics, per-person income for Hispanics is actually lower because Hispanics tend to have larger families.

Racial differences in poverty persist despite the recent economic upturn. Although most poor people are white, blacks remained disproportionately poor followed by Hispanics and then whites. In 1987, the poverty rate for blacks was 33.1 percent or 9.6 million compared with 28.2 percent or 5.4 million for Hispanics compared with 10.5 percent or 21.4 million for whites. The 1987 poverty rate among children under sixteen years old was 46.7 percent for blacks, 40.6 percent for Hispanics, and 16.2 percent for whites. (*Sta-*

Table 11–1
Median Income of White, Hispanic, and Black Families: 1972–1987 (in current dollars)

	Median Family Income		
Year	*White*	*Hispanic*	*Black*
1972	$25,107	$17,790	$14,922
1973	25,777	17,836	14,877
1974	24,728	17,594	14,765
1975	24,110	16,140	14,835
1976	24,823	16,390	14,766
1977	25,124	17,141	14,352
1978	25,606	17,518	15,166
1979	25,689	18,255	14,590
1980	24,176	16,242	13,989
1981	23,517	16,401	13,266
1982	24,603	16,227	13,598
1983	25,837	16,930	14,561
1984	27,686	18,822	15,431
1985	29,152	19,027	16,786
1986	30,809	19,995	17,604
1987	32,274	20,306	18,098

Source: Bureau of the Census, "Money Income and Poverty Status of Families and Persons in the United States: 1981," *Current Population Report,* Series P-60, no. 134 (July 1983), Table 3, and U.S. Bureau of the Census, *Current Population Reports,* Series P-60, no. 154, "Money, Income and Poverty States of Families and Persons in the U.S.: 1985 (Advance Data from the March, 1986 Current Population Survey)," U.S. Government Printing Office, Washington, D.C., 1986, Table 2, p. 9. "Money Income of Households, Families, and Persons in the United States: 1987," *Current Population Reports,* Series P-60, no. 162 (February 1989) Table 9, p. 32.

tistical Abstract of the U.S., 1989:454). For Hispanics, these percentages are the highest number living in poverty since the Census Bureau began collecting Hispanic figures in 1972. Hispanic poverty rates have risen alarmingly as the Hispanic presence in the United States has increased in the last decade. If current patterns continue, Hispanics will emerge in the 1990s as the nation's poorest racial ethnic group.

Poverty is especially prevalent in families headed by females. Here, race and gender inequalities combine to produce extreme hardships. More than half of the black and Hispanic families maintained by women had incomes below the poverty level in 1987. In that year, 52 percent of blacks and 52 percent of Hispanics in female-headed households lived in poverty compared with 27 percent of white families (U.S. Bureau of the Census, 1988:37).

Black and Hispanic women maintaining families had lower median earnings, lower labor force participation rates, and higher unemployment rates than white women maintaining families. These data give one explanation for the high incidence of poverty in families maintained by women. Thus, "feminization of poverty" is important in explaining some kinds of poverty, but it does not explain the persistent pattern of widening income inequality in minority families with a man and a woman present. A two-parent family is no guarantee against poverty for racial minorities. As Swinton says, "On the average, a poor black family is poorer than a poor white family. In 1985, the median black family would have needed an extra $4,424 to escape poverty as compared with $3,582 for the median white family" (Swinton, 1987:56).

Many factors explain the difference in white and minority earnings. Racial-ethnics are concentrated in the South and Southwest, where incomes are lower for everyone. Another part of the explanation is the differing age structure of minorities. They are younger, on average, than the white population. A group with a higher proportion of young people of working age will have a lower average earning level, higher rates of unemployment, and lower rates of labor force participation. But looking at racial inequalities by age reveals another disturbing pattern. The degree of inequality increases after the teenage years. Racial disparities become greater in peak earning years. This suggests that another part of the explanation for racial inequalities in earnings lies in the lack of education and skill levels required to move out of poor-paying jobs. All these explanations leave a substantial amount of inequality unexplained (Currie and Skolnick, 1988:151–155). Minorities at all levels of unemployment and education still earn less than whites due to current racial discrimination in the labor force, as we see in Chapter 16.

The gap between minority and white earnings has increased in recent years. On the average, blacks earn about 56 cents for every dollar earned by whites—a drop of about five cents in the last decade (Williams, 1987:56).

Education

Educational progress for blacks and Hispanics followed the civil rights era, but those gains in educational attainment have not closed the gap in education. For example, in the period 1975 to 1986, the proportion of whites 18 to

21 years old in high school remained at 80 percent. The percentage of blacks 18 to 21 years old in high school rose from 60 percent to 72 percent while the percentage of Hispanics for the same age category remained lower than for blacks—57 percent in 1975 and 58 percent in 1986. In 1986, 80 percent of whites were high school graduates compared with 60 percent of blacks and 57 percent of Hispanics. Table 11–2 provides data for 1987 educational attainment for whites, blacks, and Hispanics. Clearly, whites complete the most years of formal education and Hispanics the least. The 50 percent drop-out rate for Hispanics is now the highest in the nation (*Business Week*, 1989:144).

Low educational achievement has been a major barrier to the advancement of minorities. Many minority group members are becoming part of America's underclass, eligible for little more than low-paying jobs or welfare. The relatively low level of educational attainment for Hispanics and blacks is the result of several factors, including language differences, malnutrition, drug abuse, teenage pregnancy, and lack of family support. Yet many of the problems have less to do with minority students themselves and more to do with discrimination in the schools. According to the National Coalition of Advocates for Students, a child who is poor, black, or Hispanic is far more likely to be physically disciplined, suspended, expelled, or made to repeat a grade—all practices shown to increase the likelihood that a child will drop out of school. A minority child is three times as likely as a white child to end up in vocational education or in classes for the mildly mentally retarded. In effect, minority children are being "pushed out" of schools (*U.S. News & World Report*, 1987:66).

Despite similarities in the educational experiences of minority students who are poor, Hispanic students are more segregated today than black students. A study of school enrollment by the University of Chicago revealed that the percentage of Hispanic students who attend predominantly minority schools is higher than it was twenty years ago. Nationwide, the percentage of Hispanic students attending schools in which minorities made up more than half the student body increased from 54.8 in 1968 to 70.6 percent in 1984. The percentage of blacks attending predominantly minority schools fell from 76.6 percent in 1968 to 63.5 percent in 1984 (Fiske, 1987:1, 15). This growing isolation from middle-class society will further disadvantage Hispanic youth.

Table 11–2
Years of School Completed by Persons Twenty-five or Older by Race (1987)

Race	Elementary			High School		College		Median Years Completed
	0–4	5–7	8	1–3	4	1–3	4+	
White	2.0%	4.1%	5.9%	11.0%	39.2%	17.2%	20.5%	12.7
Black	5.0	8.0	5.3	18.2	37.1	15.7	10.7	12.4
Hispanic	11.9	15.2	8.1	13.9	29.0	13.3	8.6	12.0

Source: Bureau of the Census, *Statistical Abstract of the United States: 1989*, 109th ed. (Washington, D.C.: Government Printing Office, 1989), Table No. 212, p. 131.

The changing demography of race will have far-reaching effects on schools as they adjust to a student body that is more diverse than ever. By the year 2010, 38 percent of Americans under the age of 18 will be black, Asian, or other minority. In California, New York, Texas, and Florida, minority children will be a majority by 2010 (Schwartz and Exter, 1989:34).

Several additional trends are creating problems for minority students. The general movement against increased taxes hurts public schools, especially the costly programs for the disadvantaged (bilingual, Head Start, and the like). Inner-city schools, where minorities are concentrated and which are already understaffed and underfinanced, face even greater financial pressures because of the current trend to reduce federal programs to aid the disadvantaged.

Another trend that may reduce the number of minorities attending college is the increased cost of higher education. Since they are more likely to be poor than whites, minorities are less able to afford college. This decline should accelerate as the costs of education rise.

These pessimistic trends are compounded by the reality that minority members, regardless of their level of education, are underpaid compared with whites of similar education. Many of the disadvantaged, knowing that race is the significant variable keeping minorities down, have little motivation to do well in school because they regard education as having no payoff. At each education level, there is a significant difference in income between blacks, Hispanics, and whites. Yet education alone is not the answer: black high school graduates are more likely to be unemployed than are whites who drop out of high school, and blacks who earn a college degree can expect to earn almost $5,000 less annually than can white college graduates (Wickham, 1989:A–10). Given the persistence of discrimination in U.S. society, education by itself cannot eliminate the income gap between racial minorities and other Americans.

Unemployment

Unemployment rates have consistently varied by race. The National Research Council study on the status of blacks found that the unemployment levels of blacks and whites has increased since 1954 when the Supreme Court outlawed school segregation. The jobless rate of blacks is usually double the national rate, and the jobless rate of Hispanics is commonly 40 to 50 percent higher than the overall unemployment rate.

Since the 1970s, there has been a growing gap in the unemployment rates of men and women of color relative to white men and women. Although the official unemployment rate for March 1987 was 6.5 percent, the rate for blacks was 13.9 and the rate for Hispanics was 9 percent. These government rates, of course, are misleading, since they count as employed those 5.5 million who work part-time because they cannot find full-time jobs, and they do not count as unemployed the 1.17 million discouraged workers who have given up their search for work (Hershey, 1987:7). Given the low pay for jobs that minorities receive if they can find work, more of them than whites would likely become discouraged enough to stop looking for a job.

The existence of pockets of disproportionately high minority unemployment suggests great potential for social unrest. Minorities from urban slums are those most affected by few job opportunities. Table 11–3 shows that the rate of unemployment for black teenagers was critically high. Hispanic teenagers also had higher rates of unemployment than those of white teenagers. With such large percentages of minority youth unemployed, the potential for social problems is especially high. These data indicate why crime rates and out-of-wedlock births have risen in inner cities.

Type of Employment

Not only are minorities twice as likely as whites to be unemployed; those who do work are also overrepresented in jobs whose pay, power, and prestige are low. Far more blacks and Hispanics than whites are blue-collar and service workers, while whites hold a majority of the white-collar jobs, which are physically safer, better paying, more stable, and offer more chance for advancement.

Although minorities are in the least rewarding jobs, there have been positive changes since 1960. Because of greater educational attainment and affirmative action programs, nonwhites hold a greater number of management, white-collar, and upper-level blue-collar jobs than before. Despite these gains, however, a huge gap remains.

The transformation of the economy of the United States from one based on manufacturing to one based on information and services is having devastating effects on minority communities across America. The effects of economic and industrial change are most visible in three areas: (1) the trend toward unemployment, (2) the changing distribution and organization of jobs, and (3) the tendency for the jobs created to be relatively low paying.

Hispanics and blacks have suffered disproportionately from industrial job loss and declining manufacturing employment. While their employment status is declining in all regions, it is worse in areas of industrial decline. For blacks the lowest employment rates are found in the Midwest and Great

Table 11–3
Unemployment Rates by Race and Gender for 1986

Teenagers (16–19 years of age)	Rate	Adults (20 years of age and over)	Rate
Black men	34.4%	Black men	12.9%
Black women	34.9	Black women	11.1
Hispanic men	24.5	Hispanic men	7.8
Hispanic women	25.1	Hispanic women	7.7
White men	15.5	White men	4.8
White women	13.4	White women	4.6

Source: U.S. Department of Labor, Women's Bureau, "20 Facts on Women Workers" *Fact Sheet* No. 88–2 (1988).

Lakes region, that is, the old industrial heartland. The labor market status of whites has also been lowered in these areas, but the level of racial inequality has increased to scandalous levels. In Swinton's words:

> In such cities as Detroit, Buffalo, Chicago, and Cleveland, the gap between the labor market position of blacks, especially black males, and whites probably exceeds the highest levels that ever existed in the most racist of the South's cities. (Swinton, 1987:68)

Yet the new economy will be increasingly made up of people of color. Between now and the year 2000, 58 percent of the young people entering the work force will be black, Hispanic, or Asian (Kaufman, 1989:54).

Health

The differences between whites and nonwhites are revealed most vividly in the facts concerning health and life itself. On virtually every measure of health nonwhites are disadvantaged, as revealed in the following list:

- Whites live about six years longer than blacks.
- At all ages except for the very old, blacks have higher death rates and a greater incidence of disease (*News Report*, 1989:4).
- Black babies are nearly twice as likely as white babies to die within the first year (*News Report*, 1989:4).
- Although only 14 percent of the white population is without health insurance, 21.8 percent of the black population and 29 percent of the Hispanic population is without health insurance (U.S. Bureau of the Census, 1985:105).
- Racial inequalities exist in the kinds of medical care received by blacks and whites. A recent Harvard University study found that blacks used clinics and emergency rooms more, had more difficulty getting to doctors, hospitals, and clinics, and were more likely than whites to go to a different doctor than the one they saw at their last visit (Stevens, 1989:1).
- Minority children are less likely to have routine physicals—3.5 percent of white children, 4.2 percent of black children, and 9.2 percent of Hispanic children have never had a physical (*USA Today*, March 9, 1989).

CONTEMPORARY TRENDS AND ISSUES IN U.S. RACIAL AND ETHNIC RELATIONS

Growing Racial Polarization

Chapter 4 discussed the new patterns of immigration that are changing the racial composition of society. This chapter has examined the persistent discrimination that blocks opportunities for people of color. These trends combined with the expected rise in the proportion of Hispanics and Asians in the population make racial-ethnics increasingly important to the nation's well-being. As the United States becomes more multiracial, issues of race have once again become central social issues.

Race relations have surged into popular view with growing racial clashes between whites and people of color. In 1989, a black teenager was killed by a gang of white youth as he walked in Bensonhurst, a Brooklyn neighborhood. This racial slaying was reminiscent of the 1986 Howard Beach incident in which a gang of whites chased a black man onto a highway, where he was killed. These two widely publicized racial attacks are not isolated incidents of racial hatred. The Southern Poverty Law Center of Montgomery, Alabama tallied 189 race related crimes in thirty-five states and the District of Columbia in 1988, up from 100 in 1987. The membership of Ku Klux Klan and other white supremacist groups is on the rise. Racial tensions are often caused by deteriorating economic conditions—lack of jobs, housing, and other resources—that lead to minority scapegoating on the part of whites (reported in *USA Today*, August 30, 1989:1). In Florida and many parts of the West and the Southwest, perceptions that Cubans, Mexicans, and other Hispanics are taking jobs from whites have led to racial tensions. Many problems of class are leading to racial polarization.

Bigotry, however, is not confined to white working-class or poor settings. Recent headlines about racism on college campuses have surprised many Americans, yet campus racism appears to be widespread. From MIT to the University of California, Berkeley, and on campuses across the nation, racial attacks on blacks, Hispanics, and Asians reveal an extensive problem of intolerance in settings where tolerance is essential to the pursuit of knowledge.

Racial politics surfaced in the 1988 presidential campaign with Jesse Jackson's political rise. The Bush media campaign also used blacks in stereotyped roles to win votes from Dukakis. Today, racial politics are dominating many city and state elections.

The Newly Repressive Racial Order

National economic, social, and political policies have produced a new age of racial division. Since the early 1970s, a reactive restructuring of the American racial order has been in progress.

The current period of racial reaction parallels an earlier period of American history marked by growing racism and racial division. In Melendez's words:

> After 1877, a reaction set in against the major political and economic advances blacks had made in the decade and a half following the emancipation of the slaves. Termed the Black Reconstruction by the historian W. E. B. DuBois, blacks made significant gains in land ownership, voting rights, and political power. The reaction reversed many of these gains, triggering policies and sentiments which disenfranchised black voters, increased violence against blacks and intensified the economic exploitation of black workers. (Melendez, 1986:42)

The new age of reaction is marked by a massive rollback of economic, social, and political gains. Conservative economic strategies during the Reagan and Bush years dramatically accelerated the economic decline of people of color. The Reagan administration played a crucial role in dividing the United States along lines of race. Tax policies that have redistributed income from the poor to the wealthy, the shift in U.S. government spending, and the deliberate shrinking of the public sector have all had a disproportionate impact on minorities. Among the most telling changes is the dismantling of civil rights legislation that has taken place under Reagan's Supreme Court appointees. In a series of decisions in 1989, the Supreme Court has severely crippled affirmative action and other protections against discrimination for minorities and women. Other more visible expressions of the repressive racial order are the official-English measures approved in 17 states (*Business Week*, September, 1989:145), repressive immigration reform, and revived nationalism in the United States (Omi and Winant, 1983:32). The changing contours of race and ethnicity are creating new forms of racial oppression and racial conflict. Race itself is acquiring new meaning within the social and political issues of the times.

The Black Underclass: Culture or Structure?

The black urban underclass expanded in the seventies and eighties despite racial reforms. Why did conditions worsen when they should have improved? One answer is that racial minorities themselves are responsible for declining conditions; that broken families and lack of motivation in finding jobs have prevented them from taking advantage of the opportunities made by antidiscriminatory legislation. This cultural explanation is in error on many counts. It relies too heavily on cultural traits to explain poverty. It falls back on

The increase in the number of black single mothers and female-headed households is the result of the decline in the proportion of young men who have jobs.

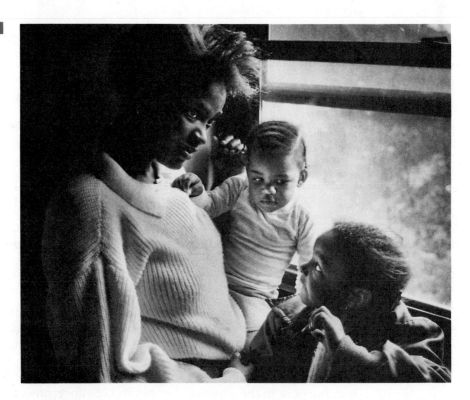

By 2010, More Than One-Third of American Children Will Be Black, Hispanic, or Asian.

By the year 2010, as many as 38 percent of Americans under the age of 18 will belong to minority groups. In seven states and the District of Columbia, more than half of children will be minorities. In an additional 19 states, at least one-quarter of children will be black, Hispanic, Asian, or other minorities.

These statistics, gleaned from several Census Bureau projection series and American Demographics' estimates, reveal that dramatic changes are in store as a diverse new generation of Americans replaces older generations dominated by non-Hispanic whites. School districts in the nation's largest states will have to adjust to a student body that is more diverse than ever. Businesses that market to children will have to adapt to a rainbow coalition of parents who are proud of their ancestry but anxious to see their children succeed in mainstream America.

By 2010, 80 percent of children in Hawaii will be nonwhite or Hispanic. "Minorities" will also form the majority of children in New Mexico (77 percent), California (57 percent), Texas (57 percent), New York (53 percent), Florida (53 percent), and Louisiana (50 percent). In the District of Columbia, 93 percent of children will be minorities by 2010.

WHERE THE KIDS ARE

New York leads the 50 states in the growth of the minority share of its youth population, rising from 40 percent to 53 percent from 1990 to 2010. California follows with an increase of 11 percentage points. Third is Texas with a rise of 10 percentage points, followed by New Mexico (9.5 percentage points) and New Jersey and Illinois (9 percentage point increase in each state).

The total youth population (all races and ethnicities combined) will grow the fastest in the Sunbelt and in the states that receive large numbers of immigrants. The only notable exceptions are New Hampshire and Utah. Between 1990 and 2010, the ten states with the fastest-growing youth populations will be New Mexico (up 22 percent); Arizona (21 percent); Alaska (18 percent); Georgia and Florida (17 percent each); California, Nevada, and New Hampshire (12 percent each); and Utah (10 percent).

In the last two decades, businesses watched the mass market explode into hundreds of demographic, lifestyle, and geographic segments. Over the next 20 years, children will lead the way toward an even more diverse future. Fast-food companies, toy manufacturers, and others that depend on the young will need to scrutinize these trends and their strategic implications. Public schools, especially, will have to meet the educational needs of increasingly diverse students. The states and local areas most blessed with children will be challenged by a profusion of races and cultures. Our children may show us the future even before they become adults.

Source: Joe Schwartz and Thomas Exter, "All Our Children," *American Demographics* (May, 1989) pp. 34–37. Reprinted with permission © American Demographics, May, 1989.

---

blaming the victim to explain patterns that are actually rooted in social structure. Economic changes in society have removed jobs and other opportunities from inner-city residents, and their families have been severely affected. This is a better explanation of persistent and concentrated poverty among blacks. It is detailed in William J. Wilson's compelling book *The Truly Disadvantaged* (1987). According to Wilson, all of the social problems of the ghetto are outgrowths of joblessness, which is due to fundamental transformations of the larger economy and the class structure of ghetto neighborhoods. The movement of middle-class black professionals from the inner city has left behind a concentration of the most disadvantaged segments of the black urban population. Meanwhile, the shift of jobs from central cities to suburbs and from the Rustbelt to the Sunbelt continues to isolate and increase the unemployment of urban blacks. These forces have led to more unemployment, more poverty, and more female-headed households among blacks, not a deviant culture, as so many would argue.

Wilson (1987) provides evidence that jobs influence the likelihood of marriage among blacks. He suggests that increasing male joblessness is a major underlying factor in the rise of black single mothers and female-headed households. Wage discrimination also works against marriage. Wilson found that men with higher incomes are more likely to be married than men with lower incomes. The underclass is largely the result of a long-term decline in the proportion of black men, and particularly young black men, who are in a position to support a family. These structural conditions make it necessary for many black women to leave a marriage or forgo marriage altogether. Adaptations to structural conditions leave black women disproportionately divorced and responsible for their children. Family structure is the consequence, not the cause, of the urban underclass.

CHAPTER REVIEW

1. Racial and ethnic stratification are basic features of American society. These forms of inequality are built into normal practices, and they exclude people from full and equal participation in society's institutions. Racial and ethnic stratification exist because certain segments of society benefit from it.

2. Race is a social category that serves as a basis for differential treatment. The concept of race is socially rather than biologically significant. Racial groups are set apart and singled out for unequal treatment.

3. An ethnic group is culturally distinct in race, religion, or national origin. That group has a common culture that is distinct from the culture of the majority. Some ethnic groups such as Jews, Poles, and Italians have distinguishing cultural characteristics that stem from religion and national origin. Since racial groups also have distinctive cultural characteristics, they are referred to as racial-ethnics.

4. Racial and ethnic groups are systematically disadvantaged by society's institutions. Both race and ethnicity are traditional bases for systems of inequality, although there are historical and contemporary differences in the societal placement of racial-ethnics and white-ethnics in this society.

5. Racial-ethnic groups that have difficulty escaping devalued states became part of the United States involuntarily and were forced into preindustrial work that was low in pay, status, and chances for upward mobility. Blacks, Chicanos, Asian Americans, and Native Americans are four such groups.

6. Blacks came to the United States involuntarily as slaves. Following the Civil War, they were freed from slavery but remained oppressed by the economic, legal, and social practices of the majority.

7. Chicanos became part of the United States involuntarily as a result of military conquest and a change in political boundaries. With few exceptions they were dispossessed of power and property. They became the major source of cheap labor in the Southwest. They continue to be the objects of discrimination today.

8. Asian Americans are more diverse than the other prominent racial minorities in the United States. Their characteristics vary according to their national origins, time of entry into the

United States, and, for the more recent immigrants, social class background.

9. The lands of the Native Americans were taken by the Europeans and their descendants by force and fraud. The Native Americans were made wards of the federal government and placed on reservations. Today, they are the poorest, lowest in educational attainment, least employed, unhealthiest, and worst-housed ethnic group in America.

10. Deficiency theories maintain that some groups are unequal because they lack some important feature common among the majority. These deficiencies may be biological (such as low intelligence), structural (such as weak family ties), or cultural (such as the "culture of poverty").

11. Bias theories place the blame for inequality on the prejudiced attitudes of the members of the dominant group. These theories, however, do not explain the discriminatory acts of the unprejudiced, which are aimed at preserving privilege.

12. Structural theories argue that inequality is the result of the politicoeconomic system that dominates and oppresses minorities. There are four main features of institutional discrimination: (1) the forces of history shape present conditions; (2) discrimination can occur without conscious bigotry; (3) this type of discrimination is less visible than individual acts of discrimination; and (4) discrimination is reinforced by the interrelationships among the institutions of society.

13. The segmented labor market is a structural source of inequality. There are two kinds of jobs: those that are secure, pay well, have fringe benefits, and offer a chance for advancement; and those that are unstable, poorly paid, and a dead end. Large numbers of minorities are found at the bottom of the labor market because of institutional discrimination, particularly in the educational and economic sectors.

14. The assimilation model—that minorities will eventually become part of the mainstream once they give up their distinctive ethnicity and learn the skills required by society—is not applicable to colonized people of color. The colonization of people means their subordination in all spheres—social, economic, and political. The superordinate group exploits the colonized for its own advantage. This exploitation traps the minority in a subordinate status.

15. Civil rights legislation improved the status of some racial-ethnics, yet the overall position of blacks and Hispanics relative to whites has not improved. Large gaps remain in work, earnings, and education. Changing conditions in the economy have contributed to the formation of an underclass in America's urban centers.

16. The racial climate of the United States is changing. Conservative economic strategies, political setbacks in the progressive legislation affecting racial-ethnics and new forms of racial violence and racial conflict signal a resurgence of a repressive racial order.

KEY TERMS

Minority group
Ethnicity
Cultural deficiency

Bias theories
Institutional racism

Colonial theory
Assimilation

STUDY QUESTIONS

1. What constitutes a minority group?
2. What is the key difference between deficiency theories and bias theories as they explain the existence of minorities?
3. Central to the order perspective's view of minority groups is that they will eventually

assimilate. What do they mean by this and why does the conflict perspective disagree with this assumption?
4. How does the social organization of society work to keep minorities subordinate?
5. What is meant by the changing demography of

race? What are the anticipated consequences of this trend for schools, employment, incidents of violence, and life chances?

6. Is the black underclass a consequence of culture or structure?

FOR FURTHER READING

Frank D. Bean and Marta Tienda, *The Hispanic Population of the United States* (New York: Russell Sage Foundation, 1987).

Dee Brown, *Bury My Heart at Wounded Knee* (New York: Bantam Books, 1970).

Vine Deloria, Jr., and Clifford M. Lytle. *American Indians, American Justice* (Austin: University of Texas Press, 1983).

Reynolds Farley, *Blacks and Whites Narrowing the Gap?* (Cambridge, MA: Harvard University Press, 1984).

Robert W. Gardner, Bryant Robey, and Peter C. Smith, "Asian Americans: Growth, Change, and Diversity." *Population Bulletin* 49 (October 1985):entire issue.

Gerald David Jaynes and Robin M. Williams, Jr., *A Common Destiny: Blacks and American Society* (Washington, DC: National Academy Press, 1989).

Harry H. L. Kitano and Roger Daniels, *Asian Americans: Emerging Minorities* (Englewood Cliffs, NJ: Prentice-Hall, 1988).

Stanley Liberson. *A Piece of the Pie: Black and White Immigrants Since 1880* (Berkeley: University of California Press, 1980).

Michael Omi and Howard Winant. *Racial Formation in the United States* (New York: Routledge & Kegan Paul, 1987).

Paul E. Peterson, ed. *The New Urban Reality* (Washington, DC: The Brookings Institution, 1985).

Clara E. Rodriguez, *Puerto Ricans: Born in the U.S.A.* (Winchester, MA: Unwin Hyman, 1989).

Stephen Steinberg. *The Ethnic Myth* (Boston: Beacon Press, 1981).

Rafael Valdivieso and Cary Davis, *U.S. Hispanics: Changing Issues for the 1990's* (Washington, DC: Population Reference Bureau, 1988).

David T. Wellman. *Portraits of White Racism* (Cambridge: Cambridge University Press, 1977).

William Julius Wilson. *The Truly Disadvantaged* (Chicago: University of Chicago Press, 1987).

Norman R. Yetman and C. Hoy Steele, eds. *Majority and Minority: The Dynamics of Racial and Ethnic Relations.* 4th ed. (Boston: Allyn and Bacon, 1985).

Chapter Twelve

Sex and Gender Stratification

*I*n the past decade, the American public has been made dramatically aware of women's rights to equality. Despite the broadening of awareness, equality for women has not been achieved.

- Although the situation is improving slowly, most women are trapped in a "pink-collar ghetto" with about 80 percent of women working in 20 out of 420 occupations.
- Women with four years of college education still have a median income below that of men with a high school diploma.
- More than half of all poor families are headed by women, and this proportion grows each year.
- Recent Supreme Court rulings on affirmative action and abortion rights have weakened legal reforms that benefit women.

The United States, like all other societies, has clear expectations for its members on the basis of sex. Women and men are assigned different expectations for personality traits, expressions of emotion, behaviors, and occupations. These classifications are so pervasive that they seem natural. It is increasingly clear that gender differentiation is not "natural" at all, but actually a product of social organization. This differentiation ranks the sexes in such a way that women are unequal in power, resources, prestige, or presumed worth. At the same time, both women and men are denied the full range of human and social possibilities. The social inequalities created by sex differentiation have far-reaching consequences for the society at large.

This chapter examines gender stratification in U.S. society at both structural and individual levels of social organization. The overriding theme is that gender inequality cuts across all aspects of life in U.S. society.

THE ROLES AND RANKING OF WOMEN AND MEN

The concept *role* is borrowed directly from the theater and is a metaphor intended to convey the idea that conduct adheres to positions (statuses) in a social system. The social system that assigns roles to women and men is the sex-gender system, which consists of two complementary, yet mutually exclusive, categories in which all human beings are placed. **Sex roles** are behaviors that are determined by the biological fact of maleness or femaleness, such as menstruation, pregnancy, lactation, erection, and seminal ejaculation. **Gender roles** are behaviors that are determined by cultural and social definitions of feminine and masculine. They contain self-concepts, psychological traits, as well as family, occupational, and political roles assigned dichotomously to each sex (Lipman-Blumen, 1984:1–2). The **sex-gender system** operates as a system of stratification by ranking and rewarding gender roles unequally. **Gender stratification** is the differential ranking and rewarding of women's and men's roles. **Sexism** refers to the individual and institutional arrangements that discriminate against women.

Are Gender Roles Based on Physiological Differences?

A controversy among scientists concerns the basis for gender roles. One school argues that there is a biogenetic foundation for the observed differences in male and female behavior, while their counterparts are convinced that the differences are explained largely by differential learning. We know that there are biological differences between the two sexes. The key question is whether these unlearned differences in the sexes contribute to the gender differences found in societies. To answer this question, let us first review the evidence for each position.

The Biological Bases for Gender Roles.   Males and females are different from the moment of conception. Chromosomal and hormonal differences make males and females physically different. These differences, for example, give the female health superiority. At every age, from conception until old age, more males than females get sick and die. Approximately 120 males are conceived for every 100 females, yet there are only 105 live male births for each 100 female births, meaning that fetuses spontaneously aborted (miscarried) or stillborn are typically males. Various studies have shown that males are more susceptible than females to respiratory, bacterial, and viral infections, hepatitis, and childhood leukemia. The explanation for females being the healthier sex is that they have twice as many of a group of genes that program the production of immunological agents (Brody, 1980). This means that females, compared to males, produce larger amounts of antibodies to combat a number of infectious agents.

Hormonal differences in the sexes are significant. The male hormones (androgens) and female hormones (estrogens) direct the process of sex differentiation from about six weeks after conception throughout life. They make males taller, heavier, and more muscular. At puberty they trigger the production of secondary sexual characteristics. In males, these include body and facial hair, a deeper voice, broader shoulders, and a muscular body. In females, puberty brings pubic hair, menstruation, the ability to lactate, prominent breasts, and relatively broad hips. Actually, males and females have both sets of hormones. It is the relative proportion of androgens and estrogens that gives one masculine or feminine physical traits.

These hormonal differences may explain in part why males tend to be more active, aggressive, and dominant than females (Baker, 1980; Maccoby and Jacklin, 1974). Studies in animals provide some evidence for this assertion. Castrated rats and monkeys, deprived of the sex hormones created by the testes, have decreased levels of aggression. When testosterone is injected into these castrated males, their aggression levels increase (Quadagno, Briscoe, and Quadagno, 1977).

Critics of the biological determinist approach have argued that research on animals is irrelevant for humans because of the importance of socialization and culture.

Biological differences that do exist between women and men are only averages, and they are often influenced by other factors. For example, although men are on the average larger than women, body size is influenced by diet and physical activity, which in turn may be influenced by culture, class, and race. Greater variation exists within one sex than between the sexes (Anderson, 1983). The sociocultural variation of sex roles suggests that pressures of society are more important than are innate physiological conditions.

The Social Bases for Gender Roles.   Gender roles are not uniform throughout the world. Every society has certain expectations for both women and men, as well as elaborate ways of producing people who are much like these expectations. The cross-cultural evidence shows a wide variation of behaviors for the sexes. Table 12–1 provides some interesting cross-cultural data from 224 societies on the division of labor by sex. This table shows that for the majority of activities, societies are not uniform in their gendered division of labor. Even activities requiring strength, presumably a male trait, are not strictly apportioned to males. In fact, activities such as burden bearing and water carrying are done by females more than by males. Even an activity like house building is not exclusively male.

While there is a wide variety in the social roles assigned to women and men, their roles "do not vary randomly" (O'Kelly, 1980:41). In most societies of the world, the domestic and familial is the world of women and that of the public and political is the world of men. These differences are due at least

Table 12–1
Gender Allocation in Selected Technological Activities in 224 Societies

	Number of Societies in Which the Activity Is Performed by:					
Activity	Males Exclusively	Males Usually	Both Sexes Equally	Females Usually	Females Exclusively	% Male
Smelting of ores	37	0	0	0	0	100.0
Hunting	139	5	0	0	0	99.3
Boat building	84	3	3	0	1	96.6
Mining and quarrying	31	1	2	0	1	93.7
Land clearing	95	34	6	3	1	90.5
Fishing	83	45	8	5	2	86.7
Herding	54	24	14	3	3	82.4
House building	105	30	14	9	20	77.4
Generation of fire	40	6	16	4	20	62.3
Preparation of skins	39	4	2	5	31	54.6
Crop planting	27	35	33	26	20	54.4
Manufacture of leather products	35	3	2	5	29	53.2
Crop tending	22	23	24	30	32	44.6
Milking	15	2	8	2	21	43.8
Carrying	18	12	46	34	36	39.3
Loom weaving	24	0	6	8	50	32.5
Fuel gathering	25	12	12	23	94	27.2
Manufacture of clothing	16	4	11	13	78	22.4
Pottery making	14	5	6	6	74	21.1
Dairy production	4	0	0	0	24	14.3
Cooking	0	2	2	63	117	8.3
Preparation of vegetables	3	1	4	21	145	5.7

Source: Adapted from George P. Murdock and Caterina Provost, "Factors in the Division of Labor by Sex: A Cross-Cultural Analysis," *Ethnology* 12 (April, 1973):207. Reprinted by permission of the publisher.

indirectly to biology. Males are physically larger and stronger. Females give birth to children and are equipped to feed the newborn children. Since women in preindustrial societies tend to have a large number of children, they are bound by biology to domestic duties. Males, however, can leave their offspring for extended periods, and therefore are logically more likely to become engaged in activities such as hunting and fighting.

The Differential Ranking of Women and Men

Male dominance refers to the beliefs, values, and cultural meanings that give higher value and prestige to masculinity than to femininity, that value males over females, men over women; and to the male control of and privileged access to socially valued resources. **Patriarchy** is the term used for forms of social organization in which men are dominant over women.

A central issue in the study of gender has been whether male dominance is universal, found in all societies across time and space. Many scholars have adopted this position, claiming that all societies exhibit some forms of patriarchy in marriage and family forms, in division of labor, and in society at large (Ortner, 1974; Rosaldo, 1974). More recently, however, scholars have challenged the universality of patriarchy by producing cases that serve as counterexamples (Shapiro, 1981). Today, the thinking in anthropology tends to follow the latter course. Sexual differentiation, it seems, is found in all societies, but it does not always indicate low female status (Rogers, 1978). Gender stratification, male dominance, and female subordination are not constants. They vary from society to society. They also vary within a given society, in different social classes, and in different racial and ethnic groups in the same society. Women may be subordinate, but they have not been passive victims of patriarchy. Like other oppressed groups, they have created various survival strategies and have often engaged in political struggles to end discrimination.

GENDER STRATIFICATION FROM THE ORDER AND CONFLICT PERSPECTIVES

The Order Perspective

From the order perspective biology, history, and the needs of society combine to separate men and women into distinctive roles. Biologically, men are stronger and women bear and nurse children. These facts have meant that men have tended to be the providers while women have "naturally" dealt with childrearing and family nurturance.

The necessity for women to nurse their infants and stay near home meant that for most of human history they have done the domestic chores while men were free to hunt and leave the village for extended periods. Thus a whole set of customs and traditions supporting men as the providers and women as the nurturers set the expectations for future generations of men and women.

Although modern technology has freed women from the necessity of staying at home and has allowed them to work at jobs formerly requiring great strength, the order theorists believe that the traditional division of labor is beneficial for society as a whole. The clear-cut expectations for each sex fulfill many needs for individuals and provide order. The traditional roles for men and women—for example, women as housekeepers and rearers of children and men as breadwinners—promote stable families and an efficient system of specialized roles with boys and girls trained throughout their youth to take their "natural" places in society.

Talcott Parsons, a major order theorist, has argued that with industrialization, the family and the role of women as nurturers and caretakers have become more important than ever before. The husband in the competitive world outside the home needs a place of affection. As women take on the "expressive" roles of providing affection and emotional support within the family, men perform "instrumental" roles outside the family that provide economic support. Not only is this division of labor practical, it is necessary because it assures that the important societal tasks are accomplished (Parsons, Bales, et al., 1955:3–9).

The Conflict Perspective

A very different view of gender emerges from the conflict perspective. Conflict theorists are critical of the order model because it neglects what is most important about gender roles, namely that they are unequal in power, resources, and prestige. According to this conflict view, gender roles are not neutral ways of meeting societies' needs but are part of the larger system of gender stratification.

Many different conflict interpretations of gender stratification may be found. All emphasize male control and domination of both women and valued resources. For example, Randall Collins has traced gender stratification in simple societies as well as those that are more complex. In simple societies, men dominate by virtue of sheer strength. As societies become more developed, male domination takes the form of control of valued economic resources. Women use their femininity to acquire resources through marriage, but they become subordinated in the process (Collins, 1972, 1975).

Most conflict theories explain gender stratification as the outcome of male control over property, the means of production, and the distribution of goods. This idea originated in the work of Friedrich Engels and Karl Marx, who viewed marriage as a means of enforcing male power and control. As societies moved beyond subsistence stages and private property developed, men instituted the monogamous family in order to pass on wealth to their biological children:

> Because of the . . . importance attached to property and inheritance, the paternity of children becomes a paramount concern of the males. The patriarchal family form arises in response to the new conditions. The wife becomes the property of the husband who can use whatever means necessary to guarantee her sexual fidelity and, thereby, the paternity of his children. (Collins, 1972:46)

Contemporary conflict theorists stress control of the distribution of goods as the crucial fact in producing gender stratification. They point out that gender stratification is greater where women's work is directed inward to the family and men's work is directed outward to trade and the marketplace (Schlegal, 1977; Friedl, 1975; Leacock, 1972). The division between domestic and public spheres of activity is particularly constraining to women and advantageous to men. The domestic and public spheres of activity are associated with different amounts of property, power, and prestige. Women's reproductive roles and their responsibilities for domestic labor limit their association with the resources that are highly valued (Rosaldo, 1980). Men are freed from these responsibilities. Their economic obligations in the public sphere assure them control of highly valued resources and give rise to male privilege. Recent studies question whether all societies have isolated women into the domestic sphere, and whether the domestic-public split is universal (McCormack, 1981). But where it does exist, it contributes to the subordination of women.

In capitalist societies the domestic-public split is even more significant, because highly valued goods and services are exchanged in the public, not the domestic, sphere. Women's domestic labor, though important for survival, ranks low in prestige and power because it does not produce exchangeable commodities (Sacks, 1974). Because of the relationship between the class relations of production *(capitalism)* and the hierarchical gender relations of its society *(patriarchy)* (Eisenstein, 1979), the United States can be defined as a capitalist patriarchy. Capitalism and patriarchy "are interrelated in complex ways and they must be analyzed together to understand the position of women" (Acker, 1980:31). Women and men are found doing different work both in the family and in the labor force. This division of labor between the sexes preserves power and prestige for men.

Gender stratification, like stratification systems based on class and race, generates privileges for some in society while denying equal access to others.

The Implications of the Conflict and Order Perspectives

A point should be made about the implications of the conflict and order perspectives on gender stratification. Each position, with its emphasis on different factors, calls for a different approach to the study of gender inequality. One consequence of the focus on gender roles by the order model has been to treat gender inequality as a problem of roles. Outmoded masculine and feminine roles are thought to be responsible for keeping women from achieving their full potential. This approach fails to recognize that gender stratification is a system of power and ranking that is found throughout the social structure (Skold, 1982).

We must distinguish between (1) a gender role approach, which focuses on learning behaviors that are defined as masculine or feminine, and (2) a structural approach, which focuses on features of social organization that produce sex inequality. The difference between the two lies in whether the individual or the society is the primary unit of analysis. The **gender roles approach** emphasizes characteristics that individuals acquire during the course of socialization, such as independent or dependent behaviors and ways of relating. The **structural approach** emphasizes factors that are external to individuals, such as the organization of social institutions, including the concentration of power, the legal system, and organizational barriers (Glazer, 1977). These approaches differ in how they view the sexes, in how they explain the causes and effects of sexism, and in the solutions they suggest for the elimination of inequality. Both the individual and the structural approaches are necessary to a complete understanding of sexism. This chapter places primary emphasis on social structure as the cause of inequality. Although gender roles are learned by individuals and produce differences in the personalities, behaviors, and motivations of women and men, essentially gender stratification is maintained by societal forms.

THE LEARNING OF TRADITIONAL GENDER ROLES

The most complex, demanding, and all-involving role that a member of society must learn to play is that of male or female.

> "Casting" takes place immediately at birth, after a quick biological inspection; and the role of "female" or "male" is assigned. It is an assignment that will last one's entire lifetime and affect virtually everything one ever does. A large part of the next 20 years or so will be spent gradually learning and perfecting one's assigned sex role; slowly memorizing what a "young lady" should do and should not do, how a "little man" should react in each of a million frightening situations—practicing, practicing, playing house, playing cowboys, practicing—and often crying in confusion and frustration at the baffling and seemingly endless task. (David and Brannon, 1980:117)

From infancy through early childhood and beyond, children learn what is expected of boys and girls, and they learn to behave according to those expectations.

The characteristics associated with traditional gender roles are those valued by the dominant society. Keep in mind that the research on gender socialization reflects primarily the experience of white middle-class persons—those who are most often the research subjects of these studies. Learning gender roles varies by race, ethnicity, and class. Still, society molds boys and girls along different lines.

The Child at Home

Girls and boys are perceived and treated differently from the moment of birth. Parents describe newborn daughters as tiny, soft, and delicate, and sons as strong and alert (Richardson, 1981:48), and interact differently with newborn daughters and sons.

How parents treat their children may be the most important factor of all in the creation of sex stereotypes. When one compares the life of the young girl with that of the young boy, a critical difference emerges: She is treated more protectively and she is subjected to more restrictions and controls; he receives greater achievement demands and higher expectations. Girl infants are talked to more. Girls are the objects of more physical contact such as holding, rocking, caressing, and kissing (Lewis, 1972). We also know that fathers, especially working-class fathers, are more concerned than mothers about their young children engaging in behaviors considered inappropriate for their sex.

Recent research compared the influence that mothers, fathers, and peers had in rewarding and punishing gendered behavior in three- and five-year-old children (Langlois and Downs, 1980). Fathers provided the strongest pressures for gender-specific behavior. In addition, they used different techniques with daughters and sons: They rewarded their daughters and gave them positive feedback for gendered behavior. With their sons they used more negative feedback and punished them for gender-inappropriate behavior. Mothers were more likely to reinforce behavior of *both* boys and girls with

Girls and boys
are treated
differently from
the moment of
birth.

rewards and positive feedback. Peers, in contrast, were more likely to use
punishment on both sexes. The researchers concluded that the combined
pattern of the three socializing agents provided a "finely tuned system" in
which fathers, mothers, and peers each make a unique contribution in reinforcing gendered behavior (Langlois and Downs, 1980). Recent research by
Jacqueline Eccles has found that parents upheld sex stereotypes more today
than they did in the 1970s, when she began her research (cited in Keegan,
1989:26).

In addition to the parents' active role in reinforcing conformity to society's gender demands, a subtler message is emitted from picture books for
preschool children that parents purchase for their children. One study of
eighteen award-winning children's books from 1967 to 1971 found the following characteristics (Weitzman et al., 1972):

- Females are virtually invisible. The ratio of male pictures to female pictures
  was 11:1. The ratio of male to female animals was 95:1.
- The activities of boys and girls varied greatly. Boys were active in outdoor
  activities, while girls were passive and most often found indoors. The
  activity of the girls typically was that of some service for boys.
- Adult men and women (role models) were very different. Men led, women
  followed. Females were passive and males active. Not one woman in these
  books had a job or profession; they were always mothers and wives.

An update of this classic study has found important changes in how girls and women are portrayed in the Caldecott books. Females are no longer invisible, they are as likely as males to be included in the books, and they have begun to move outside the home if not into the labor market. In many respects, however, female storybook characters remain consistent with traditional culture. No behavior was found to be shared by a majority of the females, whereas all males were portrayed as independent, persistent, and active. Girls expressed no career goals, and there were no adult female role models to provide any ambition. The researchers found that only one woman in the entire 1980s collection of 24 books had an occupation outside of the home, and she worked "as a waitress at the Blue Tile Diner" (Williams et al., 1987:155).

Two books by the same author best illustrate how children's books are biased toward traditional occupational roles apportioned by sex. The first, *What Boys Can Be*, lists fourteen occupations: fireman, baseball player, bus driver, policeman, cowboy, doctor, sailor, pilot, clown, zoo manager, farmer, actor, astronaut, and president (Walley, n.d.). The book *What Girls Can Be* also lists fourteen occupations: nurse, stewardess, ballerina, candyshop owner, model, actress, secretary, artist, nursery school teacher, singer, dress designer, bride, housewife, and mother (Walley, n.d.).

Before formal schooling, parents often send their child to day-care centers and nursery schools. The teachers there serve as surrogate parents, also reinforcing traditional gender roles. A study of fifteen preschools found that teachers act and react in quite different ways to boys and girls. The teachers, for example, responded over three times as often to males as to females who hit or broke things. Boys were typically punished by a loud public reprimand, but girls were taken aside for a soft rebuke. In task-learning situations boys were twice as likely as girls to receive individual instructions on how to do things. Summarizing their study, the researchers noted:

> As nursery-school children busily mold clay, their teachers are molding behavior. Unwittingly, teachers foster an environment where children learn that boys are aggressive and able to solve problems, while girls are submissive and passive. The clay impressions are transient, but the behavioral ones last into adulthood and present us with people of both sexes who have developed only parts of the psychological and intellectual capabilities. (Serbin and O'Leary, 1975:57)

The past decade has undoubtedly seen changes in parents' sex-stereotyped attitudes. Unfortunately, attitude changes do not always translate into changes in behavior. Psychologist Beverly Fagot recently completed a study in which she compared parents' attitudes and their behavior toward their two-year-old children. Although parents' attitudes were not gender-stereotyped, their behavior often contradicted the attitudes they had expressed. They still treated their daughters and sons differently in important areas of development (Deckard, 1983:55).

Differences can be found even where gender roles are changing and socialization is becoming more flexible or androgynous. Androgyny refers to the integration of traditional feminine and masculine characteristics. Jeanne Brooks-Gunn at The Educational Testing Service in Princeton, New Jersey, recently conducted a study of "masculine," "feminine," and "androgynous" mothers. The androgynous mothers were self-reliant as well as tender, affectionate as well as assertive. Although they encouraged nurturing and independent behavior in their daughters, they did not promote nurturing in their sons. One can thus speculate that in the next generation, some females will be androgynous but that men will still be socialized in the traditional way (Shreve, 1984:43).

The Child at Play

According to the great social psychologist George Herbert Mead, through play and game activities children develop a sense of who they are and what the expectations of others and of society are. If Mead's contention is correct, these activities should also contribute to the preservation of sex-role distinctions by stressing particular social skills and capacities for boys and others for girls. Janet Lever studied this possibility among fifth graders, most of whom were white and middle class. Her research found that boys, more than girls (1) played outdoors; (2) played in larger groups; (3) played in age-heterogeneous groups; (4) were less likely to play in games dominated by the opposite gender; (5) played more competitive games; and (6) played in games that lasted longer (Lever, 1976).

These differences in play by gender reinforce the traditional roles: Boys play at competitive games that require aggressiveness and toughness, whereas girls tend to play indoors with dolls and play-acting scenarios of the home. Lever's conclusions suggest that the skills and patterns of relating developed by girls are different from those developed by boys. These gender differences may be most characteristic of white middle-class children. An important study on black adolescent girls by Joyce Ladner has shown that black girls develop in a more independent fashion (Ladner, 1971).

Formal Education

By the time they graduate from high school, youngsters have each spent approximately thirteen thousand hours in the classroom. Obviously, school has a profound influence on a child's world. The question to be answered in this section is: To what degree do the schools contribute to channeling people into narrow roles according to gender? To answer this question, we examine several areas: curriculum, textbooks, teacher-student interactions, sports, female role models, and counseling.

Curriculum.   Home economics, business education, shop classes, and vocational agriculture have traditionally been rigidly segregated by gender. Reflecting society's expectations, schools taught girls childrearing, cooking, sewing, and secretarial skills. Boys, on the other hand, were taught mechanics, woodworking, and other vocationally oriented skills. These courses were usually segregated by custom and sometimes by official school policy.

Many of these gender-segregated patterns persist even though Title IX of the Education Amendments Act, passed in 1972, prohibits all forms of sex discrimination in educational institutions. Over the past two decades, Title IX has had little impact in changing the rules and policies that perpetuate the unequal treatment of males and females in the public schools. For example, a 1983 investigation of New York City's vocational schools, undertaken for the U.S. Department of Education, revealed instance after instance of officials ignoring directives to reduce sex discrimination. The survey found that eleven of New York's twenty-one vocational schools had 95 percent or more male enrollment (Purnick, 1983). Examples of unequal treatment of girls and boys could undoubtedly be found in schools throughout the country. In one Huron Valley, Michigan, school, for instance, descriptions of a particular course were nearly identical, but one class was called "Slimnastics" and the other "Body Conditioning." The physical education department of the school told counselors that one was for girls and one was for boys, and that is how they were scheduled (Power, 1981:6).

Textbooks.   The content of textbooks transmits messages to readers about society, about children, and about what adults are supposed to do. For this reason, individuals and groups concerned about the potential for sexist bias in schools have looked carefully at how males and females are portrayed in textbooks assigned to students. Their findings provide a consistent message: Textbooks commonly used in American schools are overtly and covertly sexist. Sexism has become a recent concern of publishers, and a number have created guidelines for creating positive sexual and racial images in educational materials.

Stereotypes abound in textbooks. Several dozen studies have documented the existence of sex stereotypes in textbooks. Males appear more frequently in stories with "active mastery themes" in which the central characters display such qualities as ingenuity, creativity, bravery, perseverance, achievement, adventurousness, curiosity, autonomy, and self-respect. In stories with themes of "passivity" and "dependency" girls have tended to appear more frequently than boys. Another way in which males and females have been stereotyped is in the range of their occupational roles. One study found that males were shown in about six times as many different occupations as females. Females were shown as either job holders or mothers, rarely both (National Organization of Women, 1972).

Students also learn values and expectations in a hidden curriculum that is deeply gendered. We can see this curriculum at work in the content of textbooks and other educational materials. There is a conspicuous absence of women in elementary school textbooks. When women are mentioned, it is usually in terms of traditional feminine roles: for example, Florence Nightingale for nursing; Betsy Ross for sewing; Dolly Madison and Jackie Kennedy Onassis for being married to famous men (Renzetti and Curran, 1989:88).

An extensive survey of the words used in elementary texts revealed that *he* occurred three times as often as *she,* and that *boy* occurred twice as often as *girl.* In an interesting switch, however, *wife* was found three times more than the word *husband.* This pattern is not necessarily inconsistent, because the emphasis on wife suggests that society heavily stresses that role, whereas the husband's role is not so important.

Textbooks, then, have given official sanction to the subordinate roles that society imposes on women in real life.

Teacher-Student Interactions.   Even when girls and boys are in the same classrooms, they are educated differently. Teachers react differently to girls and boys; they have different kinds of contact with them and different expectations for them.

Research suggests that girls and boys have to act differently to get attention from their teachers. Serbin and colleagues found that girls who were physically close to their teachers receive more attention than boys who were physically close; boys who were aggressive received more attention than girls who were aggressive (Serbin et al., 1973). Another study of second graders found that teachers made more contacts with girls during reading classes and with boys during mathematics classes (Leinhardt, Seewald, and Engel, 1979). These findings reveal a hidden curriculum of gender socialization.

Studying classroom interaction at all levels for more than a decade, Myra Sadker has found that male students received more attention from teachers and are given more time to talk in class than are female students. Even though boys are more assertive than girls—eight times more likely to call out answers—Sadker found that teachers also called on boys more often and gave them more positive feedback than girls received. Boys also received more precise feedback from teachers, such as praise, criticism, or help with the answers they gave in class (Reported in Keegan, 1989:26). Most researchers in this and other studies have found that boys get more attention whether the teachers are male or female.

The Reinforcement of Gender in School Sports.   Sport in American schools has historically been almost exclusively a male preserve. This observation is clearly evident if one compares by sex the number of participants, facilities, support of school administrators, and financial support.

Such disparities are based on the assumption that competitive sport is basically a masculine activity and that the proper role of girls is that of spectator and cheerleader. What is the impact on a society that encourages its boys and young men to participate in sports while expecting its girls and young women to be spectators and cheerleaders? The answer is that sport thereby serves to reinforce societal expectations for males and females. Males are to be dominant and aggressive—the doers—while females are expected to be passive supporters of men, attaining status through the efforts of their menfolk. As Gilbert and Williamson observe:

> The overemphasis on protecting girls from strain or injury, and underemphasis on developing skills and experiencing teamwork, fits neatly into the

The much greater participation of girls and women in sports since 1975 is an important change that should have positive consequences for them.

pattern of the second sex. Girls are the spectators and the cheerleaders. They organize the pep clubs, sell pompoms, make cute, abbreviated costumes, strut a bit between halves and idolize the current football hero. This is perfect preparation for the adult role of women—to stand decoratively on the sidelines of history and cheer on the men, who make the decisions. (Gilbert and Williamson, 1973:73)

A very important consequence of minimizing sport participation for women is that approximately one-half of the population is denied access to all that sport has to offer (enjoyment, teamwork, goal achievement, ego enhancement, social status, competitiveness, and character building). School administrators, school boards, and citizens of local communities have long assumed that sports participation has general educational value. If so, then clearly girls should also be allowed to receive the benefits.

In June 1975 the federal government set forth guidelines to equalize opportunities for females in education. Every school that receives federal aid is affected: 2700 colleges and universities and 16,000 public school districts. With respect to sport, these guidelines insist that schools integrate their physical education classes; provide athletic supplies, equipment, facilities, and travel allowances for women equal to those of men; sponsor separate women's teams for contact sports if requested; and allow women and men to participate together on teams in noncontact sports.

The results of the legislation guaranteeing women equal opportunity in school sports are mixed. On the positive side, athletic programs on both the high school and the college level were opened to women. There has been a tremendous increase in the number of women's teams. Some women's sports have become popular with spectators as well. Women are beginning to have an opportunity to achieve recognition by participating in physical competitive activities (Richmond-Abbott, 1983:169). But coed sports have not been successful in attracting girls largely because they still do not offer males and females equal opportunities (Monagan, 1983).

Many schools have coed gym classes, where students learn game-playing skills, but when games are played competitively, teams tend to be of a single sex. Girls play softball; boys play baseball. The popular argument is that on coed teams, even in noncontact sports, boys will dominate and girls will feel mismatched (Louie, 1989:29).

Today, the critical issue is one of differential financial support for the two sexes. Women's sports and women's teams typically have inferior facilities, equipment, and uniforms, lower-paid coaches, less access to desirable practice fields and hours, less money for athletic scholarships, and, in general, fewer perquisites than their male counterparts (Weitzman, 1984:186).

Female Role Models in Education.   A subtle form of gender role reinforcement in education is found in the types of jobs held by men and women. The pattern is the familiar one found in hospitals, business offices, and throughout the occupational world: Women occupy the bottom rungs, and men are in the prestigious and decision-making positions. Women make up a large percentage of the nation's classroom teachers but a far smaller percentage of school district superintendents. In 1986 women comprised 81.9 percent of all elementary school teachers, almost half of all secondary school teachers (49.1 percent), and 42.6 of all school administrators (*USA Today,* 1987:B4).

As the level of education increases, the proportion of women teachers declines. In 1985, thirteen years after the Office of Civil Rights issued guidelines spelling out the obligations of colleges and universities in the development of affirmative action programs, the proportion of women in college faculties was only 35 percent (*The American Woman, 1987–88*:30). In the academic world a definite prestige and pay pyramid extends from lowly instructorships to full professorships. Women tend to be lower in academic rank than men, make less money (even when statistically controlling for academic level), are less likely to have tenure, and are virtually excluded from administrative positions.

Today at the University of Michigan, the first university to incorporate an affirmative action plan for hiring and promotion of women, the distribution of women among faculty ranks remains distinctly pyramidal; the lower the rank, the higher the proportion of women. In virtually every college and department at Michigan, dramatic disparities exist in gender representation on the faculty. Out of 2238 professors, 386 are women, a scant 16.9 percent of the faculty. In 1987 only 7.5 percent of all full professors were women. Furthermore, only 19.6 percent of all associate professors were women, and 27.9 percent of all assistant professors were women (*Michigan Daily,* 1987:6).

More than half the students in colleges and universities in the United States are women. But on most campuses women are left with few role models. Male students, too, should have outstanding women among their mentors, according to Dr. Muriel Ross, University of Michigan Professor of Anatomy,

> so that the next generation will understand that femaleness and excellence are not a rare simultaneous occurrence. Male faculty members need to see their female colleagues as achievers, in order to better prepare women to compete successfully in the world of business and industry (*Ann Arbor News,* 1983)

Counseling. A fundamental task of school guidance personnel is to aid students in their choice of a career. This function involves testing students for their occupational preference and aptitude and advising them on course selection and what kind of post–high school training they should get. The guidance that students receive on career choice tends to be biased. High school guidance counselors may channel male and female students into different (i.e., gender stereotyped) fields and activities. There is evidence that gender stereotyping is common among counselors and that they often steer females away from certain college preparatory courses, especially in mathematics and the sciences (Renzetti and Curran, 1989:93).

In the past, aptitude tests have themselves been sex-biased, listing occupations as either female or male. Despite changes in testing, counselors may inadvertently channel students into traditional gendered choices.

Socialization as Blaming the Victim

The discussion so far shows clearly the many ways in which gender differences are learned. As philosopher Simone de Beauvoir (1970) has argued, women are created, not born. Thus, socialization appears useful for "explaining" women. However, the socialization perspective on sexism can be misused in such a way that it blames women themselves for sex inequality. A critique of the socialization perspective by Elaine Enarson and Linda Peterson contends that, when used uncritically, socialization diverts attention from the oppression imposed by the dynamics of contemporary social structure:

> Misuse of the concept of socialization plays directly into the Blaming the Victim ideology; by focusing on the victim, responsibility for "the woman problem" rests not in the social system with its sex-structured distribution of inequality, but in socialized sex differences and sex roles. (Peterson and Enarson, 1974:8)

Not only is the cause of the problem displaced; so are the solutions. Enarson and Peterson concluded:

> Rather than directing efforts toward radical social change, the solution seems to be to change women themselves, perhaps through exhortation ("If we want to be liberated, we'll have to act more aggressive . . .") or, for example, changing children's literature and mothers' child rearing practice. (Peterson and Enarson, 1974:8)

This raises the critical question: If the socialization perspective is limited and perhaps biased, what is a better way of analyzing gender inequality? In answering this question, let us look at the ways in which male dominance affects our society.

THE REINFORCEMENT OF MALE DOMINANCE

Male dominance is both a socializing and a structural force. It exists at all levels of society, from the interpersonal interactions of women and men, to the gender patterning that is found in all cultural forms and social institutions. This section describes the interpersonal and institutional reinforcement of male dominance.

Language

Language perpetuates male dominance by ignoring, trivializing, and sexualizing women. Use of the pronoun *he* when the sex of the person is unspecified and of the generic term *mankind* to refer to humanity in general are obvious examples of how the English language ignores women. Common sayings like "that's women's work" (as opposed to "that's men's work!"), jokes about women drivers, phrases like "women and children first," or "wine, women, and song" (Adams and Ware, 1979) are trivializing. Women, more than men, are commonly referred to in terms that have sexual connotations. Terms referring to men ("studs," "jocks") that do have sexual meanings imply power and success, while terms applied to women ("broads," "dogs," "chicks") imply promiscuity or being dominated. In fact, the term promiscuous is usually applied only to women, although its literal meaning applies to either sex (Richmond-Abbott, 1983:115). Terms such as dogs and chicks tell us a great deal about how women are regarded by society. Their cumulative effect is illustrated in the following passage:

> In her youth she is a "chick" and then she gets married and feels "cooped up" and goes to "hen parties" and "cackles" with her women friends. Then she has her "brood" and begins to "henpeck" her husband. Finally, she turns into an "old biddy." (Nilson, in Richmond-Abbott, 1983:115)

Interpersonal Behavior

Day-to-day interaction between women and men perpetuates male dominance. Gender differences in conversational patterns reflect differences in power. Women's speech is more polite than men's. Women end statements with tag questions ("don't you agree?" "you know?") (Lakoff, 1975:14–15). Men are more direct, interrupt more, and talk more, notwithstanding the stereotype that women are more talkative. Men also have greater control over what is discussed (Parlee, 1979). Another indication of women's lack of power lies in the work they do to keep conversations going. Fishman (1978) studied male-female conversations and found that women work harder in conversations, even though they have less control over the subject matter. Males typically initiate interaction with women; they pursue, while females wait to be asked out.

Male dominance is also sustained by various forms of nonverbal communication. Men take up more space than women, touch women without permission more than women touch men. Women, on the other hand, engage in more eye contact, smile more, and generally exhibit behavior associated with low status. Gender differences in nonverbal behavior may be traced to differences in power, and these differences strengthen the system of dominance and privilege that exists (Henley, 1977).

Mass Communications Media

The mass media (television, newspapers, magazines, movies, and popular magazines) reflect society's assumptions about gender. Since the 1950s women's portrayal in magazines has become less monolithic. With the rise of feminism, many magazines devoted attention to women's achievements. Alongside these magazines for the "new woman" many "ladies magazines" continue to define the lives of women in terms of men—husbands or lovers. Many newspapers have refused to treat women on their own terms. It was only in 1986 that the *New York Times* adopted the title Ms. in its pages.

Several studies have demonstrated that highly stereotyped behavior characterizes both children and adult programming as well as commercials. Male role models are provided in greater numbers than female, with the exception of daytime soap operas in which men and women are equally represented. The imbalance has also been found with respect to occupations of men and women. Males are represented as occupying a disproportionately high percentage of the work force, a greater diversity of occupations, and higher-status jobs. Sex typing of behavior and personal characteristics during prime-time television has also been found in the following areas (see McGhee and Frueh, 1980:179–188):

- Females tend to be much younger than males and are more likely to be depicted as being married or "about to be married."
- Females are more likely to be cast in a leading role when some family or romantic interest is central to the plot.
- Males are more likely to be cast in serious roles; females are more likely to be cast in comic or light roles.
- Males are more likely to initiate violence, females are most likely to be victims.
- Females are less likely to get away with violence when they do demonstrate it.
- Females tend to be depicted as more attractive, happier, warmer, more sociable, fairer, more peaceful, and more useful. Males tend to be represented as smarter, more rational, more powerful, more stable, and more tolerant.

Images of women on television have improved in recent years. The National Commission on Working Women reports increasing diversity of characters portraying working women as television's most significant improvement in the past decade. According to the report, however, that trend may not continue, as new shows begin to return to homemakers and "pretty sidekicks" (Henry, 1988:1). For every contemporary show that includes positive images of women, there are numerous other shows in which women are sidekicks to men, sexual objects, or helpless imbiciles (Andersen, 1988:25–26).

Television commercials also present the sexes in stereotyped ways. A review of the research on television advertising has shown, for example, that (1) almost all commercials with voice-overs are spoken or sung by men; (2) men have a wider variety of roles than women; (3) the roles depicted for females are typically family roles; (4) women tend to be doing activities in the home that benefit men; (5) women tend to be inside the home and men outside; (6) women are younger than men; and (7) in commercials during children's programming, women and girls are seen less often than men and boys (see Butler and Paisley, 1980:103–114).

The sexism prevalent in advertising can be very subtle, as Erving Goffman has noted:

> (1) Overwhelmingly a woman is taller than a man only when the man is her social inferior; (2) a woman's hands are seen just barely touching, holding or caressing—never grasping, manipulating, or shaping; (3) when a photograph of men and women illustrates an instruction of some sort the man is always instructing the woman—even if the men and women are actually children (that is, a male child will be instructing a female child); (4) when an advertisement requires someone to sit or lie on a bed or a floor that someone is almost always a child or a woman, hardly ever a man; (5) when the head or eye of a man is averted it is only in relation to a social, political, or intellectual superior, but when the eye or head of a woman is averted it is always in relation to *whatever* man is pictured with her; (6) women are repeatedly shown mentally drifting from the scene while in close physical touch with a male, their faces lost and dreamy, "as though his aliveness to the surroundings and his readiness to cope were enough for both of them";
> (7) concomitantly, women, much more than men, are pictured at the kind of psychological loss or remove from a social situation that leaves one unoriented for action (e.g., something terrible has happened and a woman is shown with her hands over her mouth and her eyes helpless with horror). (Goffman, 1979:viii)

The advertising industry has been slowly modifying this image, since it has realized the potential buying power of larger numbers of working women, who have become targets of advertising campaigns designed to sell everything from three-piece suits to scotch. The underlying message is that women were discriminated against in the past but that mistake has been remedied (Gordon, 1983). One cigarette advertiser directed an entire campaign to such a segment of the market with a slogan—"You've come a long way, baby"—intended to reach the "new woman." Such advertising actually exploits women, though, by masking their position in society (women, as we shall see, have not come such a long way), by trivializing them ("baby"), and by fostering excessive consumption. The advertising aimed at the "new woman" places additional stresses on women and at the same time upholds male privilege. According to a University of Michigan report:

> When a television commercial shows a woman breezing in from her job to sort the laundry, or pop a roast in the oven, it reinforces the notion that it's all right for a woman to pursue a career, as long as she can still handle the housework. (University of Michigan, 1981)

Advertising aimed at such women increasingly relays the message that they should be superwomen, managing multiple roles of wife, mother, career woman, and so on, and be glamorous as well. Such multifarious expectations are not imposed on men. A recent cologne advertisement illustrates well the new expectations placed on employed women. Appealing to the "24-hour woman," the advertisement suggested that she "bring home the bacon, fry it up in a pan, and never let him forget he's a man." Under the guise of liberation, advertisers contribute to women's oppression by reinforcing the notion that domestic labor, child rearing, and pleasing men are women's responsibilities.

Although women comprise 52 percent of the U.S. population, a 1989 study of the front pages of ten large daily newspapers found that only 11 percent of the people mentioned in articles were women, 27 percent of articles were written by women, and 24 percent of photographs were of women, usually with a spouse or children. The study also looked at network newscasts and found that women reported 22 percent of the stories on CBS, 14 percent on NBC, and 10 percent on ABC. Women were the focus of 13 percent of the stories on ABC, 10 percent on CBS, and 8 percent on NBC (*USA Today,* April 11, 1989:2B).

Religion

The customs, beliefs, attitudes, and behaviors that discriminate against women are clearly reinforced by organized religion. Despite important differences in religious doctrines, there are similarities in views about gender. Limiting discussion to the Judeo-Christian heritage, let's examine some of the teachings from the Old and New Testaments regarding the place of women. The Old Testament clearly established male supremacy in a number of ways. To begin, God is believed to be a male. Women were obviously meant to be second to males because Eve was created from Adam's rib. According to the Scriptures, only a male could divorce a spouse. A woman who was not a virgin at marriage could be stoned to death. Girls could be purchased for marriage. Even employers were enjoined to pay women only three-fifths the wages of men: "If a male from 20 to 60 years of age, the equivalent is 50 shekels of silver by the sanctuary weight; if it is a female, the equivalent is 30 shekels" (Leviticus 27:4). As Gilman notes:

> The Old Testament devotes inordinate space to the listing of long lines of male descent to the point where it would seem that for centuries women "begat" nothing but male offspring. Although there are heroines in the Old Testament—Judith, Esther and the like—it's clear that they functioned like

the heroines of Greek drama and later of French: as counterweights in the imaginations of certain sensitive men to the degraded position of women in actual life. The true spirit of the tradition was unabashedly revealed in the prayer men recited every day in the synagogue: "Blessed art Thou, O Lord . . . for not making me a woman." (Gilman, 1971:51)

The New Testament generally continued the tradition of male dominance. Jesus was a male. He was the son of a male God, not of Mary, who remained a virgin. All the disciples were male. The great leader of the early church, the Apostle Paul, was especially adamant in arguing for the primacy of the male over the female. According to Paul, "the husband is supreme over his wife," "woman was created for man's sake," and "women should not teach nor usurp authority over the man, but to be silent."

Contemporary religious thought reflects this heritage. Some conservative denominations severely limit or even forbid women from any decision making. Others allow women to vote but limit their participation in leadership roles.

There are, however, some indications of change. Recently, the National Council of Churches called for elimination of sexist language and the use of "inclusive language" in the Revised Standard Version of the Bible. Terms such as *man, mankind, brothers, sons, churchmen,* and *laymen* would be replaced by neutral terms that include reference to female gender.

Women are pursuing equal rights in all denominations and faiths, and the sexual revolution is causing upheaval and resistance at every level of organized religion. The number of American women ordained to "full ministry" that is, preaching the word and administering the sacraments nearly doubled in the past decade. In 1987 women made up almost 8 percent of the clergy in denominations ordaining women (Cornell, 1989:106). In 1986, 26 percent of Protestant theological students were women. The number of female rabbis in the nation has grown, climbing to 130 in 1986 (Goldman, 1986:E6). Despite reluctance of established churches, women are making advances in religious status and changing the face of the ministry.

The Law

That the law has been discriminatory against women is beyond dispute. One need only to recall that women were specifically denied the right to vote prior to the passage of the Nineteenth Amendment. Less well known, but very important, was the 1824 Mississippi Supreme Court decision upholding the right of husbands to beat their wives (the U.S. Supreme Court finally prohibited this practice in 1891). Another interesting case that shows the bias of the legal system is *Minor* v. *Happerset* (1874). Here the Supreme Court ruled that the "equal protection" clause of the Fourteenth Amendment did not apply to women. Another ruling by the Supreme Court, at the time of the early feminist Susan B. Anthony, ruled that women were entitled to counsel, but that it must be male counsel.

During the past three decades, legal reforms and public policy changes have begun to place women and men on more equal footing. Some laws that focus on employment include the 1963 Equal Pay Act, Title VII of the 1964

Civil Rights Act, and the 1978 Pregnancy Discrimination Act. The 1974 Educational Amendments Act calls for gender equality in education. Other reforms have provided the framework for important institutional changes. For example, sexist discrimination in the granting of credit has been ruled illegal, and discrimination against pregnant women in the work force is now prohibited by the law. Affirmative action has remedied some kinds of gender discrimination in employment, sexist discrimination in housing is prohibited, and the differential requirements by gender as traditionally practiced by the airline industry have been eliminated. The force of these new laws, however, depends on their enforcement as well as on the interpretation of the courts when they are disputed.

Legal discrimination remains in a number of areas. There are still problems with Social Security and other pension programs. State laws vary considerably concerning property ownership by spouses, welfare benefits, and the legal status of homemakers. Legal reforms to reduce gender inequality have been dealt major setbacks by recent Supreme Court decisions in the areas of abortion and affirmative action. In July 1989, the Supreme Court narrowed its 1973 landmark *Roe* v. *Wade* decision that had established the right to abortion. *Roe* v. *Wade* was considered a major breakthrough for women, giving them the ultimate right to control their bodies. Although several later decisions by the Court reaffirmed this principle, the 1989 decision limited the constitutional right to abortion by ruling that the states may impose substantial restrictions on the availability of abortion. The new ruling weakens the framework established by *Roe* v. *Wade*. It allows states to restrict abortion at any stage of pregnancy, including the first three months. This decision curtails abortion rights and moves the abortion battleground to state legislatures.

Other Supreme Court decisions have also contributed to the dismantling of progressive legislation for women. In the Civil Rights Act of 1964, the Court had upheld affirmative action programs to end race and sex discrimination in employment. A series of recent rulings, however, place the burden

Reprinted by permission of Grimmy, Inc.

LOOK GUYS...WHY DON'T WE JUST SAY THAT ALL MEN ARE CREATED EQUAL...AND LET THE LITTLE LADIES LOOK OUT FOR THEMSELVES?

of proof on those who file bias suits. By shifting the burden of proof to women and minorities, discrimination will be difficult to abolish.

The June 1982 defeat of the Equal Rights Amendment represents a major setback to women's newly won rights. The amendment reads, "Equality of rights under the law shall not be denied or abridged by the United States or by any state on account of sex." What the amendment would have done is to render unconstitutional all state and federal laws and practices that treat men and women unequally. It would have prohibited all levels of government from discriminating against women in public employment and in job-training programs. Ratification would have declared equality of the sexes a national policy and would have provided a sound constitutional basis for challenging sex discrimination.

Politics

Women's political participation has always been different from that of men. Women received the right to vote in 1920, when the Nineteenth Amendment was ratified. Today, although women vote in about the same proportions as men, they make up a very small percentage of officeholders.

Between 1981 and 1989 the number of women in the U.S. Senate remained at 2 and the number of women in the U.S. House of Representatives increased from 19 to 25 (*Statistical Abstract of the U.S.*, 1989:252). The largest increases in women's elective political participation since 1975 have occurred at the county and local levels. In 1987, women held 20.5 percent of local offices and 12.5 percent of the offices in state legislatures (*Statistical Abstract of the U.S.*, 1989:256) (see Table 12–2). Women are also gaining prominence in the nation's cities. Six major urban centers are run by a woman. Eighty-two women were mayors of cities with populations exceeding 30,000 in 1986, compared with 37 in 1975 (Phillips, 1986:4B).

Despite these gains the United States ranks among the worst in denying women access to political leadership. It bears repeating that in America's two-hundred-year history, there has never been a woman president, there has

Table 12–2
Women in Selected Elective Office (1975–1987)

Elected Officeholders	Percentage Female							Number of Women	
	1975	1977	1979	1981	1983	1986	1987	1986	1987
Members of U.S. Congress	4	3	3	3	4	5	5	25	25
Statewide elective officials	10	8	11	11	13	14	14	42	43
Members of state legislatures	8	9	10	12	13	15	16	1101	1156

Source: Center for the American Woman and Politics, *Women in Elective Office* (May 1986), and unpublished data. Cited in *The American Woman 1987–88* (New York: Norton, 1987), p. 313. Reproduced from *The American Woman 1987–88*. A Report in Depth, edited by Sara E. Rix, by permission of W. W. Norton & Company, Inc. Copyright © 1987 by the Women's Research and Education Institute of the Congressional Caucus for Women's Issues.

been only one female justice of the Supreme Court, and the proportion of women in Congress has not reached 5 percent (Katzenstein, 1984:14).

Voting studies of the 1980 and 1984 elections demonstrated that women voted differently from men. This gender gap—measurable differences in the way women and men vote and view political issues—appears to continue today, with women tending to vote for liberal candidates and issues more than men. The gender gap appears to have more to do with the economic deprivation of certain groups of women than with a gender-specific political stance.

STRUCTURED GENDER INEQUALITY

In this discussion of structured gender inequality, we examine specific processes that limit women's access to highly valued resources and thereby "place" them in subordinate roles and activities. Women's oppression in both the work world and the family is part of the reinforcing systems of capitalism and patriarchy.

Occupational Distribution

In the past five decades, the proportion of women in the labor force has changed dramatically. In 1940, less than 20 percent of the female population age sixteen and older was in the labor force. By 1987, 58 percent of black women (6.5 million), 56 percent of white women (45.5 million), and 52 percent of Hispanic women (3.4 million) were in the labor force (U.S. Department of Labor, 1988).

Since 1980, women have taken 80 percent of the new jobs created in the economy. If this pace continues, women will make up most of the work force by the turn of the century (Hacker, 1986:26).

Who is today's working woman? She may be, whatever her age, a nurse or a secretary or a factory worker or a department store clerk or a public school teacher. Or she may be—though it is far less likely—a physician or the president of a corporation or the head of a school system. Hers may be the familiar face seen daily behind the counter at the neighborhood coffee shop, or she may work virtually unseen, mopping floors at midnight in an empty office building. The typical woman worker is a wage earner in clerical, service, manufacturing, and some technical jobs that pay poorly, give her little possibility for advancement, and little control over her work.

Women's surge into the labor force has taken place in "pink-collar" occupations, those that are predominantly female. The capitalist system's new demand for workers in service and clerical jobs has been met by women. Throughout the 1970s and the 1980s, women were clustered in a relatively small number of occupations defined as female jobs—clerical workers, retail sales workers, sewers and stitchers, waitresses, private household workers, nurses, and noncollege teachers. Women make up more than 70 percent of retail salespersons and of noncollege teachers. The other occupations listed are more than 80 percent female. Job segregation is extreme and persistent, with most occupations male-dominated and very few integrated.

A National Research Council study has concluded that the overall degree of sex segregation is a remarkably stable phenomenon; it has not changed much since 1900. This stability is surprising in light of the enormous changes that have taken place in the structure of the economy (see Chapter 13), the turnover in occupations as obsolete occupations disappear and new ones develop; the narrowing of educational differentials between women and men; and the increasing similarity in the work patterns of women and men over their lifetimes (Reskin and Hartmann, 1986:1). Some characteristics of women's participation remain amazingly resistant to change: their concentration in sex-typed jobs, their disproportionate share of low-ranking positions, and their low earnings relative to those of men with similar training and experience.

Media coverage of women's gains in traditionally male jobs is often misleading. Between 1970 and the late 1980s, small reductions have occurred in the overall extent of sex segregation in the labor force. For example, in blue-collar fields gains look dramatic at first glance, with the number of women in blue-collar jobs rising by 80 percent in the 1970s. But the increase is so high because women were virtually excluded from these occupations until then. In 1987, only 3 percent of machinists, 1 percent of carpenters, and 0.6 percent of auto mechanics were women (*Statistical Abstract of the U.S.*, 1989:389).

The years 1970 to 1985 found 290,000 more women in the fields of law, medicine, journalism, and higher education. By 1985 the percentage of women in the group the census classifies as "executive, administrative, and managerial" had grown (Hacker, 1986:31). Today, women fill nearly one-third of all management positions (up from 19 percent in 1972), but most are stuck in jobs with little authority and relatively low pay (Hymnowitz and Schellhardt, 1986:1–D). Despite recent progress in the prestige professions, there are far fewer women in these jobs than men. In 1987, only 19.7 percent of lawyers, 19.5 percent of doctors, and 37.1 percent of university or college teachers were women (*Statistical Abstract of the U.S.*, 1989:388). Although women have made inroads in the high-paying and high-prestige professions, they still occupy the least professional specialties, and they face barriers to their entry into and advancement through the professions.

As the economy is being transformed from its traditional manufacturing base to a base in service and high technology, men and women are affected differently. Industrial jobs are taken away from men, and more women are employed in service jobs. The Bureau of Labor Statistics expects that through 1995 nearly 75 percent of new jobs will come from service-producing sectors of the economy (Wayne, 1984).

Along with service work, clerical work is projected to increase at faster rates than all other occupational categories. The explosion of services would appear to benefit women by expanding employment opportunities as keypunchers, salesclerks, food service workers, secretaries, and cashiers. But the full effect of economic restructuring on women must take into account the low wage levels and the limited opportunities for advancement that will characterize service work in the new economy (see Table 12–3).

Part-time work is often sought by women as a way of combining earning a living and raising a family. Yet three-fourths of women who work part-time

Table 12–3
Twenty Occupations with the Largest Projected Absolute Growth (1978–1990)

Occupation	Percentage Female 1980[a]	Growth in Employment 1978–1990 (in thousands)	Percentage Growth 1978–1990
Janitors and sextons	17.3%	671.2	26.0%
Nurses' aides and orderlies	87.5	594.0	54.6
Sales clerks	71.1	590.7	21.3
Cashiers	86.6	545.5	36.4
Waiters/waitresses	89.1	531.9	34.6
General clerks, office	80.1	529.8	23.4
Professional nurses	96.5	515.8	50.3
Food preparation and service workers, fast food restaurants	66.9	491.9	68.8
Secretaries	99.1	487.8	21.0
Truck drivers	2.2	437.6	26.2
Kitchen helpers	66.9	300.6	39.0
Elementary school teachers	83.7	272.8	21.4
Typists	96.9	262.1	26.4
Accountants and auditors	36.2	254.2	32.7
Helpers, trades	NA	232.5	25.0
Blue-collar workers, supervisors	10.8	222.1	17.4
Bookkeepers, hand	90.5	219.7	23.7
Licensed practical nurses	97.3	215.6	43.9
Guards and doorkeepers	12.4	209.9	35.5
Automotive mechanics	.6	205.3	24.3

NA = not available.

[a]Approximate, due to the use of different occupational classifications in sources.

Source: Data from the U.S. Department of Labor, Bureau of Labor Statistics, reported in Barbara F. Reskin and Heidi I. Hartmann, eds., *Women's Work, Men's Work* (Washington, DC: National Academy Press, 1986):33.

are in low-paying sales, service, and clerical occupations (*The American Woman, 1987–88*:134).

Earning Discrimination

The earning gap between women and men has been widely documented. Although there was a slight narrowing of the earnings difference during the past ten years, women workers do not approach earnings parity with men even when they worked in similar occupations.

In 1987 the average working woman earned 70 cents for every dollar earned by a man. This income differential has remained at about the same level throughout the past two decades. The earnings gap persists for several reasons:

- Women are concentrated in lower-paying occupations.
- Women enter the labor force at different and lower-paying levels than men.

- Women as a group have less education and experience than men; therefore, they are paid less than men.
- Women tend to work less overtime than men.

These conditions explain only part of the earnings gap between women and men. They do not explain why women workers earn substantially less than men workers with the same number of years of education and with the same work histories, skills, and work experience.

Two research scientists at the University of Michigan have examined the income gap to determine whether it can be explained by differences in job qualifications of men and women. Although findings do reveal some differences between the sexes in accumulated job experiences, taken together, they account for only about one-third of the existing wage gap. Corcoran and Duncan found that a large part of the wage gap can be explained by institutional sex discrimination in the labor market that obstructs women's access to the better-paying jobs through hiring or promotion or simply paying women less than men in any job (IRS Newsletter, 1982).

America's educated women are not being compensated fairly. In 1986, the median income of women with four years of college education ($22,410.) was still below that of men with only a high school diploma ($24,701) (U.S. Department of Labor, 1988).

Differential earning can be found even within occupational classification. Fully employed women, when compared with fully employed men, are consistently underpaid by thousands of dollars when equal in educational attainment or type of occupation. A national survey found that most professional women do not earn even $25,000 a year. Fifty-six percent earn less than $15,000, one-third earn between $15,000 and $24,999, and a mere 10 percent earn $25,000 or more (Townsend, 1985:5).

Double Discrimination: Race and Gender

If women are disadvantaged due simply to their sex, minority women are doubly disadvantaged. For every dollar earned by a white man in 1985, black women earned 56 cents and Hispanic women earned 53 cents (National Committee on Pay Equity, 1987). Black and Hispanic women are overrepresented in low-paying, low-status jobs. They tend to have few fringe benefits, poor working conditions, high labor turnover, and little chance of advancement. Black and Hispanic women are clustered in service jobs such as cooks, dishwashers, food counter and fountain workers, cleaning service workers, waitresses, nurses' aides and child care workers. Because of their race, black and Hispanic women are crowded into society's "dirty work" sectors. The gender system works with and through the system of racial stratification to place women of color at the bottom of the work hierarchy. (See Table 12–4.)

Pay Equity

Most new jobs in the near future are expected to open up in traditionally female occupations. Thus, limited progress will be made in integrating oc-

Table 12–4
**Occupations
with the
Highest
Concentration
by Race/
Ethnicity/
Gender**

Workers	Occupations
Black men	Stevedores, garbage collectors, longshore equipment operators, baggage porters
Black women	Private household workers, cooks, housekeepers, welfare aides
Hispanic men	Farm workers, farm supervisors, elevator operators, concrete finishers
Hispanic women	Graders and agricultural workers, housekeepers, electrical assemblers, sewing machine operators
Asian men	Physicians, engineers, professors, technicians, baggage porters, cooks, launderers, longshore equipment operators
Asian women	Marine life workers, electrical assemblers, dressmakers, launderers
Native American men	Marine life workers, hunters, forestry (except logging), fishers
Native American women	Welfare aides, child care workers, teachers' aides, forestry (except logging)
White men	Airplane pilots, sales engineers, firefighting supervisors, electrician supervisors
White women	Dental hygienists, secretaries, dental assistants, occupational therapists

Source: Pay Equity: An Issue of Race, Ethnicity, and Sex (Washington, D.C.: National Committee on Pay Equity, February 1987), p. 4. Reprinted by permission.

cupations over the next decade. Although considerable evidence suggests that traditionally female jobs pay less because it is women rather than men who do them, the law does not presently view such differences as discrimination. To combat this problem, equal-rights activists are striving to close the wage gap between women's jobs and men's jobs by mounting a fight for pay equity. The goal of pay equity is to raise pay levels for occupations in which women and minorities predominate. Raises would be accomplished by subjecting jobs to a rational evaluation that would assess their "worth" in terms of skills and responsibilities of the work itself. Because pay equity calls for jobs of comparable value to be paid the same, it is also called comparable worth (Hacker, 1986; Sociologists for Women in Society, 1986).

How would employers use sex- and race-neutral criteria to set equal wages for workers in different but equally demanding occupations? Employers would set their own pay scales, but pay scales would be based on the work itself. The pay scales would be set up by using *job evaluation systems.* In job evaluation the employer and employees (and union, when there is a collective-bargaining agreement) select the criteria on which wages should be based—such as skill, effort, responsibility, working conditions—and decide how much to weigh each factor. Points are assigned for every job in a company according to its evaluation system, so that a job's total score represents its worth to the employer. Very different jobs in the same company may have similar scores. These scores are used to set *salary ranges* for each job, so that jobs with the same score fall into the same salary range. The idea of job evaluation is not new; at present, about two-thirds of all U.S. workers are employed in establishments that use some form of job evaluation to set wages. However, employers often use separate wage scales for predominantly male and predominantly female jobs (Sociologists for Women in Society, 1986) (see Panel 12–1).

A decade of lobbying for Pay Equity has brought women and minorities in the public sector more than $450 million in wage and salary gains. According to the National Committee on Pay Equity, 20 state governments have negotiated pay increases. The prospects for achieving further pay increases for women and minorities in the 1990s are bright because these groups will represent the majority of new entrants into the job market (*USA Today*, October 10, 1989:1). However, pay equity proponents lost an important case in California (1989) when the judge ruled that the plaintiffs must prove discriminatory intent, which is what the Supreme Court has ruled in several cases (1989) involving Affirmative Action. This ruling, too, allows discrimination to continue unabated.

The Organization and Operation of Work

There has been a widespread view that women's status in the labor force was a result of their socialization, their low aspirations, and their greater commitments to family than to work. New sociological research has found that the economic system, not individual characteristics, structures the position of women. Let us examine the organization of the labor force that assigns better jobs and greater rewards to men and positions of less responsibility with lower earning to women.

The differential placement of women and men stems from forces in American capitalism. The capitalist labor market is divided into two separate segments with different characteristics, different roles, and different rewards. The primary segment is characterized by stability, high wages, promotion ladders, opportunities for advancement, good working conditions, and provisions for job security. The secondary market is characterized by low wages, fewer or no promotion ladders, poor working conditions, and little provision for job security.

Women's work tends to fall in the secondary segment. Clerical work, the largest single occupation for women, has many of the characteristics associated with the secondary segment. The office provides a good example of segmentation by gender. According to Glenn and Feldberg:

> We observe two separate groups of office jobs, divided by sex. Some jobs are clearly "female" (typists, secretaries, key punchers); others are clearly "male" (vice president, product manager, sales manager). Furthermore, groups of jobs are organized into a hierarchy and the "clerical" staff is a largely female

Facts about Pay Equity

IS PAY EQUITY FAIR?

The point of pay equity is not to eliminate inequality in wages, but to eliminate wage inequality that is based on sex or race. Jobs that are more difficult or valuable should be rewarded accordingly. However, job evaluation studies by employers and state civil service systems have repeatedly shown that women's jobs are underpaid relative to their evaluation scores. Basing wages on workers' personal characteristics rather than on the worth of the job is unfair.

WILL PAY EQUITY COST SO MUCH IT WILL WEAKEN THE ECONOMY?

Implementing pay equity will cost less than many fear. For example, the cost of doing so in Minnesota was less than 4 percent of the state's payroll budget. Moreover, taxpayers already share the cost of women's artificially low wages. A Department of Labor study calculated that about half of the families living in poverty would not be poor if their female wage-earners were

paid as much as similarly qualified men. Pay equity will save tax dollars spent assisting employed women and minorities whose wages are lowered by discrimination.

WILL PAY EQUITY MEAN GOVERNMENT INTERFERENCE IN PRIVATE FIRMS?

Pay equity would *not* require national or statewide wage-setting systems. Employers would continue to set wages, but they would have to do so in a nondiscriminatory way according to their own job evaluation systems.

WILL IMPLEMENTING PAY EQUITY LOWER WHITE MEN'S WAGES?

Under the Equal Pay Act and Title VII, courts have consistently held that an employer may not lower any employee's pay to eliminate wage discrimination. Pay equity will mean raises for *all* workers who work in occupations that have been underpaid. Since these tend to be women, pay equity will reduce the wage gap between predominantly male and female occupations.

---

hierarchy. Each hierarchy is made up of jobs graded by level representing steps in a career. When a person takes a job she/he occupies not only that particular job, but also a step on a particular career ladder. A person who starts on the clerical career ladder may move up the ranks as she/he gains experience, but she/he rarely is allowed to cross over into a different ladder. Occasionally one hears of a clerk or secretary who becomes an officer in a company. Such stories generate excitement precisely because each is a freak occurrence. (Glenn and Feldberg, 1984:314)

Today's office is in the midst of change, described variously as "office automation," "the electronic office," and "the office of the future." Women are an overwhelming majority of office workers—workers in the occupation group identified as "administrative support, including clerical"—and they are particularly affected by changes in this workplace. Advances for business are not always advances for women, though, whose work is becoming more

WHY DON'T WOMEN AND MINORITIES CHANGE TO HIGHER PAYING JOBS?

Race and sex discrimination continue to exclude women and minorities from many jobs. Moreover, jobs traditionally reserved for white men could not begin to absorb the millions of women and minorities who work in sex- and race-segregated jobs. Even if enough jobs existed, many mature workers lack the credentials or specific skills they require. Schools and the media continue to channel young people into occupations that have been labelled "appropriate" for their sex and race.

WHAT CAN YOU DO TO PROMOTE PAY EQUITY?

- Inform yourself (see organizations and references below). Work to inform others, in the classroom, through letters to the editor, and talks to community groups. Write your legislators, supporting your opinions with facts.
- If you do research on race or sex segregation or wage differences, share your findings with public legislators.
- Organize workshops, conferences, letter-writing campaigns.

- Press for job evaluation studies and pay equity on your job, in your union or employees' organization, and in your city and state government.
- Contact and support labor, women's and civil rights organizations working for pay equity. These include the American Association of University Women; the American Civil Liberties Union; the American Federation of State, County and Municipal Employees; the Business and Professional Women's Foundation; the Coalition of Labor Union Women; the League of Women Voters; the Mexican-American Women's National Association; the National Conference of Puerto Rican Women; the National Education Association; the National Organization for Women; 9 to 5; the National Association of Working Women; the Service Employees International Union.

These and other groups belong to the National Committee of Pay Equity (NCPE). For further information, contact the NCPE at 1201 Sixteenth Street, N.W., Washington, D.C. 20036, 202/822–7304.

Source: Sociologists for Women in Society, "Facts About Pay Equity" (April, 1986).

repetitious and subject to impersonal supervision. Machung has described word processing and the deskilling of clerical work:

> Working face to face with a T.V. screen all day long, operators, especially those in large centers, have few social contacts, except with each other. Unlike secretaries who are highly visible at front desks, word processing operators are virtually invisible. Isolated from the rest of the corporation by their dress (frequently more casual), their age (frequently younger), and their race (frequently minority), they work anonymously under fluorescent lighting in crowded back offices and windowless rooms. A supervisor usually handles all contacts with areas of the center; operators never see the person whose letter or paper they have typed. . . . Unlike secretaries who are known by their first names and friendly manners, word processing operators are virtually unknown. Many have taken the jobs to escape the stigmatization and subordination of secretarial work, only to find themselves even more faceless and nameless. (Machung, 1984:129)

Gendered work can be found even in the professions. In medicine women may no longer be concentrated in the low-prestige specialties such as pediatrics and obstetrics gynecology; but except for general surgery, their numbers are not increasing in the more prestigious areas of medicine. Women lawyers are engaged in low-prestige specialties with a large proportion of female clients.

Although women are increasingly entering managerial and administrative jobs in private industry, they tend to be clustered in areas more traditionally open to females: public relations, personnel, and other staff jobs; consequently, they earn less than men with the same background.

Structural changes now occurring within the professions are creating a split between prestige jobs and a new category of more routinized jobs that are "professional" in name only. Carter and Carter have shown that women are concentrated in the new, more routinized sectors of professional employment, but the upper tier of relatively autonomous work continues to be male-dominated, with only token increases in female employment (Carter and Carter, 1981).

Changes in the organization of three professions—medicine, college teaching, and law—have degraded women's work. In medicine the growth of hospital-based practice has paralleled women's admission to the profession. Women doctors are more likely than men to be found in hospital-based practice, which provides less autonomy than the more traditional office practice. In college and university teaching, demand is greatest in two-year colleges with heavy teaching responsibilities that leave little time or energy for writing and publishing—the keys to academic career advancement. And in law, women's advancement to prestigious positions is being eroded by the growth of the legal clinic where much legal work is routinized. Women have made important inroads into the professions, but because of structural changes occurring in many professions, the occupations to which women have gained access in recent years no longer have the same meaning in terms of economic or social status that they once possessed. Although they require a fair amount of formal schooling, many professional positions have become low paying, routine, and dead-end, much like other occupations employing larger numbers of women.

People have long assumed that women's and men's behavior in work settings is different and that women's behavior accounts for their lack of career advancement. Men are thought to be more ambitious, task-oriented, and work-involved; women are considered less motivated, less committed, and more oriented to work relationships than to work itself. Recent research, however, has pointed to the importance of the effect of people's location or placement in work settings and its effect on behavior.

Rosabeth Moss Kanter's important research on men and women in the corporate world reveals that structural position can account for what appear to be "sex differences" in organizational behavior. Hierarchical structures of opportunity and power shape women's and men's work behavior. People in low-mobility or blocked situations (regardless of their sex) tend to limit their aspirations, seek satisfactions in activities outside work, dream of escape, and create sociable peer groups in which interpersonal relationships take over other aspects of work. The jobs held by most women workers tend to be associated with shorter chains of opportunity. What has been considered typical women's behavior can be explained by their structural position (Kanter, 1977:129–163).

Just as hierarchical structures track women and men, other processes contribute to gender stratification. In the professions, for example, sponsor-protégé systems and informal interactions among colleagues limit women's mobility. Cynthia Epstein points to the importance of sponsorship in training personnel and ensuring leadership continuity. Women are less likely to be acceptable as protégés. Furthermore, their sex status limits or excludes their involvement in the buddy system or the old-boy system (Epstein, 1970). These informal interactions create alliances that can further chances for social mobility, but they are systematically blocked for women. Clearly, the work situations of women are different from those of men. In Acker's words:

> The question, Why aren't women more assertive, more ambitious, more career oriented? is essentially a question about why women aren't more like men, and it assumes that they work in the same world as men. We could assume . . . that women live and work in a different culture-structural environment from that of men. In this environment they are viewed as outsiders in a place where they are not expected to be. They are also seen as people who are by definition either too passive or too aggressive—people who have a proper place in supportive but not in leadership roles. (Acker, 1978:151)

Women and Men in Families

Women's status in the family parallels their status in other social institutions. This is readily apparent from the kind of work they do. In the role of wife and mother, a woman earns no money for her household chores of cleaning, ironing, cooking, sewing, and caring for the needs of the household members. Although this work is necessary, it is low in prestige and it is unpaid. Apportioning domestic labor and child rearing to women upholds male privilege by freeing men from such responsibilities.

Although many wife-husband relationships are moving toward equality, men continue to exercise greater marital power. The higher the husband's occupational status, the higher his income, and the higher his overall status, the greater his power. Such resources are acquired outside the family. We have seen that women's opportunities to acquire these resources are much more limited then those of men: American families are still patriarchal. Family life tends to be subordinate to demands of the male-husband role.

THE COSTS AND CONSEQUENCES OF SEXISM

Who Benefits?

Clearly, gender inequality enters all aspects of social life in the United States. This inequality is profitable to certain segments of the economy, and it also gives privileges to individual men.

Capitalists derive extra profits from paying women less than men. Women's segregation in low-paying jobs produces higher profits for certain economic sectors; namely, those where most of the labor force is female. Women who lack the economic support of husbands and who are in the wage labor force on only a temporary basis have always been a source of easily exploitable labor. These women provide a significant proportion of the marginal labor force needed by capitalists to draw upon during upswings in the business cycle and to release during downswings (Edwards, Reich, and Weisskopf, 1978:333).

Gender inequality and male dominance are suited to the needs of the economy in other ways as well. Capitalism involves not only the accumulation of capital but also the maintenance of labor power. The physical and emotional labor of maintaining wage workers must be done. The unpaid work that women do inside the home keeps capitalism going, servicing its workers both physically and emotionally. Women do domestic labor and child rearing, but they also do the emotional work, building and maintaining interpersonal relationships and ensuring the stability of children and men so they can function in a capitalistic society (Edwards, Reich, and Weisskopf, 1978:334).

Because domestic work and emotional work are assigned to women, individual men gain leisure and service and the opportunity to pursue their own interests or careers. If women tend to men's "existence needs," such as cooking and taking care of clothing, men gain time at women's expense:

> He reads the evening paper and his wife fixes dinner. He watches the news or an informative television show and she washes the dishes. He retires to his study (or his office or his shop or a soft chair) and she manages the children. Men gain leisure time at the expense of the oppression of women. This is a very fundamental privilege which accrues to the division of labor (or lack of division) in the home. (Newton, 1973:121)

This domestic division of labor, in turn, can limit women's occupational participation and advancement. Women burdened with domestic duties have less time or energy left over to devote to careers. Thus, the domestic division of labor reinforces the division of labor in the labor force: men's occupational superiority is upheld. The interaction of the two interlocking systems of capitalism and patriarchy has created a vicious cycle of domination and subordination.

The Social and Individual Costs

Gender inequality generates benefits for certain segments of society, but ultimately society and individual women and men pay a high price. Sexism diminishes the quality of life for all Americans. Our society is deprived of half of its resources when women are denied full and equal participation in its institutions. If women are systematically kept from jobs requiring leadership, creativity, and productivity, the economy will obviously suffer. The pool of talent consisting of half the population will continue to be underutilized and underproductive, in effect constituting a massive "brain drain" for the society. This potential for creativity and leadership is lost because of the barriers that keep women "in their place." As Robertson has summarized it:

> Any society that ascribes low status to some of its members on such arbitrary grounds as race, caste, or sex is artificially restricting the economic contribution of part of the population. To be fully efficient, a modern industrial economy must allow social mobility on the grounds of merit, not restrict it on the grounds of an irrational ascribed status. (Robertson, 1977:306)

Sexism also produces suffering for millions. We have seen that individual women pay for economic discrimination. Their children pay as well, especially if employed mothers are unmarried, separated, divorced, or forced by economic circumstances to buttress the earnings of their husbands.

Due to rising divorce rates, women are increasingly likely to carry primary responsibility for supporting themselves and their children. At the same time most women remain in the secondary labor force with wages too low to support themselves, let alone a family. Women now head 28 percent of America's 91 million households. Characteristics of women who head families include higher unemployment, lower educational attainment, more dependent children, and lower earnings when compared with other groups. In 1987, the median income of a female head of household was $17,000 for a white woman, $9,700 for a black woman, and $10,200 for a Hispanic woman (Crispell, 1989:29).

The costs of the undeserved pay gap between women and men is great, especially in families where fathers are absent. A 1977 government study found that if working women were paid what similarly qualified men earn, the number of poor families would decrease by half (Sexton, 1977). A difference between male and female poverty is that male poverty is often the consequence of unemployment and a job is an effective remedy; female poverty often exists even when a woman works full-time.

The impoverishment of women is costly to society. Households headed by women account for 83 percent of all AFDC (Aid to Families with Dependent Children) recipients, 70 percent of all food stamp households, 60 percent of those using Medicaid, 66 percent of households using subsidized housing, and 67 percent of all legal service clients (Stallard, Ehrenreich, and Sklar, 1983:47).

All women pay a psychological price for sexism. The devaluation of women by society can create identity problems, low self-esteem, and a general sense of worthlessness, particularly as women age. Middle-aged and older women in U.S. society face two problems from which men are relatively exempt. The first problem is the loss of sexual attractiveness. The second problem is the loss of their primary role—the bearing and raising of children.

Given the occupational patterns of our society, men generally gain in prestige and power as they age. They therefore tend to retain or even enhance their attractiveness to women. The reverse, however, is not the case (Bell, 1984). The result is that widowed or divorced men tend to remarry younger women. Widowed or divorced women either remain single or marry older men. Consequently, although the male-female ratio is approximately 1:1 in the forty-five to sixty-four age bracket, there are three times as many single, divorced, and widowed women as there are single, divorced, and widowed men in that age category. Those women who worked inside the home for husbands and children can become "displaced homemakers" through the death, separation, or divorce of a husband.

Sexism also denies men the potential for full human development. Occupational segregation by sex denies employment opportunities to men who wish to enter such fields as nursing, grade school teaching, or secretarial work. Eradication of sexism would benefit such males. It would benefit all males who have been forced into stereotypic male behavioral modes. In learning to be men, boys express their masculinity through physical courage, toughness, competitiveness, and aggression. Expressions typically associated with femininity, such as gentleness, expressiveness, and responsiveness, are seen as undesirable for males. In rigidly adhering to gender expectations, males pay a price for their masculinity. As Pleck puts it:

> The conventional expectations of what it means to be a man are difficult to live up to for all but the lucky few and lead to unnecessary self-deprivation in the nest when they do not measure up. Even for those, who do, there is a price: they may be forced, for example, to inhibit the expression of many emotions. (Pleck, 1981:69)

Male inexpressiveness can hinder communication between husbands and wives, between fathers and children; it has been labeled a "tragedy of American society" (Balswick and Peck, 1971). Certainly, it is a tragedy for the man himself, crippled by an inability to show the best part of a human being—his warm and tender feelings for other people (Balswick and Collier, 1976:59).

Ideally, men and women should be able to integrate traditionally feminine and traditionally masculine traits. Such flexibility of gender, or androgyny, would permit all people to be either rational or emotional, either assertive or yielding, depending on what is appropriate to the situation.

FIGHTING THE SYSTEM

Feminist Movements in the United States

Gender inequality in this society has led to feminist social movements. Three stages of feminism have been aimed at overcoming sex discrimination. The first stage grew out of the abolition movement of the 1830s. Working to abolish slavery, women found that they could not function as equals with their male abolitionist friends, and they became convinced that women's freedom was as important as freedom from slavery. In July 1848 the first convention in history devoted to issues of women's position and rights was held at Seneca Falls, New York. Participants in the Seneca Falls convention approved a declaration of independence, asserting that men and women are created equal, and that they are endowed with certain inalienable rights.

During the Civil War feminists for the most part turned their attention to the emancipation of blacks. After the war and the ratification of the Thirteenth Amendment abolishing slavery, feminists were divided between those seeking far-ranging economic, religious, and social reforms, and those seeking voting rights for women. The second stage of feminism gave priority to women's suffrage. The women's suffrage amendment, introduced into every session of Congress from 1878 on, was ratified on August 26, 1920, nearly three-quarters of a century after the demand for women's suffrage had been made at the Seneca Falls convention. From 1920 until the 1960s feminism was dormant. "So much energy had been expended in achieving the right to vote that the woman's movement virtually collapsed from exhaustion" (Hole and Levine, 1979:554).

Feminism was reawakened in the 1960s. Social movements aimed at inequalities gave rise to an important branch of contemporary feminism. The civil rights movement and other protest movements of the 1960s spread the ideology of equality. But like the early feminists, women involved in political protest movements found that male dominance characterized even movements seeking social equality. Discovering injustice in freedom movements, they broadened their protest to such far-reaching concerns as health care, family life, and relationships between the sexes.

Another strand of contemporary feminism emerged among professional women who discovered sex discrimination in earnings and advancement. Formal organizations, such as the National Organization of Women, evolved seeking legislation to overcome sex discrimination (Freeman, 1979).

These two branches of contemporary feminism gave rise to a feminist consciousness among millions of American women. As a consequence, during the 1960s and early 1970s many changes occurred in the roles of women and men. However, periods of recession, high unemployment, and inflation in the late seventies fed a backlash against feminism. The contemporary women's movement may be the first in American history to face the opposition of an organized antifeminist social movement. From the mid-1970s a coalition of groups calling themselves profamily, prolife, and anti-ERA emerged. These groups have drawn from right-wing political organizations and the Moral Majority to oppose feminist gains in reproductive, family, and antidiscrimination policies (Sapiro, 1986:972). In addition, many gains have been set back by opposition to affirmative action programs and other equal-rights policies. Thus, sexism persists and continues to affect the lives of all women and men.

Social Structure and Equality

An important question is whether gender equality is compatible with present political economic conditions. We have seen that the form of the economy and the distribution of power (capitalist patriarchy) produces gender inequality at all levels of American society. Acker observes:

> Many serious feminists believe that neither equality nor liberation can emerge within the capitalist economic system—a system in which the primary objective is profit making rather than equality and improvement of the conditions of life for all. They contend that as long as the unequal situation of women

Women and Workforce 2000

Several emerging trends in the economy and the labor force today will shape and characterize the work force of the future. Significant among them are an aging work force, greater numbers of women, minorities and immigrants in the work force, a declining pool of youth, a continuing shift to the service producing sector, and an increasing demand for workers with high skills.

LABOR FORCE OUTLOOK

Today, more than 53 million women age 16 and over comprise 45 percent of the total labor force. Although the labor force will grow more slowly than in the past, there will be 139 million persons in the labor force in the year 2000, an increase of 21 million from 1986. Women, minorities, and immigrants will account for 90 percent of the increase. It is projected that women's share of the labor force will increase to 47 percent in 2000.

Women will be the major source of new entrants into the labor force over the next 13 years. They will account for 63 percent of the net labor force growth or 13.2 million women by 2000. The number of black women will increase by 2.1 million or 16 percent and account for one-tenth of the overall labor force growth.

The number of Hispanic women in the labor force by the year 2000 is projected to reach 5.8 million, an increase of 85 percent. This projected 1986 to 2000 increase is more than that of white and black women's increases combined. Hispanic women will account for about 13 percent of the increase in the total labor force by 2000. In addition, about 1 out of 10 women entrants will be of Asian, American Indian, Alaskan Native, or other descent.

The labor force will be older by the year 2000. While the number of workers between the ages of 20 and 34 will decline by 4.6 million, the number between 45 and 54 will increase by 12.8 million. Half of the women in the labor force will be between the ages of 35 and 54. This is a shift from 1986 when the majority of women in the labor force were between the ages of 25 and 44. There will be a net increase of workers aged 16 to 19 between 1986 and 2000, but there will be a substantial, immediate (short term) decline in these workers between 1986 and 1995. . . .

does not interfere with production and profits, little will be done to effect real changes. (Acker, 1978:155)

Because structural problems are largely invisible, we must understand how individual lives are bound up with structural events.

Individual women and men seeking change will continue to discover that no matter how they struggle for equality, the sexism that is rooted in our culture and our social institutions will continue to affect them. Thus, the insights of sociology have become increasingly significant in the continuing struggle for women's equality.

CHAPTER REVIEW

1. American society, like other societies, assigns different expectations to women and men, and these expectations are ranked in favor of males. Male dominance refers to the fact that men have greater prestige, power, and privileges than women.

2. The pressures of society are more important than innate biological differences in the forma-

OCCUPATIONAL OUTLOOK

Of the eleven occupations which are projected to increase by more than 400,000 jobs by 2000, women held more than 80 percent of those jobs in six occupational categories in 1986. These 11 occupations are expected to account for 30 percent of job growth to 2000.

The three broad occupation groups with the most highly trained workers, (executive, administrative, and managerial; professional specialty; and technician and related support) will account for 40 percent, or 8 million, of the job growth between 1986 and 2000. In 1986, women held 43.8 percent of such jobs. Black women accounted for 7 percent and Hispanic women 3 percent.

The occupation group with the greatest increase, 5.4 million, is service workers. This job category, dominated by women who accounted for 61 percent of the service jobs in 1986, is within the group of jobs requiring the least skills. . . .

Source: U.S. Department of Labor, Women's Bureau, "Facts on U.S. Working Women," Fact Sheet No. 88–1 (January 1988), excerpts from pp. 1–4.

Occupations with Largest Job Growth, 1986–2000 (Numbers in thousands)

Occupation	1986 Employment		New Jobs
	Number	Percent Women	
Salespersons, retail	3,579	59.5	1,201
Waiters and waitresses	1,702	85.1	752
Registered nurses	1,406	94.3	612
Janitors, cleaners (incl. maids and housekeeping cleaners)	2,676	42.7	604
General managers and top executives	2,383	na	582
Cashiers	2,165	82.9	575
Truck drivers, light and heavy	2,211	4.3	525
General office clerks	2,361	80.5	462
Food counter, fountain and related workers	1,500	na	449
Nursing aides, orderlies, and attendants	1,224	90.5	433
Secretaries	3,234	99.0	424

Source: U.S. Department of Labor, Bureau of Labor Statistics, *Monthly Labor Review,* September 1987.

tion of sex roles and the ranking of traits associated with the sexes.

3. Conflict and order perspectives provide different explanations of the origin and persistence of the gender system. Order theorists emphasize division of labor and social integration, while conflict theorists emphasize male control of economic resources and women's inequality.

4. Many sociologists have viewed gender inequality as the consequences of behavior learned by individual women and men. More recently sociologists have explained sex inequality as a consequence of the way in which society is structured. The thesis of this chapter is that while socialization accounts for the acquisition of gender, the systems of capitalism and patriarchy in our society "place" females and males in different and unequal positions.

5. The gender system is reinforced through language, interpersonal behavior, mass communication, religion, the law, and politics.

6. The occupational concentration of women in a few sex-typed occupations contrasts with that of men who are distributed throughout the occupational hierarchy; and women, even with the same amount of education and when doing the same work, earn less than men in all occupations.

7. Labor market segmentation is the basic source of gender inequality in the labor force. Work opportunities for women tend to concentrate in a secondary market that has few advancement opportunities, fewer job benefits, and lower pay.

8. The position of women in families parallels their status in the labor force. Their responsibil-

ity for domestic maintenance and child care frees individual men from such duties and supports the capitalist economy.

9. Sexism deprives society of the potential contributions of half of its members, creates poverty among families headed by women, and limits the capacities of all women and men.

10. Feminist movements aimed at eliminating inequality have created significant changes at all levels of society, but because sexism is deeply embedded in the social structure, its elimination will require a fundamental transformation of American society.

KEY TERMS

Sex roles
Gender roles
Sex-gender system

Gender stratification
Sexism
Patriarchy

Gender roles approach
Structural approach

STUDY QUESTIONS

1. In explaining sex inequality order theorists emphasize the gender roles approach whereas conflict theorists focus on structural factors. Compare and assess these two approaches.
2. What are the mechanisms that reinforce male dominance in society?

3. The incomes of men and women differ significantly. Why?
4. Have recent Supreme Court decisions increased or reduced gender inequality?
5. Who benefits from gender inequality?

FOR FURTHER READING

Margaret L. Andersen, *Thinking about Women.* 2d ed. (New York: Macmillan, 1988).

Lourdes Beneria and Catharine R. Stimpson (eds.), *Women, Households and The Economy* (New Brunswick, NJ: Rutgers University Press, 1987).

Ann Bookman and Sandra Morgan (eds.), *Women and the Politics of Empowerment* (Philadelphia: Temple University Press, 1988).

Beth B. Hess and Myra Marx Feree, *Analyzing Gender: A Handbook of Social Science* (Beverly Hills, CA: Sage Publications, 1987).

Rochelle Lefkowitz and Ann Withorn, *For Crying Out Loud, Women and Poverty in the United States.* (New York: Pilgrim Press, 1986).

Margarita B. Melville (ed.), *Twice a Minority, Mexican American Women* (St. Louis: Mosby, 1980).

Barbara F. Reskin (ed.), *Sex Segregation in the Workplace* (Washington, D.C.: National Academy Press, 1984).

Barbara F. Reskin and Heidi I. Hartmann, *Women's Work, Men's Work* (Washington, D.C.: National Academy Press, 1986).

La Frances Rodgers-Rose, *The Black Woman.* (Beverly Hills, Calif.: Sage Publications, 1980).

Anne Helton Stromberg and Shirley Harkess, *Women Working* (Mountain View, CA: Mayfield Press, 1988).

Chapter Thirteen

The Economy

*B*etween 1978 and 1987, the poorest fifth of American families became eight percent poorer, and the richest fifth became 13 percent richer. That leaves the poorest fifth with less than five percent of the nation's income, and the richest fifth with more than 40 percent. This widening gap can't be blamed on the growth in single-parent lower-income families, which in fact slowed markedly after the late 1970s. Nor is it due mainly to the stingy social policy of the Reagan years. Granted, Food Stamp benefits have dropped in real terms by about 13 percent since 1981, and many states have failed to raise benefits for the poor and unemployed to keep up with inflation. But this doesn't come close to accounting for the growing inequality. Rather, the trend is connected to a profound change in the American economy as it merges with the global economy. And because the merging is far from complete, this trend will not stop of its own accord anytime soon.

It is significant that the growth of inequality shows up most strikingly among Americans who have jobs. Through most of the postwar era, the wages of Americans at different income levels rose at about the same pace. Although different workers occupied different steps on the escalator, everyone moved up together. In those days poverty was the condition of *jobless* Americans, and the major economic challenge was to create enough jobs for everyone. Once people were safely on the work force escalator, their problems were assumed to be over. Thus "full employment" became a liberal rallying cry, while conservatives fretted over the inflationary tendencies of a full-employment economy.

In recent years working Americans have been traveling on two escalators—one going up, the other going down. In 1987 the average hourly earnings of nonsupervisory workers, adjusted for inflation, were lower than in any year since 1966. Middle-level managers fared much better, although their median real earnings were only slightly above the levels of the 1970s. Executives, however, did spectacularly well. In 1988 alone, CEOs of the hundred largest publicly held industrial corporations received raises averaging almost 12 percent. The remunerations of lesser executives rose almost as much, and executives of smaller companies followed close behind.

Between 1978 and 1987, as the real earnings of unskilled workers were declining, the real incomes of workers in the securities industry (investment bankers, arbitrageurs, and brokers) rose 21 percent. Few investment bankers pocket anything near the $50 million lavished yearly upon the partners of Kohlberg, Kravis, Roberts & Company, or the $550 million commandeered last year by Michael Milken, but it is not unusual for a run-of-the-mill investment banker to bring home comfortably over a million dollars. Partners in America's largest corporate law firms are comparatively deprived, enjoying average yearly earnings of only $400,000 to $1.2 million.

Meanwhile, the number of impoverished *working* Americans climbed by nearly two million, or 23 percent, between 1978 and 1987. The number who worked full time and year round but were poor climbed faster, by 43 percent. Nearly 60 percent of the 20 million people who now fall below the Census Bureau's poverty line are from families with at least one member in full-time or part-time work.

The American economy, in short, is creating a wider range of earnings than at any other time in the postwar era. The most basic reason, put simply, is that America itself is ceasing to exist as a system of production and exchange separate from the rest of the world. One can no more meaningfully speak of an "American economy" than of a "Delaware economy." We are becoming but a region—albeit still a relatively wealthy region—of a global economy, whose technologies, savings, and investments move effortlessly across borders, making it harder for individual nations to control their economic destinies.*

Source: Robert B. Reich, "As the World Turns: U.S. Income Inequality Keeps on Rising," *The New Republic* 200 (May 1, 1989), p. 23. Reprinted by permission of the publisher.

The final five chapters of this book describe the fundamental institutions of society. As noted in Chapter 2, **institutions** are social arrangements that channel behavior in prescribed ways in the important areas of social life. They are interrelated sets of normative elements—*norms, values,* and *role* expectations—that the people making up the society have devised and passed on to succeeding generations in order to provide solutions to society's perpetually unfinished business.

The institutions of society—family, education, religion, polity, and economy—are interrelated. But while there are reciprocal effects among the institutions, the economy and the polity are the core institutions. The way society is organized to produce and distribute goods and services and the way power is organized are the crucial determinants of the way the other institutions are organized. We begin, then, with a chapter on the economy followed by a chapter on the polity. The remaining three chapters focus on the supporting institutions of the family, education, and religion. Each of these institutions is strongly affected by the form of the economy and power arrangements in the contemporary United States.

The task of this chapter is to describe the American economy. Four areas are emphasized: the domination of huge corporations, the maldistribution of wealth, the structural transformation of the economy, and the current economic crises. We begin, though, with a brief description of the two fundamental ways societies can organize their economic activities.

CAPITALISM AND SOCIALISM

All the ways that industrialized societies organize their economic activities can be divided into one of two fundamental forms: *capitalism* and *socialism*. Each of these types will be examined in its pure form (that is, how it might exist in ideal circumstances). Although no society has a purely capitalist or socialist economy, examining these ideal types provides examples of extremes so that we can assess the American economy more accurately.

Capitalism

Capitalism is an economic system based on the private ownership of property. Several crucial conditions must be present for pure capitalism to exist. The first is private ownership of property. Individuals are encouraged to own, not only private possessions, but most important, the capital necessary to produce and distribute goods and services. In a purely capitalist society there would be no public ownership of any potentially profitable activity.

The pursuit of personal profit is the second essential ingredient of capitalism. This goal implies that individuals are free to maximize their personal circumstances. Most important, the proponents of capitalism argue that this profit-seeking by individuals has positive consequences for the society. Thus, the act of seeking individual gain through personal profit is considered morally acceptable and socially desirable.

Competition is the mechanism that keeps individual profit-seeking in check. Potential abuses such as fraud, faulty products, and exorbitant prices are negated by the existence of competitors who will soon take business away from those who violate good business judgment. So, too, economic inefficiency is minimized as market forces cause the inept to fail and the efficient to succeed.

These three elements—private property, personal profit, and competition—require a fourth condition if true capitalism is to work. This is a government policy of laissez-faire (literally, to leave alone). The government must allow the marketplace to operate unhindered. This requires a minimum of government interference in economic life. Any government intervention in the marketplace will, argue capitalists, distort the economy by negatively affecting incentives and freedom of individual choice. If left unhindered by government, the profit motive, private ownership, and competition will achieve the greatest good for the greatest number. This "greatest good" is translated into individual self-fulfillment and the general material progress of society.

Socialism

Socialism is an economic system where the means of production are owned by the people for their collective benefit. The three principles of socialism are democratism, egalitarianism, and public ownership of the means of production. True socialism must be democratic. Representatives of a socialist state must be answerable and responsive to the wishes of the public they serve. Nations that claim to be socialist but are totalitarian violate this fundamental aspect of socialism. The key to differentiating between authentic and spurious socialism is to determine who is making the decisions and whose interests are being served. Thus, it is a fallacy to equate true socialism with the politicoeconomic systems found in the Soviet Union, the People's Republic of China, or Cuba. These societies are socialistic in some respects; that is, their material benefits are more evenly distributed than those in the United States. But their economies and governments are controlled by a single political party in an inflexible and authoritarian manner, although the Soviet Union appears to be moving toward more democracy. Although these countries claim to have democratic elections, in fact the citizens have no electoral choice but to "rubber-stamp" the candidates of the ruling party. The people are denied civil liberties and freedoms that should be the hallmark of a socialist society. In a pure socialist society democratic relations must operate throughout the social structure: in government, at work, at school, and in the community.

The second principle of socialism is egalitarianism: equality of opportunity for the self-fulfillment of all; equality rather than hierarchy in decision making; and equality in sharing the benefits of society. Thus, there is a fundamental commitment to achieving a rough parity by leveling out gross inequities in income, property, and opportunities. The key is a leveling of advantages so that all citizens receive the necessities (food, clothing, medical care, living wages, sick pay, retirement benefits, and shelter).

The third feature of socialism is public ownership of the means of production. The people own the basic industries, financial institutions, utilities, transportation, and communication companies. The goal is serving the public, not making profit. Thus, a purely socialist government requires central planning to provide, at the least possible individual and collective cost, the best conditions to meet the material needs of its citizens. Planning also aims to achieve societal goals such as protecting the environment, combating pollution, saving natural resources, and developing new technologies. Public policy is decided through the rational assessment of the needs of society and how the economy might best be organized to achieve them. In this situation the economy must be regulated by the government, which acts as the agent of the people. The government sets prices and wages; important industries are run at a loss if necessary. Dislocations such as surpluses or shortages or unemployment are minimized by central planning. The goal is to run the economy for the good of the society.

THE CORPORATION-DOMINATED ECONOMY

The American economy has always been based on the principles of capitalism; however, the present economy is far removed from a free enterprise system. There are two important discrepancies between the ideal system and the real one we operate in. The American economy is no longer based on competition among more or less equal private capitalists. It is now dominated by huge corporations that, contrary to classical economic theory, control demand rather than being responsive to the demands of the market. However well the economic system might once have worked, the increasing size and power of corporations disrupt it. This calls into question just what is the appropriate economic form for a modern industrialized society. We examine the consequences of concentrated economic power domestically and internationally, for they create many important social problems. The second contradiction of American economic life is the existence of what has been called corporate socialism: the dependence of corporations on governmental largesse, contracts, and regulation of the market for profit. We examine these developments in turn.

Monopolistic Capitalism

Karl Marx, more than 100 years ago when bigness was the exception, predicted that capitalism was doomed by several inherent contradictions that would produce a class of people bent on destroying it. The most significant of these contradictions for our purposes is the inevitability of monopolies.*

---

*Marx prophesied that capitalism carried the seeds of its own destruction. In addition to resulting in monopolies, capitalism (1) encourages crises—inflation, slumps, depressions—because the lack of centralized planning will mean overproduction of some goods and underproduction of others; (2) encourages mass production for expansion and profits but in so doing a social class, the proletariat, is created that has the goal of equalizing the

Marx hypothesized that free enterprise would result in some firms becoming bigger and bigger as they eliminate their opposition or absorb smaller competing firms. The ultimate result of this process is the existence of a monopoly in each of the various sectors of the economy. Monopolies, of course, are antithetical to the free-enterprise system because they, not supply and demand, determine the price and the quality of the product.

For the most part, the evidence in American society upholds Marx's prediction. Most sectors of the American economy are dominated by **shared monopolies.** Instead of a single corporation controlling an industry, the situation is one in which a small number of large firms dominate an industry. When four or fewer firms supply 50 percent or more of a particular market, a shared monopoly results, which performs much as a monopoly or cartel would. Most economists agree that above this level of concentration—a four-firm ratio of 50 percent—the economic costs of shared monopoly are most manifest. Government data show that a number of industries are highly concentrated (e.g., each of the following industries has four or fewer firms controlling at least 60 percent of the market: light bulbs, breakfast cereals, turbines/generators, aluminum, chocolate/cocoa, photography equipment, brewing, guided missiles, and roasted coffee).

This trend toward ever-greater concentration among the largest American business concerns has accelerated because of two activities—mergers and interlocking directorates.

Megamergers.   In 1978 the sale of conglomerate mergers cost approximately $5 billion. By 1986 the amount had increased to an astonishing $190 billion. The federal government encouraged these mergers by relaxing the antitrust law enforcement on the grounds that efficient firms should not be hobbled.

This trend toward megamergers has at least four negative consequences: (1) it increases the centralization of capital, which reduces competition and raises prices for consumers; (2) it increases the power of the huge corporations over workers, unions, and governments; (3) it diminishes the number of jobs; and (4) it is nonproductive. Jim Hightower emphasizes this last point:

> In the last three years [1983–1986], 9,000 companies changed owners at a cost of nearly half a trillion dollars. For what? Not for new plants, products or jobs, but for paper shuffling, for lawyers, accountants, brokers, bankers and big investors—hundreds of millions of dollars paid in nonproductive fees to achieve nonproductive ends. (Hightower, 1987:25)

The amount of money brokers make on these deals can be incredible. At the extreme, Michael Milken, as an employee of Drexel Burnham Lambert, Inc.,

---

distribution of profits; (3) demands the introduction of labor-saving machinery, which forces unemployment and a more hostile proletariat; and (4) will control the state, the effect of which is that the state will pass laws favoring the wealthy, thereby incurring the further wrath of the proletariat. All these factors increase the probability of the proletariat building class consciousness, which is the condition necessary before class conflict and the ushering in of a new economic system (Marx, 1967).

created high-risk junk bonds to finance leveraged buyouts; he was paid $550 million in 1987 for his services.

> More than half a billion dollars a year is $1.5 million a day. We're counting all 365 days because Mr. Milken often works seven days a week, even during vacation. That's a bit over $107,000 an hour, based on his normal 14-hour day. The 42-year-old financier's 1987 compensation, paid for his 1986 work, was more than the gross national product of the Republic of Guyana, whose 779,000 citizens produced only about $460 million in goods and services in 1985. (Swartz, 1989:1)

Defenders of a free and competitive enterprise system should attack the existence of monopolies and shared monopolies as un-American. There should be strong support of governmental efforts to break up the largest and most powerful corporations. Nearly two decades ago, Mark S. Green offered the following commentary:

> Huey Long once prophesied that fascism would come to the United States first in the form of antifascism. So too with socialism—*corporate* socialism. Under the banner of free enterprise, up to two-thirds of American manufacturing has been metamorphosed into a "closed enterprise system." Although busi-nessmen spoke the language of competitive capitalism, each sought refuge for himself: price-fixing, parallel pricing, mergers, excessive advertising, quotas, subsidies, and tax favoritism. While defenders of the American dream guarded against socialism from the left, it arrived unannounced from the right. (Green, 1972:4)

Interlocking Directorates.   Another mechanism for the ever-greater concentra-tion of the size and power of the largest corporations is **interlocking director-ates,** the linkage between corporations that results when an individual serves on the board of directors of two companies (a direct interlock) or when two companies each have a director on the board of a third company (an indirect interlock). Such arrangements have great potential to benefit the interlocked companies by reducing competition through the sharing of information and the coordination of policies. As a Senate report has put it:

> Personal interlocks between business leaders may lead to a concentration of economic or fiscal control in a few hands. There is in this the danger of a business elite, an ingrown group inpervious to outside forces, intolerant of dissent, and protective of the status quo, charting the direction of production and investment in one of several industries. (U.S. Senate, 1978:6)

In 1914 passage of the Clayton Act made it illegal for a person to serve simultaneously on the corporate boards of two companies that were in direct competition with each other. Financial institutions and indirect interlocks, however, were exempt. Moreover, the government has had difficulty in deter-mining what constitutes "direct competition." The result is that despite the prohibition, interlocking directorates are widespread. For example, there is a direct interlock between AT&T and Citicorp, linking a customer of financial services and a lending institution. Indirect interlocks, even among competi-tors, are commonplace. IBM and AT&T, for example, are competitors in telecommunications equipment and services, yet in 1976 they were indirectly linked through common memberships on the boards of twenty-two other companies.

Evidence of the proliferation of interlocking directorates is substantial. In 1976, for example, each of the thirteen largest corporations (holding one-eighth of the nation's corporate assets) had an average of 4.5 direct and 122.5 indirect links with the other twelve (Jung, Purdy, and Eitzen, 1981). Obviously the potential for cohesiveness, common action, and unified power is strong among the directors linked in this tight network.

Instead of functioning as a free enterprise system, then, the U.S. economy is controlled by huge corporations (see Table 13–1) that have political power to guarantee their privileged positions. These companies need not be concerned with sound business principles and quality products, because there is no real threat of competition. In other words, the concentration of industrial wealth means that the principles of free enterprise cannot work. Nevertheless, many large corporations devote considerable efforts to convincing the public that the American economy *is* competitive despite the evidence. Many advertisements depict the economy as an Adam Smith style of free market with competition among innumerable small competitors. This, however, is a dream world. Competition does exist among the mom-and-pop stores, but these stores control only a minute portion of the nation's assets. The largest

Table 13–1
The Fifteen Largest U.S. Companies, Ranked by Sales, Assets, and Profits (1988)

Company (by Rank)	Sales (Millions of Dollars)	Assets (Millions of Dollars)	Assets Rank	Profits (Millions of Dollars)	Profits Rank
General Motors	$121,817	$163,820	2	$4,632.1	4
Ford Motor	92,446	143,150	3	5,300.2	2
Exxon	80,868	74,293	14	5,260.0	3
IBM	59,681	73,037	15	5,491.0	1
Sears, Roebuck	50,251	77,952	12	909.5	38
General Electric	49,773	110,865	6	3,386.0	5
Mobil	48,198	38,820	31	2,087.0	6
Chrysler	35,472	48,562	23	1,050.2	32
AT&T	35,210	35,152	36		
Texaco	33,544	26,337	57	1,304.0	18
DuPont	32,514	30,719	42	2,190.0	7
Citicorp	32,024	297,666	1	1,698.0	12
K Mart	27,550	12,126	130	802.9	49
Philip Morris	25,860	36,960	34	2,064.0	9
Chevron	25,196	33,968	37	1,768.0	11

Source: Excerpted by permission of *Forbes* magazine, May 1, 1989. © Forbes, Inc., 1989.

assets are located among the very large corporations, and competition there is virtually nonexistent.

Multinational Corporations

The thesis of the previous section is that there is a trend for corporations to increase in size resulting, eventually, in huge enterprises that join with other large companies to form effective monopolies. This process of economic concentration provides the largest companies with enormous economic and political power. Another trend—the globalization of America's largest corporations—makes their power all the greater. This fact of international economic life has very important implications for social problems, both domestically and abroad.

There has been a tendency of late for U.S. corporations to increase their foreign investments sharply. Why are U.S. corporations shifting more and more of their total assets outside of the United States? The obvious answer is that the rate of profit tends to be higher abroad. Resources necessary for manufacture and production tend to be cheaper in many other nations, and labor costs are substantially lower. Wages in general are much lower than in the United States, and unions are nonexistent.

The consequences of this shift in production from the United States to outside this country are significant. Most important is the drying up of many

Many U.S. corporations increase their size and thus their profits by doing business abroad, where their rate of profits tends to be higher.

semi- and unskilled jobs. The effects of the increased unemployment are twofold: increased welfare costs and increased discontent among those in the working class. We return to this problem of domestic job losses through overseas capital investments later in this chapter when deindustrialization is discussed.

The problems of domestic unemployment exacerbated by overseas investment are the problems of lost revenues through taxes and a negative balance of payments. Tax revenues are lost because corporations can escape domestic taxes by having goods produced overseas and by undervaluing exports and overvaluing imports. Indirectly, taxes are also lost by increased unemployment. The balance-of-payments problem is aggravated by the flow of investment money overseas and the purchase of goods produced in foreign countries.

Another result of the twin processes of concentration and internationalization of corporations is the enormous power wielded by the gigantic multinational corporation. In essence, the largest corporations control the world economy. Their decisions to build or not to build, to relocate a plant, to start a new product, or to scrap an old one have a tremendous impact on the lives of ordinary citizens in the countries they operate from and invest in.

In their desire to tap low-wage workers the multinational corporations have tended to locate in poor countries. On the surface this would appear to have positive consequences for these nations (e.g., by providing a higher standard of living and access to modern technology). Unfortunately, this has not been the case. One reason is that the profits generated in these countries tend to be expatriated back to the United States in the form of dividends. Second, global companies do not have a great impact in easing the unemployment of the poor nations because they use advanced technology whenever feasible, and this reduces the demand for jobs. Third, the multinational companies tend to exploit the natural resources of the poor countries. An important consequence of this abuse is that exploited countries are beginning to unite in order to curb the abuses of the corporations. The Organization of Petroleum Exporting Countries (OPEC) was formed to demand higher prices in order to compensate for many years of exploitation and to achieve independence from the multinationals. Organizations are being formed also among the countries exporting copper, tin, bauxite, coffee, and tea. Unfortunately, these efforts, although directed at the multinational companies, are paid for by the U.S. consumer because the U.S. companies merely raise their retail prices accordingly.

Finally, multinational corporations tend to meddle in the internal affairs of other nations in order to protect their investments and maximize profits. Two examples of this activity are: (1) the active involvement of IT&T in the overthrow of the socialist government in Chile and (2) the support of various oil companies to keep the Reza Shah in power in Iran. The multinationals have paid millions in bribes and political contributions to reactionary governments and conservative leaders in countries like South Korea, Bolivia, Taiwan, Japan, and Italy (Parenti, 1988:147).

CAPITALISM AND INEQUALITY

Inequality is endemic to capitalism. In the competition for profits there are winners and losers. We have seen how corporate wealth is concentrated through shared monopolies and interlocking directorates. Individuals, too, are advantaged or disadvantaged by the structure of capitalism. Let's consider four additional manifestations of inequality that occur in the contemporary American version of capitalism—the concentration of private wealth, the concentration of want and misery, the segmented labor market, and the capitalist patriarchy.

Concentration of Private Wealth

Capitalism generates inequality. Wealth is concentrated not only in the largest corporations but also among individuals and families. The top 10 percent of American households hold 86 percent of the total net financial assets in the United States; the top 2 percent have 54 percent of the total personal assets. In sharp contrast, 55 percent of all American households had no net financial assets (Rose, 1986:31).

A few families are fabulously wealthy and colossal in corporate magnitude. Michael Parenti describes the holdings of the DuPonts and the Rockefellers:

> The DuPont family controls eight of the largest defense contractors and grossed over $15 billion in military contracts during the Vietnam war. The DuPonts control ten corporations that each have over $1 billion in assets, including General Motors, Coca-Cola and United Brands, along with many smaller firms. The DuPonts serve as trustees of scores of colleges. They own about forty manorial estates and private museums in Delaware alone, and, in an attempt to keep the money in the family, have set up thirty-one tax-exempt foundations. The family is frequently the largest contributor to Republican presidential campaigns and has financed right-wing and antilabor . . . causes.
>
> Another powerful family enterprise, that of the Rockefellers, . . . extends into just about every industry in every state of the Union and every nation in the non-socialist world. The Rockefellers control five of the twelve largest oil companies and four of the largest banks in the world. They finance universities, churches, "cultural centers," and youth organizations. At one time or another, they or their close associates have occupied the offices of the president, vice-president, secretaries of State, Commerce, Defense, and other cabinet posts, the Federal Reserve Board, the governorships of several states, key positions in the Central Intelligence Agency (CIA), the U.S. Senate and House, and the Council on Foreign Relations. (Parenti, 1988:13–14)*

---

*Copyright © 1988 by St. Martin's Press, Inc. From *Democracy for the Few*, fifth edition. By Michael Parenti. Reprinted with permission of St. Martin's Press, Inc.

Concentration of Want and Misery

The inequality generated by a capitalist economy has a dark side. Summarizing the 1987 data on poverty (found in Chapter 10), 13.5 percent of the population (32.5 million Americans) were below the poverty line. According to the National Council on Economic Opportunity, another 30 million were on the edge of poverty. The data indicate that the poor are concentrated among certain social categories, especially people of color and families headed by women.

Again, summarizing from earlier chapters, research strongly substantiates how the "life chances" of the poor are jeopardized by their lack of resources. The fewer the resources available, the greater are the possibilities for any of the following to occur:

- Premature births and babies born mentally retarded because of prenatal malnourishment;
- Below average life expectancy;
- Death from tuberculosis, influenza, pneumonia, cancer of the stomach, lung, bronchus, and trachea, and accidents;
- Impaired health because of differences in diet, sanitary facilities, shelter, and medical care;
- More frequent and longer periods of illness;
- An arrest, conviction, and serving of a longer sentence for a given violation;
- A lower than average level of educational attainment;
- Spouse and child abuse, divorce, and desertion.

Thus, the economic position of a family has very telling consequences on the probability of good health, educational attainment, justice, and a stable marriage.

Segmented Labor Market

The **segmented labor market** refers to the division of the capitalist economy into two separate sectors that have different characteristics, different roles, and different rewards for laborers within each (see Piore, 1975; Bonacich, 1976; Berg, 1981; Gordon, Edwards, and Reich, 1982). The primary sector is composed of large, bureaucratic organizations with relatively stable production and sales. Jobs within this sector require developed skills, are relatively well paid, occur in good working conditions, and are stable. Within this sector there are two types of jobs. The first type, those in the upper tier, are high-status professional and managerial jobs. The pay is very good for the highly educated persons in these jobs, who have a high degree of personal autonomy; the jobs offer variety, creativity, and initiative. Upward mobility is likely for those who are successful. The second type, the lower-tier jobs within the primary sector, are held by working-class persons. The jobs are either white-collar clerical or blue-collar skilled and semiskilled. The jobs are repetitive and mobility is limited. The jobs are relatively secure because of unionization, although much more vulnerable than those in the upper tier.

When times are difficult, these workers tend to be laid off rather than terminated.

The secondary economic sector is composed of marginal firms where product demand is unstable. Jobs within this sector are characterized by poor working conditions, low wages, few opportunities for advancement, and little job security. Little education or skill is required to perform these tasks. Workers beginning in the secondary sector tend to get locked in because they lack the skills required in the primary sector, and they usually have unstable work histories. A common interpretation of this problem is that secondary sector workers are in these deadend jobs because of their pathology—poor work history, lack of skills, and lack of motivation. Such an explanation, however, blames the victim (Edwards, 1975). Poor work histories tend to be the result of unemployment caused by the production of marginal products and the lack of job security. Similarly, these workers have few, if any, incentives to learn new skills or stay for long periods with an employer because of the structural impediments to upward mobility. And, unlike the primary sector, workers in the secondary sector are more likely to experience harsh and capricious work discipline from supervisors, primarily because there are no unions.

The significance of this dual labor market is twofold. First, placement in one of these sectors corresponds with socioeconomic status, which tends to be perpetuated from generation to generation. And second, its existence reinforces racial, ethnic, and gender divisions in the labor force. White males, while found in both segments, tend to predominate in the upper tier of the primary sector. White females tend to be clerks in the lower tier of the primary sector, and white ethnics tend to be overrepresented in the production lines of the lower tier of the primary sector. Males and females of color are found disproportionately in the secondary sector. This explains why unemployment rates for blacks and Hispanics are consistently twice as high as that for whites. It explains the persistent wage differences found by race and gender. It also explains the vast overrepresentation of people of color and women living in poverty. Referring to women, Ehrenreich and Stallard have argued that occupational segregation makes a crucial difference:

> For women, employment is not necessarily an antidote to poverty. The jobs that are available to us are part of the problem. The list is familiar—clerical work, sales, light manufacturing, and the catchall category, "service work," which includes nurse's aides and grade-school teachers, waitresses, and welfare caseworkers. Only 20 out of 420 listed occupations account for 80 percent of employed women, and it is this occupational segregation that accounts for women's low average earnings. In general, "women's work" not only pays less than men's but is less inflation proof. . . . The extreme occupational segregation of women in our society makes for a crucial difference between women's poverty and men's. For men, poverty is often a consequence of unemployment, and is curable by getting a job. But for women, concentrated in the low-wage stratum of the work force, a job may not be a solution to poverty. According to the National Advisory Council on Economic Opportunities,

"poverty among hundreds of thousands of women already working under-lines the failure of the 'job' solution. Of the mothers working outside the house who headed households with children less than 18 years old in 1978, more than one quarter had incomes below the poverty level." (Ehrenreich and Stallard, 1982:220)

Similarly, people of color are doubly disadvantaged:

The combination of racial [disadvantage] with the primary-secondary seg-mentation compounds the immobility, low wages, and poor working condi-tions of the large number of black workers [and we would add Hispanics, Native Americans, and others of color] who participate in the secondary labor market. On the whole they are considerably worse off than the white poor and the near poor who work in the secondary sector. (Baron, 1975:205)

Capitalist Patriarchy

Closely tied to segmented labor markets is the phenomenon of *capitalist patriarchy*. Although male supremacy (patriarchy) existed before capitalism and is found in noncapitalist societies today, a strong relationship between the two helps to explain the present oppression of women in U.S. society (Eisenstein, 1979). Current sex inequality results from a long history of pa-triarchal social relations where men have consciously kept women in subor-dinate roles at work and in the home. Men as workers consistently have acted in their own interests to retain power and to keep women either out of their occupations or in subordinate and poorly paid work roles. Historically through their unions, males insisted that the higher-status and better-paying jobs be exclusively male. They lobbied legislatures to pass legislation suppor-tive of male exclusiveness in occupations and in opposition to such equali-zation measures as minimum wages for women. Also, the male unions prevented women from gaining the skills that would lead them to equal paying jobs. The National Typographical Union in 1854, for example, insisted that women not only be refused jobs as compositors but that they not be taught the skills necessary to be a compositor (Hartmann, 1976).

Throughout U.S. history, capitalists have used sex inequality in the work-place to their advantage. Women were hired because they would work for less money than men, which made men all the more fearful of women in the workplace. Capitalists even used the threat of hiring cheaper women to take the place of more expensive men to keep the wages of both sexes down and to lessen labor militancy.

In contemporary U.S. society, capitalism and patriarchy interact to op-press women. Males and females are accorded different, and unequal, posi-tions in church, government, school, work, and family activities. Looking only at work, women and men do different work both in the family and in the labor force. This division of labor between the sexes preserves the differ-ential power, privilege, and prestige of men. In monetary terms, in 1987 the average female employee earned 65 percent of the average male employee's salary. This difference is even more substantial than it appears at first glance. It means, for example, that the gap in lifetime earnings between males and females is approximately $500,000 if they are high school graduates and $1.6 million if they are college graduates. When the type of work is considered, women are vastly overrepresented in nonleadership and limited-mobility jobs (see Chapter 12 for a more comprehensive discussion). Both of these examples—percentage of income and type of work—give men power over women in the public and private spheres.

THE STRUCTURAL TRANSFORMATION OF THE ECONOMY

There have been two fundamental turning points in human history, and we are in the midst of the third.* The Neolithic revolution began about 8,000 B.C., marking the transition from nomadic pastoral life, where the animal and vegetable sources of food were hunted and gathered, to life in settlements based on agriculture. During this phase of human existence cities were built, tools were created and used, language, numbers, and other symbols became more sophisticated, and mining and metal working were developed.

The second fundamental change, the industrial revolution, began in Great Britain in the 1780s. While the Neolithic agricultural revolution took almost ten thousand years to run its course, the second lasted but two hundred years. And the industrial revolution really involved three distinct but related technological revolutions, each of which brought fundamental changes to the economy, the relationship of people and work, family organization, and the like. The first phase lasted about sixty years in Great Britain and involved primarily the application of steam power to textiles, mining, manufacturing, and transportation. The second phase in the industrial revolution occurred between 1860 and 1910 largely in the United States, Great Britain, and Germany. It was marked by a significant cluster of inventions and discoveries—the use of oil and electricity as energy sources for industry and transportation, the telephone and telegraph, motor cars and airplanes, and the first plastics. The final stage of the industrial revolution is still in progress and involves the major technological breakthroughs of atomic fission and fusion, supersonic aircraft and missiles, television, biotechnology, and computers. This third phase of the industrial revolution is giving way to a new era. Whereas employment throughout the industrial revolution was dominated by manufacturing, the new era is characterized by a shift in employment toward service occupations and the collection, storage, and dissemination of information (Jones 1982; Baca Zinn and Eitzen, 1987:76–77).

Each of these surges in invention and technological growth had major implications for the economy and other societal institutions and for individuals and families within society. The next two sections describe the forces transforming American society and the special conditions that are making this turning point in history different, much different, from the previous two.

---

*This section on the structural transformation of the economy is from Stanley Eitzen/Maxine Baca Zinn, *The Reshaping of America: Social Consequences of the Changing Economy*, © 1989, pp. 1–12. Reprinted by permission of Prentice-Hall, Inc., Englewood Cliffs, New Jersey.

The Interrelated Forces Transforming America

Several powerful forces are converging in the United States that are transforming its economy, redesigning and redistributing jobs, exacerbating inequality, reorganizing cities and regions, and profoundly affecting families and individuals. These forces are (1) technological breakthroughs in microelectronics, (2) the globalization of the economy, (3) capital flight, and (4) the shift from an economy based on the manufacture of goods to one based on information and services.

The New Technologies Based on Microelectronics.   The computer chip is the technology transforming the United States toward a service/information economy. Micro-based systems of information allow for the storage, manipulation, and retrieval of data with speed and accuracy unknown just a few years ago. Computer transactions are measured in multiples of picoseconds (pico means one trillionth). Information can be sent instantaneously via communications satelite throughout the world in microseconds. Parallel processing with supercomputers gives machines the ability to reason and make judgments. Computer-aided design (CAD) permits engineers to design and modify an incredible array of products in three dimensions very quickly. Computer-aided manufacturing (CAM) is replacing traditional manufacturing with conventional machines and workers. The problem with these industrial robots is that while they increase productivity, they displace rather than create jobs (Oxford Analytica, 1986:232). Moreover, the use of robotics will replace the higher-paid semiskilled workers, not the unskilled manual workers. "Thus, the continuing use of robots will result in a minimal increase in the number of skilled positions, a significant reduction of the middle layer of semi-skilled positions and a substantial increase in the number of manual workers at the base of the skill hierarchy. The overall effect is a deskilling of the workforce" (Dassbach, 1986:59).

Globalization of the Economy.   Because of the size of the domestic market, the relative insulation of the Pacific and Atlantic Oceans, and superior technological expertise, the American economy throughout most of this century has been relatively free from the competitive pressures from abroad. This has changed dramatically since about 1970. The United States, once the world's industrial giant, has lost its premier status.

> In 1960, the United States led the world in per capita gross domestic product (GNP less income from abroad) by a comfortable margin. In 1980, the United States stood eleventh among nonsocialist countries, and the leader outpaced the United States by 39 percent. U.S. steel production accounted for 26 percent of the world's total output in 1960, while Japan's was just over 6 percent. By 1980 Japan was at 15.5 percent and the United States at only 14.0 percent. In 1967, the States built more cars and trucks than the rest of the nonsocialist world combined. By 1982, the United States was third behind Japan and Europe. (Dolbeare, 1986:62)

Examined another way, again comparing the twenty years from 1962 to 1982, automobile imports to the United States rose from 1.9 percent to 22.8 percent; in consumer electronics from 18.5 to 42.1 percent; communications and electronic equipment up from 1.3 percent to 13 percent; textiles from 4.0 to 15.4 percent; and shoes and leather from 5.3 to 43.5 percent (Dolbeare, 1986:63). Put in a closer time frame, in 1982 some 10.8 percent of all goods and services purchased in the United States were imported. By 1987, it had increased to 13.6 percent (Karmin 1987).

This competition from abroad means reduced profits to U.S. corporations. Their typical response has been to cut costs by demanding concessions from workers, reducing the labor costs as the semiconductor industry did when sixty-five thousand workers were laid off over a two-year period because of the intense competition with Japan (Koepp, 1986). Many corporations in the hardest hit areas such as steel just shut down plants completely, throwing thousands of employees out of work and the communities in which they were located into difficult dislocations. Another strategy used by U.S. corporations was to compete as strongly as possible. Massive investment has occurred in the automobile industry (General Motors spent $40 billion from 1980 to 1984), for example, but these monies were spent on labor-saving devices, which, of course, did little to help workers (Oxford Analytica, 1986:211–212).

Capital Flight. Private businesses in their search for profit make crucial investment decisions. The term **capital flight** refers to the investment choices that involve the movement of corporate monies from one investment to another. This takes several forms: (1) investment overseas, (2) plant relocation within the United States, and (3) mergers, which we have already considered. While these investment decisions may be positive for the recipients of the move, they also take investment away (disinvestment) from others (workers and their families, communities, and suppliers).

Overseas investment by U. S. firms. U.S. multinational corporations have invested heavily in foreign countries. In 1984 the direct investment by U.S. based firms in foreign countries amounted to $233.4 billion, up from $192 billion in 1980, and $16 billion in 1950 (Vernon, 1986). "The total overseas output of American multinational corporations is now larger than the gross domestic product of every country in the world except the United States and the Soviet Union" (Bluestone and Harrison, 1982:42). The foreign revenues of the largest U.S. based multinationals in 1985, for example, were Exxon, 68.1 percent of their total revenues; Mobil, 57.2 percent; Texaco, 47.2 percent; and I.B.M., 43 percent (*Forbes,* 1986:207).

Corporate capital is invested overseas because manufacturing overseas is profitable, mainly because of cheap and nonunionized labor and the relative lack of the kind of regulations found in the United States that the companies believe to be excessive and expensive on such matters as pollution and worker safety. The primary reason, though, is greater profit from lower wages. For example, there are over eleven hundred U.S. owned plants—owned by corporations such as Ford, General Motors, RCA, Zenith, and Westinghouse—located in Northern Mexico close to the U.S. border (these plants are called maquiladoras). U.S. corporations are allowed to ship raw materials, components, equipment, and machinery to Mexico duty free. They are delivered to factories in Mexico and then assembled by laborers working for 75 cents an hour (1987 wages). The finished products are then exported back to the United States with duty paid only on the value added. Obviously, the corporations profit greatly from such an arrangement.

Relocation of business. Corporate administrators may decide to move their business to another locality. Such decisions involve what is called plant migration or more pejoratively, "runaway shops." The decision may be to move the plant to Mexico, as we have seen, to the Caribbean (all baseballs for major league baseball, for example, are manufactured in Haiti), or to the Far East, where many U.S. plants involved in textiles, electronics assembly, and other labor-intensive industries are located.

Capital is also moved within the United States as corporations shut down operations in one locality and start up elsewhere. Profit is the motivation for investment in a new place and disinvestment in another. Corporations move their plants into communities and regions where wages are lower, unions are weaker or nonexistent, and the business climate more receptive (that is, there are lower taxes and greater government subsidies to the business community).

Regardless of whether plants are moved within the United States or to foreign countries, there are consequences to individuals and communities. Plant closures are devastating. Workers in the affected plants are suddenly unemployed and so, too, may be many in the affected communities whose jobs were directly and indirectly tied to that plant (such as transportation, supplies, and services). Also, real estate, banking, schools, and other areas are adversely affected. The local governments can no longer provide the same level of services because of a lower tax base. The recipient communities benefit from the increase in jobs, greater tax revenues, and the image of growth and progress. The boom communities, however, often cannot meet the greater demand for new roads, sewage treatment, schools, hospitals, recreation facilities, and housing that the new plants engender.

From Manufacturing to Services. Manufacturing, the backbone of the U.S. economy in this century, is no longer dominant. In 1947 employment in the service sector of the economy reached 50 percent, and now it is over 70 percent. Whereas people mostly worked at producing goods, now they tend to be doing work in offices, banking, insurance, retailing, health care, education, custodial work, restaurant work, security, and transportation.

Overall manufacturing has remained relatively stable, but within this sector about twenty industries have experienced steady declines since 1975. These "sunset" industries (for example, steel, tires, shoes) have declined in both output and employment (Kutscher and Personick 1986). More than fifteen hundred plants in these industries have closed permanently since 1975.

A large number of jobs in the steel industry have been lost with the permanent closure of plants.

And, literally, millions of jobs have been lost that will not be replaced. The Labor Department reported, for example, that 2.3 million manufacturing jobs disappeared from January 1980 through the end of 1984 and that 90 percent of these jobs most likely will never return (reported in Noble 1985). Moreover, the data suggest that this trend will continue. Peter Drucker, the esteemed management expert, has predicted that by the year 2015 as many as fifteen million manufacturing jobs will have evaporated and only about 5 to 10 percent of the work force will be holding manufacturing jobs—roughly equivalent to the proportion now engaged in agriculture (cited in Hart, 1983:11).

The "sunrise" industries, which are characterized by increased output and employment, are involved in the production of "high tech" products (computers, communications equipment, medical instruments, fiber optics, bioengineering, and robotics). These industries are creating many new and exciting products. The employees are typically highly skilled, but "only a very small number of very highly trained workers are needed to provide the technical breakthroughs critical to industry—less than 10 percent of all jobs through 1995. The rest of the jobs will be routine, and new labor-saving technologies will cause workers to be 'de-skilled'" (Oxford Analytica, 1986:252). The production workers in high tech, unlike those in heavy industry, tend to be nonunionized and to be paid relatively low wages and benefits.

The third category of manufacturing involves those industries that have gained in output but have lost employment (for example, food processing, metal products, industrial machinery, and automobiles). The source of this seeming incongruity (high productivity with a loss in employment) is automation, a topic we will discuss shortly.

To repeat, the manufacturing sector of the economy overall has been relatively stable. But this stability masks a massive redistribution of job opportunities with declines in some industries (steel, for example, has lost jobs steadily since 1975 and is projected to drop another 20 percent between 1984 and 1995) and increases in the high-tech industries. But the redistribution of jobs and opportunities is not only within the manufacturing sector. The major change is in the growth of the service sector of the economy.

From 1970 to 1985 some thirty million jobs were created. Most of these were in the service sector—from professional and administrative to clerical and service workers. About one half of these jobs were "bad" jobs in the sense that they involved few skills, were poorly paid, had little responsibility attached to them, and provided poor job security. They have been typically filled by teenagers, women, racial minorities, and the poorly educated. Oxford Analytica, a group of scholars from Oxford, England, commissioned by three major U.S. corporations to project trends in the United States, predicted that "the likely distribution between 'good' and 'bad' jobs in the future will not be an improvement on that of the past decade. Most of the new jobs will be service jobs and many of those will be 'bad' jobs with attendant problems of poor payment" (1986:251). Table 13-2 provides job projections from the U.S.

Table 13–2 **What Jobs Will Be Expanding Most**	Job Category	Growth in Jobs 1982–1995
	Building custodians	779,000
	Cashiers	744,000
	Secretaries	719,000
	Office clerks	696,000
	Salesclerks	685,000
	Registered nurses	642,000
	Waiters, waitresses	562,000
	Teachers (elementary)	511,000
	Truckdrivers	425,000
	Nursing aides, orderlies	423,000
	Accountants, auditors	344,000
	Auto mechanics	324,000
	Blue-collar supervisors	319,000
	Kitchen helpers	305,000
	Guards, doorkeepers	300,000

Source: U.S. Department of Labor Statistics, "Employment Projections for 1995," Bulletin No. 2147 (March 1984):43.

Department of Labor that reveal the likelihood of most new jobs being in the "bad" category of the service sector.

Age of Discontinuity

Every new era poses new problems of adjustment, but this one differs from the agricultural and industrial eras. The earlier transformations were gradual enough for adaptation to take place over several decades, but conditions are significantly different now. The rate of change is phenomenal and unprecedented. There is a global economy now in which communication is instantaneous and capital is incredibly mobile. The potential work force in the United States is expanding (women and minorities) at the very time when technology combines with other forces to reduce jobs. These factors, which are discussed in this section, result in considerable discontinuity and disequilibrium (Jones, 1982:4–39).

Technology.   There are several aspects regarding technology that make this era different than the preceding ones. First, new technologies, some quite revolutionary, are being developed rapidly. These have potentials that can be positive and negative and many that are unforeseen. Lasers and fiber optics, for example, have a wide variety of applications as components in telecommunications systems, information processing, and entertainment (three-dimensional television). Fiber optics will increase the capacity of communications networks and make them more efficient. These technologies will generate considerable investment, render other technologies obsolete, generate new jobs, and destroy others.

Biotechnology is just beginning to effect changes in a wide range of industries—foods, agriculture, fuel, pharmaceuticals, chemicals, waste treatment, and natural resource recovery. The changes occurring in this field are rapid and far reaching. This is a field of tremendous growth potential (Oxford Analytica, 1986:233–234). Its future consequences for the economy and jobs are unknown.

Of greatest significance for our purposes are the technological changes directly affecting work and workers. For the most part, the new technologies, especially those related to computers, are reducing jobs and wages. The cost of technology in the microchip field has fallen dramatically relative to the cost of labor. "Despite inflation and the rising cost of resources, the price of each unit of performance in micro-technology is 100,000 times cheaper than it was in 1960. 'Miniaturization' has destroyed the historic relationship between the cost of labor and the cost of technology, permitting exponential growth with insignificant labor output" (Jones, 1982:36). The declining cost of computing power is illustrated by what has happened in personal computers. "A 1977 state-of-the-art personal computer processed 100,000 machine instructions per second and came with 64 kilobytes of main memory and 160 kilobytes of disk storage. A 1987 machine not only costs much less, but also has 20 times the processing power, 20 times the main memory and 500 times the disk storage capacity. The price of storing a single digital unit of data in a memory chip fell from one-tenth of a cent in 1976 to one-thousandth of a cent in 1986, and it will keep dropping by about 35 percent per annum" (Forester, 1987:2).

The capacity of microchips staggers the imagination. Microchips increased their capacity to store information ten thousand times between 1971 and 1980, and the pace continues. We now have "superchips" with one million transitors per chip. "Before the end of the century gigabit—one billion components per chip—integration may be possible" (Forester, 1987:2). The incredible storage and speed capabilities of modern computers is almost beyond comprehension. "Imagine . . . two computers conversing with each other over a period. They are then asked by a human being what they are talking about, and in the time he takes to pose the question, the two computers have exchanged more words than the sum total of all the words exchanged by human beings since *Homo sapiens* first appeared on earth 2 or 3 million years ago" (Simons, 1985:165).

Microprocessors, of course, are programmable, making robots possible. Robots can, for example, cut materials, weld, paint, and assemble. These robots, unlike human workers, do not get bored or tired, go on strike, require cost of living increases, or bicker among themselves. Not surprisingly, corporate managers are purchasing robots to replace workers at an accelerating rate. Robots are drastically altering the workplace. For example, robots perform more than 98 percent of the spot welding on Ford's Taurus and Sable cars. And at a General Dynamics plant in Fort Worth, Texas, one robot drills 550 holes in the vertical tail fins of an F-16 plane in three hours, a job that takes three workers eight hours to do (Bock, 1987:46). The result of this trend, of course, is fewer and fewer industrial jobs and for the workers who remain, less and less leverage in bargaining with management. A University of Michigan study has predicted that robots will displace 4.3 percent of the industrial work force—roughly 200,000 jobs—by 1990. Robotics manufacturing, meanwhile, will create only about 44,500 jobs by 1995 (*New York Times*, 1986).

Robotics are not just mechanical menials. They can be equipped with a multitude of sensors for vision, touch, and proximity. They can react to these sensory inputs and adapt. Even more incredible, they can be linked (computer-integrated manufacturing or CIM) into one comprehensive, integrated manufacturing system. In short, robots and computer-controlled machines will work together to plan, schedule, transport, control inventory, and perform many, if not most, of the manufacturing operations that used to require human skills.

The elimination of jobs because of superautomation is not limited to industrial factories. Offices are increasingly electronic. Engineers and architects now draw three-dimensional designs, then update, test, and store them almost instantaneously. In agriculture, there are robot fruit pickers and sheepshearers, computerized irrigation systems that use sensors to calculate water and fertilizer needs in different parts of a field, and automated chicken houses. Retail stores, banks, and brokerage houses use on-line transaction processing to obtain instant information and to conduct transactions. Laser scanning and bar codes are transforming the physical handling of goods by retailers and wholesale distributors. As a final example of technological change affecting jobs, there is the widespread use of televisions, telephones, and personal computers for the purposes of home banking and shopping.

Today's technology is different from that occurring at other stages in history. We now have "smart machines." As Jones has put it: "Computers can be programmed to parallel human mental processes—including the exercise of judgment and intuition. Machines have never before posed a challenge to mental (or white-collar) work: no steam engine could play chess, no slide rule could converse" (Jones, 1982:37). Throughout history technological changes have tended to increase overall productivity, and although there were considerable dislocations to workers in some fields, employment actually increased overall. In the past the introduction of machines extended the capacity of the labor force. The machines of the past (for example, sewing machines, typewriters, telephones, and motor vehicles) were designed to have one operator for each machine. Not only were they designed to have at least one operator per machine, they required other workers to make, sell, and maintain them. Now, however, there has been a significant shift toward labor-displacing technology in which machines are designed to reduce, if not eliminate, human labor. "Much technological innovation in the past was 'labor-complementing'—it extended the capacity of the existing labor force, and the machines themselves changed the nature of work. *But there has been a significant shift to 'labor-displacing' technology where low-cost machines are specifically intended to reduce, if not eliminate, labor inputs*" (Jones, 1982:39; emphasis added).

The effects of technology on social organization are not random or aimless. The costs and benefits are not shared equally by all members of society. For this reason, "there is no such thing as technological change pure and simple" (Smith, 1987:7). Technology is shaped by the prevailing social, demographic, and political conditions. Technology is part of the social relations of production that can assume the particular forms given it by the most powerful and forceful people in society (Noble, 1977:xxii).

The Global Economy.   The profound transformation in the international economy is another factor making this time in history different from the previous transitions. For thousands of years caravans have moved across the land, and ships have sailed along the winds and currents. People explored, conquered, and exploited other peoples and their resources; but the pace was slow, and the interaction among different nations muted by time and space. Now, however, there is instant communication around the globe, and transportation anywhere is only a day away rather than six months or more as was once the case. These dramatic advances in communication and transportation have at least two important ramifications. First, technological advances now diffuse rapidly. During the industrial revolution technological change was quite slow (although rapid compared to previous epochs). The first steam-powered cotton mill in the United States, for example, began in 1847, sixty-three years after its adoption in Britain. Now technological breakthroughs in one country rapidly spread to other nations.

The second consequence of advances in transportation and communications is the enhanced mobility of capital. As Harrison and Bluestone put it: "The ability to move managers and key components at nearly the speed of sound by jet and to move money and the information needed to coordinate production at nearly the speed of light enables capital, as never before, to go anywhere in the world" (*Working Papers,* 1983:43). Corporations of almost any size now make plans regarding raw materials, workers, and markets across national boundaries. "The globe is the unit of planning" (Coates, 1986:539). Corporations seek cheap labor, which means a transfer of jobs—millions of jobs—to other nations. Americans now buy more foreign goods than foreigners buy ours, driving down the number of American jobs and the wages of American workers. America's economic, political, and even military power, supreme since World War II, is now seriously threatened by the globalization of the economy.

Demography.   Three population facts—declining overall growth, disproportionate growth by racial minorities, and much greater participation by women in the work force—combine to make this time in economic history different from other stages. Let us examine each of these demographic trends briefly.

A major source of economic growth during the industrial revolution has been rapid population growth in the technologically advanced countries. Construction, the provision of services, and the like provided a significant source of employment especially in the rapidly growing urban centers. Since about 1970, however, population growth (births minus deaths) has stabilized in some countries and actually declined in others. This fact provides a further impetus for corporations to seek markets and workers in other countries.

While the fertility rate for whites has declined significantly in the United States, the rate for racial minorities has remained about the same. This imbalance, combined with the massive influx of legal and illegal immigrants, has led to the disproportionate growth of racial minorities. Throughout American history racial minorities have been denied equality in education and jobs. They have been relegated to the semiskilled and unskilled jobs in agriculture, in the mines, in construction, in the packing plants, and on the production lines. This bias continues today at a time when these are the declining and obsolete jobs, made unnecessary in a society increasingly committed to knowledge, high technology, and education. This puts immigrants at a distinct disadvantage—more so than at any time in history—and so, too, are the racial minorities already here but locked in poverty by institutional racism, blighted neighborhoods with inferior services (especially education), and fewer and fewer jobs.

Another major demographic trend contributing to the uniqueness of the present economic transformation is the entry of women into the work force on a massive scale. In 1950 about one third of the women held jobs outside the home, now more than two-thirds do, and the proportion is growing. This change is directly related to shifts in the economy, especially the expansion of the service sector. Two-thirds of the jobs created since 1975 have been taken by women. In fact, it is precisely this great increase in women's paid work that has been a primary factor in the rise of service jobs. These changes, combined with the economic requirements of families (high cost of housing, education, and the like), have made women's labor force participation a permanent phenomenon and have contributed to their greater autonomy.

There are two related problems resulting from the permanent addition of many millions of women to the work force. First, this influx of workers has and is occurring at the very time that the number of jobs in the relatively high-pay industrial sector is declining. Second, women, for the most part, are competing against each other for the expanding number of jobs at the low-paying end of the service/information sector. During the 1970s the service sector of the economy grew by fourteen million jobs and three fourths of these were filled by women new to the labor force. These jobs tended to be temporary, part-time, and low paying. They were not associated, typically, with skill and achievement but rather tended to require obedience, dependence, and repetitiveness. In short, although there are exceptions, most working women have jobs consistent with traditional gender expectations.

These factors—microelectronic innovation, the global economy, and demography—combine to make the present turning point in history unique. The old answers no longer apply, yet few economists and other social scientists are confronting this reality. The thinking of most "has been shaped by the axioms of the Industrial Revolution, and they are unable to entertain the possibility of radical discontinuity with the past. . . . Attempts to apply old remedies to a new situation are as futile as attempting to use a Ptolemaic world-view to interpret an Einsteinian universe" (Jones, 1982:39).

In sum, this current transformation of the economy has important and sometimes wrenching consequences for workers, families, minorities, communities, society, and the world economy. It is imperative that we understand this complex economic phenomenon.

CAPITALISM IN CRISIS

The Negative Consequences of Private Profitability over Social Need

We have written elsewhere (Eitzen with Baca Zinn, 1989) that the problems of American society are in large measure the result of the form of the economy. This is illustrated by the role of capitalists as they seek profit in the climate engendered by the economic transformation just discussed. Entrepreneurs, as they seek to maximize profit, shut down plants, reduce work forces, replace workers with machines, or threaten to move operations overseas to force workers to accept lower wages and benefits. They also continue to pollute the environment and fight government attempts to enforce worker and consumer safety. These entrepreneurs, corporate boards of directors, and corporate executives have no allegiance to consumers, workers, or the communities in which their operations are located. Their ultimate loyalty is to the bottom line. Parenti describes this fundamental logic of capitalism and capitalists:

> Capitalism's purpose is not to create jobs; in fact, capitalists are constantly
> devising ways of eliminating jobs in order to cut labor costs. Nor is its pur-

pose to build communities, for capitalists will build or destroy communities as investment opportunities dictate. Nor is capitalism dedicated to protecting the family or traditional life, for no system in human history has been more relentless in battering down ancient practices and destroying both rural and urban homegrown cultures. Nor is capitalism intent upon protecting the environment on behalf of generations yet to come; for corporations will treat the environment like a septic tank in order to cut production costs and maximize profits without regard for future generations or for the generation enduring it all today. Nor can we say that capitalists are committed to economic efficiency as such, since they regularly pass on their hidden diseconomies to the public in the form of overproduction, overpricing, pollution, unemployment, population dislocation, harmful products, and personal injury. And as the military budget shows, they actively court waste and duplication if it brings fatter contracts and bigger profits.

Capitalism has no loyalty to anything but its own process of capital accumulation, no loyalty to anything but itself. Nor could it be otherwise if one wished to survive as a capitalist; for the first law of the market is to make a profit off other people's labor or go out of business. Private profitability rather than social need is the determining condition of capital investment. (Parenti, 1986:1–2)

Can society continue to allow capitalists the freedom to make investment decisions unfettered by the concerns of society? Can corporations pollute the environment and produce waste with impunity? Should businesses be allowed to shut down a plant without sufficient warning and compensation to the affected workers and communities? Should taxes be levied on robots with the monies spent on job retraining of workers displaced by them? As we see in the next chapter, the close relationship between economic power and political power appears to preclude the government curbs on the abuses created by capitalists. And the rationale provided by many for the lack of governmental control of business will likely be that capitalism is not the problem but really the solution to society's problems—if allowed to operate without restraints.

The Lack of Economic Planning

The inability of governments to plan adequately for energy shortages indicates a weakness of free enterprise economies. The capitalist philosophy dating back to Adam Smith is that the government should stay out of economic affairs. According to this view, the marketplace will force businesses to make the decisions that will best benefit them, and indirectly the citizenry. Yet when the government does receive valuable information with which it could make decisions to avert future crises, the strong tendency in the United States is to remain aloof. For example, in 1951 President Harry Truman named a commission to plan what the country should do about the likelihood of scarce resources in 1975. The commission, although underestimating the problems, foresaw the trends accurately. The report called for immediate efforts to conserve energy, for ways to safeguard outside oil sources, and for massive increases in energy output. The report was not implemented.

Ironically, the government is involved in central planning in the areas of space exploration and defense. As one commentator has said:

> The U.S. launched Mariner 10 on Nov. 3, 1973, and it flew to Venus and then to Mercury, which it circled for a total of a billion miles. It performed magnificently and sent back photographs. That took years of planning. But planning for a thing like that is one thing. Social planning and foreseeing energy shortages before they happen, that is different, and to some, slightly sinister. (TRB, 1975:2)

The issue of central planning revolves around whether the society is able *and* willing to respond to present and future social problems. Is a capitalist society capable of meeting the problems of poverty, unemployment, social neglect, population growth, energy shortages, environmental damage, and monopoly? Robert Heilbroner, a distinguished economist, has argued that we will not prepare for the problems of the future: "the outlook is for what we may call 'convulsive change'—change forced upon us by external events rather than by conscious choice, by catastrophe rather than by calculation" (Heilbroner, 1974:132).

The lack of central planning points to the undemocratic nature of U.S. society. It is commonly believed that the people, through their economic choices, actually govern business decisions. While this is partially true, it ignores the manipulation of the public by business interests through advertising and other "hypes" (Ewen, 1976). Neither the public nor its elected representatives are involved in the economic decisions of the giant corporations—and these decisions often have dire consequences domestically and internationally.

As Andrew Hacker has argued:

> The power to make investment decisions is concentrated in a few hands, and it is this power which will decide what kind of a nation America will be. Instead of government planning there is boardroom planning that is accountable to no outside agency; and these plans set the order of priorities on national growth, technological innovation, and ultimately, the values and behavior of human beings. Investment decisions are sweeping in their ramifications—no one is unaffected by their consequences. Yet this is an area where neither the public nor its government is able to participate. (Hacker, 1970:52)

The lack of central planning is also a result of the resistance of powerful interest groups in society. Short-term goals such as employment for labor groups or profit for corporations lead special interests to block government efforts to meet future needs. Thus, the power of the economic dominants in society has the effect of superseding the interests of the nation, as we see in the next chapter.

Panel 13–1 outlines some major current and future problems facing U.S. society. In particular, society has a major problem in replacing its infrastructure. How does society tackle this mammoth and expensive project? It will take money, societal planning, and the conversion of corporate enterprises from one type of economic activity to another. Can we do it? Economist Richard Bartel shows how it might be done.

Economic Planning to Solve Future Problems

Investment is the key, as economists know very well, to economic growth and material progress. History records how the creation of physical and human capital drives the wealth of nations.

Yet even some economists tend to think of investment in narrow terms—private spending on business plant and equipment. We often forget about additions to the stock of public infrastructure—spending on roads, bridges, mass transportation, airports, waterways, water supply, waste disposal facilities, and other public utilities. And equally neglected, but perhaps even more important in explaining the advance of human progress, is investment in human capital: spending on education, acquiring skills, and accumulating knowledge through research and development. These are powerful, though intangible, investments. Yet still a fourth dimension to investment comes to mind: changes in our stock of natural resources and the environment put light on how investment depletes, enhances, or sustains this part of the nation's productive capital.

A broad consensus among economists points to the collapse of investment in the 1980s as a striking departure from American historical experience since World War II. . . . When the downtrend in investment is viewed from the perspective of the nation's infrastructure, human capital needs, and deteriorating environment, a radical reversal of the 1980s performance becomes an urgent matter.

Most recently 327 American economists joined with researchers at Washington's Economic Policy Institute in decrying the growing "deficiency of public investment in our people and our economic infrastructure." They see the investment shortfall—a "third deficit," joining the still persistent trade and budget deficits—as crippling U.S. competitiveness in the world economy.

Looking at U.S. outlays for public works over the last twenty years, the collapse in infrastructure spending is stunning. Spending on highways, mass transportation, airports, waterways, water supply, and waste disposal facilities has plunged from some 2.3 percent of GNP to about 1 percent in 1988. Capital spending on public works, measured as a percentage of private capital spending, has also been cut in half. As a result, the stock of *infrastructure* capital per worker has declined, even though the *private* capital stock per worker has continued to rise. U.S. population has continued to climb, generating growing demands for the services provided by an eroding public infrastructure. Exploding population in some sunbelt regions and suburban sprawl are rapidly outstripping the infrastructure. In the rustbelt and the urban Northeast, aging infrastructure is literally crumbling. Bridges and roadways are collapsing, and sewage is polluting major water supplies. Employers in the Northeast, for example, have long complained that a deteriorating public transportation system is dragging down the productivity of their commuting workers.

ECONOMICS OF CONVERSION

How can we close the investment deficit? Where do we get the productive resources in an economy that saves relatively little and is now operating at near full employment? In looking for the answers, GNP budgeting is a useful tool. We will have to shift resources from conspicuous consumption to productive investment. The economics of conversion will provide an analytical approach . . . to these problems that both the United States and the Soviet Union will have to confront. Converting from guns to butter now offers distinct possibilities since the door is open to halting the East-West arms race.

The amounts needed for net new public investment are really not so outlandish: the Economic Policy Institute calls for some $30 billion in fiscal 1990—½ percent of GNP—to come from new tax revenues and savings from other areas of excess spending.

But the guns-to-butter conversion requires some tough political/economic decisions on the part of elected officials on Capitol Hill and in the White House. Votes on defense spending usually hinge on their economic impact on local communities, and their employment, incomes, and profits, rather than on the contribution of a specific weapon or program to a strong U.S. defense. . . .

Some actual numbers help to illustrate the dilemma faced by Congressmen, businessmen, and workers. The Stealth B-2 bomber, for example, produced by Northrop, carries a pricetag of $530 million per plane, and the total program involves 12,000 jobs. Scrapping this one program clearly creates hardships for companies, workers, and their local communities. That may be true unless these workers can be readily trained to produce useful products, employing the plant and equipment that Northrop would otherwise have to close down. Thus, the need for a conversion program. Clearly there are many capital goods that Northrop could conceivably produce to help close

the public infrastructure deficit—rapid transit, fuel efficient buses, for example. . . .

A conversion program not only requires a list of new products and projects that achieve worthwhile national goals, but it means mastering and applying new technology and imparting new skills to production workers, engineers, and managers. A good case in point is the new high-speed rail line now being planned to run between Houston and Dallas. German and French manufacturers are in hot competition for the job. Even the Japanese are laggards in that race. The Europeans have developed the leading technology and the French, in particular, have undisputed practical experience in running a high-tech, high-speed rail line. This year, the French have cut down the time to travel the 300 miles from Paris to Lyons with the TGV to two hours. U.S. producers have neither the technology, expertise, nor practical experience in building and running such a railroad.

There are many other examples that one can cite from U.S. auto manufacturing, computers, machine tools, and steel, but the point is simple. Investment in high-tech public infrastructure means private-sector engagement, applying and refining new technologies, and workers and managers acquiring new skills. There is a synergistic process that in the end will feed into better productivity growth and improved competitiveness in world markets.

Source: Reprinted with permission of publisher, M. E. Sharpe, Inc. 80 Business Park Drive, Armonk, New York 10504 USA, from the September/October 1989 issue of *Challenge.*

CHAPTER REVIEW

1. Economic activity involves the production and distribution of goods and services.

2. There are two fundamental ways society can organize its economic activities—capitalism and socialism.

3. Capitalism in its pure form involves: (a) the private ownership of property; (b) the pursuit of personal profit; (c) competition; and (d) a government policy of allowing the marketplace to function unhindered.

4. Socialism in its pure form involves: (a) democracy throughout the social structure; (b) equality—equality of opportunity, equality rather than hierarchy in making decisions, and equality in sharing the benefits of society; and (c) efficiency in providing the best conditions to meet the material needs of the citizens.

5. Marx's prediction that capitalism will result in an economy dominated by monopolies has been fulfilled in the United States. But rather than a single corporation dominating a sector of the economy, the United States is characterized by the existence of *shared monopolies*—where four or fewer corporations supply 50 percent or more of a particular market.

6. Economic power is concentrated in a few major corporations and banks. This concentration has been accomplished primarily through mergers and interlocking directorates.

7. The power of America's largest corporations is increased by their international activities. Multinational corporations have important consequences: (a) decline in domestic jobs; (b) crippling of the power of unions; (c) hurting the government through lost revenues in taxes and a negative balance of payments; (d) increased power of corporations over the world economy and world events; and (e) exploitation of workers and natural resources in Third World countries.

8. Inequality is endemic to capitalism. Corporate wealth and private wealth are highly concentrated. Poverty, too, is concentrated disproportionately among people of color and in households headed by women. Two features of contemporary society promote these inequities: (a) the segmented labor market; and (b) capitalist patriarchy.

9. The economy of the United States is in the midst of a major structural transformation—from one based on manufacturing to one based on the collection, storage, and dissemination of information.

10. Deindustrialization refers to the movement of capital by corporations and banks away from manufacturing and toward the production of information and services. This occurs in four ways: (a) by corporations using excess profits to purchase other companies rather than modernize their plants; (b) by banks making loans to only the successful companies (foreign or domestic); (c) by firms shifting their operations overseas; and (d) by corporations closing plants in one part of the country and opening them elsewhere.

11. American capitalism is facing three crises: (1) the structural transformation of the economy; (2) the primacy of profit over human considerations; and (3) the lack of central planning to solve current problems and anticipate future ones.

12. Two facts about institutions of society are especially important: (a) although they are interrelated, the economy is the most dominant and shapes each of the other institutions; and (b) the particular way that an institution is organized is at once a source of stability and a source of problems.

KEY TERMS

Institution	Shared monopoly	Segmented labor market
Capitalism	Interlocking directorate	Capital flight
Socialism		

STUDY QUESTIONS

1. What are the mechanisms within the American economy that work against the capitalist ideal of free enterprise?
2. Why is inequality endemic to capitalism?
3. The structural transformation of the economy is having dramatic consequences. What social categories are most disadvantaged by these changes? Why?
4. A major assumption of conflict theorists is that capitalism is a primary source for many social problems. Parenti's critique of capitalism on pages 363–364 is an example of this approach. Do you agree or disagree? Why?

FOR FURTHER READING

Barry Bluestone and Bennett Harrison, *The Deindustrialization of America* (New York: Basic Books, 1982).

D. Stanley Eitzen and Maxine Baca Zinn (eds.), *The Reshaping of America: Social Consequences of the Changing Economy* (Englewood Cliffs, NJ: Prentice-Hall, 1989).

Michael Harrington, *Decade of Decision* (New York: Simon & Schuster, 1980).

Bennett Harrison and Barry Bluestone, *The Great U-Turn: Corporate Restructuring and the Polarizing of America* (New York: Basic Books, 1988).

Barry Jones, *Sleepers Awake! Technology and the Future of Work* (Melbourne: Oxford University Press, 1982).

Robert Lekachman, *Greed is Not Enough: Reaganomics* (New York: Pantheon, 1982).

National Conference of Catholic Bishops, *Economic Justice for All: Pastoral Letter on Catholic Social Teaching and the U.S. Economy* (Washington, D.C.: National Conference of Catholic Bishops, 1986).

James O'Connor, *The Fiscal Crisis of the State* (New York: St. Martin's Press, 1973).

Michael Parenti, *Power and the Powerless* (New York: St. Martin's Press, 1978).

William Ryan, *Equality* (New York: Vintage Books, 1982).

Albert Szymanski, *The Capitalist State and the Politics of Class* (Cambridge, MA: Winthrop, 1978).

Chapter Fourteen

Power and Politics

*I*n Washington, D.C. there are about 15,000 lawyers, association executives, public relations experts, and technical workers who are lobbyists. These lobbyists work on behalf of interest groups to influence legislators and regulatory agencies. Lobbyists' tactics include supplying information, doing favors, providing entertainment, giving campaign contributions, flooding Congress with telegrams, and furnishing transportation.

The phenomenon of lobbying can be interpreted in two opposite ways—*each of which illustrates a fundamental view of the distribution of power for the whole society.* The first view is that lobbying is the essence of democracy, as competing pressure groups each present their best case to the decision makers. These officials, faced with these countervailing forces, tend to compromise and make decisions most beneficial to the public.

In contrast, others view lobbying as another instance of the privileged few consistently getting their way. Interest groups are not equal in power. Some have enormous power and are not challenged by effective opposition. For example, the American Petroleum Institute speaks for 350 corporations and has an annual lobbying budget of $30 million. Also, the United States Chamber of Commerce has a $20 million budget and represents 89,500 corporations and 2,500 local communities. These and other business-oriented lobbies are extremely well organized and financed. Their opposition is negligible. Clearly, from this perspective, power in Washington is centralized and represents the powerful few.

The compelling question of this chapter is: Who are the real power wielders in American society? Is it an elite, or are the people sovereign? The location and exercise of power are difficult to determine, especially in a large and complex society such as the United States. Decisions are necessarily made by a few people, but in a democracy these few are to be representatives of the masses and therefore subject to their influence. But what of nonrepresentatives who aid in shaping policy? What about the pressure on the decision makers by powerful groups? What about those pressures on the decision makers which are so diffuse that the leaders may not even know who is applying the pressure?

MODELS OF THE NATIONAL POWER STRUCTURE

There are two basic views of the power structure—the **elitist model** and **pluralist model**. The elitist view of power is that there is a pyramid of power. Those persons at the apex control the rest of the pyramid. The pluralists, on the other hand, see power as dispersed rather than concentrated. Power is broadly distributed among a number of organizations, special interests, and the voters. This chapter is devoted to the examination of different elitist and pluralist conceptions of power in the United States. As we survey each, the fundamental question we should ask ourselves is: How does this model mesh with the facts of contemporary America? Does the model portray things as they are or as they should be?

Pluralist Models

Pluralism I: Representative Democracy. Many Americans accept the notion promoted in high school civics books that the United States is a "government of the people, by the people, for the people." **Democracy** is the form of government in which the people have the ultimate power. In a complex society of over 250 million persons, the people cannot make all decisions; they must elect representatives to make most decisions. So, decision making is concentrated at the top, but it is to be controlled by the people who elect the decision makers. This model is shown in Figure 14–1.

The most important component of a democratic model is that the representatives, because they are elected by the people, are responsive to the wishes of the people. This model, however, does *not* conform to reality. The United States is undemocratic in many important ways. The people, although

Figure 14–1
Representative Democracy

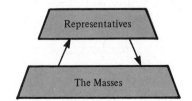

they do vote for their representatives every few years, are really quite powerless. For example, who makes the really important decisions about war and peace, economic policies, and foreign policy? The people certainly do not. The record shows that many times the American people have been deceived when the object was to conceal clandestine illegal operations, mistakes, undemocratic practices, and the like. These illicit activities have been carried out by Democratic and Republican presidents alike. The last section of this chapter, which describes political deviance, provides many examples of official government deceit.

Not only have the people in the United States been misinformed, but the basic democratic tenet that the public be informed has also been defied. On the one hand, Congress has shown its contempt for the electorate by the use of secret meetings. The executive branch, too, has acted in secret. Recent presidents have gone months without a press conference, have used "executive privilege" to keep presidential advisors from testifying before congressional committees, and have refused to debate opponents in election campaigns.

Many persons who are appointed rather than elected wield tremendous power. Technical experts, for example, evaluate extremely complicated issues; they can virtually dictate to the president and Congress what is needed for defense, shoring up the economy, or winning friends abroad, because they are the experts. The coterie of advisors may convince the president to act in particular ways. The members appointed to the regulatory agencies have tremendous power to shape various aspects of the economy.

Perhaps one of the most undemocratic features (at least in its consequences) of the U.S. political system is a result of how campaigns are financed. Political campaigns are expensive, with money needed to pay for staff, direct-mail operations, phone banks, polling, computers, consultants, and media advertising. The 1988 campaigns for Congress and president cost $1.2 billion overall including monies from the federal government (each major presidential candidate received about $70 million in public funds), individuals, political parties, and political action committees (PACs). The average victorious Senate candidate spent $3 million in 1988 (up from $1.2 million in 1978).

These expensive campaigns are funded by the candidates' wealth, individual contributions, and (in the case of congressional candidates) money donated from special interest groups through PACs. In 1974 PACs gave $12.4 million to congressional candidates; in 1976 they gave $22.6 million, which increased to $35 million in 1978, $45 million in 1980, $80 million in 1982, $100 million in 1984, $130 million in 1986, and $151 million in 1988.

The increasingly higher sums given to congressional candidates have led some cynics to comment that we have "the best Congress money can buy" (Stern, 1988). The PACs are formed to represent interests such as labor unions, doctors, realtors, auto dealers, teachers, and corporations. Each PAC may give up to $5,000 to any candidate in a primary and another $5,000 in a general election. As *U.S. News & World Report* editorialized, "PACs of every ilk have a way of contributing their allowed $5,000 chunks to candidates who either have voted 'right' or had better do so shortly" (Stone, 1978:112).

In addition to PACs, special interests can funnel money to political parties at the national, state, and local levels or to other private organizations that are technically independent of the candidates. These gifts are not covered by the federal election laws and thus are unlimited.

It is difficult to prove conclusively that receiving campaign contributions from a special interest buys a vote, but there is some indirect evidence that special interest groups gain an advantage through campaign contributions.

- In the 1988 election, $8.4 million was given to 53 candidates for the House of Representatives *who were running unopposed.* House Speaker James Wright, for example, ran without an opponent yet received $566,000 from PACs.
- Some PACs give money to both sides in an election (see Panel 14–1).
- Some PACs contribute after the election to the candidate they opposed but who won anyway.

As the *Dallas Times Herald* editorialized:

> The power of PAC money threatens increasingly to turn Members of Congress into legalized political prostitutes. It drives them to sell to the highest bidders their one most easily and legally salable product—access. But worst of all, it erodes the public's confidence in the integrity of the congressional system. (quoted in Wertheimer, 1986:60)

There are many examples of how PAC money seemed to make a difference in legislation passed or defeated. Two cases make the point. In 1982 the National Automobile Dealers' Association opposed a proposed law suggested by the Federal Trade Commission that would require used-car dealers to disclose known defects to potential buyers. The dealers' association, through various PACs, distributed campaign contributions of more than $840,000 to more than 300 senators and representatives, 85 percent of whom voted against the used-car rule, killing it by a greater than two-to-one margin (*The Nation*, 1982; see also Green, 1984). Another example concerns a congressional vote on whether to fund the Clinch River nuclear breeder reactor in 1981. Ralph Nader's Public Citizen's Congress Watch noted that the five companies involved in designing and building the reactor contributed about $280,000 to members of Congress. Of eleven representatives receiving more than $3,000, ten voted to build the reactor (the other was absent at the time of the vote); of those representatives who received $1,500 to $3,000, 76 percent voted for the project; and of those representatives who did not receive any money, 71 percent voted to kill it (Pike, 1982).

Money presents a fundamental obstacle to democracy because only the interests of the wealthy tend to be served. It takes money and lots of it to be a successful politician. The candidate must either be rich or be willing to accept contributions from other people. In either case, the political leaders will be part of or beholden to the wealthy.

PACs Play Both Sides of Fence

Like gamblers betting on both entries in a two-horse race, political action committees are giving money to Democratic and Republican candidates in the same campaign.

A Common Cause study, released today, found 274 PACs "double giving" in seven Senate races last fall.

Most backed both candidates before the election, but nearly a quarter hedged their bets by making postelection contributions to the winner after first backing only the loser.

"Double-giving PACs are not interested in the outcome of an election," said Common Cause President Fred Wertheimer. "They just want to make sure they've bought access and influence with a member of Congress."

Officials at Federal Express Corp.—whose PAC gave money to all 14 candidates in the seven races studied—disagree.

"A company as big as Federal Express, with significant operations in every state, with revenues approaching $4 billion, doesn't have to worry about access," said Douglas Buttrey, manager of government affairs. "We've never had trouble talking to any member about anything we've wanted to talk about."

His explanation for backing both candidates: "We're a bipartisan PAC. . . . We supported many of the Senate candidates when they held other offices. Does that mean we can't support them now because we've also supported their opponent in the past?"

But University of Virginia political scientist Larry Sabato, author of *PAC Power,* says, "PACs give money for access. They need access to elected officials, not losers, so rationally it (double-giving) makes sense. But it looks like rank influence-peddling and appearances matter in politics."

Common Cause, a liberal-oriented reform group and frequent critic of the political power of PACs, picked seven close races—four where incumbents lost and three open seats—where "double-giving" was most likely. Incumbents get three-quarters of all PAC money.

Double donations in the Senate. A total of 274 political action committees gave to both sides in the seven 1988 Senate races in the study. The biggest "double givers":

Amount	Political action committee
$83,500	Federal Express Corp.
$80,000	National PAC
$51,500	American Bankers Association
$38,900	Union Pacific Corp.
$34,250	American Telephone & Telegraph Co.
$28,500	American Dental Association
$18,300	Philip Morris Inc.
$15,200	General Electric Co./Gelco Corp.
$11,350	Coca-Cola Co.
$10,575	Grumman Corp.
$10,000	Americans for Good Government Inc.
$ 7,110	Wexler, Reynolds, Harrison and Schule Inc.

Closely related to the financing of campaigns is the process by which political candidates are nominated. Being wealthy or having access to wealth is essential for victory because of the enormous cost. This means that the candidates tend to represent a limited constituency—the wealthy.

The two-party system also works to limit choices among candidates to a rather narrow range. Each party is financed by the special interests—especially business.

When all of these direct and indirect gifts (donations provided directly to candidates or through numerous political action committees of specific corpo-

How the money was distributed. Here's what winners and losers in the seven campaigns got from the same political action committees (winners listed first):

State	Candidates	Amount from same PACs
Connecticut	Democrat Joseph Lieberman	$55,500
	Republican Lowell Weicker	$83,405
Florida	Republican Connie Mack	$186,749
	Democrat Buddy MacKay	$146,918
Mississippi	Republican Trent Lott	$168,450
	Democrat Wayne Dowdy	$147,860
Montana	Republican Conrad Burns	$114,036
	Democrat John Melcher	$122,827
Nebraska	Democrat Bob Kerrey	$156,505
	Republican David Karnes	$156,852
Nevada	Democrat Richard Bryan	$113,291
	Republican Chic Hecht	$155,723
Washington	Republican Slade Gorton	$118,325
	Democrat Mike Lowry	$48,150

Source: Bob Minzesheimer, "PACs Play Both Sides of Fence," *USA Today* (May 9, 1989), p. 6A. Copyright 1989 *USA Today.* Excerpted by permission.

rations and general business organizations) are combined, the power elite can be seen to provide the great bulk of the financial support to both parties at the national level, far outspending the unions and middle status liberals within the Democrats, and the melange of physicians, dentists, engineers, real-estate operators and other white-collar conservatives within the right wing of the Republican Party. (Domhoff, 1979:148)

Affluent individuals and the largest corporations influence candidate selection by giving financial aid to those sympathetic with their views and withholding support from those who differ. The parties, then, are constrained to choose candidates with views congruent with the monied interest.

Pluralism II: Veto Groups.   Although some groups have more power than others and some individuals have more power than others, the power structure in the United States is viewed according to the "veto groups" model as a plurality of interest groups (Reisman, 1950:213–217). Each interest group (for example, the military, labor, business, farmers, education, medicine, law, veterans, the aged, blacks, and consumers) is primarily concerned with protecting its own interests. The group that primarily exercises power varies with the issue at stake. There is a balance of power, since each "veto group" mobilizes to prevent the others from actions threatening its interests. Thus, these groups tend to neutralize each other.

The masses are sought as an ally (rather than dominated, as is the case in the various elitist models) by the interest groups in their attempts to exert power over issues in their jurisdiction. Figure 14–2 shows the relationship between the various levels in this model.

This pluralist model assumes that there are a number of sectors of power. The most powerful persons in each are usually wealthy—probably upper class. But, the pluralist view is that the upper class is not a unified group—there is considerable disagreement within the upper-class category because of differing interests. Power is not concentrated, but is viewed as a shifting coalition depending upon the issue. The basic difference between pluralists and elitists is on the question of whether there is a basic unity or disagreement among the powerful from different sectors (basically, those who are wealthy enough to be upper class).

There are several criticisms of this pluralistic model stemming from the knowledge that it, like the other pluralistic model (for representative democracy), is an idealized conception of the distribution of power—as such, it does not conform with reality and is subject to question on several grounds. First, is the power structure so amorphous that power shifts constantly from one power source to another? Second, are the interest groups so equal in power that they neutralize each other? The special bias of this view is that it does not give attention to the power differentials among the various interest

Figure 14–2
Veto-Groups
Model

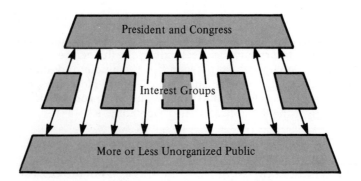

groups. It is absurd to claim that the power of big business is neutralized by the countervailing power of farmers. A more probable occurrence is that there is a hierarchy of power among these "veto groups."

A final criticism is that the leaders in each sector come disproportionately from the upper economic strata. If this assertion is correct, the possibility of a power elite that transcends narrow interest groups is present, since they may know each other, tend to intermarry, and have similar economic interests (as we will see later).

The pluralist models are not altogether faulty. There are a number of possible power centers that often compete for advantage. Shifting coalitions are possible. There are instances when selected officials are responsive to public opinion. However, it seems to this observer that most of the evidence supports an elitist view, although each of the three types described below also has its faults.

Elitist Models

The elitist views of societal power are usually structured quite similarly to those of Karl Marx. For Marx, economics was the basis for the stratification system (that is, unequal distribution of rewards including power). The economic elite, because of similar interests (that is, keeping the status quo) and limited social interaction patterns, is a unified group. The economic elite controls the state and its inhabitants.

Implicit in the Marxian conception of the powerful is the notion of conspiracy. The elite manipulate the masses through religion, nationalism, control of the media, and control of the visible governmental leaders (Marx and Engels, 1947:39).

Power Elite I: The Thesis of C. Wright Mills.   C. Wright Mills's view of the American structure of power posits that the key persons in three sectors—the corporate rich, the executive branch of the government, and the military—all combine to form a **power elite** that makes all important decisions (Mills, 1956).

The elite is a small group of persons who routinely interact together. They also, as Mills assumed, have similar interests and goals. The elite is the power elite because the members have key institutional positions—that is, they command great authority and resources in specific and important sectors, and each sector is dependent upon the other sectors.

There are three levels in Mills's pyramid of power. The uppermost is the power elite—composed of the leaders of three sectors. Mills implied that of the three, the corporate rich are perhaps the most powerful (first among "equals"). The middle level of power is comprised of local opinion leaders, the legislative branch of government, and the plurality of interest groups. These bodies, according to Mills, do the bidding of the power elite. The third level is the powerless mass of unorganized people who are controlled from above. They are exploited economically and politically. The three levels of power are depicted in Figure 14–3.

Figure 14–3
**Mills's Pyramid
of Power**

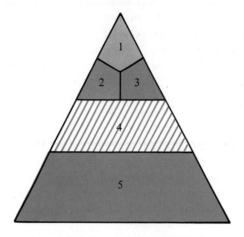

(Legend: 1, corporate rich; 2, executive branch; 3, military leaders; 4, leaders of interest groups, legislative branch, local opinion leaders; 5, unorganized masses.)

Mills believed that the power elite was a relatively new phenomenon resulting from a number of historical and social forces that have enlarged and centralized the facilities of power, making the decisions of small groups much more consequential than in any other age (Mills, 1968).

The two important and related factors giving rise to the recent emergence of the power elite are: (1) the means of power and violence are now infinitely greater than they were in the past, and (2) they are also increasingly centralized. The decisions of a few become ultimately crucial when they have the power to activate a system that has the capability of destroying hundreds of cities within minutes. Transportation, communication, the economy, the instruments of warfare are examples of several areas that have become centralized—making a power elite possible. The federal government taxes, regulates, and passes laws so that the lives of almost all Americans are affected. This same bureaucratic process is evident in the military, where decisions are more and more centralized. The Pentagon, which oversees the largest and most expensive feature of the government, is a relatively new phenomenon. The economy in the United States was once composed of many, many small productive units that were more or less autonomous. But over time the number of semiautonomous economic units has dwindled through mergers, interlocking directorates, and chainstores, putting the financial squeeze on the small businessperson. The result is that the economy has become dominated by less than 200 giant corporations.

The tremendous advances in transportation and communication have made it much more likely that the persons holding key positions in the political, economic, and military hierarchies can be in contact with each other if they wish to do so. If, as Mills assumed, they have similar interests, then they must be in contact so that their activities can be coordinated to the best mutual advantage.

The key decision makers also have instruments to influence the masses, such as television, public relations firms, and techniques of propaganda that are unsurpassed in the history of humankind. Hence, if there is a power elite and they want to manipulate the masses to accept their decisions, they have the instruments of mass persuasion at their disposal.

Mills also contended that the importance of institutions has shifted. Whereas the family and religion were once the most important American institutions, they (along with education) have become subordinate to the three power institutions of the economy, polity, and military—thus making the leaders of these three domains the power elite. Mills said, "Families and churches and schools adapt to modern life; governments and armies and corporations shape it; and, as they do so, they turn these lesser institutions into means for their ends" (Mills, 1968:267). For example, religious institutions supply chaplains to the armed forces, where they increase the effectiveness of the combat units by raising morale. Schools train persons for their places in the giant corporations. Fathers and sons are sometimes taken from their homes to fight and die for their country. And, Mills said, the symbols of these lesser institutions are used to legitimate the decisions of the power elite who dominate the powerful institutions.

A most important impetus for the formation of the power elite was World War II. U.S. participation in a war worldwide in scope and where the possibility of defeat was very real meant, among other things, that a reorganization of various sectors had to be accomplished. The national government, particularly the executive department, had to be granted dictatorial powers so that the war could be conducted. Decisions had to be made quickly and in secret, two qualities not compatible with a democracy. The nation's corporations had to be mobilized for war. They made huge profits. Finally, the military became very prominent in decision making. Their expertise was essential to the making of wartime strategy.

Following World War II, the United States was faced with another threat, the spread of communism. This meant, in effect, that the executive department, the corporations, and the military did not shift back to their peacetime ways. The military remained in the decision-making process, the corporations remained dependent upon lucrative defense contracts, and the executive branch continued to exercise its autonomous or at least semiautonomous powers.

All these factors, according to Mills, ensured that the domains of the polity, economy, and military were enlarged and centralized. Decisions made in each of these domains became increasingly crucial to all citizens, but particularly to the leaders of the other key domains. The result had to be a linkage between the key persons in each domain. It was in their interests to cooperate. Since each sector affected the others, the persons at the top of each hierarchy had to interact with the leaders from the other sectors, so that the actions and decisions would benefit all. Thus, they have come to form a triangle of power, an interlocking directorate of persons in the three key domains making coordinated decisions—a power elite.

An important ingredient in Mills's view is that the elite is a self-conscious cohesive unit. This unity is based on three factors: psychological similarity, social interaction, and coinciding interests.

1. *Psychological similarity.* The institutional positions men and women occupy throughout their lifetimes determine the values they will hold. For example, career military men hold certain values by virtue of being socialized into the military subculture. The famous quote that "What's good for General Motors is good for the country" by Secretary of Defense (under President Eisenhower) Charles Wilson is also indicative of this probability. Thus, for Mills, the psychology of these leaders is largely shaped by the values they develop in their institutional roles. Additionally, the psychological similarity among the members of the elite is derived from their similar social origins and style of life.

2. *Social interaction.* Mills stated that the ruling elite are involved in a set of overlapping groups and intricately connected cliques.

   The people of the higher circles may also be conceived as members of a top social stratum, as a set of groups whose members know one another, see one another socially and at business, and so, in making decisions, take one another into account. The elite, according to this conception, feel themselves to be, and are felt by others to be, the inner circle of "the upper social classes." They form a more or less compact social and psychological entity; they have become self-conscious members of a social class. People are either accepted into this class or they are not, and there is a qualitative split, rather than merely a numerical scale, separating them from those who are not elite. They are more or less aware of themselves as a social class and they behave toward one another differently from the way they do toward members of other classes. They accept one another, understand one another, marry one another, tend to work and to think if not together at least alike. (Mills, 1956:11; see also Domhoff, 1975)

3. *Coinciding interests.* A third unifying condition hypothesized by Mills is the existence of similar interests among the elite. The interest of the elite is, among other things, maintenance of the capitalist system with themselves at the top. Additionally, the government needs adequate defense systems, to which the military agree and which the corporations gladly sell for a profit. The huge corporations have large holdings in foreign countries. They therefore expect the government to make policy decisions that will be beneficial (profitable) for American interests. These similar interests result in a unity and a need for planning and coordination of their efforts. Since each sector affects the other, the persons at the top of each hierarchy must interact with leaders of the other sectors so that their actions will benefit all. Top decisions, Mills argued, thus become coordinated decisions.

Empirical Evidence for the Existence of a Military-Industrial Power Elite. Mills postulated that there was an interlocking directorate uniting key persons in the business, military, and economic sectors. The relationships among the three are therefore:

There is much evidence supporting the linkages for each of the three relationships pictured above.

On the surface the federal government appears to have great power over business—through taxation, the power of the regulatory agencies (for example, Federal Trade Commission, Interstate Commerce Commission, and Securities and Exchange Commission), the power to determine interest rates and the flow of money, and so on. But who are the people who wield power in the executive branch of government? The evidence is that they tend to be wealthy businesspeople (Mills, 1956; Domhoff, 1967). The leaders either are rich or they are dependent upon contributions from the wealthy. The important appointees of the president (cabinet members, members of regulatory agencies, Supreme Court justices, ambassadors) most often are executives in the large corporations, corporation lawyers, or bankers. The implication is clear, if Mills was correct, that the linkage between the executive branch and business is very strong and that the leaders in both areas are alike in attitudes and actions because of similar interests.

The Defense Department is dependent upon Congress for money, including the appropriations for new programs. The Defense Department, according to the Constitution, must be headed by a civilian appointed by the president and approved by the Senate. The president is also Commander-in-Chief of the Armed Forces, and the final authority for important policy decisions.

The alliance between the government and the military is not a one-way relationship, however, since Congress and the executive department are influenced in many ways by the military. Frequently, they must rely upon the testimony of military experts, and the assessment of America's spy network determines to a significant degree what course of action the government will take. Furthermore, the Pentagon has thousands of public relations people around the world. Part of their job is to convince the public and governments of the importance of the Pentagon's programs and of the need for new weaponry.

Government officials also are pressured by state and local governments to maintain and/or increase military expenditures in local areas. In fiscal 1988, California had $23.46 billion in military contracts; Virginia, $10.24 billion; and Texas, $9.0 billion. These states were followed by New York with $7.7 billion; Massachusetts, $7.2 billion; and Missouri, $5.51 billion (Schneider, 1989). The other revenues generated locally by military payroll and other expenditures affect all segments of local communities—businesspeople, teachers, homeowners, factory workers, and professionals. Even universities benefit, some very substantially, from military spending. In fiscal 1988, for example, the top seven university recipients of defense contracts were MIT ($403.7 million), Johns Hopkins University ($353.9 million), University of California ($66.3 million), Carnegie Mellon ($50.0 million), Penn State ($46.8), University of Texas ($46.0 million), and Georgia Tech ($41.1 million) (*Chronicle of Higher Education*, 1989:A16). Because so many benefit from military spending one critic of the military-industrial complex, Senator William Proxmire from Wisconsin, suggested that the system should rather be called the "military-industrial-bureaucratic-labor-intellectual-technical-academic complex" (Proxmire, 1970). Proxmire's label indicates the interconnectedness and extent of military dominance in American life.

But while all of these groups exert pressure on governmental officials to continue huge outlays for defense, the greatest coercion comes from business (hence the term "military-industrial complex"). In many respects the military cannot be separated from business. The military needs weapons, ammunition, vehicles, clothing, and other materials. Industries gladly supply them for a profit.* The needs of both are apparently rarely satiated. The military continually seeks more sophisticated weaponry and delivery systems, while industry seeks more contracts and profits.

In the United States, the pressure applied to governmental decision makers by the military has reaped great monetary benefits for large military contractors. Business prospers handsomely because, as we have seen, all the risks of military contract business are underwritten by the taxpayers. Profits are higher than in the competitive consumer market. Because weapon systems rapidly become technologically obsolete, there is a constant demand for new generations of such systems, resulting in endless demand and profit. Finally, each new weapon system is more sophisticated than its predecessor, making weapons production profits escalate (Parenti, 1978:86).

It appears that fear of communism, need for an adequate defense, *and* pressures from the military, local government officials, businessmen, and corporations have helped to keep military budgets very high since World War II. This raises questions about what constitutes an adequate budget for defense. The current Pentagon budget is bigger than those of the Soviet Union and China combined. Moreover, the American stockpile of weapons is capable of killing all of the earth's beings many times over.

But instead of reducing the budget or at least maintaining it at its present level, Congress increases the budget yearly. This growth is due in part to inflation and the costs of an all-volunteer army, but it also results from the Pentagon and its corporate friends seeking larger expenditures for more sophisticated weaponry and delivery systems. For example, the military budget following the U.S. withdrawal from Vietnam *increased.* When President Bush was faced with a thawing of the Cold War early in his presidency, he requested an *increase* in military spending.

The greatest impetus for huge outlays for defense comes from business. The military continually seeks more sophisticated weaponry and delivery systems, while industry seeks more contracts and profit. But why is industry so interested in obtaining governmental contracts? The answer is that producing goods for the military is more profitable, less competitive, and more susceptible to control through lobbying in Washington and other forms of influence than commercial work. For example, the general rule that govern-

---

*The ten companies with the most money from defense contracts in 1987 were McDonnell ($7.7 billion), General Dynamics ($7.0 billion), General Electric ($5.8 billion), Lockheed ($5.6 billion), General Motors ($4.1 billion), Raytheon ($3.8 billion), Martin Marietta ($3.7 billion), United Technologies ($3.6 billion), Boeing ($3.5 billion), and Grumman ($3.4 billion).

ment purchases be made through competitive bids is suspended in most cases for the procurement of military items.

Slightly more than half of Pentagon contracts are awarded *without* competitive bidding. Thus, there is little motivation for a company to keep its bid low, and some contractors make huge profits. In addition to minimal competition, defense contractors receive other benefits from the government, which unnecessarily increases their profits and the cost of the projects. The Pentagon provides all or part of the research and development funds. The contractors often are provided land, buildings, and equipment. Most significant, if a defense contractor has been inefficient, miscalculating, or even fraudulent in its cost estimates, resulting in cost overruns, the government often absorbs all or part of the additional cost.

The willingness of the Pentagon to pay whatever the contractors ask has led to some gross overpricing. For example, in a $1.8 billion contract for nuclear submarines, General Dynamics was alleged to have padded the bills by $544 million (Larsen, 1987). Other examples of extreme overpricing include the following: (1) the Pentagon was billed $9,609 for a simple Allen wrench that would have cost 12 cents in a hardware store; (2) a $1 washerlike spacer cost the Pentagon $9,800 each; and (3) a $5 tool carried a Pentagon price tag of $1,100.

What does it take to get a contract, if it is not being the lowest bidder? The answer is not easy, for there are many possibilities, including superior design, more efficient programs, performance on schedule, and better quality control. Perhaps more important is convincing a few key people in the Pentagon. A good deal of time and money is spent in trying to influence these people. Not the least of these methods is the practice in industry of hiring former military officers. The General Accounting Office found that about 30,000 people with the rank of Army major or higher had left the Pentagon in 1983 and 1984 and more than 6,000 of these persons later worked for companies doing business with the Pentagon (Cushman, 1986).

The defense corporations and the military also curry the favor of powerful legislators by building plants or moving military bases to their districts. When Mendel Rivers, for example, was chairman of the House Armed Services Committee, his district in Charleston, South Carolina, became economically blessed by a naval station, a shipyard, an air base, an army depot, a missile plant, a mine-warfare center, and defense industries that accounted for 60 percent of the economic activity in his district (Etzioni, 1984:106).

The gist of these assertions is that there are tremendous profits to be made in defense contracting, and many, if not most, of the risks are borne by the government. The irony is that this is in opposition to the free-enterprise system. Apparently, U.S. capitalism is, in fact, a form of corporate socialism where very large corporations receive government aid while smaller business ventures must operate on the principle of "survival of the fittest."

Much of Mills's argument seems to fit with the realities of American politics. Certainly the men at the top of the key sectors wield enormous power. The last several decades have seen shifts in this power with the decline of the role of Congress and the rise in military clout.

There are some elements in Mills's thesis, however, that are not consistent with the facts. First, Mills believed that the three subelites that comprise the power elite are more or less equal, with the corporate rich probably having the most power. The equality of these groups is not proved. Certainly, the military seems second-rate compared with the executive branch, Congress, and the large corporations. Military leaders are influential only in their advisory capacities and their ability to convince the executive branch and Congress. What looks like military power is often actually the power of the corporations and/or the executive branch carried out in military terms. In the view of many observers (especially Domhoff, as we see in the next section), the business leaders comprise the real power elite. While this is debatable, the fact is that they far surpass the military in power, and since the executive branch is composed of ex-businesspeople, the logical conclusion is that business interests prevail in that sector as well.

Conflict occurs among the three sectors. There is often bitter disagreement between corporations and the government, between the military and the executive branch, and between the military and some elements in the business community. How is this conflict to be explained if, as Mills contended, the power elite is a group that acts in concert, with joint efforts planned and coordinated to accomplish the agreed-on goals? There is a good deal of empirical evidence that the heads of the three major sectors do *not* comprise a group.

Mills relegates a number of powerful (or potentially powerful) forces to the middle ranges of power. What about the power of pressure groups that represent interests other than business or the military? Certainly organized labor, farmers, professional organizations such as the American Medical Association, and consumers exert power over particular issues. Sometimes business interests even lose. How is this to be explained?

Finally, is Congress only in the "middle level" of the power structure? In Mills' view, Congress is a rubber stamp for the interests of business, the executive branch, and the military. Congress is apparently not composed of "puppets" for these interests, although the laws most often seem to favor these interests. But Congress does have its mavericks, and some of these persons, by virtue of seniority, exert tremendous power (for either the blockage or passage of legislation). Should not the key congressional leaders be included in the power elite? The problem is that they often have interests that do not coincide with those of the presumed "elite."

Power Elite II: Domhoff's "Governing Class" Theory.   While in the Mills view, power is concentrated in a relatively small, cohesive elite, G. William Domhoff's model of power is more broadly based in a "governing class." Domhoff (1983) defined this **"governing class"** as the uppermost social group (approximately 0.5 percent of the population), which owns a disproportionate amount of the country's wealth and contributes a disproportionate number of its members to the controlling institutions and key decision-making groups of the country. This status group is composed mainly of rich businessmen and their families, many of whom are, according to Domhoff's convincing evidence, closely knit through stock ownership, trust funds, intermarriages, private schools, exclusive social clubs, exclusive summer resorts, and corporation boards.

The "governing class" in Domhoff's analysis controls the executive branch of the federal government, the major corporations, the mass media, foundations, universities, and the important councils for domestic and foreign affairs (for example, the Council on Foreign Relations, Committee for Economic Development, National Security Council, National Industrial Conference Board, the Twentieth Century Fund). If they can control the executive branch, this governing class can probably also control the very important regulatory agencies, the federal judiciary, the military, the Central Intelligence Agency, and the Federal Bureau of Investigation.

The "governing class" has greater influence (but not control) than any other group upon Congress and state and local governments. These parts of the formal power structure are not directly controlled by the "governing class" in Domhoff's analysis, but since he claims that such a class controls the executive and judicial branches, the Congress is effectively blocked by two of the three divisions of government. Thus, U.S. foreign and domestic policies are initiated, planned, and carried out by members and organizations of a power elite that serves the interests of an upper class of rich businesspeople. Decisions are made that are considered appropriate for the interests of the United States—a strong economy, an adequate defense, and social stability. While perhaps beneficial to all Americans, policies designed to accomplish these goals especially favor the rich. Consequently, U.S. corporations overseas are protected, foreign trade agreements are made that benefit U.S. corporations, and the tax structure benefits corporations or the very wealthy (by means of allowances for oil depletion, for capital gains and capital losses, for depreciation of equipment, and for other business expenses).

Domhoff has demonstrated in detail the manner in which the governing class interacts (which we have already examined in Chapter 10). Once he established the interlocking ties brought about by common interests and through interaction, he cited circumstances that show the impact of individuals and subgroups within the elite upon the decision-making structure of the United States. To mention a few:

- Control of presidential nominations through the financing of political campaigns: The evidence is clear that unless candidates have large financial reserves or the backing of wealthy persons, they cannot hope to develop a national following or compete in party primaries.
- Control of both major political parties: Even though the Democratic Party is usually considered the party of the common man, Domhoff shows that it, like the Republican Party, is controlled by aristocrats (Parenti, 1982).
- Almost total staffing of important appointive governmental positions (cabinet members, members of regulatory agencies, judges, diplomats, and presidential advisors): These appointees are either members of the upper class or persons who have held positions in the major corporations, and are thereby persons who accord with the wishes of the upper class.

As a result of the circumstances above (and others), all the important foreign and domestic decisions are seen as made by the governing class. Domhoff's view of the power structure is reconstructed graphically in Figure 14–4.

In many ways, Domhoff's model of the U.S. power structure was a refinement of the one posited earlier by Mills. Domhoff's assessment of the power structure was similar to Mills's in that they both: (1) view the power structure as a single pyramid; (2) see the corporate rich as the most powerful interest group; (3) relegate Congress to a relatively minor role and place the executive branch in an important role in the decision-making process; and (4) view the masses as being dominated by powerful forces rather than having much grass-roots power.

The major difference between the views of Mills and Domhoff is that Domhoff has asserted the complete ascendancy of the upper class to the apex of power. The executive branch is controlled by upper-class businesspeople, industrialists, and financiers rather than the two groups being more or less equal partners in the power elite, as Mills saw it. Moreover, the placement of the military in the pyramid of power is quite different. Mills saw the military as part of the alliance of the "troika," while Domhoff saw the military as having much less power and being dominated by the corporate rich through the executive branch.

Figure 14–4
Domhoff's View of the Structure of Power

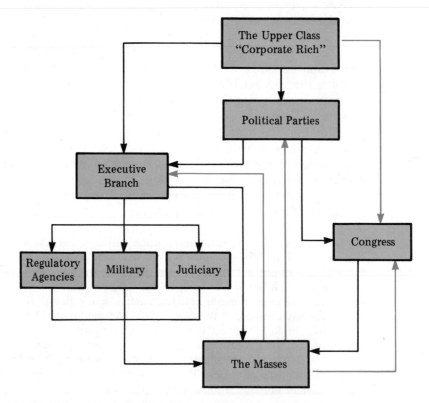

(Legend: black line, control; color line, influence.) This model is based on our interpretation of Domhoff and is therefore subject to minor errors in emphasis.

The graduates of prestigious colleges and universities will take their places in positions of power in the government and the largest corporations.

Domhoff's book is quite persuasive, but there are also several criticisms that should be mentioned. First, much of Domhoff's proof is in the form of listing the upper-class pedigrees of presidential advisors, cabinet members, ambassadors, regulatory agency members, and so on. While persons in these positions are disproportionately from upper-class backgrounds (as evidenced by their attendance at prestige schools, their membership in exclusive social clubs, and their placement in the various social registries), we are given no proof that these persons actually promote the interests of the corporate rich. This is an assumption by Domhoff that appears reasonable, but it is an oversimplification. There is always the possibility of wealthy persons' making decisions on bases other than economics, such as religious or moral altruism or civil rights or human rights. Thus, Domhoff's assumption is one of Marxian economic determinism, and as such is subject to the criticism of oversimplification of a complex process. While an economic motive of some kind may explain a great deal of social behavior, its operation with other prestige factors may be very complex, and it will not explain all of human behavior.

Although Domhoff had denied his belief in an upper-class conspiracy, his books strongly suggest that he does hold this view, at least implicitly. The upper class is shown to get its way either by force or fraud. His chapter on social legislation showed, for example, that workmen's compensation, Social Security, and collective bargaining were accomplished not by pressure from working people, but because the upper class felt it was in their long-range economic interest to pass such seemingly socialistic legislation. Domhoff,

By permission of
Johnny Hart and
News Group
Chicago, Inc.

therefore, viewed the efforts of the upper class (assuming that they indeed form an elite) as only self-seeking, never altruistic. Moreover, the power of labor and other pressure groups in the forming of social legislation was virtually ignored (Domhoff, 1970).

Power Elite III: Parenti's "Bias of the System" Theory (Parenti, 1978, 1988). Commonly we think of the machinery of government as a beneficial force promoting the common good. While the government can be organized for the benefit of the majority, it is never neutral. The state regulates; it stifles opposition; it makes and enforces the law; it funnels information; it makes war on "enemies" (foreign and domestic); and its policies determine how resources are apportioned. And in all of these areas, the government is generally biased toward policies that benefit the wealthy, especially the business community.

Power in the United States is concentrated among those who control the government and the largest corporations (see Dye, 1979). This assertion is based on the assumption that power is not an attribute of individuals but rather of social organizations. The elite in U.S. society is composed of those persons who occupy the power roles in society. The great political decisions are made by the president, the president's advisors, cabinet members, the members of regulatory agencies, the Federal Reserve Board, key members of Congress, and the Supreme Court. The individuals in these government command posts have the authority to make war, raise or lower interest rates, levy taxes, dam rivers, and institute or withhold national health insurance.

Once economic activity was the result of many decisions made by individual entrepreneurs and the heads of small businesses. Now a handful of companies have virtual control over the market place. The decisions by the boards of directors and the management personnel of these huge corporations determine employment and production, consumption patterns, wages and prices, the extent of foreign trade, the rate at which natural resources are depleted, and the like.

The few thousand persons who comprise this power elite tend to come from backgrounds of privilege and wealth. It would be a mistake, however, to equate personal wealth with power. Great power is only manifested through decision making in the very large corporations or in government. We have seen that this elite exercises great power. Decisions are made by the powerful and these decisions tend to benefit the wealthy disproportionately. But the power elite is not organized and conspiratorial.

The interests of the powerful (and the wealthy) are served, nevertheless, because of the way society is organized. This bias occurs in three ways—by their influence over elected and appointed governmental officials at all levels; through systemic imperatives; and through the ideological control of the masses.

As we saw in an earlier section, the wealthy are able to receive favorable treatment by actually occupying positions of power or by having direct influence over those who do. The laws, court decisions, and administrative decisions tend to give the advantage.

More subtly, the power elite can get its way without actually being mobilized at all. The choices of decision makers are often limited by various **systemic imperatives** (the economic and social constraints on decision makers, which promote the status quo). Whoever is in power is constrained in their decision making by tradition and by economic imperatives. There are pressures on the government to do certain things and not to do others. Inevitably, this bias favors the status quo, allowing those with power to continue. For example, no change is always easier than change. The current political and economic systems have worked and generally are not subject to question, let alone change. In this way the laws, customs, and institutions of society resist change. Thus the propertied and the wealthy benefit while the propertyless and the poor continue to be disadvantaged.

In addition to the inertia of institutions, there are other systemic imperatives that benefit the power elite and the wealthy. One such imperative is for the government to strive to provide an adequate defense against our enemies, which stifles any external threat to the status quo. Moreover, this means that Congress, the president, and the masses tend to support large appropriations for defense, which provides extraordinary profit to many corporations. In addition, the government will protect our multinational companies in their overseas operations, which, of course, promotes a healthy and profitable business climate for them. Domestically, government policy is also shaped by the systemic imperative for stability. The government promotes domestic tranquility by squelching dissidence.

Power is the ability to get what one wants from someone else. This can be achieved by force or by getting that someone to think and believe in accordance with your interests. "The ability to control the definition of interests is the ability to define the agenda of issues, a capacity tantamount to winning battles without having to fight them" (Parenti, 1978:41). This is accomplished by the schools, churches, and families in society. The schools, for instance, consciously teach youth that capitalism is the only correct economic system. This is indoctrination with conservative values that achieves a consensus among the citizenry concerning the status quo. In other words, the people tend to accept the system, even though it may work against their interests (false consciousness). Through the very powerful socialization process each of us comes to accept the system, obey the law, favor military solutions, and accept the present arrangements in society because they seem the only options that make sense. Thus, there is a general consensus on what is right—and wrong. In sum, the dominance of the wealthy is legitimized. "The interests of an economically dominant class never stand naked. They are enshrouded in the flag, fortified by the law, protected by the police, nurtured by the media, taught by the schools, and blessed by the church" (Parenti, 1978:84).

Finally, the belief in democracy works to the advantage of the power elite, as Parenti has noted in the following passage:

> As now constituted, elections serve as a great asset in consolidating the existing social order by propagating the appearances of popular rule. History demonstrates that the people might be moved to overthrow a tyrant who shows himself provocatively indifferent to their woes, but they are far less inclined to make war upon a state, even one dominated by the propertied class, if it preserves what Madison called "the spirit and form of popular government." Elections legitimate the rule of the propertied class by investing it with the moral authority of popular consent. By the magic of the ballot, class dominance becomes "democratic" governance. According to the classical theory of democracy, the purpose of suffrage is to make the rulers more responsive to the will of the people. But history suggests the contrary: more often the effect and even the intent of suffrage has been to make the enfranchised group more responsive to the rulers, or at least committed to the ongoing system of rule. In the classical theory, the vote is an exercise of sovereign power, a popular command over the rulers, but it might just as easily be thought of as an act of support extended by the electorate to those above them. Hence, an election is more a *surrender* than an *assertion* of popular power, a gathering up of enpowering responses by the elites who have the resources for such periodic harvestings, an institutionalized mechanism providing for the regulated flow of power from the many to the few in order to legitimate the rule of the few in the name of the many. (Parenti, 1978:201)

THE CONSEQUENCES OF THE NATIONAL POWER STRUCTURE

The way power is concentrated in American society raises the question—who benefits? At times most everyone does, but for the most part, the decisions made tend to benefit the wealthy. Whenever the interests of the wealthy clash with those of other groups or even the majority, the interests of the wealthy are served. As examples, examine carefully how the president and Congress deal with the problems of energy shortages, inflation, or deflation. Who is asked to make the sacrifices? Where is the budget cut—are expenditures for the military reduced or are funds for food stamps slashed? When the Congress considers tax reform, after the roar of rhetoric recedes, which groups benefit by the new legislation or by the laws that are left alone? When a corporation is found guilty of fraud, violation of antitrust laws, bribery, or whatever, what are the penalties? How do they compare with the penalties for crimes committed by poor individuals such as "welfare chiselers," and thieves? When there is an oil spill or other ecological disaster caused by huge enterprise, what are the penalties? Who pays for the cleanup and the restoration of nature? The answers to these questions are obvious—the wealthy benefit at the expense of the less well-to-do. In short, the government is an institution made up of people—the rich and powerful or their agents—who seek to maintain their advantageous positions in society.

Before we examine the bias of the system in the contemporary scene, let's briefly describe its continuation throughout American history (from Parenti, 1983:60–75; Wolfe, 1978:21–50). The government's policy has primarily, although not exclusively, favored the needs of the corporate system.

The Founding Fathers were wealthy members of the upper class. The Constitution they wrote gave the power to people like themselves—property owners (see Panel 14–2). This bias continued throughout the nineteenth century as bankers, railroad entrepreneurs, and manufacturers joined the landed gentry to make the power elite. The shift from local business to large-scale manufacturing during the last half of the nineteenth century saw a concomitant increase in governmental activity in the economy. Business was protected from competition by protective tariffs, public subsidies, price regulation, patents, and trademarks. Throughout that century when there was unrest by troubled miners, farmers, and laborers, the government inevitably took the side of the strong against the weak. The militia and federal troops were used to crush the railroad strikes. Antitrust laws, which were not used to stop the monopolistic practices of business, were invoked against labor unions. President Cleveland's Attorney General, Richard Olney, a millionaire owner of railroad stocks,

> used antitrust laws, court injunctions, mass arrests, labor spies, deputy marshals and federal troops against workers and their unions. From the local sheriff and magistrate to the President and the Supreme Court, the forces of "law and order" were utilized to suppress the "conspiracy" of labor unions and serve "the defensive needs of large capitalist enterprises." (Parenti, 1983:78; see also Josephson, 1938)

The Framers of the Constitution: Plotters or Patriots?

The question of whether the framers of the Constitution were motivated by financial or national interest has been debated ever since Charles Beard published *An Economic Interpretation of the Constitution* in 1913. Beard believed that the "founding fathers" were guided by their class interests. Arguing against Beard are those who say that the framers were concerned with higher things than just lining their purses. True, they were moneyed men who profited directly from policies initiated under the new Constitution, but they were motivated by a concern for nation building that went beyond their particular class interests, the argument goes. To paraphrase Justice Holmes, these men invested their belief to make a nation; they did not make a nation because they had invested. "High-mindedness is not impossible to man," Holmes reminds us.

That is exactly the point: high-mindedness is a common attribute among people even when, or especially when, they are pursuing their personal and class interests. The fallacy is to presume that there is a dichotomy between the desire to build a strong nation and the desire to protect wealth and that the framers could not have been motivated by both. In fact, like most other people, they believed that what was good for themselves was ultimately good for the entire society. Their universal values and their class interests went hand in hand, and to discover the existence of the "higher" sentiment does not eliminate the self-interested one.

Most persons believe in their own virtue. The founders never doubted the nobility of their effort and its importance for the generations to come. Just as many of them could feel dedicated to the principle of "liberty for all" and at the same time own slaves, so could they serve both their nation and their estates. The point is not that they were devoid of the grander sentiments of nation building but that *there was nothing in their concept of nation that worked against their class interest and a great deal that worked for it.*

People tend to perceive issues in accordance with the position they occupy in the social structure; that position is largely—although not exclusively—determined by their class status. Even if we deny that the framers were motivated by the desire for personal gain that moves others, we cannot dismiss the existence of their class interest. They may not have been solely concerned with getting their own hands in the till, although enough of them did, but they were admittedly preoccupied with defending the wealthy few from the laboring many—for the ultimate benefit of all, as they understood it. "The Constitution," as Staughton Lynd noted, "was the settlement of a revolution. What was at stake for Hamilton, Livingston, and their opponents, was more than speculative windfalls in securities; it was the question, what kind of society would emerge from the revolution when the dust had settled, and on which class the political center of gravity would come to rest."

The small farmers and debtors who opposed a central government have been described as motivated by self-serving, parochial interests—unlike

During this time approximately 1 billion acres of land in the public domain (almost one-half the present size of the United States) were given to private individuals and corporations. The railroads in particular were given huge tracts of land as a subsidy. These lands were and continue to be very rich in timber and natural resources.

This active intervention of the government in the nation's economy during the nineteenth century was almost solely on the behalf of business.

The government did exercise laissez-faire in regard to the needs of the common people, giving little attention to poverty, unemployment, unsafe working

the supposedly higher-minded statesmen who journeyed to Philadelphia and others of their class who supported ratification. How or why the wealthy became visionary nation builders is never explained. In truth, it was not their minds that were so much broader but their economic interests. Their motives were neither higher nor lower than those of any other social group struggling for place and power in the United States of 1787. They pursued their material interests as single-mindedly as any small freeholder—if not more so. Possessing more time, money, information, and organization, they enjoyed superior results. How could they have acted otherwise? For them to have ignored the conditions of governance necessary for the maintenance of their enterprises would have amounted to committing class suicide—and they were not about to do that. They were a rising bourgeoisie rallying around a central power in order to protect their class interests. Some of us are quite willing to accept the existence of such a material-based nationalism in the history of other countries, but not in our own.

Finally, those who argue that the founders were motivated primarily by high-minded objectives consistently overlook the fact that the delegates repeatedly stated their intention to erect a government strong enough to protect the haves from the have-nots. They gave voice to the crassest class prejudices and never found it necessary to disguise the fact—as have latter-day apologists—that their uppermost concern was to diminish popular control and resist all tendencies toward class equalization (or "leveling," as it was called). Their opposition to democracy and their dedication to moneyed interests were unabashedly and openly avowed. Their preoccupation with their class interests was so pronounced that one delegate, James Wilson of Pennsylvania, did finally complain of hearing too much about how the sole or primary object of government was property. The cultivation and improvement of the human mind, he maintained, was the most noble object—a fine sentiment that evoked no opposition from his colleagues as they continued about their business.

If the founders sought to "check power with power," they seemed chiefly concerned with restraining mass power, while assuring the perpetuation of their own class power. They supposedly had a "realistic" opinion of the rapacious nature of human beings—readily evidenced when they talked about the common people—yet they held a remarkably sanguine view of the self-interested impulses of their own class, which they saw as inhabited largely by virtuous men of "principle and property." According to Madison, wealthy men (the "minority faction") would be unable to sacrifice "the rights of other citizens" or mask their "violence under the forms of the Constitution." They would never jeopardize the institution of property and wealth and the untrammeled uses thereof, which in the eyes of the framers constituted the essence of "liberty."

Source: Copyright © 1988 by St. Martin's Press, Inc. From *Democracy for the Few,* fifth edition. By Michael Parenti. Reprinted with permission of St. Martin's Press, Inc.

conditions, child labor, and the spoliation of natural resources. (Parenti, 1988:72)*

The early twentieth century was a time of great governmental activity in the economy, which gave the appearance of restraining big business. However, the actual result of federal regulation of business was to increase the power of the largest corporations. The Interstate Commerce Commission, for instance, helped the railroads by establishing common rates to replace ruin-

*Reprinted by permission of the publisher, St. Martin's Press.

ous competition (Huntington, 1965). The federal regulations in meat packing, drugs, banking, and mining weeded out the weaker cost-cutting competitors, leaving a few to control the markets at higher prices and higher profits (Renshaw, 1968). Even the actions of that great "trust-buster," Teddy Roosevelt, were largely ceremonial.

World War I intensified the governmental bias toward business. Industry was converted to war production. Corporate interests became more actively involved in the councils of government. Governmental actions clearly favored business in labor disputes. The police and military were used against rebellious workers because strikers were treated as efforts to weaken the war effort and therefore treasonous.

The New Deal is typically assumed to be a time when the needs of those impoverished by the Great Depression were paramount in government policies. But the central dedication of the Franklin Roosevelt administration was to *business recovery* rather than *social reform* (Renshaw, 1968:85). Business was subsidized by credits, price supports, bank guarantees, stimulation of the housing industry, and the like. Welfare programs were instituted to prevent widespread starvation, but even these humanitarian programs also worked to the benefit of the big business community. The government provided jobs, minimum wages, unemployment compensation, and retirement benefits, which obviously aided those in dire economic straits. But these programs were actually promoted by the business community because of benefits to them. The government and business favored social programs at this time not because millions were in misery but because of the threat of violent political and social unrest. Two social scientists, Piven and Cloward, after a historical assessment of government welfare programs, have determined that the government institutes massive aid to the poor *only* when the poor constitute a threat (Piven and Cloward, 1971a). When large numbers of people are suddenly barred from their traditional occupations, the legitimacy of the system itself may be questioned. Crime, riots, looting, social movements bent on changing the existing social, political, and economic arrangements become more widespread. Under this threat, relief programs are initiated or expanded by the government to diffuse the social unrest. During the Great Depression, Piven and Cloward contend, the government remained aloof from the needs of the unemployed until there was a surge of political disorder. Added proof for Piven and Cloward's thesis is the contraction or even abolishment of public assistance programs when stability is restored.

The historical trend for government to favor business over less powerful interests continues in current public policy. Let's look at some examples.

Subsidies to Big Business

There is a general principle that applies to the government's relationship to big business—business can conduct its affairs either undisturbed by or encouraged by government, whichever is of greater benefit to the business community. The following are some illustrative cases in which governmental decisions benefited business:

- In 1979 the Chrysler Corporation, after sustaining losses of $207 million in the previous year, appealed to the government and received $1.5 billion in loan guarantees. The government's aid to Chrysler is typical—if the company is big enough. Earlier in the 1970s, Penn Central received $125 million when it faced bankruptcy, and the government guaranteed Lockheed $250 million in new bank loans. In other celebrated cases the banking industry and certain large banks have received large sums of government aid. In 1983 the International Monetary Fund was bailed out with $8 billion in federal monies to offset the bad debts incurred by U.S. bank loans to Third World nations. Also, in 1984, when Continental Bank of Illinois was on the brink of bankruptcy, the federal government put together a $7.5 billion rescue package (Parenti, 1988:83). In 1987 the government bailed out two Texas financial concerns—$970 million to Houston's First City Bancorporation and $1.3 billion to Vernon Savings. This bailout of savings and loans was only the beginning as it may cost as much as $500 billion.
- State and local governments provide businesses with a variety of subsidies such as low-interest loans, tax-free financing, subsidized employee training, and tax breaks to entice them to locate in their jurisdictions.
- Quotas are placed on imports of beef, wheat, oil, and other products to protect the profits of American industry.
- A number of major U.S. corporations such as DuPont, General Motors, Ford, Exxon, and ITT owned factories in enemy countries during World War II. These factories produced products for the Axis war effort. "After the war, rather than being prosecuted for trading with the enemy, ITT collected $27 million from the U.S. government for war damages inflicted on its German plants by Allied bombings. GM and Ford subsidiaries built the

Danziger in Used Cartoons © 1988 TCSPS.

bulk of Nazi Germany's heavy trucks which served as 'the backbone of the German Army transportation system.' GM collected more than $33 million in compensation for damages to its war plants in enemy territories. Ford and other multinational corporations collected lesser sums." (Snell, 1974:14–16; see also Di Baggio, 1976; Borkin, 1978; Higham, 1983).

- The federal government directly subsidizes the shipping industry, railroads, airlines, and exporters of iron, steel, textiles, paper, and other products.
- Government-regulated industries such as trucking and railroads result in excess prices and profits. The federal government maintains "prices at noncompetitive, monopolistic levels in 'regulated' areas of the economy at an estimated annual cost of $80 billion to American consumers" (Parenti, 1983:92).
- From 1965 to 1967 several major petroleum companies leased acreage in Alaska for oil exploration, paying $12 million for leases worth at least $2 billion. In another oil lease auction, the companies paid the government $900 million for lands that were expected to be worth some $50 billion within a decade (Parenti, 1983:93).
- The government develops new technologies at public expense and then turns them over to private corporations for their profit. This transfer occurs routinely with nuclear energy, synthetics, space communications, and mineral exploration. For example, taxpayers spent $20 billion to develop the satellite communications system, which was later put under the control of AT&T (in 1982). Similarly, in 1982, two major corporations built a synthetic fuel plant, with the government paying 98 percent of the $4.5 billion cost (Parenti, 1988:83–84). A variation of this government subsidy to business occurs with universities as the linkage. Universities are permitted to sell to companies exclusive licenses on discoveries made under a company's sponsorship. "This adds up to a fat public subsidy for private business. In 1988, the federal government allocated approximately $7 billion to universities for research and development. That same year, corporations bought control of many of the fruits of that research for a puny $750 million" (Bourke, 1989:495).

Perhaps the best illustration of how business benefits from government policies is the fact that corporations pay a much smaller percentage of their income taxes than do individuals. They legally escape much of the tax burden through a number of loopholes (e.g., investment tax credit, accelerated depreciation, and capital gains). Some corporations are able to escape taxes altogether—even when they are profitable—because of these tax subsidies.

Foreign Policy for Corporate Benefit

The operant principle here is that "foreign policy seems to be carried on in the light of the needs of the munitions makers, the Pentagon, the CIA, and the multinational corporations" (Hutchins 1976:4). Several examples make this point. First, military goods are sold overseas for the profit of the arms merchants. Sometimes arms are sold to both sides in a potential conflict, the argument being that if we did not sell them the arms, then the Russians would, so we might as well make the profits.

The government has supported foreign governments that are supportive of American multinational companies regardless of how tyrannical these governments might be. The Reza Shah's government in Iran, Chiang's regime in China, Chung Hee Park's dictatorship in South Korea, and Ferdinand Marcos's rule in the Philippines are four examples of this tendency.

The U.S. government has directly intervened in the domestic affairs of foreign governments to protect American corporate interests. Intervention has occurred routinely in Latin America: Guatemala in 1954, the Dominican Republic in 1962, Chile and Uruguay in 1973, and most recently, Nicaragua. As Parenti has characterized it:

> Sometimes the sword has rushed in to protect the dollar, and sometimes the dollar has rushed in to enjoy the advantages won by the sword. To make the world safe for capitalism, the United States government has embarked on a global counterrevolutionary strategy, suppressing insurgent peasant and worker movements throughout Asia, Africa, and Latin America. But the interests of the corporate elites never stand naked; rather they are wrapped in the flag and coated with patriotic appearances. (Parenti, 1988:94)*

The Powerless Pay the Burden

Robert Hutchins, in his critique of American governmental policy, characterized the basic principle guiding internal affairs as: "Domestic policy is conducted according to one infallible rule: the costs and burdens of whatever is done must be borne by those least able to bear them" (Hutchins, 1976:4). Let's review several examples of this.

When threatened by war the government institutes a military draft. A careful analysis of the draft reveals that it is really a "tax on the poor." During the height of the Vietnam War, for instance, only 10 percent of men in college were drafted, although 40 percent of draft-age men were in college. Even for those educated young men who ended up in the armed services, there was a greater likelihood of their serving in noncombat jobs than for the non-college-educated. Thus, the chances for getting killed while in the service were about three times greater for the less educated than for the college educated (Zeitlin, Lutterman, and Russell, 1977; Baskir and Strauss, 1978). Even more blatant was the practice that occurred legally during the Civil War. The law at that time allowed the affluent who were drafted to hire someone to take their place in the service.

The poor, being powerless, can be made to absorb the costs of societal changes. In the nineteenth century the poor did the back-breaking work that built the railroads and the cities. Today they are the ones pushed out of their homes by urban renewal, the building of expressways, parks, and stadia (Gans, 1971).

The government's attempts to solve economic problems generally obey the principle that the poor must bear the burden. A common "solution" for runaway inflation, for example, is to increase the amount of unemployment.

---

*Reprinted by permission of the publisher, St. Martin's Press.

Domestic and International Terrorism

There can be no doubt that terrorism will continue into the next century. It is the primary way in which the weak and disenfranchised can ensure that their voices will be heard and that governments will feel the pressure to meet their demands, even when they are counter to the will of the majority. It is a war of psychology and perception. The terrorist's message to the targeted government is, "No matter how big and powerful you are, no matter how small we are, we can hurt you if you don't do what we want." . . . [Modern terrorists have a new range of weapons]:

- **Stinger hand-held rockets.** Small, light, and powerful, Stingers can be used—with almost no training—to knock out an airplane.
- **Computer viruses.** Viruses are programs that destroy data stored in a computer's memory. It is relatively easy for a programmer to write a program that will tell the computer to erase its memory or otherwise render its programs useless. What makes these viruses so hard to trace is that they often contain timing instructions, so that it might be months between the time a virus is introduced and the time it is triggered. The programmer simply embeds the codes into an otherwise harmless program, then tries to get the program into a victim's computer.
- **Electromagnetic pulse generators.** Put a pulse generator on the power line to an important computer, and the pulse will wipe out the data in the computer's memory.

- **Chemical and biological weapons.** Chemical weapons range from old-fashioned poison in the water and nerve gas to a new Liquid Metal Embrittlement agent (LME). Applied with a felt-tip type pen, LME is a clear, invisible substance that changes the chemical structure of a metal so that it is no longer resilient and flexible. The result: The metal can fracture under stress. Trucks, airplanes, or bridges would be vulnerable to catastrophic failure without advance warning. . . .
- **Nuclear weapons.** Technically, it is horrifyingly easy to produce an atomic bomb: Actual plans for building a bomb have been printed several times. The hardest part is obtaining the teaspoonful of weapons-grade plutonium that will produce an explosion the size of that produced by the Hiroshima bomb. Nuclear energy plants produce this substance as waste material. Though waste-storage sites and transports are closely guarded, there is at least 100 pounds of plutonium missing from various sites and shipments around the world. That's not very much over the course of the 40+ years since the development of nuclear power, but it means that it is possible that there are terrorists in possession of both the knowledge and the materials to build atomic bombs.

THE COMING RISE IN DOMESTIC TERROR

The biggest change in low-intensity conflict in the next decade will be an explosion in the inci-

Of course the poor, especially minorities (whose rate of unemployment is consistently twice the rate for whites), are the ones who make the sacrifice for the economy. This "solution," aside from being socially cruel, is economically ineffective because it ignores the real sources of inflation—excessive military spending, excessive profits by energy companies (foreign and domestic), and administered prices set by shared monopolies, which, contrary to classical economic theory, do not decline during economic downturns (Harrington, 1979).

More fundamentally a certain level of unemployment is maintained continuously, not just during economic downturns. Genuine full employment for

dence of domestic terror in the United States. Security measures currently in place around the world will help slow the spread of international terrorism, but the frustrated in the United States will begin to take their cue from terrorists abroad. Some of the groups that have already begun terrorist-type actions include:

- **Antiabortionists.** Planned Parenthood offices and women's health clinics that offer abortion have already been bombed. Attacks will get worse because religious groups believe that God's law puts them above civil law and other people's rights.
- **Drug dealers.** Terrorism by drug dealers will aim at breaking the resistance of city and state governments and law enforcement agencies. It will be sponsored by organized crime and "disorganized crime"—the kind of crazed violence observed in crack users that stuns those who haven't seen it. The methods may be inspired by the international terrorists, but the organized-crime armies have been trained and weaned in Colombian drug wars.

    The U.S. government can muster tremendous resources to fight terrorism within its borders, and national leaders have always had to deal with threats from other countries. Few city mayors or state governments, however, are psychologically prepared or fiscally and strategically able to deal with sustained pressure from terrorism.

- **Counterterror from the right.** In Colombia, people who got tired of police inability to

deal with terrorism have formed death squads to "help out" the police. The same thing could happen in the United States. . . .

U.S. law enforcement authorities will have their hands full coping with the new tide of domestic terrorism in the next century. Swamped by this flood of stateside terrorism, local governments and police forces will press the federal government to enact laws that allow extraordinary measures to be taken in certain situations. The new legislation will define terrorism and clarify the duties of federal and state authorities. Meanwhile, the decriminalization of drugs will take away the motivation for drug merchants to conduct a terrorist war against law enforcement authorities. After a number of attacks on industrial sites, the United States will finally get smart and post security forces around computer centers, reservoirs, electrical power stations, and phone switching stations.

Make no mistake about it: Terrorism is here to stay because it is still a useful tool for conveying an old message. It will take 10 to 15 years before the United States can get its act together to end the new terrorism. In the meantime, the best remedy against future terrorism is better preparation now: The United States must prepare psychologically, socially, and militarily. Security systems in the public and private sectors must be rethought—and hard questions about laws and theories of justice must be asked.

Source: Marvin J. Cetron, "The Growing Threat of Terrorism," *The Futurist* 23 (July/August 1989): 20–24. Reprinted by permission of the publisher.

all job seekers is a myth. But why, since all political candidates extol the work ethic and it is declared national policy to have full employment? Economist Robert Lekachman (1979) has argued that it is no accident that we tolerate millions of unemployed persons. The reason is that a "moderate" unemployment rate is beneficial to the affluent. Among these benefits are: (1) people are willing to work at humble tasks for low wages; (2) the children of the middle and upper classes avoid the draft as the unemployed join the volunteer army; (3) the unions are less demanding; (4) workers are less likely to demand costly safety equipment; (5) corporations do not have to pay their share of taxes because local and state governments give them concessions to lure them to their area; and (6) the existing wide differentials between white males and the various powerless categories such as females, teenagers, Hispanics, and blacks are retained.

"Trickle Down" Solutions

Periodically the government is faced with the problem of finding a way to stimulate the economy during an economic downturn. One way to accomplish this goal is to spend federal monies through unemployment insurance, government jobs, and housing subsidies. In this way the funds go directly to those most hurt by shortages, unemployment, inadequate housing, and the like. Opponents of such plans advocate that the subsidies should go directly to business, which would help the economy by encouraging companies to hire more workers, add to their inventories, and build new plants. Thus, by subsidizing business in this way, the advocates argue, everyone benefits. To provide subsidies to businesses rather than directly to needy individuals is based on the assumption that private profit maximizes the public good.

There are two possible reasons government officials tend to opt for these "trickle down" solutions. First, because they tend to come from the business class, government officials believe in the conservative ideology that says what is good for business is good for America. The second reason for the pro-business choice is that government officials are more likely to hear arguments from the powerful. Since the weak, by definition, are not organized, their voice is not heard or, if heard, not taken seriously in decision-making circles.

Although the government most often opts for "trickle-down" solutions, such plans are not very effective in fulfilling the promise that benefits will trickle down to the poor. The higher corporate profits generated by tax credits and other tax incentives do not necessarily mean that companies will increase wages or hire more workers. What is more likely is that corporations will increase dividends to the stockholders, which further exacerbates the existing problem of the maldistribution of resources. Job creation is also not guaranteed because companies may use their newly acquired wealth to purchase labor-saving devices. If so, then the government programs will actually have widened the gulf between the "haves" and the "have-nots."

In summary, this view of power argues that the power of wealthy individuals and the largest corporations is translated into public policy that disproportionately benefits the power elite. Throughout American history there has been a bias that pervades government and its policies. This bias is perhaps best seen in the aphorism once enunciated by President Calvin Coolidge and repeated by President Reagan: "The business of America is business."

CONCLUSION

Power is unequally distributed in all social organizations. In our examination of the structure of power at the societal level, two basic views were presented—the pluralist and the elitist. The former is consistent with the world view of order theorists, while the latter is congruent with the way conflict theorists perceive reality (see Table 14–1).

One glaring weakness of many pluralists and elitists is that they are not objective. Their writings tend often to be polemics because so much effort is spent attempting to prove what they believe is the nature of the power structure. The evidence is presented so as to ensure the absolute negation of the opposite stance. This points to a fundamental research problem. Are the data reliable? Are our observations distorted by bias? Sociologists or political scientists are forced in the study of power to rely on either the perceptions of others (who are presumed to be knowledgeable) or their own observations, which are distorted by not being present during all aspects of the decision-making process. Unfortunately, one's perceptions are also affected by one's model (conflict or order). Ideological concerns often cause either faulty perceptions or a rigidity of thought that automatically rejects conflicting evidence.

The task for sociologists is to determine the real distribution of power with our ideological distortion. Given these problems with objectivity, we must ask ourselves: (1) What is the power structure really like? (2) What facts are consonant with the pluralist model and what facts fit the elitist model? With these questions in mind, let us enumerate some conditions of societies that affect the distribution of power.

All societies are composed of different segments. The bases for segmentation may be sex, age, race, religion, physical prowess, social class, occupational specialty, or special interest. The extent of segmentation and the degree of competition among such groups are variables. It is safe to assume that most segmented parts of a society would hope for and work toward greater power (and therefore advantage) in that society (although some may not if they have been socialized to accept their role and to accept that attempts to change it would bring serious religious or other sanctions).

Table 14–1
Assumptions of the Order and Conflict Models about Politics

Order Model	Conflict Model
1. People in positions of power occupy bureaucratic roles necessary for the rational accomplishment of society's objectives.	1. People in positions of power are motivated largely by their own selfish interests.
2. The state works for the benefit of all. Laws reflect the customs of society and ensure order, stability, and justice—in short, the common good.	2. The state exists for the benefit of the ruling class (law, police, and courts protect the interests of the wealthy).
3. Pluralism: (1) competing interest groups; (2) majority rule; (3) power is diffused.	3. Power is concentrated (power elite).

The second basic condition of societies is that they all require some coordination among the various segments. The more complex the society, the greater the problem of coordination. Complex societies also require rapid decision making. Both of these requirements—rapid decision making and coordination—mean that decision making *must* be concentrated in a few persons. It is an empirical question as to whether power is concentrated in one or several elites or whether the "people" retain power while not actually making most decisions.

Finally, the degree of power centralization is a variable. The logical range is from absolute equality of all individuals and groups on the one hand to total power in one person or group on the other. All societies are found somewhere between these two extremes. Various factors affect change in the degree of power centralization. As Mills noted, World War II and the Cold War were important factors giving increased power to the executive branch and the military sector of American society. Force and fraud may also be used by certain individuals and groups to increase their power.

These conditions are accepted by elitists and pluralists. Where both of these theorists go wrong is in their distorted interpretations of the real world. Let us examine the *real* situation which, hopefully, will aid in the formulation of a more realistic view of the power structure. First, what is there about the elitist position that fits reality?

- The executive branch has a tremendous amount of power, particularly in foreign affairs. Congress has tried to reassert its historic role, but the executive branch continues to have great power in this area. Some examples are: sending the military forces to various places, fighting undeclared wars, diplomatic decisions, and CIA activities.
- There is no question but that the wealthy in America have great influence in Congress and in the executive branch. This influence is accomplished through campaign contributions, control of the political parties, occasional bribes, and through being either elected or appointed to high offices. It is also fair to say that American foreign and domestic policy is, for the most part, based on the assumption that if business interests benefit, all Americans benefit.
- Even if there are a number of different sectors of power present (the pluralist position), the leaders of each are almost universally wealthy, members of the establishment who more or less favor the status quo. This is true, for example, in industry, in banking, for labor, and for the farm bloc. Because of great wealth they probably have some interests in common (the economic status quo, an adequate defense system, protecting U.S. interests abroad, and an expanding economy).

What is there about the pluralist position that fits reality?

- There are many separate power structures. Each operates generally within its own sphere of influence—the AFL-CIO in labor, the AMA in medicine, the NEA in public education, the NAM for large business concerns, and so forth. Each tries to influence Congress and the executive branch on issues affecting it. Within each of these domains there is a hierarchy of power. A powerful elite then makes decisions and in other ways influences its public (and this influence is often reciprocal).

- The various power structures are unequal in power. The economic elite is the most powerful. But there are shifting coalitions that may at times effectively counterbalance the unequal power of the corporate rich. Or one group may band with the corporate rich against some other coalition.
- Pressure groups exert a tremendous influence on decision making. They may be organized or diffuse, but they can and do bring change. Blacks, migrant workers, young people, the aged, consumers, have by individual and collective efforts caused a shift in policy on occasion.

A realistic view of the power structure must incorporate the valid points mentioned above from both pluralistic and elitist views. The resulting model of power hinges on the empirical answer to the basic question: how democratic is the political process in U.S. society?

CHAPTER REVIEW

1. In answering the question: Who are the real power wielders in American society? there are two contrasting answers from pluralists and elitists.

2. The "representative democracy" version of pluralism emphasizes that the people have the ultimate power. The people elect representatives who are responsive to the people's wishes. This version ignores the many instances in which the people have been deliberately misled by their leaders, secrecy, and the undemocratic manner in which election campaigns are funded.

3. The "veto groups" version of pluralism recognizes the existence of a number of organizations and special interest groups that vie for power. There is a balance of power, however, with no one sector getting its way. The groups tend to neutralize each other resulting in compromise. Critics of this view of power argue that it is an idealized version that ignores reality. The interest groups are not equal in power. Power does not shift from issue to issue. Also, at the apex of each of the competing groups are members of the upper class, suggesting the possibility of a power elite.

4. C. Wright Mills's view of power is that there is a power elite composed of the top people in the executive branch of the federal government, the military, and the corporate sector. Although these persons represent different interests they

tend to perceive the world alike because of their similar social class backgrounds and similar role expectations; because they interact socially; because their children go to the same schools and intermarry; and because they share similar interests. There is considerable evidence for the linkages among these three sectors. There are some problems with this view, however. The equality of these three groups is not a fact. There is conflict among the three sectors. There are other sectors of power that are ignored.

5. G. William Domhoff's view of power is that there is a governing class—the uppermost social class. The very rich control the nation's assets, control the corporations, are overrepresented in the key decision-making groups in society, and through contributions and activities they control both major political parties. The major criticism of this view is that while the people in key positions tend to have upper-class pedigrees, there is no evidence that these people actually promote the interests of the corporate rich.

6. Michael Parenti's "bias of the system" view is another elitist theory. The powerful in society (those who control the government and the largest corporations) tend to come from backgrounds of privilege and wealth. Their decisions tend to benefit the wealthy disproportionately, but the power elite is not organized and conspiratorial. The interests of the wealthy are served, neverthe-

less, by the way society is organized. This bias occurs by their influence over elected and appointed officials, systemic imperatives, and through the ideological control of the masses.

7. The pluralist model of power is congruent with the order model: (a) People in powerful positions work for the accomplishment of society's objectives; (b) The state works for the benefit of all; and (c) Power is diffused through competing interest groups.

8. The elitist model of power fits with the conflict model: (a) People in powerful positions are motivated largely by selfish interests; (b) The state exists for the benefit of the ruling class; and (c) Power is concentrated in a power elite.

9. Neither the pluralists nor the elitists have the correct vision of the power structure. A realistic view of the power structure must incorporate the valid points of each model.

KEY TERMS

Elitist view of power
Pluralist view of power
Democracy

Power elite
Governing class

Systemic imperatives
Power

STUDY QUESTIONS

1. How does the way political campaigns are financed have undemocratic consequences?
2. Summarize the three variations of the conflict view of politics by Mills, Domhoff, and Parenti. Which variation most closely approximates politics in contemporary United States? Why? Or, alternatively, is each variation incorrect? If so, why?

3. How have government decisions tended to increase the gap between the "haves" and the "have-nots"?
4. What is your reaction to Panel 14–2? In short, were the framers of the Constitution providing a document that would insure the advantage of their social class or was their primary concern democracy?

FOR FURTHER READING

Paul A. Baran and Paul M. Sweezy, *Monopoly Capital* (New York: Monthly Review Press, 1968).

Ronald Brownstein and Nina Easton, *Reagan's Ruling Class* (New York: Pantheon, 1983).

Center for Popular Economics, *Economic Report of the People* (Boston: South End Press, 1986).

Kenneth M. Dolbeare, *Democracy at Risk: The Politics of Economic Renewal*, Revised Edition (Chatham, NJ: Chatham House, 1986).

G. William Domhoff, *Who Rules America Now: A View for the '80s* (Englewood Cliffs, NJ: Prentice-Hall, 1983).

Amitai Etzioni, *Capital Corruption: The New Attack on American Democracy* (New York: Harcourt Brace Jovanovich, 1984).

Martin N. Marger, *Elites and Masses: An Introduction to Political Sociology,* 2nd ed. (Belmont, CA: Wadsworth, 1987).

C. Wright Mills, *The Power Elite* (New York: Oxford University Press, 1956).

Marvin E. Olsen (ed.), *Power in Societies* (New York: Macmillan, 1970).

Michael Parenti, *Power and the Powerless* (New York: St. Martin's, 1978).

Philip M. Stern, *The Best Congress Money Can Buy* (New York: Pantheon, 1988).

Howard Zinn, *A People's History of the United States* (New York: Harper and Row, 1980).

Chapter Fifteen

Families

*T*he American family does not exist, rather we are creating many American families, of diverse styles and shapes. In unprecedented numbers, our families are unalike: we have fathers working while mothers keep house; fathers and mothers both working away from home; single parents; second marriages bringing children together from unrelated backgrounds; childless couples, unmarried couples, with and without children; gay and lesbian parents. We are living through a period of historic change in American family life.

The upheaval is evident everywhere in our culture. Babies have babies, kids refuse to grow up and leave home, affluent Yuppies prize their BMWs more than children, rich and poor children alike blot their minds with drugs, people casually move in with each other and out again. The divorce rate has doubled since 1965, and demographers project that half of all first marriages made today will end in divorce. Six out of 10 second marriages will probably collapse. One-third of all children born in the past decade will probably live in a stepfamily before they are 18. One out of every four children today is being raised by a single parent. About 22 percent of children today were born out of wedlock; of those, about a third were born to a teenage mother. One out of every five children lives in poverty; the rate is twice as high among blacks and Hispanics.

Most of us are still reeling from the shock of such turmoil. Americans—in their living rooms, in their boardrooms and in the halls of Congress—are struggling to understand what has gone wrong. We find family life worse than it was a decade ago, . . . and we are not sanguine about the next decade. An astonishing two thirds of all mothers are in the labor force, roughly double the rate in 1955, and more than half of all mothers of infants are in the work force.

Parents feel torn between work and family obligations. Marriage is a fragile institution—not something anyone can count on. Divorce has left a devastated generation in its wake, and for many youngsters, the pain is compounded by poverty and neglect. While politicians and psychologists debate cause and solution, everyone suffers. Even the most traditional of families feel an uneasy sense of emotional dislocation. Three decades ago the mother who kept the house spotless and cooked dinner for her husband and children each evening could be confident and secure in her role. Today, although her numbers are still strong—a third of mothers whose children are under 18 stay home—the woman who opts out of a paycheck may well feel defensive, undervalued, as though she were too incompetent to get "a real job." And yet the traditional family retains a profound hold on the American imagination.*

Source: Jerold K. Footlick, "What Happened to the Family?" From *Newsweek,* 1990 Special Edition, © 1990, Newsweek, Inc. All rights reserved. Reprinted by permission.

American families are in flux. Social changes are creating upheavals in our families, and these changes have led to concerns about the demise of the family. When we understand the social context within which families exist, we are better able to make sense of family changes.

This chapter examines the family as a social institution and relates families to society as a whole. Families in the United States are diverse, with regional, social class, religious, racial, and ethnic differences; nonetheless, distinct patterns can be found in family life. The connections between family and society is revealed as we describe with broad brush strokes family life in past times. The theme of the chapter is that families are not isolated units free from outside constraints but that social forces outside the family affect life inside families.

THE MYTHICAL AMERICAN FAMILY

Family life is difficult to think about objectively. Our perceptions are clouded by our own family experiences, by cultural ideals about family, and paradoxically, by the very familiarity of family life. Because the family is familiar, we tend to take it for granted, to view it as "natural." Other obstacles have handicapped the study of the family: "It is morally sacred, and it is secret," (Skolnick, 1983:33). The family is not merely a social institution, it is associated with a larger societal morality of good and right. It is, at the same time, the most private of all society's institutions. The norm of privacy gives the family a secret quality that exists alongside its familiarity. To a greater extent than ever before, family life goes on behind closed doors (Laslett, 1977). The family is a "backstage" area where people can be relaxed and behave in ways they would not in public (Goffman, 1959). According to Arlene Skolnick, this privacy accounts for the deceptive quality of family life:

> Privacy results in pluralistic ignorance—we have a backstage view of our own families, but can judge others only in terms of public presentation. The gap between public norms and private behavior can be wide; marital relationships tend to be even more private and invisible than those between parents and children. (Skolnick, 1979:300)

We have little direct knowledge of what goes on behind closed doors, but we do know what family life *should* be. "Family" in American society is a symbol, a visual image of adults and children living together in mutually satisfying and harmonious ways. Family evokes warmth, caring, physical and psychological nurturance in a setting apart from the troubled world. Tufte and Meyerhoff have described the image of the contemporary family in the following way:

> It is quintessentially the private (and some feel the only contemporary private) opportunity for vulnerability, trust, intimacy, and commitment, for lasting, pleasant and peaceful relations, for fullness of being in the human realm. The family thus is located as the physical site for a vast (and repressed) range of human expression, the valid arena (and again perhaps the only arena) where quality of life is a concern. It is in the family that we find the opportunity for psychologically bearable, nonexploitive personal life. (Tufte and Meyerhoff, 1979:17–18)

This image characterizes the family as a refuge from an impersonal world, a place of intimacy, love, and trust where individuals may escape the competition of dehumanizing forces in modern society. Lasch (1977) named this image a "haven in a heartless world," and described it as a glorification of private life made necessary by the deprivations experienced in the public world. In this image, family and society are set apart. Relations inside the family are idealized as nurturant while those outside the family, especially in business and work, are seen as competitive.

Relationships between husbands and wives and between parents and children are especially idealized in the family image. The ideal states that families are formed in the marriage of one man and one woman who will satisfy each other's emotional and physical needs till death do them part. When children are added to this exclusive dyad, then "parenting" becomes the natural extension of the husband and wife relationship. Parents mold and shape happy children (who will become successful adults) by providing "proper" child care (Birdwhistell, 1980).

This view assumes a division of labor based on sex: "a breadwinner husband, freed for and identified with activities in a separate sphere, and a full-time mother defines as the core of the family" (Thorne, 1982:4). It also assumes a single uniform family experience for all members of society. This image of the family is mythical in many respects.

To begin, full-time homemakers are found in few families. Now, more women work outside the home than do not, and dual-earner families outnumber traditional families two to one. In 1987, only 10 percent of families had a working husband, a full-time housewife, and one or more children. Divorced, separated, widowed, and never-married persons head 13 million families (one out of every five) in the United States. Four out of these five are headed by a woman. Six percent of all women expect never to have children, about 5 to 10 percent of the U.S. population will never marry, and about 12 percent of adults live alone. Thus, the living arrangements of more than 90 percent of all households differ from the traditional family form (Levitan, et al., 1988:8).

And what of the "perpetually happy family" set apart from the harsh realities of the world? This myth ignores the persistent effects of economic conditions (e.g., poverty or near poverty, unemployment or underemployment, downward mobility or the threat of downward mobility). It ignores the social inequalities (racism, sexism, ageism) that prevent certain kinds of people from experiencing the good things in life. And this erroneous view masks the inevitable problems that arise in intimate settings (tensions, anger, and even violence in some instances).

The popular wisdom that we are witnessing a breakdown of the family is based on a mythical family of the past. Part of this myth holds that there were three generations living under one roof or in close proximity. The reality of past family life was quite different. Families of the past were not necessarily more stable or more harmonious than families of the present. Desertion by spouses, the presence of illegitimate children, and the existence of other conditions that are considered "modern" problems existed in the past as well—and the image of the three-generational family is also a false stereotype. Few examples of this "classical family of western nostalgia" (Goode, 1983:43) have been found by family historians.

Whereas we once assumed that there was a prevailing type of family in different periods of history, new research has discovered that factors such as economics, race, and demographics have always produced diversity in family patterns.

FAMILIES IN CONTEMPORARY AMERICAN SOCIETY

The Family in Capitalism

The historical development of the family in the United States shows an interrelationship with the economic structure of society. Industrialization with the development of capitalism moved the center of production from the domestic unit to the workplace. Men went off to earn a wage in factories and offices while women remained in the home to nurture their children. When the workplace became separated from the home, the family became a private domain, and the modern family type emerged.

The modern family is characterized by its dependence on the economic market, its privacy, and its sharply divided gender system. Zaretsky (1976) has shown how in capitalism the split between work and home is related to another split—one between personal life and public life. The development of subjective and personal realms encourages consumerism. The pursuit of personal life becomes a central purpose of the modern family. It is now an emotional retreat—a specialized institution focusing on the socialization of young children and the stabilization of adult personalities through identity and emotional gratification.

The separation of public and private worlds creates yet another division—division between women's and men's roles and activities. Women are identified with family roles of consumption, emotional support, and child care while men are identified with "public" activities. This patriarchal ordering is suited to the capitalist economy. Capitalism depends on the maintenance of labor power. The domestic labor and emotional work that women do in families enables male workers to function in a capitalist economy.

The emergence of the breadwinner–homemaker pattern is an important development, but it has been a distinctly white middle-class phenomenon. It has never applied to immigrants and people of color who have rarely been afforded opportunities to earn a family wage. Research has found that people deprived of resources by society have often used their families to adapt to adversities and to changing social conditions.

As the nation's economy industrialized, wave after wave of immigrants filled the industrial labor force. Through working for wages, they became an integral part of the economy and society. Immigrant families were crucial in assisting their newly arrived kin and other members of their ethnic groups to adapt to the new society. Many immigrants came to America in family groupings or they sent for families once they were established in cities. Kin assisted in locating jobs and housing and providing other forms of support. Contrary to the typical portrayal of immigrants, their transplanted kinship and ethnic bonds did not disintegrate, but rather were maintained and regenerated in the new society (see Vecoli 1964; Early, 1983).

The developing capitalist economy did not provide equal opportunities for all. People of color were prevented from becoming part of the industrial labor force by a complex web of forces called *internal colonialism* (see Chapter 11) (Blauner, 1972). Blacks and Chicanos were forced to be laborers in nonindustrial sectors of the economy. They were brought to this society to work in unfree, unskilled labor systems that were tightly controlled. Slavery destroyed West African kinship systems and assaulted the families that developed among the slaves by breaking them up when it suited the owners' economic interests. Chicano families, on the other hand, were adversely affected by migratory labor, but they were able to retain considerable strength due to different, less-total forms of control and the proximity to their native land. In both cases, systems of racial control shaped much of family life. In neither case was the family institution destroyed.

The family in contemporary society is an ideal that implies a private, autonomous retreat set apart from society. This image obscures the real relationship between families and the economy. A better way of understanding the interconnection is to distinguish between family and household. A **family** involves blood ties among husbands, wives, and children; a household is a material or economic unit (Andersen, 1983b:114). The **household** is a unit in which people pool resources and perform certain tasks. "They are units of production, reproduction, and consumption. They are residential units within which people and resources get distributed and connected" (Rapp, 1982:170). Households vary in membership, composition, and the resources they have for living, a fact not recognized by the concept "family." "Family" implies a single form, but the reality of household diversity enables us to see how families exist within an economic system.

The Changing Composition of Households and Families

Households are defined by the census bureau as taking one of three general forms: family, **nonfamily,** and **single-person households.** First, family households consist of two or more persons living together who are related by birth or marriage. The most common family household is a married couple with or without children in the home. A single parent with one or more children also comprises a family household. Second, nonfamily households consist of two or more unrelated individuals who share living quarters. They can be non-married couples, of the same or opposite sex. Third, single-person households are individuals who live alone in their own separate residential units (Hacker, 1983:93).

Over the years, U.S. households have changed in several important ways. Households have become smaller and less complex, and there has been a trend toward independent living among young unmarried persons, the elderly, and mothers with no current spouse (Thornton and Freedman, 1983:29). Between now and the year 2000, households made up of married couples will increase only slightly in number, while other types of households will increase dramatically. Fewer households will have children present. No one household arrangement will be "typical." Instead, a very diverse world of households, families, and individual life histories is emerging (Masnick and Bane, 1980:4–9). Figure 15–1 highlights predicted shifts in American households as we move toward the year 2000. Two changes deserve special attention: (1) the increase in the number of families with employed wives, and (2) the increase in the number of families headed by women.

More than half (56 pecent) of all married women were in the labor force in 1987 compared with 40 percent in 1972 (U.S. Department of Labor, 1988). The increase in women's labor force participation has had major effects on family life. It has lowered birth rates and provided women with economic resources that must often be balanced with traditional domestic responsibilities.

The large increase in the number of families headed by women is one of the most important social developments of the recent past. In 1970, female-headed families were 10 percent of all families. Divorce, separation, and premarital births have *doubled* the proportion of single-parent households in

Figure 15–1
Census Figures Predict Shift in Household Composition

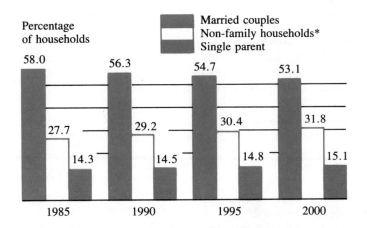

Census Bureau as used in Paul Clancy, "Census Figures Predict Shift in Household Composition," *U.S.A. Today.* (May 29, 1986):3–A. Copyright, 1986 *USA Today.* Reprinted with permission.

the past fifteen years. In 1987, almost 11 million families were headed by women. These families accounted for nearly 17 percent of all families in the United States, compared with 13 percent in 1975. There were proportionately more female-headed families in the black population than in any other category. By 1987, women headed 42.3 percent of black families, 23.9 percent of Hispanic families, and 13.5 percent of white families (U.S. Department of labor, 1988).

There is a clear relationship between the household composition and its economic well-being. Women with children but no husband lack the economic resources of dual-earner families. The earnings gap found in all occupations makes female-headed households especially vulnerable. Table 15–1 depicts the low median income of female householders when compared to husband-wife families.

Stratification and Family Life

In previous chapters, we have examined the structures of inequality that distribute resources and rewards. These hierarchies of stratification—class, race, and gender—"place" families and individuals in the larger society, and they produce distinctive patterns in family living. In this section, we examine the effects of social class on families in the United States.

Families are embedded in a class hierarchy. Furthermore, the family is the principal unit in the social class system. Most children will have the same life chances as their parents. The "haves" will pass on their advantages to their children, and likewise, the "have-nots" will transmit their disadvantages to their offspring. A family's placement in the class system is the single most important determinant of family life.

Table 15–1
Median Income by Race and Type of Family (1987)

	Median Income
All Races	
Married couple families	$34,700
Wife in labor force	40,422
Male householder, no wife present	24,804
Female householder, no husband present	14,620
White	
Married couple families	$35,295
Wife in labor force	41,023
Male householder, no wife present	26,230
Female householder, no husband present	17,018
Black	
Married couple families	$27,182
Wife in labor force	33,333
Male householder, no wife present	17,455
Female householder, no husband present	9,710
Hispanic	
Married couple families	$24,677
Wife in labor force	31,354
Male householder, no wife present	19,411
Female householder, no husband present	9,805

Source: Department of Commerce, U.S. Bureau of the Census. "Money, Income and Poverty Status of Families and Persons in the U.S." *Current Population Reports,* P–60, No. 161 (March 1988).

Households in different classes, Rapp says, "vary systematically in their ability to hook into, accumulate, and transmit wealth, wages, or welfare" (Rapp, 1982:170). This variation is closely related to the connections that households and families have with other social institutions. The social networks or relationships outside the family—at work, school, church, voluntary associations—produce differential access to society's resources, and they produce class and racial differences in families.

Among the middle class, households are based on a relatively stable and secure resource base. Therefore, according to Rapp, the

> families that organize such households have boundaries that conform closely to the nuclear family ideal of autonomy and self-support. When exceptional economic resources are called for, nonfamilial institutions usually are available in the form of better medical coverage, expense accounts, credit at banks, and so on. (Rapp, 1982:181)

These links with nonfamily institutions are precisely the ones that distinguish life in middle-class families from families in other economic groups. The strongest links are with the occupations of middle-class family members, especially those of the husband-father. Occupational roles greatly affect family roles and the quality of family life (Schneider and Smith, 1973). Occupations are part of the larger opportunity structure of society: Those that are highly valued and carry high income rewards are unevenly distributed. The amount of the paycheck determines how well a given household can acquire the resources needed for survival and perhaps for luxury. (See Table 15–1 for a breakdown of median income by race and type of family.) The job or occupation that is the source of the paycheck connects families with the opportunity structure in different ways.

In the working class, resources are dependent on hourly wages acquired in exchange for labor. When such hourly wages are insufficient or unstable, individuals in households must pool their resources with others in the larger family network. Pooling of resources may involve exchanging baby-sitting, sharing meals, or lending money. Pooling represents an attempt to cope with the limitation of resources that are necessary for survival (Rapp, 1982:176), and it requires that the boundaries of the family be expanded.

At the lower levels of the class hierarchy survival is especially dependent on pooling resources with a wide network of people that become, in effect, "family." The lower one moves in the class structure, the more uncertain and difficult survival through wage work becomes and the more important the kin network becomes in providing subsistence over time. Much has been written about these networks among poor black families: "extremely flexible, and fluctuating groups of people committed to resource pooling, to sharing, to mutual aid, who move in and out from under one another's roofs" (Rapp, 1982:177). The fluctuating boundaries of families among working-class and poor people should not be considered unstable. Rather, they organize and sustain the limited resources that they have available. Even the black single-parent family, which has sometimes been criticized as "disorganized" or even "pathological," is often embedded in a functioning kinship network. These networks should not be romanticized, but neither should they be considered deviant (Cherlin and Furstenberg, 1983:10). Chicano families also exhibit strong and persistent kinship bonds that provide socioeconomic and emotional support (Baca Zinn, 1983). Looking at these families without racist assumptions, we see that variation in family organization is a way of adapting to harsh conditions. In Rapp's words:

> The very poor have used their families to cement and patch tenuous relations to survival; out of their belief in "family," they have invented networks capable of making next-to-nothing go a long way. It isn't the family that is deficient, but the relationship between household and productive resources. (Rapp, 1982:180)

What is most important about the differences in family boundaries is that they arise out of different kinds of linkages with institutions that are *consequences* of class position, not causes of that position. Lacking economic resources to purchase services from specialists outside the family, poor people turn to relatives and exchange these services. This family network then becomes a crucial institution in both the working class and the lower class.

Middle-class families with husbands (and perhaps wives) in careers have both economic resources and built-in ties with supportive institutions such as banks, credit unions, medical facilities, and voluntary associations. These ties are intrinsic to some occupations and to middle-class neighborhoods. They are structurally determined. Such institutional linkages strengthen the autonomy of middle-class families. Yet the middle class is shrinking, and many middle-class families are without middle-class incomes because of changes in the larger economy. Changes in family structure have also contributed to the lowering of family income. High divorce rates, for example, create many more family units with lower incomes.

In contrast to the economic autonomy of the middle class, many blue-collar jobs lack ties that would link family with work and other institutions. Thus, the boundaries of the middle-class family are more circumscribed because institutional ties support a degree of autonomy from kin. But the stable working class is also threatened since millions of manufacturing workers continue to be the victims of deindustrialization. More than 11 million of them lost jobs between 1979 and 1984, and half the workers who found new jobs took pay cuts (Congressional Office of Technology Assessment, cited in *U.S. News & World Report,* 1986a:41). Kin have become the lifeline for millions of families with displaced workers. Families lower in the socioeconomic hierarchy display more openness of boundaries simply because kinship resources must be maximized in the absence of other forms of institutional support.

Turning to the upper class, we find that family boundaries are more open than those of the middle class, even though class boundaries are quite closed. Among the elite, family constitutes not only a nuclear family but also the extended family. The elite are described as having multiple households (Rapp, 1982:182). The concerns and much of day-to-day life exist within the larger context of a network of relatives (Dyer, 1979:209).

The institutional linkages of the elite are national in scope. Families in various sections of the country are connected by such institutions as boarding schools, exclusive colleges, exclusive clubs, and fashionable vacation resorts. In this way the elite remains intact, and the marriage market is restricted to a small (but national) market (Blumberg and Paul, 1975:69).

Family life of the privileged is privileged in every sense, as Stein, Richman, and Hannon report:

> Wealthy families can afford an elaborate support structure to take care of the details of everyday life. Persons can be hired to cook and prepare meals and do laundry and to care for the children. (Stein, Richman, and Hannon, 1977:9)

The vast economic holdings of these families allow them to have a high degree of control over the flow of rewards and resources and to enjoy freedoms and choices not normally available to other families in society. As a result, these families maintain privileged access to life chances and lifestyles.

Kinship ties, obligations, and interests are more extended in classes at the two extremes than they are in the middle (McKinley, 1962:22). In the upper extreme and toward the lower end of the class structure, kinship networks serve decisively different functions. At both extremes they are institutions of resource management. The kin-based family form of the elite serves to preserve inherited wealth. It is intricately tied to other national institutions that control the wealth of society. The kin-based family form of the working and lower classes is a primary institution through which individuals participate in social life as they pool and exchange their limited resources to ensure survival. It is influenced by society's institutions, but it remains separate from them.

Structural Transformation and Family Life

The transformation of the economy brought about by new technologies, the globalization of the economy, capital flight, and deindustrialization has profoundly affected families and will continue to do so in the forseeable future. As the need for certain kinds of labor diminishes, more and more working-class and middle-class families are the victims of economic dislocation. Families are affected when their resources are reduced, when they face economic and social marginalization, and when family members are unemployed or underemployed. (This section is adapted from Baca Zinn and Eitzen, 1990:148–152.)

What does downward mobility mean for families? Katherine Newman describes the experience of the downwardly mobile middle class:

> They once "had it made" in American society, filling slots from affluent blue-collar jobs to professional and managerial occupations. They have job skills, education, and decades of steady work experience. Many are, or were, home-owners. Their marriages were (at least initially) intact. As a group they savored the American dream. They found a place higher up the ladder in this society and then, inexplicably, found their grip loosening and their status sliding. Some downwardly mobile middle-class families end up in poverty, but many do not. Usually they come to rest at a standard of living above the poverty level but far below the affluence they enjoyed in the past. They must, therefore, contend not only with financial hardship but with the psychological, social, and practical consequences of "falling from grace, of losing their proper place" in the world. (Newman, 1988:8)

Downward mobility is devastating in American society not only because of the loss in economic resources but also because self-worth is so closely connected to occupation. Loss of occupational status also ravages those people affected because Americans tend to interpret this as the fault of the downwardly mobile.

Downward mobility also occurs within the stable working class whose links with resource-granting opportunity structures has always been tenuous. Many downwardly mobile families find successful coping strategies to deal with their adverse situations. Some families develop a tighter bond to meet their common problems. Others find support from families in similar situations or from their personal kin networks. For many families, however, downward mobility adds tensions that make family life especially difficult. Family members experience stress, marital tension, and depression. Newman has suggested that these conditions are normal given the persistent tensions generated by downward mobility. Although many families experience some degree of these pathologies and still somehow endure, some families disintegrate completely under the pressure, experiencing physical brutality, incapacitating alcoholism, desertion, and even suicide (Newman, 1988:134–140).

The new technology may affect families in other ways. The redistribution of jobs has displaced many workers and placed many millions, as we have seen, in low-wage, service jobs, often without traditional benefits. These kinds of jobs include contingent work such as part-time work, temporary work, and home-based work—jobs disproportionately held by women. We focus here on **home-based work**—women working for pay in their homes. (The following discussion is from Christensen, 1988.)

Home-based work includes word processing, typing, editing, accounting, telemarketing, sewing, laundry, and child care. Women often opt for home-based work because the flexibility permits them to combine work and family obligations. Employers contract women to do home work because they pay only for work delivered, they avoid unions, and they do not pay for benefits such as health insurance, vacation and sick leaves, and pensions.

There are positive and negative consequences of home-based work. On the positive side, home-based work allows flexibility and independence not found in most jobs. On the negative side, the pay is typically low, and the strains engendered from combining the work and parent roles may be overwhelming. Children, spouses, neighbors, the telephone, household tasks, and other home distractions hinder productivity—and pay. "Working at home eliminates the boundary between work and family so that women often find they never leave their work" (Christensen, 1988:5). Thus, the combination of work and family in the home setting engenders a form of claustrophobia for some people. This feeling is exacerbated by the common problem of isolation. Working alone for powerful others means that home-based workers are denied the fair pay and appropriate fringe benefits that most other workers receive.

CHANGING FAMILY ROLES

Marriage

Marriage is still very much the norm, with about 19 of 20 Americans eventually marrying. However, the number of marriages is declining. From 1982 to 1989 the number of marriages per thousand population declined from 10.5 to 9.6, the lowest since 1977. This relatively low rate is partly a function of people marrying later. In 1960, the median age at first marriage was 22.8 years for men and 20.3 years for women. This contrasts with the 1988 statistics of 25.9 years for men and 23.6 years for women. Changes in marriage patterns have contributed to a decline in the number of married-couple households. Between 1970 and 1987, the share of married couples fell from 70.5 percent of the nation's households to 58 percent (Levitan, 1988:19–25).

American marriages are thought to be characterized by relative equality between the spouses. This idyllic view of marriage fails to take into account the impact of the gender system on the marital relationship. As noted in Chapter 12, women and men are assigned different roles that are unequally ranked. This difference constitutes the foundation on which marriage rests.

As a result of the gender system, men and women experience marriage and the family in different ways.

Jessie Bernard's classic work on marriage revealed that every marital union actually contains two marriages—and that the two do not always coincide (Bernard, 1973). When researchers ask husbands and wives identical questions about their marriages, they often get quite different replies even on fairly simple, factual questions. Bernard coined the concept "his" and "her" marriage to describe the differences in women's and men's experiences. Generally, differences reveal that men seem to be happier in marriage than women and that marriage is better for men than for women. This finding will be surprising to many because of the stereotype that women get most of their fulfillment through marriage. Bernard has examined the advantages of marriage and found that men gain more than women in marriage. Comparing married and unmarried men of the same background, she found that in psychological, social, health, and labor market characteristics, married men were better off. Furthermore, married women express more unhappiness than married men. According to Bernard and other social scientists, this problem of unhappiness can be explained by the legal, social, and personal changes that take place in women's lives when they become wives. Taking on the role of housewife creates dependency and affects women's self-esteem (Bernard, 1973). Housewives exhibit much higher rates of such dysfunctional mental symptoms as anxiety, paranoia, and phobias than do either married men or single women.

Though couples marry for togetherness, the reality of marriage is such that many activities of the spouses are segregated. Women, whether they work outside of the home or not, are responsible for domestic and childrearing activities while men pursue their work or other interests. Not only are women and men required to fill separate role activities, but the activities are governed by different gender ideologies or different beliefs about womanhood and manhood. According to sociologist Arlie Hochschild, traditional gender ideologies lead women to identify with home and family, while men identify with work and career (Hochschild, 1989:15). Wives and husbands, even though they live in the same physical space, experience differently the social world of the family.

Roles themselves, as well as how wives and husbands feel about them, can create a vast gulf between spouses. As they go about their separate activities, they may find they have less and less to talk about. This is especially true in blue-collar families, where roles are traditionally segregated. Lack of economic resources make it difficult for wives and husbands to go out by themselves, and so they spend time with relatives in sex-segregated activities (the men watch a ballgame on television while the women prepare meals and watch over children). Leisure time spent in the home includes little real interaction. The following excerpt from Lillian Rubin's study of working-class families illustrates the separateness of wives and husbands:

> Frank comes home from work; now it's about five, because he's been working overtime every night. We eat right away, right after he comes home. Then, I don't know. The kids play a while before bed, watch t.v., you know, stuff like that. Then, I don't know . . . maybe watch more t.v. or something like that. I

don't know what else—nothing, I guess. We just sit, that's all. The husband: I come home at five and we have supper right away. Then, I sit down with coffee and a beer and watch t.v. After that, if I'm working on a project I do that for a while. If not, I just watch t.v. (Rubin, 1973:124).

The quality of marital relationships is strongly influenced by class position. The three positive attributes most frequently mentioned by working-class women in Rubin's study were "He's a steady worker, he doesn't drink, he doesn't hit me" (Rubin, 1973:93). Not one woman in the professional middle-class families mentioned these qualities when answering the same question. They tended to focus on such issues as intimacy, sharing, and communication and, while expressed in subtle ways, on the comforts, status, and prestige, that their husbands' occupations afford. Rubin comments on the difference in working-class marriages:

> Does this mean that working-class women are unconcerned about the emotional side of the marriage relationship? Emphatically it does not. It says first that when the material aspects of life are problematic, they become dominant as issues acquiring solutions, and second, that even when men are earning a reasonably good living, it is never "taken for granted" when financial insecurity and marginality are woven into the fabric of life. (Rubin, 1973:94)

While marriages in this society differ in many ways, marriage as an institution has remained patriarchal. **Marital power** is the ability to control the spouse and to influence or control family decisions and activities. Husbands in all social classes have greater power than wives, although we find important differences in the operation of marital power. The classic study of marital power by sociologists Blood and Wolfe found that power was related to the resources that partners bring to the marriage. Resources are anything that a person brings to the marriage that enables the family to satisfy needs: for example, money, education, attractiveness, and social status. They found that the higher the husband's status in occupation, income, and education, the greater decision-making power he had in the family. Husbands with white-collar occupations had greater power than husbands with blue-collar occupations (Blood and Wolfe, 1960). Still, the stereotype of the egalitarian middle-class marriage persists partly because the middle class has a more egalitarian *ideology.*

Actually, the ideology and the actual distribution of power are at odds. As Goode has commented:

> Lower-class men concede fewer rights ideologically than their women in fact obtain, and the more educated men are more likely to concede more rights ideologically than they in fact grant (Goode, 1963:21).

Blood and Wolfe concluded that marriages would eventually become more equal as wives acquired more resources. Other sociologists have argued that marriages will likely remain male dominated because men automatically have greater resources than women. Better job opportunities and earnings are built into the structure of society and then carried into the private family where men can dominate with little outright effort (Gillespie, 1972). In order to change the unequal distribution of marital power, women would have to better or at least equal their husband's resources. This may be occurring in some couples where wives have high-status and high-paying occupations. Currently, 20 percent of the wives in two-income families earned more than their husbands (Hochschild, 1989:93). Women whose incomes exceed their husbands' are more likely than the average wife to have no minor children at home, to have completed college, and to be employed in professional specialties or executive, administrative, or managerial occupations (U.S. Census Bureau, reported in the *New York Times,* May 11, 1986:E7). This new type of marriage, however, has created what Hochschild calls a "stalled revolution," one that got wives out of the home but has resulted in limited changes in the gendered division of labor. In most marriages women remain responsible for housekeeping and child care. We will return to this topic.

Marital patterns have changed over time by breaking the rule that "first comes love, then comes marriage, then comes baby, in a baby carriage." Two further changes are important. First, out-of-wedlock childbearing has increased substantially. The rate of premarital conceptions has almost doubled during the past quarter century. Out-of-wedlock births accounted for 22 percent of births in 1988. This rate doubled from a decade earlier. Most out-of-wedlock births were to teens and women under 25 (Dunn, 1989:1). Second, the emergence of childless couples has become an important demographic trend. The number of young childless couples increased by 75 percent between 1967 and 1985. In 1988, 22 percent of women in their thirties had never had children (Wessel, 1989:B1). Although childless couples remain a minority, their rapid growth represents an alternative to the traditional family.

Divorce and Remarriage

Even though most Americans marry, all marriages do not last forever; some eventually are dissolved. The divorce rate doubled from 1950 to 1982, then leveled off slightly by 1985. (See Table 15–2.) Still, half of all marriages will end in divorce. In 1987, nearly 1.2 million divorces and annulments were granted, for a rate of 21 per 1,000 married couples. The U.S. divorce rate is by far the world's highest—more than triple the Japanese rate and at least double the divorce rates in the other major industrial democracies except England (Levitan, 1988:26).

The high divorce rate has contributed to the growing number of single-parent families discussed earlier. Three-fifths of all divorces involve couples with children living at home. In at least nine out of ten cases, the wife retains custody of the children after a separation. Although joint custody has received much attention in the press, national data show that it is still uncommon (Cherlin and Furstenburg, 1983:8).

Divorce and marital separation are not evenly distributed through the population but vary according to social and economic characteristics. The following are some generalizations about divorce in the United States:

1. Half of all divorces occur during the first seven years of marriage.
2. The divorce rate is related to economic conditions. the rate increases during prosperity. Apparently this is due to unwillingness to break up a marriage when wives and children will need greater economic support.

Table 15–2
Increasing
Rate of
Divorce
(1860 to 1988)

Year	Number of Divorces	Divorce Rate per Thousand People	Divorce Rate per Thousand Marriages	Percentage of Marriages Begun in Each Year Ending in Divorce
1860	7,000	.3	1	—
1870	11,000	.3	2	7%
1880	20,000	.4	2	10
1890	33,000	.5	3	10
1900	56,000	.7	4	12
1910	83,000	.9	5	14
1920	171,000	1.6	8	18
1930	196,000	1.6	7	24
1940	265,000	2.0	9	25
1950	385,000	2.5	10	30*
1960	393,000	2.2	7	39*
1970	708,000	3.5	15	48*
1980	1,189,000	5.2	23	49*
1988	1,161,000	4.8	21	49*

*Projections

Sources: Leonard Beeghley and Jeffrey W. Dwyer, "Social Structure and the Divorce Rates." Paper presented at the annual meetings of the American Sociological Association, Atlanta (August, 1988); and "Population Update," *Population Today* 16 (June 1988), p. 9.

3. The younger the age at marriage of the partners, the greater the likelihood of divorce. "Women whose first marriage ended in divorce have been, on the average, about two years younger when they entered marriage than married women of the same age who have not been divorced" (Glick, 1975:9).
4. The higher the income, the less the likelihood of divorce.
5. The higher the education for males, the lower the incidence of divorce. In contrast to males, a more complicated pattern is found for women. The highest rate of divorce is found among the least educated women, followed by those with postgraduate degrees. The lowest rates were found for those women with high school and college educations.
6. About four out of every five of those persons who obtain a divorce will remarry, with men more likely than women to do so (Carter and Glick, 1976:403).
7. The divorce patterns for blacks and Hispanics differ significantly from those of whites. Hispanics are slightly more prone to divorce than are whites, and blacks are very much more likely to divorce than are either of the other two categories.

There are many reasons for the increased divorce rate. Some of these are: increased independence (social and financial) of women; deindustrialization that eliminates many jobs for men and makes women's employment necessary; women's inequality; greater tolerance of divorce by religious groups; and reform of divorce laws, especially the adoption of no-fault divorce in many states (that is, one spouse no longer has to prove that the other was at fault in order to obtain a divorce). An important reason is the striking change in public attitudes toward divorce. While divorce is a difficult step and one that commands sympathy for the partners and children, "it is no longer considered a violation of public decency. Whether the individual is viewed as the sinner or as sinned against, divorce is generally accepted today as one possible solution for family difficulties" (Goode, 1976:529).

There is however, growing recognition that divorce treats women and children unfairly. Leonore Weitzman's study of divorce reform (1985) has uncovered some unanticipated consequences of no-fault divorce. Despite its gender-neutral rules, no-fault divorce increased the economic vulnerability of women by depriving them of equitable economic settlements. The problem is that the courts assume that husband and wife are equal at the time of divorce. This assumption ignores the economic inequalities created during marriage. The rules do not compensate wives for their years of homemaking and support while husbands moved ahead, in their careers. What of wives' lost educational opportunities, impaired earning capacities, lost job seniority, and lost pension benefits? Husbands' career assets are almost always superior to those of wives. Weitzman's study shows that

> on the average, divorced women and the minor children in their households experience a 73 percent decline in the first year after divorce. Their former husbands, in contrast, experienced a 42 percent rise in their standard of living. (Weitzman 1985:xii)

Divorce does not mean a permanent withdrawal from the marriage arena. Approximately one-third of marriages each year involve a previously married bride, and a smaller proportion involve grooms who have been married before. The probability of remarriage is affected by several important variables, such as age, gender, socioeconomic status, and race. Age is significant for women but not for men. The older a woman at the time of divorce, the lower her chances of remarriage. More men than women remarry, and they are more likely than women to marry soon after divorce. This is because divorced women who seek remarriage are disadvantaged over men because the size of the pool of potential male spouses is small. One reason for this shortage in available men is the shorter life expectancy for men than for women. The second and more important reason for this imbalance is the propensity for men to remarry younger women (Baca Zinn and Eitzen, 1990:375).

The race of the divorced who remarry is a significant factor, with blacks taking longer to remarry, if they do at all. Larry Bumpass and Ronald Rindfuss (1979:61) found, for example, that after divorce two-thirds of white mothers but only one-fifth of black mothers with children under age 18 will remarry within five years of the divorce. Another national study found that among divorced women two-thirds of the white women but only one-third of the black women had remarried (Thornton, 1977). This finding is contrary to the observation that the poor tend to remarry soon after they divorce.

By adding a male income, remarriage may solve the economic problems many single-parent families face. It may also relieve the many burdens of running a household alone. Remarriage also frequently involves blending together two families into one, a process that is complicated by the absence of clear-cut ground rules for how to accomplish the merger. Families formed by remarriages can become quite complex, with children from either spouse's previous marriage and/or from the new marriage, along with numerous sets of grandparents, stepgrandparents, and other kin and quasi-kin (Cherlin and Furstenburg, 1983:8).

The Interdependence of Work and Family Roles

The belief that work and family roles operate independently of each other is referred to by Rosabeth Moss Kanter as **"the myth of separate worlds."** Many people do not recognize that the institutions of the economy and the family are linked together and dependent on one another in numerous ways (Kanter, 1977). The economy provides jobs with varying amounts of social status and economic resources for the family and in this way sets limits on its standard of living. The family supplies skilled workers to the economy. The segmented labor force imposes different constraints on families such as the amount of time spent working and the scheduling of work, which determine the amount of time workers can spend with their families. In addition, work has psychological costs and benefits that influence family interaction. Family roles, especially the traditional roles of wife and mother, influence labor force participation and commitment to work (Mortimer and London, 1984). Extensive research on work and family in recent years has given us new information on the overlapping worlds of work and family (the following is adapted from Baca Zinn and Eitzen, 1990:190–195).

For the first time in history, more women are in the labor force than out of it. In 1987, 52 percent of mothers of children under the age of one were working compared with 32 percent 10 years earlier (see Panel 15–1). Although vast numbers of women in the work force have transformed families and the workplace, women still face a double standard. For women, the demands of the family intrude into their work. If an emergency or irregularity arises requiring a choice between the family or work, the family usually takes priority. For men, the relationship is reversed. Work takes priority over the family. Many men bring work home with them or use their time at home to recuperate from the stresses they face in the workplace. This gendered and uneven relationship to work and family has been termed the *work-family role system* by Joseph Pleck (1977). This system reinforces traditional division of labor in both work and family.

Although more and more wives share the provider role, husbands do not often share the family labor. This fact has produced for wives what Hochschild has called "the second shift," in an era of social transition. She interviewed 50 couples and asked:

> Who did how much of a wide variety of household tasks. I asked who cooks? Vacuums? Makes the beds? Sews? Cares for plants? Sends Christmas or Hanukkuh cards? I also asked: Who washes the car? Repairs household appliances? Does the taxes? Tends the yard? I asked who did most household planning, who noticed such things as when a child's fingernails needed clipping, cared more how the house looked or about the change in a child's mood. (Hochschild, 1989:6)

Which Mothers Are Working: Four Profiles

The most remarkable growth in the female labor force in the postwar period has been among women with very young children. Between 1976 and 1985, especially large increases were experienced by mothers with newborns who were (1) 30 to 44 years old; (2) white; (3) divorced, separated or widowed; and (4) who had completed a year or more of college. Conversely, black women, high school dropouts, and young, unwed mothers had modest gains in labor force participation.

Some of this change can be summarized in the four profiles of American mothers presented below, which compare labor force participation rates in 1976 and 1985, based on a statistical analysis of survey data on mothers with newborn babies.

1. **The Young Mother:** A young married white woman, whose first child was born before she was 24 years old. Her formal education stopped with high school graduation. The chance of her returning to work within a year of the birth of her child was 34 percent in 1975; in 1985, it was 54 percent, a substantial increase.

2. **The Delayed Childbearer:** A married white woman whose first child was born after age 24 and who completed some years of college. Forty-four percent of the women in this category worked in 1976. By 1985, this percentage had risen to 64 percent.

3. **The Unmarried Mother:** A white woman, aged 25 to 44, from the growing ranks of the formerly married. A high school graduate with two or more children, her chances of working within a year of the birth of her last child doubled in the past decade from 27 to 54 percent.

4. **The Young Single Mother:** A black woman, 18 to 24 years old, with two or more children. She has not married, nor has she finished high school. Her chances of working have actually decreased over the past decade, from 34 to 31 percent, and in relative terms, she has lost ground to her contemporaries. While less common than the other women profiled here, she is not atypical of a growing percentage of women with out-of-wedlock births.

Source: Martin O'Connell and Donald E. Bloom, *Juggling Jobs and Babies: America's Child Care Challenge,* Washington, D.C.: Population Reference Bureau (1987): 6–7. Reprinted by permission of the publisher.

Hochschild found that women were much more deeply torn between the demands of work and family than were their husbands. The additional hours that working women put on the second shift of housework, she calculated, add up to an extra month of work each year! Even though social class is important in determining how the household labor gets done (more affluent families can afford to purchase more labor-saving services), Hochschild has found that social class, race/ethnicity, and personality give limited clues about who does and does not share the second shift. Gender is paramount. This finding is repeated in study after study.

In spite of the stresses of work and family, wives who work outside of the home report that they are happier than are housewives, even though the demands on them are greater (Richmond-Abbot, 1983:275). Work has a profound effect on a woman's sense of self-worth, her feelings of being in charge

Even though positive consequences can arise from women's employment, one fundamental problem remains unsolved: child care.

of her life, and her chance of avoiding depression and anxiety (Baruch, Barnett, and Rivers, 1983). Working wives have additional resources that they can use to have a greater say in important family decisions, and in this way they can alter the traditional balance of family power.

Even though these positive consequences can arise from women's employment, one of the most fundamental problems remains unsolved: child care. In recent years the increase in women's employment has been greatest among women with very young children. Sixty-four percent of all children between the age of three and five spend part of their day in facilities outside of the home. Mothers are left to work out their own arrangements for child care, and often they are unsatisfactory.

It is often assumed that maternal employment adversely affects children. However, the separation of mother and child for brief periods is not harmful if adequate substitute care is provided. Kristin A. Moore and Isabell Sawhill have reviewed a number of studies and found that the children of employed mothers compare favorably in intellectual and social development with the children of mothers at home. Furthermore, employed mothers tend to stress independence in their children (Moore and Sawhill, 1984).

The changing connections between work and family pose new problems for women and men, for work institutions, and for the family. Sex inequality in the workplace and in the home lies at the heart of these problems. The challenges of combining work and family are experienced differently by women and men.

Children and Adolescents

American society purports to value children highly. Yet one of the most distressing developments of the past decade is the rise in child poverty. Children are disproportionately poor. Almost a quarter of all American children live below the poverty line and for minority children the statistics are one in two. The increased proportion of children living in poverty is linked to the growth in female-headed households.

Childhood and adolescence are experienced differently by class, race, and type of family. These conditions produce varied relationships between parents and children. A primary responsibility of parents is to teach their children the attitudes, values, and behaviors considered appropriate by the parents (and society). This teaching ensures that more children will be reared to take socially acceptable niches in the society when they reach adulthood. Parents, therefore, are important socialization agents in the child's formative years.

However, the belief that early family experience is the most powerful influence in a child's life is not supported by evidence. Arlene Skolnick points to two serious flaws in this notion: the assumption that the child is passive, and the assumption that parents exert influence in a vacuum (Skolnick and Skolnick, 1983:11). To begin with, children are not passive. They come into the world with unique temperaments and characteristics. Parents have greater power and authority than children, yet children can also shape parents. Second, the assumption of parental determinism is not well founded. Parents are not simply independent agents who train children, free of outside influences. For example, an employed parent may behave quite differently than an unemployed one, becoming more depressed, defensive, or physically abusive. Indirectly, parents communicate to their children what to worry about. The stresses or supports parents find in the neighborhood, the workplace, and the economy, all influence children (Skolnick and Skolnick, 1983:11).

A number of work-related factors affect parents and their interactions with children (the following is adapted from Baca Zinn and Eitzen, 1989:310–311). Some of these factors are the level of job satisfaction, promotions or demotions, transfer to a new community, the level of pay, work schedules, job-related stress, layoffs or threatened layoffs, sexual harassment at work, job discrimination, and both parents in the work force.

The influence of parents on their children is diminished by a number of other outside forces as well. When both parents work, preschool children will be cared for by someone other than the parents. Once the child is school age, the school (teachers, policies, and curriculum) becomes an important socialization agent, sometimes in opposition to the wishes of the parents. Peers become increasingly important to youth especially in adolescence and they often have a profound influence on their values and behaviors. Religious ideology can become salient and again this may not always be congruent with the ideology of parents (as evidenced by the attempts by parents to "depro-

I Want a Wife

I belong to that classification of people known as wives. I am A Wife. And, not altogether incidentally, I am a mother.

Not too long ago a male friend of mine appeared on the scene fresh from a recent divorce. He had one child, who is, of course, with his ex-wife. He is obviously looking for another wife. As I thought about him while I was ironing one evening, it suddenly occurred to me that I, too, would like to have a wife. Why do I want a wife?

I would like to go back to school so that I can become economically independent, support myself, and, if need be, support those dependent upon me. I want a wife who will work and send me to school. And while I am going to school I want a wife to take care of the children. I want a wife to keep track of the children's doctor and dentist appointments. And to keep track of mine too. I want a wife to make sure my children eat properly and are kept clean. I want a wife who will wash the children's clothes and keep them mended. I want a wife who is a good nurturant attendant to my children, who arranges for their schooling, makes sure that they have an adequate social life with their peers, takes them to the park, the zoo, et cetera. I want a wife who takes care of the children when they are sick, a wife who arranges to be around when the children need special care, because, of course, I cannot miss classes at school. My wife must arrange to lose time at work and not lose the job. It may mean a small cut in my wife's income from time to time, but I guess I can tolerate that. Needless to say, my wife will arrange and pay for the care of the children while my wife is working.

I want a wife who will take care of *my* physical needs. I want a wife who will keep my house clean, A wife who will pick up after me. I want a wife who will keep my clothes clean, ironed, mended, replaced when need be, and who will see to it that my personal things are kept in their proper place so that I can find what I need the minute I need it. I want a wife who cooks the meals, a wife who is a *good* cook. I want a wife who will plan the menus, do the necessary grocery shopping, prepare the meals, serve them pleasantly, and then do the cleaning up while I do my studying. I want a wife who will care for me when I am sick and sympathize with my pain and loss of time from school. I want a wife to go along when our family takes a vacation so that

gram" children they feel have been brainwashed by religious cults). The media's depiction of violence, sexual mores, recreational drugs, alternative life-styles, and social issues such as abortion, war, evolution, and capital punishment may persuade or provide justifications for some youth to choose ways different from their parents.

The most crucial outside variable, however, is social class. The amount of economic resources available to a family and the degree of esteem the family members receive from others outside the family are of ultimate importance to the child's well-being, self-concept, and opportunities.

Most basically, social class position provides for the child's life chances. The greater the family's economic resources, the better the chance to live past infancy, to be in good health, to receive a good education, to have a satisfying job, to avoid being labeled a criminal, to avoid death in war, and to live the "good life." Negatively, this means that millions of the nation's children are denied these advantages because they were born to parents who were unemployed, underemployed, stuck in the lower tier of the segmented labor mar-

someone can continue to care for me and my children when I need a rest and change of scene.

I want a wife who will not bother me with rambling complaints about a wife's duties. But I want a wife who will listen to me when I feel the need to explain a rather difficult point I have come across in my course of studies. And I want a wife who will type my papers for me when I have written them.

I want a wife who will take care of the details of my social life. When my wife and I are invited out by my friends, I want a wife who will take care of the babysitting arrangements. When I meet people at school whom I like and want to entertain, I want a wife who will have the house clean, will prepare a special meal, serve it to me and my friends, and not interrupt when I talk about the things that interest me and my friends. I want a wife who will have arranged that the children are fed and ready for bed before my guests arrive so that the children do not bother us.

And I want a wife who knows that sometimes I need a night out by myself.

I want a wife who is sensitive to my sexual needs, a wife who makes love passionately and eagerly when I feel like it, a wife who makes sure that I am satisfied. And, of course, I want a wife who will not demand sexual attention when I am not in the mood for it. I want a wife who assumes the complete responsibility for birth control, because I do not want more children. I want a wife who will remain sexually faithful to me so that I do not have to clutter up my intellectual life with jealousies. And I want a wife who understands that *my* sexual needs may entail more than strict adherence to monogamy. I must, after all, be able to relate to people as fully as possible.

If, by chance, I find another person more suitable as a wife than the wife I already have, I want the liberty to replace my present wife with another one. Naturally, I will expect a fresh, new life; my wife will take the children and be solely responsible for them so that I am left free.

When I am through with school and have a job, I want my wife to quit working and remain at home so that my wife can more fully and completely take care of a wife's duties.

My God, who *wouldn't* want a wife?

Source: Judy Syfers, "I Want a Wife," *Ms.* (December 1979):144. Copyright © 1970 by Judy Syfers. Reprinted by permission.

ket, handicapped, victims of institutional racism or sexism, divorced or separated, or otherwise disadvantaged.

Significantly, the family's resources and educational achievements affect how children perceive themselves. These acscribed characteristics (along with race/ethnicity and gender) place children in the perceptions of others, which in turn gives children an understanding of their worth. If they have favored characteristics, they are very likely to gain nourishment from the social power and esteem that come from high social position. But the children of the poor and minorities find they are devalued by persons outside the immediate family and kin network, which can have a profound effect on their psyches and behavior regardless of the efforts of their parents (Kagan, 1977:35).

About 13 percent of the total population is between the ages of thirteen and nineteen years. This is a very significant category in American society for several reasons. first, teenagers are a strong economic force. For example, they account for more than one-fourth of phonograph record sales and more than one-third of movie audiences. They spend collectively an enormous amount of money on clothes and toiletries. As they shift from fad to fad, fortunes are made and lost in the clothing and entertainment industries.

The rise of a service economy has produced a new demand for service workers. This trend has recently begun to capture the attention of family researchers. By the 1980s, three out of four high school seniors were working an average of 18 hours a week and bringing home more than $200 a month. their earnings went mostly to discretionary items such as cars, stereos, "extra" clothing, concert tickets, and drugs. Researchers at the University of Michigan found that less than 11 percent of high school seniors save all or most of their earnings for long-term purposes. This has created for many a "premature" affluence, an unrealistic level of discretionary income that is impossible to maintain at college unless they have extravagant parents (Woodward, 1989:57).

The stage of adolescence in U.S. society is a period of stress and strain for many teens. The most important reason is that it is an age of transition from one social status to another. There is no clear line of demarcation between adolescence and adulthood. Are people considered adult when they can get a full-time job, when they are physically capable of producing children, or when they can be drafted for military service? There is no clear distinction. Most primitive societies, by contrast, have "rites of passage" that often seem cruel and barbaric but do serve the function of clearly identifying the individual as a child or an adult. Adulthood in American society is unclear. Surely much of the acting out by adolescents in the United States can be at least partially explained by these status ambiguities.

The Aged

The population of the United States is increasingly older:

- In colonial times, the median age was 16. Now it is 32 years. "What is new is the rapid pace of aging. By 2010, the median is expected to be almost 39 years; by 2050 at least 43 years" (Taeuber, 1988:591).
- In 1955, the average life expectancy was 69.6 years of age. By 1980, it was 73.6 years, and it will be over 80 years of age by 2000 (Monk, 1988).
- In 1900, 4 percent of all people in the United States were 65 years of age or older. In 1980, the proportion had increased to 11.3 percent; by 2000 it will be 15 percent; and by 2030 it will be over 20 percent.
- Between 1960 and 1980 the number of children under age 15 *declined by 7 percent.* Meanwhile, the number of people aged 65 years and over *increased by 54 percent* (Preston, 1984).

There are several important implications in the trend toward an increasingly elderly population in the United States. First, it means that an ever larger number of Americans are moving into a devalued, stigmatized, and oppressed social category. To be old in U.S. society is to be considered unnecessary because one is a nonproducer in a society that values productivity. This newly acquired devalued status by an individual often has negative consequences for self-esteem and may lead to depression, withdrawal from social relationships, and confusion over role expectations.

A second ramification of the aging trend involves the financial burden on the old and the nonold. Typically when people retire from work they must lower their expenditures because their Social Security and other pension benefits are significantly less than were their wages. Many elderly persons and couples must now live in near-poverty or poverty conditions. Widows are especially disadvantaged because of a bias in the Social Security system—a widow receives 82.5 percent of her deceased husband's benefits. The marginal financial status of the elderly is alleviated sometimes by their children who supplement their parents' income with contributions or who invite the parents to move in with them. In either case the family is affected by the lowering of discretionary income or by the distruption of family patterns through the intrusion of new members in the home.

Most significantly, the increasing numbers of elderly will place a tremendous burden on the younger generation to finance their retirement. This is the result of a major shift in the dependency ratio—the number of workers compared with the number of Social Security recipients. In 1960 this ratio was 5 to 1 but this will drop to 2 to 1 by the year 2035. This demographic fact increases the financial burden progressively onto the workers, which may have either of two consequences. On the one hand, the ever higher taxes on workers to finance Social Security will reduce the workers' level of affluence and increase their hostility toward the aged. On the other, political agitation by workers may reduce their taxes and the benefits to the elderly, further lowering the incomes of the elderly and increasing their ill will toward the young.

An ever-aging population has a third consequence: it affects marital relationships in several fundamental ways. An obvious result is that the longer people live, the greater the likelihood that marriage will end in divorce or separation. Several generations ago the average marriage ended with the death of one spouse (usually the wife because of complications during childbirth) after only 20 years of marriage or so. Now, the average couple could live 20 to 30 years after the last child leaves home. Obviously, with couples increasing their potential living time together from 20 to 50 years, the potential for marital conflict and an eventual rift is enhanced.

Marital relationships are also affected by women outliving men by an average of seven years. This means not only that there are five times as many widows as widowers but also that elderly women will have fewer chances than elderly men to remarry. In Colorado, for example, similar to the case nationwide, women outnumber men in the widowed category 5 to 1 in the 75-and-older category; and there are four women for every man in that age group among persons living alone (never married, widowed, divorced, or separated) (Kreck, 1983).

Another consequence of the graying of America also has an impact on the family—the longer life expectancy has made grandparents a regular part of children's growing up (Skolnick, 1983:396–398). The four-generation family is now relatively commonplace as over one-half of all persons 65 and over have great-grandchildren (Shanas, 1980). This was not true in the past. Nor was there a time in the American past when the elderly lived with their children in a close knit, loving, and revered relationship, as is commonly believed (Laslett, 1976). The elderly today tend to live apart from their children although there are strong ties with them, frequent interaction, and help in times of difficulty.

VIOLENCE IN FAMILIES

The family has two faces. On the positive side, it is a haven from an uncaring, impersonal world, a place where love and security prevail. The family members love each other, care for each other, and accept each other under all circumstances. However, there is another side to the family. The presence of tension and discord can be found in all families at various phases in the family life cycle. The intensity that characterizes intimate relationships can give way to conflict. Some families resolve the inevitable tensions that arise in the course of daily living, but in other families conflict gives way to violence.

Although the family is based on love among its members, the way it is organized encourages conflict. (The following discussion is adapted from Baca Zinn and Eitzen, 1990:165–166). First, the family, like all other social organizations, is a power system; that is, power is unequally distributed between parents and children and between spouses, with the male typically dominant. Second, parents have authority over their children. They feel they have the right to punish children in order to shape them in the ways they consider important. Third, since marriage is between a woman and a man, it sets the stage for a "battle of the sexes." Gender differences may not present a problem in some homes where there is a basic agreement on gender roles, but for many couples these problems can become a constant source of stress.

Unlike most organizations where activities and interests are relatively narrow, the family encompasses almost everything. Thus, there are more "events" over which a dispute can develop. Moreover, there is a vast amount of time during each day when family members can interact. Extensive exposure increases the probability of disagreements, irritations, violations of privacy, and the like, which increase the risk of violence.

Not only is the range of activities greater in the family than in other social organizations, but the feelings are also more intense. As Richard Gelles and Murray Straus have put it:

> There is . . . a greater intensity of involvement in family conflict. Love, paradoxically, gives the power to hurt. So, the degree of distress felt in conflicts with other family members is likely to be much greater than if the same issue were to arise in relation to someone outside the family. (Gelles and Straus, 1979:35)

Family privacy is another characteristic that enhances the likelihood of violence. The rule in our society that the home is private has two negative consequences. First, it insulates the family members from the protection that society could provide if a family member gets too abusive. And second, the rule of privacy often prevents the victims of abuse from seeking outside help.

Violence in the family presents the ultimate paradox—the physical abuse of loved ones in the most intimate of social relationships. The bonds between wife and husband, parent and child, and adult child and parent are based on love, yet for many these bonds represent a trap in which they are victims of unspeakable abuses.

Although it is impossible to know the extent of battering that takes place in families, the problem these forms of violence represent is not trivial. The threat of violence in intimate relationships exists for all couples and for parents and children. For those who do not cope well, the result is the abuse by the strong of the weak. But violence in the family is not only a problem of family units. It represents an indictment of society, its institutions, and the cultural norms that support violence.

THE MODERN FAMILY FROM THE ORDER
AND CONFLICT PERSPECTIVES

From the order perspective, the nuclear family (composed of father, mother, and their children) serves important survival functions for society (e.g., replacement of members, regulation of sexual behavior, socialization of new members, care and protection of members). Many functions that were performed by the family in past times have been taken over by other social institutions. Today, the family's primary functions are to socialize children and provide stabilization for adult family members. According to this view, the family operates most effectively when a division of labor is present in the nuclear family. Women fill the expressive or emotional roles and men fill the instrumental or economic roles. The trend toward greater depersonalization in society (living in densely populated cities and working in bureaucracies) is countered by families serving as havens (Parsons, Bales, et al., 1955). Thus, the isolated nuclear family is an important adaptation making an achievement-oriented industrial society workable. In this way, the family "fits" with other social institutions and contributes to the maintenance of social order.

From the conflict perspective, the family is shaped by the demands of capitalism. At the macro level, the family is a vital part of the capitalist economy because it produces both workers and consumers to keep the economy going. The family is one of the primary mechanisms for perpetuating social inequality. Wealth is locked up in elite families and then passed down through intergenerational inheritance. This limits the resources and opportunities of those who are lower in the socioeconomic hierarchy. As we have seen, families pass on their advantages and disadvantages to their offspring. While this transmission of social class position promotes stability in society—which the order theorists cherish—it also promotes inequality based on *ascribed status*.

The family serves the requirements of capitalism in still another way: by idealizing the realm of the "personal." This serves the economy through heightened consumerism, and it also supports the interests of the dominant class by promoting false consciousness. The family is one of the primary socialization agents of youth, and as such it promotes the status quo by transmitting the culture of society. Children are taught to accept the inequalities of society as "natural," and they are taught to accept the political and economic systems without question. However, these very systems may need reform (or even transformation) to increase the likelihood of their serving the needs of everyone in society.

The family, from the conflict perspective, is not necessarily the haven posited by the order theorists. At the micro level, conflict is generated by: (1) female resistance to male domination; and (2) the demands of work and economic hardships that work against intimacy and companionship between spouses. Thus, the modern family is not a tranquil institution, but one fraught with potential and actual conflict.

Conflict theorists argue that the isolated nuclear family has positive consequences for capitalism, but it is highly negative for individuals (Zaretsky, 1976). The economic system benefits when employers are able to move individuals from place to place without great disruption. The economy is served when employers do not have to worry about satisfying the emotional needs of workers. Finally, the system benefits when the family is isolated and therefore cannot affect society.

This has negative consequences for individuals, the conflict theorists maintain, because the family has sole responsibility for maintaining a private refuge from an impersonal society and for providing personal fulfillment, and is thus structured to fail. The demands are too great. The family, alone, cannot provide for all the emotional needs of its members, although its members try to fulfill these needs through consumerism, "the joy of sex," and child-centered activities. Conflict theorists would argue that society should be restructured so that personal fulfillment, identity, and other individual needs are met not only in the family but also in the community, at work, and in the other institutions of society.

FAMILIES OF THE FUTURE

We have examined a number of marriage and family trends of the late 1970s and 1980s that have interesting implications for the future of families. Some of the most important are:

- The proportion of couples living together outside of marriage is increasing.
- Individuals are marrying later.
- Couples are having fewer children.
- The number of childless couples is rising.
- An ever-greater proportion of wives is working outside the home.
- The divorce rate continues to be high.
- The proportion of dual-provider families is rising.
- The fastest-growing family type is the household maintained by a woman with no husband present.

Do these trends indicate that the nuclear family is dying? We can safely predict that some form of the nuclear family will characterize U.S. society for the foreseeable future. Still, changes in marital and family life will create different life patterns for children and adults. Cherlin and Furstenburg predict that many children born in the 1980s will follow this sequence of living arrangements: live with both parents for several years, live with their mothers after their parents divorce, live with their mothers and stepfathers, live alone for a time in their early twenties, live with someone of the opposite sex without marrying, get married, get divorced, live alone again, get remarried, and end up living alone once more following the death of their spouses (Cherlin and Furstenburg, 1983:8–9).

Estimates are that about one-half of all young children alive today will spend some time in a single-parent family before they reach eighteen years of age; about nine out of ten will eventually marry and then divorce; and about one out of three will marry, divorce, and then remarry (Cherlin and Furstenburg, 1983).

Although the nuclear family will continue to exist, there will be increasing diversity in patterns of family living.

CHAPTER REVIEW

1. The family is one of the most idealized of all of society's institutions. There are disparities between common images of the family and real patterns of family life. New research has given us a better understanding of the American family in the past and present.

2. Family diversity became pronounced as society incorporated European immigrants and racial ethnics. Immigrants used their families to assist them in adapting to industrial work and urban living. Racial minorities were excluded from equal participation in the developing capitalistic economy; their families made survival possible for them.

3. The modern family is characterized by privacy and sharply segregated age and sex roles. Household size has declined and household composition has become increasingly diverse. More families now have only one spouse in residence than ever before.

4. Families are embedded in a class hierarchy. Different social classes have different links with institutions that can provide resources for family support, which creates variation in household and family structure. These variations also produce differences in forms of marital interaction and patterns of socialization. Class position is the most important determinant of the quality of family life.

5. The changing nature of work has a direct impact on the family. Dual-provider families have increased problems with child care, the alloca-tion of family tasks, and role overload. At the same time, employed wives report high values of their own well-being.

6. Although work and family are interdependent, husbands give priority to jobs over families, and employed wives give priority to families over their jobs. Sexism in the larger society reinforces sex segregation and patriarchy in families. Women and men experience the family in different ways, and men benefit more than women from family arrangements.

7. The family is not a tranquil institution, but one fraught with potential and actual conflict.

8. The divorce rate continues to rise in American society. The reasons for this trend are: increased social and financial independence of women; increased affluence; greater tolerance of divorce by religious groups; passage of no-fault divorce laws; and a change toward leniency in the public attitude toward divorce.

9. Adolescence is a difficult time in American society for many young people and their parents. The fundamental reason for this is that these people are in a transitional stage between childhood and adulthood with no clear distinction to indicate when adulthood is reached.

10. The aged also experience ambivalence because they are in a transitional stage between work and death. Moreover, they are the objects of discrimination in a youth-oriented society.

11. The family is a major source of violence in American society. One-fourth of all the murders

in the United States involves the killing of spouses, parents, and children. Wife abuse is most common in low-income families.

12. Order theorists view the family as a source of stability for individuals and society. The traditional division of labor by sex contributes to social order.

13. Conflict theorists argue that the traditional family supports capitalism but is detrimental to individuals. The family is a major source of false consciousness, and the primary agent by which the system of social stratification is perpetuated.

14. A number of trends indicate that the American family is changing: for example, high divorce rate, the rising number of childless marriages, and the fact that the fastest-growing family type is the household with no man present.

KEY TERMS

Family
Household
Nonfamily household

Single-person household
Home-based work

Marital power
Myth of separate worlds

STUDY QUESTIONS

1. What are the myths about U.S. families?
2. What is the relationship between capitalism and family patterns?
3. Explain the statement: "Families are embedded in a class hierarchy." What are the consequences of this fact for families?

4. What is the relationship between the family and work?
5. What are the consequences for families of an aging population?
6. Contrast the differing views of families by order and conflict theories.

FOR FURTHER READING

Maxine Baca Zinn and D. Stanley Eitzen, *Diversity in Families,* 2nd ed. (New York: Harper and Row, 1990).

David T. Ellwood, *Poor Support, Poverty in the American Family* (New York: Basic Books, 1988).

Kathleen Gerson, *Hard Choices* (Berkeley: University of California Press, 1985).

Naomi Gerstel and Harriet Engel Gross, *Families and Work* (Philadelphia: Temple University Press, 1987).

Arlie Hochschild, *The Second Shift* (New York: Viking, 1989).

Sar Levitan, Richard S. Belous, and Frank Gallo, *What's Happening to the American Family?* (Baltimore: The Johns Hopkins University Press, 1988).

Charles H. Mindel and Robert W. Habenstein, *Ethnic Families in America*, 3rd ed. (New York: Elsevier, 1988).

Martin O'Connell and David E. Bloom. *Juggling Jobs and Babies: America's Child Care Challenge* (Washington, D.C.: Population Reference Bureau, February 1987).

Lillian Breslow Rubin. *Worlds of Pain: Life in the Working-Class Family.* (New York: Basic Books, 1976).

Ruth Sidel. *Women and Children Last: The Plight of Poor Women in Affluent America.* (New York: Penguin Books, 1986).

Arlene S. Skolnick and Jerome H. Skolnick, eds. *Family in Transition.* 6th ed. (Boston: Little, Brown, 1988).

Chapter Sixteen

Education

On an average morning in Chicago, about 5,700 children in 190 classrooms come to school only to find they have no teacher. Victimized by endemic funding shortages, the system can't afford sufficient substitutes to take the place of missing teachers. . . .

The odds these [mostly] black kids in Chicago face are only slightly worse than those faced by low-income children all over America. Children like these will be the parents of the year 2000. Many of them will be unable to earn a living and fulfill the obligations of adults; they will see their families disintegrate, their children lost to drugs and destitution. When we later condemn them for "parental failings," as we inevitably will do, we may be forced to stop and remember how we also failed them in the first years of their lives.

It is commonplace that a society reveals its reverence or contempt for history by the respect or disregard that it displays for older people. The way we treat our children tells us something of the future we envision. The willingness of the nation to relegate so many of these poorly housed and poorly fed and poorly educated children to the role of outcasts in a rich society is going to come back to haunt us.

Source: Reprinted by permission of Jonathan Kozol, "The New Untouchables," *Newsweek* 114 (Winter/Spring 1990), p. 48. Copyright © 1990.

This chapter is divided into four sections. The first describes the characteristics of American education. The second focuses on how corporate society reproduces itself through education—in particular, how the schools socialize youth in accordance with their class position and point them toward factory, bureaucratic, or leadership roles in the economy. The third section describes the current role of education in perpetuating inequality in society. The final section summarizes the chapter by looking at education from the order and conflict perspectives.

THE CHARACTERISTICS OF AMERICAN EDUCATION

Education as a Conserving Force

The formal system of education in U.S. society (and in all societies) is conservative, since the avowed function of the schools is to teach newcomers the attitudes, values, roles, specialties, and training necessary to the maintenance of society. In other words, the special task of the schools is to preserve the culture, not to transform it. Thus, the schools indoctrinate their pupils in the culturally prescribed ways. Children are taught to be patriotic. They learn the myths, the superiority of their nation's heritage, who are the heroes and who are the villains. Jules Henry has put it this way:

> Since education is always against some things and for others, it bears the burden of the cultural obsessions. While the Old Testament extols without cease the glory of the One God, it speaks with equal emphasis against the gods of the Philistines; while the children of the Dakota Indians learned loyalty to their own tribe, they learned to hate the Crow; and while our children are taught to love American democracy, they are taught contempt for the totalitarian regimes. (Henry, 1963:285–286)

There is always an explicit or implicit assumption in American schools that the American way is the only really right way. When this assumption is violated on the primary and secondary school level by the rare teacher who asks students to consider the viability of world government, or who proposes a class on the life and teachings of Karl Marx or about world religions, then strong enough pressures usually occur from within the school (administrators, school board) or from without (parents, the American Legion, Daughters of the American Revolution) to quell the disturbance. As a consequence, creativity and a questioning attitude are curtailed in school, as Parenti points out forcefully:

> Among the institutions . . . , our educational system looms as one of the more influential purveyors of dominant values. From the earliest school years, children are taught to compete individually rather than work cooperatively for common goals and mutual benefit. Grade-school students are fed stories of their nation's exploits that might be more valued for their inspirational nationalism than for their historical accuracy. Students are instructed to believe in America's global virtue and moral superiority and to fear and hate the

Great Red Menace. They are taught to hold a rather uncritical view of American politico-economic institutions. One nationwide survey of 12,000 children (grades two to eight) found that most youngsters believe "the government and its representatives are wise, benevolent and infallible, that whatever the government does is for the best."

Teachers concentrate on the formal aspects of representative government and accord little attention to the influences that wealthy, powerful groups exercise over political life. Teachers in primary and secondary schools who wish to introduce radical critiques of American politico-economic institutions do so often at the risk of jeopardizing their careers. High school students who attempt to sponsor unpopular speakers and explore dissident views in student newspapers have frequently been overruled by administrators and threatened with disciplinary action.

School texts at the elementary, high-school, and even college levels seldom give but passing mention to the history of labor struggle and the role of American corporations in the exploitation and maldevelopment of the Third World. Almost nothing is said of the struggles of indentured servants, of Latino, Chinese, and European immigrant labor, and of small farmers. The history of resistance to slavery, racism, and U.S. expansionist wars is largely untaught in American schools at any level. One learns that the Soviet Union is to blame for all cold-war tensions. (Parenti, 1988:37–38)*

Mass Education

Americans have a basic faith in education. This faith is based on the assumption that a democratic society requires an educated citizenry so that individuals may participate in the decisions of public policy. It is for this reason that they not only provide education for all citizens, but also compel children to go at least to the eighth grade or until age sixteen (although this varies somewhat from state to state).

It is hard to quarrel with the belief that all children should be compelled to attend school, since it should be for their own good. After all, the greater the educational attainment, the greater the likelihood of larger economic rewards and upward social mobility. However, to compel a child to attend school for six hours a day, five days a week, forty weeks a year, for at least ten years, is quite a demand. The result is that many students are in school for the wrong reason. The motivation is compulsion, not interest in acquiring skills or curiosity about their world. This involuntary feature of American schools is unfortunate since so many school problems are related to the lack of student interest.

As a result of the goal of and commitment to mass education, an increasing proportion of persons have received a formal education. In 1940, for example, 38 percent of Americans aged 25 to 29 years had completed high school. This proportion increased to 74 percent in 1970 and 86 percent in 1987 (*Statistical Abstract*, 1989: 130).

---

*Reprinted by permission of the publisher, St. Martin's Press.

Local Control of Education

Although the state and federal governments finance and control education in part, the bulk of the money and control for education comes from local communities. There is a general fear of centralization of education—into a state-wide educational system or, even worse, federal control. Local school boards (and the communities themselves) jealously guard their autonomy. Since, as it is commonly argued, local people know best the special needs of their children, local boards control allocation of monies, curricular content, and the rules for running the schools, as well as the hiring and firing of personnel.

There are several problems with this emphasis on local control. First, tax money from the local area traditionally finances the schools. Whether the tax base is strong or weak has a pronounced effect on the quality of education received (a point we shall return to later in this chapter). Second, local taxes are almost the only outlet for a taxpayers' revolt. Dissatisfaction with high taxes (federal, state, and local) on income, property, and purchases is often expressed at the local level in defeated school bonds and school tax levies. Third, because the democratic ideal requires that schools be locally controlled, the ruling body (school board) should represent all segments of that community. Typically, however, the composition of school boards has overrepresented the business and professional sectors and overwhelmingly underrepresented blue-collar workers and various minority groups. The result is a governing body that is typically conservative in outlook and unresponsive to the wishes of people unlike themselves. Fourth, local control of education may mean that some communities will ban books considered classics by most educators. (Favorite targets are, for example, *The Catcher in the Rye* by J. D. Salinger and John Steinbeck's *Grapes of Wrath.*) In 1988, for instance, there were 142 incidents in 42 states of attempted or successful censorship in schools (Mydans, 1989). Similarly, the local school boards may use textbooks that support religious fundamentalism or some other narrowly shared belief. A final problem with local control is the lack of curriculum standardization across school districts. Families move on the average of once every five years (and the rate is probably higher for families with school-age children), and the large numbers of children moving from district to district often find a wide variation in curriculum and graduation requirements.

The Competitive Nature of American Education

It is not surprising that the schools in a highly competitive society are competitive. Competition extends to virtually all school activities. The compositions of athletic teams, cheerleading squads, "pompon squads," debate teams, choruses, drill teams, bands, and dramatic play casts are almost always determined by competition between classmates. Grading in courses, too, is often based on the comparison of individuals ("grading on a curve") rather than on measurement against a standard. To relieve boredom in the classroom, teachers often invent competitive games such as "spelling baseball," or "hangman." In all these cases, the individual learns at least two lessons: (1) your classmates are "enemies," for if they succeed, they do so at your expense; and (2) fear of failure is the great motivator, not intellectual curiosity or love of knowledge.

The "Sifting and Sorting" Function of Schools

Schools play a considerable part in choosing the youth who come to occupy the higher-status positions in society. Conversely, school performance also sorts out those who will occupy the lower rungs in the occupational prestige ladder. Education is, therefore, a selection process. The sorting is done with respect to two different criteria: a child's ability and his or her social class background. Although the goal of education is to select on ability alone, ascribed social status (the status of one's family, race, and religion) has a pronounced effect on the degree of success in the educational system. The school is analogous to a conveyor belt, with people of all social classes getting on at the same time but leaving the belt in accordance with social class—the lower the class the shorter the ride (see Panel 16–1).

The Preoccupation with Order and Control

Most administrators and teachers share a fundamental assumption that school is a collective experience requiring subordination of individual needs to those of the school (this section is taken from Silberman, 1970:122–157). American schools are characterized, then, by constraints on individual freedom. The school day is regimented by the dictates of the clock. Activities begin and cease on a timetable, not in accordance with the degree of interest shown or whether students have mastered the subject. Silberman characterizes this as the "tyranny of the lesson plan," meaning that teachers too often see the lesson plan as the end rather than as a means to an end. Another indicator of order is the preoccupation with discipline (that is, absence of unwarranted noise and movement, and concern with the following of orders).

In their quest for order schools also demand conformity in clothing and hair styles. Dress codes are infamous for their constraints on the freedom to dress as one pleases. School athletic teams also restrict freedom, and these restrictions are condoned by the school authorities. Conformity is also demanded in what to read, where to set the margins on the typewriter, and how to give the answers the teacher wants.

The many rules and regulations found in schools meet a number of expressed and implicit goals. The school authorities' belief in order is one reason for this dedication to rules: teachers are rated not on their ability to get pupils to learn but rather on the degree to which their classroom is quiet and orderly. The community also wants order. A survey of high school students' parents found that nearly two-thirds believe that "maintaining discipline is

Cooling Out the Failures

Although our schools can be a golden avenue of opportunity for those who succeed in them, they are also the arena in which many confront failure that condemns them to the more subservient positions in our society. How are those who "fail" handled so they do not become bitter revolutionaries intent on overthrowing the system that so brutally used them?

"Cooling out" is the process of adjusting victims to their loss. When someone has lost something that is valuable to him, it leads to intense frustration. This frustration and its accompanying anger are dangerous to society because they can be directed against the social system if the social system is identified as being responsible for the loss. But our educational system is insidiously effective, and many who fall within it (perhaps most), never even need to be cooled out. They learn early in grade school that they are stupid and that higher education is meant for others. They suffer miserably in school as they continue to be confronted year after year with

more evidence of their failure, and they can hardly wait until they turn sixteen so they can leave for greener pastures. Such persons are relieved to end their educational miseries and need no cooling out.

For those who do need to be cooled out, however, a variety of techniques is used. The primary one makes use of the ideology of individualism. To socialize students into major cultural values means to teach them more values than conformity and competition. . . . Two other major values students consistently confront in our educational system are the ideologies of individualism and equal opportunity. They are taught that people make their own way to the top in a land of equal opportunity. Those who make it do so because of their own abilities, while those who do not make it do so because of a lack of ability or drive on their own part. They consequently learn to blame themselves for failure, rather than the system. It was not the educational system that was at fault, for it was freely offered. But it was the fault of the individual who failed to make proper use of that which society offered him. Individualism provides amazing stabilization for the maintenance

more important than student self-inquiry" (Silberman, 1970:145). An important reason is that schools operate on the assumption of distrust. As Christopher Jencks has observed, "The school board has no faith in the central administration, the central administration has no faith in the principals, the principals have no faith in the teachers, and the teachers have no faith in the students" (quoted in Silberman, 1970:133). The consequence of this distrust is a self-fulfilling prophecy. When teachers are not treated as professionals (not consulted on matters that concern them most, required to punch time clocks), they do not act as professionals. When students are treated as slaves, they do not develop into self-reliant, self-motivated individuals. An excerpt from a famous (or infamous) book entitled *The Student as Nigger* dramatizes the demands for order in American schools.

> [Students] haven't gone through twelve years of public school for nothing. They've learned one thing and perhaps only one thing during those twelve years. They've forgotten their algebra. They've grown to fear and resent literature. They write like they've been lobotomized. But Jesus, can they follow orders! . . . Students don't ask that orders make sense. They give up expecting things to make sense long before they leave elementary school. Things are true because the teacher says they're true. At a very early age we all learn to

of our social system, for it results in the system going unquestioned as the blame is put squarely on the individual who was himself conned by the system.

If this technique of cooling out fails to work, as it does only in a minority of cases, other techniques are put into effect. Counselors and teachers may point out to the person that he is really "better suited" for other tasks in life. He may be told that he will "be happier" doing something else. He might be "gradually disengaged" from the educational system, perhaps be directed to alternate sources of education, such as vocational training.

The individual may also be encouraged to blame his lack of success on tough luck, fate, and bad breaks. In one way or another, as he is cooled out, he is directed away from questioning the educational system itself, much less its relationship to maintaining the present class system and his subservient position within it. . . .

Finally, the malcontent-failure has the example before him of those from similar social class circumstances as his own who did "make it." This becomes incontrovertible evidence that the fault does lie with himself and not the system, for if they could make it, so could he. This evidence of those who "made it" is a powerful cooling out device, as it directly removes any accusatory finger that might point to the educational and social systems.

Having our educational system set up in such a way that some lower class youngsters do manage to be successful and are able to enter upper middle class positions serves as a pressure valve for our social system. In the final analysis, it may well be this pressure valve which has prevented revolutions in our country—as the most able, the most persistent, and the most conforming are able to rise above their social class circumstances. And in such instances, the educational system is pointed to with pride as representing the gateway to golden opportunity, freely open to all.

Source: James M. Henslin, Linda K. Henslin, and Steven D. Keiser, "Schooling for Social Stability: Education in the Corporate Society," in *Social Problems in American Society.* James M. Henslin and Larry T. Reynolds, eds., 2nd ed. (Boston: Allyn and Bacon, 1976):311–312. Reprinted by permission of the publisher.

accept "two truths," as did certain medieval churchmen. Outside of class, things are true to your tongue, your fingers, your stomach, your heart. Inside class things are true by reason of authority. And that's just fine because you don't care anyway. Miss Wiedemeyer tells you a noun is a person, place or thing. So let it be. You don't give a rat's ass; she doesn't give a rat's ass. The important thing is to please her. Back in kindergarten, you found out that teachers only love children who stand in nice straight lines. And that's where it's been at ever since. (Farber, 1970:92)

The paradoxes listed below indicate the many profound dilemmas in U.S. education. They set the foundation for the remaining sections of this chapter, which deal with the crises facing education and with some alternative modes.

- Formal education encourages creativity but curbs the truly creative individual from being too disruptive to society.
- Formal education encourages the open mind but teaches dogma.
- Formal education has the goal of turning out mature students but does not give them the freedom essential to foster maturity.
- Formal education pays lip service to meeting individual needs of the students but in actuality encourages conformity at every turn.

Reprinted with permission from *Love is Hell.* © 1983. By Matt Groening, Pantheon Books a Division of Random House, New York.

- Formal education has the goal of allowing all students to reach their potential, yet it fosters kinds of competition that continually cause some people to be labeled as failures.
- Formal education is designed to allow people of the greatest talent to reach the top, but it systematically benefits certain categories of people regardless of their talent: the middle- and upper-class students who are white.

THE POLITICAL ECONOMY OF EDUCATION IN CORPORATE SOCIETY

Americans want to believe that their society is a meritocratic one in which the most intelligent and talented people rise to the top. Because public schools are free and available to everyone, individuals can go as high as their ability and drive will take them. In this view education is the great equalizer, providing opportunities for everyone to develop his or her full potential. This section and the next argue that this belief is a myth. The truth is that schools reinforce inequality in society (this section is taken from Bowles, 1977; Bowles and Gintis, 1973; Spring, 1972; and Carnoy, 1975). This belief, besides being a myth, has an especially negative outcome: it tends to blame or credit individuals for their level of failure or success without considering the aspects of the social structure that impel or impede their progress (another instance of blaming the victim). Thus, it results in praise of the system and condemnation of individuals who are defined as losers.

The Role of Education in Corporate Society

The schools perform several vital functions for the maintenance of the prevailing social, political, and economic order. Education, along with the institutions of the family and religion, has a primary responsibility for socializing newcomers to the society. A second function of education is the shaping of personalities so that they are in basic congruence with the demands of the society. In other words, one goal of the educational system of any society is to produce people with desired personality traits (such as competitiveness, altruism, bravery, conformity, or industriousness, depending on the culture and organization of the society). A third function is preparing individuals for their adult roles. In U.S. society this means preparing individuals for the specialized roles of a highly complex division of labor. It also means preparing youngsters for life in a rapidly changing world. Early in American history the primary aims of schooling were teaching the basics of reading, writing, spelling, and arithmetic, so that adults in an agrarian society could read the Bible, write letters, and do simple accounting. Modern society, on the other hand, demands people with specialized occupational skills, with expertise in narrow areas. The educational system is saddled with providing these skills in addition to the basics. Moreover, the schools have taken over the teaching of citizenship skills, cooking, sewing, and even sex education—skills and knowledge that were once the explicit duty of each family to transmit to its offspring.

Contemporary schools go beyond these functions, however. They exist to meet the needs of the economy by providing employers with a disciplined and skilled labor force and a means to control individuals in order to maintain political stability. A review of the changing role of the school in American history can make this role clear (Bowles, 1977).

When most Americans were farmers and artisans, the schools had a relatively simple task because the skills society required were essentially unchanged from generation to generation and were generally learned at home. As the economy changed to a factory system in urban settings, the family became less important as an agent of economic socialization, and the school grew in importance. Work became specialized, technology changed rapidly, and work was done in large organizations with rigid authority structures. The workers were no longer in control of their own labor but were controlled by the owners of the factories. Thus, workers were placed in potentially oppressive and alienating work situations. This was a concern to capitalists because the workers might unite to challenge the existing system. Stability was also threatened by the rising numbers of immigrants who entered the United States to live in urban centers and work in factories.

According to radical educational historians, mass public education was perceived by those in power as the answer to these problems in a changing society, for the church and family were no longer effective in teaching the skills and uniformity in belief necessary for an effective and tractable work force.

> An ideal preparation for factory work was found in the social relations of the school: specifically, in its emphasis on discipline, punctuality, acceptance of authority outside the family, and individual accountability for one's work. The social relations of the school would replicate the social relations of the work-place, and thus help young people adapt to the social division of labor. Schools would further lead people to accept the authority of the state and its agents—the teachers—at a young age, in part by fostering the illusion of the benevolence of the government in its relations with citizens. Moreover, be-cause schooling would ostensibly be open to all, one's position in the social division of labor could be portrayed as the result not of birth, but of one's own efforts and talents. (Bowles, 1977:139)

Social Class Biases of the Educational System

Through their curricula, testing, bureaucratic control, and emphasis on com-petition, the schools reflect the social class structure of society by processing youth to fit into economic slots quite similar to those of their parents. As the educational system rapidly expanded during the nineteenth and early twen-tieth centuries, a system of class stratification emerged within the schools (Katz, 1968). As the high schools opened to youth of all social classes, the older curriculum, which provided a standard education for all, was sup-planted by the "progressive" notion that school should be tailored to meet the individual needs of each child. While this makes obvious sense, the effects of the new curriculum tended to provide vocational school tracks for children of working-class families and preparation for college for children of professionals. Such a division was not blatant, because "objective" tests were used to decide the program for each child. Though seemingly fair, these tests were biased. The IQ test, for example, is clearly biased to reward children who have had middle-class experiences (Kagan, 1973). Thus, they unfairly legitimate a hierarchical division of labor by separating individuals into dif-ferent curricula, with different expectations, which in turn then fulfill the prophecy of the original test scores. Moreover, they serve to reconcile people to their eventual placement in the economic system (Bowles and Gintis, 1976:74).

The amount of schooling one has is directly correlated with economic success in society. Thus, schools act as society's gatekeepers. But the way in which the schools work biases the outcome, as we have seen. Two "rules-of-the-school" games serve to buttress this further. The first is that

> excellence in schooling should be rewarded. Given the capacity of the upper class to define excellence in terms on which upper class children tend to excel (for example, scholastic achievement), adherence to this principle yields ine-galitarian outcomes (for example, unequal access to higher education) while maintaining the appearance of fair treatment. Thus the principle of rewarding

excellence serves to legitimize the unequal consequences of schooling by associating success with competence. At the same time, the institution of objectively administered tests of performance serves to allow a limited amount of upward mobility among exceptional children of the lower class, thus providing further legitimation of the operations of the social system by giving some credence to the myth of widespread mobility. (Bowles, 1977:148)

The second "rule of the game" is the principle that elementary and secondary schooling should be financed largely from local revenues. This principle is supported on the seemingly logical grounds that the local people know what is best for their children. The effect, however, is to perpetuate educational inequalities. The next section catalogs the reasons for this and the many other ways education reinforces inequality.

EDUCATION AND INEQUALITY

Education is presumed by many to be the great equalizer in U.S. society—the process by which the disadvantaged get their chance to be upwardly mobile. The data in Table 16–1 show, for example, that the higher the educational attainment, the higher the income. But these data do not in any way demonstrate equality of opportunity through education. They show clearly that blacks and Hispanics with the same educational attainment as whites receive lower economic rewards. For example, the average family income for whites with householders who have an eighth-grade education is *more* than the average for Hispanics who have one to three years of high school and within one thousand dollars of black families where the householder is a high school graduate. These differences reflect discrimination in society, not just in schools. This section examines how the schools help perpetuate class and race inequities.

The Relation between School Success and Socioeconomic Status

The evidence that educational performance is linked to socioeconomic background is clear and irrefutable. The advantages of the children of the rela-

Table 16–1
Average Family Income by Education and Race (1987)

Highest Educational Attainment	Average Family Income		
	White	Black	Hispanic
Less than 8 years	$19,825	$16,396	$17,500
8 years	22,550	17,958	19,160
1–3 years high school	27,335	17,018	22,475
High school graduate	34,437	23,695	28,286
1–3 years college	41,142	30,019	34,408
College graduate	54,118	36,860	45,617
5 or more years college	65,187	50,624	60,312

Source: Bureau of the Census, "Money Income of Households, Families and Persons in the United States: 1987," *Current Population Reports,* Series P–60, no. 162 (February 1989), Table 14, pp. 49–52.

tively affluent over those of the poor are enormous, as seen in the following illustration from a study by the Carnegie Council on Children:

> Jimmy is a second grader. He pays attention in school, and enjoys it. School records show he is reading slightly above grade level and has a slightly better than average I.Q. Bobby is a second grader in a school across town. He also . . . enjoys school and his test scores are quite similar to Jimmy's. Bobby is a safe bet to enter college (more than four times as likely as Jimmy) and a good bet to complete it—at least twelve times as likely at Jimmy.
>
> Bobby will probably have at least four years more schooling than Jimmy. He is twenty-seven times as likely as Jimmy to land a job which by his late forties will pay him an income in the top tenth of all incomes. Jimmy has one chance in eight of earning a median income.
>
> These odds are the arithmetic of inequality in America. . . . Bobby is the son of a successful lawyer whose annual salary of $35,000 puts him well within the top 10 percent of the United States income distribution in 1976. Jimmy's father, who did not complete high school, works from time to time as a messenger and a custodial assistant. His earnings, some $4,800, put him in the bottom 10 percent. (Kempton, 1979:8–9)

The research of Bowles and Gintis also makes the point that socioeconomic background determines how much education one receives. They found that people in the lowest 10 percent in socioeconomic background *with the same average IQ scores* as those in the highest 10 percent will receive an average of 4.9 fewer years of education (Bowles and Gintis, 1976:31).

Christopher Jencks and his associates have added to the work of Bowles and Gintis, providing the most current and methodologically sophisticated analysis of the determinants of upward mobility in their book *Who Gets Ahead?* (Jencks et al., 1979). Among their findings is that educational attainment, especially graduation from college, is very important to later success; but it is not so much what one learns in school, as the obtaining of the credentials that counts. Most important, the probability of high educational attainment is closely tied to family background.

Inequality in education occurs also along racial lines (which is closely related to socioeconomic status). In 1987, for example, 77 percent of white adults were high school graduates compared with only 63.4 percent of black adults, and 50.9 percent of Hispanic adults* (*Statistical Abstract*, 1989:133). The Coleman report, an analysis of all third-, sixth-, ninth-, and twelfth-grade pupils in 4,000 schools, noted that whites surpass blacks in various achievement areas and that the gaps increase the longer they remain in school (Coleman et al., 1966). Clearly, the school is to blame, for in no instance is the initial gap narrowed. Moreover, the increasing gaps are *understated*, because there is a greater tendency for the people of lowest aptitude among the minority groups to drop out of school.

---

*There are major differences among Hispanics in educational attainment by country of origin: 45 percent of adult Mexicans (Chicanos) have graduated from high school compared with 54 percent for Puerto Ricans, and 62 percent of Cubans.

William Ryan has summarized the situation as follows:

The school is better prepared for the middle-class child than for the lower-class child. Indeed, we could be tempted to say further that the school experience is tailored for, and stacked in favor of, the middle-class child. The cause-and-effect relationship between the lack of skills and experiences found among lower-class children and the conditions of lower-class life has yet to be delineated. So far, explanations of this relationship have been, at best sketchy, and have been based on casual observation. We know poor and middle-class children exhibit certain differences in styles of talking and thinking, but we do not know yet why or how these differences occur.

We do know, however, that these differences—really differences in *style* rather than ability—are not handicaps or disabilities (unlike barriers to learning such as poor vision, mild brain damage, emotional disturbance or orthopedic handicap). They do represent inadequate *preparation* for the reality of the modern urban school. They are, in no sense, cultural or intellectual defects. (Ryan, 1976:35–36)*

How is the educational system stacked in favor of middle- and upper-class children and against children from the lowest classes?† At least four interrelated factors explain why the education system tends to reinforce the socioeconomic status differentials in the United States: finances, curriculum, segregation, and personnel.

Finances.   Though not a guarantee of educational equality, if schools spent approximately the same amount of money per pupil, this would be a significant step toward meeting that goal. This has not been accomplished nationwide, because wealthier states are able to pay much more per pupil than are poorer states. Table 16–2 provides a state-by-state comparison in per pupil expenditures for 1987–88, which is correlated with teacher salary and pupil/teacher ratio. Also reported in that table is one measure of student performance, average state scores on college admission tests, which also is roughly correlated with state spending. Because the federal government provides only about 7 percent of the money for public schools, equalization from state to state is impossible as long as the states vary in wealth and commitment to public education.

The disparities in per-pupil expenditures within a given state are also great, largely because of the tradition of funding public schools through property taxes. This procedure is discriminatory because rich school districts can spend more money than poor ones on each student, and at a *lower* taxing rate.

---

*Reprinted by permission of the publisher.

†We have phrased the question to focus on the system, not the victims, contrary to the typical response, which is to focus on the **"cultural deprivation"** of the poor. That approach attacks the home and culture of poor people. It assumes that these people perform inadequately because they are handicapped by their culture. Observers cannot, however, make the value judgment that a culture is "deprived." They can note only that their milieu does not prepare children to perform in schools geared for the middle class. In other words, children of the poor and/or minority groups are not nonverbal—they are very verbal, but not in the language of the middle class.

Table 16–2
Education Spending by State and Educational Performance (1987–1988)

	Expenditure per Pupil	Average Teacher Salary	Dropout Rate	Combined SAT Scores	Percentage Tested
Alabama	$2,573 (49)*	$23,320 (42)*	29.8 (18)*	993**	6%
Alaska	8,010 (1)	40,424 (1)	33.3 (11)	934	30
Arizona	3,544 (35)	27,388 (24)	35.6 (7)	968	11
Arkansas	2,733 (46.5)	20,340 (50)	22.5 (34)	1001	4
California	3,728 (30)	33,092 (5)	33.9 (10)	906	38
Colorado	4,147 (18)	28,651 (19)	26.3 (25.5)	980	17
Connecticut	5,435 (5)	33,515 (4)	19.5 (41)	912	69
D.C.	5,742 (4)	36,465 (2)	44.5 (1)	842	54
Delaware	4,825 (9)	29,575 (13)	29.9 (17)	910	50
Florida	3,794 (25)	25,382 (28)	41.4 (2)	893	38
Georgia	3,374 (39)	26,177 (26)	37.5 (5)	840	49
Hawaii	3,787 (26)	28,785 (17)	29.2 (19)	891	47
Idaho	2,585 (48)	22,783 (44)	21.2 (38)	975	7
Illinois	4,106 (19)	29,735 (11)	24.3 (30)	984	14
Indiana	3,556 (34)	27,386 (25)	26.3 (25.5)	874	47
Iowa	3,808 (24)	24,867 (30)	13.6 (46)	1089	3
Kansas	3,933 (21.5)	24,364 (32)	17.9 (43)	1042	5
Kentucky	2,733 (46.5)	24,274 (34)	32.6 (13)	998	6
Louisiana	3,069 (44)	20,885 (48)	39.9 (3)	982	5
Maine	3,850 (23)	23,425 (40)	20.7 (39)	899	46
Maryland	4,717 (10)	30,829 (8)	25.5 (29)	914	50
Massachusetts	5,145 (7)	30,019 (10)	23.5 (32)	909	66
Michigan	4,353 (14)	32,926 (6)	37.6 (4)	972	11
Minnesota	4,180 (17)	29,620 (12)	9.4 (51)	1003	7
Mississippi	2,350 (51)	20,669 (49)	35.2 (8)	909	66
Missouri	3,472 (36)	24,703 (31)	25.6 (28)	992	11
Montana	4,194 (16)	23,798 (38)	13.8 (47)	1009	9
Nebraska	3,756 (29)	23,246 (43)	13.3 (48)	1033	6
Nevada	3,573 (32)	27,600 (22)	27.9 (21)	923	17

Thus, suburban students are more advantaged than are students from the inner city; districts with business enterprises are favored over agricultural districts; and districts blessed with natural resources are better able to provide for their children than are districts with few resources. In Texas, for example, the residents of Edgewood Independent school district, a poor, mostly Hispanic area in San Antonio, the property taxes of almost $1 per $100 of assessed valuation raises $3,596 per student. Another Texas school district, Santa Gertrude, which is rich in oil, has property taxes of 8 cents per $100 of assessed valuation, yet spends $12,000 per student (Tifft, 1989). Examined another way, the 150,000 students living in the poorest districts of Texas receive educations costing half of their 150,000 wealthiest counterparts (Wise and Gendler, 1989).

	Expenditure per Pupil	Average Teacher Salary	Dropout Rate	Combined SAT Scores	Percentage Tested
New Hampshire	3,933 (21.5)	24,019 (36)	27.3 (23)	938	57
New Jersey	5,953 (3)	30,778 (19)	22.8 (33)	892	65
New Mexico	3,558 (33)	24,351 (33)	28.3 (20)	1009	8
New York	6,497 (2)	33,600 (3)	37.1 (6)	894	62
North Carolina	3,129 (41)	25,073 (29)	32.2 (14.5)	838	47
North Dakota	3,437 (37)	21,660 (47)	11.6 (49)	1067	3
Ohio	3,671 (31)	28,778 (18)	17.2 (44)	954	16
Oklahoma	3,099 (42)	22,006 (45)	27.4 (22)	1006	5
Oregon	4,337 (15)	27,750 (21)	27.2 (24)	928	42
Pennsylvania	4,616 (11)	28,961 (16)	21.3 (37)	891	52
Rhode Island	4,985 (8)	32,858 (7)	30.6 (16)	898	61
South Carolina	3,237 (40)	24,241 (35)	33.1 (12)	832	49
South Dakota	3,097 (43)	19,750 (51)	20.3 (40)	1076	3
Tennessee	2,827 (45)	23,785 (39)	32.2 (14.5)	1011	8
Texas	3,409 (38)	25,655 (27)	34.9 (9)	875	32
Utah	2,415 (50)	23,882 (37)	19.4 (42)	1043	4
Vermont	3,399 (13)	23,397 (41)	22.0 (36)	914	54
Virginia	3,780 (28)	27,436 (23)	26.0 (27)	907	51
Washington	3,964 (20)	27,980 (20)	22.2 (35)	951	19
West Virginia	3,784 (27)	21,736 (46)	23.8 (31)	954	7
Wisconsin	4,523 (12)	29,206 (15)	15.6 (45)	909	10
Wyoming	5,201 (6)	29,378 (14)	10.7 (50)	1016	5

*Parentheses indicate rank order.
**SAT averages by state are somewhat misleading for several reasons, especially the wide variation in the proportion of high school students taking the exam. For example, only 3 percent of high school seniors took the SAT in South Dakota, but 69 percent did in Connecticut. See Brian Powell and Lala Carr Steelman, "Variations in State SAT Performance: Meaningful or Misleading?" *Harvard Educational Review* (November 1984); and Albert Shanker, "Another Look at States' SAT Ranking," *The New York Times* (January 6, 1985):E7.

Sources: data supplied by the U.S. Department of Education and the College Board.

The U.S. Supreme Court in *San Antonio* v. *Rodriquez* (1973) ruled that even though there were unequal expenditures in Texas, these disparities did not violate the Constitution. In effect, the Court ruled that this was a matter for the individual states to decide.

Several states, led by California, have made strides to right inequities in school financing. In 1976, the California Supreme Court declared in *Serrano* v. *Priest* that the state's system of school finance violated the state and federal constitutional guarantees for the right of citizens to equal protection under the law. By 1988, California had equalized finances so that "95.6 percent of all students attend districts with a per-pupil revenue limit within an inflation adjusted . . . band [$238] of the statewide average for each district type (Wise and Gendler, 1989:15). Gradually, the courts in other states have ruled that their school financing needs revamping. In 1989, the Texas Supreme Court ruled unanimously that the state's unequal method of school finance was unconstitutional. Similar cases are pending in Alaska, Minnesota, North Dakota, Montana, Oregon, Tennessee, and New Jersey. Thus, the trend indicates a move to greater equality, which will have significant consequences.

> It equalizes the capacity of poor districts to secure the services of a sufficient number of teachers, even to bid for the services of highly qualified teachers. It permits schools from poor districts to exercise the same choice— Shall we offer Latin or Russian? Shall we buy computers or microscopes?— that schools from wealthy districts now enjoy. It ensures, to the extent that is possible, that educational opportunity is independent of the wealth of one's parents and neighbors.
>
> Improving education for children in poor school districts would benefit them and the nation. A future physicist is as easily born in Jersey City as in Princeton, a future pianist in Edgewood as in Alamo Heights. But it is not only potential luminaries that are lost; it is part of an entire generation of citizens whose potential contributions are stunted by the inadequacy of the education they are provided. School finance reform cannot solve all of the problems of education, but it can equalize the opportunities that the state provides. To continue to distribute better education to children in rich districts and worse education to children in poor districts is only to exacerbate the inequalities that children bring to school. To equalize educational opportunity is to redress some of the accidents of birth. (Wise and Gendler, 1989:37)

Family Economic Resources. Family finances have important consequences for academic achievement and for translating these achievements into success following formal education (this section is dependent on *Children's Defense Fund,* 1989:68–77). Poor parents, most without health insurance, are unable to afford prenatal care, which increases the risk of babies born at low birthweight, a condition that may lead to learning disabilities. As these poor children age, they are less likely to receive adequate nutrition, decent medical care, and a safe and secure environment. These deficiencies increase the probability of poor children being less alert, less curious, and less able to interact effectively with their environment than are healthy children. Children of the affluent are also advantaged by being more likely to attend early childhood development programs, which prepare children for school. "In 1986, for example, two out of three four-year-olds in families with annual incomes of $35,000 or more were enrolled in some type of preschool program, compared with only four out of 10 four-year-olds in families with incomes less than $10,000" (*Children's Defense Fund,* 1989:73).

Poor children are more likely than the children of the affluent to attend schools with poor resources, which, as we have seen, means that they are less likely to receive an enriched educational experience. Similarly, most poor young people live in communities where

> opportunities to apply academic skills and build new ones are either not available or not accessible. The lack of community resources is especially destructive during the summer months, the time when children doing least well

in school (a group that is disproportionately poor) slide backward the farthest. Recent research shows that most of the learning gap between poor and nonpoor children is due to this summer learning loss. (*Children's Defense Fund*, 1989:74).

Poor teens are more likely than their more affluent peers to fall behind in school. Among 16-year-olds who have lived at least half of their lives below the poverty line, 40 percent have repeated at least one grade, a rate twice as great as for those whose families had never lived in poverty (*Children's Defense Fund*, 1989:69).

The level of affluence also affects how long children will stay in school, because schools, even public schools, are costly. There are school fees (many school districts, for example, charge fees for participation in music, athletics, and drama), supplies, meals, transportation, and other costs of education. These financial demands pressure youngsters from poorer families to drop out of school prematurely to go to work. The children from the middle and upper classes, not constrained by financial difficulties, tend to stay in school longer, which means better jobs and pay in the long run. In 1985, for example, about 60 percent of all high school dropouts came from families with incomes of less than $15,000, while only 16 percent came from families with incomes of $30,000 or more. Because minorities are overrepresented among the poor, their dropout rate is disproportionate to whites—33 percent of minority students drop out of high school compared with 17 percent of whites (Horn, 1987).

These children [dropouts]—most of them poor, black or Hispanic—are America's educational underclass. While middle-class kids enjoy gleaming laborato-

A significant and disturbing trend is the declining enrollment of blacks in colleges and universities.

ries and computers, these children struggle in an educational Third World where supplies are shoddy, teachers are baffled by a barrage of different languages, and discrimination handicaps even the brightest and most willing child. From this classroom ghetto, it's a short journey to the world of adults trapped in joblessness and poverty. (Horn, 1987:66)

The affluent also give their children educational advantages, such as home computers, travel experiences abroad and throughout the United States, visits to zoos and libraries, and various cultural activities. Another advantage available to the affluent is the hiring of tutors to help children having difficulty in school or to transform already good students into outstanding ones. One tutor in the state of Washington said "One hundred percent of the children I tutor are from wealthy families. I charge $40 an hour" (quoted in Warren, 1988:24).

The well-to-do also have the option of sending their children to private schools (about 12 percent of American children attend these schools). Parents send their children to private schools for many reasons. Some do so for religious reasons. Some choose private schools because private schools, unlike public schools, are selective in who they let in, so parents can ensure that their children will interact with children similar to theirs in race (some private schools were expressly created so that white children could avoid integrated public schools) and social class. Similarly, private schools are much more likely than are public schools to get rid of troublesome students (those with behavioral problems and low-achievers), thereby providing an educational environment more conducive to achievement. Finally, the most elite private schools provide a demanding education *and* entree to the most elite colleges and universities, which, in turn, lead to placement in top positions in the professional and corporate occupational worlds.

Obtaining a college degree is a most important avenue to later success. One's family finances are directly related to whether one attends college and, if so, what type. The cost of higher education, always out of reach of the poor, rose twice the rate of inflation during the 1980s. The result was that by 1988 the full costs at a private college were $12,924 per student (about 40 percent of a median-family's income) and $5,823 at a public college (almost 20 percent of median-family income) (Gwynne, 1988). These high costs, which continue to rise, coupled with declining scholarship monies, preclude college not only for the able poor but increasingly for children of the working and lower-middle classes as well. An indicator of this trend is the declining enrollment of blacks in colleges, from 33 percent of black high school graduates in 1975 to 20 percent in 1986.

Behind the decline is shortage of money. Since 1980, while college costs have outstripped the inflation rate, requirements for financial aid have tightened. A decade ago, most black students who needed money could get government grants covering nearly 75 percent of their college costs. Now, most aid is in the form of loans. Grants, on average, cover only 45 percent of the costs, which in some schools run to $15,000 to $20,000 a year. (Taylor, 1987:75)

The ability to pay for college reinforces the class system in two ways. We have just seen that the lack of money shuts out the possibility of college for some students. For those who do attend college, money stratifies. The poorest, even those who are talented, are most likely to attend community colleges, which are the least expensive but emphasize technical careers and are therefore limiting in terms of later success. Those students with greater resources are likely to attend public universities. Finally, those with the greatest financial backing are the most likely to attend elite and prestigious private schools (see Panel 16–2). It is important to note that, although ability is an important variable, it is money not ability that places college students in this stratified system. For example, "some less qualified students from upper-class families are able to attend elite universities because of admission programs that favor the children of alumni and the children of big contributors to the university's fund-raising campaigns" (Coleman and Cressey, 1990:103).

Curriculum.   American schools are essentially middle or upper class. The written and spoken language in the schools, for example, is expected to be middle class. For children of the poor, however, English (at least middle-class English) may be a second language. English is clearly a second language for many Hispanic youngsters, making their scores on tests and success in U.S. schools especially problematic. Standardized tests often ask the student to determine how objects are similar. For those students whose first language is Spanish, this presents a problem. "Spanish, which separates words into masculine and feminine categories, tends to emphasize the differences between objects. This interferes with tasks that require the subject to describe how objects are similar" (Philippus, 1989:59). The schools, in general, have failed to recognize the special needs of these and other bilingual students, which results in their overall poor student performance.

In these and other matters, the curriculum of the schools does not accommodate the special needs of the poor. To the contrary, the schools assume that the language and behaviors of the poor are not only alien but wrong—things to be changed. This assumption denigrates the ways of the poor and leads to loss of ego strength (a trait already in short supply for the poor in a middle-class world).

The curriculum also is not very germane to the poor child's world. What is the relevance of conjugating a verb when you are hungry? What is the relevance of being able to trace the path of how a bill becomes law when your family and neighbors are powerless? Irrelevancy for the poor is also seen in the traditional children's primers, which picture middle-class surroundings and well-behaved blond children. There is little effort at any educational level to incorporate the experience of slum children in relation to realistic life situations of any kind. Schools also have a way of ignoring real-life problems and controversial issues. Schools are irrelevant if they disregard topics such as race relations, poverty, and the distribution of community power.

The typical teaching methods, placement tests, and curricula are inappropriate to children from poor families. This factor, along with the others

The Costs and Consequences of a Harvard Education

Our son came home for the holidays from one of the best (and most costly) colleges in the country and began two days of catching up—telephoning friends from his high school, one of the best (and most costly) private schools in the country.

"Wow!" he said excitedly after one call. "Seven seniors at Dalton made early admissions at Harvard. The numbers are really going up."

The numbers that are going up in the United States in the 1980s are the numbers of the children of wealthy and influential elites who are getting the big break: admission to the elite schools.

Rest in peace, "Equal Opportunity." Those words are being reduced to a cynical slogan, an Orwellian perversion spouted by the people running the country to give their own children the best shots at running it 30 years from now. The most successful (and distressing) victory for the Reagan Revolution has been in the battle to cut both federal aid for college tuition and federal pressure to admit minority students to colleges. With people of color and salary pushed down, there is again more opportunity to be equally shared by families that can afford tuition and board now approaching $20,000 a year.

It's supply-side education: The best educations are supplied to the children of those capable of supplying $20,000 per student per year. Or more, I have been told by college admissions officers that the worst pressure on them these days is to admit more and more of the dimwit children of alumni capable of contributing $100,000 or more to universities needing more private money because they're receiving less federal money. If Rupert IV gets in, Rupert III kicks in—and there is no room for some kid named Bernie or Mary Catherine.

What that means for the American future can be demonstrated by the American past. The graduates of America's best schools have always run the country. If the children of the rich get into Harvard—as they always did until democratization began in the 1960s (and is now being ended)—they become the presidents of the banks, the colleges and the country.

The consistency of that pattern has been shown by statistics compiled by Prof. Philip Harry Burch Jr. of Rutgers University. From 1789 to 1980, he found, more than one-quarter of the United States' "high federal officials"—Cabinet level and Supreme Court justices, for example—have been graduates of only three universities: Harvard, Yale, Princeton. And, on the Cabinet level alone, for instance, that proportion has been increasing in recent years—in case you're wondering what chance your daughter has of becoming Treasury secretary.

As the numbers for the rich go up, the numbers for everyone else have to go down. That is not always easy to document but it does show up in statistics showing that there has been a decrease during the Reagan years in the number of children going to college whose parents did not. And, of course, there has been a decrease in the number of minority-group students. The percentage of blacks in Harvard freshman classes fell from 8.7 percent to 6.3 percent in the past four years—at a time when black admission test scores rose dramatically. What didn't rise was black family income—and income is the new criterion for admission.

It is not fashionable these days for whites to concede that they might have the same problems as blacks. But unless you are rich, you do have problems if you have large ambitions for your children. The best test of equal opportunity in America is not whether anyone can grow up to be president, it is whether anyone's son or daughter can get into Harvard. Or Yale. Or Princeton.

We're returning to the good old days—a time, in a phrase used recently by Dr. Bernard W. Harleston, president of the City University of New York, of: "Education for and of the Elite."

Source: Richard Reeves, "Could Your Kid Go to Harvard?" *Denver Post*, Dec. 31, 1984. Reprinted with permission of Universal Press Syndicate, © 1984.

mentioned earlier, results in failure for a large proportion of these youngsters. They perceive themselves (as do others in the system) as incompetents. As Silberman has put it:

> Students are not likely to develop self-respect if they are unable to master the reading, verbal, and computational skills that the schools are trying to teach. Children must have a sense of competence if they are to regard themselves as people of worth; the failure that minority-group children, in particular, experience from the beginning can only reinforce the sense of worthlessness that the dominant culture conveys in an almost infinite variety of ways, and so feed the self-hatred that prejudice and discrimination produce. Chronic failure makes self-discipline equally hard to come by; it is these children's failure to learn that produces the behavior problems of the slum school . . . and not the behavior problems that produce the failure to learn. (Silberman, 1970:67).

Silberman's discussion of the problems of minority-group children can be broadened to include all poor children (who are, after all, also a minority group). The poor of all races experience prejudice and discrimination. They quickly learn that they are considered misfits by the middle class (teacher, administrator, citizen).

Segregation

American schools tend to be segregated by social class, both by neighborhood and, within schools, by ability grouping. Schools are based in neighborhoods that tend to be relatively homogeneous by socioeconomic status. Racial and economic segregation is especially prevalent at the elementary school level, carrying over to a lesser degree in the secondary schools. Colleges and universities, as we have seen, are peopled by a middle- and upper-class clientele. Thus, at every level, children tend to attend a school with others like themselves in socioeconomic status and race. This results more often in unequal facilities, since rich districts provide more than poor districts do for their pupils. Moreover, within districts, the schools labeled "lower class" tend to get a disproportionately smaller slice of the economic pie than "middle-class" schools.

Tracking and Teachers' Expectations

Although segregation according to the socioeconomic composition of neighborhoods is by no means complete, the tracking system within the schools achieves this to a large extent. **Tracking** (also known as ability grouping) sorts students into different groups or classes according to their perceived intellectual ability. The decision is based on grades and teachers' judgments but primarily through standardized tests. The result is that children from poor families and from ethnic minorities are overrepresented in the slow track while children from advantaged backgrounds are disproportionately in the middle and upper tracks. The rationale for tracking is that it provides a better fit between the needs and capabilities of the student and the demands and opportunities of the curriculum. Slower students do not retard the progress of brighter ones, and teachers can adapt their teaching more efficiently to the level of the class if the students are relatively homogeneous in ability. The special problems of the different ability groups, from "gifted" to "retarded," can be dealt with more easily when groups of students share the same or similar problem.

Although these benefits may be real, tracking is open to serious criticisms. First, students in lower tracks are discouraged from producing up to their potential. They tend to be given repetitive and unchallenging tasks. Students labeled as "low-ability" tend to get a curriculum empty of ideas (Rachlin, 1989). They are given low-level work that increases the gap between them and the higher tracks. Rather than seeing the remedial track as a way to get students "up to speed," many "teachers see themselves as weeders, getting rid of the kids who can't make it, rather than nurturers trying to make all grow to their potential" (Rachlin, 1989:52). Second, students in the upper track develop feelings of superiority while those in the lower track tend to define themselves as inferior. As early as the second grade students know where they stand on the "smart or dumb" continuum and this profoundly affects their self-esteem (Tobias, 1989:57). These psychological wounds can have devastating effects. Third, the low-track students are "tracked to fail." The negative labels, low teacher expectations, poor education resources (the highest track is much more likely to have access to computers, for example), and the fact that teachers typically do not want to teach these classes (there is a subtle labeling among teachers regarding who gets to teach what level), all lead to a high probability of failure among students assigned to the lowest tract. Given all of these negatives, it is not surprising that students who are "discipline problems" or who eventually drop out come disproportionately from the low track. Fourth, the tracking system is closely linked to the stratification system—that is, students from low-income families are disproportionately placed in the lowest track, resulting in a reinforcement of the social class structure. If this criticism is correct, the tracking system so prevalent in U.S. schools denies equality of educational opportunity and thus is contrary to the ideal of the school system as open and democratic.

Finally, and most telling, recent research calls into serious question whether tracking has educational value. Research at the Johns Hopkins University found, for example, that "given the same curriculum in elementary and middle-grade schools, there is no difference in achievement between advanced students in a tracked school and students in the top third of a class made up of students with varying abilities" (cited in Rachlin, 1989:52). The Carnegie Corporation in a report assessing the state of middle-grade schools advocated "abolishing tracking on the grounds that it discriminates against minorities, psychologically wounds those labeled slow, and doesn't work" (cited in Rachlin, 1989:51).

The tracking system appears to not accomplish its educational goals, but it is powerful in its negative effects. There are four principal reasons this system stunts the success of students who are negatively labeled.

Stigma.   Assignment to a lower track carries a strong **stigma** (a label of social disgrace). Such students are labeled as intellectual inferiors. Their self-esteem wanes as they see how others perceive them and behave toward them. Thus, individuals assigned to a track other than college prep perceive themselves as "second class," as unworthy, stupid, and in the way. Clearly, assignment to a low track is destructive to a student's self-concept.

The Self-Fulfilling Prophecy. This effect is closely related to stigma. If placed in the college-prep track, students are likely to receive better instruction, have access to better facilities, and be pushed more nearly to their capacity than those assigned to other tracks. The reason is clear: the teachers and administration *expect* great things from the one group and lesser things from the other. Moreover, these expectations are fulfilled. Those in the higher track do better and those in the lower track do not. These behaviors justify the greater expenditures of time, faculties, and experimental curricula for those in the higher track—thus perpetuating what Merton has called a "reign of error" (Merton, 1957:421–436).

An example comes from a controversial study by Rosenthal and Jacobson. Although this study has been criticized for a number of methodological shortcomings, the findings are consistent with theories of interpersonal influence and with the labeling view of deviant behavior. In the spring of 1964, all students in an elementary school in San Francisco were given an IQ test. The following fall the teachers were given the names of children identified by the test as potential academic spurters, and five of these were assigned to each classroom. The "spurters" were chosen by means of a table of random numbers. The only difference between the "experimental group" (those labeled as "spurters") and the "control group" (the rest of the class) was in the imaginations of the teachers. At the end of the year all the children were again tested, and the children from whom the teachers expected greater intellectual gains showed such gains (in IQ and grades). Moreover, they were rated by their teachers as being more curious, interesting, happy, and more likely to succeed than the children in the control group (Rosenthal and Jacobson, 1968).

The implications of this example are clear. Teachers' expectations have a profound effect on students' performance. When students are overrated, they tend to overproduce; when they are underrated, they underachieve. The tracking system is a labeling process that affects the expectations of teachers (and fellow students and parents). The limits of these expectations are crucial in the educational process. Yet the self-fulfilling prophecy can work in a positive direction if teachers have an unshakable conviction that their students *can* learn. Concomitant with this belief, teachers should hold *themselves,* not the students, accountable if the latter should fail (Silberman, 1970:98). Employed in this manner, the self-fulfilling prophecy can work to the benefit of *all* students.

Future Payoff.   School is perceived as relevant for those students going to college. Grades are a means of qualifying for college. For the non-college-

Educating the Class of 2000

The high-school graduating class of 2000 is with us already; its members entered kindergarten in September 1987. . . .

PREPARING FOR 2000

The class of 2000 will need a far better education simply to get a decent job. In part, this is because today's fast-growing employment areas—the ones where good jobs can be found—are fields such as computer programming, health care, and law. They require not only a high-school diploma, but advanced schooling or job-specific training.

By contrast, less than 6 percent of workers will find a place on the assembly lines that once gave high-school graduates a good income; the rest will have been replaced by robots. Instead, service jobs will form nearly 90 percent of the economy. A decade ago, about 77 percent of jobs involved at least some time spent in generating, processing, retrieving, or distributing information. By the year 2000, that figure will be 95 percent, and that information processing will be heavily computerized.

Traditional jobs also call for more familiarity with technology; even a department store sales clerk must be "computer literate" enough to use a computerized inventory system. Approximately 60 percent of today's jobs are open to applicants with a high-school diploma; among new jobs, more than half require at least some college. By the year 2010, virtually every job in the country will require some skill with information-processing technology.

Beyond that, simply living in modern society will raise the level of education we all need. By the year 2000, new technology will be changing our working lives so fast that we will need constant retraining, either to keep our existing jobs or to find new ones. Even today, engineers find that half of their professional knowledge is obsolete within five years and must go back to school to keep up; the rest of us will soon join them in the classroom. Knowledge itself will double not once, not twice, but four times by the year 2000! In that single year, the class of 2000 will be ex-

posed to more information and knowledge than their grandparents experienced in a lifetime.

Schools will have to meet these new demands. . . .

TRAINING FOR THE FUTURE

Solving the problems of conventional education is only one half of the task. America will also need a much stronger system of vocational education if it is to meet the challenge of the years to come. On average, the next generation of workers will have to make no fewer than five complete job changes in a lifetime, not counting the multiple tasks (which will also be changing) associated with each respective job. This is a mandate for continuous retraining.

In the future, vocational training will be just as crucial as traditional education. If schools fail to turn out well-educated high-school and college graduates, more and more young people will find themselves unqualified for any meaningful career, while millions of jobs go begging for trained people to fill them. If schools and businesses fail to retrain adults for the growing technical demands of their jobs, millions of conscientious workers will find their careers cut short, and the skilled work they should have done will be exported to countries like Japan and Taiwan, where educational systems definitely are up to the task.

EDUCATION FOR THE CLASS OF 2000

America's school system today is clearly overburdened, even by the traditional demands placed on it. How can the school system be strengthened to bring high-quality education to all members of the class of 2000? And what can be done about the growing demand for adult education in the years to come? Over half a dozen measures come to mind, most of them embarrassingly simple:

- Lengthen the school day and year. In any field, you can get more work done in eight hours than in six, in 10 days than in seven. Japan's school year consists of 240 eight-hour days. America's averages 180 days of about 6.5 hours. So let's split the difference: Give us 210 seven-hour school days a year.

- Cut the median class size down from 17.8 to 10 students. Naturally, this means hiring more teachers. This will give teachers more time to focus on the *average* student. . . .
- Computerize. Computer-aided learning programs are already replacing drill books; as software improves, they will begin to replace some kinds of textbooks as well. . . .
- Tailor courses to the needs of individual students. Individualized educational programs (IEPs) are already used in many schools; they suggest which skills the student should practice and recommend ways of testing to make sure they have been learned. But far more is possible. . . .
- Promote students based on performance, not on time served in class. Students starting school in 2000 will move up not by conventional grade levels, but by development levels, ensuring that each child can work on each topic until it's mastered.
- Recruit teachers from business and industry, not just university educational programs. Get chemists to teach chemistry, accountants to teach arithmetic, and so on. These specialists could become teachers in areas where teachers are scarce. Give them the required courses in education necessary to meet teaching standards. But start by making sure that would-be teachers actually know something worth teaching.
- Set new priorities for school systems that today are overregulated and underaccountable. In many communities, the curriculum is so standardized that teachers in any given course on any given day will be covering the same material. It's time to cut through that kind of red tape and give teachers the right to do the job they supposedly were trained for. Then make teachers and their supervisors responsible for the performance of their students. Teachers who turn out well-educated students should be paid and promoted accordingly. If students don't ad-

vance, neither should their would-be educators.
- Bring business and industry into the public school system. Corporations must train and retrain workers constantly, and that requirement will grow ever more pressing. The obvious answer is for them to contract with schools to do the teaching. The money earned from such services can go toward teachers' salaries and investments in computers, software, and such things as air conditioning needed to keep schools open all year.

   For students not headed toward college, businesses may also provide internships that give high school students practical experience in the working world they are about to enter. When public schools turn out graduates who haven't mastered reading, writing, or math, business suffers.
- Finally, if Americans really want quality education they must be willing to pay for it. . . .

Today's education system cannot begin to prepare students for the world they will enter on graduation from high school. By 2030, when the class of 2000 will still be working, they will have had to assimilate more inventions and more new information than have appeared in the last 150 years. By 2010, there will be hardly a job in the country that does not require skill in using powerful computers and telecommunications systems.

America needs to enact all the reforms outlined above, and many others as well. It is up to concerned citizens, parents, and teachers to equip our children with the knowledge and skills necessary to survive and thrive in the twenty-first century. In [any] election year, education should be a major political issue, for time is running out: The class of 2000 is already with us.

Source: Marvin J. Cetron, "Class of 2000," *The Futurist* 22 (November/December 1988): 9–15. Reprinted by permission of the publisher.

bound student, however, school and grades are far less important for entry into a job. At most they need a high school diploma, and grades really do not matter as long as one does not flunk out. Thus, non-college-bound students often develop negative attitudes toward school, grades, and teachers. These attitudes for students in the lower tracks are summed up by sociologist Arthur Stinchcombe:

> Rebellious behavior is largely a reaction to the school itself and to its prom-ises, not a failure of the family or community. High school students can be motivated to conform by paying them in the realistic coin of future advan-tage. Except perhaps for pathological cases, any student can be motivated to conform if the school can realistically promise something valuable to him as a reward for working hard. But for a large part of the population, especially the adolescent who will enter the male working class or the female candidates for early marriage, the school has nothing to offer. . . . In order to secure con-formity from students, a high school must articulate academic work with careers of students. (quoted in Schafer, Olexa, and Polk, 1972:49).

As we have seen, being on the lower track has negative consequences. These students are more rebellious both in school and out and do not partic-ipate as much in school activities. Finally, what is being taught is often not relevant to their world. Thus, we are led to conclude that many of these students tend to feel that they are not only second-class citizens but perhaps even pariahs. What other interpretation is plausible in a system that disad-vantages them, shuns them, and makes demands of them that are irrelevant?

The Student Subculture.   The reasons given above suggest that a natural reac-tion of persons in the lower track would be to band together in a subculture that is antagonistic toward school. This subculture would quite naturally develop its own system of rewards, since those of the school are inaccessible. David Hargreaves, in *Social Relations in a Secondary School,* showed this to be the case in an English secondary school that incorporated tracks (or "streams," as they are called in England): Boys in the high stream were drawn to the values of the teachers, while lower-stream boys accorded each other high status for doing the opposite of what the teacher wanted.

These factors show how the tracking system is at least partly responsible for that fact that those in the lower tracks are relatively low achievers, un-motivated, uninvolved in school activities, more prone to drop out of school, and to break school or community rules. To segregate students either by ability or by future plans is detrimental to the students labeled as inferior. It is an elitist system that needs to be reevaluated and changed. Tracking is a barrier to equal educational opportunity for lower-income and other minority students who are disproportionately assigned to the lowest track. It is an elitist system that for the most part takes the children of the elite and edu-cates them to take the elite positions of society. Conversely, children of the nonelite are trained to recapitulate the experiences of their parents. In a presumably democratic system that prides itself on providing avenues of up-ward social mobility, such a system borders on immorality (Oakes, 1985).

In conclusion, inequality in the educational system causes many people to fail in American schools. This phenomenon is the fault of the schools, not of the children who fail. To focus on these victims is to divert attention from the inadequacies of the schools. The blame needs to be shifted.

> We are dealing, it would seem, not so much with culturally deprived children as with culturally depriving schools. And the task to be accomplished is not to revise, and amend, and repair deficient children but to alter and transform the atmosphere and operations of the schools to which we commit these children. Only by changing the nature of the educational experience can we change its product. (Ryan, 1976:60)*

EDUCATION FROM THE ORDER AND CONFLICT PERSPECTIVES

From the order perspective, schools are of crucial importance in maintaining social integration. They are a vital link between the individual and society, deliberately indoctrinating youth with the values of society, and teaching the skills necessary to fit into society. Most important, the schools sift and sort children so that they will find and accept their appropriate niche in the societal division of labor.

The conflict perspective emphasizes that the educational system reinforces the existing inequalities in society by giving the advantaged the much greater probability of success (in grades, in achievement tests, in IQ tests, in getting an advanced education; all of which translate into economic and social success outside school). Conflict adherents also object to the "**hidden curriculum**" in schools—that is, learning to follow orders, to be quiet, to please persons in authority regardless of the situation. In short, students learn to fit in, to conform. This may be functional for society and for students who will act out their lives in large bureaucracies, but it is not conducive to personal integrity and to acting out against situations that ought to be changed.

---

*Reprinted by permission of the publisher.

CHAPTER REVIEW

1. The American system of education is characterized by: (a) conservatism—the preservation of culture, roles, values, and training necessary for the maintenance of society; (b) belief in mass education; (c) local control; (d) competition; (e) reinforcement of the stratification system; and (f) preoccupation with order and control.

2. The belief that American society is meritocratic, with the most intelligent and talented at the top, is a myth. Education, instead of being the great equalizer, reinforces social inequality.

3. Schools perform a number of functions that maintain the prevailing social, political, and economic order: (a) socializing the young; (b) shaping personality traits to conform with the demands of the culture; (c) preparing youngsters for adult roles; and (d) providing employers with a disciplined and skilled labor force.

4. The curricula, testing, bureaucratic control, and emphasis on competition in schools reflect the social class structure of society by processing youth to fit into economic slots similar to those of their parents.

5. The schools are structured to aid in the perpetuation of social and economic differences in several ways: (a) by being financed principally through property taxes; (b) by providing curricula that are irrelevant to the poor; and (c) by tracking according to presumed level of ability.

6. The tracking system is closely correlated with social class; students from low-income families are disproportionately placed in the lowest track. Tracking thwarts the equality of educational opportunity for the poor by generating four effects: (a) stigma, which lowers self-esteem; (b) self-fulfilling prophecy; (c) a perception of school as having no future payoff; and (d) a negative student subculture.

KEY TERMS

Cultural deprivation   Stigma
Tracking   Hidden curriculum

STUDY QUESTIONS

1. Formal education reinforces the status quo. Should it? Must it? Should there be some point in the educational process when schools promote a critical assessment of society? If so, when?

2. What is meant by the "political economy of education"?

3. How does the formal system of education reinforce the social stratification system in society?

4. Contrast the order and conflict perspectives on formal education.

FOR FURTHER READING

Education: General

Samuel Bowles and Herbert Gintis, *Schooling in Capitalist America: Educational Reform and the Contradictions of Economic Life* (New York: Basic Books, 1976).

Martin Carnoy, ed., *Schooling in a Corporate Society: The Political Economy of Education in America*, 2nd ed. (New York: David McKay, 1975).

John I. Goodlad, *A Place Called School* (New York: McGraw-Hill, 1983).

Jules, Henry, *Culture Against Man* (New York: Random House [Vintage Books], 1963).

John Holt, *The Underachieving School* (New York: Dell Publishing, 1972).

Christopher J. Hurn, *The Limits and Possibilities of Schooling*, 2nd ed. (Boston: Allyn and Bacon, 1985).

Frank Musgrove, *School and the Social Order* (New York: John Wiley, 1979).

Charles E. Silberman, *Crisis in the Classroom* (New York: Random House, 1970).

Peter W. Cookson, Jr., and Caroline Hodges Persell, *Preparing for Power: America's Elite Boarding Schools* (New York: Basic Books, 1985).

Paulo Freire, *Pedagogy of the Oppressed*, Myra Bergman Ramos, trans. (New York: Seabury Press, 1970).

Christopher Jencks et al., *Who Gets Ahead? The Determinants of Economic Success in America* (New York: Basic Books, 1979).

Jerome Karabel and A. H. Halsey, eds., *Power and Ideology in Education* (New York: Oxford University Press, 1977).

Jennie Oakes, *Keeping Track: How Schools Structure Inequality* (New Haven: Yale University Press, 1985).

Joel Spring, *The Sorting Machine* (New York: Longman, 1976).

Adam Yarmolinsky, Lance Liebman, and Corinne S. Schelling, eds., *Race and Schooling in the City* (Cambridge, MA: Harvard University Press, 1981).

Education and Inequality

Randall Collins, *The Credential Society: A Historical Sociology of Education and Stratification* (New York: Academic Press, 1979).

Chapter Seventeen

Religion

*A*ll human beings
have an innate need to tell and hear stories and to have a story to live by.
Religion, whatever else it has done, has provided one of the main ways
of meeting this abiding need. Most religions begin as clusters of stories,
embedded in song and saga, rite and rehearsal. Go back as far as the bloody
Babylonian epic of Gilgamesh or to Homer's accounts of the gods and heroes
of Hellas. Or read the tales told by Bantu priests, Cheyenne holy men or
Eskimo shamans. They are all, in their own way, stories. The Hebrew
Scriptures are largely stories; so is the New Testament. Rabbis, saints, Zen
masters and gurus of every persuasion convey their holy teachings by jokes,
kōans, parables, allegories, anecdotes and fables. There has never been a
better raconteur than Jesus of Nazareth himself."

Source: Harvey Cox, *The Seduction of the Spirit: The Use and Misuse of People's Religion* (New
York: A Touchstone Book, Simon and Schuster, 1973):9.

Religion is a ubiquitous phenomenon that has a tremendous impact on any society and its members. It is part of a large social system, affected by and affecting the other institutions of the society—that is, patterns of the family, the economy, education, and the polity. Since religious trends may be responses to fundamental changes in society, and some religious ideas may constrain social behaviors in a narrowly prescribed manner, the understanding of any society is incomplete unless one comprehends the religion of that society.

But, what is religion? The variety of activities and belief systems that have fallen under this rubric is almost infinite (see Panel 17–1). There are some elements essential to religion, however, that allow us to distinguish it from other phenomena (taken from Nottingham, 1954:1–11). A starting point is that religion is created by people (that is, it is a part of culture). It is an integrated set of ideas by which a group attempts to explain the meaning of life and death. Religion is also a normative system, defining immorality and sin as well as morality and righteousness. Let us amplify some of these statements further.

- Religion deals with the ultimate of human concerns—the meaning of life and death. It provides answers as to the individual's place in society and in the universe.
- There is an emphasis on human conduct. There are prescriptions for what one ought to do as well as the consequences for one's misconduct.
- There is a distinction between the sacred and the secular. Some objects and entities are believed to have supernatural powers and are therefore treated with respect, reverence, and awe. What is sacred and what is not is a matter of belief. The range of items believed to be sacred is limitless. They may be objects (idols, altars, or amulets), animals or animal totems, parts of the natural world (mountains, volcanos, or rivers), transcendental beings (gods, angels, devils), or persons (living or dead, such as prophets, messiahs, or saints) (see Panel 17–2).
- Because the sacred is held in awe, there are beliefs (theologies, cosmologies) and practices (rituals) to express and reinforce proper attitudes among believers about the sacred. The set of beliefs attempts to explain the meaning of life. Moreover, these beliefs present a set of guidelines for action toward the sacred, and toward one's fellows. Ritual, with its symbolism and action, evokes common feelings among the believers (awe, reverence, ecstasy, fear), which lead to group unity.
- An essential ingredient of religion is the existence of a community of believers. There must be a social group that shares a set of beliefs and practices, moral values, and a sense of community (a unique identity).

One important consequence of a group of persons having the same religious heritage and beliefs is unity. All believers, whether of high or low status, young or old, are united through the sharing of religious beliefs. Thus, religion, through the holding of common values to be cherished, sins to be avoided, rules to be followed, and symbols to be revered, integrates. Group unity is also accomplished through the universal feeling that God or the gods look upon this particular group with special favor (the ethnocentric notion

The Cargo Cult of Melanesia

Some religions prophesy a radical change in the future (the end of the world, the 1000-year reign of Christ, or a return to some golden age). One such "millenarian movement" is the cargo cult of Melanesia. The islands in Melanesia have been visited throughout history by foreigners in sailing ships, steamships, and airplanes. Each time the visitors brought riches unknown to the island people. The natives were greatly impressed by these goods, which they believed were being manufactured and sent to them by their ancestors.

The natives were most impressed with the cargo brought to the islands by plane during World War II (canned food, clothing, tools, radios, watches, guns, and motorcycles.) When the war ended, however, the supplies were used up and not replaced by new shipments. The island prophets proclaimed that if airstrips were built, these would entice back the planes with their fabulous cargo. As a result, the natives have built airstrips in the jungle, complete with hangars, radio shacks, beacon towers, and airplanes (all made out of bamboo sticks and leaves). The airports are staffed 24 hours a day, with bonfires set at night to serve as beacons for the expected cargo planes.

Thus, 40 years or so after World War II, the natives await the phantom cargo that will hail the beginning of a new age. When the planes finally arrive their lives will be filled with riches and plenty. They will be reunited with their deceased ancestors, heralding the beginning of heaven on earth.

---

that "God is on our side"). An example of this is found in a verse of the national anthem of Great Britain:

> O lord our God, arise
> Scatter our enemies
> And make them fall.
> Confound their politics,
> Frustrate their knavish tricks,
> On thee our hopes, we fix,
> God save us all.

Another consequence of religion is that it constrains the behavior of the community of believers, thus providing a social control function. This is accomplished in two ways. First, there are explicit rules to obey which if violated will be punished. Second, in the process of socialization, children internalize the religious beliefs and rules. In other words, they each develop a conscience which keeps them in line through guilt and fear.

A final positive consequence of religion—positive in the sense that it aids in uniting persons— is the legitimation of social structures that have profane origins (Berger, 1967b:343-344). There is a strong tendency for religious beliefs to become intertwined with secular beliefs, thereby providing religious blessings to the values and institutions of society. In American society, for example, private property and free enterprise have become almost sacred. Democracy, too, is believed to be ordained by God.

The very same religious bases that promote group integration also divide. Religious groups tend to emphasize separateness and superiority, thereby defining others as inferior ("infidels,""heathens,""heretics," or "nonbeliev-

Holy Tortilla

Lake Arthur, N.M.—The woman crawled on her knees from the railroad tracks in this tiny southern New Mexico town down the dirt road to the house of Maria and Eduardo Rubio.

She came in to worship, then crawled out beyond the tracks and disappeared.

The Rubios were not surprised. They have accepted that the Lord works in mysterious ways. And so have the 10,190 pilgrims who since Oct. 5, 1977, have made their way to the modest Rubio home in the middle of southeastern New Mexico's beanfields.

Mrs. Rubio was making lunch for her husband, a farmhand, on that October afternoon. That's when the face of Jesus appeared on a tortilla frying in her skillet.

She called her sister to witness the "miracle," and awakened Eduardo, who was taking a nap.

"She was crying," recalled Blanca Rubio, 21, one of the family's six children. "He told her to go to the church and the priest blessed it."

Word of the event spread. The Rubios erected a wall in their living room to separate the television and the couch from a shrine to the holy object. A family from a town about 50 miles away donated a specially built altar topped by a hollow square about 10 inches deep.

Inside that square rests a spray of lavender and white plastic flowers, which Mrs. Rubio changes occasionally, a wad of cotton simulating a cloud, and the tortilla. In a square-inch of burn marks on it, some see the profile of a long-haired man with a likeness to some depictions of Jesus.

On the wall above the altar, and beside a velvet painting of a weeping Jesus, are a string of *milagros*—small metal emblems depicting arms, legs, hearts, eyes and other ailing body parts believers want hung for healing near the tortilla.

Sometimes it works, Mrs. Rubio said in Spanish. "A lady about 55 years old came here a couple of years ago in a wheelchair. She was paralyzed and promised to walk here all the way from Artesia once a year if she was cured.

"She was, and made her first walk last year," Mrs. Rubio claimed.

The oil refineries of Artesia are about 11 miles south of Lake Arthur.

Each weekend, someone prays for a sick relative or expresses gratitude for a recovery at the shrine of the tortilla. "Just yesterday, a neighbor's son pulled out of a coma, and she came by to offer thanks," said Mrs. Rubio.

More than a hundred letters have come to Lake Arthur, a few from as far as Europe, asking the Rubios' prayers to remedy a hundred kinds of suffering.

Source: Steve Chawkins, "Holy Tortilla: Burden or Blessing?" *Rocky Mountain News* (June 6, 1982): 10. Reprinted from the *Rocky Mountain News*, Denver.

ers"). This occurs because each religious group tends to feel it has the way (and perhaps the only way) to achieve salvation or reach nirvana or whatever the goal.

Religious differences accentuate the differences among societies, denominations, and even within local churches. Since religious groups have feelings of superiority, there may be conflict brought about by discrimination, competition for converts, or feelings of hatred. Also, because religious ideas tend to be strongly held, groups may split rather than compromise. Liberals and fundamentalists, even within the same religion, denomination, or local church, will, doubtless, disagree on numerous issues. A common result, of course, is division.

A major divisive characteristic of religion is its tendency, through established churches, to accept the acts of the state. American churches, for example, have condoned such things as slavery, segregation, white supremacy, and war.* Within the church, there have always been those who spoke out against the church's cohabitation with the secular. This ability of the church to rationalize the activities of the state no matter how onerous has split many churches and denominations. The slavery issue, for example, split Baptists into American Baptists and Southern Baptists.

Conflict itself can occur between religious groups (with the sanction of each religion). Recent world history gives bloody evidence of this occurrence (for example, Moslems versus Hindus in India and Pakistan, Moslems versus Jews in the Middle East, Catholics versus Protestants in Northern Ireland). Religious conflict has also occurred within the United States at various times. Confrontations between Catholics and Protestants, between warring sects of Muslims (Black Muslims versus Sunni Muslims), as well as Protestants and Jews, have been fairly commonplace. Clearly, religious values are reason enough for individuals and groups to clash.

CLASSICAL SOCIOLOGY'S DIFFERING INTERPRETATIONS OF RELIGION

The great classical sociologists—Emile Durkheim (1858–1917), Karl Marx (1818–1883), and Max Weber (1864–1920)—wrote perceptively about religion. From different perspectives and asking different questions, each theorist adds to our sociological understanding of the differing consequences of religion on society and its members.

Religion from the Order Perspective of Emile Durkheim

Durkheim, the French sociologist, wrote *The Elementary Forms of Religious Life* in 1912 (1965). This classic work explored the question of why religion is universal in human societies. He reasoned that religion must help to maintain society. Durkheim studied the religion of the Australian aborigines to understand the possible role of religion in societal survival.

Durkheim found that each aborigine clan had its own totem, an object it considered sacred. The totem—a kangaroo, lizard, tree, river, or rock formation—was sacred because the clan believed that it symbolized the unique qualities of the clan. Two of Durkheim's interpretations are important in this regard. First, people bestow the notion of the sacred onto something, rather than that object being intrinsically sacred. Second, what the group worships

---

*Actually, the church has sometimes actively pursued some of these policies. The Puritan Church of the early settlers condoned witch hunts. The defeat of the Native Americans was justified by most Christian groups on the grounds that they were heathens and in need of white man's religion. Finally, most religious denominations sought Biblical rationalizations for slavery (van den Berghe, 1967:82).

is really society itself. Thus, people "create" religion.* Because the members of a society share religious beliefs, they are a moral community and as such the solidarity of the society is enhanced.

The society is held together by religious rituals and festivals in which the group's values and beliefs are reaffirmed. Each new generation is socialized to accept these beliefs, ensuring consensus on what is right and wrong. Religion, then, whether it be among the pre-industrial Australian aborigines, the Muslims of the Middle East, the Buddhists of Asia, or the Christians of North America, serves the same functions of promoting order and unity.

Religion from the Conflict Perspective of Karl Marx

Whereas Durkheim interpreted the unity achieved through religion as positive, Marx viewed it as negative. Religion inhibits societal change by making existing social arrangements seem right and inevitable. The dominant form of economics in society, the type of government, the law, and other social creations are given religious sanction. Thus, the system remains stable, which the order theorists see as good, when it perhaps should be transformed to meet the needs of all of the people.

Religion promotes the status quo in other ways. The powerless are taught to accept religious beliefs that are against their own interests. The Hindus, for example, believe that it is the person's duty to accept his or her caste. Failure to do so will result in being reincarnated to a lower caste or even as an animal. Christianity proclaims that the poor should accept their lot in this life for they will be rewarded in Heaven. In short, somehow oppression and poverty are reinterpreted by religion to be a special form of righteousness. Thus, religion is the ultimate tool to promote false consciousness.

Max Weber's View of Religion and Social Change

Max Weber disagreed fundamentally with Marx's notions that (1) religion impeded social change by being an opiate of the masses and by encouraging the oppressed to accept their lot and (2) economic considerations superseded ideology. Weber's classic, *The Protestant Ethic and the Spirit of Capitalism* (1958, first published in 1904), refuted Marx on both grounds. Weber demonstrated that the religious beliefs of John Calvin (1509–1564) were instrumental to the rise of capitalism in Europe. The Calvinist doctrine of predestination was the key. Because God, by definition, knows everything, God knows who will go to heaven (the elect) and who will be condemned to hell *even before they are*

---

*This raises an important question: Do we create God or is there a supernatural somewhere that human beings grope to find? Durkheim is correct in stating that religion is a social product. This universal response, however, does not prove or disprove the existence of a God or Gods. Sociologists as individuals may have strong religious beliefs, but as sociologists they focus on the complex interrelationship between religion and society.

born. This view was disconcerting to believers because it meant that one's future was locked in. Calvinists dealt with their anxiety by emphasizing economic success as the indicator to themselves and others of being one of God's elect. The rationale for this emphasis was that surely God would reward the chosen in this life as well as in the afterlife. This belief, then led Calvinists to work very hard, to live frugally, to accumulate savings, and to invest those savings in more land, equipment, and labor. Thus, the particular religious beliefs of the Calvinists were conducive to the development of capitalism in Europe and later among the colonies in America. Religious ideology in this case led to economic change.

SOME DISTINCTIVE FEATURES OF AMERICAN RELIGION

Civil Religion

One feature of American religion, traditionally, has been the separation of Church and State (established by the First Amendment to the Constitution). This is both a consequence and the cause of the religious diversity found in the United States. There is a relationship between religion and the state in America, but it differs from the usual conception of one dominant church that is inseparable from the state. In many respects, God and Country are conceived by most Americans as one. This has been labeled the civil religion of the United States (Bellah, 1967).

America's **civil religion** is seemingly antithetical to the constitutional demand for separation of Church and State. The paradox is that on the one hand the government sanctions God (the Pledge of Allegiance has the phrase, "one nation, under God" the phrase, "In God We Trust," is stamped on all money; every presidential inaugural address except Washington's second has mentioned God; and present-day presidents have regularly scheduled prayer breakfasts), while at the same time declaring it illegal to have prayer and/or religious instruction in the public schools. The basis for the paradox is that the civil religion is not a specific creed. It is a set of beliefs, symbols, and rituals that is broad enough for all citizens to accept. The God of the civil religion is all things to all people. One thing is certain—politicians, if they want to be successful, must show some semblance of piety by occasionally invoking the blessings of this nondenominational, nonsectarian God.

There are several central themes of the civil religion that are important for the understanding of American society. First, there is the belief that God has a special destiny for the United States. This implies that God is actively involved in history and, most important, that America has a holy mission to carry out God's will on earth. John F. Kennedy phrased this message well in the conclusion to his inauguration address: "With a good conscience our only sure reward, with history the final judge of our deed, let us go forth to lead the land we love, asking His blessing and His help, but knowing that here on earth God's work must truly be our own" (Bellah, 1967:1–2). This belief has been the source of self-righteousness in foreign relations. It has allowed

Americans to subdue the "pagan" Indians, win the frontier, follow a policy of manifest destiny, and defeat fascism. Currently, the defeat of communism is seen as a holy crusade. President Reagan, for example, exorted Americans to understand that Communism was evil and that God wanted us to be strong. Thus, he invoked Scripture to justify a strong defense:

> I found myself wanting to remind you of what Jesus said in Luke 14:31: "Oh, what king, when he sets out to make [war]—or meet another king in battle will not first sit down and take counsel whether he is strong enough with 10,000 men to encounter the one coming against him with 20,000. Or else, while the other is still far away, sends a delegation and asks the terms of peace." I don't think the Lord that blessed this country, as no other county has ever been blessed, intends for us to have to someday negotiate because of our weakness. (quoted in Pierard and Linder, 1988:280)

A second aspect of the civil religion is maintenance of the status quo. The God of civil religion is more closely allied to law and order than to changing the system. Thus, civil religion tends strongly toward uncritical endorsement of American values and the system of stratification. Order and unity are the traditional ways of God, not change and dissent. Thus, public policy tends to receive religious sanction.

At the same time, however, the civil religion enjoins Americans to stand up for certain principles—freedom, individualism, equal opportunity. Consequently, there are occasions when current governmental policy or the policy of some group is criticized because it does not measure up to certain ideals. The civil religion of America, then, accomplishes both the **priestly** (acceptance of what is) and the **prophetic** (challenging the existing system) **roles of traditional religion,** with emphasis, however, on the former.

The Variety of Religious Belief

Some societies are unified by religion. All persons in such societies believe the same religious ideas, worship the same deities, obey the same moral commandments, and identify strongly with each other. Superficially, through its civil religion, the United States appears to be homogeneous along religious lines. Moreover, 86 percent of Americans in 1986 were Christian (*Gallup Report*, 1987:18). The range of attitudes and beliefs among American Christians, however, is fantastically wide. Among Roman Catholics, for example, there are radical priests, nuns, and parishioners who disobey the instructions of bishops, cardinals, and even the Pope. At the same time, however, there are Catholics who rigidly adhere to all the rules set down by the church authorities. The range within Protestantism is even greater. Many Protestants believe that the Bible is to be taken literally, word for word; for others, the Bible is purely allegorical. Some religious groups have so much faith in the healing power of religion that their members refuse to see physicians under any circumstances. Within Protestantism are Amish, Hutterites, Quakers, high-church Episcopalians, Pentecostal Holiness groups, Congregationalists, and even snake handlers.

Religious Organization

Very broadly, American religious organizations can be divided according to their secular commitments into two categories—churches and sects (Troeltsch, 1931).

Religious groups have a choice—to reject and withdraw from the secular society, or to accommodate to it. The basis for a decision to reject the social environment is maintenance of spiritual and ethical purity. Such a choice, by definition, entails withdrawal from the world, thereby consciously avoiding any chance to change it. The opposite choice—accommodation—requires compromise and the loss of distinctive ideals but it also means that the groups can influence the larger society. The accommodation or resistance to the secular world is the fundamental difference between a church and a sect.

The **church,** as an ideal type, has the following attributes:

- The tendency to compromise with the larger society and its values and institutions.
- Membership tends to occur by being born to parents who belong. Membership, moreover, takes place through infant baptism, which implies that all members are "saved."
- A hierarchy of authority, with those at the top being trained for their vocation.
- Acceptance of a diversity of beliefs, since the membership is large, and for many the scriptures are interpreted metaphorically rather than literally.
- There is a tolerance of the popular vices.

A **sect** in its perfect form is exactly opposite a church in every way.

- There is a fundamental withdrawal from and rejection of the world. A sect is a moral community separate from and in many ways hostile toward the secular world (see Scanzoni, 1980).
- Membership is only through a "conversion" experience. Membership is therefore voluntary and limited to adults. Hence, adult baptism is the only accepted form of baptism.
- Organization is informal and unstructured. Ministers are untrained. They became ministers by being "called" from the group.
- The belief system is rigid. The Bible is the source and it is interpreted literally. The goal of the membership is spiritual purity as found in the early Christian Church.
- There are rigid ethical requirements restraining the members from the popular vices of drinking, smoking, card playing, dancing, and cursing.

The church–sect dichotomy does not exhaust all the possibilities. Some religious groups would fit somewhere in between—as institutionalized sects. These groups (for example, Mormons, Disciples of Christ, and Southern Baptists) incorporate features of both a church (trained leadership, some accommodation to the larger society) with the sectlike attributes of adult baptism, and an unwillingness to compromise on some theological questions.

For our purposes, however, the church–sect dichotomy, while oversimplifying the situation, is useful in two ways: to depict a form of social change, and to show why certain categories of persons are attracted to one type and not the other.

The church–sect dichotomy illustrates an important sociological phenomenon—the very process of organization deflects away from the original goal of the group. A group may form to pursue a goal such as religious purity, but in so doing it creates a new organization, which means that some of the group's energies will be spent in organizational maintenance. Consequently, a sect may form with the explicit intention of eliminating a hierarchy and a codification of beliefs. Patterns of behavior emerge, however, as certain practices are found to be more effective. In particular, the selection of ministers tends to become routinized, and a system of religious instruction for children is developed so that they will learn the catechism in the proper sequence. Sects, then, tend to become churches. This is illustrated by the type of leader found in each. Often a sect is formed by a charismatic person and his followers. This person is followed because he is believed to possess extraordinary qualities of leadership, saintliness, gifts of prophecy, or ability to heal. What happens to such an organization when this leadership is gone? The organization is faced with a crisis of succession. Groups typically find ways to pass on the **charisma** (the extraordinary attributes) of the original leader. This process is called the **routinization of charisma** (whereby an organization attempts to transmit the charisma of the former leader to a new one). This is done by either: (1) selection of the successor by the original charismatic leader, (2) designation of a successor by the group closest to the original leader ("disciples"), (3) hereditary transmission, or (4) transmission of charisma by ritual ("laying on of hands") (Weber, 1947:358–366). In this last instance there is the recognition of a charisma of office—that is, whoever holds the position possesses charisma. When this occurs, the organizational machinery is advanced enough to move the group away from its sectlike qualities toward a church. The important sociological point here is that organizations seldom remain the same. The simple tends to become complex. But the process does not stop at complexity; as the original goal of the sect (religious purity with the necessity of separation from the world) is superseded when the organization gets larger and more bureaucratic, some persons will become dissatisfied enough to break away and form a new sect. Thus, the process tends to be cyclical.

Increased bureaucratization (and subsequent splintering) is characteristic of modern urban society. This leads us to a final consideration relative to the church–sect dichotomy—the motivation to join sects. At the risk of oversimplification, we can identify two important features of sects that help explain why some categories of persons are especially prone to join sects rather than churches. The first is that a sect (more so than a church) may provide a total world of meaning and social identity, and a close circle of persons to whom members can turn when troubled. The sect provides precisely those things missing in the lives of many urban dwellers. They find meaning in a meaningless world. They find friends in a sea of strangers. They find stability in a setting that is rapidly undergoing change. Thus, the alienated are especially attracted to sects. So, too, are new migrants to the city. In the city, they are confronted with a variety of new and difficult problems—industrialized work, work insecurity, loss of kinship ties, and disruption of other primary group ties. The sects, unlike the established city churches, appeal to such persons by their form of worship, emphasis on individual attention, and lack of formal organization appeal (Yinger, 1961:21–25).

A second variable affecting attraction to a sect or church is social class. Generally, low-status persons tend to be attracted to sects rather than churches because religious status is substituted for social status (or as the Bible puts it, "and the last shall be first"). It makes sense for persons of low social or economic status to reject this world and the religious bodies that accommodate to it. Such persons would be especially attracted to a religious group that rejects this world and assures its followers that in the next world "true believers"—those who are religiously pure—will have the highest status. The sect represents to its followers a reaction against or escape from the dominant religious and economic systems in society. It is a protest against the failure of established churches to meet the needs of marginal groups (Pope, 1942:140). The sect, moreover, rejects the social class as irrelevant and, in fact, a system of rewards that is in exact reverse order from God's will.*

Churches, on the other hand, attract the middle and upper classes. Since these persons are successful, they obviously would not turn to a religious organization that rejects their world. As Max Weber said more than fifty years ago:

> Other things being equal, classes with high social and economic privilege will scarcely be prone to evolve the ideas of salvation. Rather, they assign to religion the primary function of legitimizing their own life pattern and situation in this world. (Weber, 1963:107)

Both the sect and the church, consequently, have well developed theodicies (Berger, 1967a). A **theodicy** is a religious legitimation for a situation that otherwise might cause guilt or anger (such as defeat in a war or the existence of poverty among affluence). Sects tend to have a theodicy of suffering—i.e., a religious explanation for their lack of power and privilege. Churches must explain the inequalities of society, too, but their emphasis is on legitimation of possessing power and privilege. This tendency to develop theodicies has the important social function of preserving the status quo. Churches convince their adherents that all is well, that one should accept one's fate as God-given. This makes people's situations less intolerable and the possibility of revolution remote—the suffering know they will be rewarded, while the guilt of the well-off is assuaged. Consequently, there is no reason to change the system.

---

*It is incorrect to say, however, that all lower-class persons who are alienated will join religious sects in order to attack the establishment. Their estrangement may lead them to join other kinds of social movements (e.g., labor or political) or toward social isolation.

Religion and Patriarchy

The great religions and their leaders have consistently taught that women were secondary to men. Consider the following examples of this thought, which supported men as God's chosen leaders:

- One hundred women are not worth a single testicle.
  —Confucius (551–479 BC)
- In childhood a woman must be subject to her father; in youth to her husband; when her husband is dead, to her sons. A woman must never be free of subjugation.
  —The Hindu Code of Manu (circa 100 AD)
- If . . . the tokens of virginity are not found in the young woman, then they shall bring out the young woman to the door of her father's house, and the men of the city shall stone her to death with stones because she has wrought folly . . . so you shall purge the evil from the midst of you.
  —Deuteronomy 22:20-21 (Old Testament)
- Blessed art thou, O Lord our God and King of the Universe, that thou didst not create me a woman.
  —Daily prayer (ancient and contemporary) of the Orthodox Jewish male
- Let a woman learn in silence with all submissiveness. I permit no woman to teach or to have authority over men; she is to keep silent.
  —I Timothy 2:11-15 (New Testament)
- Men are superior to women.
  —The Koran (circa 650 AD)
- Women should remain at home, sit still, keep house, and bear and bring up children. . . .
  —Martin Luther (1438–1546)
- Woman in her greatest perfection was made to serve and obey man, not rule and command him.
  —John Knox (1505–1572)

Given these pronouncements we should not be surprised that women traditionally have not held positions of spiritual leadership within organized religion. But these statements were made long ago at historical times when women were clearly subservient to men in all aspects of society. However, this patriarchal tradition continues. Women are formally denied the role of pastor, minister, priest, or rabbi in the Missouri Synod Lutheran Church, The Greek Orthodox Church, the Church of Latter Day Saints, The Catholic Church, the Southern Baptist Church, and Orthodox Judaism. In other denominations there have been bitter fights over this matter, with some dissidents breaking away to form separate organizations, when women were allowed to become ministers. The majority of Protestant denominations now have women in the ministry, as do Reformed and Conservative Judaism. About 8 percent of all U.S. clergy are women and about one-fourth of seminary students are women.

Serious questions remain: Will congregations accept women clergy in the same way they do men? Will women clergy be called to lead the largest and most prestigious congregations? Will the hierarchy in the various denominations promote women to the highest offices? And, will some religious groups continue to deny women the clergy role?

Source: The quotations were taken from a list compiled by Meg Bowman, "Why We Burn: Sexism Exorcised," *The Humanist* 43 (November/December 1983):28–29.

The Relationship between Socioeconomic Status and Religion

The dominant religion in the United States, Christianity, stresses the equality of all people in the sight of God (with some notable exceptions; see Panel 17-3). All persons, regardless of socioeconomic status, are welcomed in Christianity. We might expect, therefore, that the distribution of members by socioeconomic status within any denomination would be randomly distributed.

We might also assume that the organization of any local congregation would ignore status distinctions. Although these two assumptions seem to have surface validity, the empirical situation refutes them.

We have seen that sects and churches tend to have a social class bias—the lower the socioeconomic status, the greater the probability of belonging to a sect. There also seems to be a ranking of denominations in terms of the socioeconomic status of their members. Although there is always a range of the social classes within any one denomination, there is a modal status that characterizes each. The reasons for this are varied: the proportion of members living in rural or urban areas, which immigrant groups brought the religion to the United States and during what historical period, the appeal of the religious experience (ritual, evangelism, close personal ties, salvation, legitimation of the social system, or attacks on the establishment). This last point is especially important because "life conditions affect men's religious propensities, and life conditions are significantly correlated with the facts of stratification in all societies" (O'Dea, 1966:60).

There is a relationship between socioeconomic status and denominational affiliation. Table 17–1 presents data from a national sample that orders the major Protestant denominations by decreasing status.

Even though Table 17–1 shows that the denominations can be ranked by socioeconomic status, it is clear that each denomination includes persons of high, middle, and lower status. As Demerath has stated, "Episcopalians may be *relatively* upper class, but more than 40 percent are from the lower class. Baptists may be *relatively* lower class, but they claim their Rockefellers as well" (Demerath, 1965:3).

Local churches, even more so than denominations, tend to be homogeneous in socioeconomic status. This is partly the result of residential patterns—that is, neighborhoods are relatively homogeneous by socioeconomic status and the local churches are attended mostly by persons living nearby. Another reason, and perhaps just as important, is the tendency for persons to want to belong to organizations composed of persons like themselves. They do not want to feel out of place, so they are attracted to churches where the members have the same lifestyle (for example, speech patterns, clothing tastes, and educational backgrounds). The result, then, is that persons belonging to a particular denomination will often seek out the local congregation in the city where they feel most comfortable. To paraphrase Broom and Selznick (1968:321), "although rich and poor, educated and uneducated are members of one denomination, they tend to worship under different roofs."

There is some range, however, in every local church. Probably no one congregation is comprised totally of persons from exactly the same status niche. Although the status differentials may be minimal within a local congregation, they are evidently important to the parishioners. The rule is that the higher the socioeconomic status of the member, the greater his or her influence in the running of the local church. There is greater likelihood that such persons will be elected or appointed to office (elder, deacon, trustee, Sunday school superintendent) and that their opinions will carry greater weight than persons of lower social status. This may be partly a function of

Table 17-1
Socioeconomic Profiles of Religious Denominations: (1986)

	Jewish	Episcopalian	Presbyterian	Methodist	Lutheran	Catholic	Christian	Baptist
Education								
College graduate	42%	34%	34%	21%	19%	16%	15%	10%
College incomplete	25	35	26	26	27	26	21	18
High school graduate	27	22	30	33	33	37	35	35
Less than high school	4	9	10	20	21	21	29	37
Income								
$40,000 and over	29	31	30	18	20	18	13	11
25,000–39,999	21	20	26	23	26	26	12	19
15,000–24,999	20	20	11	23	24	21	28	22
Under $15,000	16	20	30	30	27	29	41	44

Source: "Religion in America," *The Gallup Report*, No.259 (April 1987):24–27. Reprinted by permission.

the disproportionately large financial contributions by the more well-to-do, but the important point here is that the secular world intrudes in the organization of each local congregation.

The common indicators of religious involvement—church membership, attendance at church services, and participation in the church's activities—all demonstrate a relationship to socioeconomic status. On each of these measures, persons of high status are more involved than those of low status. Unfortunately, these are not very good measures of religiosity, although often assumed to be. The problem is that upper-class persons are much more likely to join and actively participate in all sorts of organizations. The joining of churches and attending services are but the manifestations of a more general phenomenon—the tendency for middle- and upper-class persons to be "joiners" while lower-class individuals tend to isolate themselves from all types of organizations. The spuriousness of the relationship between socioeconomic status and "religiosity" is more clearly seen when we analyze the importance of religion to persons of varying socioeconomic circumstances, as well as differences in religious beliefs and the degree to which church activities are secular by social class.

Goode, after comparing white-collar church members with working-class church members, found that while the former were more likely to belong and participate in formal activities of the church, the latter were in fact more religious.

> They participate less in formal church activities, but their religious activity does not appear to be nearly so secularized. It is more specifically religious in character. This is indicated by the fact that on a number of other religious dimensions, dimensions not dependent on extraneous nonreligious variables, individuals of manual-status levels appear to display a considerably higher level of religious response. This is true particularly of psychological variables, such as religious "salience," the greater feeling that the church and religion are great forces in the lives of respondents. It is also true for "religiosity" as measured by a higher level of religious concern, and for religious "involvement," the extent to which the individual is psychologically dependent on some sort of specifically religious association in his life. (Goode, 1966:111)

Table 17–2 presents evidence for the "secularization of religion" by the upper classes and the difference by level of education on religious beliefs. Examination of Table 17–2 reveals that the lower the educational status of the respondent, the more likely the respondent is to hold conservative religious beliefs. This means, in effect, that the middle- and upper-status categories have tended to abandon the bases of Christianity.

In summary, there is a rather complex relationship between socioeconomic status and religion. Although the relatively poor and uneducated are more likely to be indifferent to religion than the better educated and financially well-off, those who are religious tend to make religion a more integral part of their lives than better-off persons. They go to church more for religious than secular reasons. They believe much more strongly that the well-to-do in the fundamental beliefs as expressed in the Bible. Thus, we have the paradox that on many objective measures of religious involvement—church

Table 17–2
Religious Beliefs and Educational Attainment

	Level of Education		
	College	High School	Grade School
Percent responding true to "My religious faith is the most important influence in my life."	56	72	81
Percent responding true to "I believe in the divinity of Jesus Christ."	74	87	94
Percent believing the Bible is the literal word of God.	21	40	56
Percent responding true to "I constantly seek God's will through prayer."	51	69	86

Source: The Gallup Report, *Religion in America,* Report nos. 201–202 (June–July 1982), adapted from a number of tables, pp. 112, 114, 122, and 174. Reprinted by permission.

attendance and participation in formal church activities—the middle- and upper-status persons exceed those of less status, whereas if importance of religion in the lives of the individual is considered, the poor who go to church outstrip their more economically favored brethren.

RELIGIOUS TRENDS

Religion in U.S. society is a paradox. On the one hand, religion seems to be losing its vitality. The data show that in the past 30 years or so there has been a downward trend and recently a leveling off in regular church attendance (see Table 17–3). Protestants during this period have stayed near the 41 percent attendance level while the percentage of Catholics attending church at least once a week has fallen from 72 percent in 1954 to 49 percent in 1986. The data also show that the percentage of young adults attending church regularly has fallen and that the largest denominations—Episcopal, Methodist, and Presbyterian—are falling in both attendance and membership.

Table 17–3
Percentage Attending Church during Average Week (1954–1987)

1954	46	1963	46	1972	40	1981	41
1955	49	1964	45	1973	40	1982	41
1956	46	1965	44	1974	40	1983	40
1957	47	1966	44	1975	40	1984	40
1958	49	1967	43	1976	41	1985	42
1959	47	1968	43	1977	41	1986	40
1960	47	1969	42	1978	41	1987	40
1961	47	1970	42	1979	40		
1962	46	1971	40	1980	40		

Source: The Gallup Report, no. 259 (April 1987):38; and The Gallup Report, no. 288 (September 1989), p.19. Reprinted by permission.

On the other hand, however, there are indications that Americans are just as religious as ever and in some areas there is even dramatic growth. On the first point, Americans have consistently and overwhelmingly believed in God. Gallup has reported that 94 percent of adult Americans believe in God or a universal spirit, which is the highest rate found in the nations of North America and Europe. Similarly, more Americans (71 percent) believe in life after death than do these other nations. (Canada is the next highest at 54 percent and West Germany the lowest with only one-third of adults accepting this belief; Gallup poll, cited in *Public Opinion*, 1979:37).

Contrary to the experience of the mainline churches, some religious groups are growing rapidly in members and interest. The fastest growing in percentage gain is the Mormon Church with a national growth of 40 percent from 1973 to 1983. More significant because of their growing numbers nationwide and their political leverage, are the evangelical denominations and sects.

In this section we highlight three major trends of U.S. religion: (1) the decline of the mainline churches; (2) the rise of the evangelicals; and (3) the new political activism of the evangelicals and the decline of religious pluralism. Because social conditions have led to these shifts, the focus is on the societal conditions that have given impetus to these trends.

Decline of the Mainline Denominations

Together, the mainline denominations of the United Church of Christ (which includes most Congregationalists), Presbyterians, Episcopalians, United Methodists, and the Disciples of Christ (Christian) have suffered membership losses of 5.2 million from 1965 to 1988, a time when the U.S. population rose by 47 million (Ostling, 1989). At the same time, the Mormons, black Protestant groups, and the conservative evangelical groups have increased membership substantially.

The reasons for the decline in the mainline denominations are not altogether clear, but the following appear plausible. These denominations have lost their vitality as they have become more and more churchlike (and have moved away from the qualities characterizing sects). The beliefs within these churches have become so pluralistic that to many people the faith seems "watered down." Many churchgoers want authority but they too often receive only more ambiguity. The mainline churches also have lost members because of a preoccupation with political and social issues at the expense of an emphasis on an old-fashioned faith and biblical teachings for personal growth.

Because other parts of society emphasize rationality, efficiency, and bureaucracy, many persons seek a religion that will emphasize feelings and fellowship. However, the mainline churches, for the most part, are just as impersonal and ossified as the other bureaucracies in society.

The Catholic Church has been especially vulnerable to losses in attendance. In this case, the rigidity of the Catholic hierarchy is partly responsible. The Church has taken strong stances against contraception, abortion, and divorce. Many Catholics feel that the Church authorities are out of step with contemporary life. The Catholic and some other traditional churches have also lost credence with some for their refusal to accept women in leadership roles. This patriarchal emphasis by some churches, however, is a positive attraction for some individuals, as we will see later.

An interesting recent development has been the defection of many Hispanic Catholics for evangelical Protestant denominations (the following is taken from Suro, 1989). Surveys indicate that approximately 20 percent of Hispanic Americans identify themselves as Protestant, with about 60,000 joining Protestant denominations each year. There are several reasons for this shift away from traditional membership patterns. First, the emotional power of the evangelicals appeals to many whites and Hispanics alike. Second, Hispanic Catholics often find linguistic and cultural barriers in the Church. Only 2 percent of Catholic priests (less than 2,000), for example, are Hispanic. Meanwhile, the Southern Baptists, to name just one evangelical denomination, has 2,300 Hispanic pastors and 500 more in seminary training. Finally, critics charge that Hispanic Americans suffer various forms of discrimination within the American Catholic Church. These charges include the failure of the Church hierarchy to encourage religious vocations among Hispanic Americans, a hesitancy to elevate Hispanic priests to higher posts, and a reluctance to accept rituals meaningful to Hispanics, such as devotions to the Virgin of Guadelupe.

Rise of Christian Fundamentalism

Beginning in the late 1960s there has been a rise in Christian fundamentalism. Although there are variations among fundamentalists, there is a set of beliefs they tend to share.

> Most simply put, [Christian fundamentalism] refers to the world view of people who think that the Bible is the inerrant word of God and who have accepted Jesus Christ as their Lord and Savior. But [it] goes beyond acceptance of such fundamentals of the faith. It involves at least the idea that the Bible and a person's relationship with Jesus provide answers to most personal and social problems—the biblically based world view is in principle all-encompassing. Fundamentalists are especially concerned about upholding a tradition, about maintaining the true faith in a defensive reaction against a perceived threat. On the basis of the fundamentals of faith and morality, they also wish to bring the wider culture back to its religious roots, to restore the Christian character of American society: the tenets of the faith are presumed to have implications for social change. (Lechner, 1989:51)

There are two categories of fundamentalists—evangelicals and pentecostals. Evangelicals emphasize a personal relationship with Jesus, public declaration of their faith, and spreading the faith to nonbelievers. Pentecostals share these beliefs with fundamentalists and also emphasize the active presence of the Holy Spirit in lives and church services. Their church services are very emotional (crying, laughing, shouting, applauding, moving about) with special emotional experiences involving faith healing and "speaking in tongues."

Both of these strands of religious fundamentalism are growing rapidly in American society. This growth caught many religious observers and sociologists by surprise because they assumed that modernizing societies undergo processes that tend to make religion increasingly irrelevant to the affairs of society (Lechner, 1989). What, then, are the reasons for this unforeseen rise?

The most obvious reason the fundamentalists are increasing in number is their great emphasis on converting other people to their faith. They stress this activity because Christ commanded "Go ye into all the world and preach the gospel to every creature."

Second, fundamentalist congregations emphasize community. The people are friendly, accepting, and caring in a world that for many people is unfriendly, unaccepting, and uncaring. Thus, the fundamentalists tend to provide for many people the ingredients they find missing in the mainline churches and in the other impersonal bureaucracies of which they are a part.

Third, the fundamentalists offer "the truth." They believe intensely that they are right and others are wrong. In a society characterized by rapid change and a plurality of ideas and choices, many people seek authority, a foundation to provide consistency and constancy in their lives. The fundamentalists provide a rigid set of beliefs based on the infallibility of the Bible as the word of God.

A fourth appeal of the fundamentalists is their insistence that society has made wrong choices and that we must go back to laws and customs based on biblical truths. Thus, fundamentalism offers not only a critique of modern society but also an action program based on its set of absolute beliefs. They

Pentecostals believe that the Holy Spirit is an active presence in their services, resulting in very emotional behaviors by the parishoners.

fight, then, for practices consistent with their view of the Christian family and the Christian society. The political beliefs that emanate from this view are, for example, strong opposition to abortion (see Panel 17–4), women's equality, homosexual rights, evolution taught in the schools, and sex education in the schools and strong support for prayer in the schools, a strong military, capital punishment, capitalism, and patriotism.

Finally, the fundamentalists have increased their popularity through an emphasis on modern marketing techniques (e.g., direct mail advertising), radio, and television. This type of ministry, which is particularly effective in reaching the disabled and the elderly, began with the advent of radio in the 1920s and expanded greatly with the growth of television in the 1950s and 1960s, cable television in the late 1970s, and satellite transmission in the 1980s.

The Electronic Church

The enormity of the impact of religious television (which is almost exclusively fundamentalist in doctrine—Robert Schuller, whose message is personal growth, optimism, and achievement, is the only major exception) is seen in the number of people affected and the amounts of money generated (Hadden and Shupe, 1988). In 1989, for example, 336 television stations and 1,485 radio stations in the United States were owned by religious organizations (Applebome, 1989). In 1987, the Christian Broadcasting Network was carried by 7,353 cable systems and watched by an estimated 4.4 million persons daily; the money raised by the electronic evangelists was estimated to be about $2 billion; and evangelists Jimmy Swaggart and Oral Roberts were watched by 3.6 million and 1.1 million a day, respectively. In sharp contrast, scholars estimate that Jesus, in his lifetime, preached to no more than 30,000 persons.

The success of this electronic church has been enhanced by the use of sophisticated methods, such as professional production of programs, showmanship, computerized mailing lists, and "personalized" letters written by computers. The successful televangelists have combined the communication technologies used in entertainment, business, and politics to reach and manipulate their audiences with the greatest effectiveness.

The electronic church began faltering in 1987 after a series of publicized scandals involving Jim Bakker (convicted in 1989 of defrauding his followers of $3.7 million, as well as confessing to sexual improprieties), Jimmy Swaggart (who confessed to hiring prostitutes to pose for him), and the outrageous claims of Oral Roberts (e.g., claiming that if he did not receive $8 million by the first of the month God would "call him home"). Many people questioned the credibility of these preachers and television evangelists in general, and the overall contributions and the number of viewers declined significantly. Comparing viewers in February 1986 with those in November 1988, the number of households watching the five major television evangelists—Jimmy Swaggart, Oral Roberts, Jerry Falwell, Pat Robertson, and Robert Schuller—dropped almost in half (Buchert, 1989). Similarly, the money dropped significantly, as evidenced by the bankruptcy of Jim Bakker's Heritage USA. Oral Roberts, with $25 million in debts, closed his hospital and medical school in

What Does It Mean To Be Prolife?

One tenet of Christian fundamentalism is a pro-life philosophy, that is opposition to abortion. Fundamentalists differ in how they define this position. Some have suggested that it also include opposition to anything that destroys life: nuclear weapons, economic injustice, environmental pollution, and the like. Ronald J. Sider, the author of the excerpt below, is executive director of JustLife and Evangelicals for Social Action and professor of theology and culture at Eastern Baptist Theological Seminary in Philadelphia. He argues that evangelicals should be consistent in their prolife position:

> Abortion is wrong. Both the Bible and biology point away from the modern notion that the fetus is merely a physical appendage of the mother rather than an independent human being. We must act on the belief that from the moment of conception, we are dealing with a human being created in the image of God. We must stop aborting millions of unborn babies each year.
>
> But if annually aborting millions is wrong, then walking down a path that increases the likelihood of the ultimate abortion, where a nuclear exchange obliterates hundreds of millions of people, is also wrong.

Most evangelical Christians stand within the just-war tradition. Under certain circumstances, the just-war tradition permits killing to promote justice and peace. But the just-war tradition teaches that aiming at civilians is murder. Nuclear weapons are clearly targeted at civilians as well as military and industrial targets located in the middle of population centers. Precisely because using nuclear weapons targeted at noncombatants would be murder, prolife people must redouble their efforts to reverse the nuclear arms race. Adm. Hyman Rickover, the man who built America's nuclear navy, declared when he retired that we will destroy ourselves if we do not abolish nuclear weapons. Even President Ronald Reagan, who clearly does not espouse pacifism, endorsed the goal of a nuclear-free world. Prolife people should work hard for bilateral and multilateral, verifiable steps to move toward that goal.

> Similarly, if human life is precious, then it is a terrible sin to stand idly by in suffocating affluence when we could prevent the death by malnutrition and starvation of 12 million children each year. And yet some Christians urge us to focus all or most of our attention on combating abortion, apparently placing concern for the poor in a category that is less urgent.

Tulsa, and Pat Robertson estimated a loss in revenues of $21 million the first year after the scandals of the others were publicized. But while some televangelists have fallen in popularity, others have risen. Mother Angelica, for example, began a television ministry in 1981 with $200 and now runs a $5 million network that reaches 14 million households on 570 television stations and continues to grow. After early losses following the 1987 scandals, some television ministries have rebounded. Robert Schuller's "Hour of Power," which lost $8 million after the Bakker scandal, was by 1989 the top-rated show, with more than 1.6 million viewers and with record donations (*U.S. News & World Report*, 1989). Sociologist Jeffrey Hadden has said that despite the recent setbacks, television preaching will continue to thrive:

> The public that is deeply committed to religious broadcasting represents about a fifth of the population. But while these viewers' loyalty may be to a particular television preacher at any given time, what they are really commit-

Nor does the list of consistently prolife issues end with abortion, the nuclear-arms race, and poverty. In the United States alone, 350,000 persons die prematurely each year because of cigarette smoking. William Pollin, director of the U.S. National Institute on Drug Abuse, pointed out recently that these 350,000 deaths from smoking are "more than all other drugs and alcohol abuse deaths combined, seven times more than all automobile fatalities per year, . . . and more than all American military fatalities in World War I, World War II, and Vietnam put together." The global death toll from cigarette smoking already runs in the tens of millions.

Alcoholism enslaves 10 million Americans. Their personal tragedies entangle another 30 million family members, close friends, and co-workers in a hell of crippling car accidents, fires, lost productivity, and damaged health that cost the nation $120 billion annually.

Racism in India, South Africa, and South Philadelphia maims and kills. More than 200,000 black children in affluent South Africa die every year of starvation.

The rape of our environment, finally, is also a prolife issue. The United States loses three million acres of agricultural land each year. Annually, erosion carries away 6.4 billion tons of topsoil—enough to cover all cropland in Maine, New Hampshire, Vermont, Massachusetts, Connecticut, Rhode Island, New York, New Jersey, Pennsylvania, Delaware, Maryland, Alabama, California, and Florida with one inch of soil. Since farming began in North America, one-third of all our topsoil has been lost forever. Every day, erosion and development remove enough productive land to feed 260,000 for a year. In a world of hunger and starvation, that is a prolife issue.

A hasty survey of the current religious scene in the United States might lead one to despair of any realistic possibility of promoting this consistent prolife agenda. But that would be a superficial judgment. Increasingly today, especially in the churches, there is a growing movement of Christians who care about justice and freedom, the sanctity of unborn life and the lives of the poor, the family and the environment, an end to murder on the highways, and concern over the nuclear-arms race.

In short, if biblical norms set the Christian's agenda, then we will reject one-issue approaches in favor of a commitment to all that for which God has a concern.

Source: Ronald J. Sider, "Abortion Is Not the Only Issue," *Christianity Today* (July 14, 1989): 28–32. Reprinted by permission.

ted to is religion. When one minister falls, it doesn't alter their basic faith; all they have to do is change the channel. (quoted in Applebome, 1989:12)

THE ROLE OF MAINLINE CHURCHES: COMFORT OR CHALLENGE?

The fundamentalists have become active politically. They have worked hard to elect politicians supportive of their political agenda and to pressure legislators, governors, and presidents to bring the United States back to a morality based on biblical principles as they interpret them. At the local level, fundamental activists have directed their efforts to changing schools (for school prayer, against the teaching of evolution and sex education, against teachers they have labeled as "secular humanists"). They have sometimes been successful in banning books they feel are contrary to their religious beliefs.

The political activism among the fundamentalists is much like that among the clergy in the mainline churches. The difference is that whereas fundamentalist congregations are relatively homogeneous in religious and political ideologies, the mainline congregations are much more pluralistic. This pluralism places the clergy in a precarious position, a dilemma brought about by the two contradictory roles (analogous to order and conflict approaches to the social order) of the church—to comfort the afflicted and to afflict the comforted (or to comfort and to challenge). The comforting role is one of aiding individuals in surmounting trials and tribulations of sickness, the death of loved ones, financial woes, social interaction with family, neighbors, colleagues, or enemies. The church aids by such means as pastoral counseling and collecting and distributing food and clothing to the needy. Another way the church comforts the afflicted is through providing a rationale for suffering (*theodicy*), the consequence of which is sanctification of the status quo.

Three related criticisms of the comforting function are immediately apparent. First, some would say that the church (and the clergy) have allowed this function to supersede the other role of challenger. Second, if the church would do more challenging and less comforting, evils such as poverty would be reduced. By helping people to accept an imperfect society, the church preserves the status quo—that is, the injustice and inequality that caused the problems in the first place. In this way, religion *is* an opiate of the masses because it convinces them to accept an unjust situation rather than working to change it from below. Third, the comfortable will not feel guilty, thereby preventing them from working to change the system from above.

The other function of the church—to challenge—is the injunction to be an agent of social protest and social reform. The church, through its pronouncements and leadership, seeks to lead in the fight to right the inequities of the society. A fundamental problem is in winning the support of the members. Change is almost by definition controversial, since some persons benefit under the existing social arrangements. When the church takes a stand against racial segregation, abortion, war, the abuses of business or labor, some members will become alienated. They may withdraw their financial support or even leave the church. The church, of course, has a commitment to its members. Since it cannot afford to lose its membership, the church may compromise its principles. Such an action, however, may make others angry at the church because of its hypocrisy. Consequently, the church is in the unenviable position of trying to keep a very precarious balance between compromise and purity.

Of course, the clergy vary in their interpretation of the role of the church. They are truly people in conflict. There are conflicting expectations of the clergy from all sides (resulting in role conflict). The church hierarchy expects the clergy to behave in a particular way (consider the rules issued by the Catholic hierarchy, for example). Most parishioners will doubtless favor the comforting role. Most joined the church to be comforted (if poor, to know they will be rewarded later; if rich, to have their wealth and power legitimized). In a survey 5,000 persons were asked what qualities of leadership they looked for in their religious leaders. The findings were clear—regardless of denomination people favored clergy who behave responsibly, counsel well in personal crisis, present a decorous appearance, and preach the Bible with competence. An awareness of social problems was far down the list of priorities, but even then the response was tempered with the qualifier that while clergy should be aware of social problems, they should not be actively engaged in solutions to them (Schuller, Strommen, and Brekke, 1981). Although they are a minority in most congregations, some parishioners wish the clergy to take stands on controversial issues and work for social change. A final source of the clergy's role conflict arises from their own definition of the role. These various expectations, and the resulting role conflict on the clergy, amount to one reason why they may drop out. Another is that if they take a stand (or do not), they may automatically alienate a segment of the parish and perhaps the church hierarchy. They may, consequently, be forced to resign.

Those who do not resign may solve their dilemma by being noncontroversial. This non-boat-rocking stance is all too familiar and results in another problem—irrelevancy. By not talking about social problems, one in fact legitimates the status quo. Hence, the inequities of the society continue, since the moral force of the churches is mainly quiet.

Not all clergy are content with the emphasis on comfort. As noted in the previous section, increasing numbers of clergy have become politically active on the "moral" issues of abortion, homosexuality, pornography, and the like. Typically, though, this view of morality ignores the social problems of inequalities and injustices. Other clergy are not content to let the church con-

Christianity's Future

The twenty-first century will be a period of challenge and change for Christianity in Western Europe and North America. Theological, political, demographic, and economic developments will force the church in these countries to:

- Accept the role of a minor player in shaping societies and cultures.
- Amend its understanding of orthodoxy and orthopraxis (the body of practices accepted or recognized as correct by the church).
- Take a back seat in the management of world evangelization.

The church in these countries will find, to a large extent, its agenda set by others. From a global perspective, the structural changes in world Christianity in the period from World War I to 2025 will prove to be more dramatic than any change in Christianity since the Protestant Reformation in the sixteenth century. . . .

SEVERING TIES BETWEEN CHURCH AND STATE

In first-world countries, the church will be viewed by governments as a social-service institution similar to most other social institutions. No special status or favor will be granted to Christianity. No preferential tax treatment will be given to churches. Religious chaplaincies will be eliminated. The use of religious conscientious objection will not be recognized by law. And no advocacy of religion in publicly funded institutions will be permitted. In short, the special status of the church in the eyes of governments will be all but eliminated . . . .

THE CHANGING COMPOSITION OF THE CHURCH

By the year 2025, Christians in first world countries will comprise slightly less than one-fourth of all the world's Christians. Three-fourths of the cardinals of the Roman Catholic Church will be from less-developed countries. Among evangelical Christians, 70 percent will be from less-developed countries. More Christians will speak Spanish than any other language.

Two sets of factors will interact to contribute to these trends. First, the population of most underdeveloped countries will continue to grow rapidly for at least the next 50 years. This is particularly true of Latin America and sub-Saharan Africa. Since most of the growth of Christianity is due to natural growth of the population and since recruitment is also running at high rates in many underdeveloped countries, the growth in numbers of Christians in the underdeveloped world will be dramatic.

On the other hand, populations in the developed world will grow slowly (or even decline) as birth rates hover around zero-population-growth rates. Further, church membership is actually declining in many first-world countries. Putting these factors together, the percentage of Christians outside North America and Western Europe will be significantly higher than at present.

Today, approximately 68 percent of the world's Christians are Caucasoid, and 47 percent are considered white. By the 2025, the percentages of Caucasoids and whites among Christians will fall at least to 50 percent and 30 percent, respectively. . . .

THE TREND TOWARD LOCAL AUTONOMY

For the last 100 years, almost 90 percent of the world's full-time foreign missionaries have come from Europe and North America. A vast host of individuals has gone around the world, spreading the Christian message, developing church organizations, and offering programs of social service in education, medicine, and economic assistance. This massive infusion of the Christian religion has been very successful, resulting in educated and dedicated clergy and Christian lay leaders in most denominations in many developing countries.

Further, in most Christian denominations, nominal if not full control of the church has passed to the local church. These churches are, in turn, sending out missionaries—some back to first-world countries. By the year 2025, perhaps as many as 50 percent of the world's full-time Christian missionaries will come from underdeveloped countries.

THE DOMINANT THEOLOGICAL ISSUES OF THE TWENTY-FIRST CENTURY

Four theological issues will be dominant in the twenty-first century. First, Christians in underdeveloped countries will be concerned about the relationship between the Christian faith and their local social, political, and economic situation. Second, many national and independent churches will extend the boundaries of Christian orthodoxy. Third, there will be significant cult movements based on charismatic personalities. And fourth, there will be considerable controversy over the emphasis to be placed on either rational or mystical approaches to faith.

Most Christians in developing countries will not separate their understanding of the Christian faith from the desire to improve their lot vis-à-vis economics and politics. The practical results of Christianity will be a dominant theme in the *Weltanschauung* [world view] of Christians in developing countries. The twentieth century discussions about liberation theology will continue and grow as this strain of Christian theology takes strong root.

Nationalism and the desire to chart their own course will lead many Christian groups in developing countries to eliminate ties that placed them in subservience to groups in other countries. Without such ties, the nationalist churches will have difficulty maintaining both orthodoxy and continuity with historical Christianity. As time goes by, there will be greater diversity in world Christianity as the boundaries of orthodoxy are expanded in now-unknown ways.

Without strong ties to historical orthodoxy and to the larger Christian community, many Christian groups will come under the sway of charismatic personalities who will lead these groups into cultish practices, moving the groups further outside Christian orthodoxy.

Finally, because of the influence of mysticism in many non-Christian religions and a growing interest in mysticism in the West, the mystical elements of religion will come into more prominence in the church. While many in first-world countries will maintain a rationalist approach to Christianity, they will increasingly find themselves in the minority among the world's Christians.

PREPARING FOR TOMORROW'S CHANGES

It is clear that the main action in Christianity is moving from developed to underdeveloped countries. This structural changes should not be viewed as dangerous to Christianity. . . .

Certainly, the twenty-first century will be challenging for Christians in general and for first-world Christians in particular. The world's Christian church will be considerably different in the year 2025 from what it is now. But Christians can look to the future with optimism: There is the potential that the twenty-first century church will be more vital and more relevant to a greater number of people than ever before.

Source: Samuel L. Dunn, "Christianity's Future," *The Futurist* 23 (March–April 1989): 34–37. Reprinted by permission.

tinue to perpetuate injustice by not speaking and acting out. They are committed to a socially relevant church, one that seeks social solutions to social problems.

A recent trend appears to be a resurgence in religious activism on social issues, not only by religious fundamentalist groups opposed to such things as sex education in the schools, gay rights, and the Equal Rights Amendment, but also by the leadership in the mainline churches. The leaders in almost every mainline religious organization have gone on record as opposing the government's budget cuts to the disadvantaged, U.S. military aid to dictatorships, and the arms race. For example, the bishops of the Roman Catholic Church in the United States have formally challenged the fundamental assumptions and strategies of the U.S. defense system (such as the deployment of the MX missile, the doctrine of nuclear deterrence, and increased expenditures for the military). Justifying this new wave of social concern by the church, Joseph Bernardin, the Archbishop of Chicago, has said:

> Some people say we shouldn't talk politics and that we should address ourselves to truly religious issues. Well, it's not as simple as all that. It's our responsibility to address the moral dimension of the social issues we face. These issues, of course, do have a political dimension as well as a moral dimension. I don't deny that, but that doesn't mean we're not permitted to talk about them. But our perspective must always be from the moral or ethical dimension. I reject out of hand that we have taken a leftward swing. What we are trying to do is focus on the teaching of the Gospel as we understand it, and to apply that teaching to the various social issues of the day. Our central theme is our respect for God's gift of life, our insistence that the human person has inherent value and dignity. (quoted in *Time*, 1982:77, see also National Conference of Catholic Bishops, 1986)

But political stands from the general leadership of a denomination are viewed quite differently from political activism by local ministers or priests. When local ministers or priests speak out, participate in marches, work for integrated housing, and demonstrate against excessive militarism, most of the parishioners become upset. As a result, the socially active clergy often become the objects of discrimination by their parishioners. Another consequence is that the laity trust their clergy less and less. As behavior in one area is questioned—e.g., social activism—church members are likely to withdraw confidence in others as well. Finally, churches have divided on this issue. Some want social action instead of just pious talk. Others want to preserve the status quo. The hypocrisy found in many churches forces splits, the formation of underground churches, or total rejection of Christianity as the source of social action. Others may leave because they feel that the church has wandered too far from the beliefs upon which the faith was founded. This dilemma accelerates the current dropout problem—by parishioners and clergy alike. The problem (if the senior author may here interject his bias) seems to be that for the most part those who drop out are the social activists who leave the church with a residue of "comforters." If this is the case, the future of the church is bleak unless there is a reversal and prophets of social action ascend—an unlikely possibility given the propensity of most parishioners for the message of "comfort" over the message of "challenge."

RELIGION FROM THE ORDER AND CONFLICT PERSPECTIVES

As usual, order and conflict theorists view this social phenomenon—religion—very differently. Also, as usual, the unity and diversity found within this institution suggest that both models of society are partially correct.

Adherents of the order model emphasize the solidarity functions of religion. Religion helps individuals through times of stress and it benefits society by binding people together through a common set of beliefs, reaffirmed through regularly scheduled ceremonial rituals.

Conflict theorists acknowledge that religion may unify in small societies but in diverse societies religious differences divide. Religious conflict occurs commonly at all levels, however, from intersocietal religious warfare, to schisms in local congregations. From the conflict perspective, religious unity within a society, if it does occur, has negative consequences. Such unity is used to legitimate the interests of the powerful (for example, slavery, racial segregation, conquest of "pagans," and war). Similarly, the interests of the powerful are served if the poor believe that they will be rewarded in the next life. Such a "theodicy" prevents revolutions by the oppressed and serves, as Marx suggested, as "an opiate of the masses."

CHAPTER REVIEW

1. Religion is socially created and has a tremendous impact on society. It is an integrated set of beliefs by which a group attempts to explain the meaning of life and death. Religion defines immorality and sin as well as morality and righteousness.

2. The consequences of religion are unity among the believers, conformity in behavior, and the legitimation of social structures. Religion also divides. It separates believers from nonbelievers, denominations, religions, and even the members of local religious groups.

3. Emile Durkheim, an order theorist, explored the question of why religion is universal. He reasoned that what any group worships is really society itself. The society is held together by religious rituals and festivals in which the group's values and beliefs are reaffirmed.

4. Karl Marx, a conflict theorist, saw religion as inhibiting social change by making existing social arrangements seem right and inevitable.

Religion further promotes the status quo by teaching the faithful to accept their condition—thus religion is the ultimate tool to promote false consciousness.

5. Max Weber, contrary to Marx, saw religious ideology as the catalyst for economic change. He demonstrated this with his analysis of the relationship between Calvinist ideology (predestination) and the rise of capitalism.

6. Civil religion is the belief that God and Country are one. God is believed to have a special destiny for the United States. Order and unity are thus given religious sanction.

7. Although most Americans identify with Christianity, there is a wide variety of religious belief in American society.

8. American religious organizations can be divided according to their secular commitment into two categories. A *church* tends to compromise with the larger society, tolerates popular vices, and accepts a diversity of beliefs. A *sect*, in sharp

contrast, rejects the world. It is a moral community with rigid ethical requirements and a narrow belief system.

9. A *theodicy* is a religious legitimation for a situation that otherwise might cause guilt or anger. Sects tend to have a theodicy of suffering, explaining their lack of power and privilege. Churches have theodicies that legitimate the possession of power and privilege.

10. There is a relationship between socioeconomic status (SES) and religion: (a) the lower the SES, the greater the probability of belonging to a sect; (b) there is a relationship between SES and denominational affiliation; (c) the higher the SES of the member, the greater his or her involvement and influence in the local church.

11. One trend is the decline in the mainline denominations. These churches are often bureaucratic and impersonal. Their beliefs are pluralistic. The Catholic Church is losing members because its stands against contraception and divorce are out of tune with contemporary life.

12. Another trend is the rise of Christian fundamentalism. The two categories of fundamentalists are evangelicals and pentecostals. They are alike except that pentecostal congregations are more emotional—personally experiencing the Holy Spirit. Fundamentalists are growing (while the mainline churches are declining) because (a) they emphasize evangelism; (b) they tend to be friendly, accepting, and caring communities; (c) they have the "truth" based on the infallibility of the Bible; (d) they offer a critique of modern society and a prescription for its change back to a God-centered society; and (e) they use modern marketing techniques and radio and television.

13. The "electronic church" is almost exclusively fundamentalist in religious doctrine. This form of outreach has been enormously successful in raising money (about $2 billion annually) and meeting the needs of many followers. Although scandals among some of the televangelists in 1987 had adverse effects on this movement, they appear to be temporary.

14. The contemporary mainline Christian churches are faced with a basic dilemma brought about by its two contradictory roles—to comfort the afflicted and to afflict the comforted. The comforting function is criticized because it focuses on helping the individual but ignores the problems of society. The challenging function— the injunction to be an agent of social protest and social reform—is criticized because it is divisive, alienating some members who disagree with the position taken. The evidence is clear that the majority of clergy are opting for the "comforting" function over the "challenging" function.

15. The order model emphasized the solidarity functions of religion, which they interpret as good.

16. From the conflict perspective, religious beliefs have negative consequences because they sanctify the status quo. That is, religion legitimates the interests of the powerful while also justifying the existence of inequality. Thus, revolutionary activity by the oppressed is suppressed by religion because it serves, as Marx suggested, as "an opiate of the masses."

KEY TERMS

Civil religion	Church	Routinization of charisma
Priestly role of religion	Sect	Theodicy
Prophetic role of religion	Charisma	

STUDY QUESTIONS

1. What are the social consequences for a community of believers?
2. Explain the contradiction that religion is both a source of stability *and* a source of conflict.
3. Contrast the views of religion by Durkheim, Marx, and Weber.
4. Is religion generally supportive of existing class and gender hierarchies? Give evidence to support your position.
5. Explain the contrast in growth patterns by the mainline denominations and the more fundamentalist denominations.

FOR FURTHER READING

Robert N. Bellah, *The Broken Covenant: American Civil Religion in Time of Trial* (New York: Seabury Press, 1975).

Peter L. Berger, *A Rumor of Angels: Modern Society and the Rediscovery of the Supernatural* (Garden City, NY: Doubleday [Anchor Books],1970).

Harvey Cox, *Religion in the Secular City* (New York: Simon & Schuster, 1984).

Mary Douglas and Steven M. Tipton (eds.), *Religion and America: Spirituality in a Secular Age* (Boston: Beacon, 1983).

Jeffrey K. Hadden and Anson Shupe, *Televangelism: Power and Politics on God's Frontier* (New York: Henry Holt and Company, 1988).

Robert C. Liebman and Robert Wuthnow (eds.), *The New Christian Right* (New York: Aldine, 1983).

National Conference of Catholic Bishops, *Economic Justice for All: Pastoral Letter on Catholic Social Teaching and the U.S. Economy* (Washington, DC: United States Catholic Conference, Inc. 1986).

Richard V. Pierard and Robert D. Linder, *Civil Religion and the Presidency* (Grand Rapids, MI: Zondervan Publishing House, 1988).

Keith A. Roberts, *Religion in Sociological Perspective* (Homewood, IL: Dorsey, 1984).

Rodney Stark and William Sims Bainbridge, *The Future of Religion: Secularization, Revival, and Cult Formation* (Berkeley: University of California Press, 1985).

Epilogue

*A*ny analyst of society has the option of emphasizing either the social system as a smoothly functioning unit or the disunity and lack of harmony within it. American society for the most part does work rather smoothly. If we examine the whole of history, we must conclude that the system has improved in many respects. But this society has severe problems—the persistence of poverty, racial and sexual discrimination, injustice, violence, and the intransigence of the institutions to change, to name but a few. We must recognize that U.S. society has many paradoxical dichotomies—unity and disunity, affluence and poverty, freedom and oppression, stability and change.

The topics selected for this book, the order in which they were presented, and the emphases have tended to focus on the problems, faults, and weaknesses of U.S. society. This strategy was employed because these aspects of society are often minimized, but more important, because the society needs reform. Since institutions are made by people, they can be changed by people. As long as there are problems, we cannot be content with the status quo. A full understanding of the complex nature of society must, however, precede the implementation of social change. That has been one goal of this book.

The primary purpose of any sociology book is to make the reader more perceptive and more analytical regarding social life. We hope you have gained new perspectives and new insights about our society from the reading and thinking required for analyzing U.S. society. We hope that you will build on this knowledge in a lifelong quest to understand better this complex system called U.S. society and to work for its improvement.

Glossary

Accommodation. Acceptance of one's position in a situation without struggle.

Achieved status. A position in a social organization attained through personal effort.

Ageism. Discrimination against the elderly.

Aggregate. A collection of individuals who happen to be at the same place at the same time.

Alienation. An individual's feeling of separation from the surrounding society.

Altruistic suicide. The sacrificing of one's life for the good of the group.

Androgyny. Having the characteristics of both males and females.

Anomie. Durkheim's term that indicates a social condition characterized by the absence of norms or conflicting norms. At the individual level, the person is not sure what the norms are, which leads to a relatively high probability of suicide.

Anticipatory socialization. Learning and acting out the beliefs, norms, and values of a group before joining it.

Argot. The specialized or secret language peculiar to a group.

Ascribed status. Social position based on such factors as age, race, and family over which the individual has no control.

Assimilation. The process by which individuals or groups voluntarily or involuntarily adopt the culture of another group, losing their original identity.

Baby boom. A term referring to a 15-year period in American history following World War II in which an extraordinary number of babies were born.

Bias theory. An explanation that blames the prejudiced attitudes of majority members for the secondary status of the minority.

Blaming the victim. The belief that some individuals are poor, criminals, or school dropouts because they have a flaw within them.

Bourgeoisie. Marx's term for the class of persons that owns the means of production in a capitalist society.

Bureaucracy. A system of administration that is characterized by specialized roles, explicit rules, and a hierarchy of authority.

Bureaucratization. The trend toward greater use of the bureaucratic mode of organization administration within society.

Capitalism. The economic system based on private ownership of property, guided by the seeking of maximum profits.

Capitalist patriarchy. A condition of capitalism

where male supremacy keeps women in subordinate roles at work and in the home.

Case study. The research strategy that involves the detailed and thorough analysis of a single event, community, or organization.

Caste system. The closed system of social stratification. Membership is fixed at birth and is permanent.

Caveat emptor. The Latin phrase that means "let the buyer beware."

Charisma. The extraordinary attributes of an individual that enable the possessor to lead and inspire without the legal authority to do so.

Church. The highly organized, bureaucratic form of religious organization that accommodates itself to the larger society.

Civil religion. The set of religious beliefs, rituals, and symbols outside the church that legitimates the status quo.

Class. Ranking in a stratification system based on economic resources.

Class consciousness. Karl Marx's term that refers to the recognition by persons in a similar economic situation of a common interest.

Class segregation. Barriers that restrict social interaction to the members of a particular social class.

Cloning. The artificial production of genetically identical offspring.

Cohabitation. The practice of living together as a couple without being married.

Commune. A small, voluntary community characterized by cooperation and a common ideology.

Conflict model, perspective. A view of society that posits conflict as a normal feature of social life, influencing the distribution of power and the direction and magnitude of social change.

Consensus. Widely held agreement on the norms and values of society.

Conspicuous consumption. The purchase and obvious display of material goods to impress others with one's wealth and assumed status.

Constraint. The state of being controlled by some force.

Control group. A group of subjects in an experiment who are not exposed to the independent variable but are similar in all other respects to the group exposed to the independent variable.

Cooptation. The process by which representatives of a potentially destabilizing subgroup are incorporated into the leadership or management level of an organization to avert problems.

Corporate crime. The illegal and/or socially harmful behaviors that result from the deliberate decisions of corporate executives in accordance with corporate goals.

Correlation. The degree of relationship between two variables.

Counterculture. A subculture that fundamentally opposes the dominant culture.

Crime. An act that is prohibited by the law.

Cultural deficiency theories. Explanations that argue that some flaw in a social group's way of life is responsible for their secondary status.

Cultural deprivation. An ethnocentric term implying that the culture of another group is not only deficient but also inferior.

Cultural relativity. Customs of another society must be viewed and evaluated by their standards, not by an outsider's.

Cultural tyranny. The socialization process forces narrow behavioral and attitudinal traits on persons.

Culture. The knowledge that the members of a social organization share.

Culture of poverty. The view that the poor are qualitatively different in values and life-styles from the rest of society and that these cultural differences explain continued poverty.

Deferred gratification. The willingness to sacrifice in the present for expected future rewards.

Deflation. The part of the economic cycle when the amount of money in circulation is down, resulting in low prices and unemployment.

Deindustrialization. The widespread, systematic diversion of capital (finance, plant, and equipment) from investment in the nation's basic industries into service and knowledge sectors of the economy or overseas.

Democracy. The form of government where the citizens participate in government, characterized by competition for office, public officials being responsive to public opinion, and the citizenry having access to reliable information upon which to make their electoral choices.

Demography. The scientific study of the size,

composition, and changes in human populations.

Dependent variable. A variable that is influenced by the effect of another variable (the independent variable).

Deprogramming. The process where persons believed to be "brainwashed" by cults are abducted and retrained against their will.

Derogation. Discrimination in the form of words that put a minority "down."

Deviance. Behavior that violates the expectations of society.

Dialectic. The clash between conflicting ideas and forces.

Differential association. The theory that a person becomes deviant because of an excess of definitions favorable to the violation of societal expectations over definitions supporting the norms and values.

Direct social control. Direct intervention by the agents of society to control the behavior of individuals and groups.

Discrimination. To act toward a person or group with partiality, typically because they belong to a minority.

Division of labor. The specialization of economic roles resulting in an interdependent and efficient system.

Dual career marriage. A marriage in which a husband and wife are both employed outside the home.

Dysfunction. A consequence that is disruptive for the stability and cohesion of the social organization.

Economy. The institution that ensures the maintenance of society by producing and distributing the necessary goods and services.

Egalitarianism. Fundamental belief in equality.

Ego. According to Freud, the conscious, rational part of the self.

Egoistic suicide. Persons lacking ties to social groups are, Durkheim found, more susceptible to suicide than those with strong group attachments.

Elitist view of power. The assumption that power is concentrated in a few rather than dispersed (the pluralist view).

Epistemology. The philosophical position that all reality is socially constructed.

Ethnic group. A social group with a common culture distinct from the culture of the majority because of race, religion, or national origin.

Ethnocentrism. The universal tendency to deprecate the ways of persons from other societies as wrong, old-fashioned, or immoral and to think of the ways of one's own group as superior (as the only right way).

Ethnomethodology. The subdiscipline in sociology that studies the everyday living practices of people to discover the underlying bases for social behavior.

Eugenics. The attempt to improve the human race through the control of hereditary factors.

Experimental group. A group of subjects in an experiment who are exposed to the independent variable, in contrast to the control group, which is not.

False consciousness. In Marxian theory, the idea that the oppressed may hold beliefs damaging to their interests.

Family. A particular societal arrangement whereby persons related by ancestry, marriage, or adoption live together, form an economic unit, and raise children.

Feminization of poverty. This refers to the relatively large number of female headed households living in poverty.

Feral children. Children reputedly raised by animals, who have the characteristics of their peers (animals) rather than human beings.

Fertility. The frequency of actual births in a population.

Folkways. Relatively unimportant rules that if violated are not severely punished.

Function. Any consequence of a social arrangement that contributes to the overall stability of the system.

Functional integration. Unity among divergent elements of society resulting from a specialized divisions of labor.

Functionalism (the order perspective). The theoretical perspective that emphasizes the order, harmony, and stability of social systems.

Gender. Refers to the cultural and social definition of feminine and masculine. Differs from sex, which is the biological fact of femaleness or maleness.

Gender roles' approach to sexual inequality. The understanding of gender differences that emphasize the characteristics that individuals learn in the socialization process.

Gender stratification. The differential ranking and rewarding of women's and men's roles.

Generalized other. Mead's concept that refers to the internalization of the expectations of the society.

Genetic engineering. The scientific effort to manipulate DNA molecules in plants and animals.

Glossolalia. The emotional religious experience involving the incoherent "speaking in tongues."

Governing class. G. William Domhoff's model of power that posits that the very wealthy in society contribute a disproportionate number of people to the controlling institutions and key decision-making groups.

Group. A collection of people (two or more) who, because of sustained interaction, have evolved a common culture.

Hedonism. The pursuit of pleasure and self-indulgence.

Hidden curriculum. That part of the school experience that has nothing to do with formal subjects but refers to the behaviors that schools expect of children (obedience to authority, remaining quiet and orderly, etc.).

Hierarchy. The arrangement of people or objects in order of importance.

Home-based work. Women working for pay in their homes.

Horizontal mobility. Changes in occupations or other situations without moving from one social class to another.

Household. A residential unit of unrelated individuals who pool resources and perform common tasks of production and consumption.

Id. Freud's term for the collection of urges and drives persons have for pleasure and aggression.

Ideal type. An abstraction constructed to show how some phenomenon would be characterized in its pure form.

Ideological social control. The efforts by social organizations to control members by controlling their minds. Societies accomplish this, typically, through the socialization process.

Ideology. The shared beliefs about the physical, social, or metaphysical world.

Independent variable. A variable that affects another variable (the dependent variable).

Individual racism. Overt acts by individuals of one race to harm a member or members of another race.

Inflation. The situation when too much money purchases too few goods, resulting in rising prices.

Institution. Social arrangement that channels behavior in prescribed ways in the important areas of societal life.

Institutional derogation. This occurs when the normal arrangements of society act to reinforce the negative stereotypes of minority groups.

Institutional discrimination. When the social arrangements and accepted ways of doing things in society disadvantage minority groups.

Institutional process. The concept designating the forces that resist change, which emanate from the assumed human need for certainty and stability.

Institutional racism. When the social arrangements and accepted ways of doing things in society disadvantage a racial group.

Institutional sexism. When the social arrangements and accepted ways of doing things in society disadvantage females.

Institutional violence. When the normal workings of the society do harm to a social category.

Instrumental process. The search for technological solutions to human problems as an impetus for change.

Interest group. A group of like-minded persons who organize to influence public policy.

Intergenerational mobility. The difference in social class position between a son and his father.

Internalization. In the process of socialization society's demands become part of the individual, acting to control his or her behavior.

Intragenerational mobility. The movement by an individual from one social class to another.

Labeling theory (societal reactions). The explanation of deviant behavior that stresses the importance of the society in defining what is illegal and in assigning a deviant status to particular individuals, which in turn dominates their identities and behaviors.

Latent consequence, function. An unintended consequence of a social arrangement or social action.

Life chances. Weber's term that refers to the chances throughout one's life cycle to live and experience the good things in life.

Looking-glass self. Cooley's concept that refers to the importance of how others influence the way we see ourselves.

Machismo (macho). An exaggerated masculinity, evidenced by male dominance, posturing, physical daring, and an exploitative attitude toward women.

Macro level. The large-scale structures and processes of society, including the institutions and the system of stratification.

Majority group. The social category in society holding superordinate power and who successfully impose their will on less-powerful groups (minority groups).

Male chauvinism. Exaggerated beliefs about the superiority of the male and the resulting discrimination.

Manifest consequence, function. An intended consequence of a social arrangement or social action.

Marginality. The condition resulting from taking part in two distinct ways of life without belonging fully to either.

Marital power. The ability to control the spouse and to influence or control family decisions and activities.

Material technology. Refers to the technical knowledge needed to use and make things.

Matriarchal family. A family structure in which the mother is dominant.

Meritocracy. A system of stratification in which rank is based purely on achievement.

Micro level. The social organization and processes of small-scale social groups.

Military-industrial complex. The term that refers to the direct and indirect relationships between the military establishment (the Pentagon) and the corporations.

Minority. A social category composed of persons that differ from the majority, are relatively powerless, and are the objects of discrimination.

Modal personality type. A distinct type of personality considered to be characteristic of the members of a particular society.

Model. The mental image a scientist has of the structure of society. This influences what the scientists look for, what they see, and how phenomena are explained.

Monogamy. The form of marriage in which an individual may not be married to more than one person at a time.

Monopolistic capitalism. The form of capitalism prevalent in the contemporary United States, where a few large corporations control the key industries, destroying competition and the market mechanisms that would ordinarily keep prices low and help consumers.

Monopoly. When a single firm dominates an industry.

Mores. Important norms, the violation of which results in severe punishment.

Mortality rate. The frequency of actual deaths in a population.

Multinational corporation A corporation that operates in more than one country.

Myth of peaceful progress. The incorrect belief that throughout American history disadvantaged groups have gained their share of power, prosperity, and respectability without violence.

Myth of separate worlds. The belief that work and family roles operate independently of each other.

Nominalist. A philosophical position that a group is nothing more than the sum of its parts.

Nomos. Literally, meaningful order. The opposite of anomie.

Norm. This part of culture refers to rules that specify appropriate and inappropriate behavior (in other words, the shared expectations for behavior).

Nuclear family. A kinship unit composed of husband, wife, and children.

Nuptiality. The proportion of married persons.

Ontology. The philosophical position that accepts the reality of things because their nature cannot be denied.

Order model, perspective. The conception of society as a social system characterized by cohesion, consensus, cooperation, reciprocity, stability, and persistence.

Paradigm. The basic assumptions a scientist has of the structure of society (see **Model**).

Participatory socialization. The mode of socialization in which parents encourage their children to explore, experiment, and question.

Patriarchal family. A family structure in which the father is dominant.

Patriarchy. A form of social organization in which males dominate females.

Peer group. Friends usually of the same age and socioeconomic status.

Peter Principle. The view that most people in an organization will be promoted until they eventually reach their level of incompetence.

Pluralism. A situation in which different groups live in mutual respect but retain their racial, religious, or ethnic identities.

Pluralist view of power. The diffuse distribution of power among various groups and interests.

Political crime. Crime either against the state (the order model's view) or crime by the state (the conflict model's view).

Polity. The societal institution especially concerned with maintaining order.

Population implosion. The trend for people to live in ever-denser localities (the movement of people from rural areas to the urban regions).

Poverty. A standard of living below the minimum needed for the maintenance of adequate diet, health, and shelter.

Power. The ability to get what one wants from someone else.

Power elite. Mill's term for the coalition of the top echelon of military, executive branch of the federal government, and business.

Prestige. The respect of an individual or social category as a result of their social status.

Primary deviance. The original illegal act preceding the successful application of the "deviant" label.

Primary group. A small group characterized by intimate, face-to-face interaction.

Progressive tax. A tax rate that escalates with the amount of income.

Proletariat. Marx's term for the industrial workers in a capitalistic society.

Protestant ethic (Puritan work ethic). The religious beliefs, traced back to Martin Luther and John Calvin, which emphasize hard work and continual striving in order to prove that one is "saved" by material success.

Psychosurgery. A form of brain surgery used to change the behavior of the patient.

Pygmalion effect. Students placed in a track are treated by teachers in a way which ensures that the prophecy is fulfilled.

Race, racial group. A group socially defined on the basis of a presumed common genetic heritage resulting in distinguishing physical characteristics.

Racism. The domination and discrimination of one racial group by the majority.

Radical nonintervention. Schur's term referring to the strategy of leaving juvenile delinquents alone as much as possible rather than processing (and labeling) them through the criminal justice system.

Random sample. The selection of a subset from a population so that every person has an equal chance of being selected.

Realist. The philosophical position that a group is more than the sum of its parts (referring to the emergence of culture and mechanisms of social control that affect the behavior of members regardless of their personalities).

Recidivism. Reinvolvement in crime.

Reference group. A group to which one would like to belong and toward which one therefore orients his or her behavior.

Reform movement. A social movement that seeks to alter a specific part of society.

Regressive tax. A tax rate that remains the same for all persons, rich or poor. The result is that poor persons pay a larger proportion of their wealth than affluent persons.

Reliability. The degree to which a study yields similar results when repeated.

Religion. The social institution that encompasses beliefs and practices regarding the sacred.

Repressive socialization. The mode of socialization in which parents demand rigid conformity in their children, enforced by physical punishment.

Resistance movement. The organized attempt to reinforce the traditional system by preventing change.

Revolutionary movement. The collective attempt to bring about a radical transformation of society.

Rites of passage. The ritual whereby the society recognizes the adult status of a young member.

Role. The behavioral expectations and requirements attached to a position in a social organization.

Role performance (role behavior). The actual

behavior of persons occupying particular positions in a social organization.

Routinization of charisma. The process by which an organization attempts to transmit the special attributes of the former leader to a new one. This is done by various means, for example, "laying on of hands" and the old leader choosing a successor.

Sacred. That which inspires awe because of its supernatural qualities.

Sample. A representative part of a population.

Sanction. A social reward or punishment for approved or disapproved behavior.

Secondary deviance. Deviant behavior that is a consequence of the successful application of the deviant label.

Secondary group. A large, impersonal, and formally organized group.

Sect. A religious organization, in contrast to a church, that tends to be dogmatic, fundamentalistic, and in opposition to "the world."

Secular. Of or pertaining to the world; the opposite of sacred.

Segmented labor market. The capitalist economy is divided into two distinct sectors, one where production and working conditions are relatively stable and secure; the other is composed of marginal firms where working conditions, wages, and job security are low.

Segregation. The separation of one group from another.

Self-esteem. The opinion of oneself.

Self-fulfilling prophecy. An event that occurs because it was predicted. The prophecy is confirmed because people alter their behavior to conform to the prediction.

Sex-gender system. A system of stratification that ranks and rewards gender roles unequally.

Sexism. The individual actions and institutional arrangements that discriminate against women.

Sex role. The learned patterns of behavior expected of males and females by society.

Sexual stratification. A hierarchical arrangement based on gender.

Shared monopoly. When four or fewer companies control 50 percent or more of an industry.

Sibling. A brother or sister.

Significant others. Mead's term referring to those persons most important in the determining of a child's behavior.

Social class. A number of persons who occupy the same relative economic rank in the stratification system.

Social control. The regulation of human behavior in any social group.

Social Darwinism. The belief that the principle of the "survival of the fittest" applies to human societies, especially the system of stratification.

Social determinism. The assumption that human behavior is explained exclusively by social factors.

Social differentiation. The process of categorizing persons by some personal attribute.

Social inequality. The ranking of persons by wealth, family background, race, ethnicity, or sex.

Social interaction. When individuals act toward or respond to each other.

Socialism. The economic system where the means of production are owned by the people for their collective benefit.

Socialization. The process of learning the culture.

Socialization agents. Those individuals, groups, and institutions responsible for transmitting the culture of society to newcomers.

Social location. One's position in society based on family background, race, socioeconomic status, religion, and other relevant social characteristics.

Social mobility. The movement by an individual from one social class or status group to another.

Social movement. A collective attempt to promote or resist change.

Social organization. The order of a social group as evidenced by the positions, roles, norms, and other constraints that control behavior and ensure predictability.

Social problem. There are two types of social problems: (1) societally induced conditions that cause psychic and material suffering for any segment of the population; and (2) those acts and conditions that violate the norms and values of society.

Social relationship. When two or more persons engage in enduring social interaction.

Social stratification. When people are ranked in

a hierarchy that differentiates them as superior or inferior.

Social structure. The patterned and recurrent relationships among people and parts in a social organization.

Social system. A differentiated group whose parts are interrelated in an orderly arrangement, bounded in geographical space or membership.

Social technology. The knowledge necessary to establish, maintain, and operate the technical aspects of social organization.

Society. The largest social organization to which individuals owe their allegiance. The entity is located geographically, has a common culture, and is relatively self-sufficient.

Socioeconomic status (SES). The measure of social status that takes into account several prestige factors, such as income, education, and occupation.

Sociology. The scholarly discipline concerned with the systematic study of social organizations.

Stagflation. The contemporary economic phenomenon that combines the problems of inflation and deflation—high prices, high unemployment, wage-price spiral, and a profits squeeze.

Status. A socially defined position in a social organization.

Status anguish. A fundamental concern with the contradictions in the individual's status set.

Status group. Persons of similar status. They view each other as social equals.

Status inconsistency. The situation in which a person ranks high on one status dimension and low on another.

Status withdrawal. The loss of status that occurs with downward mobility.

Stereotype. An exaggerated generalization about some social category.

Stigma. A label of social disgrace.

Structural approach to sexual inequality. The understanding of gender differences resulting from factors external to individuals.

Structural theories of racial inequality. Explanations that focus on the institutionalized patterns of discrimination as the sources of the secondary status of minorities.

Structured social inequality. This refers to the patterns of superiority and inferiority, the dis-

tribution of rewards, and the belief systems that reinforce the inequities of society.

Subculture. A relatively cohesive cultural system that varies in form and substance from the dominant culture.

Subsidy. Financial aid in the form of tax breaks or gifts granted by the government to an individual or commercial enterprise.

Suburb. A community adjacent to a city.

Superego. Freud's term that refers to the internalization of society's morals within the self.

Survey research. The research technique that selects a sample of people from a larger population in order to learn how they think, feel, or act.

Symbol. A thing that represents something else, such as a word, gesture, or physical object (cross, flag).

Synthesis. The blending of the parts into a new form.

Systemic imperatives. The economic and social constraints on the decision makers in an organization, which promote the status quo.

Technology. The application of science to meet the needs of society.

Theodicy. The religious legitimation for a situation that might otherwise cause guilt or anger (such as defeat in a war or the existence of poverty among affluence).

Tracking. A practice of schools of grouping children according to their scores on IQ and other tests.

Transcience. Toffler's term that refers to the rapid turnover in things, places, and people characteristic of a technological society.

Underemployment. Being employed at a job below one's level of training and expertise.

Undocumented immigrant. Immigrants who have entered the United States illegally.

Urbanism. The ways in which city life characteristically affects how people feel, think, and interact with one another.

Urbanization. The trend referring to the movement of people from rural to urban areas.

Urban region (megalopolis, conurbation, strip city). The extensive urban area that results when two or more large cities grow together until they are contiguous.

Validity. The degree to which a scientific study measures what it attempts to measure.

Value neutrality. The attempt by scientists to be absolutely free of bias in their research.

Values. The shared criteria used in evaluating objects, ideas, acts, feelings, or events as to their relative desirability, merit, or correctness.

Variable. An attitude, behavior, or condition that can vary in magnitude from case to case (the opposite of a constant).

Voluntary association. Organizations that people join because they approve of their goals.

Wealthfare. Receipt by the affluent of financial aid and/or services from the government.

Welfare. Receipt of financial aid and/or services from the government.

White flight. Whites leaving the central cities for the suburbs to avoid interaction with blacks, especially the busing of children.

References

Acker, Joan. 1973. "Women and Stratification: A Case of Intellectual Sexism," *American Journal of Sociology* 78 (January):936–945.

——————. 1978. "Issues in the Sociological Study of Women's Work," in *Women Working,* Ann H. Stromberg and Shirley Harkess (eds.). Palo Alto, CA: Mayfield, pp. 134–161.

——————. 1980."Women and Stratification: A Review of the Recent Literature," *Contemporary Sociology* 9 (Winter).

Acuña, Rudolfo. 1972. *Occupied America*. San Francisco: Canfield.

Adams, Karen L., and Norma C. Ware. 1979. "Sexism and the English Language: The Linguistic Implications of Being a Woman," in *Woman: A Feminist Perspective,* 2nd ed., Jo Freeman (ed.). Palo Alto, CA: Mayfield.

Alm, Richard. 1984. "As Defense Billions Pour into the Economy," *U.S. News & World Report* (March 12):58.

Andersen, Margaret L. 1983. *Thinking About Women, Sociological and Feminist Perspectives.* New York: Macmillan.

——————. 1988. *Thinking about Women,* 2nd ed. New York: Macmillan.

Anderson, Jack. 1983. "Plans to Test Adolescents Smack of 1984," *Rocky Mountain News* (October 13):106.

Anderson, Walt. 1973. "Breaking Out of the Establishment Vise," *Human Behavior* 2 (December):10–18.

Ann Arbor News. 1983. (September 8).

Antonovsky, Aaron. 1967. "Social Class, Life Expectancy and Overall Mortality," *Millbank Memorial Fund Quarterly* 45 (April):31–73.

Appelbaum, Richard P. 1989. "The Affordability Gap," *Society* 26 (May/June):6–8.

Applebome, Peter. 1989. "Scandals Aside, TV Preachers Thrive," *New York Times* (October 8):12.

Asch, Solomon E. 1958. "Effects of Group Pressure upon the Modification and Distortion of Judgments," in *Readings in Social Psychology,* 3rd ed., Eleanor E. Maccoby, Theodore M. Newcomb, and Eugene L. Hartley (eds.). New York: Holt, Rinehart and Winston.

Asimov, Isaac. 1981. "Disassembling the Assembly Line," *American Way* (May):13–14.

Associated Press. 1971. " 'He' Could Stir Women's Lib Nightmare" (November 6).

——————. 1976. "Jungle Boy Remains More Like Monkey," (May 15).

——————. 1987. "Applicants Lie to Employers to Land Jobs," (September 3).

——————. 1989. "Lobotomies Proposed for Criminals," (June 22).

Aufderheide, Pat. 1989. "Re-Regulating Sleazy Kid Stuff," *In These Times* (August 2–29):28.

——————. 1981. "Sociological Theory in Emergent Chicano Perspectives," *Pacific Sociological Review* 24 (April):255–272.

——————. 1982. "Urban Kinship and Midwest Chicano

Families: Evidence in Support of Revision," *De Colores Journal* 6 (Summer):85–98.

————. 1983. "Familism among Chicanos: A Theoretical Review," *Humboldt Journal of Social Relations* 10 (Spring):224–238.

————, and D. Stanley Eitzen. 1990. *Diversity in Families,* 2nd ed. New York: Harper and Row.

Baker, Mary Anne. 1980. "How Are We Born Different?" in *Women Today,* Mary Anne Baker, et al. (eds.). Monterey, CA: Brooks/Cole.

Balint, M. 1957. *The Doctor, His Patient, and the Illness.* New York: International Universities Press.

Balswick, Jack, and Charles Peck. 1971. "The Inexpressive Male: A Tragedy of American Society," *Family Coordinator* 20:363–368.

————, with James Lincoln Collier. 1976. "Why Husbands Can't Say 'I Love You,' " in *The Forty-Nine Percent Majority,* Deborah S. David and Robert Brannon (eds.). Reading, MA: Addison-Wesley.

Baltzell, E. Digby. 1958. *Philadelphia Gentlemen: The Making of a National Upper Class.* New York: Free Press.

Banfield, Edward C. 1974. *The Unheavenly City Revisited.* Boston: Little, Brown.

Barker, Eugene C. 1965. *Mexico and Texas, 1821–1835.* New York: Russell and Russell.

Barnouw, Victor. 1979. *Culture and Personality,* 3rd ed. Homewood, IL: Dorsey.

Baron, Harold M. 1975. "Racial Domination in Advanced Capitalism," in *Labor Market Segmentation,* Richard C. Edwards, et al. (eds.). Lexington, MA: D. C. Heath.

Barrera, Mario. 1979. *Race and Class in the Southwest: A Theory of Racial Inequality.* Notre Dame: University of Notre Dame Press.

Barringer, Felicity. 1989. "America's Head Count Sets Battle Lines for Congress's Seat Count," *New York Times* (September 3):E4.

Baruch, Grace, Rosalind Barnett, and Caryl Rivers. 1983. "Happiness Is a Good Job," *Working Woman* (February):75–78.

Baskir, Laurence M., and William A. Strauss. 1978. *The Draft, The War, and the Vietnam Generation.* New York: Knopf.

Baum, Martha. 1972. "Love, Marriage, and the Division of Labor," in *Family, Marriage, and the Struggle of the Sexes,* Hans Peter Dreitzel (ed.). New York: Macmillan.

Beauvoir, Simone de. 1970. *The Second Sex,* H. M. Parshley, trans. New York: Bantam.

Becker, Howard S. 1963. *The Outsiders: Studies in the Sociology of Deviance.* New York: Free Press.

————. 1967. "Whose Side Are We On?" *Social Problems* 14 (Winter):239–247.

Begus, Sarah. 1984. "Votes for Women," *The Women's Review of Books* 2 (October):3.

Bellah, Robert N. 1967. "Civil Religion in America," *Daedalus* 96 (Winter):1–21.

Benokraitis, Nijole, and Joe R. Feagin. 1974. "Institutional Racism: A Review and Critical Assessment of the Literature." Paper presented at the American Sociological Association, Montreal (August).

Berardo, Felix. 1968. "Widowhood Status in the United States," *The Family Coordinator* 17 (July):191–203.

Berg, Ivar (ed.). 1981. *Sociological Perspectives on Labor Markets.* New York: Academic Press.

Berger, Peter L. 1963. *Invitation to Sociology: A Humanistic Perspective.* Garden City, NY: Doubleday Anchor Books.

————. 1967a. *The Sacred Canopy.* New York: Doubleday.

————. 1967b. "Religious Institutions," in *Sociology,* Neil J. Smelser (ed.). New York: John Wiley.

————. 1975. "Religion and World Construction," in *Life as Theatre,* Dennis Brissett and Charles Edgley (eds.). Chicago: Aldine.

————, and Hansfried Kellner. 1975. "Marriage and the Construction of Reality," in *Life as Theatre,* Dennis Brissett and Charles Edgley (eds.). Chicago: Aldine.

————, and Thomas Luckman. 1967. *The Social Construction of Reality.* Garden City, NY: Doubleday.

Bernard, Jessie. 1973. *The Future of Marriage.* New York: Bantam.

Bernay, Elayn, 1978. "Affirmative Inaction and Other Facts, Trends, Tactics for Academic Life," *Ms.* (November).

Berreman, Gerald D. 1960. "Caste in India and the United States," *American Journal of Sociology* 66 (September):120–127.

Bierstedt, Robert. 1974. *The Social Order,* 4th ed. New York: McGraw-Hill.

Birdwhistell, Ray L. 1980. "The Idealized Model of the American Family," in *Marriage and the Family in a Changing Society,* James M. Henslin (ed.). New York: Free Press.

Blau, Francine D. 1979. "Women in the Labor Force: An Overview," in *Woman: A Feminist Perspective,* 2nd ed., Jo Freeman (ed.). Palo Alto, CA: Mayfield.

————, and Carol L. Jusenius. 1976. "Economists' Approaches to Sex Segregation in the Labor Market," in *Women and the Workplace,* Martha Blaxall and Barbara Regan (eds.). Chicago: University of Chicago Press.

Blau, Peter M., and Otis Dudley Duncan. 1967. *The American Occupational Structure.* New York: John Wiley.

————, and Marshall W. Meyer. 1971. *Bureaucracy in Modern Society,* 2nd ed. New York: Random House.

————, and W. Richard Scott. 1962. *Formal Organiza-*

tions: A Comparative Approach. San Francisco: Chandler.

Blauner, Robert. 1972. Racial Oppression in America. New York: Harper & Row.

Blood, Robert O., and Donald Wolfe. 1960. Husbands and Wives. New York: Free Press.

Bloom, David E., and Neil G. Bennett. 1986. "Childless Couples," American Demographics (August):23–54.

Bluestone, Barry, and Bennett Harrison. 1982. The Deindustrialization of America. New York: Basic Books.

Blumberg, Paul M., and P. W. Paul. 1975. "Continuities and Discontinuities in Upper-Class Marriage," Journal of Marriage and Family 37 (February).

Blumer, Herbert, 1951. "Collective Behavior," in New Outline of the Principles of Sociology, Alfred McClung Lee (ed). New York: Barnes and Noble, pp. 167–222.

Bock, Gordon. 1987. "Limping Along in Robot Land." Time (July 13):46–47.

Bonacich, Edna. 1976. "Advanced Capitalism and Black/White Relations in the United States: A Split Labor Market Interpretation," American Sociological Review 41:34–51.

Boocock, Sarane S. 1975. "Is U.S. Becoming Less Child Oriented?" National Observer (February 22):12.

Borkin, Joseph. 1978. The Crime and Punishment of I. G. Farben. New York: Free Press.

Bourke, Jaron. 1989. "Mergermania," The Nation (October 30):495.

Bouvier, Leon F. and Robert W. Gardner. 1986. "Immigration to the U.S.: The Unfinished Story," Population Bulletin 41 (November): entire issue.

Bowen, Ezra. 1986. "A Courtroom Clash over Textbooks," Time (October 27):94.

Bowles, Samuel. 1972. "Schooling and Inequality from Generation to Generation," Journal of Political Economy (May–June).

————. 1977. "Unequal Education and the Reproduction of the Social Division of Labor," in Power and Ideology in Education, Jerome Karabel and A. H. Halsey (eds.). New York: Oxford University Press, pp. 137–153.

————, and Herbert Gintis. 1973. "I.Q. and the U.S. Class Structure," Social Policy 3 (January–February):65–96.

————. 1976. Schooling in Capitalist America. New York: Basic Books.

Boyd, Malcolm. 1976. "Does God Have a Candidate?" The Progressive 41 (November).

Brackman, Harold, and Steven P. Erie. 1986. "The Future of the Gender Gap," Social Policy 16 (Winter):5–11.

Branscombe, Art. 1982. "Court Upholds School Finance Law," The Denver Post (May 25):A1–8.

Briggs, Kenneth A. 1981. "Study Documents Growing Impact of Female Clergy," The Dallas Morning News (November 15):A28.

Brody, Jane E. 1980. "Genetic Explanations Offered for Women's Health Superiority," The New York Times (January 20):C1–5.

Bronfenbrenner, Urie. 1958. "Socialization and Social Class in Time and Space," in Readings in Social Psychology, E. E. Maccoby, T. M. Newcomb, and E. L. Hartley (eds.). New York: Holt, Rinehart and Winston, pp. 400–425.

Bronowski, J. 1978. The Common Sense of Science. Cambridge, MA: Harvard University Press.

Bronson, Gail, 1984. " 'Made Abroad'—A Label You Can't Escape," U.S. News & World Report (November 19):83.

Broom, Leonard, and Philip Selznick. 1968. Sociology, 4th ed. New York: Harper & Row.

Brophy, Beth. 1986. "Middle-Class Squeeze," U.S. News & World Report (August 18):36–41.

Brown, Dee. 1971. Bury My Heart at Wounded Knee. New York: Holt, Rinehart and Winston.

Buchert, Wendy. 1989. "Sex Scandals Hurt All Television Ministries," USA Today (March 23):13A.

Bukovinsky, Janet. 1982. "A Wife Is Abused Every 18 Seconds, FBI Says," Rocky Mountain News (March 9):38, 42.

Bumpass, Larry, and Ronald R. Rindfuss. 1979. "Children's Experience of Marital Disruption," American Journal of Sociology 85 (July):49–65.

Burnham, David. 1989. "The Abuse of Power: Misuse of the I.R.S.," New York Times Magazine (September 3): 25–27, 50–52, 58–59.

Burnham, Linda. 1986. "Has Poverty Been Feminized in Black America?" For Crying Out Loud: Women and Poverty in the U.S., Rochelle Lefkowitz and Ann Withorn (eds.). New York: Pilgrim, pp. 69–83.

Business Week. 1989. "Hispanics, A Nation within a Nation," (September 25):144–145.

Butler, Matilda, and William Paisley. 1980. Women and the Mass Media. New York: Human Sciences Press.

Cabib, Amalia, 1981. "Indians of the Americas: Refugees in Their Own Land," Intercom 9 (June):3.

Cain, Bruce, and Roderick Kiewiet. 1986. "California's Coming Minority Majority," Public Opinion (February–March):50–52.

Caldwell, Carol. 1977. "You Haven't Come a Long Way, Baby," New York Times (June 10):57–62.

Cannon, Lynne Weber, and Stella Warren. 1983. "Feminization of Poverty," Newsletter. Memphis: Center for Research on Women (April):2–3.

Caplan, Nathan, and Stephen D. Nelson. 1973. "On Being Useful: The Nature and Consequences of Psychological Research on Social Problems," American Psychologist 28 (March):199–211.

Carey, Max L. 1976. "Revised Occupational Projections to 1985," Monthly Labor Review (November):15–16.

Carmichael, Stokely, and Charles V. Hamilton. 1967.

Black Power: The Politics of Liberation in America. New York: Random House.

Carnegie Foundation Report. 1981. Cited in "Hispanics Make Their Move," *U.S. News & World Report* (August 24):64.

Carnoy, Martin (ed.). 1975. *Schooling in a Corporate Society: The Political Economy of Education in America,* 2nd ed. New York: David McKay.

Carroll, John B. (ed.). 1956. *Language, Thought, and Reality: Selected Writings of Benjamin Lee Whorf.* Cambridge, MA: MIT Press.

Carter, Hugh, and Paul C. Glick. 1976. *Marriage and Divorce: A Social and Economic Study,* rev. ed. Cambridge, MA: Harvard University Press.

Carter, Michael J., and Susan Boslego Carter. 1981. "Women Get a Ticket to Ride after the Gravy Train has Left the Station," *Feminist Studies* 7:477–504.

Chafetz, Janet Saltzman. 1974. *Masculine/Feminine or Human?* Itasca, IL: F. E. Peacock.

Chambliss, William J. 1969. *Crime and the Legal Process.* New York: McGraw-Hill.

_____. 1973. "The Saints and the Roughnecks," *Society* 11 (November–December):24–31.

_____. 1974. *Functional and Conflict Theories of Crime,* Module 17. New York: MSS Modular Publications.

_____. 1976. "Functional and Conflict Theories of Crime: The Heritage of Emile Durkheim and Karl Marx," in *Whose Law, What Order? A Conflict Approach to Criminology,* William J. Chambliss and Milton Mankoff (eds.). New York: John Wiley.

Chaze, William L. 1986. "Living Dangerously," *U.S. News & World Report* (May 19):19–23.

Cherlin, Andrew, and Frank F. Furstenburg, Jr. 1983. "The American Family in the Year 2000," *The Futurist* 17 (June).

Children's Defense Fund. 1989. *A Vision for America's Future.* Washington, DC: Children's Defense Fund (entire issue).

Chiricos, Theodore G., Philip D. Jackson, and Gordon P. Waldo. 1972. "Inequality in the Imposition of the Criminal Label," *Social Problems* 19 (Spring):553–572.

Chiswick, Barry R. 1985. "Immigrants in the U.S. Labor Market," in *Majority and Minority,* Norman R. Yetman (ed.). Boston: Allyn and Bacon, pp. 401–407.

Christensen, Kathleen. 1988. *Women and Home-Based Work.* New York: Henry Holt.

Christian Century, The. 1980. "The God-Language Bind" (April 16):430–431.

Christian Science Monitor, The. 1984. "Jobs for the Future" (October 22):19.

Chronicle of Higher Education. 1989. "Fact File: Defense Department Contracts to Non-Profit Organizations, Fiscal 1988," (June 7):A16.

Church, George J. 1985. "A Melding of Cultures," *Time* (July 8):36–41.

Churchill, Ward, and Jim Vander Wall. 1988. *Agents of Repression: The FBI's Secret Wars Against the Black Panther Party and the American Indian Movement.* Boston: South End Press.

Cimons, Marlene. 1989. "Study Says Poor Die Needlessly from Cancer," *Los Angeles Times* (July 18):1.

Clark, Ramsey. 1970. *Crime in America: Observations on Its Nature, Causes, Prevention and Control.* New York: Simon and Schuster.

Coakley, Jay J. 1986. *Sport in Society: Issues and Controversies,* 3rd ed. St. Louis: Times Mirror/Mosby.

Coates, Joseph F. 1986. "Twenty-Twenty Vision." *Vital Speeches of the Day* 52 (June 15):536–540.

Cohen, Albert K. 1955. *Delinquent Boys: The Culture of the Gang* Glencoe, IL: Free Press.

_____. 1966. *Deviance and Control.* Englewood Cliffs, NJ: Prentice-Hall.

Cole, George F. 1973. *Politics and the Administration of Justice.* Beverly Hills, CA: Sage.

Cole, Stephen. 1975. *The Sociological Orientation: An Introduction to Sociology.* Chicago: Rand McNally.

Coleman, James S. 1961. *The Adolescent Society.* New York: Free Press.

_____, et al. 1966. *Equality of Educational Opportunity.* Washington, D.C.: Government Printing Office.

Coleman, James William, and Donald R. Cressey. 1990. *Social Problems,* 4th ed. New York: Harper and Row.

Collins, Randall. 1972. "A Conflict Theory of Sexual Stratification," in *Family, Marriage and the Struggle of the Sexes,* Hans Peter Dreitzel (ed.). New York: Macmillan.

_____. 1975. *Conflict Sociology.* New York: Academic Press.

_____. 1988. "Women and Men in the Class Structure," *Journal of Family Issues* 9 (March):27–50.

Comer, Lee. 1978. "Women and Class, the Question of Women and Class," *Women's Studies International Quarterly* 1:165–173.

Commission on Population Growth and the American Future. 1972. *Population and the American Future.* New York: New American Library.

Conklin, Ellis A. 1986. "Immigrant Tide Turns L.A. Area into Alien Stew," *The Flint Journal* (June 16):D5.

Cook, James. 1981. "The American Indian Through Five Centuries," *Forbes* (November 9).

Cooley, Charles Horton. 1964. *Human Nature and the Social Order.* New York: Schocken.

Cornell, George. 1989. "Women in 'Full Ministry' Nearly Double in Decade," *Rocky Mountain News* (May 27):106.

Correia, Eddie. 1986. "The Reagan Assault on Antitrust," *Multinational Monitor* 7 (February 15):3–7.

Coser, Lewis. 1966. *The Functions of Social Conflict.* New York: Free Press.

Cox, Harvey G. 1977. "Why Young Americans Are

Buying Oriental Religions," *Psychology Today* (July):36–42.

Crispell, Diane. 1989. "In Charge," *American Demographics* (September):27–29.

Crutsinger, Martin. 1986. "40% of Wealth Controlled by 12% of Families," *The Flint Journal* (July 28):1.

Currie, Elliott, and Jerome H. Skolnick. 1984. *America's Problems: Social Issues and Public Policy.* Boston: Little, Brown.

_____. 1988. *America's Problems: Social Issues and Public Policy,* 2nd ed. Boston: Little, Brown.

Cushman, John H. 1986. "Pentagon-to-Contractor Job Shift Is Profiled," *The New York Times* (August 31):37.

Cutler, James E. 1905. *Lynch-Law: An Investigation into the History of Lynching in the United States.* New York: Longmans, Green.

Cuzzort, R. P. 1969. *Humanity and Modern Sociological Thought.* New York: Holt, Rinehart, and Winston.

Dahl, Robert. 1961. *Who Governs?* New Haven, CT: Yale University Press.

Dahrendorf, Ralf. 1959. *Class and Class Conflict in Industrial Society.* Stanford, CA: Stanford University Press.

_____. 1968. "Out of Utopia: Toward a Reorientation of Sociological Analysis," *American Journal of Sociology* 64 (September).

Dassbach, Carl H. A. 1986. "Industrial Robots in the American Automobile Industry." *Insurgent Sociologist* 13 (Summer):53–61.

David, Deborah S., and Robert Brannon. 1980. "The Male Sex Role," in *Family in Transition,* 3rd ed., Arlene S. Skolnick and Jerome H. Skolnick (eds.). Boston: Little, Brown.

Davies, James A. 1966. "Structural Balance, Mechanical Solidarity, and Interpersonal Relations," *Sociological Theories in Progress I,* Joseph Berger, Morris Zelditch, Jr., and Bo Anderson (eds.). Boston: Houghton Mifflin.

Davis, Cary, Carl Haub, and JoAnne Willette. 1983. "U.S. Hispanics Changing the Face of America," *Population Bulletin* 38 (June): entire issue.

Davis, Kingsley. 1940. "Extreme Social Isolation of a Child," *American Journal of Sociology* 45 (January):554–564.

_____. 1948. *Human Society.* New York: Macmillan.

_____, and Wilbert E. Moore. 1945. "Some Principles of Stratification," *American Sociological Review* 10 (April):242–249.

Davis, Nanette J. 1975. *Sociological Constructions of Deviance Perspectives and Issues in the Field.* Dubuque, Iowa: Wm. C. Brown.

Deckard, Barbara Sinclair. 1983. *The Women's Movement,* 3rd ed. New York: Harper and Row.

Degler, Carl. 1980. *At Odds: Women and the Family in America from the Revolution to the Present.* New York: Oxford University Press.

De Lone, Richard H. 1979. *Small Futures: Children, Inequality, and the Limits of Liberal Reform.* New York: Carnegie Council on Children. Cited in Patricia McCormack, "Economic Gap between Classes," *Rocky Mountain News* (August 22):66.

Demerath, N. J. III. 1965. *Social Class in American Protestantism.* Chicago: Rand McNally.

Demos, John. 1977. "The American Family of Past Time," in *Family in Transition,* 2nd ed., Arlene S. Skolnick and Jerome H. Skolnick (eds.). Boston: Little, Brown.

Dentler, Robert A., and Kai T. Erickson. 1959. "The Functions of Deviance in Groups," *Social Problems* 7 (Fall):98–107.

Denver Post, The. 1982. " 'Male Job' Concept Vanishing" (December 13):C1.

_____. 1989. "Babies of Parents Lacking Insurance Face More Risks," (August 24):44.

Dessler, Gary. 1987. "Report Describes Worker Time Theft," *Denver Post* (January 18):E2.

Detroit Free Press. 1986. "Study Finds 1 in 5 Births Are to Unwed Mothers" (July 29):5A.

Devens, Richard W., Carol Boyd Leon, and Debbie L. Sprinkle. 1985. "Employment and Unemployment in 1984: A Second Year of Strong Growth in Jobs," *Monthly Labor Review* (February):3–15.

Diamond, Stuart. 1985. "U.S. Toxic Mishaps in Chemicals Put at 6,928 in 5 Years," *New York Times* (October 3):1, 13.

_____. 1986. "Chernobyl Rouses Bad Memories, New Fears," *New York Times* (May 4):E3.

Di Baggio, Thomas. 1976. "The Unholy Alliance," *Penthouse* (May):74–91.

Dibble, Ursula, and Murray S. Straus. 1980. "Some Social Structure Determinants of Inconsistency Between Attitudes and Behavior: The Case of Family Violence," *Journal of Marriage and Family* 42 (February).

Dolbeare, Kenneth M. 1986. *Democracy at Risk: The Politics of Economic Renewal,* rev. ed. Chatham, NJ: Chatham House.

Dollars and Sense. 1987. "Income Distribution: Going to Extremes," No. 131 (November):22.

Domhoff, G. William. 1967. *Who Rules America?* Englewood Cliffs, NJ: Prentice-Hall.

_____. 1970. *The Higher Circles: The Governing Class in America.* New York: Random House.

_____. 1975. "How Fat Cats Keep in Touch," *Psychology Today* 9 (August):44–48.

_____. 1979. *The Powers That Be: Processes of Ruling Class Domination in America.* New York: Random House.

_____. 1983. *Who Rules America Now?* Englewood Cliffs, NJ: Prentice-Hall.

Donner, Frank. 1971. "The Theory and Practice of

American Political Intelligence," *New York Review of Books* 16 (April 22):27–39.

_____. 1985. "Travelers' Warning for Nicaragua," *The Nation* (July 6–13):13–14.

Dorris, Michael A. 1981. "The Grass Still Grows, the Rivers Still Flow: Contemporary Native Americans," *Daedalus* 110 (Spring):43–69.

Doyle, Jack, and Paul T. Schindler. 1974. "The Incoherent Society," paper presented at the American Sociological Association, Montreal (August 25–29).

Duncan, Greg J. 1984. *Years of Poverty, Years of Plenty: The Changing Economic Fortunes of American Workers and Families.* Ann Arbor: Institute of Social Research.

Dunn, William. 1989. "Housing Debate: Save It, Raze It," *USA Today* (April 19):3A.

_____. 1989. "Mini-Boom: Births at 25-Year High," *USA Today* (June 22):1A.

Durkheim, Emile. 1951. *Suicide,* reprinted ed. Glencoe, IL: Free Press.

_____. 1958. *The Rules of Sociological Method,* 8th ed., Sarah A. Solovay and John H. Mueller, trans. Glencoe, IL: Free Press.

_____. 1960. *The Division of Labor in Society,* George Simpson, trans. New York: Free Press.

_____. 1961. *The Elementary Forms of Religious Life,* Joseph Ward Swain, trans. New York: Macmillan.

_____. 1965. *The Elementary Forms of Religious Life.* New York: Free Press.

Dye, Thomas R. 1976. *Who's Running America? Institutional Leadership in the United States.* Englewood Cliffs, NJ: Prentice-Hall.

Dyer, Everett D. 1979. *The American Family: Variety and Change.* New York: McGraw-Hill.

Early, Frances H. 1983. "The French-Canadian Family Economy and Standard of Living in Lowell, Massachusetts, 1870," in *The American Family in Social Historical Perspective.* 3rd ed., Michael Gordon (ed.). New York: St. Martin's, pp. 482–503.

Edgley, Charles, and Ronny E. Turner, 1975. "Masks and Social Relations," *Humboldt Journal of Social Relations* 3 (Fall–Winter).

Edmondson, Brad. 1985. "Southern California Gas's 88 Languages," *American Demographics* 7 (July).

Edwards, Richard C. 1975. "The Social Relations of Production in the Firm and Labor Market Structure," in *Labor Market Segmentation,* Richard C. Edwards et al. (eds.). Lexington, MA: D. C. Heath, pp. 3–26.

_____, Michael Reich, and Thomas E. Weisskopf. 1978. "Sexism," in *The Capitalist System,* 2nd ed. Englewood Cliffs, NJ: Prentice-Hall.

Ehrenreich, Barbara. 1986. "Two, Three, Many Husbands," *Mother Jones* (July–August):8.

_____, and Karin Stallard. 1982. "The Nouveau Poor," *Ms.* (August).

_____. 1989. *Fear of Falling: The Inner Life of the Middle Class.* New York: Pantheon.

Eisenstein, Zillah. 1979. "Developing a Theory of Capitalist Patriarchy and Socialist Feminism," in *Capitalist Patriarchy and the Case for Socialist Feminism.* Zillah R. Eisenstein (ed.). New York: Monthly Review Press, pp. 5–40.

_____. 1982. "The Sexual Politics of the New Right: Understanding the 'Crisis of Liberalism' for the 1980's," *Signs* 7 (Spring):567–588.

Eitzen, D. Stanley. 1967. "A Conflict Model for the Analysis of Majority-Minority Relations," *Kansas Journal of Sociology* 3 (Spring):76–89.

_____, and George H. Sage. 1989. *The Sociology of North American Sport,* 4th ed. Dubuque, IA: Wm. C. Brown.

_____, and Maxine Baca Zinn. 1989. "The Forces Reshaping America," in *The Reshaping of America,* D. Stanley Eitzen and Maxine Baca Zinn (eds.). Englewood Cliffs, NJ: Prentice-Hall, pp. 1–13.

Ekman, Paul, Wallace V. Friesen, and John Bear. 1984. "The International Language of Gestures," *Psychology Today* 18 (May):64–69.

Epstein, Cynthia Fuchs. 1970. *Woman's Place.* Berkeley: University of California Press.

Erickson, Kai T. 1966. *Wayward Puritans: A Study in the Sociology of Deviance.* New York: John Wiley.

Ermann, M. David, and Richard J. Lundman (eds.). 1978. *Corporate and Governmental Deviance.* New York: Oxford University Press.

Eshleman, J. Ross. 1988. *The Family,* 5th ed. Boston: Allyn and Bacon.

Eskey, Kenneth. 1986. "Minorities Trail Whites in Net Worth," *The Rocky Mountain News* (July 19).

Estrada, Leobardo F., et al. 1981. "Chicanos in the United States: A History of Exploitation and Resistance," *Daedalus* 110 (Spring):103–131.

Etzioni, Amitai. 1984. *Capital Corruption: The New Attack on American Democracy.* New York: Harcourt, Brace, Jovanovich.

Ewen, Stuart. 1976. *Captains of Consciousness: Advertising and the Social Roots of the Consumer Culture.* New York: McGraw-Hill.

Farber, Jerry. 1970. *The Student as Nigger.* New York: Pocket Books.

Farberman, Harvey, and Erich Goode. 1973. *Social Reality.* Englewood Cliffs, NJ: Prentice-Hall.

Farris, Robert, and H. Warren Dunham. 1939. *Mental Disorders in Urban Areas.* Chicago: University of Chicago Press.

Farrell, M. P., and S. Rosenberg. 1981. *Men at Midlife.* Boston: Auburn House.

Feagin, Joe R. 1972. "Poverty: We Still Believe That God Helps Those Who Help Themselves," *Psychology Today* 6 (November):101–110, 129.

_____. 1984. *Racial and Ethnic Relations.* Englewood Cliffs, NJ: Prentice-Hall.

_____. 1986. *Social Problems,* 2nd ed. Englewood Cliffs, NJ: Prentice-Hall.

Feigelson, Jeremy. 1982. "Our Next War: Who Will Fight It?" *Civil Rights Quarterly* 14 (Spring):16–21.

Festinger, Leon, Henry W. Riecken, Jr., and Stanley Schachter. 1956. *When Prophecy Fails.* Minneapolis: University of Minnesota Press.

Findlay, Steven. 1986. "Cancer Risk Higher for Poor," *USA Today* (October 7):D1.

Fischman, Joshua. 1986. "A Journey of Hearts and Minds," *Psychology Today* (July):42–47.

Fishman, Pamela M. 1978. "Interaction: The Work Women Do." *Social Problems* 25 (April):397–406.

Fiske, Edward B. 1987. "Integration Lacks at Public Schools." *New York Times* (July 26):1, 15.

FitzGerald, Francis. 1979. *America Revised: History Schoolbooks in the Twentieth Century.* Boston: Atlantic-Little, Brown.

Fleetwood, Blake. 1980. "The Tax Police: Trampling Citizens' Rights," *Saturday Review* (May):33–36.

Flora, Cornelia Butler. 1979. "Changes in Women's Status in Women's Magazine Fiction," *Social Problems* 26 (June):558–569.

Forbes. 1986. "The 100 Largest Multinationals." *Forbes* (July 28):207.

_____. 1989. "The 400 Richest People in America," (October 23):106–317.

Forester, Tom. 1987. *High-Tech Society: The Story of the Information Technology Revolution.* Cambridge, MA.: The MIT Press.

Forstall, Richard L., and Donald E. Starsinic. 1989. "Patterns of Metropolitan Area and County Population Growth: 1980–1987," *Current Population Reports,* Series P–25, No. 1039. Washington, DC: Government Printing Office.

Franklin, Deborah. 1989. "What a Child Is Given," *New York Times Magazine* (September 3):36–41, 49.

Frazier, Nancy, and Myra Pollack Sadker. 1973. *Sexism in School and Society.* New York: Harper & Row.

Freeman, Jo. 1979. "The Women's Liberation Movement: Its Origins, Organizations, Activities, and Ideas," in *Women: A Feminist Perspective,* 2nd ed. Jo Freeman (ed.). Palo Alto, CA: Mayfield, pp. 557–574.

Freud, Sigmund. 1946. *Civilization and Its Discontents.* Joan Riviere, trans. London: Hogarth Press.

Friedl, Ernestine. 1975. *Women and Men: An Anthropologist's View.* New York: Holt, Rinehart and Winston.

Friedrich, Otto. 1985. "Immigrants," *Time* (July 8):24–33.

Frieze, Irene Hanson. 1983. "Investigating the Causes and Consequences of Marital Rape," *Signs* 8 (Spring):532–553.

Fussell, Paul. 1983. *Class.* New York: Ballantine.

Gallup Report. 1987. "Religion in America," No. 259 (April): entire issue.

Gans, Herbert J. 1962. *The Urban Villagers.* New York: Free Press.

_____. 1971. "The Uses of Power: The Poor Pay All," *Social Policy* 2 (July–August): 20–24.

_____. 1979. *Deciding What's News.* New York: Pantheon.

Gardner, Robert W., Bryant Robey, and Peter C. Smith. 1985. "Asian Americans: Growth, Change, and Diversity," *Population Bulletin* 40 (October): entire issue.

Garfinkel, Harold. 1967. *Studies in Ethnomethodology.* Englewood Cliffs, NJ: Prentice-Hall.

Gay, Lance. 1983. "Pentagon Billed $9,609 for $.12 Wrench," *Rocky Mountain News* (November 2):4.

Gelles, Richard J. 1977. "No Place to Go: The Social Dynamics of Marital Violence," in *Battered Women,* Marina Roy (ed.). New York: Van Nostrand.

_____. 1979. "The Myth of Battered Husbands," *Ms.* 8 (October):65–66a, 71s–74.

Gerrard, Nathan L. 1968. "The Serpent Handling Religions of West Virginia," *Trans-action* 5 (May).

Gerson, Kathleen. 1983. "Changing Family Structure," *Journal of the American Planning Association* 49 (Spring).

_____. 1986. "Briefcase, Baby, or Both?" *Psychology* (November):31–36.

Gerth, Hans, and C. Wright Mills, 1953. *Character and Social Structure: The Psychology of Social Institutions.* New York: Harcourt, Brace, and World.

Gest, Ted. 1983. "When Employees Turn into Thieves," *U.S. News & World Report* (September 26):79–80.

Gibbs, Jack P. 1966. "Conceptions of Deviant Behavior: The Old and the New," *Pacific Sociological Review* 9 (Spring):9–14.

Gilbert, Bil, and Nancy Williamson. 1973. "Programmed to Be Losers," *Sports Illustrated* (June 11).

Gillespie, Dair. 1972. "Who Has the Power? The Marital Struggle," in *Family, Marriage, and the Struggle of the Sexes,* Hans Peter Dreitzel (ed.). New York: Macmillan, pp. 105–157.

Gilman, Richard. 1971. "Where Did It All Go Wrong?" *Life* (August 13).

Gintis, Herbert. 1979. "Who Gets Ahead?" *Saturday Review* (June 2):29–33.

Gittell, Marilyn. 1981. "Localizing Democracy out of the Schools," *Social Policy* 12 (September–October).

Glazer, Nona. 1977. "Introduction, Part Two," in *Woman in a Man-Made World,* 2nd ed. Nona Glazer and Helen Youngelson Waehrer (eds.). Chicago: Rand McNally.

Gleidman, John, and William Roth. 1980. "The Unexpected Minority," *New Republic* (February 2):26–30.

Glenn, Evelyn Nakano, and Roslyn L. Feldberg. 1979. "Clerical Work: The Female Occupation," in *Women: A Feminist Perspective,* 2nd ed. Jo Freeman (ed.). Palo Alto, CA: Mayfield.

Glick, Paul C. 1975. "Some Recent Changes in American Families," *Current Population Reports,* Series P–23, No. 52. Washington, DC: Government Printing Office.

Glock, Charles Y., Benjamin B. Ringer, and Earl R. Babbie. 1967. *To Comfort and to Challenge: A Dilemma of the Contemporary Church.* Berkeley, CA: University of California Press.

_____, and Rodney Stark. 1965. *Religion and Society in Tension.* Chicago: Rand McNally.

Goffman, Erving. 1959. *The Presentation of Self in Everyday Life.* Garden City, NY: Doubleday.

_____. 1979. *Gender Advertisements.* New York: Harper/Colophon.

Gold, Allan R. 1989. "The Struggle to Make Do without Health Insurance," *New York Times* (July 30):1,11.

Goldman, Ari L. 1986. "As Call Comes, More Women Answer," *New York Times* (October 10):E6.

Goldsen, Rose K. 1977. *The Show and Tell Machine: How Television Works and Works You Over.* New York: Delta.

Goode, Erich. 1966. "Social Class and Church Participation," *American Journal of Sociology* 72 (July).

Goode, William J. 1963. *World Revolution and Family Patterns.* New York: Free Press.

_____. 1976. "Family Disorganization," in *Contemporary Social Problems,* 4th ed., Robert K. Merton and Robert Nisbet (eds.). New York: Harcourt, Brace Jovanovich.

_____. 1984. "Idealization of the Recent Past: The United States," in *Family in Transition,* 4th ed., Arlene S. Skolnick and Jerome H. Skolnick (eds). Boston: Little, Brown, pp. 43–53.

Gordon, David M., Richard C. Edwards, and Michael Reich. 1982. *Segmented Work, Divided Workers.* Cambridge: Cambridge University Press.

Gordon, Suzanne. 1983. "The New Corporate Feminism," *The Nation* (February 5).

Gouldner, Alvin W. 1962. "Anti-Minotaur: The Myth of Value-Free Sociology," *Social Problems* 9 (Winter).

Green, Mark J. 1972. "The High Cost of Monopoly," *The Progressive* 36 (March).

_____. 1984. "When Money Talks, Is It Democracy?" *The Nation* (September 15):200–205.

Greenhouse, Steven. 1986. "The Average Guy Takes It on the Chin," *New York Times* (July 13): Section 3:1, 10.

Gutman, Herbert G. 1976. *The Black Family in Slavery and Freedom, 1750–1925.* New York: Pantheon.

Guttman, Peter. 1983. "The Subterranean Economy Five Years Later," *Across the Board* 20:24–31.

Gwynne, S. C. 1988. "Are You Better Off?" *Time* (October 10):28–32.

Hacker, Andrew. 1970. *The End of the American Era.* New York: Atheneum.

_____(ed.). 1983. *U/S: A Statistical Portrait of the American People.* New York: Viking.

_____. 1986. "Women at Work," *New York Review of Books* 33 (August 14):26–32.

Hadden, Jeffrey K. 1980. "Soul-Saving Via Video," *The Christian Century* (May 28).

_____, and Charles E. Swann. 1981. *Prime Time Preachers.* Reading, MA: Addison-Wesley.

_____, and Anson Shupe. 1988. *Televangelism: Power and Politics on God's Frontier.* New York: Henry Holt.

Hannerz, Ulf. 1969. "Roots of Black Manhood: Sex, Socialization, and Culture in the Ghettos of American Cities," *Trans-action* 6 (October).

Hareven, Tamara K. 1976. "Modernization and Family History," *Signs* 2:190–206.

_____. 1976. "Women and Men: Changing Roles," in *Women and Men: Changing Roles, Relationships and Perceptions,* Libby A. Carter, Anne Firor Scott, and Wendy Martyna (eds.). Aspen, CO: Aspen Institute for Humanistic Studies.

Harrington, Michael. 1963. *The Other America: Poverty in the United States.* Baltimore: Penguin.

_____. 1965. *The Accidental Century.* Baltimore: Penguin.

_____. 1979. "Social Retreat and Economic Stagnation," *Dissent* 26 (Spring):131–134.

Harris, Marvin. 1975. *Cows, Pigs, Wars, and Witches: The Riddles of Culture.* New York: Random House.

_____. 1978. "India's Sacred Cows," *Human Nature* 1 (February).

Harrison, Bennett, Chris Tilly, and Barry Bluestone. 1986. "Wage Inequality Takes a Great U-Turn," *Challenge* 29 (March–April):26–32.

Hart, Gary. 1983. "Investing in People for the Information Age," *The Futurist* 17 (February).

Hartjen, Clayton A. 1974. *Crime and Criminalization.* New York: Praeger.

Hartley, Shirley Foster. 1973. "Our Growing Problem: Population," *Social Problems* 21 (Fall).

Hartmann, Heidi I. 1976. "Capitalism, Patriarchy, and Job Segregation by Sex," *Signs* 1 (Spring):137–169.

Hayakawa, S. I. 1949. *Language in Thought and Action.* New York: Harcourt, Brace.

Hayes-Bautista, David E., Warner O. Schinek, and Jorge Chapa. 1984. "Young Latinas in an Aging American Society," *Social Policy* 15 (Summer):49–52.

Hayghe, H. 1979. "Working Wives' Contributions to Family Income in 1977," *Monthly Labor Review* 39:62–64.

Healy, Tim, and Peter Marshall. 1986. "Big Business Is Watching You," *In These Times* (February 26):12–13.

Heilbroner, Robert L. 1974. *An inquiry into the Human Prospect.* New York: W. W. Norton.

Henley, Nancy M. 1977. *Body Politics: Power, Sex, and*

Nonverbal Communication. Englewood Cliffs, NJ: Prentice-Hall.

Henry, Jules. 1963. *Culture against Man.* New York: Random House Vintage.

Henry, Tamara. 1988. "Working Women's TV Roles," *Philadelphia Inquirer* (December 14):7E.

Herrnstein, Richard. 1971. "I.Q." *The Atlantic* 228 (September):43–64.

———. 1973. *I.Q. in the Meritocracy.* Boston: Little, Brown.

Hershey, Robert D. 1987. "Jobless Rate Down but Growth of Jobs Also Falls," *New York Times* (April 4):7.

Higham, Charles. 1983. *Trading with the Enemy.* New York: Dell.

Hightower, Jim. 1987. "Where Greed, Unofficially Blessed by Reagan, Has Led," *New York Times* (June 21):25.

Hillam, Bruce P. 1976. "You Gave Us Your Dimes . . . ," *Newsweek* (November 1):13.

Hillkirk, John. 1983. "Computer Age Brings New Fears," *USA Today* (October 4):B1–2.

———. 1983. "Atari Move: Start of a Tragic Trend," *USA Today* (February 23):B3.

Himes, Joseph S. 1966. "The Functions of Racial Conflict," *Social Forces* 45 (September):1–10.

Himmelweit, Hilde, A. N. Oppenheim, and Pamela Vance. 1958. *Television and the Child.* London: Oxford University Press.

Hirschi, Travis. 1969. *Causes of Delinquency.* Berkeley: University of California Press.

Hoch, Paul. 1972. *Rip Off The Big Game.* New York: Doubleday.

Hochschild, Arlie. 1989. *The Second Shift.* New York: Viking.

Hodge, Robert W., Paul M. Seigel, and Peter H. Rossi. 1964. "Occupational Prestige in the United States, 1925–63," *American Journal of Sociology* 70 (November):286–302.

———, Donald J. Treiman, and Peter H. Rossi. 1966. "A Comparative Study of Occupational Prestige," in *Class, Status, and Power,* 2nd ed., Reinhard Bendix and S. M. Lipset (eds.). New York: Free Press, pp. 309–321.

Hofstadter, Richard. 1955. *Social Darwinism in American Thought,* rev. ed. Boston: Beacon Press.

Hole, Judith, and Ellen Levine. 1979. "The First Feminists," in *Women: A Feminist Perspective,* Jo Freeman (ed.). Palo Alto, CA: Mayfield.

Homans, George. 1964. "Bringing Men Back In," *American Sociological Review* 29 (December):809–818.

Horn, Miriam. 1987. "The Burgeoning Educational Underclass," *U.S. News & World Report* (May 18):66–67.

Horton, John. 1966. "Order and Conflict Theories of Social Problems as Competing Ideologies," *American Journal of Sociology* 71 (May):701–713.

Horwitz, Allan V. 1984. "The Economy and Social Pathology," *Annual Reviews of Sociology* 10. New York: Annual Reviews Inc.

Huaco, George A. 1966. "The Functionalist Theory of Stratification: Two Decades of Controversy," *Inquiry* 9 (Autumn):215–240.

Hughes, Dana, Kay Johnson, Sara Rosenbaum, and Joseph Liu. 1989. *The Health of America's Children.* Washington, DC: Children's Defense Fund.

Hughes, Everett C. 1944–1945. "Dilemmas and Contradictions of Status," *American Journal of Sociology* 50 (July/May):353–359.

Hunt, Carol. 1982. "Inequities Continued in School Finance Act," *The Denver Post* (May 11):B3.

Hunter, Floyd. 1953. *Community Power Structure.* Chapel Hill: University of North Carolina Press.

Huntington, Samuel P. 1965. "The Marasmus of the ICC," in *Bureaucratic Power in National Politics,* Francis Rourke (ed.). Boston: Little, Brown, pp. 73–86.

Hutchins, Robert M. 1976. "Is Democracy Possible?" *Center Magazine* 9 (January–February):2–6.

Hymnowitz, Carol, and Timothy D. Schellhardt. 1986. "The Glass Ceiling," *The Wall Street Journal* (March 24):1, 4.

Iglitzen, Lynn B. 1972. *Violent Conflict in American Society.* San Francisco: Chandler.

ISR Newsletter. 1982. "Why Do Women Earn Less?" Institute for Social Research, The University of Michigan (Spring/Summer).

In These Times. 1986. "Wealth Triumphs, We Lose" (August 6):14; and the data correction noted (September 3):15.

Jackson, Robert L. 1982. "Tax-Cheating Loss," *The Denver Post* (March 18):A1–7.

Janzen, David. 1974. "Love 'em and Leave 'em Alone," *The Mennonite* (June 11):390.

Jaynes, Gerald David and Robin M. Williams, Jr. 1989. *A Common Destiny: Blacks and American Society.* Washington, DC: National Academy Press.

Jeffries, Vincent, and H. Edward Ransford. 1980. *Social Stratification: A Multiple Hierarchy Approach.* Boston: Allyn and Bacon.

Jencks, Christopher, et al. 1979. *Who Gets Ahead? The Determinants of Economic Success in America.* New York: Basic Books.

Jensen, Arthur R. 1969. "How Much Can We Boost IQ and Scholastic Achievement?" *Harvard Educational Review* 39 (Winter):1–123.

———. 1980. *Bias in Mental Testing.* New York: Free Press.

Jones, Barry. 1982. *Sleepers Awake! Technology and the Future of Work.* Melbourne: Oxford University Press.

Jones. J. H. 1981. *Bad Blood.* New York: Free Press.

Josephson, Matthew. 1938. *The Politicos, 1865–1896*. New York: Harcourt, Brace.

Jung, Maureen, Dean Purdy, and D. Stanley Eitzen. 1981. "The Corporate Inner Group," *Sociological Spectrum* 1 (July–September):317–333.

Kagan, Jerome. 1973. "What Is Intelligence?" *Social Policy* 4 (July–August):88–94.

_____. 1977. "The Child in the Family," *Daedalus* 106 (Spring):33–56.

Kanter, Rosabeth Moss. 1977. *Men and Women of the Corporation*. New York: Basic Books.

Karmin, Monroe W. 1987. "Will the U.S. Stay Number One?" *U.S. News & World Report* (February 2):18–22.

_____, and Jeffrey L. Shaler. 1982. "Jobs: A Million That Will Never Come Back," *U.S. News & World Report* (September 13):55.

Kasarda, John D. 1985. "Urban Change and Minority Opportunities," in *The New Urban Reality*, Paul E. Peterson (ed.). Washington, DC: The Brookings Institution, pp. 33–67.

Kasinitz, Philip. 1984. "Gentrification and Home-lessness," *The Urban and Social Change Review* 17 (Winter):9–14.

Katz, Michael B. 1968. *The Irony of Early School Reform: Educational Innovation in Mid-Nineteenth Century Massachusetts*. Cambridge, MA: Harvard University Press.

Katzenstein, Mary Fainsod. 1984. "Feminism and the Meaning of the Vote," *Signs: Journal of Women in Culture and Society* 10 (Autumn):4–26.

Kaufman, Debra Renee. 1984. "Professional Women: How Real Are the Recent Gains?" in *Women: A Feminist Perspective*, 3rd ed., Jo Freeman (ed.). Palo Alto, CA: Mayfield, pp. 353–369.

Kaufman, Jonathan. 1989. "The Color Line," *The Boston Globe Magazine* (June 25):18–56.

Keegan, Patricia, 1989. "Playing Favorites," *The New York Times Magazine* (August 6):A26.

Keller, Helen. 1954. *The Story of My Life*. Garden City, NY: Doubleday.

Kempton, Murray. 1979. "Arithmetic of Inequality," *The Progressive* 43 (November):8–9.

Kerbo, Harold R. 1983. *Social Stratification and Inequality: Class Conflict in the United States*. New York: McGraw-Hill.

Kesey, Ken. 1962. *One Flew over the Cuckoo's Nest*. New York: Signet Books.

Key. V. O., Jr. 1949. *Southern Politics*. New York: Random House.

Kirkham, James F., Sheldon G. Levy, and William J. Crotty. 1970. *Assassination and Political Violence*. New York: Bantam.

Kitagawa, Evelyn M., and Philip M. Hauser. 1968. "Education Differentials in Mortality by Cause of Death: United States, 1960, *Demography* 5:318–353.

Kitano, Harry H. L. and Roger Daniels. 1988. *Asian Americans: Emerging Minorities*. Englewood Cliffs, NJ: Prentice-Hall.

Kittle, Robert A. 1984. "Anatomy of a Pentagon Horror Story," *U.S. News & World Report* (October 15):69.

Kluckhohn, Clyde, and D. Leighton. 1946. *The Navaho*. Cambridge, MA: Harvard University Press.

Kluckhohn, Florence, and Fred L. Strodtbeck. 1961. *Variations in Value Orientaton*. New York: Harper & Row.

Knottnerus, J. David. 1987. "Status Attainment Research and Its Image of Society," *American Sociological Review* 52 (February):113–121.

Knowles, Louis L., and Kenneth Prewitt (eds.). 1965. *Institutional Racism in America*. Englewood Cliffs, NJ: Prentice-Hall.

Koepp, Stephen. 1986. "Feeling the Crunch from Foreign Chips." *Time* (October 27):72–73.

Kohn, Melvin. 1959. "Social Class and Parental Values," *American Journal of Sociology* 64 (January):337–351.

Kotz, Nick. 1984. "The Politics of Hunger," *New Republic* 190 (April 30):19–23.

Kozol, Jonathan. 1985. *Illiterate America*. New York: New American Library.

_____. 1988. *Rachel and Her Children: Homeless Families in America*. New York: Crown.

Kramer, R. C. 1982. "Corporate Crime," in *White Collar and Economic Crime*, P. Wickman and T. Dailey (eds.). New York: Lexington, pp. 75–94.

Kreck, Carol. 1983. "Elderly Women Finding Men Scarce." *Denver Post* (January 31):1E–2E.

Kutscher, Ronald E., and Valerie A. Personick. 1986. "Deindustrialization and the Shift to Services." *Monthly Labor Review* (June):3–13.

Kuttner, Bob. 1983. "The Declining Middle," *The Atlantic Monthly* 252 (July):60–63.

Ladner, Joyce A. 1971. *Tomorrow's Tomorrow*. New York: Doubleday.

Lakoff, Robin. 1975. *Language and Woman's Place*. New York: Harper/Colophon.

Langlois, Judith H., and A. Chris Downs. 1980. "Mothers, Fathers, and Peers as Socialization Agents of Sex-Typed Play Behaviors in Young Children," *Child Development* 57:1237–1247.

Lansky, L. M. 1967. "The Family Structure Also Affects the Model: Sex Role Attitudes In Parents of Pre-school Children," *Merrill-Palmer Quarterly* 13 (April):139–150.

Lasch, Christopher. 1977. *Haven in a Heartless World*. New York: Basic Books.

Laslett, Barbara. 1977. "The Family as a Private and Public Institution: An Historical Perspective," in *The Family: Functions, Conflicts, and Symbols*, Peter Stein, Judith Richman, and Natalie Hannon (eds.). Reading, MA: Addison-Wesley, pp. 44–59.

_____. 1984. "Family Membership, Past and

Present," in *Family in Transition*, 4th ed., Arlene S. Skolnick and Jerome H. Skolnick (eds.). Boston: Little, Brown.

Lauer, Robert H. 1973. *Perspectives on Social Change*. Boston: Allyn and Bacon.

Leacock, Eleanor B. 1972. "Introduction to the 1972 Edition of Engels' *Origin of the Family, Private Property and the State*." New York: International.

Lechner, Frank J. 1989. "Fundamentalism Revisited," *Society* 26 (January/February):51–59.

Leinhardt, Gaea, Andrea Mar Seewald, and Mary Engel. 1979. "Learning What's Taught: Sex Differences in Instruction," *Journal of Educational Psychology* 71 (August):432–439.

Lekachman, Robert. 1979. "The Specter of Full Employment," in *Crisis in American Institutions*, 4th ed., Jerome H. Skolnick and Elliott Currie (eds.). Boston: Little, Brown, pp. 50–58.

Lemert, Edwin M. 1951. *Social Pathology: A Systematic Approach to the Theory of Sociopathic Behavior*. New York: McGraw-Hill.

———. 1967. *Human Deviance, Social Problems and Social Control*. Englewood Cliffs, NJ: Prentice-Hall.

Lenski, Gerhard E. 1966. *Power and Privilege: A Theory of Social Stratification*. New York: McGraw-Hill.

———. 1970. *Human Societies: A Macrolevel Introduction to Sociology*. New York: McGraw-Hill.

Lerner, Michael. 1982. "Recapturing the 'Family Issue,' " *The Nation* (February 6).

Leslie, Gerald R., Richard F. Larson, and Benjamin L. Gorman. *Introductory Sociology*, 3rd ed. New York: Oxford University Press.

Lever, Janet. 1976. "Sex Differences in the Games Children Play," *Social Problems* 23 (April):478–487.

Levitan, Sar A., Richard S. Belous, and Frank Gallo. 1988. *What's Happening to the American Family?* rev. ed. Baltimore: Johns Hopkins University Press.

Levy, Betty. 1974. "Do Schools Sell Girls Short," in *And Jill Came Tumbling After: Sexism in American Education*, Judith Stacey, Susan Bereaud, and Joan Daniels (eds.). New York: Dell, pp. 142–146.

Levy, Frank S., and Richard C. Michel. 1986. "An Economic Bust for the Baby Boom," *Challenge* 29 (March–April):33–39.

Lewis, Michael. 1972. "There's No Unisex in the Nursery," *Psychology Today* 5 (May):54–57.

Liazos, Alexander. 1972. "The Poverty of the Sociology of Deviance: Nuts, Sluts, and Preverts," *Social Problems* 20 (Summer): 103–120.

———. 1985. *Sociology: A Liberating Perspective*. Boston: Allyn and Bacon.

Liebow, Elliot. 1967. *Tally's Corner*. Boston: Little, Brown.

Lipman-Blumen, Jean. 1984. *Gender Roles and Power*. Englewood Cliffs, NJ: Prentice-Hall.

Lipset, Seymour Martin. 1963. "The Sources of the 'Radical Right,' " in *The Radical Right*, Daniel Bell (ed.). Garden City, NY: Doubleday.

Lord, Lewis J. 1987. "An Unholy War in the TV Pulpits," *U.S. News & World Report* (April 6):58–65.

Lord, Walter. 1955. *A Night to Remember*. New York: Henry Holt.

Luhman, Reid, and Stuart Gilman. 1980. *Race and Ethnic Relations*. Belmont, CA: Wadsworth.

Louis, Elaine. 1989. "Unequal Contest," *New York Times* (August 6):A28.

Lynd, Robert S., and Helen Merrill Lynd. 1937. *Middletown in Transition*, New York: Harcourt Brace Jovanovich.

McCaghy, Charles H. 1976. *Deviant Behavior: Crime, Conflict, and Interest Groups*. New York: Macmillan.

McCarthy, Sarah J. 1979. "Why Johnny Can't Disobey," *The Humanist*. (September–October).

McCartney, James. 1986. "Critical Guns Zero In on Reagan's Champion of Secret Deals," *Denver Post* (November 14):G1.

Maccoby, Eleanor E., and Carol Nagy Jacklin. 1974. "What We Know and Don't Know about Sex Differences," *Psychology Today* 8 (December):109–112.

MacCormack, Carol P. 1981. "Anthropology: A Discipline with a Legacy," in *Men's Studies Modified*, Dale Spender (ed.). Oxford: Pergamon Press, pp. 99–110.

McGahey, Rick. 1981. "In Search of the Undeserving Poor," *Working Papers* 8 (November–December): 62–64.

McGee, Reece. 1975. *Points of Departure: Basic Concepts in Sociology*, 2nd ed. Hinsdale, IL: Dryden Press.

McGhee, Paul E., and Terry Frueh. 1980. "Television Viewing and the Learning of Sex-Role Stereotypes," *Sex Roles* 6:179–188.

McGuinness, Diane. 1979. "How Schools Discriminate against Boys," *Human Nature* 2 (February):82–88.

Machung, Anne. 1984. "Word Processing: Forward for Business, Backward for Women," in *My Troubles are Going to Have Trouble with Me*, Karen Brodkin Sacks and Dorothy Remy (eds.). New Brunswick, NJ: Rutgers University Press, pp. 124–139.

McGeary, Michael G. H. and Lawrence E. Lynn, Jr. (eds.). 1988. *Urban Change and Poverty*. Washington, DC: National Academy Press.

McKinley, Donald Gilbert. 1964. *Social Class and Family Life*. Glencoe, IL: Free Press.

McLeod, Beverly. 1986. "The Oriental Express," *Psychology Today* (July):48–52.

McWhirter, Norris, and Ross McWhirter. 1972. *Guinness Book of World Records*, 11th ed. New York: Sterling.

McWilliams, Carey. 1949. *North from Mexico*. Philadelphia: Lippincott.

Maddocks, Melvin. 1977. "America's Therapy Industry," *Christian Science Monitor* (January 10):16–17.

Mann, Leo L. 1980. "School Finance Reform in Connecticut," *Phi Delta Kappan* 62 (December).

Manuel, Herschel. 1934. "The Mexican Population of Texas," *Southwestern Social Science Quarterly* 15 (June):29–51.

Marx, Karl. 1967. *Capital: A Critique of Political Economy* vol. 1. New York: International Publishers.

————, and Friedrich Engels. 1947. *The German Ideology.* New York: International Publishers.

————. 1959. *Marx and Engels: Basic Writing on Politics and Philosophy,* Lewis S. Feuer (ed.). Garden City, NY: Anchor Books.

Masnick, George, and Mary Jo Bane. 1980. *The Nation's Families: 1960–1990.* Boston: Auburn House.

Mattera, Philip. 1983. "Home Computer Sweatshops," *The Nation* (April 2).

Matza, David. 1964a. "Position and Behavior Patterns of Youth," in *Handbook of Modern Sociology,* Robert E. L. Faris (ed.). Chicago: Rand McNally.

————. 1964b. *Delinquency and Drift.* New York: John Wiley.

Mayer, Martin. 1975. "Growing Up Crowded," *Commentary* 60 (September).

Mead, George Herbert. 1934. *Mind, Self, and Society.* Chicago: University of Chicago Press.

Melendez, Edwin. 1986. "Divided America," in Center for Popular Economics, *Economic Report of the People.* Boston: South End Press.

Merry. George B. 1984. "November 6 Results: More U.S. Women in Governmental Leadership Posts," *Christian Science Monitor* (December 14):3.

Merton, Robert K. 1957. *Social Theory and Social Structure,* 2nd ed. Glencoe, IL: Free Press.

Mewshaw, Michael. 1976. "Irrational Behavior or Evangelical Zeal?" *Chronicle of Higher Education* (October 18):32.

Michels, Robert. 1966. *Political Parties,* Eden Paul and Cedar Paul, trans. New York: Free Press.

Michigan, University of. 1984. "Old at 40: Women in the Workplace," A Report from the Institute of Gerontology. Ann Arbor: University of Michigan.

————. 1985. *Affirmative Action.* Ann Arbor: University of Michigan Office of Affirmative Action.

The Michigan Daily. 1987. "Why Women Faculty Are So Few," (March 13):6–7,12.

Miller, S. M. 1972. "Confusions of a Middle-Class Husband," in *The Future of the Family,* Louise Kapp Howe (ed.). New York: Touchstone.

Miller, Walter B. 1958. "Lower Class Culture as a Generating Milieu of Gang Delinquency," *Journal of Social Issues* 14 (No. 3):5–19.

Mills, C. Wright. 1956. *The Power Elite.* New York: Oxford University Press.

————. 1959. *The Power Elite.* Fair Lawn, NJ: Oxford University Press.

————. 1968. "The Power Elite," in *Reader in Political Sociology,* Frank Lindenfeld (ed.). New York: Funk & Wagnalls, pp. 263–276.

Mitgang, Herbert. 1987. "Policing America's Writers," *The New Yorker* (October 5):47–90.

Mokhiber, Russell. 1988. *Corporate Crime and Violence.* San Francisco: Sierra Club Books.

Monagan, David. 1983. "The Failure of Coed Sports," *Psychology Today* 17 (March): 58–63.

Monk, Abraham. 1988. "Aging, Generational Continuity, and Filial Support," *The World and I* 3 (December):549–561.

Monthly Labor Reivew. 1985. "Women and Minorities: Their Proportions Grow in the Professional Work Force" (February):49–50.

Moore, Joan. 1976. *Mexican Americans.* Englewood Cliffs, NJ: Prentice-Hall.

————. 1981. "Minorities in the American Class System," *Daedalus* 110 (Spring).

————, et al. 1978. *Homeboys: Gangs, Drugs, and Prison in the Barrios of Los Angeles.* Philadelphia: Temple University Press.

Moore, Kristin A., and Isabell V. Sawhill. 1984. "Implications of Women's Employment for Home and Family Life," in *Work and Family,* Patricia Voydanoff (ed.). Palo Alto, CA: Mayfield, pp. 153–171.

Moore, Roger. 1980. "Suicide Rises as Economy Dips in Iowa," *Des Moines Register and Tribune* (September 28):A1, B3.

Moore, Wilbert E. 1969. "Social Structure and Behavior," in *The Handbook of Social Psychology,* 2nd ed., vol. IV, Gardner Lindzey and Elliot Aronson (eds.). Reading, MA: Addison-Wesley.

Mortimer, Jeylan T., and Jayne London. 1984. "The Varying Linkages of Work and Family," in *Work and Family,* Patricia Voydanoff (ed.). Palo Alto, CA: Mayfield.

Moskos, Charles C., Jr. 1975. "The American Combat Soldier in Vietnam," *The Journal of Social Issues* 31 (Fall):25–37.

Mott, Paul E. 1965. *The Organization of Society.* Englewood Cliffs, NJ: Prentice-Hall.

Murray, Charles. 1984. *Losing Ground.* New York: Basic Books.

Murray, Jim. 1976. "Vocabulary Takes on a Ruddy-Faced Look," *Rocky Mountain News* (December 9):150.

Mydans, Seth. 1989. "Book Ban in California School Strikes Down Familiar Target," *New York Times* (September 3):1, 11.

Myers, Jerome K., and Lee L. Bean. 1968. *A Decade Later: A Follow-Up of Social Class and Mental Illness.* New York: John Wiley.

Myrdal, Gunnar. 1944. *An American Dilemma.* New York: Pantheon.

The Nation. 1982. "The Death Lobby" (September 11):196–197.

National Center for Education Statistics. 1980. Cited in

"Bilingual Hispanics Do Better in School," *Phi Delta Kappan* 62 (December).

National Organization for Women. 1972. *Dick and Jane as Victims: Women on Words and Images.* Princeton, NJ: National Organization for Women.

Newman, Katherine S. 1988. *Falling from Grace: The Experience of Downward Mobility in the American Middle Class.* New York: Free Press.

News Report. 1989. "Slow Economy, Discrimination Block Opportunity for Blacks," (August/September):2–6.

Newsweek. 1970. "The Preaching and the Power," (July 20):52.

————. 1981a. (March 30):35.

————. 1981b. "Women and the Executive Suite" (September 14):65–68.

————. 1986. "The Marriage Crunch" (June 2):54–61.

Newton, Jan M. 1973. "The Political Economy of Women's Oppression," in *Women on the Move: A Feminist Perspective,* Jean Ramage Lepaluoto (ed.). Eugene: University of Oregon Press.

New York Times. 1983. (April 24):1.

————. 1985. "Technology Boom Allows Big Brother to Get Even Bigger," (October 25).

————. 1986. "Generation of Poor Growing Up in U.S. without a True Champion," (May 11):G3.

————. 1986. "Warning over Widening Income Gaps," (July 13):F11.

————. 1986. "Rise of the Robots," (January 5):3,1.

————. 1988. "Despite a 5-Year Upturn, 9.7 Million Jobs Are Lost," (December 13):A12.

Nilson, Linda Burzotta, and Murray Edelman. 1979. "The Symbolic Evocation of Occupational Prestige," *Society* 16 (March–April).

Noble, David F. 1977. *America by Design: Science, Technology and the Rise of Corporate Capitalism.* New York: Alfred A. Knopf.

Noble, Kenneth B. 1985. "U.S. Study Details Employment Shift." *The New York Times* (June 8):1,9.

————. 1986. "America's Service Economy Begins to Blossom—Overseas." *The New York Times* (December 14):E5.

North, C. C., and Paul K. Hatt. 1947. "Jobs and Occupations: A Popular Evaluation," *Public Opinion News* 9 (September):3–13.

Nottingham, Elizabeth K. 1954. *Religion and Society.* New York: Random House.

Oakes, Jeannie. 1985. *Keeping Track: How Schools Structure Inequality.* New Haven: Yale University Press.

O'Brien, John E. 1971. "Violence in Divorce Prone Families," *Journal of Marriage and the Family* 33 (November):692–698.

O'Dea, Thomas. 1966. *The Sociology of Religion.* Englewood Cliffs, NJ: Prentice-Hall.

Ogbu, John U. 1982. "Minority Education and Caste," in *Majority and Minority,* 3rd ed., Norman R. Yetman and C. Hoy Steele (eds.). Boston: Allyn and Bacon, pp. 426–439.

O'Hare, William P. 1985. "Poverty in America: Trends and New Patterns," *Population Bulletin* 40 (June): entire issue.

————. 1986. "The Eight Myths of Poverty," *American Demographics* 8 (May):22–25.

————. 1987. "America's Welfare Population: Who Gets What?" *Population Trends and Public Policy,* no. 13 (September): entire issue.

O'Kelly, Charlotte. 1980. *Women and Men in Society.* New York: Van Nostrand.

————, and Larry S. Carney. 1986. *Women and Men in Society.* 2nd ed. Belmont, CA: Wadsworth.

Oliver, Melvin L. and Thomas M. Shapiro. 1989. "Race and Wealth," *The Review of Black Political Economy* 17 (Spring):5–25.

Olsen, Marvin E. 1976. *The Process of Social Organization,* 2nd ed. New York: Holt, Rinehart and Winston.

Omi, Michael, and Howard Winant. 1983. "By the Rivers of Babylon: Race in the United States, Part One," *Socialist Review* 71 (September–October): 31–66.

————. 1983. "By the Rivers of Babylon: Race in the United States, Part Two," *Socialist Review* 72 (November–December):35–68.

Ordovensky, Pat. 1984. "Hispanic Woes Laid to Schools," *USA Today* (December 12):3A.

Orwell, George. 1946. *Animal Farm.* New York: Harcourt, Brace.

Ostling, Richard N. 1989. "Those Mainline Blues," *Time* (May 22):94–96.

Oxford Analytica. 1986. *America In Perspective: The Social, Economic, Political, Fiscal, and Psychological Trends that Will Shape American Society for the Next Ten Years and Beyond.* Boston: Houghton Mifflin.

Pachon, Harry P., and Joan W. Moore. 1981. "Mexican Americans," *The Annals of the American Academy of Political and Social Sciences* (March):111–124.

Paine, Nathaniel. 1897. "Early American Broadsides, 1680–1800," *Proceedings, American Antiquarian Society* cited in Ian Robertson, *Sociology,* 2nd ed. New York: Worth, 1981.

Parenti, Michael. 1978. *Power and the Powerless,* 2nd ed. New York: St. Martin's Press.

————. 1980. *Democracy for the Few,* 3rd ed. New York: St. Martin's Press.

————. 1982. "The Left," *The Progressive* 46 (October): 23–26.

————. 1986. *Inventing Reality: The Politics of the Mass Media.* New York: St. Martin's.

————. 1988. *Democracy for the Few,* 5th ed. New York: St. Martin's.

Parlee, Mary Brown. 1979. "Conversational Politics," *Psychology Today* 12 (May):48–56.

Parsons, Talcott, Robert F. Bales, et al. 1955. *Family,*

Socialization and Interaction Process. New York: Free Press.

Pearce, Diana. 1978. "The Feminization of Poverty: Women, Work, and Welfare," *The Urban and Social Change Review* 11:28–36.

Peter, Laurence F., and Raymond Hull, 1969. *The Peter Principle.* New York: Morrow.

Petersen, David M., and Paul C. Friday. 1975. "Early Release from Incarceration: Race as a Factor in the Use of 'Shock Probation,' " *The Journal of Criminal Law and Criminology* 66 (March):79–87.

Peterson, Linda, and Elaine Enarson. 1974. "Blaming the Victim in the Sociology of Women: On the Misuse of the Concept of Socialization." Paper at the Pacific Sociological Association, San Jose, CA (March).

Phi Delta Kappan. 1980. "Bilingual Hispanics Do Better in School," *Phi Delta Kappan* 62 (December).

Philippus, M. J. 1989. "Hispanics Fail Tests Because Tests Fail Them," *Rocky Mountain News* (June 15):59.

Phillips, Bernard S. 1971. *Social Research: Strategy and Tactics,* 2nd ed. New York: Macmillan.

Phillips, E. L., E. A. Phillips, D. L. Fixsen, and M. M. Wolf. 1973. "Behavior Shaping Works for Delinquents," *Psychology Today* 7 (June):75–79.

Phillips, Leslie A. 1986. "Leaving the House," *USA Today* (June 30):4B.

Physicians' Task Force on Hunger in America. 1985. *Hunger in America: The Growing Epidemic.* Middletown, CT: Wesleyan University Press.

Piernard, Richard V., and Robert D. Linder. 1988. *Civil Religion and the Presidency.* Grand Rapids, MI: Zondervan Publishing House.

Pike, Otis. 1982. "The Cancer of Congressmen and Campaign Funds," *The Denver Post* (August 31):B2.

Piore, Michael J. 1975. "Notes for a Theory of Labor Market Stratification," in *Labor Market Segmentation,* Richard L. Edwards et al. (eds.). Lexington, MA: D. C. Heath.

Piven, Frances Fox, and Richard A. Cloward. 1971a. *Regulating the Poor.* New York: Random House.

_____. 1971b. "The Relief of Welfare," *Trans-action* 8 (May).

Pleck, Joseph. 1977. "The Work-Family Role System," *Social Problems* 24 (April):417–427.

_____. 1981. "Prisoners of Manliness," *Psychology Today* 15 (September).

_____, G. L. Staines, and L. Laing. 1980. "Conflicts between Work and Family Life," *Monthly Labor Review* 40 (March):29–32.

Pope, Liston. 1942. *Millhands and Preachers.* New Haven, CT: Yale University Press.

Population Reference Bureau. 1986. "Anti-Asian Violence Pattern Probed, *Population Today* 14 (July–August):9–11.

Poulantzas, Nicos. 1974. *Classes in Contemporary Capitalism.* London: New Left Books.

Powell, Walter W. 1987. "Explaining Technological Change." *American Journal of Sociology* 93 (July): 185–197.

Power, Sarah Goddard. 1981. "Women, the Economy, and the Future," *Innovator* 13. University of Michigan School of Education. (September).

Powers, Edwin, and Helen Witmer. 1951. *An Experiment in the Prevention of Delinquency.* New York: Columbia University Press.

Preston, Samuel H. 1984. "Children and the Elderly: Divergent Paths for America's Dependents," *Demography* 21 (November):435–457.

Progressive, The. 1976. "Voting for What We Want" (November).

_____. 1980a. "Out of the Bottle" 44 (August):8.

_____. 1980b. An Editorial 44 (August): 27–28.

_____. 1981. "Merger Madness," 45 (September): 10–11.

Proxmire, William. 1970. *America's Military-Industrial Complex.* New York: Praeger.

Public Broadcasting System. 1984. "On Television: The Violence Factor." (October 14).

Purnick, Joyce. 1983. "State Cites City for Sex Bias at Trade Schools," *New York Times* (August 13):25, 28.

Quadagno, D. M., R. Briscoe, and J. S. Quadagno. 1977. "Effect of Perinatal Gonadal Hormones on Selected Nonsexual Behavior Patterns," *Psychological Bulletin* 84:62–80.

Quinney, Richard. 1970. *The Social Reality of Crime.* Boston: Little, Brown.

_____. 1973. *Critique of Legal Order: Crime Control in Capitalist Society.* Boston: Little, Brown.

_____. 1974. *Criminal Justice in America: A Critical Understanding.* Boston: Little, Brown.

Rachlin, Jill. 1989. "The Label That Sticks," *U.S. News & World Report* (July 3):51–52.

Rapp, Rayna. 1982. "Family and Class in Contemporary America," in *Rethinking the Family: Some Feminist Questions,* Barrie Thorne and Marilyn Yalom (eds.). New York: Longman.

Record, Jane C., and Wilson Record. 1965. "Ideological Forces and the Negro Protest," *The Annals* 357 (January):89–96.

Reich, Robert B. 1989. "As the World Turns: U.S. Income Inequality Keeps on Rising," *The New Republic* 20 (May 1):23–28.

Renshaw, Patrick. 1968. *The Wobblies.* Garden City, NY: Doubleday.

Renzetti, Claire M., and Daniel J. Curran. 1989. *Women, Men, and Society.* Boston: Allyn and Bacon.

Reskin, Barbara F., and Heidi I. Hartmann (eds.). 1986. *Women's Work, Men's Work: Sex Segregation on the Job.* Washington, DC: National Academy Press.

Richardson, Laurel Walum. 1981. *The Dynamics of Sex and Gender,* 2nd ed. Boston: Houghton Mifflin.

Richmond-Abbott, Marie. 1983. *Masculine and Feminine: Sex Roles over the Life Cycle.* Reading, MA: Addison-Wesley.

Riesman, David. 1950. *The Lonely Crowd.* New Haven, CT: Yale University Press.

Rix, Sara E. (ed.). 1987. *The American Woman 1987–88.* New York: W. W. Norton.

Robertson, Ian. 1977. *Sociology.* New York: Worth.

Robey, Bryant. 1987. "Locking Up Heaven's Door," *American Demographics* 9 (February):24–29, 55.

Robins, Natalie. 1987. "The Defiling of Writers," *The Nation* (October 10):367–372.

Rodman, Hyman. 1963. "The Lower Class Value Stretch," *Social Forces* 42 (December):205–215.

Rogers, Susan Carol. 1978. "Women's Place: A Critical Review of Anthropological Theory," *Comparative Studies in Society and History* 20 (1):123–162.

Rosaldo, Michele Zimbalist. 1974. "Women, Culture and Society: A Theoretical Overview," in *Women, Culture and Society,* Michele Zimbalist Rosaldo and Louise Lamphere (eds.). Palo Alto, CA: Stanford University Press, pp. 17–42.

————. 1980. "The Use and Abuse of Anthropology," *Signs* 5 (Spring):389–417.

Rose, Stephen J. 1986. *The American Profile Poster.* New York: Pantheon.

Rosenthal, Robert, and Lenore Jacobsen. 1968. *Pygmalion in the Classroom: Teacher Expectations and Pupils' Intellectual Development.* New York: Holt, Rinehart and Winston.

Ross, I. 1980. "How Lawless Are Big Companies?" *Fortune* 102 (December 1):56–64.

Rossi, Peter H. 1989. *Down and Out in America: The Origins of Homelessness.* Chicago: University of Chicago Press.

Rowley, James. 1986. "Policies Create More Poor," *Fort Collins Coloradoan* (December 22).

Rubin, Lillian B. 1973. *Worlds of Pain.* New York: Basic Books.

————. 1983. *Intimate Strangers.* New York: Harper and Row.

Rubington, Earl, and Martin S. Weinberg. 1973. *Deviance: The Interactionist Perspective,* 2nd ed. New York: Macmillan.

Rudolph, Barbara. 1989. "Whose Mess Is It?" *Time* (July 10):42–43.

Ryan, Barbara Haddad. 1980. "Common Cause: Special Interests Won on Nov. 4," *Rocky Mountain News* (November 16):4.

Ryan, Joanna. 1972a. "IQ—The Illusion of Objectivity," in *Race and Intelligence,* Ken Richardson and David Spears (eds.). Baltimore: Penguin.

Ryan, Mary P. 1983. *Womanhood in America: From Colonial Times to the Present,* 3rd ed. New York: Franklin Watts.

Ryan, William. 1970. "Is Banfield Serious?" *Social Policy* 1 (November–December):74–76.

————. 1972. "Postscript: A Call to Action," *Social Policy* 3 (May–June).

————. 1976. *Blaming the Victim,* rev. ed. New York: Pantheon.

Sacks, Karen. 1974. "Engels Revisited: Women, the Organization of Production, and Private Property," in *Woman, Culture, and Society,* Michelle Zimbalist Rosaldo and Louise Lamphere (eds.). Stanford, CA: Stanford University Press, pp. 207–222.

Sampson, Anthony. 1974. *The Sovereign State of ITT.* Greenwich CT: Fawcett.

————. 1977. *The Arms Bazaar: From Lebanon to Lockheed.* New York: Viking.

Sandefur, Gary. 1989. "American Indian Reservations: The First Underclass Areas?" *Focus* 12 (Spring): 37–41.

Sanderson, Stephen K. 1988. *Macrosociology: An Introduction to Human Societies.* New York: Harper and Row.

Sapiro, Virginia. 1986. *Women in American Society.* Palo Alto, CA: Mayfield.

Scanzoni, John. 1980. "Resurgent Fundamentalism: Marching Backward into the '80s?" *The Christian Century* (September 10):847–849.

Scarpitti, Frank R., and Margaret L. Andersen. 1989. *Social Problems.* New York: Harper and Row.

Schafer, Walter E., Carol Olexa, and Kenneth Polk. 1972. "Programmed for Social Class," in *Schools and Delinquency,* Kenneth Polk and Walter E. Schafer (eds.). Englewood Cliffs, NJ: Prentice-Hall.

Scheff, Thomas J. 1966. *Mentally Ill.* Chicago: Aldine.

Schlegal, Alice. 1977. *Sexual Stratification: A Cross Cultural View.* New York: Columbia University Press.

Schneider, David M., and Raymond T. Smith. 1973. *Class Differences and Sex Roles in American Family and Kinship Structure.* Englewood Cliffs, NJ: Prentice-Hall.

Schneider, Michelle. 1989. "Pentagon Spending Up in State," *Rocky Mountain News* (March 12):79.

Schuller, David S., Merton P. Strommen, and Milo L. Brekke (eds.). 1981. *Ministry in America.* Harper & Row.

Schultz, Terri. 1977. "The Handicapped, a Minority Demanding Its Rights," *New York Times* (February 13):E9.

Schur, Edwin. 1971. *Labeling Deviant Behavior: Its Sociological Implications.* New York: Harper & Row.

————. 1973. *Radical Non-intervention: Rethinking the Delinquency Problem.* Englewood Cliffs, NJ: Prentice-Hall.

————. 1980. *The Politics of Deviance.* Englewood Cliffs, NJ: Prentice-Hall.

Schwartz, Gail Garfield, and William Neikirk. 1983. *The Work Revolution.* New York: Rawson Associates.

Schwartz, Herman. 1983. "Reagan's Bullish on Bugging," *The Nation* (June 4):697–699.

Schwartz, Joe, and Thomas Exter. 1989. "All Our Children," *American Demographics* 11 (May):34–37.

Sears, Pauline S., and David H. Feldman. 1974. "Teacher Interactions with Boys and with Girls," in *And Jill Came Tumbling After.* Judith Stacey, Susan Bereaud, and Joan Daniels (eds.). New York: Dell, pp. 147–158.

Sears, Robert R., Eleanor E. Maccoby, Harry Levin, et al. 1957. *Patterns of Child Rearing.* Evanston, IL: Row, Peterson.

Sennett, Richard, and Jonathan Cobb. 1973. *The Hidden Injuries of Class.* New York: Random House Vintage.

Serbin, Lisa, and K. Daniel O'Leary. 1975. "How Nursery Schools Teach Girls to Shut Up," *Psychology Today* 9 (December).

———, K. Daniel O'Leary, Ronald N. Kent, and Ilene J. Tolnick. 1973. "A Comparison of Teacher Responses to the Preacademic and Problem Behavior of Boys and Girls," *Child Development* 44 (December):776–804.

Sexton, Patricia C. 1983. *Women and Work,* cited in *Poverty in the American Dream.* Boston: South End Press.

Shanas, Ethel. 1980. "Old People and Their Families: The New Pioneers," *Journal of Marriage and the Family* 42:9–15.

Shapiro, Judith. 1981. "Anthropology and the Study of Gender," in *A Feminist Perspective in the Academy,* Elizabeth Langland and Walter Gove (eds.). Chicago: University of Chicago Press, pp. 110–129.

Shapiro, Laura. 1977. "Violence: The Most Obscene Fantasy," *Mother Jones* 2 (December).

Sherif, Muzafer. 1958. "Group Influences upon the Formation of Norms and Attitudes," in *Readings in Social Psychology,* 3rd ed. Eleanor E. Maccoby, Theodore M. Newcomb, and Eugene L. Hartley (eds.). New York: Holt, Rinehart and Winston, pp. 219–232.

———, and Carolyn W. Sherif. 1966. *Groups in Harmony and Tension.* New York: Farrar, Straus & Giroux.

Shils, Edward A., and Morris Janowitz. 1948. "Cohesion and Disintegration in the Wehrmacht in World War II," *Public Opinion Quarterly* 12 (Summer 1948):280–315.

Silberman, Charles E. 1970. *Crisis in the Classroom.* New York: Random House.

Simon, David R., and D. Stanley Eitzen. 1990. *Elite Deviance,* 3rd ed. Boston: Allyn and Bacon.

Simpson, Peggy. 1985. "The Fight for Pay Equity," in *Crisis in American Institutions,* 4th ed., Jerome H.

Skolnick and Elliott Currie (eds.). Boston: Little, Brown, pp. 208–216.

Skinner, B. F. 1972. *Beyond Freedom and Dignity.* New York: Alfred A. Knopf.

Skold, Karen. 1982. "Book Review," *Signs: Journal of Women in Culture and Society* 8 (Winter):367–372.

Skolnick, Arlene S. 1979. "Public Images, Private Realities: The American Family in Popular Culture and Social Science," in *Changing Images of the Family,* Virginia Tufte and Barbara Meyerhoff (eds.). New Haven: Yale University Press, pp. 297–315.

———. 1983. *The Intimate Environment,* 3rd ed. Boston: Little, Brown.

———, and Jerome H. Skolnick (eds.). 1983. *Family in Transition,* 4th ed. Boston: Little, Brown.

Skolnick, Jerome. 1969. *The Politics of Protest.* New York: Ballantine Books.

———, and Elliott Currie. 1970. "Approaches to Social Problems," in *Crisis in American Institutions,* Jerome H. Skolnick and Elliott Currie (eds.). Boston: Little, Brown.

Slater, Philip. 1970. *The Pursuit of Loneliness: American Culture at the Breaking Point.* Boston: Beacon Press.

Smelser, Neil. 1962. *Theory of Collective Behavior.* New York: Free Press.

Smith, Joan. 1981. *Social Issues and the Social Order: The Contradictions of Capitalism.* Cambridge, MA: Winthrop.

Snell, Bradford. 1974. "GM and the Nazis," *Ramparts* (June):14–16.

Snow, David A., Susan G. Baker, Leon Anderson, and Michael Martin. 1986. "The Myth of Pervasive Mental Illness among the Homeless," *Social Problems* 33 (June):407–423.

Socioeconomic Newsletter. 1978. "Nation Is Divided on Welfare Attitudes," *Socioeconomic Newsletter* 3 (February):4.

Sociologists for Women in Society. 1986. "Facts About Pay Equity," (April). East Lansing: Department of Sociology, Michigan State University.

Sowell, Thomas. 1981a. *Ethnic America: A History.* New York: Basic Books.

——— 1981b. "Culture—Not Discrimination— Decides Who Gets Ahead," *U.S. News & World Report* (October 12):74.

Spaulding, Robert L. 1963. *Achievement, Creativity, and Self-Concept Correlates of Teacher-Pupil Transactions in Elementary Schools,* Cooperative Research Project no. 1352. Washington, DC: U.S. Department of Health.

Spock, Benjamin. 1947. *Baby and Child Care.* New York: Simon and Schuster.

Spring, Joel H. 1972. *Education and the Rise of the Corporate State.* Boston: Beacon Press.

Stallard, Karin, Barbara Ehrenreich, and Holly Sklar. 1983. *Poverty in the American Dream.* Boston: Institute for New Communications, South End Press.

Steadman, Henry J. 1972. "The Psychiatrist as a Conservative Agent of Social Control," *Social Problems* 20 (Fall).

Stegner, Wallace, and Page Stegner. 1978. "Rocky Mountain Country," *Atlantic Monthly* 241 (April).

Steif, William. 1979. "U.S. Government, Slowly Aiding Battered Wives," *Rocky Mountain News* (October 27):76.

Stein, Peter J., Judith Richman, and Natalie Hannon. 1977. *The Family Functions, Conflicts, and Symbols.* Reading, MA: Addison-Wesley.

Steinberg, David. n.d. "Racism in America: Definition and Analysis," in *People Against Racism.* Detroit.

Steinmetz, Suzanne K. 1977. "Wifebeating, Husband-beating—A Comparison of the Use of Violence between Spouses to Resolve Marital Conflicts," in *Battered Women: A Psychological Study of Domestic Violence,* Marina Roy (ed.). New York: Van Nostrand.

———. 1977–78. "The Battered Husband Syndrome," *Victimology* 2, nos. 3–4:449–509.

Stephens, William N. 1967. "Family and Kinships," in *Sociology,* Neil J. Smelser (ed.). New York: John Wiley.

Stevens, William K. 1989. "Racial Differences Found in Kind of Medical Care Americans Get," *New York Times* (January 1):1.

Stewart, Sally Ann. 1985. "Heart Disease Decreases as Income Goes Up," *USA Today* (February 21):D1.

Stivers, Richard. 1975. "Introduction to the Social and Cultural Control of Deviant Behavior," in *The Collective Definition of Violence,* F. James Davis and Richard Stivers (eds.). New York: Free Press.

Stone, Marvin, 1978. "Political Spending Running Wild," *U.S. News & World Report* (October 23):112.

Straus, Murray A. 1974a. "Leveling, Civility, and Violence in the Family," *Journal of Marriage and the Family* 36:13–27.

———. 1974b. "Sexual Inequality, Cultural Norms, and Wife Beating," *Journal of Marriage and the Family* 36 (February):13–30.

———. 1977. "A Sociological Perspective on the Prevention and Treatment of Wifebeating," in *Battered Women,* Maria Roy (ed.). New York: Van Nostrand.

———, and Richard J. Gelles. 1985. "Societal Change and Change in Family Violence from 1975 to 1985 as Revealed by two National Surveys." Paper presented at the American Society of Criminology, San Diego (November). Published by the Family Violence Research Program, University of New Hampshire, Durham.

———, and Suzanne K. Steinmetz. 1980. *Behind Closed Doors: Violence in the American Family.* New York: Anchor Books.

Suro, Roberto. 1989. "Switch by Hispanic Catholics Changes Face of U.S. Religion," *New York Times* (May 14):1, 14.

Sutherland, Edwin H., and Donald R. Cressey. 1966. *Principles of Criminology,* 7th ed. Philadelphia: J. B. Lippincott.

Swartz, Steve. 1989. "Why Mike Milken Stands to Qualify for Guinness Book," *Wall Street Journal* (March 31):1, 4.

Swinton, David. 1987. "Economic Status of Blacks 1986," in *The Status of Black America 1987.* New York: National Urban League.

Sykes, Gresham M. 1971. *Social Problems in America.* Glenview, IL: Scott, Foresman.

———. 1974. "Criminology: The Rise of Critical Criminology," *The Journal of Criminal Law and Criminology* 65 (June).

Szasz, Thomas. 1974. *Ceremonial Chemistry.* Garden City, NY: Doubleday.

Szymanski, Albert. 1978. *The Capitalist State and the Politics of Class.* Cambridge, MA: Winthrop.

Taeubur, Cynthia M. 1988. "Demographic Perspectives of an Aging Society," *The World and I* 3 (December):591–603.

Taylor, Ronald L. 1979. "Black Ethnicity and the Persistence of Ethnogenesis," *American Journal of Sociology* 84 (May):1401–1423.

Thorne, Barrie. 1982. "Feminist Rethinking of the Family: An Overview," in *Rethinking the Family: Some Feminist Questions,* Barrie Thorne and Marilyn Yalom (eds.). New York: Longman.

Thornton, Arland. 1977. "Decomposing the Remarriage Process," *Population Studies* 31 (July):383–392.

———, and Deborah Freedman. 1983. "The Changing American Family," *Population Bulletin* 38 (October): entire issue.

Thurow, Lester. 1982. "The Cost of Unemployment," *Newsweek* (October 4):70.

Tifft, Susan. 1989. "The Big Shift in School Finance," *Time* (October 16):48.

Tilly, Chris. 1986. "U-Turn on Equality: The Puzzle of Middle-Class Decline," *Dollars and Sense,* no. 116 (May):11–13.

Tilly, Louise A. 1982. "Women's Employment—Past, Present, and Future," University of Michigan (July).

———, and Joan W. Scott. 1978. *Women, Work, and Family.* New York: Holt, Rinehart and Winston.

Time. 1980. "Unmanning the Holy Bible" (December 8):128.

———. 1982. "Bishops and the Bomb" (November 29):77.

———. 1985. "Solo Americans" (December 2):41.

Timmer, Doug A., and D. Stanley Eitzen (eds.). 1989. *Crime in the Streets and Crime in the Suites.* Boston: Allyn and Bacon.

Tobias, Sheila. 1989. "Tracked to Fail," *Psychology Today* 23 (September):54–60.

Toffler, Alvin. 1970. *Future Shock.* New York: Bantam.

Townsend, Bickley. 1985. "Working Women," *American Demographics* 7 (January):4–6.

TRB. 1975. "The Case for More Planning," *Rocky Mountain News* (March 30):2.

————. 1978. "Why Mobil Isn't Loved," *New Republic* (October 14):3.

Troeltsch, Ernst. 1931. *The Social Teaching of the Christian Churches,* Olive Wyon (trans.). New York: Macmillan.

Tuchman, Gaye. 1979. "Women's Depiction by the Mass Media," *Signs* 4 (Spring).

Tufte, Virginia, and Barbara Meyerhoff (eds.). 1979. *Changing Images of the Family.* New Haven, CT: Yale University Press.

Tumin, Melvin M. 1953. "Some Principles of Stratification," *American Sociological Review* 18 (August): 387–393.

————. 1973. *Patterns of Society.* Boston: Little, Brown.

Turner, Ronny. n.d. Personal communication.

United Press International. 1986. "New Worth of Typical Household $33,000," United Press International (July 19).

University Record. 1981. "Perspective: On 'Superwoman,' " University of Michigan (May 2).

USA Today. 1987. "Women Still Doing Mostly 'Women's Work,' " (September 4):4B.

————. 1989. "Kids' Health: The Obstacles," (March 3):1.

————. 1989. "Media Coverage of Women 'Poor,' " (April 11):2B.

————. 1989. "Ethnic, Racial Divisions Still Deeply Rooted," (August 30):1–2.

————. 1989. "Pay Equity Lobby Helps Raise Wages," (October 20):1.

U.S. Bureau of the Census. 1983. "Marital States and Living Arrangements: March 1983," *Current Population Reports,* Series P-20, no. 389. Washington, DC: Government Printing Office.

————. 1985a. "School Enrollment—Social and Economic Characteristics of Students," *Current Population Reports,* Series P-20, no. 404. Washington, DC: Government Printing Office.

————. 1985b. *Statistical Abstract of the United States,* 106th ed. Washington, DC: Government Printing Office.

————. 1986a. "Money, Income and Poverty Status of Families and Persons in the United States: 1985," *Current Population Reports,* Series P-60, no. 154. Washington, DC: Government Printing Office.

————. 1986b. "Estimates of the Population of the United States by Age, Sex, and Race: 1980 to 1985," *Current Population Reports,* Series P-25, no. 985. Washington, DC: Government Printing Office.

————. 1988. "Money Income and Poverty Status in the U.S.: 1987," *Current Population Reports,* Series P-60, no. 161. Washington, DC: Government Printing Office.

————. 1989. *Statistical Abstract of the U.S.,* 109th ed. Washington, DC: Government Printing Office.

U.S. Commission on Civil Rights. 1979. *Window Dressing on the Set.* Washington, DC: U.S. Commission on Civil Rights.

————. 1980. *Character in Textbooks: A Review of the Literature.* Washington, DC: U.S. Commission on Civil Rights.

————. 1983. *A Growing Crisis: Disadvantaged Women and Their Children.* Clearinghouse Publication, 78 (May).

U.S. Department of Health, Education and Welfare. 1966. *Equality of Educational Opportunity.* Washington, DC: Government Printing Office.

U.S. Department of Justice. 1985. *Crime and Justice Facts, 1985.* Washington, DC: Department of Justice.

U.S. Department of Labor. 1965. *The Negro Family: The Case for National Action.* Washington, DC: Office of Policy Planning and Research.

————. 1988. "Twenty Facts on Women Workers," Office of the Secretary. Women's Bureau. Washington, DC: Government Printing Office.

U.S. News & World Report. 1986a. "Middle Class Squeeze," (August 18):36–41.

————. 1986b. "Progress and Poverty," (September 8):8.

————. 1989. "The Living Legacy of Jim Bakker," (November 6):14.

U.S. Senate, 1978. Committee on Governmental Affairs, *Interlocking Directorates among the Major United States Corporations.* Washington, DC: Government Printing Office.

Useem, Michael. 1983. "Equity and the Draft," *Working Papers* 10 (January–February):62–64.

Valdivieso, Rafael and Cary Davis. 1988. *U.S. Hispanics: Changing Issues for the 1990s.* Population Reference Bureau, No. 17 (December): entire issue.

van den Berghe, Pierre L. 1963. "Dialectics and Functionalism: Toward a Theoretical Synthesis," *American Sociological Review* 28 (October):697–705.

————. 1967. *Race and Racism: A Comparative Perspective.* New York: John Wiley.

Vanneman, Reeve, and Lynn Weber Cannon. 1987. *The American Perception of Class.* Philadelphia: Temple University Press.

Vecoli, Rudolph J. 1964. "Contadini in Chicago: A Critique of the Uprooted," *Journal of American History* 51:405–417.

Vernon, Raymond. 1986. "Multinationals Are Mushrooming." *Challenge* 29 (May–June).

Viviano, Frank. 1983. "The New Immigrants," *Mother Jones* (January):26–46.

Van Hoffman, Nicholas. 1977. "Moonies, Hare Krishnas

Are Ideal American Kids, Right?" *Rocky Mountain News* (April 8):51.

Voydanoff, Patricia (ed.). 1984. *Work and Family.* Palo Alto, CA: Mayfield.

Walker, Leonore E. 1979. *The Battered Woman.* New York: Harper & Row.

Walley, Dean. n.da. *What Boys Can Be.* Kansas City: Hallmark.

————. n.d. *What Girls Can Be.* Kansas City: Hallmark.

Walsh, Joan. 1984. "How Reagan Bridged the Gender Gap," *In These Times* (November 21):6.

Warner, W. Lloyd, and Paul S. Lunt. 1941. *The Social Life of a Modern Community.* New Haven, CT: Yale University Press.

Warren, Carol A. B., and John M. Johnson. 1973. "A Critique of Labeling Theory from the Phenomenological Perspective," in *Theoretical Perspectives on Deviance,* Jack D. Douglas and Robert Scott (eds.). New York: Basic Books.

Warren, William J. 1988. "Tutoring Becomes a Tool to Provide an Edge," *New York Times* (July 20):24.

Warriner, Charles K. 1956. "Groups Are Real: A Reaffirmation," *American Sociological Review* 21 (October): 549–554.

Wayne, Leslie. 1984. "America's Astounding Job Machine," *New York Times* (June 17):25.

Weber, Max. 1947. *The Theory of Social and Economic Organization,* A. M. Henderson and Talcott Parsons, trans. New York: Free Press.

————. 1958. *The Protestant Ethic and the Spirit of Capitalism,* Talcott Parsons, trans. New York: Scribner's.

————. 1963. *The Sociology of Religion,* Ephraim Fischoff, trans. Boston: Beacon Press.

Weinstein, Deena, and Michael Weinstein. 1974. *Living Sociology: A Critical Introduction.* New York: David McKay.

Weitzman, Lenore J. 1979. "Sex Role Socialization," in *Woman: A Feminist Perspective,* 2nd ed., Jo Freeman (ed.). Palo Alto, CA: Mayfield.

————. 1984. "Sex-Role Socialization: A Focus on Women," in *Women: A Feminist Perspective,* 3rd ed., Jo Freeman (ed.). Palo Alto, CA: Mayfield, pp. 157–237.

————. 1985. *The Divorce Revolution: The Unexpected Social and Economic Consequences for Women and Children in America.* New York: The Free Press.

————, Deborah Eifler, Elizabeth Hokada, and Catherine Ross. 1972. "Sex-Role Socialization in Picture Books for Preschool Children," *American Journal of Sociology* 77 (May):1125–1150.

Wellman, David T. 1977. *Portraits of White Racism.* Cambridge: Cambridge University Press.

Wertheimer, Fred. 1986. "A Boost for Campaign Finance Reform," *Common Cause Magazine* 12 (January–February):60.

Wessel, David. 1989. "Census Bureau Study Finds Shift in Fertility Patterns," *Wall Street Journal* (June 22):B1.

West, Cornel. 1986. "Unmasking the Black Conservatives," *The Christian Century* (July 16–23):644–648.

Westhues, Kenneth. 1982. *First Sociology.* New York: McGraw-Hill.

Wheelis, Allen. 1958. *The Quest for Identity.* New York: W. W. Norton.

Whitman, David. 1988. "America's Hidden Poor," *U.S. News & World Report* (January 11):18–24.

Whorf, B. L. 1956. "Science and Linguistics," in *Readings in Social Psychology,* E. E. Maccoby, T. M. Newcomb, and E. L. Hartley (eds.). New York: Holt.

Whyte, William Foote. 1956. *Street Corner Society: The Social Structure of an Italian Slum,* rev. ed. Chicago: University of Chicago Press.

————. 1988. *City: Rediscovering the Center.* New York: Doubleday.

Wickham, DeWayne. 1989. "Violence Shows Race Relations Still Sit on Powderkeg," *Fort Collins Coloradoan* (September 2):A10.

Wilkins, Roger. 1988. "Absence of Class," *Mother Jones* 13 (January):56.

Wilkins, Shirley, and Thomas A. W. Miller. 1985. "Working Women: How It's Working Out," *Public Opinion* (October–November):44–48.

Wilkinson, William H., and Victor W. Sidel. 1986. "Hunger in America," *The Social and Health Review,* no. 3:59–64.

Williams, J. Allen, JoEtta A. Vernon, Martha C. Williams, and Karen Malecha. 1987. "Sex Role Socialization in Picture Books: An Update," *Social Science Quarterly* 68 (March):148–156.

Williams, Juan. 1987. "Racism Revisited," *Utne Reader* (May/June):54–61.

Williams, Robin M., Jr. 1970. *American Society: A Sociological Interpretation,* 3rd ed. New York: Alfred A. Knopf.

Wilson, Everitt K. 1966. *Sociology: Rules, Roles and Relationships.* Homewood, IL: Dorsey.

Wilson, William J. 1987. *The Truly Disadvantaged: The Inner City, the Underclass, and Public Policy.* Chicago: University of Chicago Press.

————, and Kathryn M. Neckerman. 1986. "Poverty and Family Structure: The Widening Gap between Evidence and Public Policy Issues," in *Fighting Poverty,* Sheldon H. Danzinger and Daniel H. Weinberg (eds.). Cambridge, MA: Harvard University Press, pp. 209–231.

Wise, Arthur E., and Tamar Gendler. 1989. "Rich Schools, Poor Schools: The Persistence of Unequal Education," *The College Board Review,* No. 151 (Spring):12–17, 36–37.

Wise, Tim. 1989. "Weed It and Reap," *Dollars & Sense,* No. 144 (March):12–15.

Wolfgang, Marvin E., Arlene Kelly, and Hans C. Nolde. 1962. "Comparisons of the Executed and the Commuted among Admissions to Death Row," *Journal of Criminal Law, Criminology and Police Science* 53 (September).

Woodward, Kenneth L. 1989. "Young beyond Their Years," *Newsweek* (special issue on the family), (November):54–60.

Working Papers. 1983. "An Interview with Bennett Harrison and Barry Bluestone." *Working Papers for a New Society* 10 (January–February):43–51.

Wright, Erik Olin, David Hachen, Cynthia Costello, and Joey Sprague. 1982. "The American Class Structure," *American Sociological Review* 47 (December):709–726.

Wright, James D. 1989. *Address Unknown: The Homeless in America.* New York: Aldine de Gruyter.

———, and Sonia R. Wright. 1976. "Social Class and Parental Values for Children," *American Sociological Review* 41 (June):527–537.

Wrong Dennis. 1969. "The Oversocialized Conceptionalization of Man in Modern Sociology," in *Sociological Theory,* 3rd ed., Lewis A. Coser and Bernard Rosenberg (eds.). New York: Macmillan.

Yancey, William L., Eugene P. Ericksen, and Richard N. Juliani. 1976. "Emergent Ethnicity: A Review and Reformulation," *American Sociological Review* 41 (June):391–402.

Yetman, Norman R. (ed.). 1985. *Majority and Minority,* 3rd ed. Boston: Allyn and Bacon.

———, and C. Hoy Steele. 1971. "Introduction," in *Dynamics of Racial and Ethnic Relations,* Norman R. Yetman and C. Hoy Steele (eds.). Boston: Allyn and Bacon.

Yinger, J. Milton. 1961. *Sociology Looks at Religion.* New York: Macmillan.

———. 1962. "Contraculture and Subculture," *American Sociological Review* 25 (October):625–635.

Yorburg, Betty. 1983. *Families and Societies: Survival or Extinction?* New York: Columbia University Press.

Zaldivar, R. A. 1987. "Illegal U.S. Planting of Articles Told," *Des Moines Register* (October 5):1.

Zaretsky, Eli. 1976. *Capitalism, The Family, and Personal Life.* New York: Harper Colophon.

Zars, Belle, with Mary Palmer. 1986. "The Statistical Student," *Ms.* (October):30.

Zarsky, Lyuba and Samuel Bowles (eds.). 1986. *Economic Report of the People.* Boston: South End Press.

Zeitlin, Maurice, Kenneth G. Lutterman, and James W. Russell. 1977. "Death in Vietnam: Class, Poverty, and the Risks of War," in *American Society, Inc.,* 2nd ed., Maurice Zeitlin (ed.). Chicago: Rand McNally, pp. 143–155.

Zimbardo, Philip G. 1972. "Pathology of Imprisonment," *Society* 9 (April).

Zinsmeister, Karl. 1988. "Black Demographics," *Public Opinion* 10 (January/February):41–44.

Name Index

Acker, Joan, 205, 305, 331, 335, 336
Acuña, Rudolfo, 271
Adams, Karen L., 315
Algren, Nelson, 165
Amman, Jacob, 148
Andersen, Margaret L., 158, 317, 410
Anderson, Jack, 162, 301
Mother Angelica, 484
Anthony, Susan B., 319
Antonovsky, Aaron, 240
Appelbaum, Richard P., 257
Applebome, Peter, 483, 485
Aronowitz, Stanley, 161
Asch, Solomon E., 27
Aufderheide, Pat, 137

Baca Zinn, Maxine, 205, 259, 277, 353, 363, 413, 415, 421, 422, 425, 430
Baker, Mary Anne, 301
Bakker, Jim, 483, 484
Bales, Robert F., 304, 431
Baltzell, E. Digby, 233
Balswick, Jack, 334
Bane, Mary Jo, 410
Banfield, Edward C., 115, 178, 179, 180, 214, 215
Barberis, Mary, 85

Barker, Eugene C., 271
Barnett, Rosalind, 424
Barnouw, Victor, 138
Baron, Harold M., 352
Barrera, Mario, 209, 270, 271, 276
Barringer, Felicity, 80
Bartel, Richard, 365
Baruch, Grace, 424
Baskir, Laurence M., 242, 397
Beach, Frank, 96, 97
Beach, Howard, 293
Bean, Lee L., 185
Bear, John, 102
Bear, Robert, 23
Beard, Charles, 392
Beauvoir, Simone de, 314
Becker, Howard S., 8, 9, 172, 174, 185
Beeghley, Leonard, 420
Bellah, Robert N., 470
Benokraitis, Nijole, 280, 281
Berg, Ivar, 350
Berger, Peter L., 3, 6, 9, 32, 99, 100, 106, 129, 138, 466, 474
Bernard, Jessie, 417
Bernardin, Joseph, 490
Berreman, Gerald D., 243
Bierstedt, Robert, 130
Birdwhistell, Ray L., 407

Blau, Peter, 17, 18, 19, 70, 244
Blauner, Robert, 283, 409
Blood, Robert O., 418
Bloom, Donald E., 422
Bluestone, Barry, 248, 355, 361
Blumberg, Paul M., 414
Blumer, Herbert, 71
Bock, Gordon, 360
Boocock, Sarane S., 139
Bonacich, Edna, 350
Borkin, Joseph, 396
Bourke, Jaron, 396
Bouvier, Leon F., 77, 80, 84
Bowles, Samuel, 244, 245, 286, 442, 443, 444, 445, 446
Bowman, Meg, 475
Brannon, Robert, 306
Brekke, Milo L., 487
Briscoe, R., 301
Brodie, Keith H., 251, 252
Brody, Jane E., 301
Bronfenbrenner, Urie, 147
Bronowski, Jacob, 108
Brooks-Gunn, Jeanne, 309
Brophy, Beth, 247
Broom, Leonard, 476
Brown, Dee, 54
Buchert, Wendy, 483
Buck, Pearl, 165
Bumpass, Larry, 421
Burch, Philip Harry, Jr., 454

Burnham, David, 165
Burnham, Linda, 253
Burt, Cyril, 212
Bush, George, 165, 198, 293, 382
Butler, Matilda, 317
Buttrey, Douglas, 374

Cabib, Amalia, 276
Caesar, Julius, 149
Calvin, John, 112, 113, 469, 470
Cannon, Lynne Weber, 232, 236, 237, 238
Caplan, Nathan, 180, 182, 183
Capote, Truman, 165
Carmichael, Stokely, 279, 280
Carnoy, Martin, 442
Carroll, John B., 106, 107
Carter, Hugh, 420
Carter, James E., 165
Carter, Michael J., 330
Carter, Susan Boslego, 330
Castro, Fidel, 92
Cetron, Marvin J., 399, 459
Chambliss, William J., 185, 186, 200
Chawkins, Steve, 467
Chaze, William L., 65
Cherlin, Andrew, 413, 419, 422, 432, 433
Chiang Kai-Shek, 397
Chin, Vincent, 49
Chiricos, Theodore G., 186
Christensen, Kathleen, 416
Cimons, Marlene, 241
Clancy, Paul, 411
Clark, Ramsey, 187
Clement, Andrew, 160, 161
Cleveland, Grover, 391
Cloward, Richard A., 65, 89, 155, 156, 169, 170, 236, 394
Coakley, Jay J., 41, 43
Coates, Joseph F., 362
Cobb, Jonathan, 61, 209
Cobb, Ron, 8, 31, 53, 130, 217, 235, 486
Cohen, Albert K., 123, 176
Colby, William, 165
Cole, Stephen, 27, 189
Coleman, James S., 446
Coleman, James William, 453
Coles, Robert, 224
Collier, James Lincoln, 334
Collins, Randall, 233, 236, 237, 238, 304

Comer, Lee, 206
Confucius, 475
Conklin, Ellis A., 82, 83
Conniff, Ruth, 263
Cook, James, 274, 275
Cooley, Charles Horton, 130, 131, 133, 143, 188
Coolidge, Calvin, 400
Cornell, George, 319
Coser, Lewis, 51
Cox, Harvey, 464
Cressey, Donald R., 177, 453
Crispell, Diane, 333
Curran, Daniel J., 310, 314
Currie, Elliott, 34, 200, 255, 288
Cushman, John H., 383
Cutler, James E., 54
Cuzzort, R. P., 99

Dahl, Robert, 14
Dahrendorf, Ralf, 40, 46
Darrow, Clarence, 186
Darwin, Charles, 209, 210, 211, 212, 222
Dassbach, Carl H. A., 354
David, Deborah S., 306
Davies, James A., 46
Davis, Cary B., 48, 84, 270, 272
Davis, Kingsley, 127–128, 208
Davis, Nanette J., 191, 200
Deckard, Barbara Sinclair, 308
DeLone, Richard H., 244
Demerath, N. J., III, 476
Dentler, Robert A., 174
De Parle, Jason, 89
Dessler, Gary, 171
Diamond, Stuart, 65
DiBaggio, Thomas, 396
Dickson, Paul, 70
Dolbeare, Kenneth M., 354, 355
Domhoff, G. William, 152, 153, 233, 235, 375, 381, 384, 385, 386, 387, 388, 403, 404
Donner, Frank, 165, 168
Dorris, Michael A., 273, 274
Downs, A. Chris, 306, 307
Doyle, Jack, 178
Drucker, Peter, 357
DuBois, W. E. B., 293
Dukakis, Michael, 293
Dukes, Samuel L., 419, 489

DuPonts, 349
Durkheim, Emile, 18, 25, 26, 39, 41, 137, 174, 468, 469, 491
Dwyer, Jeffrey, 420
Dye, Thomas R., 388
Dyer, Everett D., 414

Early, Frances H., 409
Eccles, Jacqueline, 307
Edelman, Murray, 231
Edgley, Charles, 108
Edison, Thomas, 175
Edmondson, Brad, 82
Edwards, Richard C., 332, 350, 351
Ehrenreich, Barbara, 232, 236, 253, 333, 351, 352
Eisenhower, Dwight D., 165, 380
Eisenstein, Zillah, 305, 352
Eitzen, D. Stanley, 115, 150, 196, 205, 259, 269, 346, 353, 363, 415, 421, 422, 425, 430
Ekman, Paul, 102
Enarson, Elaine, 314
Engel, Mary, 311
Engels, Friedrich, 208, 304, 377
Epstein, Cynthia, 331
Ericksen, Eugene P., 48
Erikson, Kai, 172, 173, 174
Ermann, M. David, 165
Eshleman, J. Ross, 235
Eskey, Kenneth, 226
Estrada, Leobardo F., 270, 272
Etzioni, Amitai, 383
Ewen, Stuart, 365
Exter, Thomas, 290, 295

Fagot, Beverly, 308
Falwell, Jerry, 483
Farrakhan, Louis, 50
Farber, Jerry, 441
Farberman, Harvey, 108–109
Faulkner, William, 165
Feagin, Joe R., 205, 216, 280, 281, 285
Feigelson, Jeremy, 242
Feldberg, Roslyn L., 327, 328
Festinger, Leon, 28
Fetchit, Stepin, 281
Findlay, Steven, 241
Fishman, Pamela M., 315
Fiske, Edward B., 289

Fitzgerald, Francis, 149
Fleetwood, Blake, 165
Footlick, Jerold K., 405
Ford, Clellan, 96, 97
Ford, Gerald, 165
Forester, Tom, 360
Forstall, Richard L., 78
Franklin, Deborah, 127
Freedman, Deborah, 410
Freeman, Jo, 335
Freud, Sigmund, 99, 132, 133, 143
Friedan, Betty, 88
Friedl, Ernestine, 304
Friedrich, Otto, 80, 83
Friesen, Wallace V., 102
Frueh, Terry, 316
Furstenberg, Frank F., Jr., 413, 419, 422, 432, 433
Fussell, Paul, 239

Galarneau, Andrew, 141
Galileo, G., 71
Gans, Herbert J., 14, 136, 218, 219, 397
Gardner, Robert W., 80, 83, 273
Garfinkel, Harold, 103
Gelles, Richard, 430
Gendler, Tamar, 448, 449, 450
Gerrard, Nathan L., 29
Gerth, Hans, 240
Gibbs, Jack P., 191
Gilbert, Bil, 311
Gillespie, Dair, 418
Gilman, Richard, 318, 319
Gilman, Stuart, 267, 268, 275
Gintis, Herbert, 244, 245, 444, 446
Gitlin, Todd, 153
Glazer, Nona, 305
Glenn, Evelyn Nakano, 327, 328
Glick, Paul C., 420
Goffman, Erving, 317, 407
Gold, Allan R., 241
Goldman, Ari L., 319
Goldsen, Rose K., 137
Goode, Erich, 108–109, 478
Goode, William J., 418, 421
Gordon, David M., 350
Gordon, Suzanne, 317
Gorman, Benjamin L., 71
Gould, Stephen Jay, 210, 211
Gouldner, Alvin W., 7, 8
Graham, Hugh Davis, 52
Green, Mark J., 345, 373

Greenberg, Benjamin, 153
Greenhouse, Steven, 247
Groening, Matt, 442
Gurr, Ted Robert, 52
Gwynne, S. C., 452

Hacker, Andrew, 322, 323, 326, 365, 410
Hadden, Jeffrey K., 483, 484
Hamilton, Alexander, 392
Hamilton, Charles V., 279, 280
Hannerz, Ulf, 216
Hannon, Natalie, 414
Hargreaves, David, 460
Harleston, Bernard W., 454
Harrington, Michael, 42, 85, 86, 217, 224, 398
Harris, Marvin, 109–110
Harrison, Bennett, 248, 355, 361
Hart, Gary, 357
Hartjen, Clayton A., 177, 189, 190, 194, 195
Hartley, Shirley Foster, 74
Hartmann, Heidi I., 323, 324, 352
Hatt, Paul K., 230
Haub, Carl, 48
Hauser, Philip M., 240
Hayden, F. Gregory, 107
Healy, Tim, 161
Heilbroner, Robert, 365
Hemingway, Ernest, 165
Henley, Nancy M., 316
Henry, Jules, 436
Henry, Tamara, 317
Henslin, Linda K., 441
Henslin, James M., 441
Herrnstein, Richard, 211, 212, 213, 214, 222, 277
Hershey, Robert D., 290
Higham, Charles, 396
Hightower, Jim, 344
Hillkirk, John, 168
Himmelweit, Hilde, 154
Hirschi, Travis, 185
Hitler, Adolph, 149
Hobbes, Thomas, 56
Hoch, Paul, 43
Hochschild, Arlie, 417, 419, 422, 423
Hodge, Robert W., 231
Hofstadter, Richard, 210
Hole, Judith, 335
Holmes, Oliver Wendell, 392
Homans, George, 18

Hoover, J. Edgar, 164
Horn, Miriam, 451, 452
Horton, John, 200
Horwitz, Allan, 254
Huaco, George A., 208
Hughes, Dana, 241
Hughes, Everett C., 92
Hull, Raymond, 69
Hunter, Floyd, 14
Huntington, Samuel P., 394
Hutchings, Robert M., 396
Hutchins, Robert, 397
Hymnowitz, Carol, 323

Jacklin, Carol Nagy, 301
Jackson, Jesse, 293
Jackson, Philip D., 186
Jacobson, Lenore, 457
Janowitz, Morris, 25
Janzen, David, 185
Jaynes, Gerald David, 286
Jefferson, Thomas, 168
Jeffries, Vincent, 206
Jencks, Christopher, 244, 245, 246, 440, 446
Jensen, Arthur, 210, 211, 212, 213, 214, 222, 277
Johnson, Ben, 198
Johnson, John M., 191
Johnson, Lyndon B., 165
Jones, Barry, 353, 359, 361, 363
Jones, J. H., 197
Jones, Jim, 149
Josephson, Matthew, 391
Juliani, Richard N., 48
Jung, Maureen, 346

Kagan, Jerome, 427, 444
Kanter, Rosabeth Moss, 330, 331, 422
Karmin, Monroe W., 355
Kasarda, John D., 259
Katz, Michael B., 444
Katzenstein, Mary Fainsod, 322
Kaufman, Jonathan, 292
Keegan, Patricia, 307, 311
Keiser, Steven D., 441
Keller, Helen, 128
Kellner, Hansfried, 138
Kelly, Arlene, 187
Kempton, Murray, 446
Kennedy, John F., 165, 470
Kephart, William, 148
Kerbo, Harold, 204, 205

Kesey, Ken, 189
Key, V. O., Jr., 269, 270
King, Martin Luther, Jr., 88,
    92, 165
Kitagawa, Evelyn M., 240
Kluckhohn, Clyde, 129
Kluckhohn, Florence, 121, 277
Knottnerus, J. David, 243
Knowles, Louis L., 280
Knox, John, 475
Koepp, Stephen, 355
Kohn, Melvin, 147
Kozol, Jonathan, 224, 230, 254,
    256, 435
Kramer, R. C., 196
Kreck, Carol, 429
Kutscher, Ronald E., 356
Kuttner, Bob, 248

Ladner, Joyce, 309
Lakoff, Robin, 315
Langlois, Judith H., 306, 307
LaRouche, Lyndon, 50
Larson, Richard F., 71
Lasch, Christopher, 407
Laslett, Barbara, 407
Lastrucci, Carlo L., 284
Lauer, Robert H., 71, 89, 92
Leacock, Eleanor B., 304
Lechner, Frank J., 481, 482
Leighton, D., 129
Leinhardt, Gaea, 311
Lekachman, Robert, 399
Lemert, Edwin M., 188, 189
Lenski, Gerhard E., 44, 103
Leslie, Gerald R., 71
Lever, Janet, 309
Levine, Ellen, 335
Levitan, Sar A., 408, 416, 419
Levy, Frank S., 246, 247
Lewis, Michael, 306
Lewis, Sinclair, 165
Liazos, Alexander, 191, 192,
    232, 233, 234
Liebow, Elliot, 14, 16, 123, 216
Lincoln, Abraham, 114, 154
Linder, Robert D., 471
Lipman-Blumen, Jean, 207, 300
Livingston, William, 392
London, Jayne, 422
Long, Huey, 345
Lord, Walter, 240
Louis, Elaine, 313
Luckman, Thomas, 106, 138
Luhman, Reid, 267, 268, 275

Lundman, Richard J., 165
Luther, Martin, 112, 113, 475
Lutterman, Kenneth G., 242,
    397
Lynd, Staughton, 392
Lynn, Lawrence E., 254

McCaghy, Charles H., 191, 192
McCarthy, Sarah J., 149
Maccoby, Eleanor E., 301
McCormack, Carol P., 305
Machiavelli, Niccolo, 59, 154
McGahey, Rick, 213
McGeary, Michael G. H., 254
McGee, Reece, 4, 131, 178
McGhee, Paul E., 316
Machung, Anne, 329
MacLeish, Archibald, 165
McMurphy, R. P., 189
McWhirter, Norris, 108
McWhirter, Ross, 108
McWilliams, Carey, 271
Madison, James, 390, 393
Mahoney, Jack, 160
Malveaux, Julianne, 60
Manson, Charles, 149
Marcos, Ferdinand, 397
Marshall, Donald S., 97
Marshall, Peter, 161
Marty, Martin E., 50
Marx, Karl, 40, 41, 61, 71, 92,
    143, 144, 154, 163, 197,
    208, 209, 304, 343, 344,
    377, 387, 436, 468, 469,
    491, 492
Masnick, George, 410
Matza, David, 151, 177
Mead, George Herbert, 131,
    132, 133, 143, 309
Mead, Margaret, 97
Melendez, Edwin, 293
Mendel, Gregor, 71
Merton, Robert K., 39, 68, 177,
    178, 457
Messenger, John C., 97
Mewshaw, Michael, 173
Meyer, Marshall W., 70
Meyerhoff, Barbara, 407
Michel, Richard C., 246, 247
Michels, Robert, 46, 47
Milken, Michael, 340, 344, 345
Miller, Walter B., 178
Mills, C. Wright, 233, 240, 377,
    378, 379, 380, 381, 384,
    386, 402, 403, 404

Minzesheimer, Bob, 375
Mitgang, Herbert, 165
Mokhiber, Russell, 64
Monagan, David, 313
Monk, Abraham, 428
Moore, Joan, 270, 283
Moore, Kristen A., 424
Moore, Wilbert, 29, 30, 208
Mortimer, Jeylan T., 422
Moskos, Charles C., Jr., 25
Mott, Paul E., 46, 61
Moyers, Bill, 278
Moynihan, Daniel Patrick, 277
Murdock, George P., 302
Murray, Charles, 278
Murray, Jim, 129
Mydans, Seth, 438
Myers, Jerome K., 185
Myrdal, Gunnar, 224, 278

Nader, Ralph, 373
Nelson, Stephan D., 180, 182,
    183
Newman, Katherine, 415, 416
Newton, Jan M., 332
Nilson, Linda Burzotta, 231
Nixon, Richard, 141, 165
Noble, David F., 361
Noble, Kenneth B., 357
Nolde, Hans C., 187
North, C. C., 230
North, Oliver, 141
Nottingham, Elizabeth K., 465

Oakes, Jennie, 460
O'Connell, Martin, 423
O'Dea, Thomas, 476
O'Hare, William P., 254, 255,
    260
O'Kelly, Charlotte, 301
O'Leary, K. Daniel, 308
Olexa, Carol, 460
Oliver, Melvin L., 226
Olney, Richard, 391
Olsen, Marvin E., 17, 18, 30,
    103
Omi, Michael, 294
Oppenheim, A. N., 154
Orwell, George, 168, 169, 225
Ostling, Richard N., 480

Paisley, William, 317
Parenti, Michael, 67, 136, 151,
    155, 156–158, 159, 208,

Parenti, Michael (*cont.*)
219–220, 235, 279, 348, 349, 363, 382, 386, 388, 390, 391, 393, 395, 396, 397, 403, 404, 436, 437
Park, Chung Hee, 397
Parks, Rosa, 92
Parlee, Mary Brown, 315
Parsons, Talcott, 303, 304, 431
Patai, Raphael, 157
Paul, P. W., 414
Pearce, Diana, 253
Peck, Charles, 334
Peck, Keenen, 153
Pelton, Joseph N., 91
Perrow, Charles, 69
Personick, Valerie A., 356
Peter, Lawrence F., 69
Peterson, Linda, 314
Philippus, M. J., 453
Phillips, Bernard S., 13
Phillips, E. L., 13
Phillips, Leslie A., 321
Pierard, Richard, 471
Pike, Otis, 373
Piore, Michael J., 350
Piven, Frances Fox, 65, 89, 155, 156, 169, 170, 236, 394
Pleck, Joseph, 334, 422
Polk, Kenneth, 460
Pollin, William, 485
Poulantzas, Nicos, 236
Powell, Brian, 449
Power, Sarah Goddard, 310
Powers, Edwin, 176
Preston, Samuel H., 428
Prewitt, Kenneth, 280
Provost, Caterina, 302
Proxmire, William, 382
Purdy, Dean, 346
Purnick, Joyce, 310

Quadagno, D. M., 301
Quadagno, J. S., 301
Quinney, Richard, 163, 164, 193, 197

Rachlin, Jill, 456
Ransford, H. Edward, 206
Reagan, Nancy, 119
Reagan, Ronald, 152, 165, 257, 260, 264, 293, 294, 339, 400, 454, 471, 484
Rapp, Rayna, 410, 412, 413, 414

Record, Jane C., 120
Record, Wilson, 120
Reeves, Richard, 454
Reich, Michael, 332
Reich, Robert B., 339, 350
Renshaw, Patrick, 394
Renzetti, Claire M., 310, 314
Reskin, Barbara F., 323, 324
Reynolds, Larry T., 441
Reza Shah, 348, 397
Richardson, Laurel Walum, 306
Richmond-Abbott, Marie, 313, 315, 423
Rickover, Hyman, 484
Riecken, Henry W., Jr., 28
Riesman, David, 376
Rifkin, Jeremy, 65, 167
Rindfuss, Ronald, 421
Rivers, Caryl, 424
Rivers, Mendel, 383
Rix, Sara E., 321
Roberts, Oral, 483
Robertson, Ian, 333
Robertson, Pat, 483, 484
Robey, Bryant, 81, 83, 273
Robins, Natalie, 165
Rockefeller, John D., 114
Rockefellers, 349
Rodin, Pierre Auguste, 97
Rodman, Hyman, 216
Rogers, Susan Carol, 303
Rolufs, Linda, 161
Roosevelt, Franklin D., 164, 394
Roosevelt, Theodore, 394
Rosaldo, Michele Zimbalist, 303, 304
Rose, Stephen J., 246, 349
Rosenthal, Robert, 457
Ross, Muriel, 314
Rossi, Peter H., 231, 254
Rowley, James, 254
Rubin, Lillian, 417, 418
Rubington, Earl, 174
Rubio, Maria, 467
Rudolph, Barbara, 64
Russell, James W., 242, 397
Ryan, Joanna, 213, 214
Ryan, William, 11, 43, 180, 182, 213, 447, 461

Sabato, Larry, 374
Sacco, Nicola, 210
Sacks, Karen, 305

Sadker, Myra, 311
Sage, George H., 115, 150
Saletan, William, 167
Sandburg, Carl, 165
Sandefur, Gary, 275
Sanderson, Stephen K., 232
Sapir, Edward, 106
Sapiro, Virginia, 335
Sawhill, Isabell, 424
Scanzoni, John, 472
Scarpitti, Frank R., 158
Schacter, Stanley, 28
Schafer, Walter E., 460
Scheff, Thomas J., 189
Schellhardt, Timothy D., 323
Schindler, Paul T., 178
Schlegal, Alice, 304
Schneider, David M., 412
Schneider, Michelle, 381
Schuller, David S., 487
Schuller, Robert, 483, 484
Schur, Edwin, 174, 175, 186, 190, 191
Schwartz, Herman, 165
Schwartz, Joe, 290, 295
Schwartzman, Andrew, 152
Scott, W. Richard, 17, 18, 19
Seewald, Andrea Mar, 311
Sennett, Richard, 61, 209
Serbin, Lisa, 308, 311
Seward, William Henry, 154
Shaiken, Harley, 161
Shanas, Ethel, 429
Shanker, Albert, 448–449
Shapiro, Joseph, 88
Shapiro, Judith, 303
Shapiro, Thomas M., 226
Sharpe, M. E., 367
Shaw, George Bernard, 282
Sherif, Carolyn, 16
Sherif, Muzafer, 16, 27
Shils, Edward A., 25
Shupe, Anson, 483
Sider, Ronald J., 484, 485
Siegel, Paul M., 231
Silberman, Charles, 86, 440, 455, 457
Simon, David R., 196, 269
Singsen, Michael, 153
Skinner, B. F., 169
Sklar, Holly, 253, 333
Skold, Karen, 305
Skolnick, Arlene, 406, 407, 425, 429
Skolnick, Jerome, 34, 37, 52, 200, 255, 282, 288, 425

Slater, Philip, 87, 119, 120
Smelser, Neil, 71
Smith, Adam, 211, 346, 364
Smith, Joan, 220
Smith, Lillian, 135
Smith, Peter C., 83, 273
Smith, Raymond T., 412
Snell, Bradford, 396
Snow, David, 258
Sowell, Thomas, 276
Spencer, Herbert, 209
Spring, Joel, 442
Stallard, Karin, 253, 333, 351, 352
Starsinic, Donald E., 78
Steele, C. Hoy, 265
Steelman, Lala Carr, 449
Stein, Peter J., 414
Steinbeck, John, 165
Steinberg, David, 282
Sterling, Bruce, 199
Stern, Philip M., 372
Stevens, William K., 292
Stewart, Sally Ann, 241
Stinchcombe, Arthur, 460
Stivers, Richard, 146
Stohr, Oscar, 126
Stone, Marvin, 373
Straus, Murray, 430
Strauss, William A., 242, 397
Strodtbeck, Fred L., 121, 277
Strommen, Merton P., 487
Sullivan, Anne, 128
Suro, Roberto, 481
Sutherland, Edwin H., 177
Swaggert, Jimmy, 483
Swartz, Steve, 345
Swinton, David, 288, 292
Syfers, Judy, 427
Sykes, Gresham M., 85, 86, 197, 200
Szasz, Thomas, 108
Szymanski, Albert, 149

Taeuber, Cynthia M., 428
Taylor, Ronald L., 48
Temple, Shirley, 281
Thorne, Barrie, 407

Thornton, Arland, 410, 421
Tiefer, Leonore, 96
Tifft, Susan, 448
Tilly, Chris, 248
Timmer, Doug A., 196
Tobias, Sheila, 456
Treiman, Donald J., 231
Troeltsch, Ernst, 472
Truman, Harry S, 165, 364
Tumin, Melvin M., 205, 208
Turner, Ronny E., 108
Tyson, Tim, 252

Useem, Michael, 242

Valdivieso, Rafael, 270, 272
Vance, Pamela, 154
Van den Berghe, Pierre L., 44, 468
Vanneman, Reeve, 232, 236, 237, 238
Vanzetti, Bartolomeo, 210
Vecoli, Rudolph J., 409
Vernon, Raymond, 355

Waldo, Gordon P., 186
Walley, Dean, 308
Walton, Samuel, 226
Ware, Norma C., 315
Warren, Carol A. B., 191
Warren, William J., 452
Warriner, Charles, 18
Wayne, Leslie, 323
Weber, Max, 68, 112, 468, 469, 473, 474, 491
Weinberg, Martin S., 174
Weinstein, Deena, 173
Weinstein, Michael, 173
Weisskopf, Thomas E., 332
Weitzman, Lenore J., 307, 313, 421
Wellman, David, 278, 279
Wertheimer, Fred, 373
Wessel, David, 419
Westhues, Kenneth, 143

Wheelis, Allen, 44
Whitman, David, 254
Whorf, Benjamin, 106, 129
Whyte, William Foote, 14, 16
Wickham, DeWayne, 290
Wilder, Thornton, 165
Wilkins, Roger, 227
Willette, JoAnne, 48
Williams, J. Allen, 308
Williams, Juan, 288
Williams, Robin M., Jr., 39, 110, 113–114, 286
Williams, Tennessee, 165
Williamson, Nancy, 311
Wilson, Charles, 380
Wilson, Everett, 134
Wilson, James, 393
Wilson, William Julius, 295, 296
Wilson, Woodrow, 175
Winant, Howard, 294
Wise, Arthur E., 448, 449, 450
Wise, Tim, 171, 448, 449
Witmer, Helen, 176
Wolfe, Alan, 92
Wolfe, Donald, 418
Wolfe, Thomas, 165
Wolfgang, Marvin E., 187
Woodward, Kenneth L., 428
Wright, Erik Olin, 232, 234, 237, 238
Wright, James D., 254, 373
Wrong, Dennis, 133, 139

Yancey, William L., 48
Yetman, Norman R., 265
Yinger, J. Milton, 122, 123, 474
Yorburg, Betty, 206
Yufe, Jack, 126

Zaldivar, R. A., 166
Zaretsky, Eli, 409, 430
Zarsky, Lyuba, 286
Zeitlin, Maurice, 242, 397
Zimbardo, Philip, 22, 23
Zinn, Howard, 168
Zinsmeister, Karl, 79

Subject Index

(Page numbers in **boldface** indicate definitions of key terms.)

Abortion, 71–72, 483, 485–486
  Gallup survey of opinions,
    120–121
  right to, 320
Accommodation, **495**
Achieved status, 106, **495**
Achievement, 41, 115
Activism, 65
Adolescents, 8, 425–428, 433, 460
Advertising, 151–154, 365
  sex roles and, 317–318
Advertising Council, 152–153
Affirmative Action, 327
Africans, 72–73
Age, generation gap, 52
Aged:
  families and, 428–430, 433
  media stereotypes, 136
  population growth of, 84–85,
    93
  social roles of, 106
Ageism, **495**
Aggregate, 17, **495**
Aimore tribe, 108
Alienation, **495**
Altruistic suicide, 26, 495
American Association for
    Retired Persons
    (AARP), 84

American Creed, 118
American Indians. *See* Native
    Americans
Americans with Disabilities
    Act, 88
Amish, 22, 23, 48–49, 122, 198,
    471
  social control and, 148
Androgyny, 308–309, 334, **495**
Mother Angelica, 484
Anomic suicide, 26
Anomie, 27, 137–138, **495**
Anthony, Susan B., 319
Anticipatory socialization, **495**
Antisemitism, 54
Aphorism, 11–12
Appalachian snake handlers,
    28, 48–49, 122, 471
Arab society, 156–157
Argot, 16, **495**
Armed services, 59
Ascribed status, 106, 431, **495**
Asian Americans, 49
  education and, 264
  employment of, 292, 336
  immigration and, 82, 83, 93,
    272–273, 296–297
  internment during World
    War II, 225

  social stratification and,
    206–207
  violence and, 47, 49, 54–55,
    292–293
Assimilation, 285–286, 297, **495**
Authoritarianism, 34
Automation, 357–358, 359–361

Baby boom, **495**
Baby boom generation, 74–78,
    84, 93, 247, 261
Bakker, Jim, 483–484
Balinese, 97, 107
Bankruptcy, 78
Bias:
  cultural, 2
  data collection methods and,
    7–12, 14
  minority groups and, 278–
    279, 297
  toward business, 391–396,
    400, 403
Bias theory, **495**
Bible, 11, 22, 49, 111–112, 475,
    478–479, 482
Bill of Rights, 119
Biological determinism, 210
Biological father, 20

Biological theories:
  deviance in, 175–176
  gender roles and, 300–301,
    336–337
  minority groups and, 277,
    297
  social stratification and,
    209–215, 221, 222
Birth rates, 72–75
Blacks. *See also* Minority
    groups; Race
  bias in sports, 1, 6
  bias of law and, 186–187
  blaming the victim ap-
    proach, 11, 181, 277
  capital punishment and, 6,
    186
  cause of death and, 241
  criminal stereotype, 100
  discrimination against, 225
  divorce patterns, 420, 421
  education and, 230, 264, 282,
    288–290, 451–452, 454
  education and income of,
    445, 446
  Ellis Island occupation, 182–
    183
  employment and, 238, 283,
    292, 336–337
  exploitation of, 91–92
  female-headed households,
    216, 411
  health, 292
  immigration and, 54–55, 93,
    268–270, 296
  income levels and, 286–288,
    290, 333, 412
  institutional racism and,
    280–281
  kinship systems of, 409, 413,
    414
  low self-esteem of, 131
  marriage likelihood, 296
  media portrayals, 281
  occupational distribution,
    322, 325–326
  population growth and, 48
  positive attitudes toward, 13
  poverty among, 234, 252–
    253, 258–261, 405
  protesting inequality in
    South Africa, 37
  relative worth as a social
    group, 134–135
  segmented labor market and,
    351, 352

  sex role learning and, 309
  social roles of, 106
  social stratification and,
    206–207, 213, 285–286
  sterilization of, 159
  subjugation of, 54
  suffrage and, 269–270
  underclass among, 294–296
  unemployment and, 290–
    292, 296
  urbanization of, 79–80
  violence and, 47–48, 55, 56,
    292–293
  wealth among, 226–227
Blaming the victim, **495**
  cultural deficiency theory
    and, 277
  deviance theories and, 180–
    184, 198–199, 201
  education and, 442–443
  poverty and, 213, 214–216,
    239
  sex stratification and, 314–
    315
  valued means to achieve
    and, 115
Boren's Laws of the Bureau-
    cracy, 70
Bourgeoisie, **495**
Bracero program, 272
Brown v. *Board of Education*, 89
Bureaucracy, 66, 68–71, 93, 118,
    495
Bureaucratization, **495**
Bureau of Indian Affairs, 275
Bush, George, 165, 198, 293,
    382

Caesar, Julius, 149
Calvinism, 469–470, 491
Campus racism, 263–264, 293
Capital flight, 355
Capitalism, 61, 101, 117–118,
    120, 123, 197, **495**
  families and, 431, 432, 434
  as form of corporate social-
    ism, 384
  generation of inequality, 246
  in crisis, 363–368
  inequality and, 349–353
  monopolistic, 343–347
  patriarchy and, 352–353,
    368, 409
  primacy of profits impact,
    220
  religion and, 469–470, 491

  sex roles and, 305, 327–332,
    335, 337, 338
  social control, 154–155
  sport and, 42
Capitalist patriarchy, **495**
Capital punishment, 6, 186–
    187
Capote, Truman, 165
Cargo cult of Melanesia, 466
Carter, James E., 165
Case study, **496**
Caste system, 28, 243, 261, **496**
Castro, Fidel, 92
Caveat emptor, **496**
Census Bureau, 47, 64, 78, 79,
    81, 83, 85, 203, 226–227,
    228, 232, 240, 247, 249,
    272, 276, 287, 288, 289,
    292, 295, 340, 411, 412,
    419, 445
Ceremonials, 39
Change:
  forces for, 72–93
  ideological beliefs stifling, 71
  social movement effect, 71
  social systems and, 45, 61
  stability and, 64–94
  values, behavior and, 118
Charisma, 473, **496**
Chiang Kai-Shek, 397
Chicanos, 47, 270–272. *See also*
    Hispanics
  bias in reasoning toward, 11
  culture inequality theory,
    277
  education and, 446
  employment and, 283
  immigration and, 296
  kinship systems of, 409, 413,
    414
  violence and, 47
Children:
  child care of, 424
  divorce and, 421
  minority groups and, 295
  poverty and, 253–254, 261,
    405, 425–428
  sex role learning among,
    306–313
Chinese, 37, 71
Chinese Exclusion Act (1882),
    272–273
Church, 472–481, 485–492, **496**
"Church of the First Born,"
    28–29

Civil religion, 470–471, 491, **496**
Civil Rights Act of 1964, 320
Civil rights movement, 91, 270, 286, 294, 297, 335
Civil Service Reform Act of 1978, 195
Civil War, 54, 59
Class, 32, 224–261, **496, 501**
  child's life chances dependent on, 426
  consciousness, 209, **496**
  consequences of position in, 233–243
  deviance and, 185–187
  education and, 452
  families and, 411–412, 433
  family roles and, 416–419
  media perception of, 59, 60
  overview of levels of, 233–238
  prejudices, 393
  religion and, 474, 475–479
  segregation, **496**
  sifting and sorting in education and, 439
  social mobility and, 52
  social stratification and, 205–206, 221
  social structure and, 47
  socioeconomic differences and, 226–243
Clayton Act (1914), 345
Cleveland, Grover, 391
Cliques, 46
Cloning, **496**
Code of ethics, American Sociological Association, 10
Coercion, 45, 61, 208
Cohabitation, **496**
Colonial period, 53–54
Colonial theory, 282–283, 297
Colors, 108
Common Cause, 374
Commune, **496**
Communication, sex roles and, 315–316
Communism, 40
  power elite and, 379
  religion and, 471
  social control and, 154–155
Compartmentalization, 120
Competition, 5, 38, 114, 123, 124
  basis of social life, 61
  international, 59

sport and, 41
synthesis model and, 45
Conflict, 38
Conflicting demands, 21
Conflict model, 39–40, 62
  class and, 260–261
  deviance in, 174, 192–201
  duality of social life and, 40–41, 44–46
  education and, 461
  families and, 431–434
  gender stratification and, 303–305, 337
  law as seen by radical criminologists, 163, 169
  perspective, **496**
  politics, 401
  racial stratification, 285–286
  religion from, 469, 491, 492
  social class conception, 234–238
  socialization process power, 143, 144
  social problems in, 43–44
  social stratification and, 207–209, 222
  sport and, 41–43
  theory, 41–42, 123, 124
  use of, 61–62
Confucius, 475
Conscience, development of, 466
Consensus, 45, **496**
Conspicuous consumption, **496**
Constitution, 57, 67, 71, 111, 391–393
  education expenditures and, 449
  individual rights violated by surveillance methods, 167
Constraint, **496**
Consumerism, 409, 431
Control group, 13, 14, **496**
Cooptation, 61, **496**
Corporate crime, 195–196, **496**
Corporate socialism, 343, 345, **384**
Correlation, **496**
Counseling, and gender roles, 314
Counterculture, 118, 122, 123, 124, **496**
"Couvade," 105
Cow worship, 109–110

Crime and criminals, 119, **496**
  boom generation effect, 75
  by government, 195
  labeling theory and, 185–192
  lower class and, 178–180
  selective emphasis on deviance, 195–196
"Cross-pressures," 58
Cub Scouts, 114
Cultural deficiency theories, 277, **496**
Cultural deprivation, 180–181, 447, **496**
Cultural relativity, 109–110, 124, **496**
Cultural time, 107
Cultural tyranny, **496**
Culture, 17–18, 29, 31–32, 34–35, 96–124, **496**
  characteristics of, 98–101
  deficiency theories, 297
  deviance in, 177
  diversity in, 120–123
  minority groups and, 277–278
  shared knowledge in, 101–106
Culture of poverty hypothesis, 178, 214–216, 221–222, 234, 239, 297, **496**

Dani tribe, 29
Darrow, Clarence, 186
Data collection methods, 7–12
Declaration of Independence, 53, 57, 111, 119
Deferred gratification, 115, **496**
Deflation, **496**
Deindustrialization, **496**
Democracy, 6, 34, 101, 111–112, 120, **496**
  representative, 371–376, 403
  socialization and, 135
  to advantage of the power elite, 390
  value judgments unclear for future, 140–141
Demography, 72, 247, 362–363, 405, **496**
  racial, 289–290
Dependent variable, 13, 14, **497**
Depressions, 31, 155, 272, 394
Deprogramming, 173, 425–426, **497**
Derogation, **497**

Deviance, 171–201
    conflict theory on, 43, 197–201
    definitions of, 172–176, 200, **497**
    examples of, 171–173
    hierarchical relationship, 9
    individual as source of, 175–184
    labeling theory and, 185–192
    order (functional) theory on, 43–44, 197–201
    political, 164–165
    society as source of, 185–197
    solutions from the labeling perspective, 190–192
    sources of, 143
Dialectic, 45, **497**
Differential association, **497**
Differential reward system, 208, 209
Differentiation (segmentation), 39, 50, 62
Direct social control, 155–169, **497**
Disabilities movements, 88, 89
Disconfirmation of prophecy, 28
Discrimination, 89, 225, **286, 497**
Division of labor, 31, 34–35, 47, 56, 71, 113, **497**
    capitalist patriarchy and, 352–353
    educational system preparing individuals for, 443
    gender roles and, 301, 303, 305, 332
    marital, 407, 409, 419, 431, 434
    social stratification and, 208, 209
Divorce, 258–259, 333, 405, 406, 414, 434
    no-fault, 420–421, 433
    and remarriage, 419–422
Documents, use of, 12, 14
Domestic labor, 304–305, 331, 332
Dominant group, 123
Double-giving, 374–375, 385
Double standard, 422
Draft, 242, 399
Drugs, performance-enhancing, 198–199
Dual career marriage, **497**

Dukakis, Michael, 293
DuPonts, 349
Dyer's Law, 70
Dysfunction, 62, **497**
Dyslexia, 175

Ecology crisis, 115
Economy and economic conditions, 339–368, **497**
    corporations and, 343–348, 368
    depression, 31, 272
    dual labor market, 283
    effects of change on employment, 291
    factors transforming, 259, 261
    free enterprise outmoded, 34
    "home rule" strategy, 260
    largest U.S. companies ranked, 346
    religion and, 475–479
    structural transformation of, 353–363, 368
    suicide rates affected, 26
Edison, Thomas, 175
Education, 435–462
    characteristics of, 436–442
    class and, 243, 444–445, 450–453, 455
    college degree and, 245, 452–453
    competitive nature of, 438–439
    conserving force of, 436–437
    corporate society and, 442–445
    curriculum in, 453–455
    divorce rates and, 420
    dyslexia in, 175
    expenditures per pupil, 447–449
    failures in, 440–441, 442, 451
    future trends in, 458–459
    gender equality by law, 320
    government assistance, 255
    "hidden curriculum," 461
    inequality and, 445–461, 462
    IQ testing implications, 210–211, 213
    local control of, 438
    minority groups and, 282, 288–290
    negative student subculture and, 460–461, 462
    on mass scale, 437, 444

    order and control in, 439–442
    religious beliefs and, 479
    school as socialization agent, 425
    sex role learning and, 309–314, 329
    sifting and sorting function of, 439
    social control and, 147–149
    socialization and, 135–136, 141
    social mobility and, 244–246
    socioeconomic differences and, 228–230
    supply-side, 454
    tracking and, 243, 455–456, 460, 462
Education Amendments Act (1972), Title IX, 88, 89, 310
Egalitarianism, **497**
Ego, 133, 143, 176, **497**
Egoistic suicide, 26, **497**
Eisenhower, D. D., 165, 380
Elite, and power, 40, 371, 376–390, 401–404, **500**
Elitist view power, **497**
Employment:
    boom generation effect, 75
    discrimination prohibited by law, 195
    families and, 415
    gender and, 324–331
    geographic mobility and, 80
    immigration and, 83
    labeling stigmas and, 188–189
    legislation forbidding discrimination, 319–322, 328
    minority groups and, 268–273, 283–285
    tax revenues and, 79
Environmental crisis, 118
Epistemology, 108, **497**
Equal Rights Amendment, 6, 67, 71, 321, 490
Eskimos, 26
Ethical schizophrenia, 120
Ethnicity and ethnic groups, 113, 122, 206, 296, **497**
    assimilation theories, 285–286
    deficiency theories, 276–285
    differences among, 267–268
    ethnic studies programs, 264

social stratification and, 206–207, 265
violence and, 48, 55, 263–264
Ethnocentrism, 100–101, 110, 124, 181, **497**
Ethnomethodology, 103, **497**
Eugenics, 159, **497**
Evelyn's Rules for Bureaucratic Survival, 70
Evolution, 71
Experiment, 12, 13, 14
Experimental group, 13, 14, **497**

Fair play, 41
False consciousness, 143, 208–209, 246, 246, 390, 431, 434, **497**
religion as tool promoting, 469, 491
Falwell, Jerry, 483
Families, 405–434, **497**
aged and, 428–430, 433
background and social mobility, 245
capitalism and, 408–410
changing composition of, 410–411
children and adolescents and, 425–428, 433
class and stability of, 241
compared to households, 410
conflict perspective, 431–434
future and, 432–433
matriarchal structure, 181
myths about, 406–408
order perspective, 431–434
remarriage and, 419–422
roles in, 416–430
social control and, 147
socialization and, 133–135, 139–140
stratification and, 411–415
structural transformation of, 415–416
urban underclass and, 296
violence in, 430–431, 433–434
work and, 422–424
Farmers, 54
Fashion, 39
Fasting, 29
Faulkner, William, 165
Feminist movements, 23, 334–336, 338
Feral children, 127–128, **497**

Fertility, **497**
Fetchit, Stepin, 281
Flag desecration, 57
Folkways, 19, 34, 104, 124, **497**
Ford, Gerald, 165
Foreign policy, 396–397, 402
Fowler's Law, 70
Freedom, 111, 112
Free enterprise mentality, 34
Free enterprise system, 57, 111
Friedan, Betty, 88
Friendship patterns, 16, 18
Fries's Rebellion, 54
Function, **497**
Functional integration, 56–57, 62, **497**
Functionalism (the order perspective), 39, **497**

Gadsden Purchase, 271
Galileo, G., 71
Gang, 14, 43, 122, 123, 198
Gay rights movement, 23, 193–195, 483, 490
Gender, 299–338, **497**
employment and, 301–302, 308, 310
family roles and, 430
inequality structured by, 216–217
interdependence of work and family roles based on, 422–424
occupation and, 231, 301–303
social stratification and, 205, 207, 221, 303–305
structured inequality between, 322–331, 337
Gender roles. *See* Sex roles
Gender roles' approach to sexual inequality, **497**
Gender stratification, **498**
Generalized other, 132, 143, **498**
Gene therapy, 166–167
Genetic engineering, 159, 166–167, 169, 199, **498**
Gentrification, 256–257
German army, 24–25
Gerontological Society, 84–85
"Ghetto pathology" theme, 277–278
"Global electronic machine," 90, 91
Glossolalia, **498**

"Governing class," 385, **498**
Government:
change and, 94
regulatory controls necessary, 117
social control and, 154–155, 162–169
social stability and, 89
"Grandfather clause," 270
Gross national product (GNP), 116
Group marriage, 33
Groups, 4–5, **498**
structure of, 16–35
Guadalupe Hidalgo, Treaty of (1848), 271

Hacker's Law of Personnel, 70
Hart, Gary, 357
Health:
minority groups, 292
population growth and, 74
sex roles and, 300–301
social class and, 241
Hedonism, **498**
Hemingway, Ernest, 165
Heresy, 71
Hero worship, 57
Hidden curriculum, 461, **498**
Hierarchy, 20, 34, **498**
Hispanics, 60. *See also* Chicanos; Minority groups
divorce patterns, 420
education and, 230, 264, 288–290
education and income and, 445, 446
employment and, 292, 336–337
female-headed households, 411
immigration and, 81–83, 93, 270–272
income levels, 286–288, 290, 333, 412
occupational distribution, 322, 325–326
population growth, 48
poverty among, 234, 252, 253, 258, 260, 261, 405
religion and, 481
segmented labor market and, 351, 352
social stratification and, 206–207

Hispanics *(cont.)*
  sterilization of, 159
  unemployment and, 290–292
  urbanization of, 79–80
  violence and, 292–293
  wealth among, 226–227
Hitler, Adolf, 149
Hmong tribespeople, 49
Hobbes, Thomas, 56
Holmes, Oliver Wendell, 392
Holy Tortilla, 467
Home-based work, 416, **498**
Homestead Act of 1862, 89
Homosexuality:
  civil rights movement for ac-
    ceptance of, 23, 193–195,
    483, 490
  identification with mental
    illness, 158
Hoover, J. Edgar, 164
Hopi language, 106–107
Horizontal mobility, 244, **498**
Households, 408, 410–414, **498**
Housing, and sexist discrimi-
  nation, 320
Housing subsidy programs,
  256–257
Human Genome Project, 166–
  167
Hutterites, 122

Id, 132–133, 143, 176, **498**
Ideal type, **498**
Ideological social control, 146–
  147, 169, **498**
Ideology, 66, 71, 93, 101–102,
  103, 124, **498**
Illegitimate births, 419
Illiteracy, 228–230
Imhoff's Law, 70
Immigration, 72, 78
  education and, 443
  electronic, 91
  family structure and, 409
  legal, 48, 49
  minority groups and, 267–
    273
  repressive reform, 294
  social change and, 80–83
  undocumented, 48, 81, 83,
    93, **502**
Immigration Reform and Control Act of 1986, 81
Impersonal justice, 112

Income:
  female-headed households
    and, 333
  median 1960–87, 247
  minority groups and, 286–
    288, 290, 412, 445
  sex roles and, 324–327
  socioeconomic differences
    and, 227–228, 232
Independent variable, 13, 14,
  498
Indians, 109–110. *See also* Native Americans
Individualism, 41, 57, 117–118,
  123–124, 440
  personality types and, 138
Individual racism, 279–285,
  498
Inflation, 247, 339, 340, 351,
  359, **498**
  education expenditure and,
    449, 452–453, 454
  housing market, 256–257
  military-industrial complex
    expenditures, 382
  unemployment increase and,
    397–399
Institution, **498**
Institutional derogation, **498**
Institutional discrimination,
  217–219, **498**
Institutional process, 44, 204,
  498
Institutional racism, 279–285,
  297, 362, **498**
Institutional sexism, 252, **498**
Institutional violence, **498**
Institutions, 32–34, 66–68, 93,
  341
Instrumental process, 44, **498**
Integration, 39
Integrative forces in society,
  56–61
Intelligence, 210–211, 212–213.
  See also IQ testing
  population changes and, 74
Intercourse, 97
Interest groups, 383, 384, 403,
  498
  lack of central planning a
    result of, 365
  power structure and, 370,
    372–377
Interest group theory, 163–164

Intergenerational mobility,
  244, 261, **498**
Interlocking directorates, 344–
  347, 349, 368, 380
Internal colonialism, 409
Internalization, 99, **498**
Intimidation, governmental
  social control and, 165
Intragenerational mobility,
  244, **498**
IQ testing, 210–213. *See also*
  Intelligence
  gene therapy and, 167
  hierarchical division of labor
    legitimated by, 444
  poverty and, 280, 281
  self-fulfilling prophecies
    and, 245, 457
  socioeconomic background,
    education level, and, 446
Irish Catholic Americans, 54
Irish islanders, 97

Jackson, Jesse, 293
Japanese, sexual behavior of,
  97
Japanese-kamikaze attacks, 26
Jefferson, Thomas, 168
Jensen-Herrnstein thesis, 212–
  213, 214, 222
Jewish (Orthodox) sects, 122
Jewish people, relative worth
  as a social group, 135
"Jim Crow" laws, 269
Job evaluation system, 326
Johnson, Lyndon B., 165
Jones, Jim, 149
Judeo-Christian ethic, 57, 112,
  124
Justice system, class and, 242
Juvenile delinquency, solutions
  for deviance from the la-
  beling perspective, 190

Keller, Helen, 128
Kennedy, John F., 165, 470
Kesey, Ken, 189
King, Martin Luther, Jr., 88,
  92, 165
Kissing, 96–97
Knox, John, 475

Labeling, and deviance, 185–
  192, 201

Labeling theory, **498**
Labor disputes, 55–56
Language, 106–109, 124
  Arabian honor-shame syndrome reflected in, 156–157
  male dominance and, 315
  socialization and, 128–129, 143
Latent consequence, function, 39, 116, **498**
Law:
  discriminatory enforcement, 194–195
  gender stratification and, 319–321
  interest-group theory of, 163–164
  male dominance and, 319–321
  social control and, 163
  social institutions and, 33–34
Law and order, 119, 391
  alliance with God of civil religion, 471
Lewis, Sinclair, 165
Liberalism, 7
Life chances, 205, 240, **499**
  class and, 261, 414, 426–427
  poor and, 254, 350
  wealth and, 243
Life expectancy, 84
  class and, 240–241
  remarriage and, 421
  women compared to men, 429
Lincoln, A., 114, 154
Lobbying, for pay equity, 327
Localism, 88
Lombroso's theory, 175
Long, Huey, 345
Looking-glass self, 130–131, 143, 188, **499**
Lower class, 234
  criminal activity and, 178–180
  education and, 447, 455
  exceptional children upwardly mobile, 445
  religion and, 474–479
Lower-middle class, 233
Lower-upper class, 233
Luther, Martin, 112–113, 475

McCarran-Walter Act, 273
Machiavelli, N., 59, 154
Machismo (macho), **499**
MacLeish, A., 165
Macro level, **499**
Madison, James, 390, 393
Majority group, **499**
Male chauvinism, **499**
Manifest consequence, function, 39, 116, **499**
Manson, Charles, 149
Maquiladoras, 356
Marcos, F., 397
Marginality, 92, **499**
Marital power, 418, **499**
Marriage, 27, 32–33, 331, 405, 406
  future trends, 432–433
  sex roles and, 304
  women and, 416–419
Materialism, 110
Material progress, 116–117, 124
Material technology, **499**
"Maternal instinct," 28
Matriarchal family, **499**
Mayans, 107
Media:
  male dominance and, 316–318
  minority group member portrayals, 281–282
  occupational stereotypes and, 231
  selective perception of race and class, 59, 60
  sexual stereotype portrayals, 329
  social control and, 151–154
  social integration and, 59, 60
  socialization and, 136–137
  social problems and, 119–120
Medicine, sex roles and, 330
Men:
  differential ranking of, 302
  expectations for, 306–309
  gender expectations and, 334
  marriage and, 416–419
  reinforcement of dominance of, 302–305, 315–322, 336
Mennonite religious sect, 23
Mental illness:
  deinstitutionalization of patients, 258
  labeling stigma, 158, 185, 188–189

Mergers, 344, 368
Meritocracy, 211, **499**
Micro level, **499**
Middle class, 236, 246–249
  churches and, 474
  downwardly mobile families of, 415
  draft and, 399
  education and, 442, 447, 451–452, 455
  families and, 413–414
  family roles and, 418–419
  religion and, 475–479
Migration patterns, 78, 80, 88
Military-industrial complex, 381–384, **499**
Mind controls, 157
  by drugs, 168, 169
Minority, **499**
Minority groups. *See also* Asian Americans; Blacks; Chicanos; Hispanics; Women
  blaming the victim approach, 181
  breadwinner-homemaker pattern not applied, 409
  characteristics of, 266–267
  children and, 295
  children and adolescents and families, 427
  deficiency theories, 276–285, 297
  deprived of equal opportunities, 219
  economy's structural transformation and, 259
  educational inequality and, 445–461
  education and, 288–290
  employment and, 283–285, 325–331, 336–337
  eugenics and, 159
  families as adapting mechanism, 433
  health and, 292
  imprisonment and, 187
  income levels, 286–288, 290, 293–294
  interest groups of, 403
  IQ test results, 213, 280, 281
  low self-esteem, 131
  media stereotypes, 136
  population growth disproportionate, 362

Minority groups *(cont.)*
    potential work force expansion and, 359
    poverty and, 234, 252, 260
    religion and, 481
    segmented labor market and, 350–352, 368
    social roles, 106
    social stratification and, 206–207
    suffrage and, 269–270, 321–322, 335
    unemployment and, 288, 398–399
    urban underclass, 297
    violence and, 47–48, 52–56, 263–265, 292–293
Minor v. *Happerset* (1874), 319
Mistresses, 105–106
Modal personality type, 138–139, 143, **499**
Model, **499**
Monogamy, 27, 32–33, 44–45, 304, **499**
Monopolies, 343–344, 345, 347, 368, **499**
Monopolistic capitalism, **499**
Monotheism, 44–45
Moral Majority, 195, 335
Mores, 19, 34, 44, 104, **499**
Morrill Act of 1862, 89
Mortality rate, **499**
Multinational corporation, **499**
Myth, 44
Myth of peaceful progress, 52–56, 62, **499**
Myth of separate worlds, **499**

Nader, Ralph, 373
National Caucus on Black Aged, 84–85
National Committee to Preserve Social Security and Medicare, 84–85
National Council of Senior Citizens, 84–85
National Council on Aging, 84–85
National Institutes of Health, 166–167
Nationalism, 66, 294, 489
    and sport, 150
    material-based, 393
National Origins Act of 1924, 268, 273

Native Americans, 122, 273–276, 297
    Alcatraz Island occupation, 182–183
    conquest reinforced by established religion, 149, 468
    education and, 230
    employment of, 336
    land seizure, 89, 196, 225
    language, 106–107, 128–129
    media portrayals, 281
    personality types and, 138–139
    poverty among, 234, 260
    segmented labor market and, 352
    sterilization of, 159
    violence and, 47–48, 54, 56
    visions expected, 172
Navajo, 108
    language, 128–129
New rich class, 233
Nixon, Richard, 141, 165
Nominalist, 18, **499**
Nomos, 138, **499**
Norms, 18–21, 23, 30, 34–35, 124, **499**
    classification of, 104
    counterculture, 123
    data collection, 10
    determining what is deviant, 200
    deviance and, 43, 172
    group membership and, 59
    institutional, 32, 33
    internalized through socialization, 133, 136
    language and, 128–129
    preserved by sport, 151
    privacy within the family, 407, 433
    reform movements and, 92
    societal, 101–106
    suicide regulations, 26–27
    supporting violence, 431
North, Oliver, 141
Nuclear family, **499**
Nuptiality, **499**

Observation, 12–14
Occupation:
    family roles and quality determined by, 412–413
    future job growth (1986–2000), 336–337

gender stratification and, 308
    largest projected absolute growth (1978–1990), 324
    projected growth 1982–1995, 358
    religious affiliation and, 478
    sex-biased aptitude testing and, 314
    sex roles and, 310, 337
    sex stratification and, 301–302, 322–331
    socioeconomic differences and, 230–239
    specialization and interaction tendencies, 46–47
Old rich class, 233
Order model, 37, 39, 62
    crime and, 195–196
    deviance in, 174, 197–201
    duality of social life and, 44–46
    education and, 461
    families and, 431–434
    gender stratification and, 303–305, 337
    integrative forces in society, 56–57
    perspective, **499**
    politics, 401
    racial stratification, 285–286
    religion from, 468, 491, 492
    social class conception, 233–234
    socialization process power, 143, 144
    social problems in, 43–44
    social stratification and, 207–209, 222
    sport and, 43
    theory, 41, 62
    use of, 61–62

Pakistanis, 28
Paradigm, **499**
Parkinson's Laws, 70
Parks, Rosa, 92
Participant observation, 122
Participatory socialization, **499**
Patriarchal family, **500**
Patriarchy, 207, 302–303, 331, 332, 335, 433, **500**
    capitalistic, 352–353, 409
    religion and, 475, 481
    sex roles and, 337
Patriotism, 42

Pay equity, 324–331, 337
Peaceful progress, 52–56, 62
Peer group, **500**
Pension programs, 78, 429
  sex roles and, 320
Personality, 3–4
  economic success and, 245–246
  group effect on, 18
  looking-glass self and, 130–131, 143
  psychoanalytic view of, 132–133, 143
  shaped by education, 443
  socialization and, 126–144
  taking role of other and, 131–132, 143
  variables and status, 21
Personnel control, 160–161
Peter Principle, 69, 70, **500**
Phone monitoring, 160–161
Pluralism, **500**
Pluralist view of power, **500**
Polarization, 61
Political action committees (PACs), 372–375
Political crime, 195–196, **500**
Political machines, 39
Political parties, 50
Politics:
  sex roles and, 321–322
  shifting attitudes and, 6–7
  two-party system, 67–68
Polity, 33–34, **500**
Pollution, 104, 115, 116, 119
Polyandry, 33
Polygamy, 33
Population:
  growth in, 72–85, 93
  implosion, 78–79, **500**
  social change and, 72–85
  violence and, 48
Posttest, 13
Poverty, 8, **500**
  aged and, 429
  benefits of, 218–220
  bias of law and, 193
  capital punishment and, 186
  children and, 253–254, 261, 425–428
  culture of, 182
  divorce patterns and, 421
  economic system and, 339–340, 350
  employment and, 351–352
  extent of, 249–254

feminization of, 252–253, 259, 288, 333, 429, **497**
homelessness analyzed, 255–261
imprisonment and, 187
minority groups and, 252, 260, 286–288, 405
myths about, 254–255
occupational ranking and, 237–238
present-time orientation, 214–216
sex roles and, 333
sickness and absences, 218–219
social stratification and, 213
student-worker alliance at Duke Univ., 250–252
tax policies and, 397–400
Power, **500**
  differential, and racially motivated violence, 265
  inequalities in, 45
Power elite, 40, 371, 377–390, 401–404, **500**
Power structure, 14, 370–414
  consequences of, 391–404
  degree of centralization, 402
  elitist models of, 371, 376–390, 400–404
  marital, 418, **499**
  pluralist models of, 371–377, 400–404
  sex roles and, 315–316
  veto groups and, 376–377, 403
  violence and, 38
Predestination, 112, 469, 491
Prejudice:
  minority groups and, 278–279
  socialization and, 134–135
Presidential Commissions on Civil Disorders and Violence, 56
Pressure groups, 85
Prestige, **500**
Pretest, 13
Primary deviance, 188, 191, **500**
Primary group, 24–25, 30, 35, **500**
Prisoners, 186–188
Private property, 44–45, 117–118
Privilege, 206

Professional managerial class, 235–237
Progress, 115–116, 123–124
Progressive tax, **500**
Proletariat, 237, 238, 343, 344, **500**
Prolife philosophy, 484–485
Protest, 50–51
Protestant ethic (Puritan work ethic), 112, 113, 124, **500**
Proverb, 11–12
Proxmire, W., 382
Psychoanalytic theory, personality development in, 132–133, 143
Psychological theories of deviance, 176–177
Psychosurgery, 158–159, 168, 169, **500**
"Public service" advertising (PSA), 152–153
Pygmalion effect, **500**

Race, racial group, 206, 296, **500**
  deficiency theories, 276–285
  differentiation criterion, 47
  earning discrimination, 325–327
  education, inequality and, 445–461
  family life affected by control, 409
  income levels and, 412
  inequality structured by, 216–217
  media perception of, 59, 60
  segregation, 120
  social stratification and, 205–207, 221, 265, 285–286
  violence and, 263–265, 292–293
  wealth and, 226–227
Racism, 1, 4, 6, 47–48, 181–182, 279–286, 292–293, 485, **500**
  biological superiority theories, 213
  institutional, 221
  on college campuses, 263–264
Radical nonintervention, 190, **500**
Rand Corporation, 83
Random sample, **500**

Rayburn's Rule, 70
Reagan, Nancy, 119
Reagan, Ronald, 152, 165, 257, 260, 264, 293, 294, 339, 400, 454, 471, 484
Realist, 18, **500**
Recidivism, 181, 187, **500**
Reference group, 99, **500**
Reformatories, 34
Reform movement, 90, 92, 94, **500**
Regionalism, 47, 52, 113, 120–121
Regressive tax, **500**
Reliability, in data collection, 10, **500**
Religion and religious groups, 71, 464–492, **500**
    beliefs and, 465
    bigotry, 50
    civil religion in, 470–471, 491
    class and, 474
    conflict perspective, 469, 491, 492
    consequences of, 491
    electronic church in, 483–487, 492
    ethnocentric notion, 465–466
    future trends, 488–489
    health and, 28–29, 35
    male dominance and, 318–319
    order perspective, 468–469, 491, 492
    organization of, 472–474
    patriarchy and, 475, 481
    pluralism, 49
    political activism and, 487–491
    regimes, 34
    rituals and, 465, 473, 481, 491
    role of, 485–491
    sacred and, 465, 468, **501**
    social change and, 469
    social control and, 149
    socialization and, 141–142
    socioeconomic status and, 475–479, 492
    sociology's interpretations of, 468–470, 491
    state acts accepted by, 467–468
    suicide rate affected, 25–26
    trends in, 465, 479–485, 492

variety of beliefs in, 44, 66, 471
    violence and, 48–50, 468
Repressive socialization, **500**
Resistance movement, 71–72, 93, **500**
Revolutionary movement, 92, 94, **500**
    impeded by sport, 150
Revolutionary War, 53–54
Reward-punishment system, 24, 35, 51, 111, 146
    deviance and, 174
    sex roles and, 306–307
Reza Shah, 348, 397
Rickover, Hyman, 484
Riesman's Law, 70
Rigg's Hypothesis, 70
Rites of passage, 428, **500**
Roberts, Oral, 483
Robertson, Pat, 483, 484
Robertson's Second Order Rule of Bureaucracy, 70
Rockefeller, J. D., 114
Rockefellers, 349
Rodin, P. A., 97
Roe v. *Wade*, 320
Role, **500**. *See also* Social roles
Role performance (role behavior), **500**
Roosevelt, F. D., 164, 394
Roosevelt, T., 394
Rotation system, U.S. army, 25
Routinization of charisma, 473, **501**
Rubio, Maria, 467
Ruling class, 235
Runaway shops, 356
Russians, stereotypes and, 100

Sacred, **501**. *See also* Religion and religious groups, sacred and
Sample, 9–11, 12–13, 120, **501**
San Antonio v. *Rodriguez* (1973), 449
Sanction, 24, 35, **501**
Sandburg, Carl, 165
Sanity, 157
Schools. *See* Education
Schuller, Robert, 483–484
Science and medicine, social control and, 156–162, 169
Scientific reasoning, 284

Secondary deviance, 188, 189, 191, **501**
Secondary group, 24–25, 30, 35, **501**
Sect, 472–474, 491–492, **501**
Secular, **501**
Segmented labor market, 350, **501**
Segregation, **501**
Self, 129
Self-esteem, **501**
    affected by personnel control, 161
    deviance and, 178
Self-fulfilling prophecy, 462, **501**
    education and, 213–214, 440, 444, 457
    labeling and deviant behavior, 192
    tracking by ability related, 218
Self-reliance, 118
Serrano v. *Priest* (1976), 449
"Service observation," 160–161
Sex-gender system, 207, **501**
Sexism, 300, 305, 331–334, 338, 433, **501**
    school textbooks and, 310–311
Sex roles, 6, 207, 299–338, **501**
    concept of, 300
    constraints of, 23
    costs of sexism in, 1, 331–334, 338
    gender role concept, 300
    gender stratification, 300, 303–305
    learning, 306–315
    physiological differences and, 300–302
    socialization and, 142
Sexual behavior, 96–97
    Arab society and social control of, 156–157
    groups and, 27, 29
    regulated by institutions, 33
Sexual revolution, 319
Sexual stratification, **501**
Sharecropping agreements, 269
Shared monopoly, 344, 345, 349, 368, **501**
Shaw, G. B., 282
Shays's Rebellion, 54
Shunning, 23

Sibling, **501**
Significant others, 132, **501**
Skinner, B. F., 169
Slavery, 5, 54, 55, 225, 268–269
   religion and, 149, 467–468
Slum neighborhoods (ghettos),
   14, 47–48, 122, 214–215,
   277, 279–280
Small business owners, 237
Smith's Principles of Bureau-
   cratic Tinkertoys, 70
Snakebite, 28–29
Social class, **501**. *See also* Class
Social conditioning, 210–211
Social control, 23–24, 30, 145–
   169, **501**
  agents of, 146–155, 158, 169
  direct, 155–169, **497**
  socialization and, 169
Social Darwinism, 184, 209–
   210, 212, 221, 222, **501**
Social definitions, 108
Social determinism, 3–4, **501**
Social differentiation, 204, 221,
   501
Social groups:
  behavior and, 29–30
  convictions and, 28, 35
  health and, 28–29, 35
  membership, 62
  perceptions and, 27, 35
  primary, 24–25, 30, 35
  secondary, 24–25, 30, 35
  sexual behavior and, 29
  social integration and, 58
  structure of, 16–35
  subgroups of, 52
  suicide and, 25–27
Social inequality, **501**
Social interaction, 17, 34, 124,
   501
Socialism, 341–343, 345, 368,
   501
Socialization, 99, 124, 126–144,
   501
  agents of, 133–137, 143, 425,
    431, **501**
  differences among individu-
    als and, 137–143
  and feral children, 127–128
  language and, 128–129
  social control and, 169
Social location, **501**
Social mobility, 117, 261, **501**
  buddy system and women,
    331

class and, 243–249
education and, 446
families and, 415
socialization and, 142
sport and, 150
Social movement, 71, 93, 94,
   501
Social organization, 17–35, 40,
   501
Social problem, 43, 62, **501**
Social relationship, 17, **501**
Social roles, 30, 34, 35, 124
  behavior and, 18–19
  institutional expectations,
    32, 33
  shared knowledge and, 101–
    102, 106
  socialization and, 142–143
  status and, 19–23
Social Security Administration, 78
Social stratifications, 32, 39,
   203–222, **501**
  concepts in, 204–207
  deficiency theories, 209–217
  inequalities in, 45
  religion and, 475–479
  sport and, 42
  structural discrimination
    theories, 279–285
  structural theories, 297
  theories of, 207–222
  tracking and, 455–456
Social structure, 17, 34, **502**
  culture and, 98
Social system, **502**
  change in, 65–66
  duality in, 66, 93
  forces for stability in, 66–72
  society as, 30–31, 38–40, 45
Social technology, **502**
Societal integration, 124
Societal scripts, 103
Society, 30, **502**
  culture of, 31–32
  deviance and, 177–178, 185–
    197
  integrative forces in, 56–62
  model, 38
  "noble lie," 109
  problems and their institu-
    tions, 33
  as social system, 30–31, 45
  sociological perspective on,
    1–2

Socioeconomic status (SES),
   502
Sociological methods, 7–15
  data collection in, 7–12
  data sources in, 12–14
Sociological perspective, 1–15
  assumptions, 2–15
  deviance in, 177
  problems with, 5–7
Sociology, definition of, 17, **502**
South Africans, 37
Sovereign state, 44–45
Specialization, 113
Sport:
  bias in, 1, 6
  interrelated with national-
    ism, 150
  order and conflict models
    and, 41–43
  scandals, 115
  sex roles and, 311–313
  social control and, 150–151
Stability, forces for, 93
Stagflation, **502**
Statistical techniques, in data
   collection, 13, 14
Status, 19–23, 30, 34–35, 106,
   502
  changes in, 22–23
  differentials, 47
  effect on family as socializ-
    ing agent, 139
  material progress and, 117
  and role, 19
Status anguish, 92, 94, **502**
Status group, **502**
Status inconsistency, 92, **502**
Status quo, 43, 62
  constraints in respect to
    deviance, 193
  favored by "bias of the
    system" theory, 389
  justification of, 103
  lack of satisfaction with, 116
  preservation of, 66, 67, 68,
    93, 278
  rule violations and, 174
  sanctified by religion, 149,
    486, 490–492
  social reform efforts
    thwarted, 197
  social workers and, 236
Status withdrawal, 93, **502**
Steinbeck, John, 165
Stereotypes, **502**

Stereotypes *(cont.)*
  occupations and, 231, 308, 310, 314
  portrayed in television media, 136–137
  sexual, 306, 314, 317
Sterilization, 159
Stigma, 180, 188–189, 457, 462, **502**
Street crimes, 195–196
Stress-related illnesses, caused by personnel control, 160–161
Structural approach to sexual inequality, **502**
Structural-functional model, 39
Structural theories of racial inequality, **502**
Structured social inequality, **502**
Subculture, 43, 122–124, 460–462, **502**
Subsidy, **502**
Suburbs, 79, **502**
Success, economic, 114, 119, 124, 217
Suffrage, and minority groups, 269–270, 321–322, 335
Suicide, 25–27, 39
Superego, 99, 133, 143, 176, 181, **502**
Surveillance methods, 160–161
  government exertion of social control, 164–168
Survey research, 12–14, **502**
Swaggart, Jimmy, 483
Symbols, 35, 57, 98, 101–102, 124, **502**
Synthesis, **502**
Systemic imperatives, 67, 389, **502**

Taboos, 44
Tax policies, and the poor, 271, 397–400
Teachers:
  sex roles and, 311–314
  tracking and expectations of, 457, 460, 462
Technology, 5, 33, 124, 354, 359–361, 368, **502**
  change and, 78, 85–91, 93–94
  educational training and retraining for, 458–459

gender stratification and, 301–302
  material, 103
  relation to progress, 116, 124
  shared knowledge and, 101–102, 103
  social, 103
Telemetry, 168
Temiar people, 108
Temple, Shirley, 281
Terrorism, 398–399
Theodicy, 474, 486, 491, 492, **502**
Tiananmen Square massacre, 37
Time, language symbols for, 106–107
Title IX legislation, 88, 89, 310
Tiv, 107
Totem, 468
Tracking methods, 218, 243, 245, 455–456, 460, 462, **502**
Tradition, 6, 29–30, 35, 44, 122
Transcience, **502**
Trobriander, 107
Truman, Harry S, 164, 364
Twinning, 105
Twins, studies of, 126, 212

Underemployment, **502**
Undocumented immigrant, 48, 81, 83, 93, **502**
Unemployment, 333
  dual labor market and, 351
  homelessness and, 258–259, 261
  inflation and, 397–400
  minority groups and, 288, 290–292
  multinational corporations and, 348
  social problems and, 295–296
U.S. army, 25
U.S. Civil Rights Commission, 49
U.S. Congress, 67–68
U.S. Supreme Court, 80, 119, 269, 274, 294, 327, 391
Upper class, 403
  churches and, 474
  draft and, 399
  education and, 442, 444–445
  family boundaries of, 414
  kinship ties, 414

power elite and, 385–387
  religion and, 475–479
Upper-lower class, 233–234
Upper-middle class, 233
Upper-upper class, 233
Urbanism, **502**
Urbanization, 78–80, 93, **502**
Urban region (megalopolis, conurbation, strip city), **502**

Vail's First Axiom, 70
Validity, in data collection, 10, **502**
Value neutrality, 7–8, 14, 42, **503**
Values, 18, 24, 34, 35, 110–124, **503**
  behavior and, 118–120
  consensus of, 62
  consistency of, 113
  counterculture, 123
  determination of, 110–111
  dominant, 113
  dual system, 180
  from the order and conflict perspectives, 123
  inconsistencies, 118
  institutional, 32, 33
  integration and consensus on, 57
  internalized through socialization, 133
  language and, 128–129
  listlessness blamed on lack of clarity, 140–141
  portrayed by media, 136–137
  reform movements and, 92
  shared knowledge and, 101–102, 106
  social factors for, 124
  social integration and social problems and, 111–113
Variable, 13, **503**
Vertical mobility, 244, 261
Veto groups, 376–377, 403
Vietnam War, 25, 49, 51, 59, 83
Violence, 37–38
  division and, 46
  families and, 430–431, 433–434
  institutional, 37
  mass, 53
  myth of peaceful progress and, 52–56, 62, **499**

police brutality, 37
power structure and, 38
religion and, 468
vandalism and, 37–38, 55
Voluntary association, **503**

WASP supremacy, 54
Wealth, 431
socioeconomic differences
and, 226–227
Wealthfare, 255, **503**
Welfare programs, 394, **503**
decrease in, 228
dependency, 277, 278
poverty and, 254–255, 260–
261
repatriation of Chicanos
and, 272
social control and, 155–156,
169
White flight, 79, **503**
Whites:
education and, 230, 288–290
employment and, 238
female-headed households,
411

income levels of, 286–288,
333, 412
occupational distribution,
322, 325–326
unemployment of, 291–292
wealth among, 226–227
Whiskey Rebellion, 54
Wilder, Thorton, 165
Williams, Tennessee, 165
Wilson, Woodrow, 175
Wolfe, Thomas, 165
Women:
differential ranking of, 302
employment and, 322, 336–
337, 362–363, 433
expectations for, 306–309
heading households, 333,
410–411, 425
in labor force, 75
laws prohibiting sexual discrimination, 319–320
marriage and, 304, 416–419
media portrayals of, 136,
281, 316–318
politics and, 321–322
poverty and, 252–253, 261,
429

role models for, 308, 310,
313–314, 316–317
role of wife, 426–427
suffrage of, 321–322
violence and, 319
working mother profiles, 423
Women's movement, 23, 334–
336, 338
Workers:
deskilling of, 354
home-based, 416
poverty among, 254–255
profiles of mothers, 423
Work-family role system, 422–
424
Working class, 237
Workplace surveillance, 160–
161
Work Rules, 70
World War II, 24–26, 54

Yancos, 108

Zero population growth (ZPG)
rate, 73